HUMAN RELATIONS IN ORGANIZATIONS

APPLICATIONS AND SKILL BUILDING

EIGHTH EDITION

HUMAN RELATIONS
IN ORGANIZATIONS

APPLICATIONS AND SKILL BUILDING

EIGHTH EDITION

Robert N. Lussier, Ph.D.
Springfield College

McGraw-Hill
Irwin

Boston   Burr Ridge, IL   Dubuque, IA   New York   San Francisco   St. Louis
Bangkok   Bogotá   Caracas   Kuala Lumpur   Lisbon   London   Madrid   Mexico City
Milan   Montreal   New Delhi   Santiago   Seoul   Singapore   Sydney   Taipei   Toronto

HUMAN RELATIONS IN ORGANIZATIONS: APPLICATIONS AND SKILL BUILDING
Published by McGraw-Hill/Irwin, a business unit of The McGraw-Hill Companies, Inc., 1221 Avenue of
the Americas, New York, NY, 10020. Copyright © 2010, 2008, 2005, 2002, 1999, 1996, 1993, 1990 by The
McGraw-Hill Companies, Inc. All rights reserved. No part of this publication may be reproduced or distributed in any form or by any means, or stored in a database or retrieval system, without the prior written
consent of The McGraw-Hill Companies, Inc., including, but not limited to, in any network or other electronic storage or transmission, or broadcast for distance learning.

Some ancillaries, including electronic and print components, may not be available to customers outside the
United States.

This book is printed on acid-free paper.

1 2 3 4 5 6 7 8 9 0 DOW/DOW 0 9

ISBN 978-0-07-338153-4
MHID 0-07-338153-5

Vice president and editor-in-chief: *Brent Gordon*
Publisher: *Paul Ducham*
Director of development: *Ann Torbert*
Managing development editor: *Laura Hurst Spell*
Editorial assistant: *Jane Beck*
Vice president and director of marketing: *Robin J. Zwettler*
Associate marketing manager: *Jaime Halteman*
Vice president of editing, design and production: *Sesha Bolisetty*
Senior project manager: *Susanne Riedell*
Lead production supervisor: *Carol A. Bielski*
Designer: *Matt Diamond*
Senior media project manager: *Allison Souter*
Cover design: *Matt Diamond*
Typeface: *10/12 Times Roman*
Compositor: *Macmillan Publishing Solutions*
Printer: *R. R. Donnelley*

Library of Congress Cataloging-in-Publication Data
Lussier, Robert N.
    Human relations in organizations : applications and skill building / Robert N.
Lussier. — 8th ed.
        p. cm.
    Includes bibliographical references and index.
    ISBN-13: 978-0-07-338153-4 (alk. paper)
    ISBN-10: 0-07-338153-5 (alk. paper)
    1. Organizational behavior. 2. Interpersonal relations. I. Title.
HD58.7.L86 2010
658.3—dc22
                                                    2009023838

I would like to dedicate this book to my wife, Marie, and our children, Jesse, Justin, Danielle, Nicole, Brian, and Renee, for their loving support.

PREFACE

In his book *Power Tools,* John Nirenberg asks: "Why are so many well-intended students learning so much and yet able to apply so little in their personal and professional lives?" Is it surprising that students can neither apply what they read nor develop skills when most textbooks continue to focus on reading about concepts and examples, rather than taking the next step and teaching them how to apply what they read and develop the skills required for using the concepts? Russ Ackoff, editor of *Academy of Management Learning & Education,* says we should be teaching students to learn how to learn. Pfeffer and Sutton, authors of *The Knowing–Doing Gap,* conclude that the most important insight from their research is that knowledge that is actually implemented is much more likely to be acquired from learning by doing than from learning by reading, listening, or thinking. *I wrote this book to give students the opportunity to learn how to learn by doing through applying the concepts and developing skills used in their personal and professional lives.*

I wrote the first edition back in 1988, prior to AACSB and SCANS called for skill development and outcomes assessment, to help professors develop their students' ability to apply the concepts and develop organizational behavior/human relations skills. Unlike competitors, I don't just tell you about the concepts. With networking, for instance—the way most people get jobs and promotions today—I tell you step-by-step how to network and provide you with self-assessment exercises, application exercises, skill development exercises, and often, videos. So rather than simply knowing the concepts, you can actually develop skills.

But is the skills approach any good? This is the eighth edition, and each edition has sold more copies. John Bigelow compared skills texts in his article, "Managerial Skills Texts: How Do They Stack Up?" in the *Journal of Management Education,* and he gave *Human Relations in Organizations* a top rating for a general OB course. *Reviewers continue to say it is the best "how to work with people" textbook on the market.* Although competing texts now include exercises, reviewers continue to say that no competitor offers the quality and quantity of application and skill-building material.

ENGAGING NetGen STUDENTS

Today's traditional students are being called the Digital Millennial or NetGen learners. Being brought up on the Internet, they have different preferred learning styles than students in prior generations. NetGens prefer active, collaborative, and team-based learning.[1] *Human Relations in Organizations,* Eighth Edition, is designed to be flexible enough to be used with the traditional lecture method, while offering a wide range of engaging activities to select from that best meet students' and professors' educational goals and preferred teaching/learning styles. Below is a list of learning preferences of NetGens and how this text can be used to engage them both in and out of the classroom.

NetGen Learning Preference	How *Human Relations in Organizations* Engages NetGens
Reading: Students prefer active learning to reading.	Students find the text easy to read and understand.
Relevance and the real world: NetGens need to be sold on why they are learning the material. They prefer to know, "What's in it for me?" And they prefer learning about the real world.	Real-world examples of actual people and organizations occur throughout the chapters and the end-of-chapter cases. Work Applications features ask the students to state how their real-world organizations use the text concepts.

[1] Erika Matulich, Raymond Papp, & Diana Haytko, "Continuous Improvement Through Teaching Innovations: A Requirement for Today's Learners," *Marketing Education Review,* 18(1) 2008: 1–7.

NetGen Learning Preference	How *Human Relations in Organizations* Engages NetGens
Breaks and feedback: Students need frequent study breaks and want to know how they are doing.	The text presents concepts followed by application material so that students can break up the reading while applying the concepts and getting feedback. Boxed items are not just passive reading; they engage the student to come up with an answer. Students especially like the Self-Assessment features within the chapters.
Attention and variety: Breaking class time into "chunks" helps keep their attention and improve learning.	The text is broken into "chunks," with concepts, followed by interactive applications and skill-building exercises (see below). Each section consists of a major heading with concepts and application material.
Application: Students value application of the text concepts.	The text includes 9 types of applications.
Skill-building: NetGens value developing skills they can use in their personal and professional lives.	The text includes 8 types of skill-building activities. Unlike many books with exercises that are simply discussion-based, *Human Relations* develops actual skills that can be used immediately.
Teamwork: Students are social and like to work in teams.	The applications can be discussed in groups, and the skill-building exercises are both individual and group-based.
Visual learning: NetGens prefer visual learning.	The text includes many exhibits and the book can be supplemented with PowerPoint presentations and videos that are available on the book's Web site.
Directions: Students benefit from checklists, formulas, and recipes for learning and for life.	*Human Relations* is the most "how to" textbook available, including behavioral model steps for handling common human relations issues, such as conflict, and exercises to develop skills.
Internet: NetGens are comfortable with online environments.	An Online Learning Center (www.mhhe.com/lussier8e) provides chapter review material as well as interactive exercises and videos.
Outcomes: Again, NetGens want to know how they are doing.	*Human Relations* includes a test bank with application and skill-based questions to assess various learning-level outcomes.

Source: Erika Matulich, Raymond Papp, and Diana Haytko, "Continuous Improvement Through Teaching Innovations: A Requirement For Today's Learners," *Marketing Education Review,* 18(1) 2008: 1–7.

INTEGRATION WITH FLEXIBILITY

This book continues to have a balanced three-pronged approach:

- A clear, concise understanding of human relations/organizational behavior (HR/OB) concepts (second to none);

- The application of HR/OB concepts for critical thinking in the business world (there are nine types of applications, including videos and the Test Bank and Instructor's Manual);

- The development of HR/OB skills (there are eight types of skills-activities, including videos and the Test Bank and Instructor's Manual).

In addition to this text and its supporting ancillary package to support these distinct but integrated parts, this new edition includes tests to assess student performance in all three areas. I wrote almost every application and skill exercise in this text and the Instructor's Manual to ensure complete integration and a seamless course experience.

The concepts, applications, and skill-building material are clearly identified and delineated in this preface, text, and IM/test bank. Our package offers more quality and quantity of application and skill-building material to allow professors to create their unique courses using only the features that will achieve their objectives. Thus, it is the most flexible package on the market. Next is an explanation of features to choose from for concepts, applications, and skill building.

CONCEPTS

- *Research-based and current*. The book is based on research, not opinion. The eighth edition has been completely updated. There are 1,390 new references (94.5 percent), for an average of 93 new references per chapter. Earlier references are primarily classics, such as the motivation (Maslow) and leadership (Fiedler) theories.

- *Comprehensive coverage*. The text includes more topics than most competing texts.

- *Systems orientation*. The text is organized in two ways. First, the parts of the book are based on the competency model of managerial education, building from intrapersonal skills, to interpersonal skills, to leadership skills. Second, it also follows the levels of behavior approach, going from individual, to group, to organizational levels of behavior. The systems effect is discussed throughout the book. Cases from Chapters 2 through 15 have questions based on previous chapters to integrate the concepts of multiple chapters.

- *Recurring themes*. Chapters 2 through 15 begin with a discussion of how the chapter concepts affect behavior, human relations, and performance. Most chapters include a discussion of how the concepts differ globally.

- *Pedagogy*. Each chapter contains the following: (1) Learning outcomes at the beginning and in the body of the chapter where the objective can be met. A summary of each learning outcome is given in the Review section at the end of the chapter. (2) Key terms at the beginning of each chapter and again at the end of the Review. The key terms appear in **boldface** and *are defined within the chapter in italic* so they are easy to find. (3) Chapter outlines. (4) Exhibits, some of which contain multiple concepts or theories. See Exhibits 8.7, 9.7, 9.8, and 12.7, for example. (5) Chapter Review. The unique feature of the Chapter Review is that it is active in two ways. Students first answer true/false questions. Then they must fill in the blanks with the appropriate key terms in one of three ways: from memory, from a list of key terms at the end of the review, or from the key terms at the beginning of the chapter.

- *Test Bank Assessment of Concepts*. The test bank includes true/false and multiple-choice questions for the concepts, including the key terms, presented in each chapter. The test bank also includes the learning outcomes from each chapter, which can be used as short-answer questions to test concept understanding. A summary of the learning outcomes appears in the Review, the Instructor's Manual, and the test bank.

APPLICATIONS

1. *Opening Case*. Each chapter opens with a case. Throughout the chapter, the ways the text concepts apply to the case are presented so that students can understand the application of the concepts to actual people in organizations.

CHAPTER OUTLINE

How Personality, Stress, Intelligence and Learning, Perception, and First Impressions Affect Behavior, Human Relations, and Performance

Personality

Personality Development

Personality Classification Methods

Locus of Control

The Big Five Model of Personality

The Big Five Model of Personality Has Universal Applications Across Cultures

The Myers-Briggs Type Indicator (MBTI)

Stress

What Is Stress?

Causes of Stress

Signs of Stress

Controlling Stress

Intelligence, Emotional Intelligence, and Learning

Intelligence

Emotional Intelligence

Learning Styles

The Learning Organization

Perception

The Nature of Perception

Bias in Perception

Developing Positive First Impressions

The Primacy Effect and the Four-Minute Barrier

Image Projection

---

2. *Work Applications.* Throughout each chapter there are approximately 11 questions (171 total) that require the students to apply the concepts to their own work experience. Work experience can be present or past and may include part-time, summer, or full-time employment. Work applications require the students to think critically and bridge the gap between the concepts and their world.

WORK APPLICATIONS

14. Give an example, preferably from an organization for which you work or have worked, of an individual creating a win–win situation for all parties involved. Identify all parties involved and how they were winners. Use Exhibit 10.4, Human Relations Guide to Ethical Decision Making (page 371), to help you answer the question.

3. *Application Situations.* Each chapter contains two to six boxes, each with 5 to 10 questions (325 total) that require students to apply the concept illustrated in a specific, short example. The questions develop critical thinking skills through the application process.

APPLICATION SITUATIONS

Channel Selection

AS 6–3

Select the most appropriate channel for each message.

| A. Face-to-Face | C. Meeting | E. Memo | G. Report |
| B. Telephone | D. Presentation | F. Letter | H. Poster |

_____ 11. The supervisor has to assign a new customer order to Karen and Ralph.

_____ 12. The supervisor is expecting needed material for production this afternoon. She wants to know if it will arrive on time.

_____ 13. Employees have been leaving the lights on when no one is in the stockroom. The manager wants this practice to stop.

_____ 14. The boss asked for the production figures for the month.

_____ 15. An employee has broken a rule and needs to be discouraged from doing it again.

4. *Cases—with Internet use and cumulative questions.* Each chapter has a case study from a real-world organization. At the end of the case, the organization's Web site is given so that students can visit the Web to get updated information on the case. Instructor's Manual material provides "How to Research Case Material Using the Internet" to help students. Chapters 2 through 15 include cumulative questions. Cumulative questions include concepts from previous chapters. For example, the case for Chapter 11 has five questions related to Chapter 11, followed by three questions relating to concepts from Chapters 2, 8, and 9. Thus, students continually review and integrate concepts from earlier chapters.

5. *Objective Cases.* At the end of each chapter there is a short objective case. The unique feature is the "objective" part, with 10 multiple-choice questions, followed by one or more open-ended questions. These cases require students to apply the concepts to people and organizations.

6. *Internet Exercises.* Online at <u>mhhe.com/lussier8e</u>, as well as self-testing and other features.

7. *Ethical Dilemmas.* Each chapter has one ethical dilemma presenting a situation with questionable ethical behavior. Students are asked if they think the behavior is ethical and what they would do in that situation.

8. *Communication Skills Questions.* New to this edition, there are 129 communication skills questions, an average of approximately 9 per chapter, which can be used for class discussion and/or written assignments.

9. *Test Bank Assessment of Applications and Instructor's Manual.* The test bank includes the work applications from the text as well as multiple-choice questions, similar to the Application Situations and case questions, to evaluate critical thinking skills. The Instructor's Manual includes the recommended answers for all the application features above, except the opening case, which is illustrated throughout the chapter text.

SKILL BUILDING

1. *Self-Assessment Exercises.* Each chapter has between one and five (47 total, an average of 3 per chapter) self-assessment exercises to enable students to gain personal knowledge. Some of the exercises are tied to skill-building exercises to enhance the impact of the self-assessment. All information for completing and scoring, and self-assessment, is contained within each exercise. A new feature includes determining a personality profile (in Chapter 3); in all other chapters, students find out how their personality relates to their use of the chapter concepts.

2. *Group Skill-Building Exercises.* Around 30 percent of the skill-building exercises focus primarily on small group (2 to 6 members) activities. Thus, breaking into small groups is required.

3. *Role-Play Skill-Building Exercises.* Around 10 percent of the skill-building exercises focus primarily on developing skills through behavior modeling, as discussed next. Thus, breaking into groups of three and role-playing is required.

In-Class Exercise	*Note:* This exercise is designed for groups that have met for some time. (Five or more hours are recommended.)
	Objectives: To gain a better understanding of the group structure components and how they affect group performance, and to improve group structure.
	AACSB: The primary AACSB learning standard skills developed through this exercise are teamwork and leadership; in addition, communication, reflective thinking, self-management, and analytic skills are developed.

4. *Models, Behavior Model Videos, and Skill-Building Exercises.* Throughout the book are 29 models with step-by-step instructions for handling day-to-day human relations situations. How to use several of the models is illustrated in the behavior-modeling videos. For example, students read the model in the book and watch people send messages, give praise, resolve conflicts, handle complaints, and coach an employee, following the steps in the model. After viewing the video, students role-play how they would handle these human relations situations. Students may also give each other feedback on the effectiveness of their role plays. Videos can also be used as stand-alone activities. The lecture may stop and skill-building begin in class to break up the lecture.

5. *Behavior Model Videos.* There are one or more behavior model videos (20 total) for most chapters. Behavior model videos 2 through 20 show people successfully handling day-to-day human relations situations. Videos can be followed by class discussion. Also, many videos are used in conjunction with skill-building exercises.

6. *Test Bank Assessment of Skill-Building and Instructor's Manual.* The test bank includes skill-building questions to assess skill building. The Instructor's Manual gives detailed instructions on using all skill-building exercises and answers to skill-building exercises. It also states how students can be tested on the exercises and provides instructions to give to students.

7. *Skill-Building Objectives and AACSB Competencies.* Each skill-building exercise begins by listing its objective. The objective is followed by listing the Association to Advance Collegiate Schools of Business (AACSB) competencies developed through the exercise.

SKILL-BUILDING EXERCISE 14–1

Coaching

In-Class Exercise
(Group)

Objective: To develop your skill at improving performance through coaching.

AACSB: The AACSB learning standard skills developed through this exercise are analytic skills, communication ability, and leadership.

Preparation: You should have read and understood the chapter.

Experience: You will coach, be coached, and observe coaching using the coaching model.

---

8. *Individual and Group Skill-Building Exercises.* Around 60 percent of the skill-building exercises focus primarily on individual skill building, most of which are done outside class as preparation for the exercise. However, in-class work in groups using the concepts and sharing answers can enhance skill building. Thus, the instructor has the flexibility to (1) simply have students complete the preparations outside class and during class, and then go over the answers, giving concluding remarks and/or leading a class discussion without using any small group time, or (2) spend group class time as directed in the exercise.

SKILL-BUILDING EXERCISE 14–3

Improving the Quality of Student Life

In-Class Exercise
(Individual and Group)

Objective: To experience the quality circle approach to increasing the quality of student life at your college.

AACSB: The AACSB learning standard skills developed through this exercise are analytic skills, communication ability, teamwork, and leadership.

Experience: You will experience being part of a quality circle.

Procedure 1
(8–15 minutes)

Break into groups of five or six members. Select a spokesperson. Your group is to come up with a list of the three to five most needed improvements at your college. Rank them in order of priority, from 1—most important to 5—least important. When you are finished, or the time is up, the spokesperson will write the ranking on the board. You may refer to the preparation for Skill-Building Exercise 14–2 for ideas on areas needing improvement.

SUMMARY OF INNOVATIONS

- The three-pronged approach to the text: concepts, applications, skills.
- The three-pronged test bank: concepts, applications, skills.
- Nine types of applications, clearly marked in the text, for developing critical thinking skills, including Internet exercises online.
- Eight types of skill-building exercises, clearly marked in the text, that truly develop skills that can be used in one's personal and professional lives.
- Flexibility—use all or only some of the features; select the ones that work for you.

CHANGES TO THE EIGHTH EDITION

This text's focus on continuous improvement has resulted in increased sales of each edition, making it the best-selling human relations textbook on the market. In keeping with this focus, I'm pleased to offer new and improved features for the eighth edition.

- *New References.* The text has been completely updated. There are now 1,390 new references, for a total of 1,471, which is an average of 93 per chapter. Thus, 94.5 percent of the references are new to this edition.
- *New Review Learning Outcomes.* The Review has been changed to provide a summary of the learning outcomes that appear at the beginning and within the chapter. However, the fill-in key terms section has been maintained.
- *New Review True/False Questions.* Each learning outcome summary in the review section is followed by a true/false question that relates to that section of the text. The false statements require students to correct them. Answers are given at the end of the chapter and include the corrections for the false statements, aiding in students' learning of the concepts.
- *New Communication Skills Questions.* New to this edition, there are 129 communication skills questions, an average of approximately 9 per chapter, which can be used for class discussion and/or written assignments. This new feature does not ask for a simple review of text material; these questions require critical thinking and personal opinions based on the text concepts.
- *Development of AACSB Competencies.* Chapter 1 discusses the Association to Advance Collegiate Schools of Business (AACSB), and each of the skill builders states the AACSB competencies developed through the exercise.
- *Revised Opening Section.* The opening section of each chapter, which addresses how the chapter concepts affect behavior, human relations, and performance, has been shortened to make it more concise and has been updated with all new references.
- *New Cases.* Half of the cases are new and the others have been updated.
- *New Ethical Dilemmas.* Some of the ethical dilemmas are new and the others have been updated and shortened. New questions have been added.
- *Other Improvements.* Some of the learning outcomes, exhibits, self-assessments, and skill-building exercises are new or have been revised.

SUPPLEMENTS FOR INSTRUCTORS AND STUDENTS

Online Learning Center—Instructor's Edition, www.mhhe.com/lussier8e

- *Instructor's Manual:* Written by the author, the Instructor's Manual includes the recommended answers for the application features, chapter outlines, learning outcomes, application situations, cases, and objective cases; sample answers to work applications; and support material for video cases and skill-building exercises.
- *Testbank:* Three types of questions are included—concept, application, and skill-building. Questions are also labeled with level of difficulty and text page references.
- *PowerPoint:* Slides include figures, tables, and graphics from the text, as well as additional material not found in the book.

Video DVD (ISBN 0073263478)

The Behavior Model Videos on the DVD focus on the following topics:

Overview	2:50
Learning Styles	4:20
Attitudes	5:08
Success	4:38
Response Styles	8:26
Situational Communications	5:22
Initiating Conflict Resolution	4:00
Mediating Conflict Resolution	8.35
Situational Supervision	4:45
Giving Praise	1:10
Power	3:25
Groups	7:00
Situational Problem Solving and Decision Making	7:00
Increasing Performance	3:30
Training	6:00
Coaching Model (increasing performance)	3:10
Evaluative Performance Appraisal	8:17
Developmental Performance Appraisal	5:00
Force Field Analysis	5:20
Handling Complaints	6:10

Online Learning Center—Student Edition, www.mhhe.com/lussier8e

The student site includes self-grading quizzes and chapter review materials. In addition, a premium content access code allows students to access online Self-Assessments, Test Your Knowledge exercises, and Manager's Hot Seat interactive videos.

The Manager's Hot Seat Videos Online, www.mhhe.com/MHS

In today's workplace, managers are confronted daily with issues like ethics, diversity, working in teams, and the virtual workplace. The Manager's Hot Seat videos allow students to watch as 15 real managers apply their years of experience to confront these issues. Students assume the role of the manager as they watch the video and answer multiple choice questions that pop up forcing them to make decisions on the spot. They learn from the manager's mistakes and successes, and then do a report critiquing the manager's approach by defending their reasoning. Reports can be emailed or printed out for credit.

ACKNOWLEDGMENTS

I want to thank Dr. Herbert Sherman, Professor of Management—Long Island University (Brooklyn Campus), for writing seven new cases and updating three others.

Special thanks to the reviewers of the eighth edition of my manuscript for their excellent recommendations:

Mary Hedberg, *Johnson County Community College*

Jane Bowerman, *University of Oklahoma*

Margaret Ryan, *Highline Community College*

Mofidul Islam, *Columbia Southern University*

Lydia E. Anderson, *Fresno City College*

Marilyn J. Carlson, *Clark State Community College*

John Thiele, *Cañada College*

Rachel Erickson, *National College of Business and Technology*

Thanks also to reviewers of past editions:

Daniel Bialas, *Muskegon Community College*

Cindy Brown, *South Plains College*

Robert Losik, *Southern New Hampshire University*

Daniel Lybrook, *Purdue University*

Thomas McDermott, *Pittsburgh Technical Institute*

Therese Palacios, *Palo Alto College*

Margaret V. Ryan, *Highline Community College*

Thomas J. Shaughnessy, *Illinois Central College*

Mary Alice Smith, *Tarrant County College*

Joseph Wright, *Portland Community College*

Boyd Dallos, *Lake Superior College*

Sally Martin Egge, *Cardinal Stritch University*

Brian E. Perryman, *University of Phoenix*

Glenna Vanderhoof, *Southwest Missouri State University*

Marion Weldon, *Edmonds Community College*

Lee Higgins, *Southeast Community College—Beatrice Campus*

Janet Weber, *McCook Community College*

William Weisgerber, *Saddleback College*

Andy C. Saucedo, *Dona Ana Community College*

Charleen Jaeb, *Cuyahoga Community College*

John J. Heinsius, *Modesto Junior College*

Roger E. Besst, *Muskingum Area Technical College*

Rebecca S. Ross, *Shenango Valley School of Business*

Thomas E. Schillar, *University of Puget Sound*

Rosemary Birkel Wilson, *Washtenaw Community College*

Thomas J. Shaughnessy, *Illinois Central College*

Edward J. LeMay, *Massasoit Community College*

Julie Campbell, *Adams State College*

John Gubbay, *Moraine Valley Community College*

Ruth Dixon, *Diablo Valley College*

John J. Harrington, *New Hampshire College*

Robert Wall Edge, *Commonwealth College*

Abbas Nadim, *University of New Haven*

Steve Kober, *Pierce College*

Dee Dunn, *Commonwealth College*

Marlene Frederick, *New Mexico State University at Carlsbad*

Linda Saarela, *Pierce College*

David Backstrom, *Allan Hancock College*

Rob Taylor, *Indiana Vocational Technical College*

Warren Sargent, *College of the Sequoias*

Jane Binns, *Washtenaw Community College*

Charles W. Beem, *Bucks County Community College*

Robert Nixon, *Prairie State College*

Leo Kiesewetter, *Illinois Central College*

Stephen C. Branz, *Triton College*

William T. Price, Jr., *Virginia Polytechnic Institute and State University*

Jerry F. Gooddard, *Aims Community College*

Rex L. Bishop, *Charles Community College*

Bill Anton, *DeVard Community College*

Stew Rosencrans, *University of Central Florida*

John Magnuson, *Spokane Community College*

Doug Richardson, *Eastfield College*

Thanks to the following students for suggesting improvements:

Doug Nguyen, *Truckee Meadows Community College of Nevada*

Richard Gardner, *New Hampshire College*

Peter Blunt, *New Hampshire College*

Christianne Erwin, *Truckee Meadows Community College*

Robert Neal Chase, *New Hampshire College*

Cheryl Guiff, *Taylor University Online*

CONTACT ME WITH FEEDBACK

I wrote this book for you. Let me know what you think of it. Write to me and tell me what you did and/or didn't like about it. More specifically, how could it be improved? I will be responsive to your feedback. If I use your suggestion for improvement, your name and college will be listed in the acknowledgment section of the next edition. I sincerely hope that you will develop your human relations skills through this book.

Robert N. Lussier, Professor of Management
Management Department
Springfield College
Springfield, MA 01109
413-748-3202
rlussier@spfldcol.edu

CONTENTS IN BRIEF

CONTENTS

HUMAN RELATIONS IN ORGANIZATIONS

APPLICATIONS AND SKILL BUILDING

EIGHTH EDITION

Intrapersonal Skills: Behavior, Human Relations, and Performance Begin with You

CHAPTER 1

Understanding Behavior, Human Relations, and Performance

International Business Machines (IBM) is a world-leading information technologies company, headquartered in Armonk, New York. At year-end 2007, IBM had $120.4 billion in assets, revenue of more than $98.8 billion, and a net income of $10.4 billion. IBM had 386,558 employees who require lots of effective human relations. The company's mission statement is: "At IBM, we strive to lead in the invention, development and manufacture of the industry's most advanced information technologies, including computer systems, software, storage systems and microelectronics. We translate these advanced technologies into value for our customers through our professional solutions, services and consulting businesses worldwide."[1] For more information on IBM, visit its Web site at www.ibm.com.

When Olin Ready graduated from college, he accepted his first full-time job with IBM. As he drove to work on his first day, he thought: How will I fit in? Will my peers and new boss Nancy Westwood like me? Will I be challenged by my job? Will I be able to get raises and promotions? At about the same time, Nancy was also driving to work thinking about Olin: Will Olin fit in with his peers? Will he be open to my suggestions and leadership? Will Olin work hard and be a high performer?

What would you do to ensure success if you were Olin? What would you do to ensure Olin's success if you were Nancy? Meeting employees' needs while achieving the organization's objectives is the goal of positive human relations in any organization.

WHY HUMAN RELATIONS SKILLS ARE SO IMPORTANT

Learning Outcome

1. Explain why human relations skills are important.

We begin by discussing what's in this book for you, followed by a look at some of the major myths about human relations and the realities of why human relations skills are so important. We then discuss the goal of human relations and the total person approach to human relations.

What's in It for Me?

It's natural to be thinking, What can I get from this book, or What's in it for me? This is a common question in all human relations, although it is seldom directly asked and answered. Here is the short, bottom-line answer: The better you can work with people—and that is what the course is all about—the more successful you will be in your personal and professional lives.[2] It's about relationships.[3] This may be one of the few courses you take in which you can actually use what you learn during the course in your personal life. You don't need to wait until you graduate to apply what you learn, and you can develop your human relations skills.[4] Now let's expand on what's in it for you by exploring some of the myths and realities surrounding human relations.

Myths and Reality about Human Relations

Four myths about human relations are: (1) Technical skills are more important than human relations skills; (2) it's just common sense; (3) global diversity is overemphasized; and (4) leaders are born, not made.

Myth 1: Technical Skills Are More Important Than Human Relations Skills

Some students believe that a human relations or organizational behavior (OB) course is less important than more technical courses, such as computer science and accounting. However, the reality is that in a survey of college graduates, human relations is rated among the most valuable courses taken.[5] Many students state that their human relations course is their most interesting course because it is about them.[6] In fact, human relations is about you and how you get along with your family, friends, coworkers, and everyone else you interact with.[7] Students also state that they like the course because they can use it in their day-to-day human relations immediately, in both their personal and professional lives.[8] Do you like to get your own way or to get what you want? Human relations skills will help you ethically achieve your personal and professional goals, as well as organizational goals.[9] By studying human relations, you will learn skills that will help you in situations like Nancy's and Olin's in the opening case.

People working together are the source of technological innovation.[10] Top-level managers spend about 95 percent of their time dealing with people issues and only 5 percent with technical issues.[11] Recruiters at major corporations say technical skills are not an issue; they seek job candidates with strong human relations skills.[12] The technology-oriented IBM gives the average employee 40 hours of training per year, with about 32 of those hours related to human relations.

Myth 2: Human Relations Is Just Common Sense

Some students believe that human relations is simple and just common sense. Do all the people in organizations get along and work well together? If human relations is just common sense, then why do most experienced managers cite people problems as their most troubling and problematic issue?[13] Human relations skills represent the single biggest reason for career success or failure. Personal qualities account for 85 percent of the factors contributing to job success, according to the Carnegie Foundation. Of the people fired from their jobs, 66 percent were fired because they failed to get along with people, according to the Harvard Bureau of Vocational Guidance. During the hiring process, managers want to know if you will get along and work well with their employees and customers.[14] This course explains the important topic of human behavior and helps you better understand why and how people behave in particular ways in their workplaces.[15]

Myth 3: Global Diversity Is Overemphasized

Some students believe that diversity is not important, but it is.[16] With continued global expansion, worldwide suppliers and customers, and changes in communication technology, many people are in contact with people from various cultures on a daily basis.[17] This multicultural contact increases the need for employees with good human relations skills, who can work with people with diverse backgrounds. Years ago, organizations moved to a team-based approach to management, and the trend continues on a global basis.[18] Even in American organizations that do business only in the United States, the workforce continues to become more diverse, and it will continue to do so as the number of immigrants continues to surge. It has been estimated that by the year 2030, fewer than 50 percent of the U.S. population will be white. Clearly, diversity is not overemphasized. Good human relations skills will be vital to our success in such a diverse global economy.

Myth 4: Leaders Are Born Not Made   Some students believe they can't develop their leadership skill, but they can if they work at it.[19] Effective leaders have good human relations skills; leadership training includes human relations skills.[20] The question "Are leaders born or made?" has been researched over the years. Leadership experts agree that leadership skills can be developed.[21] Virtually all the large, major corporations spend millions of dollars each year on leadership training.[22] Why would they spend all that money if human relations skills could not be developed? Regardless of your natural ability to get along and work well with people, using the material in this book, you can develop your human relations skills.

WORK APPLICATIONS

1. In your own words, explain why human relations skills are important to you. How will they help you in your career?

Throughout this book we use many important, or key, terms. To ensure that you have a clear understanding of these terms, when a key term first appears, we present it in **bold letters** with its definition *italicized*.

Goal of Human Relations

Learning Outcome

2. Discuss the goal of human relations.

The term **human relations** *means interactions among people*. When Olin Ready arrives at IBM on his first day of work, he will interact with his new boss, Nancy. Next, a variety of people will help orient and train Olin. Later, as he performs his daily tasks, Olin will interact with Nancy and his coworkers, as well as with people from other departments and with customers. Olin's success at IBM will be based on human relations, and his job satisfaction will affect his personal life.

The **goal of human relations** *is to create a win–win situation by satisfying employee needs while achieving organizational objectives*. A **win–win situation** *occurs when the organization and the employees get what they want*. When an employee asks, What's in it for me?, that employee is expressing his or her needs. When a manager expects high levels of performance from employees, that manager is identifying organizational objectives. When employees and organizational goals align, performance tends to follow.[23]

Creating a win–win situation applies to human relations at all levels, not just management–employee relations. For example, members of a department often must share the work. If Olin does not do his share of the work at IBM, he creates problems within the department. (This would be an I-win–coworkers-lose situation.) Coworker Mary may decide it is not fair that she has to do more work than Olin. Consequently, Mary may argue with Olin, slow down her performance, or complain to their boss, Nancy. Or if Olin and coworker Ray do not like each other, their dislike may affect their behavior, the human relations in the department, and the department and organization's performance. Nancy's job is to make sure the human relations within her department have a positive effect on her department's performance. Conflicts usually arise because of a lack of a win–win situation.[24] In Chapter 7, you will learn how to create win–win situations when facing conflicts.

WORK APPLICATIONS

2. Give an example, personal if possible, of a situation in which the goal of human relations was met. Explain how the individual's needs were met and how the organizational objectives were achieved.

This book discusses the goal of human relations as it applies to various topics. One goal of this book is to develop your ability to create win–win situations in a variety of settings, including your professional and personal lives.

The Total Person Approach

The **total person approach** *realizes that an organization employs the whole person, not just his or her job skills.* People play many roles throughout their lives, indeed, throughout each day. Olin, therefore, is more than just an employee; he is also a father, a member of the PTA, a scout leader, a jogger, a student, and a fisherman. At work, Olin will not completely discard all other roles to be a worker only. His off-the-job life will affect his job performance at IBM. Thus, if Olin has a bad day at work, it may not be related to his job, but to another of his life's roles. Also, a bad day at work can affect personal life satisfaction.[25]

Analog Services, 3M, Marriott, Hewlett-Packard, IBM, and numerous other organizations view employees as total people. Such organizations are trying to give employees a better quality of work life.[26] Consider Federal Express Corporation. FedEx pays good wages, offers a profit-sharing program, and maintains excellent communications with employees. Fred Smith, founder and chairman of Federal Express, states that management is interested in making FedEx a good place to work, where people are dealt with as human beings rather than as numbers.

WORK APPLICATIONS

3. Give a specific example, personal if possible, that supports the total person approach. Explain how an individual's job performance was affected by off-the-job problems.

BEHAVIOR, HUMAN RELATIONS, AND ORGANIZATIONAL PERFORMANCE

Levels of Behavior

The study of human relations looks closely at the way people behave.[27] **Behavior** *is what people do and say.* Human relations fuel behavior. The three **levels of behavior** *are individual, group, and organizational.* Human relations take place at the group and organizational levels.

Individual- and Group-Level Behavior   As Olin types a letter on the computer or fills out requisition forms, he is engaged in individual behavior. **Group behavior** *consists of the things two or more people do and say as they interact.* Individual behavior influences group behavior.[28] For example, as Olin and Mary work on a project together or attend department meetings, their actions are considered group behavior. Studying the chapters in this book, particularly Chapters 1 through 4, should help you understand and predict your own behavior, and that of others, in an organizational setting. In addition, Chapters 12 and 13 will help you gain a better understanding of how your behavior affects others, and how their behavior affects you in teams.

Organizational-Level Behavior   An **organization** *is a group of people working to achieve one or more objectives.* This book focuses on human relations in both profit and nonprofit organizations in which people work to make a living. Organizations are created to produce goods and services for the larger society. If you have ever worked, you have been a part of an organization. You also come into contact with organizations on a regular basis, such as when you go into a store, school, church, post office, or health club.

As individuals and groups interact, their collective behavior constitutes the organization's behavior.[29] Thus **organizational behavior** *is the collective behavior of an organization's individuals and groups.* IBM is an organization, and its collective behavior is based on Olin's behavior, the behavior of Nancy's department, and the behavior of all other departments combined.

This book explores all three levels of behavior. Chapters 2 through 4 focus primarily on individual behavior, Chapters 5 through 11 examine the skills influencing all three levels of behavior, and Chapters 12 through 15 focus on group and organizational behavior.

Exhibit 1.1 illustrates the three levels of behavior. The focus of level three is on the organization as a whole. At this level, the responsibility of the board of directors and the

EXHIBIT 1.1 |

Levels of Behavior

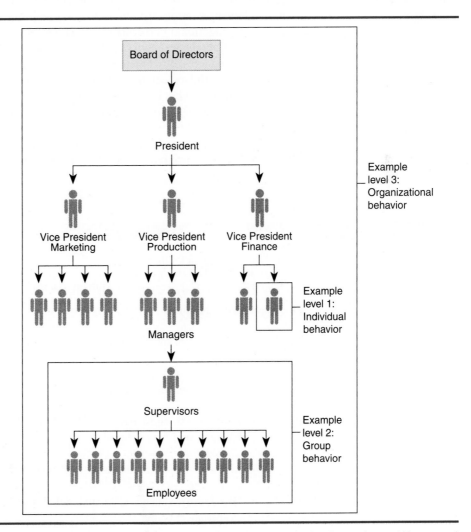

Each manager would have one or more supervisors reporting to him or her, and each supervisor would have several employees reporting to him or her.

president is to focus on the entire organization. The focus of level two is on the behavior and human relations within and between groups such as the marketing, production, and finance departments. The focus of level one is on the behavior of any one person in the organization.[30]

Exhibit 1.1 is a formal organization structure showing authority and reporting relationships. However, it does not show the multiple possible human relations that exist outside the formal structure. For example, the president could interact with any employee, an employee could interact with a manager, and a supervisor could interact with a vice president's administrative assistant.

WORK APPLICATIONS

4. Give two specific examples of your involvement in human relations—one positive and one negative. Also identify the level of behavior for each example.

The Relationship between Individual and Group Behavior and Organizational Performance

Learning Outcome

3. Describe the relationship between individual and group behavior and organizational performance.

Human relations has an effect on performance.[31] Throughout this course you will learn how human relations affects individual and group behavior, and the resulting effects on organizational performance. **Performance** *is the extent to which expectations or objectives have been met.* For example, if the objective of a production worker is to produce 100 widgets per day and the employee produces 100 widgets, performance is at the expected level. However, some workers may produce less than 100 widgets, while others may produce more than 100 widgets. Performance is usually measured on a continuum contrasted by high and low levels of performance, or ranked on a scale of 1 through 10. The same concept holds true for the entire organization. Performance is a relative term. Performance levels are more meaningful when compared to past performance or the performance of others within and/or outside the organization.[32]

APPLICATION SITUATIONS

Understanding Important Terms

AS 1–1

Identify each statement by its key term.

A. Behavior	C. Human relations	E. Performance
B. Goal of human relations	D. Organization	F. Total person approach

_____ 1. Bill and Sara are discussing how to complete a project they are working on together.

_____ 2. Julio just delivered his report to the outgoing mailbox.

_____ 3. It's 4:50 P.M. and Cindy typed the last bill to be sent out today with the 5:00 P.M. mail.

_____ 4. All the people listed above are members of an _____.

_____ 5. "Because I've been doing a good job, I got a raise; now I can buy that new car I want so badly."

EXHIBIT 1.2 | The Relationship between Individual and Group Behavior and Organizational Performance

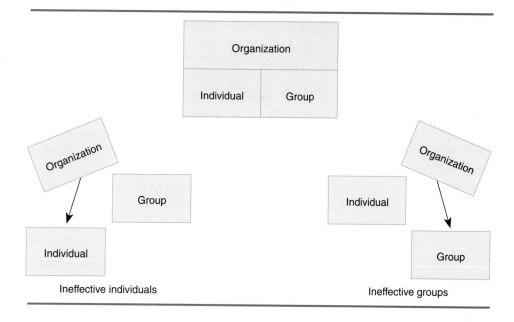

The Systems Effect   A system is a set of two or more interactive elements. The systems approach, developed by Russell Ackoff, focuses on the whole system with an emphasis on the relationships between its parts. The whole cannot be decomposed into independent subsets.[33] For our purposes, under the **systems effect** *all people in the organization are affected by at least one other person, and each person affects the whole group or organization.* The organization's performance is based on the combined performance of each individual and group. To have high levels of performance, the organization must have high-performing individuals and groups.[34] Groups are the building blocks of the organization. As a result of the systems effect, the destructive behavior of one individual hurts that group and other departments as well. In addition, the destructive behavior of one department affects other departments and the organization's performance. Systems thinking is needed to understand performance.[35]

The challenge to management is to develop high-performing individuals and groups.[36] In a sense, individuals and groups are the foundation of an organization.[37] If either is ineffective, the organization cannot stand. See Exhibit 1.2 for a graphic illustration.

The Relationship between Behavior, Human Relations, and Organizational Performance

Learning Outcome

4. Describe the relationship between behavior, human relations, and organizational performance.

The focus of this book is behavior, human relations, and performance from a systems effect perspective. People, not simply technology, are the key to increased levels of performance.[38]

WORK APPLICATIONS

5. Give two specific examples of how human relations affected your performance—one positive and the other negative. Be specific in explaining the effects of human relations in both cases.

APPLICATION SITUATIONS

Focus of Study

AS 1–2

Identify the focus of study in each statement below by selecting two answers. First select the level of behavior:

A. Individual   B. Group   C. Organizational

Then select the scope of study:

A. Behavior   B. Human relations   C. Performance

_____ _____ 6. Bill and Sara are discussing how to complete a project they are working on together.

_____ _____ 7. The management hierarchy is from the president down to the employee level.

_____ _____ 8. Carl is writing a letter to a supplier to correct an error in billing.

_____ _____ 9. The marketing department has just exceeded its sales quota for the quarter.

_____ _____ 10. IBM has just completed its income statement for the quarter.

Just as people are the foundation of the organization, behavior and human relations are the foundation supporting performance. If either is ineffective, performance will suffer.[39] Exhibit 1.3 gives a graphic illustration.

EXHIBIT 1.3 | The Relationship between Behavior, Human Relations, and Performance

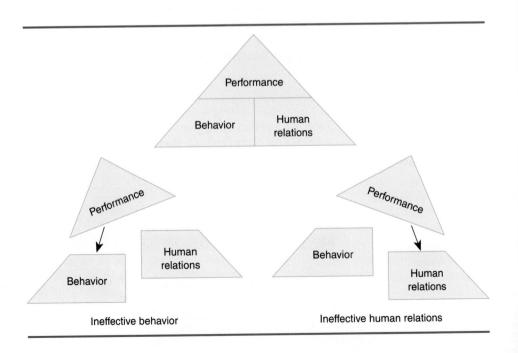

HUMAN RELATIONS: PAST, PRESENT, AND FUTURE

Human Relations Is a Multidisciplined Science

Learning Outcome

5. Briefly describe the history of the study of human relations.

Popularly called *organizational behavior* and rooted in the behavioral sciences, the science of human relations was developed in the late 1940s. It is based primarily on psychology (which attempts to determine why individuals behave the way they do) and sociology (which attempts to determine how group dynamics affect organizational performance); social psychology, economics, and political science have also contributed to organizational behavior.

During the 1950s, research in human behavior was conducted in large organizations. By the late 1970s, organizational behavior was recognized as a discipline in its own right, with teachers, researchers, and practitioners being trained in organizational behavior itself. Organizational behavior is a social science that has built its knowledge base on a sound foundation of scientific theory and research.[40] Human relations takes a practical, applied approach.[41] It attempts to anticipate and prevent problems before they occur and to solve existing problems of interpersonal relations in organizations.[42]

The Early Years: Frederick Taylor and Robert Owen

In early America, most people worked on farms or were self-employed tailors, carpenters, shoemakers, or blacksmiths. Then, during the Industrial Revolution people left the farms to work in factories that were all privately owned. The corporation form of business did not become prominent until much later. These early family-run businesses were concerned with profits, not employees, and managers viewed people only as a source of production. They did not realize how workers' needs affected production. Since the labor supply was plentiful and the cost of labor low, they could easily replace employees who had complaints. In this situation, most of the early owner-managers gave little thought to the working conditions, health, or safety of their employees. Working conditions were very poor—people worked from dawn until dusk under intolerable conditions of disease, filth, danger, and scarcity of resources. They had to work this way just to survive; there was no welfare system—you worked or you starved.

Frederick Taylor   Frederick Taylor, an engineer known as the "father of scientific management," focused on analyzing and redesigning jobs more efficiently in the late 1800s and early 1900s, which led to the idea of mass production. Scientific managers focused on production, not people.[43] They were not in touch with human behavior, assuming that workers always acted rationally and were motivated simply by money; later these were found to be false assumptions. Also, Taylor failed to recognize the social needs of employees and placed them in isolated jobs.[44]

Robert Owen   Robert Owen, a young Welsh industrialist and social theorist, in 1800 was considered the first manager-entrepreneur to understand the need to improve the work environment and the employee's overall situation. In 1920, Owen was called "the real father" of personnel administration.[45] He believed that profit would be increased if employees worked shorter hours, were paid adequately, and were provided with sufficient food and housing. He refused to employ children under the age of 11. (In the early 1800s, children went to work full-time at the age of 9.) Owen taught his employees cleanliness and temperance and improved their working conditions. Other entrepreneurs of this time period did not follow his ideas. Compared with today's conditions, Owen's were primitive—but they were a beginning.

Elton Mayo and the Hawthorne Studies

From the mid-1920s to the early 1930s, Elton Mayo and his associates from Harvard University conducted research at the Western Electric Hawthorne Plant near Chicago. The research conducted through the Hawthorne Studies has become a landmark in the human relations field. In fact, **Elton Mayo** *is called the "father of human relations."* As a consequence of these studies, several unexpected discoveries were made in regard to the human relations in organizations:[46]

1. The **Hawthorne effect** *refers to an increase in performance caused by the special attention given to employees, rather than tangible changes in the work.* During the research, Mayo changed the lighting and ventilation. To his surprise, performance went up regardless of the working conditions. Through interviews, Mayo realized that the control group during the research felt important because of all the attention it got; therefore performance increased because of the special attention given to employees. It wasn't until Mayo discovered the Hawthorne effect that he extended his study. What was to last only a few months lasted six years. With the knowledge of the results of the Hawthorne Studies, some managers used human relations as a means of manipulating employees, while others took the attitude that a happy worker is a productive worker. Studies have shown that happy workers are usually, but not always, more productive than unhappy workers. In this context, both approaches were unsuccessful at improving performance.

WORK APPLICATIONS

6. Give a specific example, personal if possible, of the Hawthorne effect. It could be when a teacher, coach, or boss gave you special attention that resulted in your increased performance.

---

2. Employees have many needs beyond those satisfied by money.

3. Informal work groups have a powerful influence within the organization. For example, work group members can band together and decide the level of production, regardless of management's standards, and influence the group to produce at that level. The group pressures members who produce more or less than the group's established production rate to conform.

4. Supervisor–employee human relations affect the quality and quantity of employee output. Employees who have positive relations with their boss are more productive than employees who do not like their boss. Having good human relations does not mean that a manager has to be popular. No relationship exists between popularity and the speed at which people are promoted.

5. Many employee needs are satisfied off the job. Managers do not always control the factors that motivate employees.

6. Employee relations affect employee performance. Employees meet social needs through their interactions with fellow employees.

The 1930s to the 1970s

During the depression of the 1930s, unions gained strength and in many cases literally forced management to look more closely at the human side of the organization and meet employees' needs for better working conditions, higher pay, and shorter hours.

During the 1940s and 1950s, other major research projects were conducted in a number of organizations. Some of the research was conducted by the University of Michigan, which conducted studies in leadership and motivation; Ohio State University, which also studied leadership and motivation; the Tavistock Institute of Human Relations in London, which studied various subjects; and the National Training Laboratories in Bethel, Maine, which studied group dynamics. Peter Drucker's management by objectives was popular in the 1950s.

During the 1960s, Douglas McGregor published Theory X and Theory Y.[47] A discussion of his theories, which contrast the way managers view employees, appears in Chapter 3. In the same time period, Eric Berne introduced transactional analysis (TA). (See Chapter 7 for a detailed discussion of TA.) Sensitivity training was popular in the 1960s.

During the 1970s, interest in human relations probably peaked. Quality circles were popular. By the late 1970s, the term *human relations* was primarily replaced with the more commonly used term *organizational behavior.*

The 1980s to the 1990s

In the 1980s, the U.S. rate of productivity was much lower than that of Japan. William Ouchi, who conducted research to determine why Japan was more productive than the United States, discovered that Japanese organizations were managed differently than U.S. organizations. While studying several U.S. organizations, Ouchi discovered that a few particularly successful firms did not follow the typical U.S. model. After years of research and investigation, Ouchi developed Theory Z.[48] **Theory Z** *integrates common business practices in the United States and Japan into one middle-ground framework appropriate for use in the United States.*

In search of excellence, Thomas Peters and Robert Waterman conducted research to determine the characteristics of successful organizations.[49] During the 1980s, their work was criticized as companies identified as excellent began to have problems. Total quality management was popular in the 1980s.

In the 1990s, the trend toward increased participation of employees as a means of improving human relations and organizational performance continued. Edward Lawler suggested the use of high-involvement management, which includes greater levels of participation at the lowest level of the organization. As a result, employees have more input into management decisions and how they perform their jobs. The use of groups and teams was popular in the 1990s.

APPLICATION SITUATIONS

Human Relations History

AS 1–3

Identify the following people with their contribution to human relations:

A. Eric Berne   C. William Ouchi   E. Tom Peters

B. Elton Mayo   D. Robert Owen   F. Frederick Taylor

_____ 11. Excellence in American corporations.

_____ 12. Theory Z.

_____ 13. Transactional analysis.

_____ 14. The father of personnel administration.

_____ 15. The Hawthorne Studies.

Current and Future Challenges in the 21st Century

Learning Outcome

6. State some of the trends and challenges in the field of human relations.

We've discussed the history of human relations; now let's briefly discuss its current and future trends and challenges. In Chapters 2 through 15, we will discuss these topics in detail.

- **Globalization, change, innovation, and speed.** CEOs rate globalization as a challenge to business leadership in the 21st century. The trend toward globalization has clearly changed the speed and the way we do business today.[50]

- **Technology.** Technology has enabled the innovation and speed we have now in the global economy; the rate of technology change will not slow down. Because technology is created by people, they have to use it effectively to compete.[51]

- **Diversity.** Due to globalization, diversity becomes more important. You need to understand how to work with people around the world.[52]

- **Learning and knowledge.** The key to success today is using knowledge effectively to continually innovate in order to compete in the new global economy.[53]
- **Ethics.** Media coverage of Enron, WorldCom, and other business scandals has heightened awareness of the need for ethical business practices, as well as new corporate governance requirements.[54]
- **Crisis.** In the wake of September 11, 2001, organizations have developed plans to prevent and/or deal with crises that may occur. Safety and security issues have led to new human relations behaviors.

As stated, we will talk more about all of these challenges in later chapters.

WORK APPLICATIONS

7. Explain how one of the above trends or challenges could personally affect your human relations.

APPLICATION SITUATIONS

Trends and Challenges of Human Relations

AS 1–4

Identify the factor in each statement as:

A. External forces   B. Changing workforce   C. Technology

_____ 16. "First we had to contend with the Japanese; now the Koreans and Chinese are serious competitors as well."

_____ 17. "The number of immigrants employed is increasing because they are the only ones applying for the jobs."

_____ 18. "Every time I look in the business section of the paper, it seems as though someone is coming out with a new or improved computer. How do I know which one to choose?"

_____ 19. "We had better do some training to help prevent getting charged with sexual harassment."

_____ 20. "These kids today don't have the dedication to come to work, and on time, like we did when we were their age."

DEVELOPING HUMAN RELATIONS SKILLS

Through gaining a better understanding of your behavior and that of others in organizations, you will be more skilled at interacting with people and better prepared to anticipate and eliminate human relations problems before they occur.[55] As you develop your human relations skills, you will be better prepared to deal effectively with specific human relations problems.[56] These skills are not gimmicks to empower you to manipulate people, and they will not offer simple solutions to the human relations problems you will face in organizations. People are complex and different, and the approach you use to solve a human relations problem with one person may not work with a different person.

This book gives you suggestions, guidelines, and models to follow. Although these guidelines do not guarantee success, they will increase your probability of successful human relations in organizations.

Wal-Mart: People or Profit?

Wal-Mart Chief Executive Lee Scott seems to have a real problem. His firm has been accused by many in the press of numerous unethical business practices dealing specifically with employees. These include hiring illegal immigrants, busting unions, locking employees in the building when taking inventory, denying meal breaks, paying subsistence level wages while providing no benefits, and following hiring practices that discriminate against employees based upon their general health.

CEO Scott has taken steps to bolster Wal-Mart's public image and address the treatment of its employees. For example, Wal-Mart's Web site states that the typical Super Center raises or gives $30,000 to $50,000 a year to local charities ranging from youth programs to literacy councils, while saving working families over $2,300 per household. Wal-Mart also claims to have competitive wages, a flexible schedule, and good benefits including family care and college tuition reimbursement.

So with all of this good news, what could be the problem? Investors looking at the firm's stock price are less than happy. Over a five-year period, Wal-Mart's stock hit a high and dropped close to its five-year low. Analysts are now claiming that CEO Scott has been paying too much attention to the company's lackluster public image and human relations, and not enough to its lackluster bottom line.

Questions

1. How is Wal-Mart trying to implement the total person approach to management?

2. How have these actions attempted to address the current and future challenges in the 21st century?

3. If you were CEO Scott, how would you address those critics who think that Wal-Mart is focusing too much on people and not enough on profits?

4. If you attended an annual Wal-Mart stockholders meeting, what would you tell CEO Scott to do?

Source: http://www.walmart.com.

As the poet Johann Wolfgang von Goethe said, "Knowing is not enough; we must apply what we learn."[57] Human relations is one of the few courses you can use immediately. Most of the material you will learn can and should be used in your daily personal life with your family, friends, and other people with whom you interact. If you presently work, use this material on the job to develop your human relations skills.

WORK APPLICATIONS

8. Do you believe that you can and will develop your human relations abilities and skills through this course? Explain your answer.

Learning Outcome

7. Explain nine guidelines for effective human relations.

Human Relations Guidelines

Are you the kind of person others enjoy being around? Find out by completing Self-Assessment Exercise 1–1. Then read on.

Self-Assessment Exercise 1–1

Likability

Select the number from 1 to 5 that best describes your use of the following behavior, and write it on the line before each statement.

(5) Usually　　(4) Frequently　　(3) Occasionally　　(2) Seldom　　(1) Rarely

_____ 1. I'm an optimist. I look for the good in people and situations, rather than the negative.

_____ 2. I avoid complaining about people, things, and situations.

_____ 3. I show a genuine interest in other people. I compliment them on their success.

_____ 4. I smile.

_____ 5. I have a sense of humor. I can laugh at myself.

**Self-Assessment
Exercise 1–1 (*continued*)**

> _____ 6. I make an effort to learn people's names and address them by name during conversations.
>
> _____ 7. I truly listen to others.
>
> _____ 8. I help other people cheerfully.
>
> _____ 9. I think before I act and avoid hurting others with my behavior.
>
> _____ 10. If I were to ask all the people I work/worked with to answer these nine questions for me, they would select the same responses that I did.
>
> To determine your likability, add the 10 numbers you selected as your answers. The total will range from 10 to 50. Place it here _____ and on the continuum below.
>
> Unlikable   10 - - - - - - - - - 20 - - - - - - - - - 30 - - - - - - - - - 40 - - - - - - - - - 50   Likable

If you want to get ahead in an organization, it is important to do a good job. But it is also important that people like you. If people like you, they will forgive just about anything you do wrong. If they don't like you, you can do everything right and it will not matter. Many hardworking, talented people have been bypassed for promotion and fired simply because their bosses or some other high-level managers didn't like them.

No one can tell you exactly how to be likable. People who try too hard are usually not well liked. However, in this section you will learn guidelines for being likable through successful human relations. The guidelines are based on the behavior of successful, likable people who possess human relations skills. Although general in nature, these guidelines apply to most situations.

The nine human relations guidelines are (1) be optimistic, (2) be positive, (3) be genuinely interested in other people, (4) smile and develop a sense of humor, (5) call people by name, (6) listen to people, (7) help others, (8) think before you act, and (9) create win–win situations.

Be Optimistic   Football coach Lou Holtz has said that you choose to be optimistic (happy) or pessimistic (sad). Happiness is nothing more than a poor memory for the bad things that happen to you. We usually find what we're looking for. If you look for, and emphasize, the positive, you will find it.[58] Most successful people are optimistic. Winston Churchill said that success is the ability to go from failure to failure without losing your enthusiasm. Again, having a poor memory for failure leads to happiness. If you catch yourself thinking or behaving like a pessimist, stop, and change to an optimistic thought or action. With time you will need to catch yourself and change behavior less frequently.

Be Positive   Praise and encourage people. People generally don't like to listen to others complain. Have you ever noticed that people ask each other, "How is it going?" but if one person starts complaining about something, the other finds an excuse for not listening. People often avoid complainers, and you should too. Associating with complainers will only depress you. Don't go around criticizing (putting people down), condemning, or spreading rumors. Do you like people to criticize you?[59]

Be Genuinely Interested in Other People   Think about the bosses you have had. Who was your favorite? Why? There is a good chance that this boss was genuinely interested in you as a person, not simply as a means of getting the job done. Think about your friends. One of the reasons you like them is that they show a genuine interest in you. One of the five main reasons managers fail is the "me only" syndrome. Managers who are preoccupied with themselves and too concerned with how much credit they get are insensitive to others. People who feel as though you don't care about them will not come through for you.[60] Do you like self-centered people?

Smile and Develop a Sense of Humor   A smile shows interest and caring. It takes fewer muscles to smile than it does to frown. The adage "Smile and the world smiles with you; weep and you weep alone" has a lot of truth to it. You have probably noticed that frowners are usually unhappy and pessimistic.

Develop a sense of humor.[61] Relax, laugh, and enjoy yourself. Be willing to laugh at yourself. Likable people do not take their jobs or themselves too seriously. Do you like people who always frown and never laugh?

Call People by Name   A person's name is the most important sound in any language. Calling people by the name they prefer shows an interest in them and makes them feel important. If you're not good at remembering names, work at it. Like any skill, it takes a conscious effort and some practice to develop.[62] One simple technique you can use to help you remember people's names when you are introduced is to call them by name two or three times while talking to them.[63] Then call them by name the next time you greet them. If you forget a person's name, whenever possible, ask someone else what it is before contacting the person. Remember that in some cultures, however, it is not polite to call a person by his or her first name. In such a culture, use last names, titles, or positions, as expected.

Listen to People   We learn more by listening than we do by talking. To truly listen we must honestly try to see things from the other person's point of view. Show respect for the other person's opinions. Don't say, "You're wrong," even when the other person is wrong. Such statements only make people defensive and cause arguments, which you should avoid. Saying you disagree has less of an emotional connotation to it. However, when you are wrong, admit it quickly and emphatically. Admitting you're wrong is not a sign of weakness and is often interpreted as a strength. However, not admitting you are wrong is often interpreted as a weakness.

Encourage others to talk about themselves. Ask them questions about themselves, rather than telling them about yourself.[64] This gives you the opportunity to listen and learn while making people feel important. Listening also shows your interest in people.[65] Do you like people who don't listen to you?

Help Others   If you want to help yourself, you can do so only by helping others. It's a basic law of success. People who use people may be somewhat successful in the short run, but those being used usually catch on. Often people who use other people are not successful in the long run. Open and honest relationships in which people help each other meet their needs are usually the best ones.[66] Help others, but don't pry when help is not welcomed. Do you like people who don't help you when you need help?

Think Before You Act   Feel your emotions, but control your behavior.[67] Try not to do and say things you will regret later. Watch your language; don't offend people. It is not always what you say but how you say it that can have a negative impact on human relations. Before you say and do things, think about the possible consequences.[68] Being right is not good enough if it hurts human relations. Conduct your human relations in a positive way.

Create Win–Win Situations   Human relations is about how we behave and treat others.[69] The goal of human relations is to create win–win situations.[70] The best way to get what you want is to help other people get what they want and vice versa. Throughout the book you will be given specific examples of how to create win–win situations.

If Olin follows these nine human relations guidelines at IBM, he will increase his chances of success. If you follow these general guidelines, you too will increase your chances of success in all walks of life. These nine guidelines are just the starting point of what you will learn in this course. For a review of the nine guidelines to effective human relations, see Exhibit 1.4.

EXHIBIT 1.4 | Nine Guidelines to Effective Human Relations

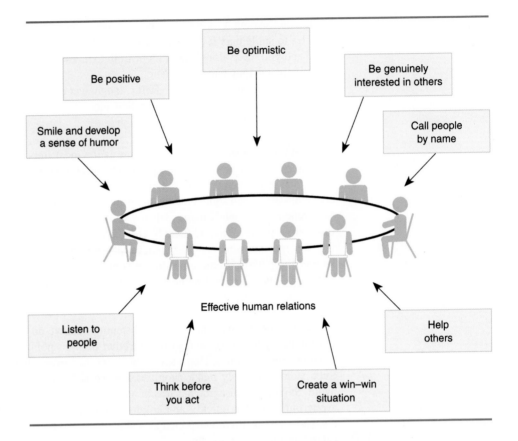

WORK APPLICATIONS

9. Which two of the nine human relations guidelines need the most effort on your part? Which two need the least? Explain your answers.

Handling Human Relations Problems

Even though you follow the human relations guidelines, in any organization there are bound to be times when you disagree with other employees.

Human relations problems often occur when the psychological contract is not met. The *psychological contract* is the shared expectations between people. At work you have expectations of the things your boss and coworkers should and should not do, and they in turn have expectations of you. As long as expectations are met, things go well. However, if expectations are not met, human relations problems occur.[71] Thus, when people share information and negotiate expectations, have clear roles, and are committed to meeting others' expectations, things go well. We'll focus on sharing information and negotiating expectations throughout this book.

When you encounter a human relations problem, you have to decide whether to avoid the problem or to solve it. In most cases, it is advisable to solve human relations problems rather than ignore them. Problems usually get worse rather than solve themselves. When you decide to resolve a human relations problem, you have at least three alternatives:

1. Change the Other Person   Whenever there is a human relations problem, it is easy to blame the other party and expect her or him to make the necessary changes in behavior to meet your expectations. In reality, few human relations problems can be blamed entirely on one party. Both parties usually contribute to the human relations problem. Blaming the other party without taking some responsibility usually results in resentment and defensive behavior. The more you force people to change to meet your expectations, the more difficult it is to maintain effective human relations.

2. Change the Situation If you have a problem getting along with the person or people you work with, you can try to change the situation by working with another person or other people. You may tell your boss you cannot work with so-and-so because of a personality conflict, and ask for a change in jobs. There are cases where this is the only solution; however, when you complain to the boss, the boss often figures that you, not the other party, are the problem. Blaming the other party and trying to change the situation enables you to ignore your own behavior, which may be the actual cause of the problem.

3. Change Yourself Throughout this book, particularly in Part 1, you will be examining your own behavior. Knowing yourself is important to good human relations. In many situations, your own behavior is the only thing you can control. In most human relations problems, the best alternative is to examine others' behavior and try to understand why they are doing and saying the things they are; then examine your own behavior to determine why you are behaving the way you are. In most cases, the logical choice is to change your own behavior. That does not mean doing whatever other people request. In fact, you should be assertive.[72] You are not being forced to change; rather, you are changing your behavior because you elect to do so.[73] When you change your behavior, others may also change.

In each chapter, there are two or more self-assessment instruments to help you better understand your behavior and that of others. It is helpful to examine behavior and to change it, when appropriate, not only throughout this course but throughout life.

WORK APPLICATIONS

10. Give a specific example of a human relations problem in which you elected to change yourself rather than the other person or situation. Be sure to identify your changed behavior.

OBJECTIVES AND ORGANIZATION OF THE BOOK

Let's discuss what we are trying to do throughout this book (objectives) and how we are going to do it (organization).

Objectives of the Book

Management gurus say that professors should be teaching students how to apply the principles learned.[74] This is the overarching objective of the book. Unlike most other courses that teach you concepts, this course takes you to the next level, as you apply the concepts and develop your human relations skills.

As indicated in the title of the book, it has a three-pronged approach to the objectives:

- To teach you the concepts and theories of human relations.
- To develop your ability to apply the human relations concepts through critical thinking.
- To develop your human relations skills in your personal and professional lives.

This book offers some unique features related to each of the three objectives; these features are listed in Exhibit 1.5. You may be tested regarding each objective. To get the most from this book, turn back to the Preface and read the descriptions of these features.

Flexibility There are so many features that your professor will most likely not use every feature with every chapter. Students have different learning style preferences.[75] There is no one right way of doing things. You have the flexibility to use your own approach. You may also use features that your professor does not include in the course requirements.

EXHIBIT 1.5 | The Three-Pronged Approach: Features of the Book

Concepts	Applications	Skill Building
Research-based and current	Opening cases	Self-assessment exercises
Comprehensive coverage	Work applications Ethical dilemmas	Skill-building objectives and AACSB
Systems-oriented	Application situations	Skill-building exercises (three types)
Learning outcomes	Cases	Behavior models
Key terms Exhibits	Objective cases	Behavior model videos
Chapter review and glossary	Internet exercises	Manager's hot seat videos

AACSB Learning Standards

It is important to develop human relations competencies.[76] So how do you know what specific leadership competencies will be important to your career success? For the answer, we have turned to the AACSB (Association for the Advancement of Collegiate Schools of Business), which gives accreditation to business schools. AACSB accreditation is highly sought after, and even the business schools that don't achieve accreditation tend to strive to meet AACSB standards.[77] Below is a list of competencies that are based on AACSB learning standards related to this course.[78]

- **Reflective thinking and self-management.** Students develop reflective thinking through identifying personal strengths and developmental needs as a first step in leading others. Self-assessment is the first step.[79] Each chapter has self-assessment exercises to help you better understand yourself and how to improve your competencies.

- **Analytic skills.** Students learn to set goals, adjust, and resolve problems and make decisions as they respond to internal and external stakeholder needs by applying knowledge in new and unfamiliar circumstances. You will learn how to write objectives in Chapter 9 and how to use participation in decision making in Chapter 13. Essentially all of the application and skill material in every chapter will help you develop your analytical skills.

- **Communication abilities.** Students learn to effectively listen, share ideas, negotiate, and facilitate the flow of information to improve performance. You will develop communication competency in Chapters 5 and 6 and negotiation skills in Chapter 11.

- **Global, multicultural, diversity, and ethical perspectives.** Students are challenged to recognize the impact of global trends on an organization, to value diversity, and to conduct business in an ethical manner. You will develop these competencies in Chapters 2 and 15. In addition, each chapter includes an Ethical Dilemma to help you develop your competency in being ethical based on a given situation.

- **Teamwork.** Students enhance group and individual dynamics in organizations to create a healthy team environment by combining talents and resources for collaboration and information sharing. You will develop team competencies in Chapters 12 and 13, as well as through the exercises in most chapters.

- **Leadership.** Students develop the capacity to lead in organizational situations. This is the focus of last two parts of the book, Chapters 8–15.

- **Strategic management.** Students learn how to develop creative strategies to guide organizations, achieve goals, minimize risks, and gain a competitive advantage. This is the ability to adapt and innovate to solve problems, to cope with unforeseen events, and to manage in unpredictable environments. Chapters 12–15 focus on these concepts, but you will develop these competencies throughout all of the chapters.

Each of the skill-building exercises indicates the AACSB learning standard skill(s) to which the exercise relates.

Organization of the Book

The book is organized in two ways. The first is by the *levels of behavior*. The parts, as well as the chapters within each part, progress from the individual, to the group, to the organizational levels of behavior.

Second, the parts of the book are based on the *domain model of managerial education*. In this model the concept of *skills* has evolved into the concept of competencies. *Competencies* are performance capabilities that distinguish effective from ineffective behavior, human relations, and performance: they are the underlying characteristics of a person that lead to or cause effective and outstanding performance. Every current competency model can be organized in terms of four competency domains: intrapersonal skills, interpersonal skills, leadership skills, and business skills.[80] The first three are human relations skills, and the last is a technical skill.

The three human relations domains, which are discussed below, as well as the levels of behavior, are reflected in the table of contents and the profile form on pages 24 to 25. This form lists the parts and the chapters within each part.

Part 1. Intrapersonal Skills: Behavior, Human Relations, and Performance Begin with You   *Intra* means "within"; thus, **intrapersonal skills** *are within the individual and include characteristics such as personality, attitudes, self-concept, and integrity.* Intrapersonal skills have also been called self-management abilities. Do you need close supervision, or can you manage yourself? Intrapersonal skills are the foundation on which management careers are built. You will learn about, apply, and develop intrapersonal skills in Chapters 2 to 4. We end the book by coming back to intrapersonal skills in Appendix A, by developing a plan for applying human relations skills.

Part 2. Interpersonal Skills: The Foundation of Human Relations   *Inter* means "between"; thus, interpersonal skills are between people, as are human relations. **Interpersonal skill** *is the ability to work well with a diversity of people.* Interpersonal skills have also been called relationship management. How well do you work with others? People with interpersonal, or human relations, skills have the ability to initiate, build, and maintain relationships; to see things from the other person's point of view; and to understand and meet others' expectations.[81] They also have good communication and conflict resolution skills.[82] Interpersonal skills are a hot topic of research because they are critical to team success.[83] Clearly, interpersonal skills are based on, and overlap to some extent, intrapersonal skills.[84] You will learn about, apply, and develop interpersonal skills in Chapters 5 through 7.

Part 3. Leadership Skills: Influencing Others and Part 4. Leadership Skills: Team and Organizational Behavior, Human Relations, and Performance   **Leadership skill** *is the ability to influence others and work well in teams.* You can be a leader without being a manager. Leadership is perhaps the most extensively studied management topic, and courses and programs directed toward training future leaders and improving leadership skills are increasing.[85] Leadership skill includes persistency and the ability to motivate others.[86] You will learn about, apply, and develop leadership skills in Chapters 8 through 15. Leadership skills are based on intrapersonal and interpersonal skills.[87] Thus, the sequence of parts in the book, as well as the chapters within each part, constitutes a logical set of building blocks for your competency and skill development.

It's time to assess your intrapersonal skills, interpersonal skills, and leadership skills. Together, these skills are called human relations skills. The following section focuses on self-assessment, an important intrapersonal skill. People with good intrapersonal skills use self-assessment as the basis for improving their human relations skills, which we will be doing throughout the book.

ASSESSING YOUR HUMAN RELATIONS ABILITIES AND SKILLS

For each of the 43 statements below, record in the blank the number from 1 to 7 that best describes your level of ability or skill. You are not expected to have all high numbers. This assessment will give you an overview of what you will learn in this course. Appendix A contains the same assessment to enable you to compare your skills at the beginning and end of the course.

Low ability/skill					High ability/skill	
1	2	3	4	5	6	7

_____ 1. I understand how personality and perception affect people's behavior, human relations, and performance.

_____ 2. I can describe several ways to handle stress effectively.

_____ 3. I know my preferred learning style (accommodator, diverger, converger, assimilator) and how it affects my behavior, human relations, and performance.

_____ 4. I understand how people acquire attitudes and how attitudes affect behavior, human relations, and performance.

_____ 5. I can describe self-concept and self-efficacy and how they affect behavior, human relations, and performance.

_____ 6. I can list several areas of personal values and state how values affect behavior, human relations, and performance.

_____ 7. I understand how to use a time management system.

_____ 8. I understand how to use time management techniques to get more done in less time with better results.

_____ 9. I know how to develop a career plan and manage my career successfully.

_____ 10. I can describe the communication process.

_____ 11. I can list several transmission media and when to use each.

_____ 12. I can identify and use various message response styles.

_____ 13. I understand organizational communications and networks.

_____ 14. I can list barriers to communications and how to overcome them.

_____ 15. I know my preferred communication style and how to use other communication styles to meet the needs of the situation.

_____ 16. I can describe transactional analysis.

_____ 17. I can identify the differences between aggressive, passive, and assertive behavior. I am assertive.

_____ 18. I can identify different conflict resolution styles. I understand how to resolve conflicts in a way that does not hurt relationships.

_____ 19. I can identify behavioral leadership theories.

_____ 20. I can identify contingency leadership theories.

_____ 21. I know my preferred leadership style and how to change it to meet the needs of the situation.

_____ 22. I understand the process people go through to meet their needs.

_____ 23. I know several content and process motivation theories and can use them to motivate people.

_____ **24.** I can list and use motivation techniques.

_____ **25.** I can identify bases and sources of power.

_____ **26.** I know how to gain power in an organization.

_____ **27.** I can list political techniques to increase success.

_____ **28.** I have 100 people I can call on for career help.

_____ **29.** I know how to open a conversation to get people to give me career assistance.

_____ **30.** I know two critical things to do during a negotiation to get what I want.

_____ **31.** I understand how to plan and conduct effective meetings.

_____ **32.** I can identify components of group dynamics and how they affect behavior, human relations, and performance.

_____ **33.** I know the stages groups go through as they develop.

_____ **34.** I understand the roles and various types of groups in organizations.

_____ **35.** I can help groups make better decisions through consensus.

_____ **36.** I know when, and when not, to use employee participation in decision making.

_____ **37.** I understand why people resist change and know how to overcome that resistance.

_____ **38.** I can identify and use organizational development techniques.

_____ **39.** I understand how to develop a positive organizational culture and climate.

_____ **40.** I understand equal employment opportunity (EEO) and the rights of legally protected groups such as minorities, people with disabilities, alcohol and drug addicts, and people with AIDS.

_____ **41.** I can define sexism and sexual harassment in organizations.

_____ **42.** I can handle a complaint using the complaint model.

_____ **43.** I understand how to plan for improved human relations.

To use the profile form below, place an X in the box whose number corresponds to the score you gave each statement above.

Review your profile form. Your lower score numbers indicate areas where behavior changes are most warranted. Select the top five areas, abilities or skills, you want to develop through this course. Write them out below. In Chapter 8, we will discuss how to set objectives. At that time you may want to return to write what you wish to learn as objectives.

Learning Outcome

8. Identify your personal low and high human relations ability and skill levels.

1.

2.

3.

Learning Outcome

9. Identify five personal human relations goals for the course.

4.

5.

As the course progresses, be sure to review your course goals and work toward attaining them.

Profile Form

	Your Score							Parts and Chapters in Which the Information Will Be Covered in the Book
	1	2	3	4	5	6	7	
								Part 1. Intrapersonal Skills: Behavior, Human Relations, and Performance Begin with You
1.								2. Personality, Stress, Learning, and Perception
2.								
3.								
4.								3. Attitudes, Self-Concept, Values, and Ethics
5.								
6.								
7.								4. Time and Career Management
8.								
9.								
								Part 2. Interpersonal Skills: The Foundation of Human Relations
10.								5. Interpersonal Communication
11.								
12.								
13.								6. Organizational Structure and Communication
14.								
15.								
16.								7. Dealing with Conflict
17.								
18.								
								Part 3. Leadership Skills: Influencing Others
19.								8. Leading and Trust
20.								
21.								
22.								9. Motivating Performance
23.								
24.								
25.								10. Ethical Power and Politics
26.								
27.								
28.								11. Networking and Negotiating
29.								
30.								

Profile Form (*continued*)

	Your Score							Parts and Chapters in Which the Information Will Be Covered in the Book
	1	2	3	4	5	6	7	
								Part 4. Leadership Skills: Team and Organizational Behavior, Human Relations, and Performance
31.								12. Team Dynamics and Leadership
32.								
33.								
34.								13. Teams and Creative Problem Solving and Decision Making
35.								
36.								
37.								14. Organizational Change and Culture
38.								
39.								
40.								15. Valuing Diversity Globally
41.								
42.								
43.								Appendix A. Applying Human Relations Skills

Don't be too concerned if your scores were not as high as you would like them to be. If you work at it, you will develop your human relations skills through this book.

This brings Chapter 1 to a close. Next is a chapter review with a glossary and more application and skill-building material to develop your human relations skills based on Chapter 1 concepts.

Videos

Manager's Hot Seat and Behavior Model Videos are available for this chapter.

Online Learning Center Resources

Go to the Internet (http://mhhe.com/lussier8e) where you will find a broad array of resources to help maximize your learning.

• Review the vocabulary.

• Try a quiz.

R E V I E W

The chapter review is organized to help you master the 10 learning outcomes for Chapter 1. First provide your own response to each learning outcome, and then check the summary provided to see how well you understand the material. Next, identify the final statement in each section as either true or false (T/F). Correct each false statement. Answers are given at the end of the chapter.

1. **Explain why human relations skills are important.**
   People are an organization's most valuable resource. It is the people who cause the success or failure of an organization. Faulty human relations skill is the most common cause of management failure.

The myths of human relations (HR) are: (1) Technical skills are more important than HR skills; (2) HR is just common sense; (3) global diversity is overemphasized; and (4) leaders are born, not made. T F

2. **Discuss the goal of human relations.**

   Organizations that can create a win–win situation for all have a greater chance of succeeding. If the organization offers everyone what they need, all benefit. Satisfying needs is not easy; rather, it is a goal to strive for, which may never be met.

   Organizations expect that employees will not let their personal lives affect their work. T F

3. **Describe the relationship between individual and group behavior and organizational performance.**

   Through the systems effect, we learn that individuals affect each other's performance and that of the group and organization. The organization is made up of individuals and groups. Its performance is based on individual and group performance.

   Human relations only takes place at the group and organizational levels. T F

4. **Describe the relationship between behavior, human relations, and organizational performance.**

   As people perform their jobs they interact. Their behavior and human relations impact their level of performance. Ineffective behavior and poor human relations have a negative effect on performance.

   One employee's behavior and human relations have little effect on the group and organization. T F

5. **Briefly describe the history of the study of human relations.**

   In the 1800s Frederick Taylor developed scientific management, which focused on redesigning jobs. Also in the 1800s Robert Owen was the first manager/owner to understand the need to improve the work environment and the employee's overall situation. Elton Mayo is called the father of human relations. In the mid-1920s to the early 1930s he conducted the Hawthorne Studies and thereby identified the Hawthorne effect, an increase in performance due to the special attention given to employees, rather than tangible changes in the work. Through the 1930s to the 1980s much attention has been paid to the human side of the organization. Teamwork and increased employee participation became popular during the 1990s.

   Thomas Peters and Robert Waterman developed Theory Z. T F

6. **State some of the trends and challenges in the field of human relations.**

   Trends and challenges in the field of human relations include: (1) globalization, change, innovation, and speed; (2) technology; (3) diversity; (4) learning and knowledge; (5) ethics; and (6) crisis.

   The rate of change and technology is slowing down. T F

7. **Explain nine guidelines for effective human relations.**

   Guidelines for effective human relations include: (1) be optimistic; (2) be positive; (3) be genuinely interested in other people; (4) smile and develop a sense of humor; (5) call people by name; (6) listen to people; (7) help others; (8) think before you act; and (9) create win–win situations.

   The goal of human relations is within guideline (7): help others. T F

8. **Identify your personal low and high human relations ability and skill levels.**

   Answers will vary from student to student.

   Most people will have the same score on most abilities and skills. T F

9. **Identify five personal human relations goals for the course.**

   Answers will vary from student to student.

   The goals you select for this course are neither right nor wrong. T F

Learning Outcome

10. Define the following 17 key terms.

10. **Define the following 17 key terms.**

    Select one or more methods: (1) fill in the missing key terms from memory; (2) match the key terms from the end of the review with their definitions below; and/or (3) copy the key terms in order from the key terms at the beginning of the chapter.

_____ are interactions among people, while the

_____ is to create a win–win situation by satisfying employee needs while achieving organizational objectives.

A(n) _____ occurs when the organization and employees get what they want.

The _____ realizes that an organization employs the whole person, not just his or her job skills.

_____ is what people do and say.

The _____ are individual, group, and organizational.

_____ is the things two or more people do and say as they interact (human relations).

A(n) _____ is a group of people working to achieve one or more objectives.

_____ is the collective behavior of its individuals and groups.

_____ is the extent to which expectations or objectives have been met.

Under the _____, all people in the organization are affected by at least one other person, and each person affects the whole group or organization.

_____ is called the "father of human relations" and conducted the Hawthorne Studies in the mid-1920s to the early 1930s, considered the first true human relations research.

The _____ refers to an increase in performance due to the special attention given to employees, rather than tangible changes in the work.

_____ integrates common business practices in the United States and Japan into one middle-ground framework.

_____ are within the individual and include characteristics such as personality, attitudes, self-concept, and integrity.

_____ is the ability to work well with a diversity of people.

_____ is the ability to influence others and work well in teams.

K E Y   T E R M S

behavior 6	interpersonal skill 21	performance 8
Elton Mayo 11	intrapersonal skills 21	systems effect 9
goal of human relations 5	leadership skill 21	Theory Z 13
group behavior 6	levels of behavior 6	total person approach 6
Hawthorne effect 12	organization 7	win–win situation 5
human relations 5	organizational behavior 7	

COMMUNICATION SKILLS

The following critical thinking questions can be used for class discussion and/or as written assignments to develop communication skills. Be sure to give complete explanations for all questions.

1. In your opinion, which myth about human relations holds back the development of human relations skills more than any of the others?

2. Which person's contribution to the history of human relations do you find to be the most impressive?

3. Which one of the trends or challenges do you believe is the most relevant to the field of human relations?

4. Which one of the nine guidelines for effective human relations do you think is the most important?

5. Of the three ways to handle human relations problems, which ones are the easiest and hardest for you?

6. Of the intrapersonal, interpersonal, and leadership skills, which one is your strongest? Your weakest?

CASE

A Changing of the Guard at Alcatel-Lucent

Alcatel-Lucent (ALU) became the leading global supplier of high-tech equipment for telecommunications networks when France's Alcatel acquired U.S. rival and technically savvy Lucent Technologies for $11.6 billion in late 2006. The company provides network switching and transmission systems for wireline and wireless networks. Serving telecom carriers and other business and government customers, the new Alcatel-Lucent organization is made up of five business units: wireline, wireless, convergence, enterprise, and services. Alcatel-Lucent's key customers include Verizon, AT&T (formerly SBC Communications), BellSouth, and China Telecom.

Former Alcatel chairman and CEO Serge Tchuruk (pronounced "cha-RUK") became chairman of the combined company; Lucent chief Patricia Russo was named CEO. Tchuruk honed a once lumbering Alcatel with broad industrial interests into a focused telecom heavyweight. He oversaw an extensive restructuring that included the sale of noncore businesses such as electrical power, engineering, nuclear power, and defense electronics. Russo, who oversaw similar streamlining measures at Lucent, was charged with turning around what has so far been a difficult integration in a slumping market.[88] Yet the company said on July 29, 2008, that these same two architects of the merger would step down, following widespread dissatisfaction with their performance. Alcatel-Lucent has cut 16,500 jobs and lost roughly $7 billion since the merger. When asked by the board of directors, Russo and Tchuruk both stated that they could not work with each other. Because they could not get along, both had to leave the company.

It was noted that Russo struggled to bring together the vastly different cultures of the two companies amid a tough business climate. Her difficulties were compounded by the fact that as the first woman to run a company listed on the CAC 40, she had to make her way in the clubby, male-dominated world where French business and politics overlap. (Alcatel-Lucent's headquarters is only a few blocks away from the Elysée presidential palace and is across the street from the headquarters of President Nicholas Sarkozy's party, the UMP.)

Ben Verwaayen, the former head of BT Group plc, a British telecommunications carrier, was appointed to succeed Patricia Russo as chief executive on September 2, 2008, and acknowledged that there remained "a divided Alcatel-Lucent." Verwaayen brings his experience of having been a customer of Alcatel-Lucent, as well as of its rivals Ericsson,

Nokia, and Huawei. He said he would spend the next few months consulting with clients as the company rethinks how it deploys its resources yet noted that they needed to move quickly to become an integrated company. Verwaayen, 56, is Dutch and speaks fluent French, in contrast to Russo, who was never entirely comfortable with the language. Alcatel-Lucent operates in 130 countries, and like many global enterprises, its language of business is English.

Thomas Langer, an analyst at WestLB in Düsseldorf, said the new team would quickly face pressure to bring results. According to Langer, "My take is that there will be another round of reorganization that will unfortunately come with more restructuring."[89]

Go to the Internet: For more information on Alcatel-Lucent, Patricia Russo, and Ben Verwaayen, and to update the information provided in this case, do a name search on the Internet and visit www.btplc.com.

1. How does this case highlight the current and future challenges of human relations in the 21st century?

2. What myths of human relations does this case challenge?

3. What should be the goal of human relations as it applies to this merger?

4. How does this case demonstrate the relationship between behavior, human relations, and organizational performance?

5. What levels of analysis are addressed in this case?

6. What new information on Alcatel-Lucent have you found on the Internet and how might that information impact your answer to the above questions?

Supervisor Susan's Human Relations

Peter has been working for York Bakery for about three months now. He has been doing an acceptable job until this week. Peter's supervisor, Susan, has called him in to discuss the drop in performance. (*Note:* Susan's meeting with Peter and/or a meeting held by Tim with Susan and Peter can be role-played in class.)

SUSAN: "Peter, I called you in here to talk to you about the drop in the amount of work you completed this week. What do you have to say?"

PETER: "Well, I've been having a personal problem at home."

SUSAN: "That's no excuse. You have to keep your personal life separate from your job. Get back to work, and shape up or ship out."

PETER: (Says nothing, just leaves.)

Susan goes to her boss, Tim.

SUSAN: "Tim, I want you to know that I've warned Peter to increase his performance or he will be fired."

TIM: "Have you tried to resolve this without resorting to firing him?"

SUSAN: "Of course I have."

TIM: "This isn't the first problem you have had with employees. You have fired more employees than any other supervisor at York."

SUSAN: "It's not my fault if Peter and others do not want to do a good job. I'm a supervisor, not a babysitter."

TIM: "I'm not very comfortable with this situation. I'll get back to you later this afternoon."

SUSAN: "See you later. I'm going to lunch."

Answer the following questions. Then in the space between questions, state why you selected that answer.

_____   1. There _____ a human relations problem between Susan and Peter.
               a. is   *b.* is not

_____   2. Susan has attempted to create a _____ situation.
               a. lose–lose   *b.* win–lose   *c.* win–win

_____   3. Susan _____ an advocate of the total person approach.
               a. is   *b.* is not

_____   4. Through the systems effect, Peter's decrease in output affects which level of behavior?
               a. individual   *c.* organizational
               b. group   *d.* all three levels

_____   5. The scope of study illustrated in this case covers:
               a. behavior   *c.* performance
               b. human relations   *d.* all three

_____   6. The focus of study by Susan is:
               a. individual/behavior   *c.* group/human relations
               b. individual/performance *d.* organizational/performance

_____   7. The focus of study by Tim should be:
               a. individual/behavior   *c.* group/human relations
               b. group/behavior   *d.* organizational/performance

_____   8. Later that afternoon Tim should:
               a. reprimand Peter
               b. talk to Peter and tell him not to worry about it

          c. bring Susan and Peter together to resolve the problem

          d. do nothing, letting Susan handle the problem herself

          e. fire Susan

_____ **9.** The major human relations skill lacking in Susan is:

          a. be optimistic

          b. smile and develop a sense of humor

          c. think before you act

          d. be genuinely interested in other people

_____ **10.** Tim _____ work with Susan to develop her human relations skills.

          a. should   *b.* should not

11. Will Peter's performance increase? If you were Peter, would you increase your performance?

12. Have you ever had a supervisor with Susan's attitude? Assume you are in Susan's position. How would you handle Peter's decrease in performance?

13. Assume you are in Tim's position. How would you handle this situation?

SKILL-BUILDING EXERCISE 1–1

Course Objectives

In-Class Excercise (Individual)

Objective: To share your course objectives.

AACSB: The primary AACSB learning standard skills developed through this exercise are reflective thinking and self-management, analytic skills, and communication abilities.

Experience: You will share your course objectives in small groups or with the entire class.

Preparation: You should have completed the self-assessment section of this chapter, including five written objectives.

Procedure 1
(5–30 minutes)

Option A: Volunteers state one or more of their course objectives to the class. The instructor may make comments.

Option B: Break into groups of three to six members and share your course objectives.

Option C1:   Same procedure as Option B with the addition of having the group select a member to share five of the group's objectives.

Option C2:   Each group's spokesperson reports its five objectives.

Conclusion: The instructor leads a class discussion and/or makes concluding remarks.

Application (2–4 minutes):   Should I change any of my objectives? If yes, rewrite it or them below.

Sharing: Volunteers give their answers to the application section.

Human Relations

In-Class Excercise
(Individual)

Objectives:

1. A. To get acquainted with the members of your permanent group and to name the group.
   B. To get acquainted with some of your classmates.

AACSB: The primary AACSB learning standard skill developed through this exercise is communication ability.

2. To get to know more about your instructor.

Experience: You will be involved in a small group discussion, and one person from each group will ask the instructor questions.

Procedure 1
(2–5 minutes)

A. Your instructor will assign you to your permanent group.
B. Break into groups of three to six, preferably with people you do not know or do not know well.

Procedure 2
(8–12 minutes)

Each group member tells the others his or her name and two or three significant things about himself or herself. After all members have finished, ask each other questions to get to know each other better.

Procedure 3
(2–4 minutes)
Permanent groups only

Everyone writes down the names of all group members. Addresses and telephone numbers are also recommended.

Procedure 4
(2–3 minutes) All groups

Each person calls all members by name, without looking at written names. Continue until all members call the others by name.

Procedure 5
(5–10 minutes)
Permanent groups only

Members decide on a name for the group; a logo is optional.

Procedure 6
(5–12 minutes)

Elect a spokesperson to record and ask your group's questions. The members select specific questions to ask the instructor under the three categories below. The spokesperson should not identify who asked which questions.

1. Questions about course expectations. (What do you hope to learn or gain from this course?)
2. Questions about doubts or concerns about this course. (Is there anything about the course that you don't understand?)
3. Questions about the instructor. (What would you like to know about the instructor to get to know him or her?)

Procedure 7
(10–20 minutes)

Each spokesperson asks the group's question under one category at a time. When all questions from category 1 are asked and answered, proceed to category 2, then to 3. Spokespersons should not repeat questions asked by other groups.

Questions (2–10 minutes):   For the groups or class.

1. Is it important to know and call people by name? Why or why not?

2. What can you do to improve your ability to remember people's names when you first meet them, and at later times?

Conclusion: The instructor may make concluding remarks.

Application (2–4 minutes):   What have I learned through this exercise? How will I use this knowledge in the future?

Sharing: Volunteers give their answers to the application section.

Human Relations Overview: OBingo Icebreaker

In-Class Exercise (Group)

Procedure
(5–10 minutes)

Objective: To get an overview of some of the many human relations topics through an icebreaker game of bingo.

AACSB: The primary AACSB learning standard skill developed through this exercise is communication ability.

Experience: You will play an interactive game of bingo related to human relations.

Go around the room and get signatures of peers who fit the descriptions in the squares on the OBingo card.

Tell the person your name, and sign only if the description really does fit you.

Each person can sign only one square on your card.

Say "bingo" when you get it.

If you get bingo before the time is up, keep getting as many signatures as you can until the time is up.

The number in the square identifies the chapter in which the topic will be covered.

Conclusion: The instructor may make concluding remarks.

Source: This exercise was adapted from Joan Benek-Rivera, Bloomsburg University of Pennsylvania. Dr. Rivera's exercise was presented at the 2002 Organizational Behavior Teaching Conference (OBTC).

HUMAN RELATIONS

OB	I	N	G	O
2. Has an introverted personality	6. Doesn't like structure	9. Is good at motivating others	11. Has a network of at least 50 people for career help	13. Likes to create new things or new ways to do things
2. Has little or no stress	7. Has an ego	9. Is a high achiever	11. Is a tough negotiator	14. Is concerned about doing a quality job
3. Has a satisfying job	7. Avoids conflict	Your name	12. Likes status symbols (name brands that show, trophy)	14. Does not like change
4. Is poor at managing time	8. Likes to be in charge	10. Does as the boss requests	12. Looks out for number one	15. Is a minority
5. Uses paraphrasing regularly	8. Uses an autocratic leader style	10. Enjoys playing organizational politics	13. Likes to solve problems	15. Has lived in a foreign country

Experiential Exercise:
Catch Participation

In-Class Exercise (Group)

Objective: To experience the need to participate in this course.

AACSB: The primary AACSB learning standard skill developed through this exercise is teamwork.

Experience: You will play catch with and without participation.

Procedure 1
(1 minute)

Break into groups of two, with one group of three, if needed. The instructor gives each group an object to catch.

Procedure 2
(1 minute)

The person with the object throws it to the partner, and the partner does not catch it. The same person picks the object up and throws it again, without its being caught.

Procedure 3
(1 minute)

The other person picks up the object and throws it back as the two play catch.

Procedure 4
(5–10 minutes)

Questions:

1. How did you feel playing catch without participation?

2. How did you feel playing with participation?

3. How does the issue of participation relate to this course?

Conclusion: The instructor may make concluding remarks.

Source: Jane-Michele Cark, president of The Q Group, JMC Marketing Communications, Toronto, Ontario, Canada, explained this experiential exercise at the 2003 Organizational Behavior Teaching Conference (OBTC).

ANSWERS TO TRUE/FALSE QUESTIONS

1. T.
2. F. Organizations employ the total person and realize that personal lives do affect work, so they try to help employees balance their work and personal lives.
3. T.
4. F. One person can have disastrous effects on both groups and organizations.
5. F. William Ouchi developed Theory Z, Peters and Waterman wrote *In Search of Excellence.*
6. F. The rate of change and technology will continue to increase.
7. F. The goal of human relations is (9): create win–win situations.
8. F. People are different and score differently.
9. T.

Personality, Stress, Learning, and Perception

After completing this chapter, you should be able to:

1. Describe the Big Five personality dimensions.

2. Explain the benefits of understanding and identifying personality profiles.

3. Describe your stress personality type.

4. List causes of stress, and describe how to be more effective at controlling stress.

5. Describe the four learning styles and know which is your preferred learning style.

6. Describe six biases affecting perception.

7. Explain the importance of first impressions and how to project a positive image.

8. Define the following 19 key terms (in order of appearance in the chapter):

personality	**divergers**
Type A personality	**convergers**
locus of control	**assimilators**
Big Five Model of Personality	**perception**
stress	**stereotyping**
stressors	**perceptual congruence**
burnout	**primacy effect**
controlling stress plan	**four-minute barrier**
intelligence	**image**
accommodators	

CHAPTER OUTLINE

How Personality, Stress, Intelligence and Learning, Perception, and First Impressions Affect Behavior, Human Relations, and Performance

Personality

Personality Development

Personality Classification Methods

Locus of Control

The Big Five Model of Personality

The Big Five Model of Personality Has Universal Applications Across Cultures

The Myers-Briggs Type Indicator (MBTI)

Stress

What Is Stress?

Causes of Stress

Signs of Stress

Controlling Stress

Intelligence, Emotional Intelligence, and Learning

Intelligence

Emotional Intelligence

Learning Styles

The Learning Organization

Perception

The Nature of Perception

Bias in Perception

Developing Positive First Impressions

The Primacy Effect and the Four-Minute Barrier

Image Projection

PepsiCo is ranked 59th in the Fortune 500 list of the biggest companies (ranked by revenue) and is 1st in the "Food and Consumer Products" category (ahead of Kraft Foods, Sara Lee, Conagra Foods, and General Mills).[1] Its two primary lines of business are snack foods (Frito-Lay is its largest unit) and beverages (Pepsi, Tropicana, Gatorade),[2] with some cereal products (Quaker Oats). Although Coca-Cola sells more carbonated soft drinks than Pepsi, PepsiCo moved into the noncarbonated beverages (bottled water, sports drinks, and teas) before Coke and it now commands half the U.S. market share, about twice as much as Coke.[3] Coca-Cola is now ranked lower (83rd) than PepsiCo in the Fortune 500 list.[4] Indian-born Indra K. Nooyi is chairman and chief executive officer of PepsiCo and, according to Fortune, Nooyi is ranked as the most powerful woman.[5] You have most likely consumed at least one of PepsiCo's products as it offers more than 100 products in nearly 200 countries and territories.[6] To learn more about PepsiCo, visit its Web site at www.pepsico.com.

June Peterson was walking alone to the lunchroom. As she walked, she was thinking about her coworker, Rod Wills. June has trouble getting along with Rod because they are complete opposites. As June walked, two general thoughts came to her mind: Why does Rod do the things he does? Why are we so different? More specific questions came to mind: (1) We do the same job—why is he so stressed out and I'm not? (2) Why am I so emotional and interested in people—while Rod isn't? (3) Why am I so eager to get involved and help—while he sits back and watches? (4) Why is Rod so quiet—while I'm so outgoing? (5) Why do I dislike routine and detail so much—while Rod enjoys it so much? (6) Why does he believe that everything that happens is because of fate—while I don't? (7) When we have to agree on a decision, why is he so slow and analytical—while I'm not? (8) Why is it that we see our jobs so differently when they are the same? (9) When I first met Rod, I thought we would hit it off fine. Why was I so wrong?

Although June's questions have no simple answers, this chapter will give you a better understanding of behavioral differences.

HOW PERSONALITY, STRESS, INTELLIGENCE AND LEARNING, PERCEPTION, AND FIRST IMPRESSIONS AFFECT BEHAVIOR, HUMAN RELATIONS, AND PERFORMANCE

Recall that in Part 1 of the book, in Chapters 2 and 3, we discuss intrapersonal skills that affect behavior, human relations, and performance. In this chapter we cover several different yet related topics, so let's start with an overview. Your *personality* affects your moods, which influence your behavior and human relations,[7] so your personality is a good predictor of your job performance.[8] Your personality also affects your level of *stress*,[9] and when you are under too much stress it tends to have a negative effect on your behavior, human relations, and job performance.[10] Your personality is also related to your level of *intelligence* and preferred method of learning, so intelligence also influences your behavior and human relations and is a good predictor of job success.[11] Finally, your personality and intelligence influence your *perception*,[12] which, in turn, affects your *first impressions* of others. Since behavior is the product of perception, it also affects human relations and performance.[13]

Throughout this chapter, you will learn how personality, stress, intelligence, perceptions, and first impressions make us similar and different. You will understand how these concepts affect your behavior, human relations, and performance and that of others, so that you can better understand yourself and others and work more effectively in teams. Intrapersonal skills are harder to develop than interpersonal and leadership skills, and since intrapersonal skills are the foundation of effective interpersonal and leadership skills,[14] you will need to give this and the next chapter your best shot.

PERSONALITY

As June Peterson's dilemma illustrates, different people behave differently in their everyday lives. Personality, or personal style, is a very complex subject, yet in our daily lives we use trait adjectives such as *warm, aggressive,* and *easygoing* to describe people's behavior.[15] *Personality* is the word commonly used to describe an individual's collection (total person) of such behavioral traits or characteristics. Personal style or **personality** *is a relatively stable set of traits that aids in explaining and predicting individual behavior.* In short, it's your total mental makeup.[16] As noted, individuals are all different, yet similar, in many ways.

Substantial progress in the development of personality theory and traits has been made.[17] In this section you will learn about personality and the personality classifications of Type A and Type B; locus of control; the Big Five Model of Personality; and the MBTI. Throughout this chapter and book, you will gain a better understanding of your personality traits, which will help explain why you and others do the things you do (behavior).

Personality Development

Why are some people outgoing and others shy, some loud and others quiet, some warm and others cold, some aggressive and others passive? This list of behaviors is made up of individual traits. *Traits* are distinguishing personal characteristics.[18] Personality development is based on genetics and environmental factors. The genes you received before you were born influence your personality traits. Your family, friends, school, and work also influence your personality. In short, personality is the sum of genetics and a lifetime of learning.[19] Personality traits, however, can be changed, with work.[20] For example, people who are shy can become more outgoing.

Personality Classification Methods

There are several personality classification methods. We discuss four of them. Let's begin here with the simple two-dimensional method Type A, Type B. A **Type A personality** *is characterized as fast moving, hard driving, time conscious, competitive, impatient, and preoccupied with work.* Because a *Type B personality* is the opposite of Type A, often it is called laid-back or easygoing. The Type A personality is commonly associated with a high level of stress, so we discuss it further in the section on causes of stress.

The next classification of personality we discuss is internal or external locus of control. Then we discuss the Big Five Model of Personality, which is the most widely accepted method of classification because of its strong research support.[21] Last comes the more complex Myers-Briggs Type Indicator (MBTI), with 16 personality types.[22]

Locus of Control

Another simple two-dimensional personality classification method is locus of control. Before we discuss it, complete Self-Assessment Exercise 2–1 to determine if you are more of an internalizer or externalizer.

Your Locus of Control

Below are five statements. In the blank beside each statement, assign 1 to 5 points based on your agreement with the statement:

Agree		Neutral		Disagree
5	4	3	2	1

_____ 1. Getting ahead in life is a matter of hard work, rather than being in the right place at the right time.

_____ 2. I determine what I do and say, rather than allowing people and situations to upset me and affect how I behave.

_____ 3. Getting a raise and promotion is based on hard work, rather than who you know.

_____ 4. I, rather than other people and situations, determine what happens to my life.

_____ 5. Students earn their grades; teachers don't determine students' grades.

_____ Total. Add the five numbers (1–5). Below, place an X on the continuum that represents your score:

Externalizer   5 – – – – 10 – – – – 15 – – – – 20 – – – – 25   Internalizer

The lower your score, the greater is your belief that you are controlled by external sources such as fate, chance, other people, or environmental situations. The higher your score, the greater is your belief that you are in control of your destiny.

There is no right or wrong score, and a simple five-question instrument may not be totally accurate, but it should be helpful. If you disagree with the score, review the questions and think about why you selected the answers.

Locus of control _is a continuum representing one's belief as to whether external or internal forces control one's destiny._ People with an external locus of control (externalizers) believe that they have little control over their performance and are closed to new experiences. Internalizers believe they are in control and are open to new experiences to improve performance.[23]

Do you believe that you determine your own career success? The message that you need to have an internal locus of control cannot be overstated; it determines your level of satisfaction with self, your stress level, and your career path. Thus, it is absolutely significant that you embrace the message that you control your own destiny.[24]

If you believe that if you try hard, it doesn't matter, that you cannot be successful, you will most likely be unhappy, give up easily, and not have a successful career. Successful people know that they are in control of their lives, and they are happy and successful because they work at it. Successful people have lots of failures, but they have a poor memory for them and keep trying. Internal locus of control can be changed.

Learning Outcome

1. Describe the Big Five personality dimensions.

The Big Five Model of Personality

Let's begin by completing Self-Assessment Exercise 2–2 to determine your personality profile. The purpose of the Big Five model is to reliably categorize most, if not all, of the traits that you would use to describe someone. The model is organized into five dimensions, and each dimension includes multiple traits.[25] The **Big Five Model of Personality** _categorizes traits into the dimensions of surgency, agreeableness, adjustment, conscientiousness, and openness to experience._ The dimensions are listed in Exhibit 2.1 and described below. Note, however, that the five dimensions are sometimes published with slightly different descriptor names.

Your Big Five Personality Profile

There are no right or wrong answers, so by being honest you can really increase your self-awareness. We suggest doing this exercise in pencil or making a copy before you write on it. We will explain why later.

Identify each of the 25 statements according to how accurately they describe you. Place a number from 1 to 7 on the line before each statement.

Like me		Somewhat like me				Not like me
7	6	5	4	3	2	1

_____ 1. I step forward and take charge in leaderless situations.

_____ 2. I am concerned about getting along well with others.

_____ 3. I have good self-control; I don't get emotional and get angry and yell.

_____ 4. I'm dependable; when I say I will do something, it's done well and on time.

_____ 5. I try to do things differently to improve my performance.

_____ 6. I enjoy competing and winning; losing bothers me.

_____ 7. I enjoy having lots of friends and going to parties.

_____ 8. I perform well under pressure.

_____ 9. I work hard to be successful.

_____ 10. I go to new places and enjoy traveling.

_____ 11. I am outgoing and willing to confront people when in conflict.

_____ 12. I try to see things from other people's points of view.

_____ 13. I am an optimistic person who sees the positive side of situations (the cup is half full).

_____ 14. I am a well-organized person.

_____ 15. When I go to a new restaurant, I order foods I haven't tried.

_____ 16. I want to climb the corporate ladder to as high a level of management as I can.

_____ 17. I want other people to like me and to be viewed as very friendly.

_____ 18. I give people lots of praise and encouragement; I don't put people down and criticize.

_____ 19. I conform by following the rules of an organization.

_____ 20. I volunteer to be the first to learn or do new tasks at work.

_____ 21. I try to influence other people to get my way.

_____ 22. I enjoy working with others more than working alone.

_____ 23. I view myself as being relaxed and secure, rather than nervous and insecure.

_____ 24. I am considered credible because I do a good job and come through for people.

_____ 25. When people suggest doing things differently, I support them and help bring about change; I don't make statements such as, "It will not work," "We never did it before," "Who else did it?" or "We can't do it."

The columns in the chart below represent specific personality dimensions. To determine _your personality profile,_ (1) place the number (1–7) that represents your score for each statement, (2) total each column (5–35), and (3) make a bar chart by marking the total scores on the vertical bars.

Surgency		Agreeableness		Adjustment		Conscientiousness		Openness to experience	
_____ 1.	35	_____ 2.	35	_____ 3.	35	_____ 4.	35	_____ 5.	35
_____ 6.	25	_____ 7.	25	_____ 8.	25	_____ 9.	25	_____ 10.	25
_____ 11.	20	_____ 12.	20	_____ 13.	20	_____ 14.	20	_____ 15.	20
_____ 16.	15	_____ 17.	15	_____ 18.	15	_____ 19.	15	_____ 20.	15
_____ 21.	10	_____ 22.	10	_____ 23.	10	_____ 24.	10	_____ 25.	10
	5		5		5		5		5
_____ Total Bar		_____ Total Bar		_____ Total Bar		_____ Total Bar		_____ Total Bar	

**Self-Assessment
Exercise 2–2 (*continued*)**

> The higher the total number, the stronger is the personality dimension that describes your personality. What are your strongest and weakest dimensions? Continue reading the chapter to find out the specifics of your personality in each of the five dimensions.

Surgency   The *surgency personality dimension* includes leadership and extroversion traits. (1) People strong in leadership, more commonly called dominance, personality traits want to be in charge. They are energetic, assertive, active, and ambitious, with an interest in getting ahead and leading through competing and influencing.[26] People weak in surgency want to be followers, and they don't like to compete or influence. (2) Extroversion is on a continuum between being an extrovert and being an introvert. Extroverts are outgoing, sociable, and gregarious, like to meet new people, and are willing to confront others, whereas introverts are shy. In Self-Assessment Exercise 2–2, review statements 1, 6, 11, 16, and 21 for examples of surgency traits. How strong is your desire to be a leader?

Agreeableness   Unlike the surgency behavior trait of wanting to get ahead of others, the *agreeableness personality dimension* includes traits related to getting along with people.[27] Agreeable personality behavior is strong when someone is called warm, easygoing, courteous, good-natured, cooperative, tolerant, compassionate, friendly, and sociable; it is weak when someone is called cold, difficult, uncompassionate, unfriendly, and unsociable. Strong agreeable personality types are sociable, spend most of their time with other people, and have lots of friends. In Self-Assessment Exercise 2–2, review statements 2, 7, 12, 17, and 22 for examples of agreeableness traits. How important is having good relationships to you?

Adjustment   The *adjustment personality dimension* includes traits related to emotional stability. Adjustment is on a continuum between being emotionally stable and being emotionally unstable.[28] Stability refers to self-control, calmness—good under pressure, relaxed, secure, and positive—and a willingness to praise others. Being emotionally unstable means being out of control—poor under pressure, nervous, insecure, moody, depressed, angry, and negative—and quick to criticize others.[29] In Self-Assessment Exercise 2–2, review statements 3, 8, 13, 18, and 23 for examples of adjustment traits. How emotionally stable are you?

Conscientiousness   The *conscientiousness personality dimension* includes traits related to achievement. Conscientiousness is on a continuum between being responsible and dependable and being irresponsible and undependable. Other traits of high conscientiousness include persistence, credibility, conformity, and organization.[30] This trait is characterized as the willingness to work hard and put in extra time and effort to accomplish goals to achieve success.[31] In Self-Assessment Exercise 2–2, review statements 4,

EXHIBIT 2.1 | Big
Five Dimensions of Traits

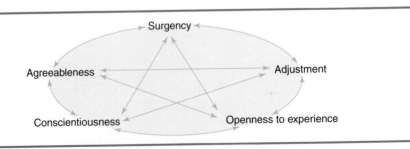

9, 14, 19, and 24 for examples of conscientiousness. Conscientiousness is a good predictor of job success.[32] How strong is your desire to be successful?

Openness to Experience   The *openness to experience personality dimension* includes traits related to being willing to change and try new things.[33] People strong in openness to experience are imaginative, intellectual, open-minded, autonomous, and creative, they seek change, and they are willing to try new things, while those who are weak in this dimension avoid change and new things.[34] In Self-Assessment Exercise 2–2, review statements 5, 10, 15, 20, and 25 for examples of openness to experience. How willing are you to change and try new things?

Learning Outcome

2. Explain the benefits of understanding and identifying personality profiles.

Personality Profiles   *Personality profiles* identify individual strong and weak traits. Students completing Self-Assessment Exercise 2–2 tend to have a range of scores for the five dimensions. Review your personality profile. Do you have high scores (strong traits) and low scores (weak traits) on some dimensions?

WORK APPLICATIONS

1. Describe your Big Five personality profile.

APPLICATION SITUATIONS

Personality Dimensions

AS 2–1

Identify the personality dimension for each of the five traits or behaviors described below.

A. Surgency   C. Adjustment   E. Openness to experience

B. Agreeableness   D. Conscientiousness

_____ 1. The manager is influencing the follower to do the job the way he, the leader, wants it done.

_____ 2. The sales rep turned in the monthly expense report on time as usual.

_____ 3. The leader is saying a warm, friendly good morning to followers as they arrive at work.

_____ 4. The leader is seeking ideas from followers on how to speed up the flow of work.

_____ 5. As a follower is yelling a complaint, the leader calmly explains what went wrong.

Think about the people you enjoy being with the most at school and work. Are their personalities similar to or different from yours? Knowing personalities can help you explain and predict others' job performance.[35] Study your boss's personality; getting along with your boss affects your career advancement.[36]

A personality assessment can help you select a job that is right for you.[37] When your personality fits well with others, you will have greater job satisfaction.[38] Rising through the ranks often requires changing personality traits to meet the demands of the new job.[39] Your personality therefore affects your career success.

Recall June's question about why she and Rod are so different. A major reason is that they have different personalities that affect their behavior, human relations, and performance. June has a Type B personality, while Rod has Type A. June is a surgency extrovert, while Rod is an introvert. Not surprisingly, June has a higher agreeableness personality dimension than Rod. They may be similar on the adjustment and conscientiousness personality dimension. June is an internalizer and more open to experience than Rod, who is an externalizer.

As you know, people are complex, and identifying a person's personality type is not always easy. Many people are in the middle of the continuum, rather than clearly at the ends. However, understanding personality can help you understand and predict behavior, human relations, and performance in a given situation.[40]

Improving Behavior, Human Relations, and Performance   Before you interact with another person, ask yourself questions like these:

- What type of personality does the other person have?
- How is he or she likely to behave in this situation during our interaction?
- How can I create a win–win situation?
- Is there anything I should or should not do to make this interaction successful? (You may want to behave differently with different people. For example, with a formal personality type, it may be best to be formal as well, especially with your boss, even if your personal style is informal.)

After such encounters, ask yourself questions like these:

- Was my assessment of the other person's personality correct?
- Did the other person behave as I predicted? If not, how was my assessment incorrect?
- Did I create a win–win situation?
- Did my behavior help the relations, and should I continue it with this person?
- Did my behavior hurt the relations, and should I discontinue it with this person?

WORK APPLICATIONS

2. Select a present or past boss and describe how his or her personality profile affected behavior, human relations, and performance in your department.

The Big Five Model of Personality Has Universal Applications Across Cultures

Studies have shown that people from Asian, Western European, Middle Eastern, Eastern European, and North and South American cultures seem to exhibit the same five personality dimensions.[41] However, some cultures do place varying importance on different personality dimensions. Overall, the best predictor of job success on a global basis is the conscientiousness dimension.[42]

The Myers-Briggs Type Indicator (MBTI)

Our fourth, and most complex, personality classification method is the Myers-Briggs Type Indicator (MBTI). The MBTI model of personality identifies your personality *preferences*. It is based on your four preferences (or inclinations) for certain ways of thinking and behaving.[43] Complete Self-Assessment Exercise 2–3 to determine your MBTI personality preference.

Self-Assessment
Exercise 2–3

Your MBTI Personality Preference

Classify yourself on each of the four preferences by selecting the one statement that best describes you:

1. *Where you focus your attention*—**Extrovert or Introvert**

_____ I'm outgoing and prefer to deal with people, things, situations, the outer world. (E)

_____ I'm shy and prefer to deal with ideas, information, explanations, or beliefs, the inner world. (I)

2. *How you take in information*—**Sensing or Intuitive**

_____ I prefer facts to have clarity, to describe what I sense with a focus on the present. (S)

_____ I prefer to deal with ideas, look into unknown possibilities with a focus on the future. (N)

3. *How you make decisions*—**Thinking or Feeling**

_____ I prefer to make decisions based on objective logic, using an analytic and detached approach. (T)

_____ I prefer to make decisions using values and/or personal beliefs, with a concern for others. (F)

4. *How you prefer to organize your life*—**Judging or Perceiving**

_____ I prefer my life to be planned, stable, and organized. (J)

_____ I prefer to go with the flow, to maintain flexibility and to respond to things as they arise. (P)

Place the four letters of preferences here _____ _____ _____ _____

There are sixteen combinations, or personality preferences, often presented in the form of a table. Remember, this indicates *preferences* only. You may also use the other traits that you did not select.

ISTJ	ISFJ	INFJ	INTJ
ISTP	ISFP	INFP	INTP
ESTP	ESFP	ENFP	ENTP
ESTJ	ESFJ	ENFJ	ENTJ

Completing Self-Assessment Exercise 2–3 gives you an idea of the types of questions included in the MBTI. There are actually multiple forms of the MBTI for various uses. For more information on the MBTI, and to complete a more detailed assessment, visit its Web site at www.myersbriggs.org. Think about your friends and family and the people you work with. What MBTI type are they? How can you improve your human relations with them based on the MBTI?

Learning Outcome

3. Describe your stress personality type.

STRESS

In this section, we discuss what stress is, problems associated with stress, causes of stress and stress as it relates to Type A and Type B personalities, signs of stress, and how to control stress.

What Is Stress?

People react to external stimuli internally. **Stress** *is an emotional and/or physical reaction to environmental activities and events.*

Situations in which too much pressure exists are known as stressors. **Stressors** *are situations in which people feel anxiety, tension, and pressure.* Stressors are events and situations to which people must adjust, and the impact of the stressor and how people react depend on the circumstances and on each person's physical and psychological

Self-Assessment Exercise 2–4

Your Stress Personality Type

Below are 20 statements. Identify how frequently each item applies to you.

(5) Usually   (4) Often   (3) Occasionally   (2) Seldom   (1) Rarely

Place the number 1, 2, 3, 4, or 5 on the line before each statement.

_____ 1. I work at a fast pace.

_____ 2. I work on days off.

_____ 3. I set short deadlines for myself.

_____ 4. I enjoy work/school more than other activities.

_____ 5. I talk and walk fast.

_____ 6. I set high standards for myself and work hard to meet them.

_____ 7. I enjoy competition, I work/play to win; I do not like to lose.

_____ 8. I skip lunch or eat it fast when there is work to do.

_____ 9. I'm in a hurry.

_____ 10. I do more than one thing at a time.

_____ 11. I'm angry and upset.

_____ 12. I get nervous or anxious when I have to wait.

_____ 13. I measure progress in terms of time and performance.

_____ 14. I push myself to the point of getting tired.

_____ 15. I take on more work when I already have plenty to do.

_____ 16. I take criticism as a personal put-down of my ability.

_____ 17. I try to outperform my coworkers/classmates.

_____ 18. I get upset when my routine has to be changed.

_____ 19. I consistently try to get more done in less time.

_____ 20. I compare my accomplishments with those of others who are highly productive.

_____ Total. Add up the numbers (1–5) you have for all 20 items. Your score will range from 20 to 100. Below place an X on the continuum that represents your score.

```
Type A   100 _ _ _ _ _ _ _ _ 80 _ _ _ _ _ _ _ _ 60 _ _ _ _ _ _ _ _ 40 _ _ _ _ _ _ _ _ 20   Type B
                    A                    A−                   B+                   B
```

The higher your score, the more characteristic you are of the Type A stress personality. The lower your score, the more characteristic you are of the Type B stress personality. An explanation of these two stress personality types follows.

characteristics. Stress is an individual matter. In a given situation one person may be very comfortable while another feels stress. For example, June and Rod have the same job, but Rod is stressed and June isn't. Too much stress over an extended period of time can have negative consequences,[44] which is discussed next.

The Positive Side   Some stress helps improve performance by challenging and motivating us.[45] Many people perform best under some pressure. When deadlines are approaching, their adrenaline flows and they rise to the occasion with top-level performance. To meet deadlines, managers often have to apply pressure to themselves and their employees.[46]

Problems Associated with Too Much Stress   Stress is a major problem as corporate downsizing requires employees to increase their job responsibilities. Too much stress affects personal health, morale, productivity, organizational efficiency, absenteeism, medical costs, and profitability.[47]

Stress also causes physical illness. It has been linked to heart problems, ulcers, asthma, diabetes, multiple sclerosis, cancer, and other maladies.[48] Stress may lead to alcohol and drug problems and even suicide. Mental stress is increasingly a reason for calling in sick, and stress can be blamed for headaches.[49] One of the major health problems today is obesity; stress also contributes to weight problems.[50]

Learning Outcome

4. List causes of stress, and describe how to be more effective at controlling stress.

Causes of Stress

There are four common stressors related to work: personality type, organizational climate, management behavior, and degree of job satisfaction. Complete the questionnaire in Self-Assessment Exercise 2–4 to determine your personality type as it relates to stress.

Personality Type   The degree to which stressors affect us is caused, in part, by our personality type. Since stress comes from within, the things we do can cause us stress.[51] As noted earlier, the Type A personality is characterized as fast moving, hard driving, time conscious, competitive, impatient, and preoccupied with work; the Type B personality is not. The 20 statements of Self-Assessment Exercise 2–4 relate to these personality types. People with Type A personalities have more stress than people with Type B personalities. If you scored 60 or above, you have a Type A personality and could end up with some of the problems associated with stress. Also, externalizer personality types are more likely to experience stress than are internalizers.

WORK APPLICATIONS

3. What was your stress personality type score and letter? Should you work at changing your personality type? Explain why or why not. Will you change?

Organizational Climate   The amount of cooperation, the level of motivation, and the overall morale in an organization affect stress levels. The more positive the organizational climate and work culture, the less stress there is.[52]

Management Behavior   Calm, participative management styles produce less stress. Tight control through autocratic management tends to create more stress. Some bosses use awful behavior; some are even abusive and have caused stress to the point of driving employees to quit their jobs.[53] Job demand stress leads to poor decision making.[54]

Degree of Job Satisfaction   People who enjoy their jobs and derive satisfaction from them handle stress better than those who do not.[55] In some cases, a change of jobs is a wise move that can lower or get rid of one of your stressors.

APPLICATION SITUATIONS

Stressors

AS 2–2

Identify the stressor in each statement below.

A. Personality type   C. Management behavior

B. Organizational climate   D. Degree of job satisfaction

_____ 6. "The morale in our department is poor."

_____ 7. "This job is OK, I guess."

_____ 8. "I'm always racing against the clock."

_____ 9. "Our priorities keep changing from week to week. It is very confusing when you're not sure what's expected of you."

_____ 10. "I work at a comfortable pace."

Signs of Stress

Some of the mild signs of stress are an increase in the rate of breathing and increased amounts of perspiration. When you continually look at the clock and/or calendar, feel pressured, and fear that you will not meet a deadline, you are experiencing stress.

When stress continues for a period of time, it tends to lead to disillusionment, irritableness, headaches and other body tension, the feeling of exhaustion, stomach problems, and depression.[56] Drinking, taking drugs, or eating or sleeping more than usual are often means of escaping stress.

People often lose interest in and motivation to do their work because of stress. Stress that is constant, chronic, and severe can lead to burnout over a period of time.[57] **Burnout** *is the constant lack of interest and motivation to perform one's job because of stress.* People sometimes experience temporary burnout during busy periods, as is the case with students studying for exams and retailers trying to cope with a holiday shopping season. However, when things slow down again, the interest and motivation come back. When the interest and motivation do not return, permanent burnout has occurred. The use of stress-controlling techniques can often prevent stress and burnout.

Controlling Stress

Controlling stress is the process of adjusting to circumstances that disrupt or threaten to disrupt a person's equilibrium. Ideally, we should identify what causes stress in our lives and eliminate or decrease it. We can better control stress by following a three-stage plan. The **controlling stress plan** *includes step 1, identify stressors; step 2, determine their causes and consequences; and step 3, plan to eliminate or decrease the stress.* Employees often require coaxing to watch their stress levels and health.[58] Below are five ways you can help eliminate or decrease stress.

Exercise   Physical exercise is an excellent way to release tension and reduce weight.[59] Many people find that exercising helps increase their ability to handle their jobs.[60] Unfortunately, the popularity of exercising has decreased. Today 70 percent of Americans don't exercise regularly, and nearly 40 percent aren't physically active at all.[61]

Aerobic exercise that increases the heart rate and maintains that rate for 20 to 30 minutes, three or more days per week, is generally considered the best type of exercise.[62] Exercises such as fast walking or jogging, biking, swimming, and aerobic dancing fall in this category. Yoga and other exercises that require you to increase your heart rate, but not to maintain that rate for 20 or more minutes, are also beneficial.

Before starting an exercise program, however, check with a doctor to make sure you are able to do so safely. Start gradually and slowly work your way up to 20 to 30 minutes—the longer the session, the better.[63]

Nutrition   Good health is essential to everyone, and nutrition is a major factor in your health. Currently, 60 percent of Americans are overweight and 30 percent are obese.[64] Obesity and related illnesses cost more than $78 billion annually in medical bills.[65] Since being overweight is stressful, you should watch how you eat and what you eat. Soda (including diet soda) has been linked to obesity. People who drink one or more sodas a day are: 31 percent more likely to be obese, 25 percent more likely to have high blood sugar, and 18 percent more likely to have high blood pressure.[66]

Watch your waistline. A pot belly with visceral fat (fat that accumulates around the internal organs) has been linked to diabetes, high blood pressure, strokes, heart disease, gallbladder disease, sleep apnea, and numerous cancers, and it triples your risk of dementia in later life. For men, the danger zone seems to be 40 inches or more. Reducing stress, exercising, and getting proper nutrition can help you control your waistline.[67]

Breakfast is considered the most important meal of the day.[68] A good high protein (eggs/yogurt), high fiber (whole-grain bread/fruit) breakfast gets you off to a good start. When you eat, take your time because rushing is stressful and leads to overeating.

Try to minimize your intake of junk food containing high levels of salt, sugar, and white flour.[69] Consume less fat, salt, caffeine (in coffee, tea, cola), alcohol, and drugs. Eat and drink more natural foods, such as fruits and vegetables, and drink plenty of water (not soda or sports drinks).[70]

Relaxation   Get enough rest and sleep. Most adults require 7–8 hours of sleep,[71] but Americans are not getting enough sleep.[72] The consequences of too little sleep can include frayed tempers, short attention spans and fuzzy thinking, health problems, and errors that cost lives. It has been estimated that sleep deprivation costs $15 billion a year in reduced productivity.[73] Here are some signs that you may need more sleep: trouble retaining information, irritability, minor illness, poor judgment, increased mistakes, and weight gain.[74]

Slow down and enjoy yourself. Have some off-the-job interests that are relaxing. Have some fun, and laugh. Some of the things you can do to relax include praying, meditating, listening to music, reading, watching TV or movies, and having hobbies.

When you feel stress, you can perform some simple relaxation exercises. One of the most popular and simplest is *deep breathing*.[75] You simply take a deep breath, hold it for a few seconds (you may count to five), and then let it out slowly. If you feel tension in one muscle, you may do a specific relaxation exercise, or you may relax your entire body, going from head to toe or vice versa. For a list of relaxation exercises that can be done almost anywhere, see Exhibit 2.2.

Positive Thinking   Be optimistic and stay positive. Optimism can be learned. Make statements to yourself in the affirmative,[76] such as I will do it. Be patient, honest, and realistic. No one is perfect. Admit your mistakes and learn from them; don't let them get you down. Have self-confidence;[77] develop your time management skills[78] (as discussed in Chapters 3 and 4). Positive thinkers are happier than negative thinkers.

EXHIBIT 2.2 | Relaxation Exercises

Muscles	Tensing Method
Forehead	Wrinkle forehead. Try to make your eyebrows touch your hairline for 5 seconds. Relax.
Eyes and nose	Close your eyes as tightly as you can for 5 seconds. Relax.
Lips, cheeks, jaw	Draw corners of your mouth back and grimace for 5 seconds. Relax.
Neck	Drop your chin to your chest; then slowly rotate your head in a complete circle in one direction and then in the other. Relax.
Hands	Extend arms in front of you; clench fists tightly for 5 seconds. Relax.
Forearms	Extend arms out against an invisible wall and push forward with hands for 5 seconds. Relax.
Upper arms	Bend elbows. Tense biceps for 5 seconds. Relax.
Shoulders	Shrug shoulders up to your ears for 5 seconds. Relax.
Back	Arch your back off the floor or bed for 5 seconds. Relax.
Stomach	Tighten your stomach muscles for 5 seconds. Relax.
Hips, buttocks	Tighten buttocks for 5 seconds. Relax.
Thighs	Tighten thigh muscles by pressing legs together as tightly as you can for 5 seconds. Relax.
Feet	Flex your feet up toward your body as far as you can for 5 seconds. Relax.
Toes	Curl toes under as tightly as you can for 5 seconds. Relax.

EXHIBIT 2.3 |

Causes of Stress and
How to Control Stress

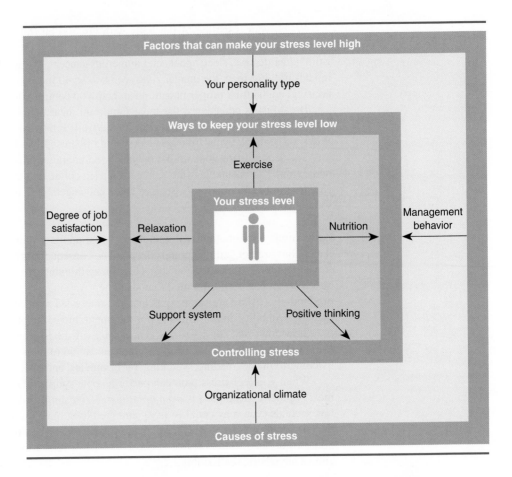

Support System   We all need people we can depend on. Have family and friends you can go to for help with your problems. Having someone to talk to can be very helpful, but don't take advantage of others and use stress to get attention. Build relationships at work.[79]

For an illustration of the causes of stress and how to control it, see Exhibit 2.3. If you try all the stress-controlling techniques and none of them work, you should seriously consider getting out of the situation. If you are experiencing permanent burnout, you should ask yourself two questions: Am I worth it? Is it worth dying for? If you answered yes and no to these two questions, a change of situation or job is advisable.

WORK APPLICATIONS

4. Following the controlling stress plan, (1) identify your major stressor, (2) determine its cause and consequences, and (3) develop a plan to eliminate or decrease the stress. Identify each step in your answer.

5. Of the five ways to eliminate or decrease stress, which do you do best? Which needs the most improvement and why? What will you do, if anything, to improve in that area?

Let's end this section with a confirmation of your lifestyle or an incentive to change it. According to a research study, if you exercise, don't smoke (or quit), drink only moderately, and eat right (lots of fruits and vegetables and limited junk food), you can live an average of 14 years longer.[80]

INTELLIGENCE, EMOTIONAL INTELLIGENCE, AND LEARNING

This section discusses the development of intelligence, learning styles, and learning organizations.

Intelligence

There are numerous theories of intelligence, many of which view intelligence as the ability to learn and the use of cognitive processes.[81] It is often called general mental ability.[82] For our purposes we will say that **intelligence** *is the level of one's capacity for new learning, problem solving, and decision making.* Today it is generally agreed that intelligence is a product of both genetics and the environment. Most scientists today believe there are at least two and perhaps as many as seven or more different components or kinds of intelligence.

People often perform at different levels for different tasks. As you know, you are good at doing some things (math, tennis, etc.) and not as good at doing others (biology, writing, etc.). Therefore, people have multiple intelligences, two of which (interpersonal and leadership) involve working with people.[83]

Intelligence is a strong predictor of many important outcomes in life, such as educational and occupational attainment.[84] Microsoft values intelligence over all other qualifications for all jobs.[85] Managers today are so busy that they often don't spend much time training employees. They expect you to be able to catch on quickly and learn on your own. Although learning new things can cause anxiety, in this fast-changing global environment, if you don't keep up, you will be left behind.[86] According to General David Petraeus, you ought to seek out-of-your-intellectual-comfort-zone experiences.[87] And yes, IQ does matter. To play in the National Football League, hopefuls must take and pass an IQ test.[88]

Emotional Intelligence

An offshoot of IQ is EQ (emotional quotient or emotional intelligence [EI]), which is clearly related to the adjustment Big Five personality dimension. Matt Goldman, cofounder of Blue Man Group, recruits and hires people with high EIs. Emotions in the workplace and emotional intelligence are hot topics. Emotional intelligence incorporates a broad range of abilities that explain workplace behavior as it relates to the way individuals manage emotions.[89] EI is part of multiple intelligences. It has been said, "IQ gets you the job, EQ gets you promoted."

There are five components of EI:[90]

1. Self-awareness (being conscious of your emotions within you; gut feelings).[91]

2. Managing emotions (not letting your emotions get in the way of getting the job done).[92]

3. Motivating yourself (being optimistic despite obstacles, setbacks, and failure).[93]

4. Empathy (putting yourself in someone else's situation and understanding that person's emotions).[94]

5. Social skills (to build relationships, respond to emotions, and influence others).[95]

As related to Parts 1 and 2 of this book, intrapersonal skills and interpersonal skills make up EI,[96] so you will develop your EI. Also, visit the Consortium for Research on Emotional Intelligence in Organizations at www.eiconsortium.org. You will learn more about dealing with emotions in Chapter 6.

You should now have a better understanding of why June and Rod are different, other than personality. June has greater emotional intelligence according to the five components of EI. Based on the opening case information, June is more outgoing, in touch with feelings, interested in people, and eager to get involved and help others, while Rod is not.

Learning Outcome

5. Describe the four learning styles and know which is your preferred learning style.

Learning Styles

Our capacity to learn new things is an important aspect of our intelligence. However, we do not all learn things in exactly the same way.[97] We will examine four styles people use when learning. Before we describe the four Kolb learning styles, determine your preferred learning style. Complete Self-Assessment Exercise 2–5 before reading on. Alice and David Kolb advocate experiential learning,[98] which we focus on in this book through skill building.

Self-Assessment Exercise 2–5

Your Learning Style

Below are 10 statements. For each statement distribute 5 points between the A and B alternatives. If the A statement is very characteristic of you and the B statement is not, place a 5 on the _____ A. line and a 0 on the _____ B. line. If the A statement is characteristic of you and the B statement is occasionally or somewhat characteristic of you, place a 4 on the _____ A. line and a 1 on the _____ B. line. If both statements are characteristic of you, place a 3 on the line that is more characteristic of you and a 2 on the line that is less characteristic of you. Be sure to distribute 5 points between each A and B alternative for each of the 10 statements. When distributing the five points, try to recall recent situations on the job or in school.

1. When learning:

_____ A. I watch and listen.

_____ B. I get involved and participate.

2. When learning:

_____ A. I rely on my hunches and feelings.

_____ B. I rely on logical and rational thinking.

3. When making decisions:

_____ A. I take my time.

_____ B. I make them quickly.

4. When making decisions:

_____ A. I rely on my gut feelings about the best alternative course of action.

_____ B. I rely on a logical analysis of the situation.

5. When doing things:

_____ A. I am careful.

_____ B. I am practical.

6. When doing things:

_____ A. I have strong feelings and reactions.

_____ B. I reason things out.

7. I would describe myself in the following way:

_____ A. I am a reflective person.

_____ B. I am an active person.

8. I would describe myself in the following way:

_____ A. I am influenced by my emotions.

_____ B. I am influenced by my thoughts.

9. When interacting in small groups:

_____ A. I listen, watch, and get involved slowly.

_____ B. I am quick to get involved.

10. When interacting in small groups:

_____ A. I express what I am feeling.

_____ B. I say what I am thinking.

Scoring: Place your answer numbers (0–5) on the lines below. Then add the numbers in each column vertically. Each of the four columns should have a total number between 0 and 25. The total of the two A and B columns should equal 25.

**Self-Assessment
Exercise 2–5 (*continued*)**

1. ____ A. ____ B.	(5)		2. ____ A. ____ B.	(5)
3. ____ A. ____ B.	(5)		4. ____ A. ____ B.	(5)
5. ____ A. ____ B.	(5)		6. ____ A. ____ B.	(5)
7. ____ A. ____ B.	(5)		8. ____ A. ____ B.	(5)
9. ____ A. ____ B.	(5)		10. ____ A. ____ B.	(5)

Totals ____ A. ____ B. (25)   ____ A. ____ B. (25)

Style   Observing   Doing   Feeling   Thinking

There is no best or right learning style; each of the four learning styles has its pros and cons. The more evenly distributed your scores are between the A's and B's, the more flexible you are at changing styles. Understanding your preferred learning style can help you get the most from your learning experiences.

Determining your preferred learning style: The five odd-numbered A statements refer to your self-description as being "observing," and the five odd-numbered B statements refer to your self-description as "doing." The column with the highest number is your preferred style of learning. Write it below:

I described myself as preferring to learn by _____.

The five even-numbered A statements refer to your self-description as being a "feeling" person, and the five even-numbered B statements refer to your self-description as being a "thinking" person. The column with the highest number is your preferred style. Write it below:

I described myself as preferring to learn by _____.

Putting the two preferences together gives you your preferred dimension of learning. Check it off below:

_____ Accommodator (combines doing and feeling).

_____ Diverger (combines observing and feeling).

_____ Converger (combines doing and thinking).

_____ Assimilator (combines observing and thinking).

Exhibit 2.4 illustrates the four learning styles.

As stated above, people learn based on two personality dimensions or types—feeling versus thinking and doing versus observing. Even though people have a preferred learning style, they cannot always use it. For example, the accommodator and converger prefer to learn by active involvement rather than by observing, while the diverger and assimilator prefer to observe rather than to be actively involved. In this course, you probably don't determine how the instructor will teach it. If the instructor spends more time in class completing and discussing skill-building exercises, the accommodators and convergers will be enjoying their preferred learning style and using their feelings or thoughts when being

EXHIBIT 2.4 | The Four Learning Styles

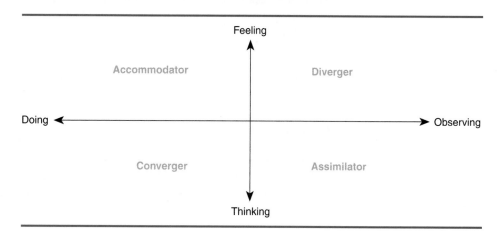

actively involved. On the other hand, if the instructor spends more class time lecturing on the material and showing films, the diverger and assimilator will be using their preferred learning style, while emphasizing feelings or thinking. Your instructor's preferred learning style will most likely influence the way he or she teaches this course.[99] For example, the author of this book is a converger, which influenced his use of a skill-building approach that includes more emphasis on thinking (than feelings) and doing (than observing); however, all four styles of learning are included. You do your best when your learning style matches the situation.[100]

Next we look at the basic characteristics of each style as well as the pros and cons associated with each.

Accommodator   People who are **accommodators** *prefer learning by doing and feeling*.

Characteristics: Accommodators tend to learn primarily from hands-on experience. They tend to act on gut feelings rather than on logical analysis. When making decisions, they tend to rely more heavily on other people for information than on their own technical analysis. Accommodators enjoy carrying out plans and being involved in new and challenging experiences. They often seek action-oriented careers such as marketing, sales, politics, public relations, and management.

Pros: Accommodators are usually good leaders, they are willing to take necessary risks, and they get things done.

Cons: Accommodators do not always set clear goals and develop practical plans. They often waste time on unimportant activities.

Diverger   People who are **divergers** *prefer learning by observing and feeling*.

Characteristics: Divergers have the ability to view concrete situations from many different points of view. When solving problems, they enjoy brainstorming. They take their time and analyze many alternatives. They tend to have broad cultural interests and like to gather information. Divergers are imaginative and sensitive to the needs of other people. They often seek careers in the arts, entertainment, and the service sector, and jobs in design, social work, nursing, consulting, and personnel management.

Pros: Divergers tend to be imaginative and are able to recognize problems. They brainstorm and understand and work well with people.

Cons: Divergers tend to overanalyze problems and are slow to act. They often miss opportunities.

Converger   The **convergers** *prefer learning by doing and thinking*.

Characteristics: Convergers seek practical uses for information. When presented with problems and making decisions, they tend to focus on solutions. Convergers tend to prefer dealing with technical tasks and problems rather than with social and interpersonal issues. They often seek technical careers in various science fields and work at engineering, production supervision, computer, and management jobs.

Pros: Convergers are usually very good at deductive reasoning, solving problems, and decision making.

Cons: Convergers tend to make hasty decisions without reviewing all the possible alternatives, and they have been known to solve the wrong problems. They often use their ideas without testing them first.

Assimilator   **Assimilators** *prefer learning by observing and thinking*.

Characteristics: Assimilators are effective at understanding a wide range of information and putting it into concise, logical form. It is more important to them that an idea or theory is logical than practical. They tend to be more concerned with abstract ideas and concepts than with people. Assimilators tend to seek careers in education, information, and science, and jobs as teachers, writers, researchers, and planners.

Pros: Assimilators are skilled at creating models and theories and developing plans.

Cons: Assimilators tend to be too idealistic and not practical enough. They often repeat mistakes and have no sound basis for their work.

After reading about the four learning styles, you should realize that there is no best learning style; each has its own pros and cons. You probably realize that you have one preferred learning style, but you also have characteristics of other styles as well. To verify your preferred learning style, you may have people who know you well fill out the self-assessment exercise as it relates to you, or have them read the four learning styles and select the one they believe is most characteristic of you. Also, we can learn about lifelong learning in college.

In addition to having different personalities and levels of emotional intelligence, June and Rod have different learning styles. June combines doing and feeling as an accommodator. Rod combines observing and thinking as an assimilator. They make decisions differently. People with similar personalities and learning styles tend to get along better than those that are different. Thus, because June and Rod are different, it is not surprising that they don't hit it off well. It takes good intrapersonal skills and interpersonal skills to get along with people who are different from you.

WORK APPLICATIONS

6. What is your preferred learning style? Are the characteristics of the style a good description of you? Explain. Can you change your learning style?

7. Think about the person you enjoy or have enjoyed working with the most. Identify that person's learning style. Is it the same as yours? What is it that you enjoy about the person?

8. Think about the person you dislike or have disliked working with the most. Identify that person's learning style. Is it the same as yours? What is it that you dislike about the person?

APPLICATION SITUATIONS

Learning Styles

AS 2–3

Identify the learning style of the people by the statements made about them.

A. Accommodator   C. Converger

B. Diverger   D. Assimilator

_____ 11. "The reason I don't like to work with Wendy is that she is slow to make decisions; she keeps analyzing the problem to death."

_____ 12. "Auto repair is a good job for Lou Ann because she enjoys fixing things and solving problems."

_____ 13. "I don't want Ted on the committee because he is a daydreamer. We can't use his ideas on the job."

_____ 14. "Ken doesn't use any standard approach like I do when selling. Ken says he feels out the customer and then decides his approach."

_____ 15. "Identify which style would be most likely to have made the comment about Ted in situation 13."

The Learning Organization

Recall from Chapter 1 the organization's need for innovation and speed to be competitive in a global environment. There is a relationship between learning, or intelligence, and innovation.[101] Jack Welch, former CEO of GE, has noted that an organization's ability to learn and translate that learning into action is the ultimate competitive advantage. When employees work together, learning and innovation are optimized. Employees learn by working together to foster some of the most important innovations.[102] To be innovative, organizations are recruiting people with the ability to continuously learn new things.[103] Probably the most important skill that college provides is the ability to continuously learn. Do not view your education as being over when you get your degree, but consider it as only the beginning. Much of what college graduates do on the job is learned at work because much of the work being done did not exist when the person was going to school. Organizations can also learn since they are based on individual learning. *Learning organizations* cultivate the capacity to learn, adapt, and change with the environment to be innovative with speed.

The learning organization focuses on improving learning and determining how knowledge is circulated throughout the organization.[104] The learning organization questions old beliefs and ways of doing things, yet it makes the learning process as painless as possible. Many researchers have demonstrated the importance of knowledge to management.[105]

What a Learning Organization Does   The learning organization learns to:

- Operate using the systems effect[106] (Chapter 1).

- Avoid making the same mistakes. Employees learn from their mistakes and don't repeat them throughout the organization; they share the knowledge of what went right and wrong and learn from every experience.[107]

- Make continuous performance improvements. Through learning, constant improvements are made. Improvements are shared with others throughout the organization to further continue improvement.[108]

- Share information. The habit of knowledge hoarding is broken. Employees are rewarded for sharing their best practices to help others improve performance throughout the organization.[109]

Organizational learning is not new; the topic has been discussed for over 30 years. Today, however, a major challenge to learning organizations is linking the learning of individual, group, and organizational levels of behavior and human relations to maximize performance.[110] The key link is the group. Teams that are effective at learning attain better performance than those that are not.[111] We'll talk more about teams and learning in Chapters 12 and 13.

PERCEPTION

In this section we discuss the nature of perception and bias in perception.

The Nature of Perception

People with different personalities perceive things differently.[112] The term **perception** *refers to a person's interpretation of reality*. In the perception process, you select, organize, and interpret all environmental stimuli through your senses. No two people experience anything exactly the same through this perception process.[113] Your perception is influenced by heredity, environment, and more specifically, by your personality, intelligence, needs, self-concept, attitudes, and values. Notice that the definition of perception refers to the "interpretation of reality." In human relations, perception is just as important as reality.[114] People often encounter the same thing and perceive it differently.[115] For example, June and Rod have the same job, but they see their job differently. In such situations, who is right?

What is the reality of any situation? We tend to believe that our perception is reality and the other party's perception is not reality. With an increasing global and diverse work environment, perception differences will continue to increase. Remember, people will behave according to their perception, not yours. So don't make the mistake of thinking that everyone thinks like you.[116]

Learning Outcome

6. Describe six biases affecting perception.

Bias in Perception

Our perception bias affects our decisions.[117] Some of the biases affecting perception are stereotypes, frame of reference, expectations, selective exposure, interest, and projection.

Stereotypes   Consider the bias of **stereotyping,** *which is the process of generalizing the behavior of all members of a group.* Stereotypes are drawn along all kinds of lines, including race, religion, nationality, and sex. Most, if not all, of us stereotype people as a way of quickly perceiving a person's behavior.[118] Women and minorities are often stereotyped in organizations.[119] Women managers have been stereotyped as being ineffective leaders. Research has shown this stereotype to be incorrect, as there is no real difference in leadership style.[120]

Much of what passes for humor (jokes) in the workplace is based on stereotypes and may be considered discrimination and harassment.[121] Such jokes usually have negative effects on human relations. Avoid sterotypes. Consciously attempt to get to know people as individuals, rather than to stereotype.[122]

Frame of Reference   Our frame of reference is our tendency to see things from a narrow focus that directly affects us. It is common for employees and management to perceive the same situation from different frames of reference.[123] For example, if managers want to make a change to increase productivity, they perceive the change as positive (ignoring the union's perception), while employees may perceive the change as negative (ignoring management's perception). Employees may view the change as a way to get more work out of them for less money when, in the broader scope, both groups may benefit from the change. Parents and their children often have frame-of-reference perception differences.

To be effective in our human relations, we should try to perceive things from the other person's frame of reference and be willing to work together for the benefit of all parties to create a win–win situation.

Expectations   Read the phrase in the triangle below:

Did you read the word *the* twice? Or, like most people, did you read what you expected, only one *the?* We perceive, select, organize, and interpret information as we expect it to appear.[124]

Over the years, a writer developed many experiential exercises that had been typed by different secretaries. However, it was common for secretaries to change the word *experiential* to *experimental* because it was the word they expected to type. Even after telling one secretary about it a few times, the secretary continued to type what she expected, rather than what was written.

Often people, especially those who know each other well, do not really listen to each other. They simply hear what they expect to hear. We have expectations of others in relationships; when they do things we don't expect or like, we have human relations problems.[125]

To improve our human relations, we must be careful to understand reality, rather than what we expect reality to be.[126]

Selective Exposure   We tend to see and hear what we want to. People sometimes selectively pick information they want to hear and ignore information they don't want to hear.[127] For example, when a manager uses the sandwich technique of telling an employee something good about performance, then switching to something negative, and then back to something good, the employee may selectively perceive the conversation as praise and ignore the negative information. Or sometimes when a manager delegates a task with a specific deadline, the employee selectively does not hear, and therefore misses the deadline.

To ensure effective human relations, we should listen to the entire message, rather than use selective exposure.

Interest   What interests you also affects how you perceive and approach things.[128] Have you ever taken a course and not liked it, while others in the class thought it was great? This difference in perception may be due to different levels of interest in the subject. Interest influences job selection.

Projection   To avoid psychological threat, people use a defense mechanism known as *projection*. Projection means attributing one's attitudes or shortcomings to others. People who steal and cheat may make statements like, "Everyone steals from the company" and "All students cheat in college." Projection may be an effective defense mechanism, but it generally does not help human relations.

WORK APPLICATIONS

9. Give an example of when you and another person experienced the same situation but perceived it differently. Which of the six biases affecting perception was responsible for the difference in perception? Explain your answer.

APPLICATION SITUATIONS

Bias in Perception

AS 2–4

Identify the particular perception bias in the statements below.

A. Stereotypes   C. Expectations   E. Interest

B. Frame of reference   D. Selective exposure   F. Projection

_____ 16. "Wayne gets on his employees' nerves because he doesn't really listen to their opinions. He thinks he knows what they want, and he makes decisions without their input all the time."

_____ 17. "Lily is always accusing others of taking long breaks, when in reality she is the violator."

_____ 18. "Ben keeps asking me about basketball. Just because I'm a tall African American doesn't mean I like the game or the L.A. Lakers."

_____ 19. "A major problem between the Arabs and Israelis is their . . ."

_____ 20. "Val has communication problems because she hears only what she wants to hear."

The term **perceptual congruence** *refers to the degree to which people see things the same way.* When people perceive things the same way, it generally has positive

Wendy's International: Does This Taste Right to You?

Wendy's competes in the burger wars against its arch rivals McDonald's and Burger King through its 6,600 restaurants. However, Wendy's wasn't doing as well as some investors would like. In fact, there was talk about it being sold.

Two major shareholders, Nelson Peltz and Peter May, asked to meet with the CEO within 48 hours to discuss their value creation plan. They did not see the firm as doing well at all and said that if their plan would be agreed to they would possibly maintain their ownership at just below 5 percent. This request for an immediate meeting was interpreted by Wendy's as an ultimatum, and John Barker (a Wendy's senior vice president) replied to Peltz and May that the CEO was too busy "managing the brand" to meet with them. He also added that similar ideas that Peltz and May had proposed had been considered in the past and rejected.

Peltz and May were outraged at the response. They were major stockholders and deserved, in their opinion, far better treatment than this. Wendy's claimed to be accessible and responsive to its individual investors. Peltz's and May's reaction to Wendy's response? Quite simple. They filed a letter of complaint with the Securities & Exchange Commission (SEC) characterizing communications with the company, or their lack thereof, as quite poor.

Peltz and May did not stop with a letter to the SEC. They helped to get the CEO canned, and they were involved in the merger of Wendy's with Triarc (the owners of Arby's) in 2008. The merger created the third largest fast-food chain, with more than 10,000 restaurants.

Questions

1. Which biases affecting perception relate to this ethical dilemma?

2. What was your first impression of each of the characters in the dilemma and their actions in this situation?

3. How might you have handled the situation differently to produce perceptual congruence if you were the CEO, the vice president, and/or Peltz and May?

4. In your opinion, does Wendy's have the right to claim that it is accessible and responsive to individual investors based upon this ethical dilemma?

Sources: Richard Gibson, "Wendy's Continues Battle with Shareholder Peltz," *Dow Jones News Wires,* December 30, 2005; http://www.wendys-invest.com/, retrieved July 1, 2008.

consequences in the organization.[129] However, perception biases also can result in lower performance.[130] The exact relationship between perceptual congruence and performance is not known. Employees who perceive management as supportive are generally happier with their jobs and perceive management's performance more favorably.[131]

For a review of the biases affecting perception, see Exhibit 2.5.

EXHIBIT 2.5 |
Biases Affecting
Perception

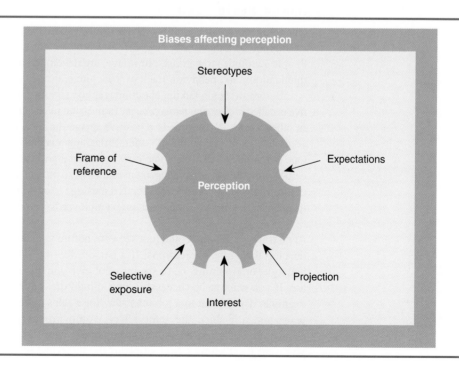

Learning Outcome

7. Explain the importance
    of first impressions and
    how to project a
    positive image.

DEVELOPING POSITIVE FIRST IMPRESSIONS

In this section we discuss first impressions: the primacy effect and the four-minute barrier. We also examine image projection.

The Primacy Effect and the Four-Minute Barrier

When we meet people, we form quick impressions of them.[132] Social psychologists call this process the primacy effect. The **primacy effect** *is the way people perceive one another during their first impressions.* It is the "enduring effect" of first impressions. Recall that our perceptions are open to six biases. These first impressions establish the mental framework within which people view one another, and they are based on personality and appearance.[133]

The **four-minute barrier** *is the time we have to make a good impression.*[134] It is also called the *four-minute sell*[135] because it is the average time during which people make up their minds to continue the contact or separate during social situations. However, in business and social situations, the time could be less. Some say first impressions are developed in six seconds, especially those based on appearances.[136]

During this short period of time, human relations will be established, denied, or reconfirmed. If our first impressions are favorable, we tend to be nice to the person and continue the contact; if not, we end the contact. In ongoing work situations, first impressions of our fellow employees set the tone for our human relations. The adage "First impressions are lasting impressions" is true for many people.[137]

First impressions usually linger, but they can be changed. Have you ever disliked someone as a result of first impressions that linger to the present time? On the other hand, can you recall meeting someone you disliked at first, but once you got to know the person, you changed your impression? Recall that June's first impression of Rod was positive, but they did not hit it off for long.

During the four-minute barrier, people's attention spans are at their greatest and their powers of retention are at their highest as people best remember what they hear first and last (recency effect). If you register negative first impressions in other people, you will have to "prove" yourself to change those impressions. It is easier to begin by projecting an image people will like.[138] Next we discuss how to project a positive image.

Image Projection

Our **image** *is other people's attitudes toward us.* Image can be thought of as being on a continuum from positive to negative. To a large extent we can control the image we project. People's attitudes toward us, our image, are developed by our appearance, nonverbal communications, and behavior. Each of these three areas is discussed separately below.

Before we begin talking about image, you should realize that image from your perspective is called *impression management.* Impression management is associated with job offers.[139] In other words, if you project a positive image during a job interview, you greatly increase your chances of getting the job offer. Projecting a negative image decreases your chances.[140] One last thing before we get into how to project a positive image: Organizations are also concerned with impression management and work to project a positive image. The image of each of the organization's employees sends a message to customers, who judge the organization by its people. The image you project as an employee has an impact on the organizational image.

Appearance   When people first see you, before you can do or say anything, they begin to develop their first impressions. If a person doesn't like the way you look, your clothes, hairstyle, or grooming, he or she may not give you the opportunity to show who you really are. If you want to be successful, you should dress appropriately for the situation.[141] For example, if you went to a job interview for a sales representative position at IBM wearing jeans and a T-shirt, the interviewer would probably decide not to hire you before asking you one question. At IBM, employees wear suits and white shirts or blouses, so if you wear these clothes, you will start the interview on a positive note. There are various dress-for-success books on the market, containing advice that can help your career progress. A simple rule to follow is to adopt the dress and grooming standards of the organization and, specifically, of the job you want. Dress like the successful people in the organization.

You will learn more tips on apparel and grooming in Chapter 4, on career management.

Nonverbal Communication   Our facial expressions, eye contact, and handshake all project our image, as does the tone and the volume of our voice.

After noticing someone's appearance, we tend to look at a person's face. Facial expressions convey feelings more accurately than words. A smile tends to say that things are OK, while a frown tends to say that something is wrong. One of the eight guidelines to human relations is to smile. It is especially important when we first meet someone; we want to project a positive, caring image.

When you first meet someone, eye contact is very important.[142] If you don't look a person directly in the eye, he or she may assume that you do not like him or her, that you are not listening, or that you are not a trusting individual. Maintaining eye contact is important, but don't make others uncomfortable by staring at them. Look in one eye, then the other; then briefly look away. Be aware, however, that in some cultures eye contact is considered differently than in North America.

In many introductions the handshake is used. Your handshake can convey that you are a warm, yet strong person. Your handshake is judged on five factors: (1) firmness—people tend to think that a firm handshake communicates a caring attitude, while a weak grip conveys indifference; (2) dryness—people don't like to hold a clammy hand; it sends a message of being nervous; (3) duration—an extended handshake can convey interest; (4) interlock—a full, deep grip conveys friendship and strength; shallow grips are often interpreted as a weakness; and (5) eye contact—you should maintain eye contact throughout the handshake.

You will learn more about nonverbal communication in Chapter 5.

Behavior   After the other person notices our appearance and nonverbal expressions, she or he observes our behavior. As stated earlier in the guidelines to effective human relations, while talking to the person, be upbeat and optimistic, don't complain, show a genuine interest in the person, smile, laugh if appropriate, call the person by name, listen, be helpful, and think before you act. Do not do or say anything that is offensive to the person. Be agreeable and complimentary. Watch your manners and be polite. During the four-minute barrier, avoid discussing controversial topics and expressing personal views about them.

Following the above guidelines on appearance, nonverbal communication, and behavior should help you develop positive first impressions. You will learn more about behavior throughout this book and more about etiquette in Chapter 10.

WORK APPLICATIONS

10. Give examples of situations when others formed a positive and a negative first impression of you. Explain the causes (appearance, nonverbal communication, behavior) of those impressions.

11. Which area of projecting a positive image (appearance, nonverbal communication, behavior) is your strongest? Which is your weakest? Explain your answers. What will you do to project a more positive image in the future?

Videos

Manager's Hot Seat and Behavior Model Videos are available for this chapter.

Online Learning Center Resources
Go to the Internet (http://mhhe.com/lussier8e) where you will find a broad array of resources to help maximize your learning.

• Review the vocabulary.

• Try a quiz.

R E V I E W

The chapter review is organized to help you master the 8 learning outcomes for Chapter 2. First provide your own response to each learning outcome, and then check the summary provided to see how well you understand the material. Next, identify the final statement in each section as either true or false (T/F). Correct each false statement. Answers are given at the end of the chapter.

1. **Describe the Big Five personality dimensions.**

   The *surgency* personality dimension includes leadership and extroversion traits; people high in surgency strive to get ahead of others. In contrast, the *agreeableness* personality dimension includes traits related to getting along with people. The *adjustment* personality dimension includes traits related to emotional stability. The *conscientiousness* personality dimension includes traits related to achievement. The *openness to experience* personality dimension includes traits related to being willing to change and try new things.

   The Myers-Briggs Type Indicator (MBTI) is a more complex personality classification method than the Big Five. T F

2. **Explain the benefits of understanding and identifying personality profiles.**

   Understanding and identifying personality profiles can help you to understand and predict behavior, human relations, and performance. One can intentionally change behavior to improve human relations and performance when working with different personality types.

   The locus of control is not part of a personality profile. T F

3. **Describe your stress personality type.**

   Student answers will vary from Self-Assessment Exercise 2–4: Your Stress Personality Type. People who have a Type A personality are characterized as fast moving, hard driving, time conscious, competitive, impatient, and preoccupied with work; those with a Type B personality are the opposite.

   The Type A personality is more prone to stress. T F

4. **List causes of stress, and describe how to be more effective at controlling stress.**

   Causes of stress include: personality type, organizational climate, management behavior, and degree of job satisfaction. We can help control stress through exercise, nutrition, relaxation, positive thinking, and support systems. To control stress one should: (1) identify stressors, (2) determine their causes and consequences, and (3) plan to eliminate or decrease the stress.

   The five ways recommended to help eliminate or decrease stress are: exercise, nutrition, relaxation, medication, and support systems. T F

5. **Describe the four learning styles and know which is your preferred learning style.**

   Accommodators prefer learning by doing and feeling. Divergers prefer learning by observing and feeling. Convergers prefer learning by doing and thinking. Assimilators prefer learning by observing and thinking. Student answers will vary.

   The converger learning style is the most effective learning style. T F

6. **Describe six biases affecting perception.**

   - *Stereotyping* is the process of generalizing the behavior of all members of a group.
   - *Frame of reference* refers to our tendency to see things from a narrow focus that directly affects us.
   - *Expectations* refers to how we perceive, select, organize, and interpret information based on how we expect it to appear.
   - *Selective exposure* means we tend to see and hear what we want to.

- Our degree of *interest* influences how we perceive things.
- *Projection* refers to our use of defense mechanisms to justify our behavior. Given a good explanation, people perceive things the same way. T F

7. Explain the importance of first impressions and how to project a positive image.

We only have up to four minutes to project a positive image. If we present a negative first impression to people, our future human relations with them can suffer. To project a positive first impression, we need to present an appropriate appearance, send positive nonverbal communications, and behave in a manner befitting the occasion.

Our perceptions are the bases for our first impressions. T F

Learning Outcome

8.   Define the following 19 key terms.

8. Define the following 19 key terms.

Select one or more methods: (1) fill in the missing key terms from memory; (2) match the key terms from the end of the review with their definitions below; and/or (3) copy the key terms in order from the key terms at the beginning of the chapter.

_____ is a relatively stable set of traits that aids in explaining and predicting individual behavior.

The _____ is characterized as fast moving, hard driving, time conscious, competitive, impatient, and preoccupied with work.

_____ is a continuum representing one's belief as to whether external or internal forces control one's destiny.

_____ categorizes traits into the dimensions of surgency, agreeableness, adjustment, conscientiousness, and openness to experience.

_____ is an emotional and/or physical reaction to environmental activities and events.

_____ are situations in which people feel anxiety, tension, and pressure.

_____ is the constant lack of interest and motivation to perform one's job because of stress.

The _____ includes step (1) identify stressors; step (2) determine their causes and consequences; and step (3) plan to eliminate or decrease the stress.

_____ is the level of one's capacity for new learning, problem solving, and decision making.

The four learning styles are _____, who prefer learning by doing and feeling; _____, who prefer learning by observing and feeling; _____, who prefer learning by doing and thinking; and _____, who prefer learning by observing and thinking.

_____ is a person's interpretation of reality.

_____ is the process of generalizing the behavior of all members of a group.

_____ refers to the degree to which people see things the same way.

The _____ is the way people perceive one another during their first impressions.

The _____ is the time we have to make a good impression.

Our _____ is other people's attitudes toward us.

K E Y   T E R M S

accommodators   52
assimilators   52
Big Five Model of
    Personality   38
burnout   46
controlling stress plan   46
convergers   52

divergers   52
four-minute barrier   58
image   58
intelligence   49
locus of control   38
perception   54
perceptual congruence   56

personality   37
primacy effect   58
stereotyping   55
stress   43
stressors   43
Type A personality   37

C O M M U N I C A T I O N   S K I L L S

The following critical thinking questions can be used for class discussion and/or as written assignments to develop communication skills. Be sure to give complete explanations for all questions.

1. Which personality traits exhibited by others tend to irritate you? Which of your personality traits tend to irritate others? How can you improve your personality?

2. Do you think that the Big Five Model of Personality or the Myers-Briggs Type Indicator is a more effective measure of personality?

3. Which cause of stress do you think is the major contributor to employee stress in organizations? What can organizations do to help eliminate or reduce employee stress?

4. Do you agree that intelligence (general mental ability) is the most valid predictor of job performance? Should organizations give an IQ test and hire based on the results? Why or why not?

5. How do you know if your perception or that of others is the correct interpretation of reality?

6. Is it ethical to judge and stereotype people based on a few seconds or minutes during first impressions? How do your first impressions help and hinder your human relations?

CASE

Ted Turner: The Mouth of the South or the Voice of Reason?

Robert Edward "Ted" Turner III (born November 19, 1938) is an American media proprietor and philanthropist. As a businessman, he is best known as the founder of the cable television network CNN, the first dedicated 24-hour cable news channel. In addition to CNN, he founded WTBS, which pioneered the superstation concept in cable television. As a philanthropist, he is well known for his $1 billion gift to support UN causes, which created the United Nations Foundation, a public charity that broadened support for the UN. Turner serves as the chairman of the board of directors for the foundation.[143]

Turner's management style and penchant for making controversial statements has earned him the nickname the "Mouth of the South." Some thought Ted Turner's resignation as vice chairman of AOL Time Warner might muffle his unruly voice in its management. But Turner let it be known that he had just begun to roar. "Only a bullet will stop me," he said in an interview with the CanWest News Service. "I couldn't do very much inside except raise my hand and object." He was once again applying his singular knack for speaking his mind, making headlines, and raising a host of questions, including whether he would further depress AOL Time Warner's stock with more sales of his own shares and would play a role in buying his favorite team, the Atlanta Braves, from the company. "Now, I have the power of the tongue," Turner told *The Globe and Mail* in Canada. "I can speak."

To AOL Time Warner's top executives, Turner's loud and often-changing views became a difficult fact of life. He was a constant center of speculation and attention, exposing internal disputes to the public, stirring up news coverage about soap operas in executive suites, and rattling the company's stock. Richard D. Parsons, chief executive of AOL Time Warner, had worked hard to keep Turner involved, calling him "my man," "Uncle Ted," and "brilliant" at the television business. But other executives and directors said they regarded Turner with a mixture of admiration and exasperation, and some rolled their eyes at his quicksilver moods.

Having left the company's management, Turner made it clear he felt himself unbound. "I waited six years to do it; I should have done it six years ago," he said in an interview, complaining that his authority within the company had steadily eroded since he sold his company. Turner made no secret of his continuing anger over AOL's ill-fated acquisition of Time Warner, which has helped drag the company's stock down more than 80 percent. Asked on the "Today" show whether someone should "go to jail" for engineering the merger, Turner responded, "There's litigation going on now, and I can't comment on that." Two people close to Turner, though, said he had even spoken rhetorically about filing a lawsuit as a shareholder himself—an obvious impossibility since, as a Time Warner director who voted for the merger, Turner would be essentially suing himself.

Turner also continued to meet frequently with Parsons and made vigorous suggestions, people close to them have said. But his views of the company can sometimes be hard to reconcile. People close to Turner have said that he liked Parsons and understood the constraints on his job, but Turner's associates have said he has also complained that Parsons was too intent on selling businesses and reducing the debt at a time when sales prices were low and borrowing was relatively inexpensive. Yet people close to the board of directors have also noted that Turner contradicted the above statement at a board meeting, urging that the company sell assets—possibly even its troubled AOL division—to regain financial flexibility.[144]

Go to the Internet: Support your answers to the following questions with specific information from the case and text, or other information you get from the Web or other sources.

1. Using Type A, Type B personality theory, describe Turner's personality.

2. Using locus of control theory, explain what Turner was trying to accomplish by being the "Mouth of the South" in terms of AOL Time Warner.

3. Using the Big Five personality theory, describe Turner's personality.

4. Assuming that Parsons felt stressed over Turner's interference, how did he try to manage the stressful situation?

5. Describe Turner's emotional intelligence using its five components.

6. What is your first impression of Turner and how might perceptual bias have impacted your perception?

Cumulative Question   7. What is the goal of human relations and how does it apply to this case?

OBJECTIVE CASE   **Personality Conflict**

Carol is the branch manager of a bank. Two of her employees, Rich and Wonda, came to her and said that they could not work together. Carol asked them why, and they both said, "We have a personality conflict." She asked them to be more specific, and this is what they told her:

RICH: Well, Wonda is very pushy; she tells me what to do all the time, and I let her get away with it because I'm a peace-loving man.

WONDA: That's because Rich is so gullible; he believes anything he is told. I have to look out for him.

RICH: We have different outlooks on life. Wonda believes that if we work hard, we can get ahead in this bank, but I don't agree. I believe you have to be political, and I'm not.

WONDA: That's because I'm motivated and enjoy working.

RICH: Motivated—is that what you call it? She's preoccupied with work. Wonda is rushing all the time, she is impatient, and she always wants to make a contest out of everything.

WONDA: If you were more cooperative, and morale was better, I would not feel stressed the way I do.

RICH: We cannot make decisions together because I am very logical and like to get lots of information, while Wonda wants to make decisions based on what she calls intuition.

WONDA: I thought working here was going to be different. I didn't know I was going to be stuck working with a person who is uncooperative.

RICH: Me? I feel the same way about you.

At this point Carol stopped the discussion.

Answer the following questions. Then in the space between questions, state why you selected that answer.

_____ 1. In Rich's first statement it appears that Wonda has a(n) _____ personality trait, while he has a(n) _____ personality trait.

      a. outgoing, reserved   *c.* conscientious, expedient

      b. aggressive, passive   *d.* imaginative, practical

_____ 2. In statement 2, it appears that Wonda is _____ and Rich is _____.

      a. shrewd, forthright   *c.* stable, emotional

      b. high, low intelligence   *d.* suspicious, trusting

_____ 3. In statement 3, it appears that Rich has an _____ locus of control while Wonda has an _____ locus of control.

      a. internal, external   *b.* external, internal

_____ 4. In statement 4, Wonda appears to be an:

      a. internalizer   *b.* externalizer

_____ 5. In statement 5, Wonda appears to have a Type _____ personality.

      a. A   *b.* B

_____ 6. In statement 6, Wonda states that _____ is the cause of her stress.

      a. personality   *c.* management effectiveness

      b. organizational climate   *d.* job satisfaction

_____ 7. In statement 7, Rich has described himself as having a(n) _____ learning style.

      a. accommodator   *c.* converger

      b. diverger   *d.* assimilator

_____ 8. In statement 7, Rich has described Wonda as having a(n) _____ learning style.

      a. accommodator   *c.* converger

      b. diverger   *d.* assimilator

_____ 9. In statement 8, the perception problem appears to be due to:

      a. stereotyping   *d.* selective exposure

      b. frame of reference   *e.* projection

      c. expectations   *f.* interest

_____ 10. Who needs to change their behavior?

      a. Rich   *b.* Wonda   *c.* both

11. Overall, are your personality, locus of control, stress type, and learning style more like Rich's or Wonda's? If you were Rich or Wonda, what would you do?

12. If you were Carol, what would you do?

Note: Carol's meeting can be role-played in class.

Learning Styles

In-Class Exercise (Group)

Objectives: To better understand your learning style and how to work more effectively with people with different learning styles.

AACSB: The primary AACSB learning standard skills developed through this exercise are reflective thinking and self-management, analytic skills, communication abilities, and teamwork.

Preparation: You should have read the chapter and determined your preferred learning style in Self-Assessment Exercise 2–5.

Procedure 1
(2–3 minutes)

The entire class breaks into four groups: The accommodators, divergers, convergers, and assimilators meet in different groups.

Procedure 2
(5–10 minutes)

Each of the four groups elects a spokesperson-recorder. Assume the class was shipwrecked on a deserted island and had to develop an economic system with a division of labor. During this process, what strengths would your group offer each of the other three groups if you were working one-on-one with them? For example, the accommodators state how they would help the divergers if they were the only two styles on the island. Then they assume the convergers and then the assimilators are the only other learning style on the island. Each group does the same. Feel free to refer to the book at any time.

Procedure 3
(5–15 minutes)

The spokesperson for the accommodators tells the other three groups how they would be helpful to that group if they were the only two styles on the island. The divergers go next, followed by the convergers, and then the assimilators.

Procedure 4
(3–7 minutes)

Break into as many discussion groups as there are members of the smallest of the four learning style groups. Each discussion group must have at least one person from all four learning styles; some will have more. For example, if the smallest group is the assimilators with five members, establish five discussion groups. If there are nine convergers, send two members to four groups and one to the remaining group. If there are six divergers, send one to four of the groups and two to one of the groups. Try to make the number of students in each discussion group as even as possible.

Procedure 5
(3–7 minutes)

Elect a spokesperson-recorder. Each group decides which learning style(s) to include in establishing the economic system. During the discussion, the instructor writes the four styles on the board for voting in procedure 6.

Procedure 6
(2–3 minutes)

The instructor records the votes from each group to be included in establishing the economic system.

Conclusion: The instructor leads a class discussion and/or makes concluding remarks.

Application (2–4 minutes):   What have I learned from this exercise? What will I do to be more open to working with people of different learning styles?

Sharing: Volunteers give their answers to the application section.

Personality Perceptions
Preparation (Group)

You should read the sections on personality traits and complete Self-Assessment Exercise 2–2. From this exercise, rank yourself below from highest score (1) to lowest score (5) for each of the Big Five. Do not tell anyone your ranking until told to do so.

_____ Surgency   _____ Agreeableness   _____ Adjustment

_____ Conscientiousness   _____ Openness to experience

In-Class Exercise

Objective: To develop your skill at perceiving others' personality traits. With this skill, you can better understand and predict people's behavior, which is helpful to leaders in influencing followers.

AACSB: The primary AACSB learning standard skills developed through this exercise are analytic skills and communication abilities.

Procedure 1
(2–4 minutes)

Break into groups of three with people you know the best in the class. You may need some groups of two. If you don't know people in the class and you did Skill-Building Exercise 1–2, Human Relations, get in a group with those people.

Procedure 2
(4–6 minutes)

Each person in the group writes down his or her perception of each of the other two group members. Simply rank which trait you believe to be the highest and lowest (put the Big Five dimension name on the line) for each person. Write a short reason for your perception, which should include some specific behavior you have observed that led you to your perception.

Name _____ Highest personality score _____ Lowest score _____

Reason for ranking _____

Name _____ Highest personality score _____ Lowest score _____

Reason for ranking _____

Procedure 3
(4–6 minutes)

One of the group members volunteers to go first to hear the other group members' perceptions.

1. One person tells the volunteer which Big Five dimensions he or she selected as the person's highest and lowest scores, and why they were selected. Do not discuss them yet.

2. The other person also tells the volunteer the same information.

3. The volunteer tells the two others what his or her actual highest and lowest scores are. The three group members discuss the accuracy of the perceptions.

Procedure 4
(4–6 minutes)

A second group member volunteers to go next to receive perceptions. Follow the same procedure as above.

Procedure 5
(4–6 minutes)

The third group member goes last. Follow the same procedure as above.

Conclusion: The instructor may lead a class discussion and/or make concluding remarks.

Application (2–4 minutes):   What did I learn from this exercise? How will I use this knowledge in the future?

Sharing: Volunteers give their answers to the application section.

SKILL-BUILDING EXERCISE 2–3

First Impressions

In-Class Exercise
(Group)

Objectives: To practice projecting a positive first impression. To receive feedback on the image you project. To develop your ability to project a positive first impression.

AACSB: The primary AACSB learning standard skills developed through this exercise are reflective thinking and self-management, analytic skills, and communication abilities.

Preparation: You should have read and now understand how to project a positive first impression.

Procedure 1
(2–4 minutes)

Pair off with someone you do not know. If you know everyone, select a partner you don't know well. Make one group of three if necessary. Do not begin your discussion until asked to do so.

Procedure 2
(Exactly 4 minutes)

Assume you are meeting for the first time. A mutual friend brought you together but was called to the telephone before introducing you. The mutual friend has asked you to introduce yourselves and get acquainted until he or she returns. When told to begin, introduce yourselves and get acquainted. Be sure to shake hands.

Procedure 3
(7–12 minutes)

Using the Image Feedback sheet below, give each other feedback on the image you projected. To be useful, the feedback must be an honest assessment of the image your partner received of you. So you answer the questions with the input of your partner.

Image Feedback

Human Relations Guidelines

1. I was optimistic _____, neutral _____, pessimistic _____.

2. I did _____ did not _____ complain and criticize.

3. I did _____ did not _____ show genuine interest in the other person.

4. I did _____ did not _____ smile and laugh when appropriate.

5. I did _____ did not _____ call the person by name two or three times.

6. I was a good _____, fair _____, poor _____ listener.

7. I was/tried to be _____ wasn't _____ helpful to the other person.

8. I did _____ did not _____ do or say anything that offended the other person.

Image Projection

Appearance:

9. My appearance projected a positive _____, neutral _____, negative _____ image to the other person.

Nonverbal communication:

10. My facial expressions projected a caring _____, neutral _____, uncaring _____ attitude toward the other person.

11. My eye contact was too little _____, about right _____, too much _____.

12. My handshake was firm _____ weak _____; dry _____ wet _____; long _____ short _____; full grip _____ shallow grip _____; with eye contact _____ without eye contact _____.

13. The behavior the other person liked most was _____.

14. The behavior the other person liked least was _____.

Overall

By receiving this feedback, I realize that I could improve my image projection by:

Perception

It is important to understand both our first impression of others and theirs of us (image). After discussing your images, do you think you made any perception errors? If yes, which one(s)?

Conclusion: The instructor leads a class discussion and/or makes concluding remarks.

Application (2–4 minutes):   What did I learn from this exercise? How will I use this knowledge in the future?

Sharing: Volunteers give their answers to the application section.

ANSWERS TO TRUE/FALSE QUESTIONS

1. T.

2. F. A personality profile includes all types of traits, depending upon the personality measurement.

3. T.

4. F. The fourth recommended method is positive thinking, not medication.

5. F. There is no one most effective learning style. We each have a preferred way of learning that works best for us.

6. F. People don't tend to "listen" to an explanation; they perceive based on their bias.

7. T.

Attitudes, Self-Concept, Values, and Ethics

After completing this chapter, you should be able to:

1. Define attitudes and explain how they affect behavior, human relations, and performance.

2. Describe how to change your attitudes.

3. List six job satisfaction determinants.

4. Determine whether you have a positive self-concept and how it affects your behavior, human relations, and performance.

5. Understand how your manager's and your own expectations affect your performance.

6. Demonstrate how to develop a more positive self-concept.

7. Identify your personal values.

8. Compare the three levels of moral development.

9. Define the following 13 key terms (in order of appearance in the chapter):

attitude	**self-efficacy**
Theory X	**self-fulfilling prophecy**
Theory Y	**attribution**
Pygmalion effect	**values**
job satisfaction	**value system**
job satisfaction survey	**ethics**
self-concept	

How Attitudes, Job Satisfaction, Self-Concept, Values, and Ethics Affect Behavior, Human Relations, and Performance

Attitudes

What Is an Attitude and Are Attitudes Important?

How We Acquire Attitudes

Management's Attitudes and How They Affect Performance

Changing Attitudes

Job Satisfaction

The Importance and Nature of Job Satisfaction

Determinants of Job Satisfaction

Job Satisfaction in the United States and Other Countries

Self-Concept

Self-Concept and How It Is Formed

Self-Efficacy

Attribution Theory and Self-Concept

Building a Positive Self-Concept

Values

Spirituality in the Workplace

Ethics

Does Ethical Behavior Pay?

How Personality Traits and Attitudes,
Moral Development, and the Situation
Affect Ethical Behavior
How People Justify Unethical Behavior

Human Relations Guide to Ethical
Decisions
Global Ethics

The mission of the American Red Cross, a nonprofit organization, is as follows: "The American Red Cross, a humanitarian organization led by volunteers, guided by its Congressional Charter and the Fundamental Principles of the International Red Cross Movement, will provide relief to victims of disasters and help people prevent, prepare for, and respond to emergencies." The Red Cross is the largest supplier of blood and blood products in the U.S.

The Red Cross is committed to saving lives and easing suffering. This diverse organization serves humanity and helps people by providing relief to victims of disaster, both locally and globally. The Red Cross gives health and safety training to the public and provides social services to U.S. military members and their families. In the wake of an earthquake, tornado, flood, fire, hurricane, or other disaster, it provides relief services to communities across the country.[1]

Rayanne was walking back to work after a meeting with her supervisor, Kent. Rayanne recalled that Kent had said she had a negative attitude and that it was affecting her performance, which was below standard. Kent had asked Rayanne if she was satisfied with her job. She had said, "No, I really don't like working, and I've messed up on all the jobs I've had. I guess I'm a failure." Kent had tried to explain how her poor attitude and negative self-concept were the cause of her poor performance. But Rayanne hadn't really listened, since work is not important to her. Rayanne has an external locus of control; thus, she believes that her poor performance is not her fault. She doesn't believe Kent knows what he's talking about. Rayanne thinks that Kent is not being ethical, that he is trying to manipulate her to get more work out of her. Is Kent's or Rayanne's analysis correct? Can Rayanne change?

HOW ATTITUDES, JOB SATISFACTION, SELF-CONCEPT, VALUES, AND ETHICS AFFECT BEHAVIOR, HUMAN RELATIONS, AND PERFORMANCE

In this chapter, we continue to focus on developing intrapersonal skills that affect behavior, human relations, and performance. We cover several different yet related topics, so let's start with an overview. *Attitudes* are critical to organizational success.[2] Our attitudes toward others, and their attitudes toward us, clearly affect our behavior, human relations, and performance.[3] Attitudes are the foundation of our *job satisfaction*.[4] Making employees happier increases their contributions, effort, and productivity;[5] plus, they stay in their jobs longer.[6] Satisfied workers have a positive impact on customers' satisfaction with the organization and its products.[7] Our *self-concept* is based on our attitude about ourself, and our confidence affects our career success[8] and overall performance in any aspect of life.[9] Our work *values* are our standards of behavior, which affect our human relations and performance.[10] *Unethical* behavior hurts both human relations and performance.[11]

Kent, in the opening case, tries to get Rayanne to understand how her poor attitude and negative self-concept are affecting her job performance, but she does not value work. Do you believe Kent is correct? Do you have a positive attitude and self-concept? Are you happy? Would you like to improve your attitude and self-concept? This chapter can help you improve.

ATTITUDES

Learning Outcome

1. Define attitudes and explain how they affect behavior, human relations, and performance.

In this section, we examine what an attitude is and the importance of attitudes, how you acquire attitudes, types of management attitudes and how they affect performance, and how to change attitudes.

What Is an Attitude and Are Attitudes Important?

An **attitude** *is a strong belief or feeling toward people, things, and situations.* We all have favorable, or positive, attitudes and unfavorable, or negative, attitudes about life, human relations, work, school, and everything else. Attitudes are not quick judgments we change easily but we *can* change our attitudes.[12] Our friends and acquaintances usually know how we feel about things. People interpret our attitudes by our behavior.[13] For example, if you make a face behind your boss's or instructor's back, peers will assume you have a negative attitude toward that person. Rayanne appears to have a negative attitude toward many things.

WORK APPLICATIONS

1. Describe your attitude about college in general and the specific college you are attending.

Attitudes are definitely important.[14] Employers place great emphasis on attitude.[15] A Xerox executive stated that organizations want to affect not only employees' behavior, but also their attitudes. J. S. Marriott, Jr., president of Marriott Corporation, stated, "We have found that our success depends more upon employee attitudes than any other single factor." This is largely due to the fact that customers evaluate service quality by the employees' attitudes; employee attitudes affect customer attitudes.[16]

How We Acquire Attitudes

Attitudes are developed primarily through experiences.[17] As people develop from childhood to adulthood, they interact with parents, family, teachers, friends, employees, and managers. From all these people, they learn what is right and wrong and how to behave.

When encountering new people or situations, you are the most open and impressionable because you usually haven't had time to form an attitude toward them.[18] Before entering a new situation, people often ask others with experience about it. This begins the development of attitudes before the encounter.[19] For example, before you signed up for this class, you may have asked others who completed the course questions about it. If they had positive attitudes, you too may have developed a positive attitude; if they were negative, you may have started the course with a negative attitude as well. Getting information from others is fine, but you should develop your own attitudes.

Management's Attitudes and How They Affect Performance

Before reading on, answer the 10 questions in Self-Assessment Exercise 3–1 to determine if you have Theory X or Theory Y attitudes.

Management Attitudes   Douglas McGregor classified attitudes, which he called *assumptions,* as Theory X and Theory Y.[20] Managers with **Theory X** *attitudes hold that employees dislike work and must be closely supervised to get them to do their work.*

Theory Y *attitudes hold that employees like to work and do not need to be closely supervised to get them to do their work.* Managers with dominant personalities often do not trust employees; thus, they have Theory X attitudes. Employee attitudes also affect managers' attitudes.[21] When managers perceive, correctly or not, negative employee attitudes, managers are quick to adopt Theory X attitudes.[22]

Over the years research has shown that managers with Theory Y attitudes tend to have employees with higher levels of job satisfaction than the employees of Theory X managers.[23] However, managers with Theory Y assumptions do not always have higher levels of productivity in their departments.

Self-Assessment Exercise 3–1

Your Management Attitudes

Circle the letter that best describes what you would actually do as a supervisor. There are no right or wrong answers.

Usually (U)   Frequently (F)   Occasionally (O)   Seldom (S)

U   F   O   S   1. I would set the objectives for my department alone (rather than include employee input).

U   F   O   S   2. I would allow employees to develop their own plans (rather than develop them for them).

U   F   O   S   3. I would delegate several tasks I enjoy doing (rather than doing them myself).

U   F   O   S   4. I would allow employees to make decisions (rather than make them for employees).

U   F   O   S   5. I would recruit and select new employees alone (rather than include employees' input).

U   F   O   S   6. I would train new employees myself (rather than have employees do it).

U   F   O   S   7. I would tell employees what they need to know (rather than everything I know).

U   F   O   S   8. I would spend time praising and recognizing my employees' work efforts (rather than not do it).

U   F   O   S   9. I would set several (rather than few) controls to ensure that objectives are met.

U   F   O   S   10. I would closely supervise my employees (rather than leave them on their own) to ensure that they are working.

To better understand your own attitudes toward human nature, score your answers. For items 1, 5, 6, 7, 9, and 10, give yourself one point for each usually (U) answer; two points for each frequently (F) answer; three points for each occasionally (O) answer; and four points for each seldom (S) answer. For items 2, 3, 4, and 8, give yourself one point for each seldom (S) answer; two points for each occasionally (O) answer; three points for each frequently (F) answer; and four points for each usually (U) answer. Total all points. Your score should be between 10 and 40. Place your score here _____. Theory X and Theory Y are on opposite ends of a continuum. Most people's attitudes fall somewhere between the two extremes. Place an X on the continuum below at the point that represents your score.

Theory X 10 – – – – – – – – – 20 – – – – – – – – – – 30 – – – – – – – – – – 40 Theory Y

The lower your score, the stronger the Theory X attitude; the higher your score, the stronger the Theory Y attitude. A score of 10 to 19 could be considered a Theory X attitude. A score of 31 to 40 could be considered a Theory Y attitude. A score of 20 to 30 could be considered balanced between the two theories. Your score may not accurately measure how you would behave in an actual job; however, it should help you understand your own attitudes toward people at work.

APPLICATION SITUATIONS

Theory X, Theory Y

AS 3–1

Identify each manager's comments about employees as:

A. Theory X   B. Theory Y

_____ 1. "Be careful with it now. I don't want you to mess it up like you did the last time."

_____ 2. "Thanks, I'm confident you will do a good job."

_____ 3. "Select the format you want to use and get it to me when you finish it."

_____ 4. "I'll be checking up on you to make sure the job gets done on time."

_____ 5. "I know you probably think it's a lousy job, but someone has to do it."

How Management's Attitudes Affect Employees' Performance   Managers' attitudes and the way they treat employees affect employees' job behavior and performance.[24] If managers have a positive attitude and expect employees to be highly productive, they will often be highly productive.[25] Research by J. Sterling Livingston and others has supported this theory.[26] It is called the *Pygmalion effect*. The **Pygmalion effect** *states that supervisors' attitudes and expectations of employees and how they treat them largely determine their performance.* In a study of welding students, the foreman who was training the group was given the names of students who were quite intelligent and would do well. Actually, the students were selected at random. The only difference was the foreman's expectations. The so-called intelligent students significantly outperformed the other group members. Why this happened is what this theory is all about.[27] The foreman's expectations became the foreman's self-fulfilling prophecy.[28]

In a sense, the Hawthorne effect is related to the Pygmalion effect because both affect performance. In the Hawthorne studies, the special attention and treatment given the workers by the management resulted in increased performance.

Through the positive expectations of others, people increase their level of performance. Unfortunately, many managers tend to stereotype and see what they expect to see: low performance. And their employees see and do as the managers expect. We all need to expect and treat people as though they are high achievers to get the best from them.[29]

Marva Collins, recognized as one of the nation's most determined and successful teachers, opened her own inner-city school where very high standards are demanded from students of all abilities. In grade school these students read Shakespeare and do hours of homework each night, while many of the public school children cannot read and do not do any homework. Many of her students have gone on to successful careers, rather than being recipients of welfare, because of the Pygmalion effect of Collins's attitude.

Although others' attitudes can affect your behavior, human relations, and performance, you are responsible for your own actions. Try to ignore negative comments and stay away from people with negative attitudes. Focus on the positives.[30]

Treat workers well and they will work harder.[31] Treat them badly and they will get even.[32] As a manager, create a win–win situation. Expect high performance and treat employees as being capable and special, and you will get the best performance from them.[33]

2. Give two examples of when your attitude affected your performance. One should be a positive effect and the other a negative one. Be sure to fully explain how your attitudes affected performance.

3. Give an example of when you lived up to (or down to) someone else's expectations of your performance (the Pygmalion effect). It could be a parent's, teacher's, coach's, or boss's expectations. Be specific.

Changing Attitudes

Learning Outcome

2. Describe how to change your attitudes.

Self-Assessment Exercise 3–2

Complete Self-Assessment Exercise 3–2. Determine your own job attitude.

Your Job Attitude

For each of the 10 statements below, identify how often each describes your behavior at work. Place a number from 1 to 5 next to each of the 10 statements.

(5) Always   (4) Usually   (3) Frequently   (2) Occasionally   (1) Seldom

_____ 1. I smile and am friendly and courteous to everyone at work.

_____ 2. I make positive, rather than negative, comments at work.

_____ 3. When my boss asks me to do extra work, I accept it cheerfully.

_____ 4. I avoid making excuses, passing the buck, or blaming others when things go wrong.

_____ 5. I am an active self-starter at getting work done.

_____ 6. I avoid spreading rumors and gossip among employees.

_____ 7. I am a team player willing to make personal sacrifices for the good of the work group.

_____ 8. I accept criticism gracefully and make the necessary changes.

_____ 9. I lift coworkers' spirits and bring them up emotionally.

_____ 10. If I were to ask my boss and coworkers to answer the nine questions for me, they would put the same answers that I did.

_____ Total: Add up the 10 numbers.

Interpreting your score. You can think of your job attitude as being on a continuum from positive to negative. Place an X on the continuum below at the point that represents your score.

Negative attitude   10 – – – – 20 – – – – 30 – – – – 40 – – – – 50   Positive attitude

Generally, the higher your score, the more positive your job attitude is. You may want to have your boss and trusted coworkers answer the first nine questions, as suggested in question 10, to determine if their perception of your job attitude is the same as your perception.

4. Based on your answers in Self-Assessment Exercise 3–2, what will you do to improve your job attitude? Be specific.

A positive job attitude is vital to career success. Your superiors and coworkers will "read" your attitudes to determine whether they can count on you to be a hardworking, quality-conscious, upbeat team player. You need to have, and to communicate, a good job attitude.[34]

Would you rather work with people who have good, moderate, or poor job attitudes? We may not be able to change our coworkers' job attitudes and behavior, but we can change our own. Review your answers to the first nine questions in Self-Assessment Exercise 3–2, and think about ways you can improve your job attitude.

Changing Your Attitudes   The environment around us influences our attitudes. Usually we cannot control our environment, but we can control and change our attitudes.[35] You can choose to be and learn to be either optimistic or pessimistic. You can choose to look for the positive and be happier and get more out of life.[36] The following hints can help you change your attitudes:

1. Be aware of your attitudes. People who are optimistic have higher levels of job satisfaction. Consciously try to have and maintain a positive attitude. Make the best of situations by looking for the positive.[37]

   If you catch yourself complaining or being negative in any way, stop and change to a positive attitude. With time you can become more positive.

2. Realize that there are few, if any, benefits to harboring negative attitudes. Negative attitudes, such as holding a grudge, can only hurt your human relations, and hurt yourself in the end.[38]

3. Keep an open mind. Listen to other people's input. Use it to develop your positive attitudes.

In the 19th century, researchers discovered that changing the inner attitudes of your mind can change the outer aspects of your life. You can gain control of your attitudes and change the direction of your life. Start today. Think and act like a winner, and you will become one. Rayanne, in the opening case, does not seem to be interested in changing her attitude. If she doesn't, Rayanne will never be successful.

Shaping and Changing Employee Attitudes   It is difficult to change your own attitudes; it is even more difficult to change other people's attitudes. But it can be done.[39] The following hints can help you, as a manager, change employee attitudes:

1. Give employees feedback.[40] Employees must be made aware of their negative attitudes if they are to change. The manager must talk to the employee about the negative attitude. The employee must understand that the attitude has negative consequences for her or him and the department. The manager should offer an alternative attitude. In the opening case, Kent has done this.

2. Accentuate positive conditions. Employees tend to have positive attitudes toward the things they do well. Make working conditions as pleasant as possible,[41] and make sure employees have all the necessary resources and training to do a good job.

3. Provide consequences. Employees tend to repeat activities or events followed by positive consequences.[42] On the other hand, they tend to avoid things followed by negative consequences. Encourage and reward employees with positive attitudes. Try to keep negative attitudes from developing and spreading.

4. Be a positive role model. If the manager has a positive attitude, employees may also.[43]

See Exhibit 3.1 for a review of how to change your attitudes and those of your employees.

EXHIBIT 3.1 |
Changing Attitudes

Changing your attitudes

Be aware of
your attitudes

Do not harbor
negative thoughts

Keep an
open mind

Shaping and changing employee attitudes

Accentuate
positive conditions

Be a positive
role model

Give employees
feedback

Provide
consequences

APPLICATION SITUATIONS

Job Attitudes

AS 3–2

Identify each employee's attitude statement as:

A. Positive   B. Negative

_____   6. "Why do I have to do it?"

_____   7. "I'd be happy to go pick up the mail for you."

_____   8. "Get out of the way. Can't you see I'm trying to get through here?"

_____   9. "It's not my fault. The guy didn't give me enough time."

_____   10. "I heard you missed your sales quota this month. Don't worry. You'll
make it up next month."

JOB SATISFACTION

In this section we discuss the importance and nature of job satisfaction, the determinants of
job satisfaction, and facts about job satisfaction.

The Importance and Nature of Job Satisfaction

A person's **job satisfaction** *is a set of attitudes toward work.* Job satisfaction is what most
employees want from their jobs, even more than they want job security or higher pay.[44]
Employees who are more satisfied with their jobs are absent less, and they are more likely
to stay on the job.[45] Low job satisfaction often contributes to wildcat strikes, work slow-
downs, poor product quality, employee theft, and sabotage.

A **job satisfaction survey** *is a process of determining employee attitudes about the
job and work environment.* High job satisfaction is a hallmark of a well-managed organization. Organizations such as the American Red Cross measure job satisfaction and work

to improve it. Today managers see a decline in employees' interest in overtime work, job dedication, attendance, and punctuality. Improving job satisfaction may lead to better human relations and organizational performance by creating a win–win situation.[46]

WORK APPLICATIONS

5. Has job or school satisfaction affected your absenteeism? Explain your answer. For example, do you attend a class or job more if you are satisfied with it or if you are dissatisfied with it?

When employees are hired, they come to the organization with a set of desires, needs, and past experiences that combine to form job expectations about work. If their expectations are met, they generally have high levels of job satisfaction. If expectations are not met, their levels of job satisfaction may be low.[47] Job satisfaction is a part of life satisfaction.[48] As Chapter 1 stated, the total person comes to work. Your off-the-job life also affects your job satisfaction, and in turn your job satisfaction affects your life satisfaction. For example, Rayanne has brought a negative attitude to work, which in turn has affected her job satisfaction.

Determinants of Job Satisfaction

Learning Outcome

3. List six job satisfaction determinants.

Job satisfaction is on a continuum from low to high. It can refer to a single employee, a group or department, or an entire organization. Notice that the definition of job satisfaction identifies an overall attitude toward work. It does so because people usually have positive attitudes about some aspects of work, such as the work itself, and negative attitudes about other aspects of work, such as pay.[49] Job satisfaction is our overall attitude toward our jobs.

There are a variety of determinants of job satisfaction. Each of these determinants may be of great importance to some people and of little importance to others.

The Work Itself   Whether a person enjoys performing the work itself has a major effect on overall job satisfaction. People who view their jobs as boring, dull, or unchallenging tend to have low levels of job satisfaction.[50] Many people want to perform work they believe is important.[51]

Pay   A person's satisfaction with the pay received affects overall job satisfaction.[52] Employees who are not satisfied with their pay may not perform to their full potential. Some employees who are dissatisfied with their pay may steal organizational resources.

Growth and Upward Mobility   Whether a person is satisfied with personal or company growth and whether the potential for upward mobility exists may affect job satisfaction.[53] Many, but not all, people want to be challenged and to learn new things. Some people want to be promoted to higher-level jobs, whether in technical or managerial fields.

Supervision   Whether a person is satisfied with the supervision received affects overall job satisfaction.[54] Employees who feel their boss does not provide appropriate direction may become frustrated and dissatisfied with work. Employees who feel their boss exerts too much control over their jobs also may feel dissatisfied.[55] The personal relationship between the boss and the employee also affects job satisfaction.[56]

Coworkers   Whether a person has positive human relations with his or her coworkers affects overall job satisfaction.[57] People who like their coworkers often have higher levels of job satisfaction than employees who dislike their coworkers.

EXHIBIT 3.2 |
Determinants of Job
Satisfaction

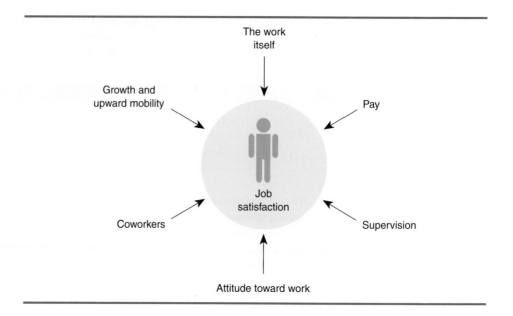

Attitude toward Work   Some people view work (attitude) as fun and interesting, while others do not. Some people have been satisfied with many different jobs, while others have remained dissatisfied in numerous work situations. People with a positive attitude toward work tend to have higher levels of job satisfaction. Personality is associated with work attitude and behavior.[58]

People differ in the ways they prioritize the above determinants of job satisfaction. A person can be highly satisfied in some areas and dissatisfied in others yet have overall job satisfaction.[59] Unfortunately, Rayanne doesn't seem happy with any of these determinants of job satisfaction. For a review of the six determinants of job satisfaction, see Exhibit 3.2.

Job Satisfaction in the United States and Other Countries

Most people start a new job with high expectations of job satisfaction, but the initial satisfaction often wears off. However, two-thirds of Americans say they would take the same job again and 90 percent are at least somewhat satisfied with their jobs.[60] Companies that work to improve job satisfaction have above-average customer service, sales, and profits because real satisfaction among employees leads to real money for the company. In a study, companies with satisfied employees posted a 3.74 percent increase in operating profit, while companies with dissatisfied workers had a 2 percent decline.[61]

There are different levels of job satisfaction across cultures. Overall, American workers are more satisfied than Japanese workers.[62] With increased global competition to increase productivity, companies need to be careful not to push employees to the point of decreased job satisfaction; such behavior can have severe negative consequences on performance.[63]

WORK APPLICATIONS

6. Consider a specific job you hold or have held. Measure your job satisfaction for the job by rating each of the six determinants of job satisfaction using a scale from 1 (not satisfied) to 5 (satisfied); then add up the total points and divide by 6 to get your average, or overall, job satisfaction level. Be sure to write down the six determinants and your ratings.

7. Has job or school satisfaction affected your performance? Explain your answer. For example, compared to your work in classes or jobs that you are satisfied with, do you work as hard and produce as much for classes or jobs that you are dissatisfied with?

APPLICATION SITUATIONS

Job Satisfaction

AS 3–3

Identify each statement by its determinant of job satisfaction:

A. Work itself   C. Growth and mobility   E. Coworkers

B. Pay   D. Supervision   F. General work attitude

_____ 11. "The boss is always on my back about something."

_____ 12. "I'd like to buy a DVD player, but my bills are piling up. I certainly
deserve more than I make."

_____ 13. "I enjoy working with my hands and fixing the machines."

_____ 14. "I'm applying for a promotion, and I think I'll get it."

_____ 15. "Pete and Ann are real jerks. I don't get along well with either of them.
They think they know it all."

SELF-CONCEPT

Learning Outcome

4. Determine whether you have a positive self-concept and how it affects your behavior, human relations, and performance.

In this section, we explain self-concept and how it is formed, self-efficacy, attribution theory and self-concept, and the steps of how to build a positive self-concept.

Self-Concept and How It Is Formed

Your **self-concept** *is your overall attitude about yourself.* Self-concept is also called *self-esteem* and *self-image.* Self-concept can be thought of as being on a continuum from positive to negative, or high to low. Do you like yourself? Are you a valuable person? Are you satisfied with the way you live your life? When faced with a challenge, are your thoughts positive or negative? Do you believe you can meet the challenge or that you're not very good at doing things?[64] If your beliefs and feelings about yourself are positive, you tend to have a high self-concept.[65] Your personality is based, in part, on your self-concept.[66]

Your self-concept includes perceptions about several aspects of yourself. You can have a positive self-concept and still want to change some things about yourself. Self-concept is your perception of yourself, which may not be the way others perceive you. Your thoughts and feelings about yourself have greater influence in determining your self-concept than does your behavior.[67] Even if individuals don't consider themselves likable, others probably do like them.

You develop your self-concept over the years through the messages you receive about yourself from others. Your present self-concept has been strongly influenced by the way others have treated you—the attitudes and expectations others have had of you (Pygmalion effect).[68] Your parents were the first to contribute to your self-concept. Did your parents build you up with statements like, "You're smart—you can do it," or destroy you with "You're dumb—you cannot do it"? If you have siblings, were they positive or negative? Your early self-concept still affects your self-concept today. As you grew through adolescence, your teachers and peers also had a profound impact on your self-concept. Were you popular? Did you have friends who encouraged you? By the time you reach adulthood in your early 20s, your self-concept is fairly well developed. However, when you take on more responsibilities, such as a full-time job, marriage, and children, your self-concept can change.[69] Your boss, for example, does or will affect your success (Pygmalion effect) and self-concept.[70]

Apparently, Rayanne came to work for Kent with a negative self-concept. Rayanne stated that she messed up on all her previous jobs, and she called herself a failure. Her self-concept, like yours, however, is dynamic and capable of changing. Kent is trying to develop a win–win situation by trying to get Rayanne to develop a more positive attitude and self-concept so that she can be happier and more productive. Rayanne can change her attitude and self-concept if she really wants to and is willing to work at it. Are you willing to develop a more positive self-concept so that you can be happier and more productive?

In addition to receiving messages from others, we also make social comparisons.[71] We compare ourselves with others all the time. You might think to yourself, Am I smarter, better looking, more successful than the people I associate with? Such comparisons can have positive or negative influences on your self-concept. Focusing on negative comparisons can cause you to have a negative self-concept and to be unhappy, so don't do it.

WORK APPLICATIONS

8. Describe your self-concept.

Learning Outcome

5. Understand how your manager's and your own expectations affect your performance.

Self-Efficacy

Self-efficacy *is your belief in your capability to perform in a specific situation.* Self-efficacy affects your effort, persistence, expressed interest, and the difficulty of goals you select. For example, if your major is business, your self-efficacy may be high for a management course but low for a language or biology course that you may be required to take.

APPLICATION SITUATIONS

Self-Concept

AS 3–4

Identify each statement as:

A. Positive   B. Negative

_____ 16. "Darn, that's the fifth mistake I've made today."

_____ 17. "Sure, I can do that. No problem."

_____ 18. "It's been three weeks, and I still cannot understand why I did not get the promotion I wanted so badly."

_____ 19. "I enjoy going on sales calls and meeting new people."

_____ 20. "I cannot do math."

Your expectations affect your performance.[72] If you think you will be successful, you will be. If you think you will fail, you will, because you will fulfill your expectations. You will live up to or down to your expectations. This expectation phenomenon is often referred to as the *self-fulfilling prophecy* and the Galatea effect.[73] The **self-fulfilling prophecy** *occurs when your expectations affect your success or failure.* Rayanne stated that she had messed up on all the jobs she had, and she called herself a failure. Is it any surprise to find that Rayanne is having problems in her new job working for Kent?

As you can see, self-efficacy and the self-fulfilling prophecy go hand in hand. Your self-efficacy becomes your self-fulfilling prophecy.

WORK APPLICATIONS

9. Give an example of when you lived up to or down to your own expectations (self-efficacy leading to self-fulfilling prophecy).

Attribution Theory and Self-Concept

Let's discuss attribution theory and how it relates to your self-concept. **Attribution** *is one's perception that the cause of behavior is either internal or external. Internal* behavior is within the control of the person, and *external* behavior is out of the person's control. When we observe others' behavior, we do not know the reason for it. So we make a judgment as to why people do the things they do. We use *distinctiveness, consistency,* and *consensus* to make our judgment. For example, your coworker Ed yells at you for a minor error you made. You ask yourself if Ed yells only when you work on a particular task (distinctiveness), if he always yells (consistency), and if others yell too (consensus). You can attribute Ed's yelling at you as just due to the situation or some personal issue bothering him and causing him to yell (external), or you can attribute it to his normal behavior (internal). If you believe the cause to be external, you may respond with positive human relations. If you believe the cause to be internal, you may yell back, which leads to negative human relations. So attribution theory is how we perceive the causes of behavior, which in turn affects our subsequent choices and behaviors.

You can improve your self-concept only if you are willing to take responsibility for your actions and change to improve. Rayanne is not willing to take responsibility for her poor performance; she says it's not her fault. Nor is she willing to change to improve. Until she takes responsibility and is willing to change, she will not improve. Are you willing to change to improve?

Building a Positive Self-Concept

Learning Outcome

6. Demonstrate how to develop a more positive self-concept.

You are the ultimate creator of your self-concept.[74] People with a positive self-concept are happier and more likable, have better relationships, and are more productive. You can always improve your self-concept, even though it is not easy to evaluate yourself and it is even more difficult to change. But as Jack Welch says, you have to take charge of yourself. Once you recognize the importance of a positive self-concept, you will see that it is worth the time and effort to improve your self-concept. You can change; you don't have to be who you were in the past or are in the present. The general guidelines below are followed by an action plan that will help you develop a more positive self-concept.

As a manager (coach, parent, teacher, friend), you can work with employees using these ideas to help them develop a more positive self-concept. One thing to keep in mind is that you need to be positive and give praise and encouragement.[75] However, real self-esteem is based on achievement, not praise for low performance.[76] If you give praise for poor performance, performance usually does not improve and it often gets worse.[77] A good example is in school when children fail and are passed anyway. Teachers say that if we keep these children back, it will hurt their self-esteem, so they pass them. As a result, these children often get through school without mastering reading and other basic skills, and that certainly does not improve their self-concept in the working world.

Kent can teach Rayanne how to improve her self-concept; he should praise her for improvements, but he should not praise her if she does not improve her performance. If Rayanne's performance does not improve and Kent takes no action, her self-concept will not improve.

General Guidelines   The following are general guidelines you can implement in your daily life to improve your self-concept:

1. View mistakes as learning experiences.[78] Realize that we all make mistakes. Talk to any successful businessperson with a positive self-concept and he or she will admit making mistakes. Jack Welch said he could fill a room with all his mistakes; he even blew up a factory. Jack didn't hide in the dugout; he always went to bat. You get some strikeouts and some hits. That's how life is. Try to be future-oriented. Don't worry about past mistakes. Dwelling on past mistakes will only have a negative effect on your self-concept.

2. **Accept failure and bounce back.**[79] Since most careers tend to zigzag upward, the ability to handle failures well can make or break a climb on the corporate ladder. Inability to rebound from disappointments is one of the main reasons managers fail. Dwelling on failure and disappointment will only have a negative effect on your self-concept. Realize that you will have disappointments but will most likely go on to bigger and better things.[80] Recall our definition of success (Chapter 1).

3. **Control negative behavior and thoughts.** Emotions, such as anger, are a part of life. You cannot control other people's behavior, nor can you completely control your emotional responses. If someone says something negative to you, you cannot be emotionless inside; however, you can control your behavior. You don't have to say something negative back to the person, yell at the person, or hit the person. Become aware of your emotions (develop your emotional intelligence), and work to control your behavior.[81]

   Your thoughts are also very important. If your thoughts are full of failure, you will fail. If you catch yourself thinking negative thoughts, be aware of what is happening and replace the negative thoughts and beliefs with positive ones, such as "I can do this. It's easy." With time you will have fewer and fewer negative thoughts. Always accept a compliment with a thank you. Don't minimize the compliment with a statement such as, "Anyone could have done it" or "It was not a big deal." Never put yourself down in your thoughts, words, or actions. If you catch yourself doing this, stop and replace the thoughts or behavior with positive ones.

4. **Tap into your spirituality.** Use any religious or spiritual beliefs you have that can help you develop a more positive self-concept: For example, think to yourself, "I am made in the image and likeness of God," or "Buddha doesn't make junk."

Action Plan for Building a Positive Self-Concept   The three-part action plan for building a positive self-concept is as follows:

Step 1:   Identify Your Strengths and Areas that Need Improvement   What are the things about yourself that you like? What can you do well? What do you have to offer other people and organizations?

What are the things about yourself or the behavior that could be improved? Be aware of your limitations. No one is good at everything. Focus on your strengths, not on your weaknesses. In areas where you are weak, get help and help others in their weak areas.

Step 2:   Set Short- and Long-term Goals and Visualize Them   Before you can get anywhere or get anything out of life, you must first determine where you want to go or what you want. Based on step 1, set some goals for the things about yourself or your behavior that you want to change for the better. Write them down in positive, affirmative language. For example, write:

- "I am calm when talking to others" (not "I don't yell at people").
- "I am a slim _____ pounds [select a weight 5 to 10 pounds less than your current weight]" (not "I must lose weight").
- "I am outgoing and enjoy meeting new people" (not "I must stop being shy").
- "I am smart and get good grades," or "I am good at my job."

Place your goals where you can review them several times each day. Put copies on your mirror, refrigerator, car visor, or desk, or record them so you can play them several times each day. Start and end each day thinking positive thoughts about yourself.

People often procrastinate because the whole goal or project seems overwhelming. When you don't know where to start, you don't do anything. Remember, success comes one step at a time. Reaching one goal helps motivate you to continue, and each success helps you develop a more positive self-concept.[82] Therefore, set short-term goals you can reach. For example, if you presently weigh 150 pounds, start with the goal "I am a slim 110 pounds," but break it up into doable parts: "I will weigh 145 pounds by XXX date," and "I will weigh 140 pounds by XXX date." Compliment and reward yourself regularly as you achieve your short-term goals. Rewards do not have to be big. When you hit the new weight, treat yourself to a small ice cream cone or a movie. Rewards will help motivate you to continue until you reach the final 110 pounds. As you continue to set and achieve short-term goals, you will continue to build your self-concept as being successful. You will learn about goal setting and motivation in Chapter 9.

Each day, visualize yourself as you want to be, as set forth in your goals. For example, picture yourself being calm when talking to a person you usually yell at. Mentally see yourself at a slim 110 pounds. Picture yourself meeting new people or being successful on the job, and so forth.

Step 3:   Develop a Plan and Implement It   What specific action will you take to improve your self-concept through changing your thoughts or behavior? Some goals take much planning, while others do not. For example, if you want to lose weight to get down to 110 pounds, you will have to do more than just imagine yourself being 110 pounds. What will be your plan to lose the weight? Exercise? Diet? What are the specifics? With other goals, such as not yelling at people, making detailed plans is not so easy. However, you can determine what it is that gets you angry and try to eliminate it. What will you do differently?

Stop comparing yourself with others and downgrading yourself, because this hurts your self-concept.[83] We can all find someone who is better than we are. Even the best are eventually topped. Set your goals, develop plans, and achieve them. Compare yourself with *you*. Be the best that *you* can be. Continue to improve yourself by setting goals, developing plans, and achieving them. Through this process, you will develop your self-concept. If you continually improve yourself, there is less chance of a midlife crisis. You are less likely to look back at your life and ask, What have I accomplished? You will know and be proud of yourself. See Exhibit 3.3 for a review of how to develop a positive self-concept.

WORK APPLICATIONS

10. Which of the four general guidelines to building a positive self-concept needs the least work? The most work? Explain your answer.

EXHIBIT 3.3 |
Developing a Positive
Self-Concept

Accept failure   Control negative
and bounce back   behavior and thoughts

View mistakes as   Tap into your
learning experiences   spirituality

1. Identify your strengths and areas that need improvement.
2. Set short- and long-term goals and visualize them.
3. Develop a plan and implement it.

VALUES

Learning Outcome

7. Identify your personal values.

In this section, we cover individual values and how they are related to, yet different from, attitudes. A person's **values** *are the things that have worth for or are important to the individual,* and a **value system** *is the set of standards by which the individual lives.* Values concern what "should be"; they influence the choices we make among alternative behaviors.[84] Values direct the form that motivated behavior will take.[85] For example, if you have three job offers, you will select the one that is of the highest value to you.

Values help shape your attitudes. When something is of value to you, you tend to have positive attitudes toward it. If something is not of value to you, you tend to have negative attitudes toward it. Since work is not important to Rayanne, it is not surprising that she has a negative attitude toward work. What is of value to you? Complete Self-Assessment Exercise 3–3 to identify your personal values in eight broad areas of life.

Self-Assessment Exercise 3–3

Your Personal Values

Below are 16 items. Rate how important each one is to you on a scale of 0 (not important) to 100 (very important). Write a number from 0 to 100 on the line to the left of each item.

Not important					Somewhat important					Very important
0	10	20	30	40	50	60	70	80	90	100

_____ 1. An enjoyable, satisfying job.

_____ 2. A high-paying job.

_____ 3. A good marriage.

_____ 4. Meeting new people, social events.

_____ 5. Involvement in community activities.

_____ 6. My religion.

_____ 7. Exercising, playing sports.

_____ 8. Intellectual development.

_____ 9. A career with challenging opportunities.

_____ 10. Nice cars, clothes, home, etc.

_____ 11. Spending time with family.

_____ 12. Having several close friends.

_____ 13. Volunteer work for not-for-profit organizations such as the cancer society.

_____ 14. Meditation, quiet time to think, pray, etc.

_____ 15. A healthy, balanced diet.

_____ 16. Educational reading, self-improvement programs, etc.

Below, transfer the numbers for each of the 16 items to the appropriate column; then add the two numbers in each column.

	Professional	Financial	Family	Social
	1. _____	2. _____	3. _____	4. _____
	9. _____	10. _____	11. _____	12. _____
Totals	_____	_____	_____	_____
	Community	**Spiritual**	**Physical**	**Intellectual**
	5. _____	6. _____	7. _____	8. _____
	13. _____	14. _____	15. _____	16. _____
Totals	_____	_____	_____	_____

**Self-Assessment
Exercise 3–3 (*continued*)**

The higher the total in any area, the higher the value you place on that particular area. The closer the numbers are in all eight areas, the more well-rounded you are.

Think about the time and effort you put forth in your top three values. Is it sufficient to allow you to achieve the level of success you want in each area? If not, what can you do to change? Is there any area in which you feel you should have a higher value total? If yes, which one? What can you do to change?

WORK APPLICATIONS

11. What is your attitude toward your personal values in the eight areas of Self-Assessment Exercise 3–3? Do you plan to work at changing any of your values? Why or why not?

Values are developed in much the same way as attitudes. However, values are more stable than attitudes. Attitudes reflect multiple, often changing, opinions. Values about some things do change, but the process is usually slower than a change in attitude. Society influences our value system.[86] What was considered unacceptable in the past may become commonplace in the future, or vice versa.[87] For example, the percentage of smokers and the social acceptance of smoking have decreased over the years. Similarly, your parents may have told you that some of your behavior would not have been tolerated in their parents' home. Value changes over the years are often a major part of what is referred to as the *generation gap.*

Business managers state that the work ethic has declined. The number of people who are not honest and do not play fair (lie, cheat, steal, etc.) has led to companies' increasingly being judged not only by their products but also by their values.[88] Thus, business success depends on achieving a balance among interests[89] or what we call the *goal of human relations:* a win–win situation. In response, companies are conducting values audits that encourage honesty and strong values.[90]

Getting to know people and understanding their values can improve human relations. For example, if Juan knows that Carla has great respect for the president, he can avoid making negative comments about the president in front of her. Likewise, if Carla knows that Juan is a big baseball fan, she can ask him how his favorite team is doing.

Discussions over value issues, such as abortion and homosexuality, rarely lead to changes in others' values. They usually just end in arguments. Therefore, we should try to be open-minded about others' values and avoid arguments that will only hurt human relations.

Spirituality in the Workplace

People want to be happy, and the level of happiness has not changed in 30 years, even though the average per capita income has more than doubled in the United States.[91] People are searching for fulfillment at work and at home.[92] Many people are seeking spirituality as a means of fulfillment in their lives. Dr. Edward Wilson, Harvard University professor and two-time Pulitzer Prize–winning expert on human nature, says, "I believe the search for spirituality is going to be one of the major historical episodes of the 21st century."[93]

Judith Neal, editor of the Web site, Spirit at Work, has defined spirituality in the workplace and developed guidelines for leading from a spiritual perspective.[94]

Defining Spirituality in the Workplace   The Latin origin of the word spirit is *spirare,* meaning "to breathe." At its most basic, then, spirit is what inhabits us when we are alive and breathing; it is the life force.

Spirituality in the workplace is about people seeing their work as a spiritual path, as an opportunity to grow personally and to contribute to society in a meaningful way. It is about

In Their Sights: The American Family Association Takes Aim at Target

The American Family Association (AFA), a Mississippi-based Christian conservative group, is successfully bringing America's culture wars into the corporate boardroom, according to *The Wall Street Journal*. Now the AFA is homing in on Target Corporation.

Why is the retailer worried about the AFA? The AFA has demonstrated its ability to mobilize large groups of Christian conservatives to its cause. That could become a serious irritant to any firm considering launching a political-style campaign to win over conservative Midwestern soccer moms. Several big corporations have already succumbed to pressure from this radical group. Ford Motor Company stopped advertising its Jaguar and Land Rover brands in gay publications when the AFA boycotted Ford for supporting gay-rights causes. The AFA also closed all of its accounts at Wells Fargo & Company because the bank contributed to a gay-rights group.

The AFA has now launched an attack on Target and other retailers for their refusal to use the word "Christmas" in any of their promotions.

Questions

1. Spirituality has become a critical force in the workplace. How does this ethical dilemma highlight spirituality from a consumer's perspective?

2. Apply the guidelines for leading from a spiritual perspective to the AFA's actions. Has the AFA abided by those guidelines?

3. In your opinion, whose behavior is unethical? The AFA, Ford, Target? Why?

4. What, if any, moral justifications are implied or inferred in this ethical dilemma?

Sources: Alan Murray, "Christian Conservatives Test Boardroom Clout," *The Wall Street Journal*, December 7, 2005, p. D1; http://investors.target.com/.

learning to be more caring and compassionate with fellow employees, with bosses, with subordinates, and with customers. It is about having integrity, being true to oneself, and telling the truth to others. Spirituality in the workplace can refer to an individual's attempts to live his or her values more fully in the workplace. Or it can refer to the ways organizations structure themselves to support the spiritual growth of employees. In the final analysis, one's understanding of spirit and of spirituality in the workplace is a very individual and personal matter.

Guidelines for Leading from a Spiritual Perspective   Here are five spiritual principles that have been useful to many leaders in their personal and professional development:

1. *Know thyself.* All spiritual growth processes incorporate the principle of self-awareness. Examine why you respond to situations the way you do.

2. *Act with authenticity and congruency.* Followers learn a lot more from who we are and how we behave than from what we say. Authenticity means being oneself, being fully congruent, and not playing a role. Managers who are more authentic and congruent tend to be more effective. Jack Welch says the mark of a good boss is candor. When you manage someone, it's about them, not you.

3. *Respect and honor the beliefs of others.* It can be very risky and maybe even inappropriate to talk about your own spirituality in the workplace. Yet if spirituality is a guiding force in your life and your leading, and if you follow the guideline of authenticity and congruency, you cannot hide that part of yourself. It is a fine line to walk. It is extremely important that employees do not feel that you are imposing your belief system (spiritual, religious, or otherwise) on them.

4. *Be as trusting as you can be.* This guideline operates on many levels. On the personal level, this guideline applies to trusting oneself, one's inner voice, or one's source of spiritual guidance. This means trusting that there is a Higher Power in your life and that if you ask, you will receive guidance on important issues.

5. *Maintain a spiritual practice.* In a research study on people who integrate their spirituality and their work, the most frequently mentioned spiritual practice is spending

time in nature. Examples of other practices are attending religious services, meditation, prayer, reading inspirational literature, hatha yoga, shamanistic practices, writing in a journal, and walking a labyrinth. These people report that it is very important for them to consistently commit to their chosen individual spiritual practice. When leaders faithfully commit to a particular spiritual practice, they are calmer, more creative, more in tune with employees and customers, and more compassionate.

Secular institutional research has found that during moments of anger and distress, turning to prayer or mediation, encouraged in nearly all religions, diminishes the harmful effects of negative emotions and stress. Also, people who attend religious services at least once a week enjoy better-than-average health and lower rates of illness, including depression.[95]

By implementing the ideas presented in this chapter, you can develop positive attitudes and a more positive self-concept, as well as clarify your values. Begin today.

ETHICS

In a recent survey, over two-thirds (71 percent) of Americans said none, few, or only some businesses operate in a fair and honest manner.[96] There is a call for increased curricular focus on business ethics.[97] Now more than ever, management ethics are being called into question.[98]

As related to values, **ethics** *refers to the moral standard of right and wrong behavior.* In this section, we discuss whether ethical behavior does pay, how personality and attitudes affect ethical behavior, how people justify unethical behavior, some ethical guidelines, the stakeholders' approach to ethics, and global ethics. Before we begin, complete Self-Assessment Exercise 3–4 to determine how ethical your behavior is.

Self-Assessment Exercise 3–4

How Ethical Is Your Behavior?

For this exercise, you will be using the same set of statements twice. The first time you answer them, focus on your own behavior and the frequency with which you use it. On the line before the question number, place the number from 1 (frequently) to 4 (never) that represents how often you have done the behavior in the past, do the behavior now, or would do the behavior if you had the chance. These numbers will allow you to determine your level of ethics. You can be honest without fear of having to tell others your score in class. *Sharing ethics scores is not part of the exercise.*

Frequently   Never

1   2   3   4

The second time you use the statements, focus on other people in an organization with whom you work or have worked. Place an O on the line after the number if you have observed someone doing this behavior. Also place an R on the line if you have reported (blown the whistle on) this behavior either within the organization or externally.

O——Observed   R——Reported

1–4   O, R

College

_____ 1. _____ Cheating on homework assignments.

_____ 2. _____ Cheating on exams.

_____ 3. _____ Passing in papers that were completed by someone else as your own work.

Self-Assessment
Exercise 3–4 (*continued*)

1–4   **O, R**

Job

_____ 4. _____ Lying to others to get what you want or to stay out of trouble.

_____ 5. _____ Coming to work late, leaving work early, or taking long breaks or lunches and getting paid for it.

_____ 6. _____ Socializing, goofing off, or doing personal work rather than doing the work that should be done and getting paid for it.

_____ 7. _____ Calling in sick to get a day off when you are not sick.

_____ 8. _____ Using the organization's phone, computer, Internet, copier, mail, car, etc., for personal use.

_____ 9. _____ Taking home company tools or equipment without permission for personal use and returning the items.

_____ 10. _____ Taking home organizational supplies or merchandise and keeping the items.

_____ 11. _____ Giving company supplies or merchandise to friends or allowing them to take the items without saying anything.

_____ 12. _____ Putting in for reimbursement for meals and travel or other expenses that weren't actually eaten or taken.

_____ 13. _____ Taking your spouse or friends out to eat or on a business trip and charging it to the organizational expense account.

_____ 14. _____ Accepting gifts from customers or suppliers in exchange for giving them business.

_____ 15. _____ Cheating on your taxes.

_____ 16. _____ Misleading customers, such as promising short delivery dates, to make a sale.

_____ 17. _____ Misleading competitors, such as pretending to be a customer or supplier, to get information to use to compete against them.

_____ 18. _____ Planting false information to enhance your chances of getting reelected.

_____ 19. _____ Selling a customer more product than the customer needs just to get the commission.

_____ 20. _____ Spreading false rumors about coworkers or competitors to make yourself look better for advancement or to make more sales.

_____ 21. _____ Lying for your boss when asked or told to do so.

_____ 22. _____ Deleting information that makes you look bad or changing information to look better than the actual results.

_____ 23. _____ Being pressured, or pressuring others, to sign off on documents that contain false information.

_____ 24. _____ Being pressured to sign off on documents you haven't read, knowing they may contain information or decisions that may be considered inappropriate, or pressuring others to do so.

_____ 25. If you were to give this assessment to a person with whom you work and with whom you do not get along very well, would she or he agree with your answers? Use 4 (yes) or 1 (no). Place the appropriate number on the line before the number 25. (No O or R responses are necessary for this question.)

Self-Assessment Exercise 3–4 (*continued*)

Other Unethical Behavior: On the lines below, add other unethical behaviors you have observed. If you reported the behavior, write an R before the behavior.

26. _____ _____

27. _____ _____

28. _____ _____

Note: This self-assessment is not meant to be a precise measure of your ethical behavior. It is designed to get you thinking about your behavior and that of others from an ethical perspective. There is no right or wrong score; however, each of these actions is considered unethical behavior in most organizations. Another ethical issue in this exercise is your honesty when rating the frequencies of your behavior. How honest were you?

Scoring: To determine your ethics score, add the numbers you recorded. Your total will be between 25 and 100. Place the number here _____ and on the continuum below place an X at the point that represents your score. The higher your score, the more ethical your behavior is; the lower your score, the less ethical your behavior is.

Unethical   25 – – – 30 – – – 40 – – – 50 – – – 60 – – – 70 – – – 80 – – – 90 – – – 100   Ethical

Does Ethical Behavior Pay?

Generally, the answer is yes. It has bottom-line benefits.[99] The unethical behavior of Enron and other companies cost many organizations and people a great deal of money directly. But indirectly, it also hurt everyone in the stock market as well as the general economy.[100] From the organizational level ethics crises at WorldCom, Conseco, Global Crossing, United Airlines, and Kmart contributed to their bankrupcies, resulting in the loss of 125,000 jobs and the destruction of assets valued at $300 billion.[101]

From the individual level, you may say that former executives made millions from their unethical behavior. However, these top executives would have made millions anyway for honest behavior: now many of them are facing prison, and they may never hold high-level positions again. With all the negative media coverage, the unethical leaders' lives will never be the same. Mahatma Gandhi called business without morality a sin.

Ethical conduct also happens to be good business.[102] Unethical behavior has long-term implications for how others trust you, your reputation, and the reputation of the organization.[103] Thus, long-term sustainable business success can only be achieved through ethical behavior.[104]

How Personality Traits and Attitudes, Moral Development, and the Situation Affect Ethical Behavior

Personality Traits and Attitudes   The use of ethical behavior is related to our individual needs and personality traits.[105] Leaders with *surgency* dominance personality traits have two choices: to use power for personal benefit or to help others. To gain power and to be *conscientious* with high achievement, some people will use unethical behavior; also, irresponsible people often do not perform to standard; they cut corners and engage in other behavior that may be considered unethical. An *agreeableness* personality, sensitive to others, can lead to following the crowd in either ethical or unethical behavior; having a high *self-concept* tends to lead to doing what the person believes is right and not following the crowd's unethical behavior. *Emotionally unstable* people and those with an external locus of control are more likely to use unethical behavior. People *open to new experiences* are often ethical.

People with *positive attitudes* about ethics tend to be more ethical than those with negative or weak attitudes about ethics.[106] The firm's internal ethical context can help or hurt employee attitudes and behavior—being ethical or unethical.[107] When you complete Self-Assessment Exercise 3–5 at the end of this section, you will have a better understanding of how your personality affects your ethical behavior.

EXHIBIT 3.4 | Levels of Moral Development

Level 3: Postconventional

Behavior is motivated by universal principles of right and wrong, regardless of the expectations of the leader or group. One seeks to balance the concerns for self with those of others and the common good. At the risk of social rejection, economic loss, and physical punishment, the individual will follow ethical principles even if they violate the law (Martin Luther King, Jr., for example, broke what he considered unjust laws and spent time in jail seeking universal dignity and justice).

"I don't lie to customers because it is wrong."

The common leadership style is visionary and committed to serving others and a higher cause while empowering followers to reach this level.

Level 2: Conventional

Living up to expectations of acceptable behavior defined by others motivates behavior to fulfill duties and obligations. It is common for followers to copy the behavior of the leaders and group. If the group (can be society, an organization, or a department) accepts lying, cheating, and stealing when dealing with customers, suppliers, the government, or competitors, so will the individual. On the other hand, if these behaviors are not accepted, the individual will not do them either. Peer pressure is used to enforce group norms.

"I lie to customers because the other sales reps do it too."

It is common for lower-level managers to use a leadership style similar to that of the higher-level managers.

Level 1: Preconventional

Self-interest motivates behavior to meet one's own needs and to gain rewards while following rules and being obedient to authority to avoid punishment.

"I lie to customers to sell more products and get higher commission checks."

The common leadership style is autocratic toward others while using one's position for personal advantage.

Source: Based on Lawrence Kohlberg, "Moral Stages and Moralization: The Cognitive-Development Approach," in *Moral Development and Behavior: Theory, Research, and Social Issues,* ed. Thomas Likona (Austin, TX: Holt, Rinehart and Winston, 1976), pp. 31–53.

Learning Outcome

8. Compare the three levels of moral development.

Moral Development A second factor affecting ethical behavior is *moral development,* which refers to understanding right from wrong and choosing to do the right thing. Our ability to make ethical choices is related to our level of moral development.[108] There are three levels of personal moral development, as discussed in Exhibit 3.4. At the first level, preconventional, you choose right and wrong behavior based on your self-interest and the consequences (reward and punishment). With ethical reasoning at the second level, conventional, you seek to maintain expected standards and live up to the expectations of others. At the third level, postconventional, you make an effort to define moral principles regardless of the leader's or group's ethics. Although most of us have the ability to reach this third level, only about 20 percent of people actually do reach it. Most people behave at the second level, conventional, while some do not advance beyond the first level, preconventional. How do you handle peer pressure? What level of moral development have you attained? What can you do to further develop your ethical behavior?

WORK APPLICATIONS

12. Give an organizational example of behavior at each of the three levels of moral development.

The Situation A third factor affecting ethical behavior is the situation.[109] Highly competitive and unsupervised situations increase the odds of unethical behavior. Unethical behavior occurs more often when there is no formal ethics policy or code of ethics and when unethical behavior is not punished. Unethical behavior is especially prevalent when it is rewarded. When we observe unethical behavior, we use attribution theory to determine if we should report it. People are also less likely to report unethical behavior (blow the whistle) when they perceive the violation as not being serious and when the potential whistle-blower is friends with the offender.

To tie together the three factors affecting ethical behavior, we need to realize that personality traits and attitudes and our moral development interact with the situation to determine if a person will use ethical or unethical behavior. In this chapter we use the individual level of analysis: Am I ethical? How can I improve my ethical behavior? At the organizational level, many firms offer training programs and develop codes of ethics to help employees behave ethically. We will talk about ethics again, as it relates to power and politics, in Chapter 10.

How People Justify Unethical Behavior

Most people understand right and wrong behavior and have a conscience, or they live by a personal code of conduct.[110] So why do good people do bad things? In most cases, when people use unethical behavior it is not due to some type of character flaw or being born a bad person. Few people see themselves as unethical. We all want to view ourselves in a positive manner. Therefore, when we do use unethical behavior, we often justify the behavior to protect our *self-concept* so that we don't have a guilty conscience or feel remorse.[111] Let's discuss several thinking processes used to justify unethical behavior.

- *Moral justification* is the process of reinterpreting immoral behavior in terms of a higher purpose. The terrorists of 9/11/01 killed innocent people, as do suicide bombers, yet they believe their killing is for the good and that they will go to heaven for their actions. People sometimes state that they have conducted unethical behavior (lying about a competitor to hurt its reputation, fixing prices, stealing confidential information, etc.) for the good of the organization and employees.[112]

    People at the postconventional level of moral development, as well as those at lower levels, may seek a higher purpose (recall Martin Luther King, Jr.). However, people at the preconventional and conventional levels of moral development more commonly use the following justifications:

- *Displacement of responsibility* is the process of blaming one's unethical behavior on others: "I was only following orders; my boss told me to inflate the figures."

- *Diffusion of responsibility* is the process of a group engaging in unethical behavior, with no one person being held responsible: "We all take bribes or kickbacks; it's the way we do business"; "We all take merchandise home." As related to conventional morality, peer pressure is used to enforce group norms.

- *Advantageous comparison* is the process of comparing oneself to others who are worse: "I call in sick when I'm not sick only a few times a year; Tom and Ellen do it all the time"; "We pollute less than our competitors do."

- *Disregard for or distortion of consequences* is the process of minimizing the harm caused by the unethical behavior: "If I inflate the figures, no one will be hurt and I will not get caught. And if I do, I'll just get a slap on the wrist anyway." Was this the case at Enron and Global Crossing?

- *Attribution of blame* is the process of claiming the victim deserved whatever happened, or the unethical behavior was caused by someone else's behavior: "It's my coworker's fault that I repeatedly hit him. He called me XXX, so I had to hit him."

- *Euphemistic labeling* is the process of using "cosmetic" words to make the behavior sound acceptable. "Terrorist group" sounds bad, but "freedom fighters" sounds justifiable. "Misleading" or "covering up" sounds better than "lying to others."

WORK APPLICATIONS

13. Give at least two organizational examples of unethical behavior and the process of justification.

Human Relations Guide to Ethical Decisions

When making decisions, try to meet the goal of human relations by creating a win–win situation for all stakeholders. Economist Alan Greenspan said, "I have found no greater satisfaction than achieving success through honest dealing and strict adherence to the view that for you to gain, those you deal with should gain as well." Some of the relevant stakeholder parties include peers, your boss, subordinates, other department members, the organization, and people and organizations outside the organization you work for as well.

Here is a simple stakeholders guide to making ethical decisions: *If, after making a decision, you are proud to tell all the relevant parties your decision, the decision is probably ethical. If you are embarrassed to tell others your decision, or if you keep rationalizing the decision, it may not be ethical.*

A second, simple guide is the golden rule: "Do unto others as you want them to do unto you." Or, "Don't do anything to anyone that you would not want them to do to you." Or, "Do to others what they want you to do."

A third guide is, when in doubt, consult ethical people who may not tell you what you want to hear. A fourth guide is the Rotary International four-way test: (1) Is it the truth? (2) Is it fair to all concerned? (3) Will it build goodwill and better friendship? (4) Will it be beneficial to all concerned?

WORK APPLICATIONS

14. Give an example, preferably from an organization for which you work or have worked, of an individual creating a win–win situation for all parties involved. Identify all parties involved and how they were winners. Use Exhibit 10.4, Human Relations Guide to Ethical Decision Making (page 371), to help you answer the question.

Global Ethics

Globalization characterizes the business transactions in which U.S. and world multinational corporations (MNCs) will increasingly participate.[113] The explosive growth of MNCs has set the stage for global business ethics to be one of the highest priorities over the coming decades. How well we come through the era of globalization will depend upon how MNCs respond to the idea that we live in one world.[114]

A difficult challenge to MNC managers is the fact that different countries have different levels of ethical standards. For example, it is unethical to give bribes in America, but it is the way in which business is conducted in some countries.[115] Managers typically have two choices. According to *universalism,* managers should make the same ethical decisions across countries, whereas *relativism* calls for decisions to be made based on the ethical standards of the particular country. Thus, the MNC manager using universalism would not give any bribes, whereas the manager using relativism would give bribes in some countries. Today, governments and MNCs are working to develop more universal ethical standards.[116] Think of the complexity of conducting business in 100 to 200 countries.

The increasing concern for global managerial ethics calls for a better understanding through cross-national comparisons. To this end, and getting back to justification of unethical behavior, researchers have found that the same justifications presented earlier are used globally.[117]

MNCs can choose their level of global corporate social responsibility (GCSR); see Exhibit 3.5 for a list of the four levels. At the World Economic Forum, corporate executives of MNCs expressed the conviction that GCSR and citizenship were the trend, which will continue with universal ethical standards.[118]

EXHIBIT 3.5 | Levels of Global Corporate Social Responsibility (GCSR) and Action

Level of GCSR	Action
4. Philanthropic	Be a good global citizen by doing what is desired by global stakeholders.
3. Ethical	Be ethical by doing what is expected by global stakeholders.
2. Legal	Be lawful by doing what is required by global stakeholders.
1. Economic	Be profitable by doing what is required by global capitalism.

Source: Adapted from A. B. Carroll, "Managing Ethically with Global Stakeholders: A Present and Future Challenge," *Academy of Management Executive* 18, 2 (2004), pp. 114–120.

Rayanne accused Kent of being unethical by trying to manipulate her into doing more work. Was Kent unethical? Before we end the discussion of ethics, complete Self-Assessment Exercise 3–5 to better understand how your personality and attitudes affect your ethical behavior, your moral development, and your justifications for using unethical behavior.

Self-Assessment Exercise 3–5

Your Personality Profile and Ethics

Return to Self-Assessment Exercise 2–2, Your Big Five Personality Profile, on page 39 and place your personality profile scores below:

Surgency _____ Agreeableness _____ Adjustment _____ Conscientiousness _____ Openness to experience _____

Review the discussion of ethics above as it relates to your personality profile. How does your personality affect your ethical behavior? Which guides for ethical decisions will you use?

_____

_____

_____

Which level of moral development have you attained? How can you improve?

_____

_____

_____

Which justifications have you used? How can you improve your ethical behavior by not using justifications?

_____

_____

_____

Videos

Manager's Hot Seat and Behavior Model Videos are available for this chapter.

Online Learning Center Resources

Go to the Internet (http://mhhe.com/lussier8e) where you will find a broad array of resources to help maximize your learning.

- Review the vocabulary.
- Try a quiz.

R E V I E W

The chapter review is organized to help you master the 9 learning outcomes for Chapter 3. First provide your own response to each learning outcome, and then check the summary provided to see how well you understand the material. Next, identify the final statement in each section as either true or false (T/F). Correct each false statement. Answers are given at the end of the chapter.

1. **Define attitudes and explain how they affect behavior, human relations, and performance.**

   Attitudes are strong beliefs or feelings toward people, things, and situations. If we have a positive attitude toward a person, our behavior and interactions with them will be different than our behavior with a person toward whom we have a negative attitude. A supervisor's attitude and expectations of an employee largely determine his or her performance. This is referred to as the Pygmalion effect. Positive attitudes tend to lead to higher levels of performance than negative attitudes, but not always.

   Theory Y attitudes are outdated. T F

2. **Describe how to change your attitudes.**

   The first thing we must do is be aware of our attitudes, and make a conscious effort to change negative attitudes into positive ones. When we catch ourselves being negative, we must stop and change to a more positive attitude. We should think for ourselves, let negative attitudes go, and keep an open mind.

   To change employee attitudes: (1) give them feedback, (2) accentuate positive conditions, (3) provide consequences, and (4) be a positive role model. T F

3. **List six job satisfaction determinants.**

   Six determinants of job satisfaction are: (1) satisfaction with the work itself, (2) pay, (3) growth and upward mobility, (4) supervision, (5) coworkers, and (6) attitude toward work.

   Most American workers are dissatisfied with their jobs. T F

4. **Determine whether you have a positive self-concept and how it affects your behavior, human relations, and performance.**

   Answers will vary from positive to negative self-concepts. Generally, people with positive self-concepts are more outgoing and have more friends than people with negative self-concepts. They also tend to have higher levels of performance.

   Your self-concept is influenced by how others treat you—their attitudes and expectations. T F

5. **Understand how your manager's and your own expectations affect your performance.**

   When supervisors and coworkers believe and act like employees will be successful, those employees usually are high performers. On the other hand, when supervisors and coworkers believe and act like employees will not be successful, they usually are not high performers. The Pygmalion effect, self-efficacy, and the self-fulfilling prophecy all hold true.

   The Pygmalion effect tends to be based on the specific situation, whereas self-efficacy and the self-fulfilling prophecy are more constant. T F

6. **Demonstrate how to develop a more positive self-concept.**

   General guidelines for developing a more positive self-concept are: (1) view mistakes as a learning experience, (2) accept failure and bounce back, (3) control negative behavior and thoughts, and (4) tap into your spirituality. An action plan for building a positive self-concept includes the following steps: (1) identify your strengths and areas that need improvement, (2) set goals and visualize them, and (3) develop a plan and implement it.

   Having a more positive self-concept can help you succeed in your personal and professional lives. T F

7. **Identify your personal values.**

   Answers will vary among students. Some personal values include professional, financial, family, social, community, spiritual, physical, and intellectual.

   Spirituality in the workplace is a fad that is decreasing in popularity. T F

8. **Compare the three levels of moral development.**

   At the lowest level of moral development, preconventional, behavior is motivated by self-interest; one seeks to gain rewards and avoid punishment. At the second level, conventional, behavior is motivated by meeting the group's expectations to fit in by copying others' behavior. At the highest level, postconventional, behavior is motivated by the desire to do the right thing, even at the risk of alienating the group. The higher the level of moral development, the more ethical the behavior.

   Most people are on the preconventional level of moral development. T F

Learning Outcome

9. Define the following 13 key terms.

9. **Define the following 13 key terms.**

   Select one or more methods: (1) Fill in the missing key terms from memory, (2) match the key terms from the end of the review with their definitions below, and/or (3) copy the key terms in order from the key terms at the beginning of the chapter.

   A(n) ———————————————— is a strong belief or feeling toward people, things, and situations.

   ———————————————— attitudes hold that employees dislike work and must be closely supervised to get them to do their work.

   ———————————————— attitudes hold that employees like to work and do not need to be closely supervised to get them to do their work.

   The ———————————————— states that management's attitudes and expectations of employees and how they treat them largely determine their performance.

   ———————————————— is a set of attitudes toward work.

   A(n) ———————————————— is a process of determining employee attitudes about the job and work environment.

   Our ———————————————— is our overall attitude about ourselves.

   ———————————————— is our belief in our capability to perform in a specific situation.

   A(n) ———————————————— occurs when your expectations affect your successes or failures.

   ———————————————— is the perception of the cause of behavior as being internal or external.

   ———————————————— are the things that have worth or are important to the individual.

   A(n) ———————————————— is the set of standards by which the individual lives.

   ———————————————— is the moral standard of right and wrong behavior.

K E Y   T E R M S

attitude 73	Pygmalion effect 75	Theory Y 74
attribution 83	self-concept 81	values 86
ethics 89	self-efficacy 82	value system 86
job satisfaction 78	self-fulfilling	
job satisfaction	prophecy 82	
survey 78	Theory X 73	

C O M M U N I C A T I O N   S K I L L S

The following critical thinking questions can be used for class discussion and/or as written assignments to develop communication skills. Be sure to give complete explanations for all questions.

1. What is your attitude toward life? Do you agree with the statement, "Life sucks, then you die"?

2. Do more managers have Theory X or Theory Y attitudes today? Be sure to give examples to back up your statements.

3. Do you really believe that you can get better results with people using the Pygmalion effect—being positive and encouraging, rather than negative and threatening? Be sure to give examples to back up your statements.

4. Do you believe that most organizations really try to provide employees with job satisfaction? Give examples of what firms do to increase job satisfaction.

5. Is having a positive self-concept really all that important?

6. What is your view of spirituality in the workplace?

7. Do most people behave ethically at work, or do they lie, cheat, and steal?

8. Which method of justifying unethical behavior do you think is most commonly used?

CASE

Coca-Cola: More Than Just a Soft Drink

Coke is the world's number one soft-drink company. The Coca-Cola Company owns four of the top five soft-drink brands (Coca-Cola, Diet Coke, Fanta, and Sprite). Its other brands include Barq's, Minute Maid, POWERade, and Dasani water. In North America, it sells *Groupe Danone's* Evian. Coca-Cola sells brands from Dr Pepper Snapple Group (Crush, Dr Pepper, and Schweppes) outside Australia, Europe, and North America. The firm makes or licenses more than 400 drink products in more than 200 nations. Although it does no bottling itself, Coke owns 35 percent of Coca-Cola Enterprises (the number one Coke bottler in the world); 32 percent of Mexico's bottler Coca-Cola FEMSA; and 23 percent of European bottler Coca-Cola Hellenic Bottling.[119]

Coke's strategic vision is the cornerstone of the firm and sets the tone for the business and work environment, as noted by Muhtar Kent, president and CEO of the firm. Coke is "committed to serving and supporting sustainable communities because our business succeeds where communities thrive. Together with our bottling partners, our business partners, and members of the communities where we operate, The Coca-Cola Company works to identify and address existing and emerging social and environmental issues, as well as potential solutions."[120]

According to Mr. Kent, this strategic vision is incorporated in the manifest for growth. "The Coca-Cola Company is on a journey. It is a bold journey, inspired by our simple desire for sustainable growth, and fueled by our deep conviction that collectively we can create anything we desire . . . The goals are simple: We will reinvigorate growth for our Company, and we will inspire our people. Likewise, our strategy is simple: We will accomplish our goals by building a portfolio of branded beverages, anchored in our icon, Coca-Cola,® and by enabling superior market execution globally and locally—aligning and leveraging the power of our global network."[121]

According to the company's Web site,

Coke is built around two core assets, its brand and its people. That's what makes working here so special. We believe that work is more than a place you go every day. It should be a place of exploration, creativity, professional growth and interpersonal relationships. It's about being inspired and motivated to achieve extraordinary things. We want our people to take pride in their work and in building brands others love. After all, it's the combined talents, skills, knowledge, experience and passion of our people that make us who we are.

Our 90,500 associates around the world live and work in the markets we serve—more than 86 percent of them outside the U.S. In this geographically diverse environment, we learn from each market and share those learnings quickly. As a result, our Company culture is ever more collaborative. From beverage concept and development to merchandising, our associates are sharing ideas across departments and markets in new ways. Consequently, our associates are increasingly enthusiastic about their work and inspired to turn plans into action.[122]

According to Mr. Kent, "Ultimately, this journey will be propelled by unleashing the collective genius of our organization that will make sustainable growth a reality. We take this journey because it is in our very nature to innovate, create and excel . . . It is who we are."[123]

Go to the Internet: For more information on Muhtar Kent and an update on the information provided in this case, do a name search on the Internet and visit http://www.coca-cola.com.

Support your answers to the following questions with specific information from the case and text, or other information you get from the Web or other sources.

1. What seems to be Muhtar Kent's attitude toward Coca-Cola's local communities, its brands, and its people?

2. Using Theory X, Theory Y, describe Mr. Kent's management attitude.

3. What determinants of job satisfaction are addressed by Mr. Kent in his description of the firm?

4. Does Coca-Cola help develop employees' self-concept?

5. How are values illustrated in this case?

6. Coca-Cola and Mr. Kent's vision statement and manifest for growth do not seem to directly address the issue of spirituality in the workplace. What guidelines could he and Coca-Cola employ to rework these statements to address the issue of workplace spirituality?

7. Coca-Cola is a multinational corporation (MNC). What level of moral development and global corporate social responsibility (GCSR) do Coca-Cola and Mr. Kent seem to be operating on?

Cumulative Questions

8. How does Coca-Cola's vision statement and manifest for growth deal with the issue of human relations (Chapter 1)?

9. Is Coca-Cola a learning organization (Chapter 2)?

OBJECTIVE CASE   ## Job Satisfaction

Kathy Barns was the first woman hired by Kelly Construction Co. to perform a "man's job." When Kathy was interviewed for the job by Jean Rossi, the personnel director, Kathy was excited to get the opportunity to prove a woman could do a man's job. During the first month Kathy never missed a day. However, in the second month she missed four days of work, and by the end of the month she came to tell Ms. Rossi she was quitting. Jean was surprised and wanted to find out what happened, so she asked Kathy some questions.

JEAN: How did your orientation for the job go?

KATHY: Well, the foreman, Jack, started things off by telling me that he was against my being hired. He told me that a woman couldn't do the job and that I would not last very long.

JEAN: Did Jack teach you the job?

KATHY: He taught me the different parts of the job by beginning with a statement about how difficult it was. Jack made comments like "I'm watching you—don't mess up." He was constantly looking over my shoulder waiting for me to make a mistake, and when I did, he would give me the old "I told you so" speech. A couple of the guys gave me some help, but for the most part they ignored me.

JEAN: Is your job performance satisfactory?

KATHY: It's not as good as it could be, but it cannot be too bad because Jack hasn't fired me. I enjoy the work when Jack leaves me alone, and I do better work, too. But it seems he's always around.

JEAN: Are you really sure you want to quit?

KATHY: *Pauses and thinks.*

Answer the following questions. Then in the space between questions, state why you selected that answer.

_____ 1. Jack had Theory _____ attitudes toward Kathy.

   a. X   *b.* Y

_____ 2. Kathy started at Kelly with a _____ job attitude.

   a. positive   *b.* negative

_____ 3. Most likely there _____ a relationship between Kathy's job satisfaction and her absenteeism.

   a. is   *b.* is not

_____ 4. The major determinant of Kathy's job dissatisfaction is:

  a. the work itself   *c.* growth and mobility   *e.* coworkers

  b. pay   *d.* supervision   *f.* general work attitude

_____ 5. Job satisfaction _____ the major reason for Kathy's performance being below her potential.

  a. is   *b.* is not

_____ 6. Jack's behavior contributed to the _____ of Kathy's self-efficacy.

  a. development   *b.* deterioration

_____ 7. The attribution cause for Kathy's lack of success at Kelly is:

  a. internal   *b.* external

_____ 8. There _____ a relationship between Kathy's job satisfaction and her quitting (turnover).

  a. is   *b.* is not

_____ 9. Kathy's _____ changed over the two months at Kelly Construction.

  a. attitude   *b.* job satisfaction   *c.* values

_____ 10. This case best illustrates:

  a. Theory X   *c.* Pygmalion effect   *e.* self-fulfilling prophecy

  b. value system   *d.* self-efficacy

  11. How could Jean have prevented this situation?

  12. What would you do if you were in Kathy's situation?

Note: Jean's meeting with Kathy can be role-played in class.

SKILL-BUILDING EXERCISE 3–1

Self-Learning

In-Class Exercise
(Individual and Group)

Objective: To better understand human behavior.

AACSB: The primary AACSB learning standard skills developed through this exercise are reflective thinking and self-management, analytic skills, and communication abilities.

Preparation: You should have completed Self-Assessment Exercises 3–1, 3–2, and 3–3 in Chapter 3.

Experience: You will share your self-learning in small groups to better understand your behavior and that of others.

Procedure 1
(5–15 minutes)

Break into groups of two or three members, and share the answers you feel comfortable sharing in Self-Assessment Exercises 3–1, 3–2, and/or 3–3. Do not pressure anyone to share anything that makes him or her uncomfortable. Focus on your similarities and differences and the reasons for them. Your instructor will tell you if you will be doing the sharing in the next section of this exercise.

Sharing: Volunteers state the similarities and differences within their group.

Conclusion: The instructor leads a class discussion and/or makes concluding remarks.

Application: What have I learned from this exercise? How will I use this knowledge in the future?

Building a More Positive Self-Concept

Preparation (Individual and Group)

This may not be an easy exercise for you, but it could result in improving your self-concept, which has a major impact on your success in life. Below, follow the three-step plan for building a positive self-concept.

You may be asked to share your plan with a person of your choice in class. Your instructor should tell you if you will be asked to share during class. If you will share during class, do not include anything you do not wish to share. Write in the space provided, using additional pages if needed. Write a separate personal plan for yourself if you do not want to share it.

Step 1. Identify your strengths and areas for improvement.
What do I like about myself?

What can I do well? (Reflect on some of your accomplishments.)

What skills and abilities do I have to offer people and organizations?

What are the things about myself or behaviors that could be improved to help me build a more positive self-concept?

Step 2. Set goals and visualize them.

Based on your area(s) for improvement, write down some goals in a positive, affirmative format. Three to five goals are recommended as a start. Once you achieve them, go on to others.

For example:

1. I am positive and successful (not: I need to stop thinking/worrying about failure).

2. I enjoy listening to others (not: I need to stop dominating the conversation).

Visualize yourself achieving your goals. For example, imagine yourself succeeding without worrying, or visualize having a conversation you know you will have, without dominating it.

Optional. If you have a negative attitude toward yourself or others—or you would like to improve your behavior with others (family, coworkers), things, or issues (disliking school or work)—try following the internationally known motivational speaker and trainer Zig Ziglar's system. Thousands of people have used this system successfully. This system can be used for changing personality traits as well.

Here are the steps to follow, with an example plan for a person who has a negative self-concept and also wants to be more sensitive to others. Use this example as a guide for developing your own plan.

1. *Self-concept.* Write down everything you like about yourself. List all your strengths. Then go on and list all your weaknesses. Get a good friend to help you.

2. *Make a clean new list, and using positive affirmations, write all your strengths.* Example: "I am sensitive to others' needs."

3. *On another sheet of paper, again using positive affirmations, list all your weaknesses.* For example, don't write, "I need to lose weight." Write, "I am a slim (whatever you realistically can weigh in 30 days) pounds." Don't write, "I have to stop criticizing myself." Write, "I positively praise myself often every day." Write, "I have good communications skills," not "I am a weak communicator." The following list gives example affirmations for improving sensitivity to others. Note the repetition; you can use a thesaurus to help.

I am sensitive to others.

My behavior with others conveys my warmth for them.

I convey my concern for others.

My behavior conveys kindness toward others.

My behavior helps others build their self-esteem.

People find me easy to talk to.

I give others my full attention.

I patiently listen to others talk.

I answer others in a polite manner.

I answer questions and make comments with useful information.

My comments to others help them feel good about themselves.

I compliment others regularly.

4. *Practice.* Every morning and night for at least the next 30 days, look at yourself in the mirror and read your list of positive affirmations. Be sure to look at yourself between each affirmation as you read. Or record the list on a tape recorder and listen to it while looking at yourself in the mirror. If you are really motivated, you can repeat this step at other times of the day. Start with your areas for improvement. If it takes five minutes or more, don't bother with the list of your strengths. Or stop at five minutes; this exercise is effective in short sessions. Although miracles won't happen overnight, you may become more aware of your behavior in the first week. In the second or third week, you may become aware of yourself using new behavior successfully. You may still see some negatives, but the number will decrease in time as the positive increases.

   Psychological research has shown that if a person hears something believable repeated for 30 days, they will tend to believe it. Ziglar says that you cannot consistently perform in a manner that is inconsistent with the way you see yourself. So, as you listen to your positive affirmations, you will believe them, and you will behave in a manner that is consistent with your belief. Put simply, your behavior will change with your thoughts without a lot of hard work. For example, if you listen to the affirmation, "I am an honest person" (not, "I have to stop lying"), in time—without having to work at it—you will tell the truth. At first you may feel uncomfortable reading or listening to positive affirmations that you don't really believe you have. But keep looking at yourself in the mirror and reading or listening, and with time you will feel comfortable and believe it and live it.

   Are you thinking you don't need to improve, or that this method will not work? Yes, this system often does work. Zig Ziglar has trained thousands of satisfied people. I tried the system myself, and within two or three weeks, I could see improvement in my behavior. The question isn't, Will the system work for you? but rather, Will you work the system to improve?

5. *When you slip, and we all do, don't get down on yourself.* In the sensitivity-to-others example, if you are rude to someone and catch yourself, apologize and change to a positive tone. Effective leaders admit when they are wrong and apologize. If you have a hard time admitting you are wrong and saying you are sorry, at least be obviously nice so that the other person realizes you are saying you are sorry indirectly. Then forget about it and keep trying. Focus on your successes, not your slips. Don't let 10 good discussions be ruined by one insensitive comment. If you were a baseball player and got 9 out of 10 hits, you'd be the best in the world.

6. *Set another goal.* After 30 days, select a new topic, such as developing a positive attitude toward work or school, or trying a specific leadership style that you want to develop. You can also include more than one area to work on.

Step 3. Develop a plan and implement it.

For each of your goals, state what you will do to achieve it. What specific action will you take to improve your self-concept through changing your thoughts or behavior? Number your plans to correspond with your goals.

In-Class Exercise

Objective: To build a more positive self-concept.

AACSB: The primary AACSB learning standard skills developed through this exercise are reflective thinking and self-management and analytic skills.

Preparation: You should have completed the three-step action plan for building a positive self-concept on the preceding pages.

Experience: In groups of two, you will share your plan to build a more positive self-concept.

Procedure 1
(2–4 minutes)

Break into teams of two. You may make a group of three if you prefer. Try to work with someone with whom you feel comfortable sharing your plan.

Procedure 2
(10–20 minutes)

Using your preparation plan, share your answers one at a time. It is recommended that you both share on each step and question before proceeding to the next. The choice is yours, but be sure you get equal time. For example, one person states, "what I like about myself." The other person follows with his or her response. After both share, go on to cover "what I do well," and so on. During your sharing, you may offer each other helpful suggestions, but do so in a positive way; remember you are helping one another build a more positive self-concept. Avoid saying anything that could be considered a put-down.

Conclusion: The instructor may lead a class discussion and/or make concluding remarks.

Application (2–4 minutes):   Will I implement my plan? If so, will I succeed at developing a more positive self-concept? What have I learned through this experience?

Giving and Accepting Compliments

In-Class Exercise (Group)

Objective: To give and accept compliments as a means to improving self-concept.

AACSB: The primary AACSB learning standard skills developed through this exercise are analytic skills and communication abilities.

Procedure 1
(2 minutes)

Preparation: Recall that one of the human relations guidelines is to help others. One way to help others is to give them compliments that will help them develop and maintain a positive self-concept. Also, as stated in this chapter, never minimize compliments, but accept them with a thank you. This exercise is based on these two points.

Experience: In groups you will give and accept compliments.

Break into groups of four to six, preferably with people you know.

Procedure 2
(4–8 minutes)

Each person in the group thinks of a sincere, positive compliment to give to each group member (for instance, make a comment on why you like the person). When everyone is ready, one person volunteers to receive first. All the other members give that person a compliment. Proceed until everyone, one at a time, has received a compliment from everyone else.

Procedure 3
(3–6 minutes)

Each group discusses the following questions:

1. How did it feel to receive the compliments? Were you tempted to—or did you—minimize a compliment?

2. How do you feel about people who give you compliments versus those who give you criticism? Is there a difference in your human relations between people in these two groups?

3. How did it feel to give the compliments?

4. What is the value of giving compliments?

5. Will you make an effort to compliment yourself and others?

Conclusion: The instructor may lead a class discussion and/or make concluding remarks. In Chapter 9, Skill-Building Exercise 9–2, Giving Praise (page 343), you can develop the skill of giving compliments.

Application: Write out your answer to question 5 above as the application question.

Ethics and Whistle-Blowing

In-Class Exercise
(Individual and Group)

*Procedure 1
(5 minutes)*

Objective: To better understand ethics and whistle-blowing.

AACSB: The primary AACSB learning standard skills developed through this exercise are reflective thinking and self-management, analytic skills, and communication abilities.

Preparation: You should have completed Self-Assessment Exercise 3–4, How Ethical Is Your Behavior?

Experience: You will share your answers to the questions below.

Briefly answer the following questions related to Self-Assessment Exercise 3–4:

1. For "College" items 1 through 3, who is harmed and who benefits from these unethical behaviors?

2. For "Job" items 4 through 24, select the three (circle their numbers) that you consider the most severe unethical behavior. Who is harmed and who benefits by these unethical behaviors?

3. If you observed unethical behavior but didn't report it, why didn't you blow the whistle? If you did, why did you report the unethical behavior? What was the result?

4. As a manager, it is your responsibility to uphold ethical behavior. If you know employees are using unethical behavior, will you take action to enforce compliance with ethical standards?

5. What can you do to prevent unethical behavior?

6. As part of the class discussion, share the "Other Unethical Behavior" you have observed. If you didn't add any, try to do so until the time is up.

Procedure 2
(15–30 minutes)

Option A: Break into groups of five or six, and share your answers to the questions. The instructor will tell the group if they should select a spokesperson to report to the entire class.

Option B: The instructor leads a discussion in which students share their answers to the questions. (The instructor may begin by going over the statements and have students who have observed the behavior raise their hands.) Then the instructor will have them raise their hands if they reported the behavior.

Conclusion: The instructor may lead a class discussion and/or make concluding remarks.

Application (2–4 minutes):   What did I learn from this exercise? How will I use this knowledge in the future?

Sharing: Volunteers give their answers to the application section.

ANSWERS TO TRUE/FALSE QUESTIONS

1. F. Theory X attitudes are outdated and being replaced with Theory Y attitudes.
2. T.
3. F. Two-thirds of Americans would take the same job again and 90 percent are at least somewhat satisfied with their jobs.
4. T.
5. F. Self-efficacy is your belief in your ability to perform in a specific situation. The Pygmalion effect and self-fulfilling prophecy are more constant.
6. T.
7. F. This was not stated in the book, and it is not true.
8. F. Most people are on the conventional level of moral development.

Time and Career Management

Whitney and Shane were talking during lunch hour in a Friendly's Restaurant in Tampa, Florida. Whitney was complaining about all the tasks she had to get done. She had all kinds of deadlines to meet. Whitney was a nervous wreck as

she listed the many tasks. After a while, Shane interrupted to say that he used to be in the same situation until he took a time management workshop that taught him to get more done in less time with better results. Shane gave Whitney the details so she could take the course. In return, Whitney told Shane about a career development course she took. It not only helped her to get the job she has now, but also to know what she wants to accomplish in the future.

Have you ever felt as though you have more to do than the time you have to do it in? Do you ever wonder about your career? If you answered yes to either of these two questions, this chapter can help you.

HOW TIME MANAGEMENT AND CAREER SKILLS AFFECT BEHAVIOR, HUMAN RELATIONS, AND PERFORMANCE

Some people may question whether time management belongs in a human relations text-book. It is here because one of the major reasons managers do not have better human relations is their lack of time.[1] If you manage your time better, you will have more time to spend developing effective human relations and creating win–win situations. Developing time management skills is also an effective way to better balance work–family life,[2] reduce stress (Chapter 2),[3] increase personal productivity,[4] and experience inner peace.[5] It is possible for you to gain control of your life by controlling your time.

Many people are concerned about their careers,[6] especially in today's environment, with so many layoffs.[7] Career planning is not just about getting a job; it's also about continually developing yourself[8] so that you can advance throughout your career.[9] Time and career management skills lead to better behavior, more effective human relations, higher levels of performance, and career success.

TIME MANAGEMENT

The term **time management** *refers to techniques designed to enable people to get more done in less time with better results.* In this section, we examine ways to analyze your present use of time, a priority determination system, ways to use a time management system, and time management techniques.

WORK APPLICATIONS

1. Why are time management skills important? How can you benefit by using the time management information discussed in this chapter?

Analyzing Time Use

Learning Outcome

1. Explain how to analyze your use of time with a time log.

The first step to successful time management is to determine current time use. People often do not realize how much time they waste until they analyze time use. Professionals say they waste at least an hour daily because they are unorganized. An analysis of how you use your time will indicate areas for improvement. Analyze your time every six months.

Time Log   The **time log** *is a daily diary that tracks activities and enables a person to determine how time is used.* You use one time log for each day. See Exhibit 4.1 for an example. It is recommended that you keep track of your daily time use for one or two typical weeks. Make 5 to 10 copies of Exhibit 4.1; you may need to change the hours to match your working hours. Try to keep the time log with you throughout the day. Fill in each 15-minute time slot, if possible. Try not to go for longer than one hour without filling in the log. Each time shown

EXHIBIT 4.1 | Time Log

Date _____

Time	
8:00	
8:15	
8:30	
8:45	
9:00	
9:15	
9:30	
9:45	
10:00	
10:15	
10:30	
10:45	
11:00	
11:15	
11:30	
11:45	
12:00	
12:15	
12:30	
12:45	
1:00	
1:15	
1:30	
1:45	
2:00	
2:15	
2:30	
2:45	
3:00	
3:15	
3:30	
3:45	
4:00	
4:15	
4:30	
4:45	
5:00	
5:15	
5:30	
5:45	

represents 15 minutes of time. Beside each time write the activity or activities completed. For example, on the 8:15 line, record the activity or activities completed from 8:00 to 8:15.

Analyzing Time Logs   After keeping time logs for 5 to 10 working days, you can analyze them by answering the following questions:

1. Review the time logs to determine how much time you are spending on your primary responsibilities. How do you spend most of your time?

2. Identify areas where you are spending too much time.

3. Identify areas where you are not spending enough time.

4. Identify major interruptions that keep you from doing what you want to get done. How can you eliminate them?

5. Identify tasks you are performing that you do not have to be involved with. If you are a manager, look for nonmanagement tasks. To whom can you delegate these tasks?[10]

6. How much time is controlled by your boss? How much time is controlled by your employees? How much time is controlled by others outside your department? How much time do you actually control? How can you gain more control of your own time?[11]

7. Look for crisis situations. Were they caused by something you did or did not do? Do you have recurring crises? How can you plan to eliminate recurring crises? Solve problems.[12]

8. Look for habits, patterns, and tendencies. Do they help or hurt you in getting the job done? How can you change them to your advantage?

9. List three to five of your biggest time wasters. What can you do to eliminate them?

10. Determine how you can manage your time more efficiently.

Multitasking   As you analyze your time, are you finding that you try to do too many things at the same time—multitasking? Research has found that people who multitask are actually less efficient than those who focus on one "complex" project at a time.[13] The brain is not actually capable of doing two things at once. Think of it as a single-screen TV. You can't watch two shows at once, but you can flip back and forth, missing some of each show; the more shows you watch, the more you miss of each one. Time is lost when switching between tasks, and the time loss increases with the complexity of the task. Managing two tasks at once reduces the brainpower available for either task, and it increases stress. Complete Self-Assessment Exercise 4–1 to determine if you are multitasking too much.

Self-Assessment Exercise 4–1

Multitasking

Identify how frequently you experience each statement.

Not frequently				Frequently
1	2	3	4	5

_____ 1. I have a hard time paying attention; my mind wanders when I'm listening to someone or reading.

_____ 2. I have a hard time concentrating; my mind is tired and does not want to work.

_____ 3. I have short-term memory loss; I forget if I did something recently.

_____ 4. I have communication problems; I have trouble clearly saying what I want to.

_____ 5. I feel stressed; I sometimes experience shortness of breath.

Add up your score (5 to 25) and place it here _____. On the continuum below, mark the point that represents your total score.

Multitasking not an issue   1 - - - 5 - - - 10 - - - 15 - - - 20 - - - 25   Possible over-multitasking

The five statements are all warning signs of over-multitasking. However, other issues, such as fatigue, could also cause these signs. Can you improve your time management by focusing more on one task at a time? If you don't like to spend much time doing one thing or get bored easily, at least try to select a good stopping point so that when you return to a task, you don't lose too much time figuring out where you left off. You can also write notes to help you quickly get back to being productive at the task when you return to it.

The remainder of this section presents ideas to help you improve your time management.

WORK APPLICATIONS

2. Identify your three biggest time wasters, preferably with the use of a time log. How can you cut down or eliminate these time wasters?

Learning Outcome

2. State the three priority determination questions and determine when an activity on the to-do list should be delegated or assigned a high, medium, or low priority.

Priority Determination

At any given time, you face having to do many different tasks.[14] One of the things that separates successful from unsuccessful people is their ability to do the important things first and the less important things later.[15] A **priority** *is the preference given to one activity over other activities.*

Tasks that you must get done should be placed on a to-do list and then prioritized, ranking the order of performance.[16] After prioritizing tasks, focus on only one at a time.[17] According to Peter Drucker, a few people seem to do an incredible number of things; however, their impressive versatility is based mainly on doing one thing at a time.

Priority Determination Questions Set priorities[18] by answering three priority determination questions. The three questions are:

1. Do I need to be personally involved because of my unique knowledge or skills? Although delegation is an important part of the manager's job, there are times when you are the only one who can do the task, and you must be involved.

2. Is the task within my major area of responsibility or will it affect the performance or finances of my department? Managers must oversee the performance of their departments and keep the finances in line with the budget.

3. When is the deadline? Is quick action needed? Should I work on this activity right now, or can it wait?[19] Time is a relative term. In one situation, taking months or even a year may be considered quick action, while in another situation a matter of minutes may be considered quick action. For example, the decision to earn a college degree may have to be made close to four years in advance. It often takes several months before applicants are told whether they have been accepted. To the admissions personnel, this may be quick action. On the production line, machine changes to make a different product may take minutes or hours, and this is considered quick action.

To summarize, **priority determination questions** *ask (1) Do I need to be personally involved? (2) Is the task my responsibility or will it affect the performance or finances of my department? and (3) Is quick action needed?*

Assigning Priorities Based on the answers to the three priority determination questions, a manager can delegate a task or assign it a high, medium, or low priority.

Delegate (D) The task is delegated if the answer to question 1 (Do I need to be personally involved?) is no. If the answer to question 1 is no, it is not necessary to answer questions 2 and 3 because a priority has not been assigned to the task. However, planning the delegation and delegating the task are prioritized.

High (H) Priority   A high priority is assigned if you answer yes to all three questions. You need to be involved, it is your major responsibility, and quick action is needed.

Medium (M) Priority   A medium priority is assigned if you answer yes to question 1 (you need to be involved) but no to either question 2 (it is not your major responsibility) or question 3 (quick action is not needed; it can wait).

Low (L) Priority   A low priority is assigned if you answer yes to question 1 (you need to be involved) but no to both questions 2 and 3. It is not your major responsibility, and quick action is not needed.

The To-Do List   The three priority determination questions are on the to-do list in Exhibit 4.2 and also appear in Application Situation 4–1 to help you develop your ability to assign priorities. The **to-do list** *is the written list of activities the individual has to complete.* Feel free to make copies of Exhibit 4.2 and use it on the job. In summary, decide what is really important, put it on your list, and find the time to do it.[20]

When using the to-do list, write each activity you have to accomplish on one or more lines and assign a priority to it. Remember that priorities may change several times during the day as a result of unexpected tasks that must be added to your to-do list.[21] Look at the high (H) priority activities and start by performing the most important one. When it's done, cross it off and select the next, until all high-priority activities are done. Then do the same with the medium (M) priorities, then the low (L) priorities. Be sure to update the priorities. As deadlines come nearer or get changed, priorities will change. With time, low priorities often become high priorities.

WORK APPLICATIONS

3. Identify at least three high priorities related to your education.

4. List at least five activities on your to-do list. Based on the three priority determination questions, prioritize each activity as H, M, L, or D.

Learning Outcome

3. List the three steps in the time management system.

Time Management System

The problem you face is not a shortage of time—we all have the same 24 hours a day—but how to use your time. Experts say that many people waste two hours a day.

The time management system that is presented in this section has a proven record of success with thousands of managers. It can also be used by nonmanagers and students. You should try it for three weeks. After that time, you may adjust it to meet your own needs.

The four major parts to the time management system are priorities, objectives, plans, and schedules:

- *Priorities.* Setting priorities on a to-do list helps increase performance.[22]
- *Objectives.* Objectives state *what* we want to accomplish within a given period of time. The manager should set objectives,[23] following the guidelines stated in Chapter 9.
- *Plans.* Plans state *how* you will achieve your objectives. They list the necessary activities to be performed.[24]
- *Schedules.* Schedules state *when* the activities planned will be carried out. You should schedule each workday.

Time management techniques all boil down to making a plan and sticking to it as much as possible. The **time management steps** *are as follows: step (1) plan each week, step (2) schedule each week, and step (3) schedule each day.*

EXHIBIT 4.2 | To-Do List

		D Delegate—no to 1 H High priority—yes to all three questions (YYY) M Medium priority—yes to 1 and 2 or 3 (YYN or YNY) L Low priority—yes to 1, no to 2 and 3 (YNN)	1 Involvement Needed?	2 Responsibility/ Performance/ Finances?	3 Quick Action/ Deadline?	 Time Needed?	 Priority
		Activity					

Source: Adapted from Harbridge House Training Materials (Boston).

Prioritizing To-Do List Activities

AS 4–1

Prioritize the following 10 activities on the to-do list of a supervisor of a production department in a large company.

Priority Determination	1	2	3	
	Do I Need to Be Involved?	Is It My Responsibility/Performance/Finances?	Is Quick Action Needed?	Deadline?	Priority
D Delegate—no to question 1					
H High priority—yes to all three questions (YYY)					
M Medium priority—yes to 1 and 2 or 3 (YYN or YNY)					
L Low priority—yes to 1, no to 2 and 3 (YNN)					

Above the questions header: **Questions**

Activity

1. John, the sales manager, told you that three customers stopped doing business with the company because your products have decreased in quality.

2. Your secretary, Rita, told you that there is a salesperson waiting to see you. He does not have an appointment. You don't do any purchasing.

3. Jan, a vice president, wants to see you to discuss a new product to be introduced in one month.

4. John, the sales manager, sent you a memo stating that the sales forecast was incorrect. Sales are expected to increase by 20 percent starting next month. Inventories are as scheduled.

5. Dan, the personnel director, sent you a memo informing you that one of your employees has resigned. Your turnover rate is one of the highest in the company.

6. Rita told you that a John Smith called while you were out. He asked you to return his call, but wouldn't state why he was calling. You don't know who he is or what he wants.

7. Sandy, one of your best workers, wants an appointment to tell you about a situation that happened in the shop.

8. John called and asked you to meet with him and a prospective customer for your product. The customer wants to meet you.

9. Tom, your boss, called and said he wants to see you about the decrease in the quality of your product.

10. In the mail you got a note from Frank, the president of your company, and an article from *The Wall Street Journal*. The note said FYI (for your information).

Source: Adapted from Harbridge House Training Materials (Boston).

Step 1: Plan Each Week   On the last day of each week, plan the coming week. Do this every week. Using your to-do list and the previous week's plan and departmental objectives, fill in the weekly planning sheet (see Exhibit 4.3). Start by listing the objectives you want to accomplish during the week. The objectives should not be routine tasks you perform weekly or daily. For example, if an employee's annual review is coming due, plan for it.

After setting a few major objectives, list the activities it will take to accomplish each objective.[25] To continue our example, you will need to make an appointment with the employee and plan to complete the performance review form. Then assign a priority to each activity.

The next two columns to fill in are the time needed and the day to schedule. To continue our example, assume it will take you 10 minutes to schedule the performance appraisal and about 1 hour to prepare for it. The day to schedule would be on Tuesday, your relatively quiet day. With time, you will learn how much you can plan for and accomplish in one week. Planning too much becomes frustrating when you cannot get it all done.[26] On the other hand, if you do not plan enough activities, you will end up wasting time and missing deadlines.[27]

Step 2: Schedule Each Week   Scheduling your week gets you organized to achieve your important objectives. You may schedule the week at the same time you plan it, or after, whichever you prefer. Planning and scheduling the week should take about 30 minutes. See Exhibit 4.4 for a weekly schedule. Make copies of Exhibits 4.3 and 4.4 for use on the job. When scheduling your plans for the week, select times when you do not have other time commitments, such as meetings. Most managers should leave some time unscheduled for unexpected events.[28] With practice, you will perfect weekly planning and scheduling. Steven Covey says, *The key to success is not to prioritize your schedule, but to schedule your priorities weekly and daily*.

Step 3: Schedule Each Day   Successful managers have daily schedules.[29] At the end of each day, you should schedule the next day. Or you can begin each day by scheduling it. This should take 15 minutes or less. Using your plan and schedule for the week, and your to-do list, schedule each day on the form in Exhibit 4.5. Make copies of it as needed on the job.

Begin by scheduling the activities over which you have no control, such as meetings you must attend, and be punctual.[30]

Leave your daily schedule flexible.[31] Most managers need about 50 percent of their time unscheduled to handle unexpected events. Don't be too optimistic; schedule enough time to do each task.[32] Many managers find that estimating the time it will take to perform a nonroutine task, and then doubling it, works well. With practice, your time estimation should improve.

Schedule your high-priority items during your prime time. Prime time is the period of time when you perform at your best. For most people this time is early in the morning. Determine your prime time and schedule the tasks that need your full attention then. Do routine things, like checking your mail, during non-prime-time hours, after high-priority items are done.

Try to schedule a time for unexpected events. Tell employees to see you with routine matters during a set time, such as 3:00 P.M. Have people call you, and call them during this set time.

Do not perform an unscheduled task before a scheduled task without prioritizing it first. If you are working on a high-priority item and a medium-priority item is brought to you, let it wait. Often, the so-called urgent things can wait.

The steps of the time management system bridge the gap between objectives, plans, and their implementation. Keep your daily schedule and to-do list with you.

Forms similar to Exhibits 4.1 to 4.5 can be purchased in pad, book, computerized, and Web versions. BlackBerrys are also popular time management tools.[33] In addition, you may copy the exhibits in the text for your own use.

EXHIBIT 4.3 | Weekly Planning Sheet

Plan for the week of _____

Objectives: (What is to be done, by when) (To + action verb + singular behavior result + target date [Chapter 9, Exhibit 9.6, page 330])

Activities	Priority	Time Needed	Day to Schedule

Total time for the week

EXHIBIT 4.4 | Weekly Schedule

Schedule for the week of _____

	Monday	Tuesday	Wednesday	Thursday	Friday
8:00 8:15 8:30 8:45					
9:00 9:15 9:30 9:45					
10:00 10:15 10:30 10:45					
11:00 11:15 11:30 11:45					
12:00 12:15 12:30 12:45					
1:00 1:15 1:30 1:45					
2:00 2:15 2:30 2:45					
3:00 3:15 3:30 3:45					
4:00 4:15 4:30 4:45					
5:00 5:15 5:30 5:45					

EXHIBIT 4.5 | Daily Schedule

Day _____   **Date** _____

8:00	
8:15	
8:30	
8:45	
9:00	
9:15	
9:30	
9:45	
10:00	
10:15	
10:30	
10:45	
11:00	
11:15	
11:30	
11:45	
12:00	
12:15	
12:30	
12:45	
1:00	
1:15	
1:30	
1:45	
2:00	
2:15	
2:30	
2:45	
3:00	
3:15	
3:30	
3:45	
4:00	
4:15	
4:30	
4:45	
5:00	
5:15	
5:30	
5:45	

APPLICATION SITUATIONS

Time Management

AS 4–2

Match each statement with its part in the time management system.

A. Priorities   C. Plans   E. Daily schedule
B. Objectives   D. Weekly schedule

_____ 11. "I set up my appointments for May 5."

_____ 12. "I know what I want to accomplish."

_____ 13. "I've decided how to get the work done."

_____ 14. "I know my major responsibilities."

_____ 15. "I've planned my week; now I'm going to . . ."

Learning Outcome

4. Identify at least three time management techniques you presently do not use but will use in the future.

Time Management Techniques

Self-Assessment Exercise 4–2 includes 68 time management techniques. They include major time wasters and ways to overcome them. Complete the exercise to determine which techniques you presently use and techniques that can help you get more done in less time with better results. Review and prioritize the items in the "Should" column. Select at least your top priority item now to work on each week. Write it on your to-do list, and schedule it, if appropriate. Once you have completed the "Should" column, do the same with the items in the "Could" and "Do" columns. Then review the "N/A" ("not applicable") column to be sure they do not apply.

Self-Assessment Exercise 4–2

Time Management Techniques This list of 68 ideas can be used to improve your time management skills. Check off the appropriate box for each item. (1) I *should* do this. (3) I *do* this now. (2) I *could* do this. (4) *Does not apply* to me.	(1) Should	(2) Could	(3) Do	(4) N/A
Planning and Controlling				
1. Set objectives—long- and short-term.				
2. Plan your week, how you will achieve your objectives.				
3. Use a to-do list; write all assignments on it.				
4. Prioritize the items on your to-do list. Do the important things rather than urgent things.				
5. Get an early, productive start on your top-priority items.				
6. During your best working hours—prime time—do only high-priority items.				
7. Don't spend time performing unproductive activities to avoid or escape job-related anxiety. It doesn't really work.				
8. Throughout the day ask yourself, "Should I be doing this now?"				
9. Plan before you act.				

	(1) Should	(2) Could	(3) Do	(4) N/A
10. Plan for recurring crises, and plan to eliminate crises.				
11. Make decisions. It is better to make a wrong decision than none at all.				
12. Have a schedule for the day. Don't let your day be planned by the unexpected.				
13. Schedule the next day before you leave work.				
14. Schedule unpleasant or difficult tasks during prime time.				
15. Schedule enough time to do the job right the first time. Don't be too optimistic on the length of time to do a job.				
16. Schedule a quiet hour(s). Be interrupted only by true emergencies. Have someone take a message, or ask people to call you back during scheduled unexpected event time.				
17. Establish a quiet time for the entire organization, department, or other group. The first hour of the day is usually the best time.				
18. Schedule large blocks of uninterrupted (emergencies only) time for projects, etc. If this doesn't work, hide somewhere.				
19. Break large (long) projects into parts (time periods).				
20. If you don't follow your schedule, ask the priority question (is the unscheduled event more important than the scheduled event?).				
21. Schedule a time for doing similar activities (e.g., make and return calls, write letters and memos).				
22. Keep your schedule flexible—allow _____ % of time for unexpected events.				
23. Schedule unexpected event time and answer mail; do routine things in between events.				
24. Ask people to see or call you during your scheduled unexpected event time only, unless it's an emergency.				
25. If staff members ask to see you—"got a minute?"—tell them you're busy and ask if it can wait until X o'clock (scheduled unexpected time).				
26. Set a schedule time, agenda, and time limit for all visitors, and keep on topic.				
27. Control your time. Cut down on the time controlled by the boss, the organization, and your subordinates.				
Organizing				
28. Keep a clean desk.				
29. Rearrange your desk for increased productivity.				
30. All non-work-related or distracting objects should be removed from your desk.				

	(1) Should	(2) Could	(3) Do	(4) N / A
31. Do one task at a time.				
32. With paperwork, make a decision at once. Don't read it again later and decide.				
33. Keep files well arranged and labeled.				
34. Have an active and inactive file section.				
35. If you file an item, put a destruction date on it.				
36. Call rather than write, when appropriate.				
37. Have someone else (delegate) write letters, memos, etc.				
38. Dictate rather than write letters, memos, etc.				
39. Use form letters and/or form paragraphs.				
40. Answer letters or memos on the document itself.				
41. Have someone read things for you and summarize them for you.				
42. Divide reading requirements with others and share summaries.				
43. Have calls screened to be sure the right person handles them.				
44. Plan before calling. Have an agenda and all necessary information ready—take notes on the agenda.				
45. Ask people to call you back during your scheduled unexpected event time. Ask when is the best time to call them.				
46. Have a specific objective or purpose for every meeting.				
47. For meetings, invite only the necessary participants and keep them only for as long as they are needed.				
48. Always have an agenda for a meeting and stick to it. Start and end as scheduled.				
49. Conclude each meeting with a summary, and get a commitment on who will do what by when.				
50. Call rather than visit, if possible.				
51. Set objectives for travel. List everyone you will meet with. Send them agendas and have a file folder for each person with all necessary data for your meeting.				
52. Combine and/or modify activities to save time.				
Leadership and Staffing				
53. Set clear objectives for subordinates with accountability—give them feedback and evaluate results often.				
54. Use your subordinates' time well. Don't make them wait idly for decisions, instructions, or materials, or in meetings.				
55. Communicate well. Wait for a convenient time, rather than interrupting your subordinates and wasting their time.				
56. Train your subordinates. Don't do their work for them.				

**Self-Assessment
Exercise 4–2 (*continued*)**

	(1) Should	(2) Could	(3) Do	(4) N/A
57. Delegate activities in which you personally do not need to be involved.				
58. Delegate nonmanagement functions.				
59. Set deadlines when delegating.				
60. Set deadlines that are earlier than the actual deadline.				
61. Use the input of your staff. Don't reinvent the wheel.				
62. Teach time management skills to your subordinates.				
63. Don't procrastinate; do it.				
64. Don't be a perfectionist; define acceptable and stop there.				
65. Learn to stay calm. Getting emotional only causes more problems.				
66. Reduce socializing without causing antisociality.				
67. Identify your time wasters and work to minimize them.				
68. If there are other ideas you have that are not listed above, add them here.				

In the opening case, Whitney could benefit from implementing the time management system and techniques presented here.

WORK APPLICATIONS

5. From the 68 time management techniques presented in Self-Assessment Exercise 4–2, list the three most important ones you should be using. Explain how you will implement each technique.

CAREER MANAGEMENT

You must take the responsibility for managing your career. If you expect others to give you jobs, raises, and promotions, they may never come your way. In this section, you will learn how to manage your career successfully. The topics covered are career stages, career planning and development, getting a job, resumes, getting raises and promotions, global careers, and apparel and grooming.

Learning Outcome

5. Describe the four career stages.

Career Stages

Before planning your career, you must consider your career stage. As people get older, they have different career stage needs.[34]

The 20s   This is the time when you are just getting started. The challenge is to prove that you have what it takes to get the job done well—and on time.[35] There is a lot of pressure to be the best. Women and minorities who seek advancement in a world dominated by men tend to feel personal pressure to try harder.[36] You must develop the job skills needed to do the present job and to prepare for advancement. Initiative is needed. Young people often have to work long, hard hours to get ahead.[37]

Today's young people have high expectations.[38] They are impatient and feel pressured to quickly advance up the corporate ladder (which is shaky at best and is better viewed as a jungle gym because you may need to go sideways or even down to find a new route to move up). Most professionals don't stay at their first job for more than three years. With today's flatter organizations, fewer management positions are available, and it takes longer to progress. Lateral moves are therefore more common than upward promotions. So don't view your career as a linear progression.[39]

The 30s   This decade is the time when managers develop expertise and show their strength as bosses.[40] They try to gain visibility with top management. In their 30s people often question their careers: Where am I going? Should I be here? Am I secure in my position? This time of doubt is especially tough on women, who must decide whether and how to combine children and careers.[41] Men especially feel trapped by financial demands and are frightened of changing careers even when they are not happy, because a change in career often requires a cut in pay to start at a lower position.[42] However, the days of working 20 to 30 years for the same organization are gone for most people. It is now common for a manager to work for many different organizations during a career.[43]

The 40s and 50s   By age 45, most managers have weathered a failure or two and know whether or not they have a shot at higher-management jobs. The majority don't make it and must accept that the race is over. In the past, people at this stage would settle into a secure middle-management job. However, times have changed. Many organizations have cut back on the number of middle-manager positions and continue to do so.[44] People in their 40s and 50s are sometimes forced to seek new employers or new careers. This can be difficult when trying to cope with growing older. As a means of getting rid of middle managers, some organizations force people to take early retirement.

The 60s and 70s   At this stage, people begin to prepare for retirement. They can pass along what they have learned and provide continuity. People at this stage make good role models and mentors. Mentors can boost young careers. Although few employees are given such an opportunity, get a mentor if you can, and then return the favor. Mentoring others can help you as well.

WORK APPLICATIONS

6. Which career stage are you in? Does the information stated about your career stage relate to your career? Explain.

Learning Outcome

6. List the five steps in the career planning model.

Career Planning and Development

There is a difference between career planning and career development. **Career planning** is *the process of setting career objectives and determining how to accomplish them.* **Career development** is *the process of gaining skill, experience, and education to achieve career objectives.* You must take responsibility for your career and develop a career plan.[45]

Most colleges and large organizations offer career planning and development services. The career planning counselor's role is not to find people jobs but to help them set realistic career objectives and plans. Many colleges also offer career placement services designed to help students find jobs. But it is the students' responsibility to obtain the job offer.

The career planning model can help you develop your own career plan. In preparation for Skill-Building Exercise 4–2, you will find working papers to guide you in the development of your own career plan. The **career planning model** *steps are these: step (1) self-assessment, step (2) career preferences and exploration, step (3) set career objectives, step (4) develop a plan, and step (5) control.*

Step 1: Self-Assessment   The starting point in career planning is the self-assessment inventory. Who are you? What are your interests, values, needs, skills, and experience? What do you want to do during your career? If you don't have the answers to these questions, most college career services offer free or low-cost tests that can help.[46]

The key to career success is to determine the following: What do you do well? What do you enjoy doing? How do you get a job that combines your interests and skills? To be successful, you need to view yourself as successful. To be successful, develop some realistic short-term objectives and achieve them.

Step 2: Career Preferences and Exploration   Based on your self-assessment, you must decide what you want from your job and career, and prioritize those wants. Career planning is not just a determination of what you want to do. It is also important to determine why you want to do these things. What motivates you? How much do you want it? What is your commitment to your career? Without the appropriate motivation and commitment to career objectives and plans, you will not be successful in attaining them.[47]

Some of the things you should consider are (1) which industry you want to work for; (2) what size organization you want to work for; (3) what type of job(s) you want in your career, including which functional areas interest you (production/operations, marketing, finance, human resources, and so on) and, if you want to be a manager, what department(s) you want to manage; (4) what city, state, or country you want to work in (people who are willing to relocate often find more opportunities); and (5) how much income you expect to earn when you start your career, as well as 5 years and 10 years from then.

Once you have made these determinations, read about your primary career area. Conduct networking interviews. Talk to people in career planning and to people who hold the types of jobs you are interested in. People in these positions can help provide information that you can use in developing your career plan. Get their advice.[48] Determine the requirements and qualifications you need to get a job in the career that interests you. Getting an internship, fieldwork position, cooperative job, part-time job, and/or summer job in your field of interest can help you land the job you want after graduation. In the long run, it is often more profitable to take a job that pays less but gives you experience that will help you in your career progression.

Step 3: Set Career Objectives   Set short- and long-range objectives,[49] using the guidelines from Chapter 9. Objectives should not simply be a listing for the next job(s). For example (assuming graduation from college in May 2011):

- To attain a sales position with a large insurance company by June 30, 2011.
- To attain a starting first-year income of $48,000.
- To attain my MBA by June 30, 2015.
- To become a sales manager in the insurance industry by June 30, 2017.
- To attain a salary of $65,000 by June 30, 2017.

Step 4: Develop a Plan   Develop a plan that will enable you to attain your objectives. A college degree is becoming more important to high school graduates for developing skills

EXHIBIT 4.6 | Career Planning Model

Step 1.   Self-assessment.
Step 2.   Career preferences and exploration.
Step 3.   Set career objectives.
Step 4.   Develop a plan.
Step 5.   Control.

and earning pay increases. This is where career development fits in. You must determine what skills, experience, and education you need to get where you want to go and plan to develop as needed. Talking to others can help you develop a career plan. You may find it helpful to use the career planning sheet from Skill-Building Exercise 4–2.

You should have a written career plan, but this does not mean that it cannot be changed. You should be open to unplanned opportunities and take advantage of them when it is in your best interest to do so.

Step 5: Control   It is your responsibility to achieve your objectives. You may have to take corrective action. Review your objectives, check your progress at least once a year, and change and develop new objectives and plans. Update your resume (to be discussed) at the same time.

Exhibit 4.6 lists the steps in the career planning model.

WORK APPLICATIONS

7. What career development efforts are you making?

APPLICATION SITUATIONS

Career Planning Steps

AS 4–3

Match each statement with its step in the career planning model.

A. 1   B. 2   C. 3   D. 4   E. 5

_____ 16. "First, I have to get my degree; then I'll apply for a management trainee position with the major banks in the Midwest."

_____ 17. "I'm very good in math and computers."

_____ 18. "I want to be a partner in a CPA firm within seven years."

_____ 19. "Once a year I sit down and reassess who I am and where I'm going."

_____ 20. "I want to get into the co-op program because I'm not sure what I want to do when I graduate. I figure it will help me decide."

Getting a Job

It has been said that getting a good job is a job in itself. In attaining any good job, you need to develop a career plan; develop a resume and cover letter; conduct research; and prepare for the interview. Networking (Chapter 11) can be helpful at each stage.[50]

Career Plan   Interviewers are often turned off by candidates who have no idea of what they want in a job and career. On the other hand, they are usually impressed by candidates with realistic career plans. Having a good career plan gives you a competitive advantage over those who do not. Doing the preparation for Skill-Building Exercise 4–2 will help prepare you for getting a job.

Resume and Cover Letter   A recruiting executive at Xerox once said that the resume is about 40 percent of getting a job. The cover letter and resume are your introduction to the organization you wish to work for. If the resume is not neat, has errors, or contains mistakes, you may not get an interview.[51] Recruiters tend to believe that a sloppy resume comes from a sloppy person.

The cover letter should be short—one page. Its purpose is to introduce your resume and to request an interview. Be careful not to be like an estimated 85 percent of people who send cover letters with errors, as you may not get an interview. The standard cover letter states the job you are applying for and summarizes your qualifications. Be sure to talk about the firm and why you want to work for it. State how the company can benefit by hiring you, and end by asking for an interview.[52]

Company information is based on research, which we discuss separately. Also, because they are so important to getting a good professional job, we also discuss resumes separately after going through the getting-a-job process.

After writing and printing your resume draft, with perfect balance for eye appeal, bold headings, and so on, have an English professor proofread it to make sure it contains no spelling or grammar errors. Then have people in the field you want to enter read it for content and suggest improvements. After it is finalized, it should be typed, printed, or copied on high-quality bond paper. Having matching personalized stationery for cover letters can impress a recruiter and get you an interview over other equally fine candidates whose resumes and letters are of low quality.

The use of a resume for part-time and summer employment can also give a positive impression that makes you stand out from the competition. Give copies to friends and relatives who can help you get a job.

Research   Research is required to determine where to send your resume. Many colleges offer seminars in job search strategies. There are also a number of articles and books on the subject. Some people take the attitude that they want to make it on their own. It's an honorable thought, but the use of network contacts can help you land the job you are looking for.[53] Most people today find jobs through networking. However, just because a friend or relative gives you a lead and recommendation, there is no guarantee that you will get the job. You still must go through the interview and land the job yourself. Help-wanted ads in newspapers and online are common places to research jobs.

Once you land an interview, but before you go to it, you should research the organization. You want to determine as much about the organization as you can.[54] For example, you should know the products and/or services it offers, know about the industry and its trends, and know about the organization's profits and future plans; www.hoovers.com may have the company information. For organizations that are publicly owned, you can get an annual report that has much of this information; they are also online at most company Web sites. If you know people who work at the organization, talk to them about these issues.

You should also develop a list of questions you want to ask the interviewer during or at the end of the interview. Asking questions is a sign of intelligence and shows interest in the organization. Two good areas to ask questions about are job responsibilities and career opportunities.

Prepare for Questions   You should also prepare to answer possible questions that you could be asked during a job interview (see Exhibit 4.7 for a list of common interview questions).[55] If you are asked to state strengths and weaknesses, don't give direct weaknesses; they should be strengths in drag. For example, don't say, "Sometimes I have trouble getting along with others." Instead say, "I'm very accomplishment-oriented, and sometimes I push people to work harder and cause some conflict."

EXHIBIT 4.7 | Common Interview Questions

Answering these questions prior to going to a job interview is good preparation that will help you get the job; written answers are better than verbal.

- How would you describe yourself?
- What two or three things are most important to you in your job and career?
- Why did you choose this job and career?
- What do you consider to be your greatest strengths and weaknesses?
- What have you learned from your mistakes?
- What would your last boss say about your work performance?
- What motivates you to go the extra mile on a project or job?
- What have you accomplished that shows your initiative and willingness to work?
- What two or three accomplishments have given you the most satisfaction? Why?
- Why should I hire you?
- What skills do you have?
- What makes you qualified for this position?
- In what ways do you think you can make a contribution to our company?
- Do you consider yourself a leader?
- How do you work under pressure?
- Why did you decide to seek a position in this company?
- What can you tell us about our company?
- What are your expectations regarding promotions and salary increases?
- Are you willing to travel and relocate?
- What are your long-range and short-range goals and objectives?
- What do you see yourself doing five years from now? Ten years from now?
- What do you expect to be earning in five years?

The Interview The interview is given the most weight in job decisions in most cases—about 60 percent, according to the Xerox recruiter. References and/or the resume will get you an interview, but how you perform during the interview usually determines if you get the job.[56] It is vital to make a very positive first impression (Chapter 2).[57] This means conveying a relaxed presence and an ability to convey accomplishments and to pique the interviewer's interest quickly. Be sure to follow job interview etiquette (Chapter 10). You also want to dress for success, which we discuss at the end of this chapter.

Many college career placement services offer workshops on how to interview for a job. Some offer mock interviews on camera that allow you to see how you conduct yourself during an interview. If this service is available, take advantage of it. During the interview, smile, be pleasant and agreeable, and offer compliments to interviewers.

After the interview, evaluate how well you did. Make some notes on what you did and did not do well. If you want the job, send a thank you letter, add anything you forgot to say, and state your interest in the job and the fact that you look forward to hearing from the interviewer. Enclose a copy of your resume.[58]

If you did not get the job, ask the interviewer how you can improve. An honest answer can be helpful in preparation for future interviews.

WORK APPLICATIONS

8. Which specific idea(s) on getting a job do you plan to use?

Resumes

Now we will get into the details of how to write a resume that will get you the job you have identified through your career plan and job search. To begin, complete Self-Assessment Exercise 4–3 to evaluate your resume, or resume knowledge.

Your Resume Evaluation

Rate either your current resume or your resume knowledge for each question as:

Describes my resume   5   4   3   2   1   Doesn't describe my resume

_____ 1. My resume is based on a good career plan.

_____ 2. My resume is customized; it's not simply a copy of some format blueprint.

_____ 3. My resume does not include the word "I," and it has incomplete sentences.

_____ 4. My resume is customized for each individual job; one size doesn't fit all.

_____ 5. My resume is neat, attractive, and free of errors.

_____ 6. My resume is one page long, or two pages max for five or more years of experience.

_____ 7. My resume has digital/Internet capabilities.

_____ 8. My most important selling points are listed first and given the most space.

_____ 9. My resume states the specific job I'm applying for; it's not a general statement.

_____ 10. My job objective includes my personal qualities and skills with the job.

_____ 11. My resume has a qualification summary, or in 10–15 seconds, the recruiter can understand the job I want and that I am qualified to do the job.

_____ 12. My resume includes accomplishments that are quantified.

_____ 13. My resume includes concrete examples of skills, not just fluff words like *communication skills, team player, driven, organization,* and *interpersonal skills.*

_____ 14. My experience includes employment by months and years; plus employer, address, telephone, and supervisor, if they want a reference.

_____ 15. My experience that is not directly related to a job applied for focuses on transferable skills related to the job.

_____ Total. Add up the number of points and place it on the continuum below.

Effective resume   75   70   60   50   40   30   20   15   Ineffective resume

The higher your score, the better are the chances of getting the job you apply for.

Let's begin by stating some general guidelines to resume writing, followed by the major parts of the resume: contact information, objective, qualification summary, education, experience, and other possible additional parts. Although there is no one right way to write a resume, most resumes do include these parts. Also, note that the advice is from experts, but you can find people who do not agree with everything presented here, or there may be exceptions to these rules. While reading about the resume, refer to Exhibit 4.8, Sample Resume.

General Resume Guidelines   It is fine to follow some resume format, but you have to customize your resume, and you should have a unique resume for each job you apply for. Resumes are written with incomplete sentences to keep them short and to the point, without stating "I." For people with less than five years of experience, a one-page resume is recommended, and two pages is the max. Today, many employers are using some form of digital/online resumes. Even if you send a print copy, many companies scan your resume. So you need to have both a print and e-resume. We will discuss the e-resume later in this section.

Your most important selling points should be the most visible. The two components of visibility are location and allocation of space. Thus, place the most job-relevant qualifications first and give them the most coverage. If you have professional full-time work

EXHIBIT 4.8 | Sample Resume

John Smith
10 Oak Street
Springfield, MA 01118
413-748-3000   jsmith@aol.com

Objective

Competitive team player with excellent sales and communication skills seeks sales position.

Qualification Summary

Degree in business with a concentration in marketing. Marketing internship and marketing research experience. Sales and customer relations experience. Increased sales by 5 percent for employer. Developed communications, sales, and leadership skills through a variety of courses and jobs. Captain of the basketball team.

Education

B.S. Business Administration/ Marketing	Springfield College, Springfield, MA 01109. Business major with a concentration in marketing. 3.0 GPA. Graduation May 2011.
Courses	Sales—developed communication skills through three class presentations.
	Sales skills developed through 10 sales role-playing exercises.
	Marketing Research—developed a questionnaire and conducted survey research for a local business, developing a customer profile to be used to target market sales promotions.
Marketing Internship	Big Y Supermarkets, 1050 Roosevelt Ave., Springfield, MA 01117, 413-745-2395. Supervisor: V.P. of Marketing John Jefferson. Worked directly for the V.P. on a variety of tasks/projects. Helped with the weekly newspaper ad inserts. Suggested a layout change that is being used. Spring Semester 2011.
Basketball Team	Member of the varsity basketball team for four years, captain senior year.

Experience

Salesperson	Eblens, 100 Cooley St., Chicopee, MA 01020, 413-534-0927. Sold clothing and footwear to a diverse set of customers. Employee of the month in July for the highest sales volume. Supervisor: Susan Miller. May to August 2010.
Landscaper	Eastern Landscaping, 10 Front St., East Longmeadow, MA 01876, 413-980-7527. Helped attract two new customers, a 5% increase. Interacted with customers and resolved complaints. Supervisor: Owner Thomas Shea. May to August 2008 and 2009.

---

experience related to the job you are applying for, list experience before education. If you are a recent college graduate with the degree as your major qualification, list education first.

Contact Information   At the top of your resume, without a heading, list your name, address, telephone, and e-mail address where you can be reached to set up an interview. Note that your telephone message and e-mail address should be appropriate for business. For example, don't use a message that begins "Hi hot stuff," or an e-mail address such as sexyjoe@aol.com.

Also, be aware that many employers do a search on social networks (i.e., Facebook and MySpace) and if they find pictures of you not behaving well, undressed or dressed sexually, or engaging in drugs and drinking, they may not hire you. So you may want to do a search on yourself and delete any material that would be inappropriate for the job you are seeking.

Objective   The objective—the job you are applying for—is critical because the rest of your resume needs to focus on your qualifications to do the job. With hundreds of resumes, recruiters don't have time to figure out what job you want or can fill. In most fields today, there are more people applying for jobs than there are actual jobs available. Companies are matching people with specific skills to related jobs, so you need to clearly state the job that you are applying for, such as sales representative.

Be sure to include with your job objective your personal qualities and skills that the employer would want. For example, don't just write: Seeking sales position. Do write: Self-starting team player with excellent time management and communication skills seeks sales position. In the resume you can provide details of your qualities and skills. You can find out desired qualities and skills by reading job descriptions.

Qualification Summary   Experts say recruiters spend only 10 to 15 seconds looking at each resume. So you need to state the job you want and that you can do the job—quickly. Start with your objective, followed by a qualification summary stating why you can do the job. The details of your qualifications should appear in the other parts of the resume.

If you have very limited job-related qualifications, you can skip this part of the resume.

Education   Throughout your resume, you want to be sure to quantify your accomplishments, such as a good GPA, and include specific examples of personal qualities and skills, such as *driven, communicator,* and *team player*. Only list high school education if your resume does not fill a full page, or if you had some outstanding accomplishments related to the job you're applying for.

- State your degree received with major, minor/concentration, and the name and address of your college/university.
- Avoid a listing of college courses. Select a few that are directly relevant to the job you are applying for, and briefly identify knowledge and skills developed to help you on the job.
- Describe internships under the education section, stating knowledge, qualities, and skills you developed that can help you on the job you are applying for.
- List any activities, such as sports and clubs. Be sure to state any leadership positions, accomplishments, and any honors received. Describe job-related qualities and skills you developed through these activities, such as goal setting and teamwork skills.

Experience   List any full-time, part-time, or summer jobs and any volunteer work.

- List job title, employer name, address, telephone number, and supervisor and/or other person, if you want the person contacted for a reference. State length of employment in both months and years.
- Describe knowledge, qualities, and skills you developed that can help you on the job you are applying for.
- State quantifiable accomplishments.

Other   List any specific skills/training (computer programs), foreign language fluency, certifications (real estate), or talents that are related to the job you are applying for—using an appropriate heading. Again, focus on knowledge, qualities, and skills you developed that can help you on the job you are applying for.

The e-Resume: As you may know, many organizations are requesting that resumes be sent electronically via e-mail. Be sure to follow their instructions. Here are a few do's and don'ts of e-resumes: (1) Do develop your resume in a word processing file. However, don't send it as an attachment. (2) Save your resume in ASCII file format; use "save as text file" in your word processing document or save your resume as a PDF file. Your resume is now an e-resume. (3) Write your cover letter in the e-mail, and then copy your e-resume in the body of the e-mail. (4) Before sending it to an employer, send it to yourself so that you can see what it looks like. If it's a mess, fix it; then resend it to yourself until it reads and looks good. (5) Send it to the employer.

Learning Outcome

7. Explain at least three tips to get ahead that you can use to improve your chances of getting a job, raises, and promotions.

Getting Raises and Promotions

This section discusses tips to help you get ahead, career paths, preparation for getting a raise or promotion, asking for a raise or promotion, changing organizations, and job shock.

Tips to Help You Get Ahead   Below are 10 ways to enhance your chances of career advancement:

- Be a top performer at your present job. If you are not successful at your present job, you are not a likely candidate for a raise or promotion.

- Finish assignments early.[59] When your boss delegates a task, finish it before the deadline. This shows initiative.

- Volunteer for extra assignments.[60] If you can handle additional work, you should get paid more, and you show your ability to take on a new position.

- Keep up with the latest technology. Request the opportunity for training. Take the time to learn to use the latest technology. Read publications that pertain to your field.

- Develop good human relations with the important people in the organization. (Follow the ideas throughout this book.)

- Know when to approach your boss. Make requests when your boss is in a good mood; stay clear when the boss is in a bad mood unless you can help resolve the reason for the bad mood.

- Be polite. Say "thank you" both orally and in writing. Sending a thank you note keeps your name in front of people.[61] Saying "please" and "thank you," "pardon me," and so on, shows concern for others.

- Never say anything negative about anyone. You never know who will find out what you've said. That "nobody" may be a good friend of an important person.

- Be approachable. Smile, and go out of your way to say hi to people. Take time to talk to people who want your help.

- Make effective presentations.[62] If you are not effective at speaking before people, get training. Join Toastmasters International.

Career Paths   A **career path** *is a sequence of job assignments that lead to more responsibility, with raises and promotions.* In organizations that have career paths, it is easier to develop a career plan, because in a sense that's what career paths are. In the fast-food industry, career paths are common. For example, management trainees start out by going to a formal training program for a few weeks; then they are assigned to a store as a trainee for six months; then they go to a different store as an assistant store manager for a year; then they become a store manager. After one year they can be promoted to a larger store. After being a store manager for five years, they are eligible for regional management positions.

Preparation for Getting a Raise or Promotion   It is very important to understand your job responsibilities and how you are evaluated by your boss, both formally and informally. Know your boss's expectations and exceed them, or at least meet them. Do what needs to be done to get a high performance appraisal. If you don't get a good performance appraisal, your chances of getting a raise or promotion will be hurt.

Chapter 14 discusses keeping a critical incidents file of the good and poor performances of employees. In reality, most bosses don't keep a written record, or they record only the negative. If you want a raise or promotion, it's your responsibility to prove that you deserve one. The way to prove it is through self-documentation.

Keep a critical incidents file of every positive thing you do that is not generally required but that helps the organization. Keeping the boss appraised of your success on a regular basis is not bragging. Some of the things to include are:

- Any additional work you now perform.
- Times when you volunteered or cooperated to help other departments.
- Ideas you suggested that helped the organization.
- Any increases in the performance of your department. Be specific. For example, productivity was up by 5 percent last year, absenteeism was down 10 percent last year, returns were down by 100 units this period, sales increased by $5,000 this quarter.
- If during the last performance appraisal you were told of areas that needed improvement, gather evidence to show how you have improved.

The first four suggestions also apply to getting a job—adding value.

If you plan to ask for a raise, state a specific amount. Check to find out what other people in similar jobs are getting for raises, and what other organizations pay their employees for similar jobs. Check Web sites (www.salaryexpert.com, www.indeed.com/salary, www.salary.com, www.payscale.com) for market rates for slaries, posted by occupation.[63] If your boss is a negotiator, start with a request for a higher raise than you expect to get. This way you can compromise and still get what you feel you deserve.

Asking for a Raise or Promotion   When asking for a raise or promotion, don't catch your boss by surprise. The best time to ask is usually during the performance appraisal process. Present your critical incidents to help you get a good review and raise.

Aspiration is an advancement-related trait. So requests for promotion should be known before a specific position is open. Your boss and the human resources or personnel department should know your career plan. Ask them where you stand, what the chances of promotion are, and when promotion may come. Have them help you prepare for a promotion.

WORK APPLICATIONS

11. Which specific idea(s) do you plan to use to help you get raises and promotions?

Changing Organizations   The choice will be yours. If you are satisfied that you are meeting your career plan with one organization, stay with it. If not, search out new opportunities elsewhere.[64] However, you should realize that it is not uncommon for a job, particularly your first full-time job, to be frustrating and not meet your expectations. It would be nice, but don't expect to be told you are doing a good job; it is expected of you. Expect to be criticized, and be open to changing.[65]

HP Crashes But the CEO Gets a Golden Parachute: Carly Fiorina and Hewlett-Packard Company

Changing organizations to get ahead is the American way of life, or so thought Carly Fiorina as she became CEO and chair of the board of Hewlett-Packard Company (HP). She worked at AT&T and Lucent Technologies and was listed by *Fortune* magazine as the most powerful woman in business for six years in a row. [yet Fiorina's tenure at HP was nothing short of a prolonged controversy. Her unpopularity at HP was amplified by her many decisions which some thought to be provoking.

Fiorina pushed through a controversial merger with rival company Compaq. The promised benefits failed to materialize, and many analysts claim that the move diluted the value of HP's otherwise profitable imaging and printer division. The company's stock price dropped.

The board had a very difficult decision to make: Should it fire Ms. Fiorina for her performance which, according to her contract, would provide her an astounding severance package estimated at over $42 million, or should it bite the bullet and continue to let HP muddle along? She was subsequently fired. In a commencement address at North Carolina Agricultural & Technical State University, Fiorina said: "The worst thing I could have imagined happened. I lost my job in the most public way possible, and the press had a field day with it all over the world. And guess what? I'm still here. I am at peace and my soul is intact." Would anyone not be at peace with $42 million in her pocket?

In hindsight, following Fiorina's exit, sales of Compaq PCs helped HP overtake Dell to become the number one PC seller.

Questions

1. Looking at the section on career management, explain why Carly Fiorina's move to HP was or was not a good career move.

2. Which career stage do you think she is in now?

3. What research should Carly Fiorina have done before taking the job at HP? How might this have helped her in her position as CEO?

4. How fair to the stockholders and former HP employees was the severance package in light of Carly Fiorina's performance as CEO?

If you are open to making a career move, have an updated resume ready and let your network of contacts know you are willing to make a move if the right opportunity comes along. Don't quit your job until you get another one, and around your boss and peers, don't publicize that you are looking for a new job.

In the opening case, Shane could benefit by developing a career plan, with a strong resume supporting his plans.

Job Shock   Few jobs, if any, meet all expectations.[66] **Job shock** *occurs when the employee's expectations are not met*. Expectations that the workplace is fair and that good work will always be recognized and rewarded are the leading cause of job shock. It is also common for employers to say, "Don't worry, we'll take care of you," and nothing happens, to your dismay. People also find part or many of their day-to-day tasks boring. Job shock has no quick cure. However, it is helpful to learn to cope with unsettling on-the-job realities by developing a "real-world" mindset. Talk to other people to find out if your situation is unique. If it's not, you probably have unrealistic job expectations. People often change jobs only to find the same frustrations they hoped to leave behind.[67] Learn to realize that your unhappiness often springs from unrealistic job expectations.[68] Developing a real-world mindset can help shield you from future shocks.

Through personal development, you can improve your human relations skills and time management skills and advance in your career. Good luck in doing so.

Global Careers

Globalization will affect your career in one way or another.[69] You could end up like William Lussier by taking a job in Europe working for a Japanese company. To advance to the top of some firms, you must leave the country and work abroad for a year or more. You could take a job working in the United States for a foreign-owned company, for example, Shell (Netherlands), Nestlé (Switzerland), Nokia (Finland), Samsung (South Korea), or Columbia Records or Aiwa (Japan). Even if you work in America for a U.S. company, there is a good chance that you will work with employees from other countries here and with employees in other countries. You will likely deal with customers or suppliers from other countries. At the least, in the corporate world, you will compete with foreign companies for business. What type of global career do you want? Regardless of your career goals, possessing good human relations skills with a diversity of people is critical to your career success.

Apparel and Grooming

Apparel and grooming play a major role in making a good first impression[70] because they send subliminal messages.[71] They are also important in maintaining your image to help you get raises and promotions. In a survey, 93 percent of managers said a person's style of dress at work influences their chances of earning a promotion.[72] Your clothes should be proper business apparel that is well coordinated, well tailored, and well maintained. Your hair should be neat, trimmed, clean, and away from your face. Clean teeth and fingernails and fresh breath are expected. Avoid tattoos, body-piercing jewelry, and flashy jewelry that shows at work.

More than 23 million American employees wear uniforms to work, from the professional level of judge to the more technical level of bank teller. Many professionals don't wear an actual uniform, but a suit or other accepted dress for specific types of jobs constitute a type of uniform. John Molloy coined the term *wardrobe engineering* to describe how clothing and accessories can be used to create a certain image. There are hundreds of image consultants, and they don't agree on everything.[73] However, here are some generally agreed-on suggestions if you want to dress for a successful career in most organizations.

Dress for the Organization and Job   Again, dress and groom like the people in the organization and specific job that you want. If you are not sure of the dress style, call or visit the organization before the job interview and find out, or at least possibly overdress, as suggested for job interviews.[74] Once you are on the job, at least dress like your peers.[75] If you are serious about climbing the corporate ladder, however, you should consider dressing like the managers.[76] Dressing like the managers can help in your career advancement.

Job Interview   As a general guide, during a job interview never underdress (such as jeans and T-shirts) and possibly overdress. As a college graduate seeking a professional job, wear a suit if managers do (tie for men), even if you will not need to wear one for the job. You may be thinking, "Why bother? No one else does." That's exactly the point. You will look more professional, like the managers, and stand out in the crowd and may have the edge on getting the job. In an actual job situation, a young applicant was asked by the interviewer why he was not dressed in a jacket and tie. The applicant responded that he was dressed like the others in the organization. The interviewer said, "There is one major difference between you and them. They already have a job here; you don't." However, some companies, like Google, advise causal clothes, and if you show up in a suit, they don't hire you.[77] So again, do some research so you know what to wear.

Wear Quality Clothes   Quality clothes project a quality image. Start with a quality suit for job interviews and important days at work, such as your first day, to develop a good first impression. Look for sales when buying apparel, but don't buy a suit, or anything else you will wear to work, unless you really like it. If you feel good about the way you look, you will generally project a more positive self-image of confidence, which will help your career. So never buy anything you don't really like, even if it is on sale, because it is not a good deal if you don't feel good about yourself when you wear it.

Dress and Groom Conservatively   The latest dress fad is often inappropriate in the professional business setting. You may not be taken seriously if you exhibit faddish or flashy apparel and grooming.

Casual Dress   What is considered casual business dress does vary.[78] In most situations, don't go to the job interview casual unless you know that is the expected apparel for the interview. In most cases, casual doesn't include jeans and T-shirts for professional employees. Dress similar to others in the firm when you get the job.

Suggestions for Men   Men may want to follow these guidelines:

- **Grooming.** If other men in the organization do not have facial hair, long hair, or wear earrings, you may consider shaving, getting a haircut, and leaving the earrings at home, at least for the job interview.
- **Suit.** The suit is still the most appropriate apparel in many organizations. A typical business suit is blue or gray, commonly dark, and stripes are acceptable. The fabric is wool, or at least a 45 percent wool blend; in warmer climates, cotton or linen suits may be acceptable, but be careful because they wrinkle easily. It is conservatively cut, and the width of the lapels and the pants are conservative in style.
- **Shirt.** The business shirt is a solid color white or light blue and may have thin stripes, though not loud. The shirt has long sleeves, and they show about ½ inch from the suit sleeves when your arms are by your side. The collar is conservative and looks good with your tie.
- **Tie.** The wrong tie can hurt the quality image of your suit. The business tie is silk and usually has some conservative design—no animals, sayings, or cartoon characters. A tie tack is not needed, but a small, conservative one is acceptable.
- **Shoes.** Conservative dark leather business shoes, not sneakers, are worn with a suit. Avoid tassels.[79] If in doubt about whether your shoes, or any other parts of your business attire, are properly conservative for business, ask a qualified sales rep.
- **Matching.** The suit, shirt, and tie all match. Be careful not to mix three sets of stripes. Generally, with a striped suit, wear a solid-color shirt. Match the color of the design in the tie to the suit and shirt. The color of the conservative belt (small, simple buckle) is the same color as your shoes. The color of the thin socks match the color of the pants (no heavy wool or white socks), and the socks are long enough so that your legs never show.

Suggestions for Women   Women may want to follow these guidelines:

- **Grooming and jewelry.** Wearing heavy makeup, such as very obvious eye shadow, dark outlined lips, and excessive-smelling perfumes, is not appropriate for business; don't wear it, at least for the job interview. Makeup should be subtle to the point that people don't think you are wearing any, and if worn, perfume should be light. Jewelry is simple and tasteful, never overdone.
- **Skirted suit.** The professional skirted wool or wool-blend suit is most appropriate; however, the conservative business dress with coordinated jacket is also acceptable. The skirt matches the blazer-cut jacket, and it reaches to just below the knee. With proper business apparel, you are not trying to make a fashion statement. Women have more color choice, but blue and gray are good for the first suit. Solids, tweeds, and plaids are acceptable, but pinstripes may make you appear as though you are trying to imitate male apparel.
- **Blouse.** The business blouse is silk or cotton and free of frills, patterns, or unusual collars; it is not low-cut. Low necklines come across as seductive, and people usually assume the sexual innuendo is intentional.[80] Do not show your cleavage, even at

business socials, because the image set forth will be lasting. You want people talking about your accomplishments, not your figure.[81] Solid colors are preferred, with a greater range of collars acceptable so long as they contrast and coordinate with the color of the suit. The collar should be equivalent to that of a man's shirt, and the top button should be open.

- **No tie, scarf optional.** It is generally agreed that a woman wearing a tie may appear as though she is trying to imitate male apparel. However, a conservative scarf is acceptable if you want to wear one.
- **Shoes.** Leather shoes match the suit and are conservative. Shoes are not a fashion statement—they are comfortable, with a moderate heel; plain pumps are a good choice.
- **Matching, and attaché case.** All apparel matches. Neutral or skin-tone pantyhose are worn with your business suit. Businesswomen carry an attaché case, which replaces a purse or handbag, whenever feasible.

If you are thinking that it is unfair to be judged by your appearance rather than for who you really are and what you can do, you are correct. However, if you haven't found out yet, life is not always fair. Fair or not, in most organizations, your appearance will affect your career success—but remember that your appearance is something over which you have control.

As we bring this chapter to a close, complete Self-Assessment Exercise 4–4 to determine how your personality affects your time and career management.

Self-Assessment Exercise 4–4

Personality and Time and Career Management

If you are *open to new experiences,* you probably are time-conscious and seek improvements. Being open and flexible, you may be good at career development.

If you have a high *agreeableness* personality, with a high need for affiliation, you may not be too concerned about time management and may freely give your time to others. However, you may need to work at saying no to requests that you don't have to do, so that you don't spread yourself too thin, you can get your own work done, and you can keep your stress level down. You also may not be too concerned about career advancement, because relationships tend to be more important to you than being a manager and climbing the corporate ladder.

If you scored high on *conscientiousness,* with a high need for achievement, you may tend to be time-conscious to achieve your goals by the dates you set. You are concerned about career success, but without a high surgency need, your concern may not be to advance in management.

If you have *surgency,* with a high need for power, you like to be in control and may need to work at trusting people and delegating to save time. You most likely have aspirations to climb the corporate ladder. But be sure to use ethical power and politics.

Action plan: Based on your personality, what specific things can you do to improve your time management and career skills?

_____

_____

Videos

Manager's Hot Seat and Behavior Model Videos are available for this chapter.

Online Learning Center Resources
Go to the Internet (http://mhhe.com/lussier8e) where you will find a broad array of resources to help maximize your learning.

- Review the vocabulary.
- Try a quiz.

R E V I E W

The chapter review is organized to help you master the 8 learning outcomes for Chapter 4. First provide your own response to each learning outcome, and then check the summary provided to see how well you understand the material. Next, identify the final statement in each section as either true or false (T/F). Correct each false statement. Answers are given at the end of the chapter.

1. **Explain how to analyze your use of time with a time log.**

   To analyze your time, keep a time log for one or two typical weeks. Then answer the 10 questions in the text to analyze areas where your time can be spent more effectively.

   Multitasking complex tasks is a good time management technique. T F

2. **State the three priority determination questions and determine when an activity on the to-do list should be delegated or assigned a high, medium, or low priority.**

   The three priority determination questions are: (1) Do I need to be personally involved? (2) Is the task my responsibility or will it affect the performance or finances of my department? and (3) Is quick action needed? An activity is high priority when you answer yes to all three questions. An activity is medium priority when you say yes to question 1 and no to either question 2 or 3. An activity is low priority when you say yes to question 1 and no to both questions 2 and 3. If the answer to question 1 is no, the activity should be delegated.

   After answering the three priority determination questions, you rank order each task on your to-do list. T F

3. **List the three steps in the time management system.**

   Following the time management system, step (1) is to plan each week, step (2) is to schedule each week, and step (3) is to schedule each day.

   Begin scheduling by listing activities over which you have no control, such as meetings. T F

4. **Identify at least three time management techniques you presently do not use but will use in the future.**

   Answers among students will vary.

   Procrastination is a time waster that leads to stress. T F

5. **Describe the four career stages.**

   The four career stages are characterized as follows. The 20s are a time for proving one's ability as one gets started. The 30s involve the development of expertise and often some questioning of one's career path. By the 40s and 50s, most managers have reached their highest level of advancement. In the 60s and 70s people begin to prepare for retirement.

   Younger people face a greater threat of being laid off; with age comes job security. T F

6. **List the five steps in the career planning model.**

   The five steps in the career planning model are: (1) self-assessment, (2) career preferences and exploration, (3) set career objectives, (4) develop a plan, and (5) control.

   Following graduation from college is a good time to begin determining career preferences and exploration. T F

7. **Explain at least three tips to get ahead that you can use to improve your chances of getting a job, raises, and promotions.**

   Answers among students will vary.

   When applying for a job, it is best not to specify a job title so that employers can match your talents to the jobs they have open. T F

8. Define the following 11 key terms.

Select one or more methods: (1) fill in the missing key terms from memory; (2) match the key terms from the end of the review with their definitions; and/or (3) copy the key terms in order from the key terms list at the beginning of the chapter.

_____ refers to techniques designed to enable people to get more done in less time with better results.

A(n) _____ is a daily diary that tracks activities, enabling you to determine how your time is used.

_____ is the preference given to one activity over other activities.

The _____ ask (1) Do I need to be personally involved? (2) Is the task my responsibility or will it affect the performance or finances of my department? and (3) Is quick action needed?

A(n) _____ is the written list of activities the individual has to complete.

The _____ are as follows: step (1) plan each week, step (2) schedule each week, and step (3) schedule each day.

_____ is the process of setting career objectives and determining how to accomplish them.

_____ is the process of gaining skill, experience, and education to achieve career objectives.

The _____ steps are these: step (1) self-assessment, step (2) career preferences and exploration, step (3) set career objectives, step (4) develop a plan, and step (5) control.

A(n) _____ is a sequence of job assignments that lead to more responsibility, with raises and promotions.

_____ occurs when the employee's expectations are not met.

K E Y   T E R M S

career development 125	job shock 135	time management 110
career path 133	priority 113	time management
career planning 125	priority determination	steps 114
career planning	questions 113	to-do list 114
model 126	time log 110	

C O M M U N I C A T I O N   S K I L L S

The following critical thinking questions can be used for class discussion and/or as written assignments to develop communication skills. Be sure to give complete explanations for all questions.

1. Based on your experience or observation, list ways in which people in organizations waste time. How can these time-wasting activities be cut back or eliminated?

2. It takes time to follow a time management system. Is the time taken worth the benefits? Will you use a time management system? Why or why not?

3. Are you a procrastinator? Are you a perfectionist? What are the pros and cons to being a procrastinator and perfectionist?

4. Have you done a career self-assessment? Was it easy or difficult? Why? Do you believe you could benefit from taking a career test? Why or why not?

5. Select a job you are interested in getting. Go online to one or more of the following Web sites to determine the compensation for the job you want: www.salaryexpert.com, www.indeed.com/salary, www.salary.com, www.payscale.com.

6. Do a job search for the job you are interested in getting. Go online to one or more of the following Web sites (or others related to your field) to find job opportunities: www.collegejournal.com (jobs and tips for new college grads); www.college recruiter.com (internships, and entry-level jobs); www.careerbuilder.com (jobs and advice); and www.monster.com (a listing of jobs).

7. From question six, or based on other sources, select an organization you would like to work for. Research the company and develop some questions in preparation for a job interview.

8. Prepare or revise your resume, and then evaluate it using Self-Assessment Exercise 4–3. How did you score? Based on your assessment, revise your resume.

9. How would you feel about working for a domestic company and competing against foreign companies? How would you feel about working for a foreign company at home? How would you feel about working in another country and, if you are interested, what countries would you be willing to work in?

10. Will your apparel and grooming really affect your career success? Why or why not?

11. What are your thoughts on women showing cleavage at work? Should cleavage be covered or shown? Why? In your opinion, is a low neckline meant to be seductive, with intentional sexual innuendo?

CASE

Building a Career by Building a Better Bear

Build-A-Bear Workshop is a unique and exceptional approach to the entertainment retail industry. The Build-A-Bear Workshop mission is to bring the teddy bear to life. An American icon, the teddy bear brings to mind warm thoughts about childhood, about friendship, about trust and comfort, and also about love. Build-A-Bear Workshop embodies those thoughts in how it runs its business every day.[82]

The teddy bear theme is carried throughout the store with original teddy bear fixtures, murals, and artwork. The store associates, known as master Bear Builder associates, share the experience with guests at each phase of the bear-making process. Regardless of age, guests enjoy the highly visual environment, the sounds, and the fantasy of this special place while they create a memory with their friends and family.[83]

Maxine Clark has been Chief Executive Bear of Build-A-Bear Workshop, Inc., since the company's inception in 1997 and has served as chair of the board of directors since the company's conversion to a corporation in April 2000. From November 1992 until January 1996, Maxine was the president of Payless ShoeSource, Inc. Prior to joining Payless, she spent over 19 years in various divisions of The May Department Stores Company in areas including merchandise development, merchandise planning, merchandise research, marketing, and product development.

Maxine Clark is one of the true innovators in the retail industry. During her 30-year career, her ability to spot emerging retail and merchandising trends and her insight into the desires of the American consumer have generated growth for retail leaders, including department, discount, and specialty stores. In 1997, she founded Build-A-Bear Workshop, a teddy-bear themed retail-entertainment experience.

Build-A-Bear Workshop and Maxine Clark are proud to be recognized in their industry. In 2008, Maxine Clark was named one of The 25 Most Influential People in Retailing by *Chain Store Age;* in 2006 she was inducted into the Junior Achievement National

Business Hall of Fame and received the 2006 Luminary Award for Entrepreneurial Achievement from the Committee of 200. She was named a Customer-Centered Leader in the 2005 Customer First Awards by *Fast Company*. Maxine was named one of the Wonder Women of Toys by *Playthings* magazine and Women in Toys, and was also one of the National Finalists in Retail for the Ernst & Young Entrepreneur of the Year in 2004. In 2005, the National Association of Small Business Investment Companies (NASBIC) made Build-A-Bear Workshop Portfolio Company of the Year, and the company was named one of the International Council of Shopping Centers' Hottest Retailers of 2004, and the Retail Innovator of the Year for 2001 by The National Retail Federation.

Maxine is a member of the board of directors of The J.C. Penney Company, Inc., where she also serves as chair of the Corporate Governance Committee. She is a member of the board of trustees of Barnes Jewish Hospital, Washington University in St. Louis, and her alma mater, the University of Georgia. She is a chair of Teach For America—St. Louis and a member of the Teach For America national board. She is also a member of the Committee of 200, a leading organization for women entrepreneurs around the world. In 2006, her first book, *The Bear Necessities of Business: Building a Company with Heart,* was published by Wiley.[84]

Go to the Internet: For more information on Maxine Clark and to update the information provided in this case, do a name search on the Internet and visit http://www.buildabear.com.

Support your answers to the following questions with specific information from the case and text, or other information you get from the Web or other sources.

1. Maxine Clark, besides being the founder and CEO of Build-A-Bear since 1997, serves on several boards of directors, chairs Teach For America—St. Louis, and has written a book discussing how one builds a company with heart. How might time management have assisted her in balancing such a demanding workload?

2. Describe Maxine Clark's career path. What stage of her career do you think she has reached?

3. Having read the description of the firm Build-A-Bear, what steps would you follow to determine if working for this firm would assist you in your career development?

4. Should apparel and grooming play a role in career progress? Do you believe that proper apparel and grooming played a role in Maxine Clark's career success? If so, how?

Cumulative Questions

5. What is the importance of human relations practices (Chapter 1) at Build-A-Bear?

6. From what you have read, define Maxine Clark's locus of control (Chapter 2).

7. Employee job satisfaction at Build-A-Bear stores would seem to be critical in creating a magical environment for the customers. What factors should Maxine Clark look at to maintain high job satisfaction (Chapter 3)?

OBJECTIVE CASE **Overworked?**

In the following discussion, Iris is a middle manager and Peggy is a first-line supervisor who reports to her.

IRIS: Peggy, I've called you into my office to speak to you again about the late report.

PEGGY: I know it's late again, but I'm so busy getting the work out that I don't have time to do it. I'm always the first to arrive for work and the last to go home. I push hard to get the job done. Sometimes I end up redoing employees' work because it's not done properly. I often get headaches and stomach cramps from working so intensely.

IRIS: I know you do. Maybe the problem lies in your time management ability. What do you usually do each day?

PEGGY: Most of each day is spent putting out fires. My employees constantly need me to help them with their work. The days just seem to speed by. Other than putting out fires, I don't do much.

IRIS: So you can't get the reports done on time because of the number of fires. What is your approach to getting the reports done on time?

PEGGY: I just wait until there are no fires to put out; then I do them. Sometimes it's after the deadline.

IRIS: You are going to have to make some definite changes if you are going to be a successful supervisor. Do you enjoy being a supervisor?

PEGGY: For the most part I do. I think I might like to move up the ladder some day. But I like the hands-on stuff; I'm not too thrilled about doing paperwork.

IRIS: If you develop your time management skills, I believe you will find that you can get the job done on time with less stress. On Monday the company is offering a time management workshop. I took the course myself; it's excellent. It really helped me a lot when I was in your position, and still does today. It teaches you a three-step approach. Do you want to attend?

PEGGY: Yes, but what about the work in my department?

IRIS: I'll cover for you. On Tuesday, I want you to come see me first thing in the morning so that we can discuss what you learned and how you are going to apply it on the job.

Answer the following questions. Then in the space between questions, state why you selected that answer.

_____ 1. Keeping a time log and using a to-do list would be helpful to Peggy.
   a. true   *b.* false

_____ 2. Peggy seems to be effective at setting priorities.
   a. true   *b.* false

_____ 3. Peggy seems to delegate _____ activities.
   a. many   *b.* few

_____ 4. Setting weekly objectives, plans, and schedules would help Peggy get the reports done on time.

    a. true   *b.* false

_____ 5. Peggy seems to have a Type _____ personality.

    a. A   *b.* B

_____ 6. Peggy appears to be in the _____ career stage.

    a. 20s   *c.* 40s and 50s

    b. 30s   *d.* 60s and 70s

_____ 7. Peggy has a career plan.

    a. true   *b.* false

_____ 8. The time management workshop is best classified as:

    a. career planning   *c.* career development

    b. career planning model   *d.* career path

_____ 9. From the case information, we can assume that this company has career paths.

    a. true   *b.* false

_____ 10. It appears that Peggy will be a good candidate for raises and promotions.

    a. true   *b.* false

11. How would you conduct the Tuesday morning session with Peggy?

SKILL-BUILDING EXERCISE 4–1

Time Management System

Preparation (Individual and Group)

Before using the time management system, you will find it helpful to keep a time log for one or two typical weeks. It is strongly recommended that you keep a time log and analyze it.

Note: For this exercise you will need copies of Exhibits 4.1, 4.3, 4.4, and 4.5. You may make photocopies of the exhibits or make your own copies on sheets of paper. While performing the steps below, refer to the text guidelines.

Step 1: Plan Your Week. Use Exhibit 4.3 to develop a plan for the rest of this week. Begin with today.

Step 2: Schedule Your Week. Use Exhibit 4.4 to schedule the rest of this week. Be sure to schedule a 30-minute period to plan and schedule next week, preferably on the last day of the week.

Step 3: Schedule Your Day.   Schedule each day using Exhibit 4.5. Do this each day, at least until the class period for which this exercise is assigned.

Be sure to bring your plans and schedules to class.

In-Class Exercise

Objective: To understand how to use the time management system to enable you to get more done in less time with better results.

AACSB: The primary AACSB learning standard skills developed through this exercise are reflective thinking and self-management and analytic skills.

Preparation: You need your completed plans and schedules.

Experience: You will share and discuss your plans and schedules for the week and your daily schedules.

Procedure 1
(5–10 minutes)

Break into groups of five or six, and share and discuss your plans and schedules. Pass them around so that you and others can make comparisons. The comparisons serve as a guide to improving future plans and schedules.

Conclusion: The instructor leads a class discussion and/or makes concluding remarks.

Application (2–4 minutes):   What did I learn from this experience? How will I use this knowledge in the future?

Sharing: Volunteers give their answers to the application section.

SKILL-BUILDING EXERCISE 4–2

Career Planning
Preparation (Individual and Group)

Answering the following questions will help you develop a career plan. Use additional paper if needed. Do not reveal anything about yourself that you prefer not to share with classmates during the in-class exercise.

Step 1: Self-Assessment

a. List two or three statements that answer the question, "Who am I?"

b. Think about two or three of your major accomplishments. (They can be in school, work, sports, hobbies, etc.) List the skills it took to achieve each accomplishment.

c. Identify skills and abilities you already possess that you can use in your career (for example, planning, organizing, communicating, leading).

Step 2: Career Preferences and Exploration

a. What type of industry would you like to work in? (You may list more than one.)

b. What type and size of organization do you want to work for?

c. List by priority the five factors that will most influence your job or career decisions (opportunity for advancement, challenge, security, salary, hours, location of job, travel involved, educational opportunities, recognition, prestige, environment, coworkers, boss, responsibility, variety of tasks, etc.).

d. Describe the perfect job.

e. What type of job(s) do you want during your career (marketing, finance, operations, personnel, and so forth)? After selecting a field, select a specific job—for example, salesperson, manager, accountant.

Step 3: Set Career Objectives

a. What are your short-range objectives for the first year after graduation?

b. What are your intermediate objectives for the second through fifth years after graduation?

c. What are your long-range objectives?

Step 4: Develop a Plan
Use the following form to develop an action plan to help you achieve your objectives.

Career Plan

Objective _____

Starting date _____   **Due date** _____

Steps (what, where, how, resources, etc.—subobjectives)	When	
	Start	**End**

In-Class Exercise

Objective: To experience career planning; to develop a career plan.

AACSB: The primary AACSB learning standard skills developed through this exercise are reflective thinking and self-management and analytic skills.

Preparation: You will need the completed preparation that serves as your career plan.

Experience: You will share your career plan with one or two classmates to help make improvements.

Procedure 1
(10–20 minutes)

Break into teams of two or three. One at a time, go through your career plans while the others ask questions and/or make recommendations to help you improve your career plan.

Conclusion: The instructor leads a class discussion and/or makes concluding remarks.

Application (2–4 minutes):   What did I learn from this experience? How will I use this knowledge in the future?

Sharing: Volunteers give their answers to the application section.

ANSWERS TO TRUE/FALSE QUESTIONS

1. F. Multitasking is effective for juggling simple, not complex, tasks.
2. F. You should not rank order tasks because you will waste time renumbering them as new ones are added.
3. T.
4. T.
5. F. In the global economy, people of all ages are being laid off.
6. F. Career preferences and explorations, such as internships, should take place during college.
7. F. Recruiters are filling jobs that have specific titles, not matching talents with jobs. Resumes without specific job titles are usually put in the reject pile.

PART 2

Interpersonal Skills: The Foundation of Human Relations

Interpersonal Communication

Sara, a manager at Sears, needs a report typed. She has decided to assign the task to David following the five steps in the message-sending process, which you will learn more about in this chapter. Here's how Sara and David communicated for each step.[1]

Step 1: Develop rapport.

SARA: David, how are you doing today?

DAVID: OK. How about you?

SARA: Fine, thanks. Is the work on schedule?

DAVID: Yes, things are running smoothly.

Step 2: State the communication objective.

SARA: David, I have a report that I'd like you to type for me.

DAVID: Let's see it.

Step 3: Transmit the message.

SARA: Here are five handwritten pages. Please print the first page on my letterhead and the others on regular bond. Place the exhibit on a separate page; it will probably be on page 3. Then run the rest.

DAVID: It sounds easy enough.

SARA: I need it for a presentation to Paul at two o'clock today, and I'd like some time to review it before then. How soon will you have it ready?

DAVID: Well, it's 10 now, and I go to lunch from 12 to 1. I've got to finish what I'm working on now, but I should have it by noon.

SARA: Good. That will allow me to look it over at noon and get it back to you at one o'clock if it needs changes.

Step 4: Check understanding.

SARA: I want to make sure I clearly explained what I need so that it will not need to be redone. Will you please tell me how you are going to do the job?

DAVID: Sure. I'm going to print it on regular bond. I'll run it until I get to the exhibit; the exhibit will be on its own page; then I will run the rest of it.

SARA: Did I mention that I wanted the first page to be on my letterhead?

DAVID: I don't remember, but I'll put page one on your letterhead.

SARA: Good!

Step 5: Get a commitment and follow up.

SARA: So you agree to type it as directed and deliver it to my office by noon today?

DAVID: Yeah, I'll get it to you before noon.

SARA: (thinking to herself as she walks back to her office): I'm confident he'll do it. But I'll follow up. If David doesn't show up by 11:55, I will be back, and he'll do it during his lunchtime.

How would you have communicated the typing job? The five steps in the message-sending process above are part of the communication process that you will learn in this chapter. Keep in mind that a diversity of people may use different communication styles.

HOW INTERPERSONAL COMMUNICATION AFFECTS BEHAVIOR, HUMAN RELATIONS, AND PERFORMANCE

Learning Outcome

1. Explain why communication skills are important.

In this chapter, we take the intrapersonal skills foundation from the first four chapters and start building interpersonal skills. Interpersonal communication skills are the foundation of human relations, as we initiate, build, and maintain relationships through communications.[2] Recall that behavior is what we do and say; thus, communication is behavior.

Clearly, communication skills are important in your personal life and for career success. According to a Stanford University study, the ability to converse with others affects career success.[3] In fact, the most important skill employers look for in new graduates is communication skills.[4] In this chapter we focus more on verbal communications, and in the next chapter we discuss written communication skills.

Our behavior during communication also affects other people's behavior and our human relations.[5] For example, if you are polite and friendly, chances are the other person will behave in a similar way. However, if you are rude, the other person may retaliate.

The general public's and the customer's perception of the organization is often based on interpersonal communications with employees. Essentially, nothing can get done in an organization without effective communications.[6] Effective communication strategies have increased productivity, improved efficiency, cut costs, improved morale, and decreased turnover. And the importance of communications will continue to increase with the global economy and the increased speed of technology and pace of conducting business.[7] In the opening case, if Sara did a good job of communicating, David should do the task correctly; if not, the task may not be done correctly and will have to be done a second time.

WORK APPLICATIONS

1. Give reasons why communication skills are important to you at work. Do not give reasons stated in the text.

2. Give a specific example in which communication affected your behavior, human relations, and performance.

THE COMMUNICATION PROCESS AND COMMUNICATION BARRIERS

Learning Outcome

2. List and explain the four steps in the communication process.

The **communication process** *consists of a sender who encodes a message and transmits it through a channel to a receiver who decodes it and may give feedback.* Exhibit 5.1 illustrates the communication process. There are also barriers to communications, and Exhibit 5.2 lists the common communication barriers.

In the opening case, Sara is the sender of an oral message about a handwritten report to be typed. David is the receiver of the message, and he responds to the message by agreeing to finish the report by noon. Below is a brief explanation of each step in the communication process; you will learn the details of each step in separate sections of this chapter.

EXHIBIT 5.1 | The Communication Process

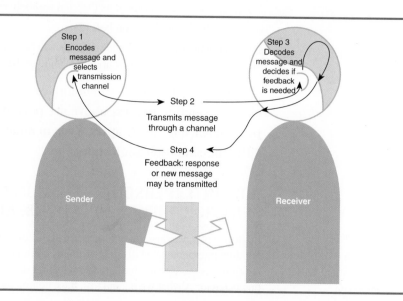

EXHIBIT 5.2 |
How Barriers Affect the
Communication Process

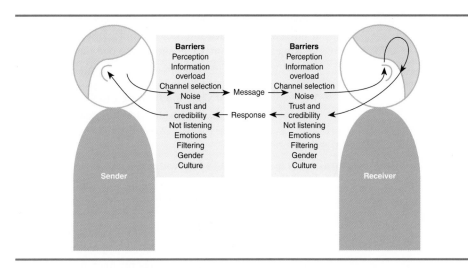

1. The Sender Encodes the Message and Selects the Transmission Channel

Encoding the Message   The *sender* of the message is the person who initiates the communication of *information and meaning that are to be communicated*. **Encoding** *is the sender's process of putting the message into a form that the receiver will understand.* You should consider the receiver of the message to determine the best way to encode the message to ensure clear transmission of the information and meaning.[8]

Perception Communication Barriers   As messages are transmitted, receivers use their perceptions to translate the messages so that they make sense to them. *Semantics* and *jargon* can be communication barriers, because the same word often means different things to different people. For example, *wicked good* can be confusing to people not familiar with the term, who do not realize it does mean "good."

Overcoming Perception Barriers   To overcome perception problems, you need to consider how the other person will most likely perceive the message and try to encode and transmit it appropriately. Thus, the choice of words is important.[9] Be careful not to use jargon with people who are not familiar with the terminology, especially people from countries with different cultures.[10]

Information Overload Communication Barriers   People have a limit on the amount of information they can understand at any given time. Information overload commonly occurs with new employees during the first few days, because they are often presented with too much information to comprehend in that period of time. With the widespread use of computers and with so much information available on the Internet, people are often dazzled and don't know what to do with all the information.[11]

Overcoming Information Overload   To minimize information overload, send messages in a quantity that the receiver can understand. When sending a message, do not talk for too long without checking to be sure the receiver understands the message as you intended. If you talk for too long, the receiver can become bored or lose the thread of the message.

Selecting the Transmission Channel   The **message** *is the physical form of the encoded information.* The message is transmitted through a channel. The three primary *communication channels* you can use are oral, nonverbal, and written; you will learn more about each channel in the next chapter.

Channel Selection Communication Barriers   Use of an inappropriate channel can result in missed communication. For example, if a manager catches an employee in the act of breaking a rule, the manager should use one-on-one, face-to-face communication. Another channel will not be as effective.

Overcoming Channel Selection Barriers   Before sending a message, give careful thought to selecting the most effective channel for the situation; you will learn how in the next chapter.

2. The Sender Transmits the Message through a Channel

As the sender, after you encode the message and select the channel, you transmit the message through the channel to one or more receivers.

Noise Communication Barriers   Noise factors during the transmission of a message can disturb or confuse the receiver. Noise is anything that interferes with message transmission. For example, a machine or people may make noise that makes it difficult to hear, the sender may not speak loud enough for the receiver to hear well, or a radio or TV may distract the receiver, causing message interpretation errors.

Overcoming Noise Barriers   To overcome noise, you need to consider the physical surroundings before transmitting the message. Try to keep noise to a minimum. If possible, stop the noise or distraction, or move to a quiet location.

3. The Receiver Decodes the Message and Decides If Feedback Is Needed

The person receiving the message decodes it. **Decoding** *is the receiver's process of translating the message into a meaningful form.* The receiver combines the message with other ideas and interprets the meaning of the message. We all decode, but we need to be careful to understand the other person's experience to truly understand the message.[12] The receiver decides if feedback, a response, or a new message is needed.[13] With oral communication, feedback is commonly given immediately. However, with written communication, it may not be necessary to reply.

Trust and Credibility Communication Barriers   During communication, receivers take into account the trust they have in the senders, as well as their credibility.[14] Managers who lack credibility and fail to create a climate of trust and openness aren't believed, no matter how hard they try to communicate.[15]

Overcoming Trust and Credibility Barriers   To improve your trust level, be open and honest with people. If people catch you in a lie, they may never trust you again.[16] To gain and maintain credibility, get the facts straight before you communicate. Send clear, correct messages. Become an expert in your area. You will learn more about developing trust in Chapter 8.

Not-Listening Barrier to Communication   People usually hear what the sender is saying, but often they do not listen to the message or understand what is being transmitted.[17] Not listening is sometimes the result of not paying attention.[18]

Overcoming Not-Listening Barriers   One method to help ensure that people listen to your message involves questioning and having them paraphrase the message back to you.[19] When listening, you should follow the listening tips presented later in this chapter.

Emotional Barriers to Communication   Everyone has emotions, such as anger, hurt, fear, sorrow, and happiness.[20] When you are emotional, it is difficult to be objective and to listen.[21]

Overcoming Emotional Barriers   When communicating, you should remain calm and be careful not to make others emotional by your behavior.[22] In the next chapter, you will learn more about emotions and how to calm an emotional employee.

4. Feedback: A Response or a New Message May Be Transmitted

After decoding the message, the receiver may give feedback to the sender. You should realize that the role of sender and receiver can change during a communication exchange; communication is often a two-way process of giving information and getting feedback.[23] Giving positive feedback increases performance.[24]

Filtering Communication Barriers   *Filtering* is the process of altering or distorting information to project a more favorable image.[25] For example, when people are asked to report progress toward objectives, they may stress the positive and de-emphasize, or even leave out, the negative side. They also may lie,[26] as did certain Enron employees.

Overcoming Filtering Barriers   To help eliminate filtering, you should treat errors as a learning experience rather than as an opportunity to blame and criticize employees.[27] You will learn about criticism in Chapter 6. Using an open-door policy can create and help support a two-way communication climate.

Here is an example of the preceding stages of the communication process: (1) a professor (sender) prepares for a class and encodes a message by preparing a lecture; (2) the professor transmits the message orally through a lecture during class; (3) the students (receivers) decode the lecture (message) by listening and/or taking notes in a meaningful way; (4) students usually have the option of asking questions (feedback) during or after class.

WORK APPLICATIONS

3. Give at least two different barriers to communication you have experienced at work. Explain the situation and how the barrier could have been overcome.

APPLICATION SITUATIONS

Communication Barriers

AS 5–1

Identify the communication barriers indicated by the statements below as:

A. Perception	D. Filtering	G. Not listening
B. Noise	E. Trust and credibility	H. Channel selection
C. Emotions	F. Information overload	

_____ 1. "You shouldn't be upset. Listen to me."

_____ 2. "Buddy, last week you took a long break. Don't do it again."

_____ 3. "That's a lot to remember; I'm not sure I got it all."

_____ 4. "Why did you say the job is going well, when you know it's not? You haven't even finished the . . . or the. . . ."

_____ 5. "I cannot hear you. Shut that thing off! Now, what did you say?"

_____ 6. "I said I'd do it in a little while. It's only been 10 minutes. Why do you expect it done now?"

_____ 7. "Why should I listen to you? You don't know what you're talking about."

Gender Conversation Differences

Research has shown that, generally, men and women converse for different reasons.[28] When they do converse, gender style becomes a barrier to communication between the sexes. Men tend to talk to emphasize status. Women tend to talk to create connections and develop relationships.[29] Women spend more time talking about their feelings and personal lives, including their families, than do men. Women who have worked together for a few weeks may know much about each other's personal lives, whereas men can work together for years and not know much about each other's personal lives.

As a result of gender diversity in conversation, men tend to complain that women talk on and on about their problems, and women criticize men for not listening. When men hear a problem, they tend to want to assert their independence and control by providing a solution. However, when women mention a problem or their feelings, it tends to be to promote closeness; they generally are not looking for advice. So men who want to improve their human relations with women need to learn to listen and give reflecting responses. You'll learn how later in the chapter.

Cross-Cultural Communication Differences

In the global economy, when conducting international business, you should be aware that cultural differences can cause barriers to communication.[30] Some of the areas of possible barriers include cultural context; social conventions; language, etiquette, and politeness; and nonverbal communication.

Cultural Context   The process of encoding and decoding is based on an individual's culture; therefore the message meaning is different for people of diverse cultures. The greater the difference in culture between the sender and receiver, the greater are the chances of encountering communication barriers. People around the globe see, interpret, and evaluate behavior differently. As a result, they act on behavior differently.[31] Thus, the chances of running into perception communication barriers increase.

Understanding high- and low-context culture differences can help you better understand potential barriers to communication and how to overcome them. The importance to which context influences the meaning individuals take from a message—not only the specific words (oral and written) but also the person's behavioral actions—varies by culture. See Exhibit 5.3 for a list of high- and low-context cultures.

EXHIBIT 5.3 |
High-Context to
Low-Context Cultures

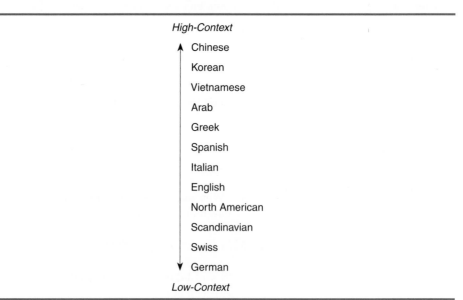

Source: Based on the work of E.T. Hall, from R.E. Dulck, J.S. Fielden, and J.S. Hill, "International Communication: An Executive Primer," *Business Horizons,* January–February 1991, p. 21.

EXHIBIT 5.4 | High-Context versus Low-Context Cultures: Communication Importance

Context	High-Context Culture	Low-Context Culture
Focus on nonverbal communications and subtle cues	X	
Focus on actual spoken and written word		X
Importance of credibility and trust	X	
Need to develop relationships	X	
Importance of position, age, seniority	X	
Use of precisely written legal contracts		X
Direct, get-down-to-business conversation		X
Managers tell employees (give orders) what to do		X

High-Context Cultures   These cultures rely heavily on nonverbal communication and subtle situational cues during the communication process; what is not said is often more important than what is actually said. People include official status, place in society, and reputation as important factors in communication.

Low-Context Cultures   These cultures rely heavily on the actual words used; nonverbal communication and subtle situational cues are not as important as what is actually said. Status, place in society, and reputation are given secondary importance to the actual words.

See Exhibit 5.4 for a list of some of the differences between high-context and low-context cultures in terms of communication. Then read on to find out how a particular culture's context level affects social conventions; language, etiquette, and politeness; and nonverbal communication.

Social Conventions   Social conventions can be a barrier to communicating with people of different countries.[32] The directness of how business is conducted varies. North Americans tend to favor getting down to business quickly and concisely. If you use this approach with the Arabs or Japanese, however, you may lose the business because they prefer a more indirect, informal chat to begin business meetings. People from the Middle East tend to talk very loudly, but this doesn't mean they are pushy or trying to intimidate you. What constitutes punctuality varies greatly around the world. North Americans and Japanese want you to be on time, while being late for a meeting with an Arab or Latin American is not viewed as negative. A Brazilian who is late for a meeting may be trying to make a proper impression, rather than showing disrespect.

Language, Etiquette, and Politeness   Even when you are speaking English to people outside North America, words mean different things, and the same thing may be called by different names (e.g., *lift* rather than *elevator,* and *petrol* rather than *gasoline*). What is considered rude in one country may not be rude in another. On an Australian airplane, if you were not in the first-class section and went to take a magazine from that section, a steward would sharply admonish you by saying, "First class, mate," rather than offering the typical explanation given in North America, "These magazines are for first-class passengers only." The steward would be surprised that you would be offended by his words.

The Japanese want to maintain interdependence and harmony. They have 16 subtle ways to say no. Rather than saying, "I don't want to buy your product," a Japanese businessperson would be more likely to say, "A sale will be very difficult." The Japanese person would think it is clear to the American that he is saying no. The American, however, would tend to reply with a statement about how the difficulty can be overcome rather than realizing the deal is off and giving up. Continuing to try to sell is an insult to the Japanese. As another example, the French tend to ask lots of questions during presentations whereas Asians do not.[33]

Nonverbal Communication   Nonverbal communication consists of messages we send without using words. It includes the setting of the communication and the facial expressions, vocal quality, gestures, and posture we use while communicating. We discuss nonverbal communication in the next chapter. Here we compare nonverbal communication globally.

Gestures do not translate well across cultures because they involve symbolism that is not shared. One gesture can mean very different things in different cultures. A raised thumb in the United States is a signal of approval, but in Greece it is an insult, meaning the same as a raised middle finger in the United States. Latin Americans and Arabs expect extensive eye contact, while Europeans would be uncomfortable and would interpret this as being stared at. Arabs, Latin Americans, and Southern Europeans want to touch, while North Europeans and North Americans don't want to be touched.

Overcoming Global Barriers   This section is not meant to teach you how to overcome all the possible barriers to global communication. The objective is to make you realize the importance of learning the cultures of other countries if you plan to do business with them successfully. Most major multinational companies train their employees to be sensitive to specific cultural differences when doing business with people from other cultures.

To help overcome global barriers to communications, you can follow these guidelines:[34]

- Believe there are differences until similarity is proved. We need to ignore our natural tendency to think that people are like us until we are sure they really are.

- Delay judgment of a person's behavior until you are sure you are being culturally sensitive. You may think a particular behavioral statement or action is inappropriate or insulting to you, but that may not be the intended meaning, or the behavior may be appropriate in the other person's culture. For example, if a Japanese businessperson gives you a gift, it is most likely a gift, not a bribe to get your business.

- Put yourself in the receiver's position. As the sender, try to decode your message with a focus on the receiver's cross-cultural differences. For example, if you don't give a Japanese businessperson a gift, you may be considered impolite and hurt your chances of developing a relationship.

- When in doubt, ask. If you are not sure what is appropriate, ask someone who knows. Then, for example, you will know to expect a gift exchange.

- Follow the other person's lead, and watch his or her behavior. For example, if a person bows, bow back. If you do or don't do something and the other person's nonverbal communication indicates discomfort, be quick to apologize and to do or avoid the behavior.

WORK APPLICATIONS

4. Describe a cross-cultural barrier to communication you have experienced. Explain the situation and how the barrier could have been overcome.

Keeping in mind the overview of the steps in the communication process and the potential barriers, let's discuss the details of sending, receiving, and responding to messages.

SENDING MESSAGES

Learning Outcome

3. List the steps in the message-sending process.

Have you ever heard a manager say, "This isn't what I asked for"? When this happens, it is usually the manager's fault. Managers often make incorrect assumptions and do not take 100 percent of the responsibility for ensuring the message has been transmitted with mutual understanding. To transmit messages effectively, managers must state exactly what they want, how they want it done, and when they need it.

Sending the message is the second step in the communication process. Before you send a message, you should carefully select the channel (we'll discuss how in the next chapter) and plan how you will send the message.

There are at least three major goals of communication. The **goals of communication** *are to influence, to inform, and/or to express feelings.* When sending a message, a person may achieve all three goals simultaneously.

Planning the Message

Before sending a message, you should plan what, who, how, when, and where. *What* is the goal of the message? What do you want as the end result of the communication?[35] Set an objective.[36] *Who* should receive the message? With the receiver(s) in mind, plan *how* you will encode the message so that it will be understood. *When* will the message be transmitted? Timing is important. Finally, decide *where* the message will be transmitted.

Sending the Message, Face-to-Face

Face-to-face communication is critical to interpersonal skills; thus, this skill influences your success.[37] It is helpful to follow the steps in the **message-sending process:** *step (1) develop rapport; step (2) state the communication objective; step (3) transmit the message; step (4) check understanding; and step (5) get a commitment and follow up.*

In the opening case, Sara followed the five steps in the message-sending process. Below is a discussion of the five steps. After reading them, return to the opening case and review the process.

Step 1: Develop rapport. Put the receiver at ease. It is usually appropriate to begin communication with small talk related to the message. It helps prepare the employee to receive the message, and to form relationships.[38]

Step 2: State the communication objective. If the goal of the business communication is to influence, it is helpful for the receiver to know the end result of the communication before getting to all the details as to why it is important.[39]

Step 3: Transmit the message. If the communication goal is to influence, tell the people what you want them to do, give instructions, and so forth. And be sure to set deadlines for completing tasks. If the goal is to inform, tell the people the information. Avoid talking too fast and giving too much detail.

Step 4: Check understanding. (1) After transmitting the message, the sender has two options. The sender can either (*a*) simply assume that the receiver understands the message and that there is mutual understanding (this is known as one-way communication) or (*b*) check to see if the message has been understood with mutual understanding. Questioning and paraphrasing are two techniques that can be used to ensure mutual understanding.[40] **Paraphrasing** *is the process of having the receiver restate the message in his or her own words.* A third technique is encouraging employees to offer comments and to make suggestions on communication[41] (These are two-way communication methods). You will learn how to use questioning and paraphrasing later in this chapter. (2) About the only time you may not want to check understanding is when the goal is to express feelings. When influencing and giving information, you should ask direct questions and/or use paraphrasing.[42] To simply ask, "Do you have any questions?" does not check understanding.

Step 5: Get a commitment and follow up. When the goal of communication is to inform or express feelings, a commitment is not needed. However, when the goal of communication is to influence, it is important to get a commitment to the action. Managers should make sure that employees can do the task and have it done by a certain time or date. In situations in which the employee does not intend to get the task done, it is better to know when sending the message rather than wait until the deadline to find out. When employees are reluctant to commit to the necessary action, managers can use persuasive power within their

EXHIBIT 5.5 | The Message-Sending Process

Step 1: Develop rapport.
Step 2: State the communication objective.
Step 3: Transmit the message.
Step 4: Check understanding.
Step 5: Get a commitment and follow up.

authority. When communicating to influence, follow up to ensure that the necessary action has been taken.

Exhibit 5.5 lists the five steps in the message-sending process.

WORK APPLICATIONS

5. Recall a present or past boss. How well did the boss send messages? Which steps in the message-sending process were followed, and which were not commonly followed?

RECEIVING MESSAGES

Important oral communication skills are following instructions and listening.[43] These skills were illustrated in the opening case. Complete Self-Assessment Exercise 5–1 to determine how good a listener you are.

Self-Assessment
Exercise 5–1

Your Listening Skills

Select the response that best describes the frequency of your actual behavior. Place the letter A, U, F, O, or S on the line before each of the 15 statements.

Almost always (A)   Usually (U)   Frequently (F)   Occasionally (O)   Seldom (S)

_____   1. I like to listen to people talk. I encourage them to talk by showing interest, by smiling and nodding and so forth.

_____   2. I pay closer attention to speakers who are more interesting or similar to me.

_____   3. I evaluate speakers' words and nonverbal communication ability as they talk.

_____   4. I avoid distractions; if it's noisy, I suggest moving to a quiet spot.

_____   5. When people interrupt me to talk, I put what I was doing out of sight and mind and give them my complete attention.

_____   6. When people are talking, I allow them time to finish. I do not interrupt, anticipate what they are going to say, or jump to conclusions.

_____   7. I tune out people whose views do not agree with mine.

_____   8. While the other person is talking or the professor is lecturing, my mind wanders to personal topics.

_____   9. While the other person is talking, I pay close attention to the nonverbal communication to help me fully understand what the sender is trying to get across.

_____ 10. I tune out and pretend I understand when the topic is difficult.

_____ 11. When the other person is talking, I think about what I am going to say in reply.

_____ 12. When I feel there is something missing or contradictory, I ask direct questions to get the person to explain the idea more fully.

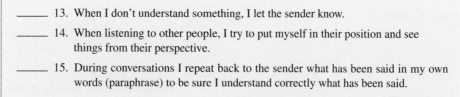

_____ 13. When I don't understand something, I let the sender know.

_____ 14. When listening to other people, I try to put myself in their position and see things from their perspective.

_____ 15. During conversations I repeat back to the sender what has been said in my own words (paraphrase) to be sure I understand correctly what has been said.

If you were to have people to whom you talk regularly answer these questions about you, would they have the same responses that you selected? Have friends fill out the questions for you and compare answers.

To determine your score, give yourself 5 points for each A, 4 for each U, 3 for each F, 2 for each O, and 1 for each S for statements 1, 4, 5, 6, 9, 12, 13, 14, and 15. Place the scores on the line next to your response letter. For items 2, 3, 7, 8, 10, and 11, the score reverses: give yourself 5 points for each S, 4 for each O, 3 for each F, 2 for each U, and 1 for each A. Place these scores on the line next to your response letter. Now add your total number of points. Your score should be between 15 and 75. Place your score here _____ and place an X on the continuum below at the point that represents your score. Generally, the higher your score, the better your listening skills.

Poor listener   15 - - - - 25 - - - - 35 - - - - 45 - - - - 55 - - - - 65 - - - - 75   Good listener

In step 3 of the communication process, the message is received. Communication does not take place unless the message is received with mutual understanding. The message cannot be received accurately unless the receiver listens.[44] When asked, "Are you a good listener?" most people say yes. In reality, 75 percent of what people hear they hear imprecisely and 75 percent of what they hear accurately they forget within three weeks. In other words, most people are poor listeners. Poor listening is caused in part by the fact that people speak at an average rate of 120 words per minute, while they are capable of listening at a rate of over 500 words per minute, which often results in wandering minds. Also, most people are not taught how listening works.

Levels of Listening

Learning Outcome

4. Explain three levels of listening.

To be a successful communicator, you need to be an effective listener.[45] There are at least three levels of listening: marginal, evaluative, and projective. See Exhibit 5.6.

1. With marginal listening, as the sender speaks, the receiver does not pay attention. Have you ever talked to someone and realized that his or her mind was "a million miles away"? The use of marginal listening results in misunderstanding and errors.

2. Evaluative listening requires the listener to pay reasonably close attention to the speaker. The receiver evaluates the speaker's remarks as correct or not and determines if he or she will continue to really listen. Once the receiver hears something he or she does not accept, listening stops, and the rebuttal is formed. Now, two ideas develop, neither of which is really communicated, rather than one idea being transmitted with mutual understanding between the sender and receiver.[46] Evaluative listening is common when the receiver feels threatened.

3. Of the three levels of listening, projective listening holds the greatest potential for mutual understanding of the message. It is important to stop talking and start listening.[47] Receivers listen carefully, utilizing their time to project themselves into the position of the sender to understand what is being said from the speaker's viewpoint.[48] Evaluation is postponed until the message is mutually understood. The receiver's attempt to stand in the sender's shoes is also called *empathic listening*.[49] To listen with empathy does not mean you have to agree with the speaker. **Empathic listening** *is the ability to understand and relate to another's situation and feelings.* Most messages have two components—feelings and content. Try to relate to both. Learning how to respond with empathy to emotional employees is covered in the next chapter.

EXHIBIT 5.6 |
Levels of Listening

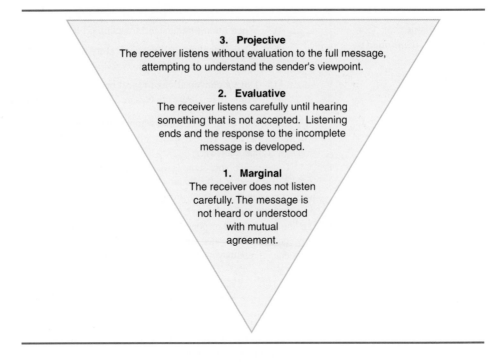

Active Projective Listening Tips

The key to effective human relations is listening.[50] People want to be listened to and understood, and if you do not listen to and understand others, they will avoid you.

To improve your listening skills, focus your attention on listening for a week by concentrating on both what other people say and their nonverbal communication. Notice if their verbal and nonverbal communication are consistent. Does the nonverbal communication reinforce the speaker's words or detract from them? Talk only when necessary so that you can listen to what others are saying. If you follow the 13 tips below, you will improve your listening skills. The tips will be presented in the sequence of the face-to-face communication process: We listen, we analyze, we speak.

Learning Outcome

5. Describe how to be an active projective listener.

Listening

1. *Pay attention.* When people interrupt you to talk, stop what you are doing and give them your complete attention. Quickly relax and clear your mind so that you are receptive to the speaker. This will get you started correctly. If you miss the first few words, you may miss the message. Commit to listening.[51]

2. *Avoid distractions.* Keep your eye on the speaker. Do not fiddle with pens, papers, or other distractions. Let your answering machine answer the phone. If you are in a noisy or distracting place, suggest moving to another spot.

3. *Stay tuned in.* While the other person is talking or the professor is lecturing, do not let your mind wander to personal topics. If it does, gently bring it back. Do not tune out the speaker because you do not like something about him or you disagree with what she is saying. If the topic is difficult, do not tune out; ask questions.[52] Do not think about what you are going to say in reply; just listen.[53]

4. *Do not assume and interrupt.* Do not assume you know what the speaker is going to say or listen at the beginning and jump to conclusions. Many listening mistakes are made when people hear the first few words of a sentence, finish it in their own minds, and miss the second half. Listen to the entire message without interrupting the speaker.

5. *Watch for nonverbal cues.* Understand both the feelings and the content of the message. People sometimes say one thing and mean something else. So watch as you listen to be sure that the speaker's eyes, body, and face are sending the same message as the verbal message.[54] If something seems out of place, clarify by asking questions.

6. *Ask questions.* When you feel there is something missing or contradictory, or you just do not understand, ask direct questions to get the person to explain the idea more fully.[55]

7. *Take notes.* Part of listening is writing important things down and documenting them when necessary so you can remember them later.[56] This is especially true when listening to instructions. You should always have something to write with, such as a pen and a notebook or some index cards.

8. *Convey meaning.* The way to let the speaker know you are listening to the message is to use verbal clues such as, "you feel . . .," "uh huh," "I see," and "I understand." You should also use nonverbal communication such as eye contact, appropriate facial expressions, nodding of the head, and sitting on the edge of the chair, leaning slightly forward to indicate you are interested and listening.

Analyzing

9. *Think.* To help overcome the discrepancy in the speed between your ability to listen and people's rate of speaking, use the speed of your brain positively. Listen actively by organizing, summarizing, reviewing, interpreting, and critiquing often. These activities will help you to actively listen at the projective level.

10. *Evaluate after listening.* When people try to listen and analyze or evaluate what is said at the same time, they tend to miss part or all of the message. You should just listen to the entire message and then come to your conclusions.

11. *Evaluate facts presented.* When you evaluate the message, base your conclusion on the facts presented rather than on stereotypes and generalities.

Speaking

12. *Paraphrase first.* Begin speaking by paraphrasing the message back to the sender. When you can paraphrase the message back correctly, you convey that you have listened and understood the other person. Now you are ready to offer your ideas, advice, solution, or decision in response to the sender of the message.[57]

13. *Watch for nonverbal cues.* As you speak, pay attention to the other person's nonverbal communication.[58] If the person does not seem to understand what you are talking about, clarify the message before finishing the conversation.

Do you talk more than you listen? To be sure your perception is correct, ask your boss, coworkers, and friends who will give you an honest answer. If you spend more time talking than listening, you are probably failing in your attempt to communicate. Regardless of how much you listen, if you follow these 13 guidelines, you will improve your communication ability and become a person that people want to listen to, instead of a person they feel they have to listen to. To become an active projective listener, take 100 percent of the responsibility for ensuring mutual understanding. Work to change your behavior to become a better active projective listener.

WORK APPLICATIONS

6. Refer to Self-Assessment Exercise 5–1 and the 13 tips to improve your listening skills. What is your weakest listening skill? How will you improve your listening ability?

APPLICATION SITUATIONS

Listen

AS 5–2

Identify each statement by its number (1 to 13) from the 13 active projective listening tips above.

_____ 8. "I'm sorry; I just saw a bird fly by. What did you say again?"

_____ 9. "Hold on; let me write this down so I don't forget it."

_____ 10. "Forgive me; I missed the beginning of what you said. Please start again."

_____ 11. "You look overwhelmed. Let me go over it again."

_____ 12. "So you want me to take this letter over to Pete in the service department now."

_____ 13. "How long do you think it will take me to get the task done?"

_____ 14. "OK, I got it. That's all I need to know."

_____ 15. "Are you finished? I can see some problems in implementing this suggestion."

RESPONDING TO MESSAGES

The fourth and last step in the communication process is responding to the message. Not all messages require a response, such as messages to inform.[59] However, when you are communicating a message face-to-face, the best way to ensure mutual understanding is to get feedback from the receiver,[60] as Sara did in the opening case. In this section, we discuss feedback and response styles.

Feedback

Learning Outcome

6. Describe how to get feedback.

Feedback *is the process of verifying messages.* Questioning, paraphrasing, and allowing comments and suggestions are all forms of feedback. Feedback when giving and receiving messages facilitates job performance.[61]

360-Degree Feedback   The performance feedback method known as *360-degree feedback* has gained wide popularity in the corporate world. The 360-degree method provides performance feedback in four directions: downward from the supervisor, laterally from peers or coworkers, upward from subordinates, and inwardly from the person getting the feedback.[62] When appropriate, customers and suppliers also provide feedback on different aspects of performance.[63] Unfortunately, feedback is not always as effective as is typically assumed,[64] and not so much the concept but the implementation of 360-degree feedback has been criticized.[65]

Getting Feedback

The Common Approach to Getting Feedback on Messages and Why It Doesn't Work   The most common approach to getting feedback is to send the entire message, followed by asking, "Do you have any questions?" Feedback usually does not follow because people have a tendency not to ask questions. There are three good reasons why people do not ask questions:

1. They feel ignorant. To ask a question, especially if no one else does, is considered an admission of not paying attention or not being bright enough to understand the issue.

2. They are ignorant. Sometimes people do not know enough about the message to know whether or not it is incomplete, incorrect, or subject to interpretation. There are no questions because what was said sounds right. The receiver does not understand the message or does not know what to ask.

3. Receivers are reluctant to point out the sender's ignorance. This is very common when the sender is a manager and the receiver is an employee. The employee fears that asking a question suggests that the manager has done a poor job of preparing and sending the message. Or it suggests that the manager is wrong.

Regardless of the reason, the result is the same: Employees don't ask questions; generally, students don't either.

After managers send their messages and ask if there are questions, they proceed to make another common error. They assume that no questions means communication is complete and that there is mutual understanding of the message. In reality, the message is often misunderstood. When "this isn't what I asked for" is the result, the task has to be repeated. The end result is often wasted time, materials, and effort.

When a message does not result in communication, the most common cause is the sender's lack of getting feedback to ensure mutual understanding.[66] The proper use of questioning and paraphrasing can help you ensure that your messages are communicated successfully.

How to Get Feedback on Messages   Below are four guidelines managers should use when getting feedback on their messages. They are also appropriate for nonmanagers.

Be Open to Feedback   First of all, managers must be open to feedback and must ask for it.[67] The open-door policy encourages feedback. When an employee asks a question, the manager needs to be responsive and patiently answer questions and explain things. There are no dumb questions, only dumb answers. The manager should make the employee feel comfortable.[68]

Be Aware of Nonverbal Communication   Managers must also be aware of their nonverbal communication and make sure that they encourage feedback. For example, if managers say they encourage questions, but when employees ask questions, they act impatient or look at the employees as though the employees are stupid, employees will learn not to ask questions. The manager must also be aware of employees' nonverbal communications. For example, if Moe, the manager, is explaining a task to Larry, the employee, and Larry has a puzzled look on his face, he is probably confused but may not be willing to say so. In such a case, Moe should stop and clarify things before going on.

Ask Questions   When you send messages, it is better to know whether or not the messages have been understood before action is taken, so that the action will not have to be changed or repeated. Direct questions dealing with the specific information you have given will indicate whether the receiver has been listening and whether or not he or she understands enough to give a direct reply. If the response is not accurate, repeating, giving more examples, or elaborating the message is needed. The manager can also ask indirect questions to attain feedback.[69] The manager could ask "how do you feel?" questions about the message. The manager could also ask "if you were me" questions, such as, "If you were me, how would you explain how to do it?" Or the manager could ask third-party questions, such as, "How will employees feel about this?" The response to indirect questions will reveal the employee's attitude and can convey misunderstandings.

Paraphrasing   The most accurate indicator of understanding is paraphrasing—asking the receiver to restate the message in his or her own words. How the manager asks the employee to paraphrase will affect the employee's attitude. For example, if the manager says, "John, tell me what I just said so that I can be sure you will not make a mistake as usual," the

McDonald's is one of the most recognized brands worldwide and has been a household name in the United States for almost fifty years. How has McDonald's become one of the most well-known firms in the world? Well, according to McDonald's, it continues to make progress on delivering a relevant restaurant experience by maintaining its focus on its most important priority—the customer.

Not everyone, however, is quite so happy in Ronald McDonald land. "A farmworkers' advocacy group is calling on fast-food leader McDonald's Corp. to pay more for the tomatoes slapped on their premium burgers so that Florida pickers can be paid more. . . . Most tomato pickers still receive roughly the same wage they did in 1978—between 40 and 45 cents for every 32-pound bucket of tomatoes. 'We are hoping McDonald's takes responsibility, the same way Taco Bell and Yum Brands did, and that it uses its power to demand a just treatment and decent pay for farmworkers,' said Gerardo Reyes, an Immokalee farmworker. The Coalition of Immokalee Workers urged consumers to pressure McDonald's to support a campaign to boost wages for more than 3,000 Florida pickers, who growers say provide about 90 percent of the nation's domestic fresh winter tomatoes." Customers appear sympathetic to the coalition's cause.

To continue to be a good community leader and obtain customer support, McDonald's should back higher tomato prices. Higher tomato prices, however, will negatively impact McDonald's operating costs because tomatoes are used in conjunction with many of its products, most notably its hamburgers, a product that it sells in the millions on a daily basis. Increased tomato prices will reduce its profit margin and/or increase the price of its burgers, a sure-fire method of wiping the smiles off of the faces of both stockholders and customers. Customers may be understanding of the Florida pickers' plight but are they willing to pay more for their burgers and salads?

Questions

1. What are the messages that McDonald's is receiving? From whom? Why are they mixed?

2. How might McDonald's, both in approach and style, respond to these messages?

3. What actions should McDonald's take to make sure that its response is understood?

4. Are you willing to pay more for McDonald's food so that it can raise the price it pays for tomatoes?

Sources: "Farmworkers Ask McDonald's to Pay More for Tomatoes," *Associated Press,* November 22, 2005; "McDonald's Corporation Investor Fact Sheet," July 22, 2008; http://www.mcdonalds.com.

---

result will probably be defensive behavior on John's part. John will probably make a mistake in fulfillment of the Pygmalion effect (as discussed in Chapter 3). Below are two examples of proper requests for paraphrasing:

- "Now tell me what you are going to do so we will be sure that we are in agreement."

- "Would you tell me what you are going to do so that I can be sure that I explained myself clearly?"

Notice that the second statement takes the pressure off the employee. The supervisor is asking for a check on her or his ability, not that of the employee. These types of requests for paraphrasing should result in a positive attitude toward the message and the manager. They show concern for the employee and for communicating effectively, as feedback builds self-esteem.[70]

WORK APPLICATIONS

7. Describe how a boss in either your present or your past used feedback. How could his or her feedback skills be improved?

8. Do you use paraphrasing now? Will you use it more, less, or with the same frequency in the future? Why?

Response Styles

Learning Outcome

7. Explain five response styles and when to use each.

Before learning about response styles, complete Self-Assessment Exercise 5–2 to determine your preferred response style.

Your Preferred Response Style

Select the response you would actually make as the supervisor in the five situations that follow:

_____ 1. I cannot work with Paul. That guy drives me crazy. He is always complaining about me and everyone else, including you, boss. Why does he have to be my job partner? We cannot work together. You have to assign someone else to be my partner.

    A. I'm sure there are things that you do that bother Paul. You'll have to work things out with him.
    B. What has he said about me?
    C. Can you give me some examples of the specific things that he does that bother you?
    D. I'll talk to Paul. I'm sure we can improve or change the situation.
    E. So Paul is really getting to you.

_____ 2. We cannot make the deadline on the Procter Project without more help. We've been having some problems. A major problem is that Betty and Phil are recent college grads, and you know they don't know anything. I end up doing all the work for them. Without another experienced person, my team will not get the job done on time.

    A. Tell me more about these problems you are having.
    B. Did you see the game last night?
    C. You are really concerned about this project, aren't you?
    D. You will have to stop doing the work and train the new people. They will come through for you if you give them a chance.
    E. Don't worry. You're a great project leader. I'm sure you will get the job done.

_____ 3. Congratulations on being promoted to supervisor. I was wondering about what to expect. After all, we go back five years as good friends in this department. It will seem strange to have you as my boss.

    A. Things will work out fine, you'll see.
    B. I take it that you don't like to see things change. Is that what you mean?
    C. Just do a good job and there will not be any problems between us.
    D. Is Chris feeling any better?
    E. Tell me how you think things will change.

_____ 4. I wish you would do something about Gloria. Because of her short, tight clothes, the men are always finding some excuse to come by here. She loves it; you can tell the way she is always flirting with all the guys. Gloria could turn this place into a soap opera if you don't do something.

    A. So you think this situation is indecent, is that it?
    B. I cannot tell Gloria how to dress. Why don't you turn your desk so you don't have to watch.
    C. Don't let it bother you. I'm sure it's innocent and that nothing is really going on. You know how these younger kids are these days.
    D. What do you think I should do?
    E. Are you feeling well today?

_____ 5. I cannot take it anymore. I've been running around like a fool waiting on all these customers and all they do is yell at me and complain.

    A. Are you going to the party tonight?
    B. What is the most irritating thing the customers are doing?
    C. With Erin being out today, it's been crazy. But tomorrow she should be back and things should be back to normal. Hang in there; you can handle it.
    D. The customers are really getting to you today, hey?
    E. I told you during the job interview that this is how it is. You have to learn to ignore the comments.

To determine your preferred response style, in the following table circle the letter you selected in situations 1 to 5. The column headings indicate the style you selected.

	Advising	Diverting	Probing	Reassuring	Reflecting
1.	A	B	C	D	E
2.	D	B	A	E	C
3.	C	D	E	A	B
4.	B	E	D	C	A
5.	E	A	B	C	D
Total	—	—	—	—	—

Add up the number of circled responses per column. The total for all columns should equal 5. The column with the highest number represents your preferred response style. The more evenly distributed the numbers are among the styles, the more flexible you are at responding.

As the sender transmits a message, how you as the receiver respond to the message directly affects communication. There is no one best response style. The response should be appropriate for the situation. You will learn five response styles.

For each alternative you will be given an example of a response to the same employee message: "You supervise me so closely that you disrupt my ability to do my job."

Advising   Advising responses provide evaluation, personal opinion, direction, or instructions. Employees often come to the manager for advice on how to do something or for the manager to make the decision. Advising tends to close, limit, or direct the flow of communication away from the sender to the receiver.

Appropriate Use of Advising Responses   Giving advice is appropriate when you are directly asked for it. However, quickly giving advice tends to build dependence. You need to develop others' ability to think things through and to make decisions. When asked for advice by employees who you believe don't really need it, ask questions such as, "What do you think is the best way to handle this situation?"

An example of a supervisor's advising responses to the employee's message is: "You need my direction to do a good job; you lack experience." Note that in this situation, advice was not asked for, but it was given anyway.

Diverting   Diverting responses switch the focus of the communication to a message of the receiver. The receiver becomes the sender of a different message. This type of response is often called *changing the subject*. Diverting responses tend to redirect, close, or limit the flow of communication.

Diverting responses used during the early stages of receiving the message may cause the sender to feel that his or her message is not worth discussing, or that the other party's message is more important.

Appropriate Use of Diverting Responses   Changing the subject is a good way to avoid arguments. When you want the job done your way, you must convey that message.

An example of a supervisor's diverting response to the employee's message is: "You've reminded me of a supervisor I once had who . . ."

Probing   A probing response asks the sender to give more information about some aspect of the message. It is useful to get a better understanding of the situation. When you are probing, "what" questions are preferred to "why" questions.

Appropriate Use of Probing Responses   Probing is appropriate during the early stages of the message to ensure understanding by getting more information.

An example of a supervisor's probing response to the employee's message is: "What do I do to cause you to say this?" not "Why do you feel this way?"

Reassuring   A reassuring response is given to be supportive and reduce the intensity of the emotions associated with the message. Essentially you're saying, "Don't worry; everything will be OK." You are pacifying the sender, which doesn't mean you are a good listener.

Appropriate Use of Reassuring Responses   A reassuring response is appropriate to use when the other person lacks confidence. Encouraging responses can help employees develop.

An example of a supervisor's reassuring response to the employee's message is: "I will not do it for much longer."

Reflecting   The **reflecting response** *paraphrases the message back to the sender to convey understanding and acceptance.* The reflecting response is used by the empathic projective listener.[71] Most messages have two components—feelings and content. A reflecting response paraphrases the message back to the sender to show him or her that the receiver understands and values and accepts him or her. The sender can then feel free to explore the topic in more depth. Empathizing has been found to affect employees' attitudes and behavior in positive ways.

Appropriate Use of Reflecting Responses   Reflecting responses are used to be empathic. The empathic responder deals with content, feelings, and the underlying meaning being expressed in the message (generally in that order). Carl Rogers, a noted psychology expert, believes that reflecting responses should be used in the beginning stages of most communication. Reflecting responses lead to mutual understanding, while developing human relations.

An example of a supervisor's reflecting response to the employee's message is: "My checking up on you annoys you!"

WORK APPLICATIONS

9. Give situations in which any two of the five response styles would be appropriate. Give the sender's message and your response. Identify its style.

APPLICATION SITUATIONS

Identifying Response Styles

AS 5–3

Below are two situations with 10 responses. Identify each as:

A. Advising   C. Probing   E. Reflecting

B. Diverting   D. Reassuring

MS. WALKER: Mr. Tomson, do you have a minute to talk?

MR. TOMSON: Sure, what's up?

MS. WALKER: Can you do something about all the swearing the men use around the plant? It carries through these thin walls into my work area. It's disgusting. I'm surprised you haven't done anything.

MR. TOMSON:

_____ 16. I didn't know anyone was swearing. I'll look into it.

_____ 17. You don't have to listen to it. Just ignore it.

_____ 18. Are you feeling well today?

_____ 19. What kind of swear words are they using?

_____ 20. You find this swearing offensive?

JIM: Mary, I have a complaint.

MARY: Sit down and tell me about it.

JIM: Being the A. D. [athletic director], you know that I use the weight room after the football team. Well, my track team has to return the plates to the racks, put the dumbbells back, and so forth. I don't get paid to pick up after the football team. After all, they have the use of the room longer than we do. I've complained to Ted [the football coach], but all he says is that's the way he finds it, or that he'll try to get the team to do a better job. But nothing happens.

MARY:

_____ 21. Before I forget, congratulations on beating Harvard.

_____ 22. You feel it's unfair to pick up after them?

_____ 23. How long has this been going on?

_____ 24. You work it out with Ted.

_____ 25. Thanks for telling me about it; I'll talk to Ted to see what's going on.

In the above two situations, which response is the most appropriate?

As we bring this chapter to a close, complete the Self-Assessment Exercise 5–3 to determine how your personality affects your communications.

Self-Assessment Exercise 5–3

Your Personality Traits and Communications

Let's tie personality traits from Chapter 2 together with what we've covered in this chapter. We are going to present some general statements about how your personality may affect your communication. For each area, determine how the information relates to you. This will help you better understand your behavioral strengths and weakness and the areas you may want to improve.

Sending and receiving messages. If you have a high *surgency* personality, you most likely are an extrovert and have no difficulty initiating communication and communicating with others. However, you may be dominating during communication and may neither listen well nor be open to others' ideas. Be careful not to use communications simply as a means to get what you want; be concerned about others and what they want. If you are low in surgency, you may be quiet and reserved in your communications. You may want to be more vocal.

If you are high in *agreeableness* personality traits, you are most likely a good listener and communicator. Your *adjustment* level affects the emotional tone of your communications. If you are high in *conscientiousness,* you tend to have reliable communications. If you are not conscientious, you may want to work at returning messages quickly. People who are *open to new experiences* often initiate communications, because communicating is often part of the new experience.

Feedback. If you have a high *surgency* personality, you have a need to be in control. Watch the tendency to give feedback but not listen to it. You may need to work at not criticizing.

Self-Assessment
Exercise 5–3 (*continued*)

If you have low surgency, you may want to give more feedback and do more coaching. If you have a high *agreeableness* personality, you are a people person and probably enjoy others. However, as a manager, you must also discipline when needed, which may be difficult for you. If you are high on *adjustment* personality traits, you may tend to give positive feedback. Low adjustment people need to watch the negative criticism. If you have a high *conscientiousness* personality with a high need for achievement, you may tend to be more concerned about your own success. This is also true of people with a high surgency personality. Remember that an important part of leadership is coaching others. If you are low in conscientiousness, you may need to put forth effort to give effective feedback. Your *openness to experience* personality affects whether you are willing to listen to others' feedback and make changes.

Action plan: Based on your personality, what specific things will you do to improve your communications?

_____

_____

_____

_____

In this chapter, you were presented with ways to help you improve your communication skills. Begin using these techniques to improve your skill level today.

Videos

Manager's Hot Seat and Behavior Model Videos are available for this chapter.

Online Learning Center Resources

Go to the Internet (http://mhhe.com/lussier8e) where you will find a broad array of resources to help maximize your learning.

- Review the vocabulary.
- Try a quiz.

R E V I E W

The chapter review is organized to help you master the 8 learning outcomes for Chapter 5. First provide your own response to each learning outcome, and then check the summary provided to see how well you understand the material. Next, identify the final statement in each section as either true or false (T/F). Correct each false statement. Answers are given at the end of the chapter.

1. **Explain why communication skills are important.**

   Communication is required for the successful completion of the organizational activities necessary to achieve objectives.

   Behavior is what we do and say; thus, communication is behavior. T F

2. **List and explain the four steps in the communication process.**

   The four steps in the communication process are: (1) The sender encodes the message and selects the transmission channel; (2) the sender transmits the message; (3) the receiver decodes the message and decides if feedback is needed; (4) feedback, in the form of a response or a new message, may be transmitted.

   Low-context cultures rely heavily on nonverbal communication and subtle situational cues during the communication process. T F

3. List the steps in the message-sending process.

The steps in the message-sending process are: (1) develop rapport, (2) state the communication objective, (3) transmit the message, (4) check understanding, and (5) get a commitment and follow up.

A good way to check understanding is to just ask, "Do you have any questions?" T F

4. Explain three levels of listening.

The three levels of listening are as follows. The *marginal listener* does not pay careful attention to the message, which results in the message either not being heard or being misunderstood. The *evaluative listener* listens carefully until he or she hears something that is not acceptable, which results in incomplete message development. The *projective listener* carefully listens without evaluation, resulting in effective communication.

Empathic listening is the ability to feel sorry for the other person's situation. T F

5. Describe how to be an active projective listener.

The active projective listener first listens to what is being said, next analyzes what has been communicated, and finally speaks by paraphrasing what has been said while watching for nonverbal cues.

Asking questions while listening is part of active projective listening. T F

6. Describe how to get feedback.

To get feedback, one must be open to feedback, be aware of nonverbal communication, ask questions, and paraphrase.

Effective managers take the time to listen to employee complaints and suggestions for change. T F

7. Explain five response styles and when to use each.

- Advising responses provide evaluation, opinion, direction, or instructions; they are used in response to a request for advice.
- Diverting responses change the subject; they are used to avoid arguments.
- Probing responses ask for more information; they are used when more information is needed.
- Reassuring responses provide support to reduce emotions; they are used to build confidence.
- Reflecting responses paraphrase back what was said to convey understanding and acceptance; they are used to empathize.

Reflecting responses should be used in the beginning stages of most communications. T F

Learning Outcome

8. Define the following 10 key terms.

8. Define the following 10 key terms.

Select one or more methods: (1) Fill in the missing key terms from memory; (2) match the key terms from the end of the review with their definitions below; and/or (3) copy the key terms in order from the key terms at the beginning of the chapter.

The _____ consists of a sender who encodes a message and transmits it through a channel to a receiver who decodes it and may give feedback.

_____ is the sender's process of putting the message into a form that the receiver will understand.

The _____ is the physical form of the encoded information.

_____ is the receiver's process of translating the message into a meaningful form.

The _____ are to influence, to inform, and/or to express feelings.

The _____ steps are (1) develop rapport, (2) state the communication objective, (3) transmit the message, (4) check understanding, and (5) get a commitment and follow up.

_____ is the process of having the receiver restate the message in his or her own words.

_____ is the ability to understand and relate to another's situation and feelings.

_____ is the process of verifying messages.

The _____ paraphrases the message back to the sender to convey understanding and acceptance.

K E Y   T E R M S

communication
  process   152
decoding   154
empathic listening   161
encoding   153

feedback   164
goals of
  communication   159
message   153

message-sending
  process   159
paraphrasing   159
reflecting response   169

C O M M U N I C A T I O N   S K I L L S

The following critical thinking questions can be used for class discussion and/or as written assignments to develop communication skills. Be sure to give complete explanations for all questions.

1. Which two barriers to communication do you believe are the most common in organizations today? What can firms do to help eliminate these two barriers?
2. Do males and females really converse differently? Do you speak about different things with your male and female friends and coworkers? If so, what do you talk about with males versus females?
3. Which is preferable, a high-context culture or a low-context culture?
4. How often do you use paraphrasing and ask others to paraphrase to ensure mutual understanding? How effective are you at paraphrasing and asking others to paraphrase, and how can you improve your paraphrasing skills?
5. Select a few friends and/or coworkers. Do you spend more time talking or listening, or do you spend an equal amount of time talking and listening when you are with them? Write down each person's name and the percentage of time you spend talking and listening. For example, 25 percent talking and 75 percent listening, 50–50, 35–65, etc. After recording the percentages, ask each person what percentage they believe you talk and listen. How accurate was your perception? Should you change the amount of time you spend talking versus listening, and if so, how will you go about changing?
6. Which response style do you believe is most commonly used at work? Should the most commonly used response style be reflecting? Why or why not?

Peter and Korby Clark: The Ranch Golf Club

The Ranch Golf Club, where every player is a special guest for the day, opened in 2001 in Southwick, Massachusetts. The Ranch's competitive advantage is the upscale public course (peak-season green fees are around $100), with links, woods, and a variety of elevations, and unsurpassed service. The Ranch is striving to be the best golf club in New England. In less than a year, the Ranch earned a four-star course rating, one of only four in New England. In the January 2003 issue of *Golf Digest*, the Ranch was rated number three in the country in the "new upscale public golf course" category, and it was ranked as the best public golf course in Massachusetts in 2007.

Prior to being a golf club, the property was a dairy farm owned by the Hall family. The Hall family wanted to turn the farm into a golf club, with the help of Rowland Bates, of Golf Realty Advisors, as project coordinator. The Halls were to provide the land, and investors would provide the capital.

Peter and Korby Clark were part owners of nearly 50 Jiffy Lubes and sold most of them to Pennzoil in 1991. At age 37, Peter Clark stopped working full-time at Jiffy Lube to assist his managing partner in six Jiffy Lubes and to develop three more in the Worcester, Massachusetts, area, which they were selling to the partner. Peter Clark spent more time coaching, being with his family, and doing community service for the Jimmy Fund.

Through the 1990s, the Clarks had a variety of opportunities to invest in new and ongoing businesses. Nothing interested the Clarks until the late 1990s. Unlike other businesses looking simply for investors, the proposal Bates offered Peter included the opportunity to create and help manage a new golf club. Although Peter played golf, it was not so much the golf that interested him, but the challenge of creating a new course and also playing an ongoing part in its management. The Clarks did not have enough capital, so they approached banks for loans. They were told that if they wanted to build more Jiffy Lubes, they could get the money, but without experience, they could not get it for a golf course. So Bates found a few more investors who would provide the additional funding, creating a one-third ownership by the Halls, one-third by the Clarks, and one-third by investors Bernard Chiu and Ronald Izen.

The Clarks were happy to have the professional golf management team of Willowbend. First, they realized that they could not create and run a successful golf club business without expertise. Neither of them had ever worked for a golf club and they only played recreational golf. Second, they would not have to manage the Ranch full time. Peter is currently the head baseball coach and assistant football coach for Agawam High School (he was also an assistant football coach for Trinity College). In 2005 Willowbend stopped managing golf courses and sold the business. By then the Clarks had gained enough experience running the Ranch and no longer needed professional management. Peter Clark increased his management role to become the managing partner, overseeing day-to-day operations. Korby works full time too.[72]

The key to success at the Ranch is clear, open communication. Peter Clark has to continually communicate with his partners and managers, and nothing takes the place of sitting down face-to-face during regular weekly meetings and listening to each other to continually improve operations. Meetings of department managers with employees focus on the importance of communicating the philosophy of unsurpassed professional service. To communicate professionalism, all employees wear Ranch uniforms and are trained on how to perform high-quality service. Even the words used are chosen to communicate professionalism. For example, the Ranch has player assistants, not rangers; golf cars, not golf carts; and a golf shop, not a pro shop.

Feedback is critical to success at the Ranch; it is how the Clarks and the other Ranch managers know if the players are getting quality service and how to improve service. The Clarks and Ranch managers and employees are open to player criticism because they realize that the only way to improve is to listen and make changes to improve performance. In fact, Peter and Korby Clark spend much of their time at the Ranch talking to players about their experiences, with the focus on listening for ways to make improvements. The Clarks and the Ranch managers set clear objectives and have regular meetings with employees to get and give feedback on how the Ranch is progressing toward meeting its objectives.

Being a small business, the Ranch does not have a formal 360-degree feedback system. However, managers who evaluate employee performance interact regularly with each employee, employee peers, the players, and other managers at the Ranch, and they use the feedback from others in their performance appraisals.

Peter Clark says there are more similarities than differences in running a Jiffy Lube business, managing a golf club, and coaching sports. The focus is the same—high-quality service. You have to treat the customer or player right. Peter uses the same three I's coaching philosophy in all three situations. You need *intensity* to be prepared to do the job right, *integrity* to do the right thing when no one is watching, and *intimacy* to be a team player. If one person does not do the job right, everyone is negatively affected. In business and sports, you need to strive to be the best. You need to set and meet challenging goals. Peter strongly believes in being positive and in the need to develop a supportive working relationship, which includes sitting down to talk and really listening to the other person.

Go to the Internet: For current information about The Ranch Golf Club, use the Internet address www.theranchgolfclub.com. You can take a virtual tour of the golf course online.

Support your answers to the following questions with specific information from the case and text, or other information you get from the Web or other sources.

1. How do the interpersonal communication skills of Peter Clark affect behavior, human relations, and performance at the Ranch?

2. Do you think Peter Clark spends more time sending or receiving messages, or an equal amount of time doing both?

3. Which level of listening does Peter Clark appear to be on?

4. Which of the 13 active projective listening tips do you think are most relevant for Peter Clark?

5. Assess Peter and Korby Clark's use of feedback.

6. Which response style do you think Peter Clark uses most often?

Cumulative Questions

7. Do you believe Peter Clark strives to meet the goal of human relations, that is, a win–win situation (Chapter 1)?

8. Assess Peter Clark's personality in relation to each of the Big Five dimensions (Chapter 2).

9. Assess Peter Clark's attitude, self-concept, values, and ethics (Chapter 3).

OBJECTIVE CASE   **Communication?**

In the following dialogue, Chris is the manager and Sandy is the employee.

CHRIS: I need you to get a metal plate ready for the Stern job.

SANDY: OK.

CHRIS: I need a ¾-inch plate. I want a ½-inch hole a little off center. No, you better make it ⅝. In the left corner I need about a ⅜-inch hole. And on the right top portion, about ⅞ of an inch from the left side, drill a ¼-inch hole. You got it?

SANDY: I think so.

CHRIS: Good, I'll be back later.

Later.

CHRIS: Do you have the plate ready?

SANDY: It's right here.

CHRIS: This isn't what I asked for. I said a ½-inch hole a little off center; this is too much off center. Do it again so it will fit.

SANDY: You're the boss. I'll do it again.

Answer the following questions. Then in the space between questions, state why you selected that answer.

_____ 1. Chris and Sandy communicated.
    a. true   *b.* false

_____ 2. Chris's primary goal of communication was to:
    a. influence   *b.* inform   *c.* express feelings

_____ 3. Chris was the:
    a. sender/decoder   *c.* sender/encoder
    b. receiver/decoder   *d.* receiver/encoder

_____ 4. Sandy was the:
    a. sender/decoder   *c.* sender/encoder
    b. receiver/decoder   *d.* receiver/encoder

_____ 5. The message transmission medium was:
    a. oral   *c.* nonverbal
    b. written   *d.* combined

_____ 6. Chris followed _____ guidelines to getting feedback on messages.
    a. open to feedback   *c.* ask questions
    b. awareness of nonverbal   *d.* paraphrasing
        communication   *e.* none of these

_____ 7. Which step(s) did Chris follow in the message-sending process? (You may select more than one answer.)
    a. step 1   *c.* step 3   *e.* step 5
    b. step 2   *d.* step 4

_____ 8. Sandy was an active listener.

      a. true   *b.* false

_____ 9. Sandy's response style was primarily:

      a. advising   *c.* probing   *e.* reflecting

      b. diverting   *d.* reassuring

_____ 10. Chris used the _____ supervisory style.

      a. autocratic   *c.* participative

      b. consultative   *d.* laissez-faire

      11. In Chris's situation, how would you have given the instructions to Sandy?

Note: Students may role-play giving instructions.

SKILL-BUILDING EXERCISE 5-1

Giving Instructions

In-Class Exercise (Group)

Objective: To develop your ability to give and receive messages (communication skills).

AACSB: The primary AACSB learning standard skill developed through this exercise is communication abilities.

Experience: You will plan, give, and receive instructions for the completion of a drawing of three objects.

Preparation: No preparation is necessary except reading the chapter. The instructor will provide the original drawings.

Procedure 1
(3–7 minutes)

Read all of procedure 1 twice. The task is for the manager to give an employee instructions for completing a drawing of three objects. The objects must be drawn to scale and look like photocopies of the originals. You will have 15 minutes to complete the task.

    The exercise has four separate parts, or steps.

1. The manager plans.

2. The manager gives the instructions.

3. The employee does the drawing.

4. Evaluation of the results takes place.

Rules: The rules are numbered to correlate with the four parts above.

1. *Planning.* While planning, the manager may write out instructions for the employee but may not do any drawing of any kind.

2. *Instructions.* While giving instructions, the manager may not show the original drawing to the employee. (The instructor will give it to you.) The instructions may be given orally, and/or in writing, but no nonverbal hand gestures are allowed. The employee may take notes while the instructions are being given but cannot do any drawing with or without a pen. The manager must give the instructions for all three objects before drawing begins.

3. *Drawing.* Once the employee begins the drawing, the manager should watch but no longer communicate in any way.

4. *Evaluation.* When the employee is finished or the time is up, the manager shows the employee the original drawing. Discuss how you did. Turn to the integration section and answer the questions. The manager writes down the answers.

Procedure 2
(2–5 minutes)

Half of the class members will act as the manager first and give instructions. Managers move their seats to one of the four walls (spread out). They should be facing the center of the room with their backs close to the wall.

Employees sit in the middle of the room until called on by a manager. When called on, bring a seat to the manager. Sit facing the manager so that you will not be able to see any manager's drawing.

Procedure 3
(15–20 minutes)

The instructor gives each manager a copy of the drawing. Be careful not to let any employees see it. The manager plans the instructions. When managers are ready, they call an employee and give the instructions. It may be helpful to use the message-sending process. Be sure to follow the rules. The employee should do the drawing on the page entitled Employee Drawing. If you use written instructions, use nonbook paper. You have 15 minutes to complete the drawing, and possibly five minutes for integration (evaluation). When you finish the drawing, turn to the evaluation questions in the integration section below.

Procedure 4
(15–20 minutes)

The employees are now the managers and sit in the seats facing the center of the room. New employees go to the center of the room until called upon.

Follow procedure 3, with the instructor giving a different drawing. Do not work with the same person; change partners.

Integration

Evaluating Questions: You may select more than one answer.

_____   **1.** The goal of communication was to:

　　　　a. influence　　　　　*b.* inform　　　　　*c.* express feelings

_____   **2.** Feedback was:

　　　　a. immediate　　　　　　　　*c.* performance-oriented

　　　　b. specific and accurate   *d.* positive

_____   **3.** The manager transmitted the message:

　　　　a. orally　　　　　　　　*c.* nonverbally

　　　　b. in writing　　　　　*d.* combined

_____   **4.** The manager spent _____ time planning.

　　　　a. too much　　　　　*b.* too little　　　　　*c.* the right amount of

The next six questions relate to the message-sending process:

_____   **5.** The manager developed rapport (Step 1).

　　　　a. true　　　　　　　　*b.* false

_____   **6.** The manager stated the communication objective (Step 2).

　　　　a. true　　　　　　　　*b.* false

_____   **7.** The manager transmitted the message _____ (Step 3).

　　　　a. effectively　　　　　*b.* ineffectively

_____   **8.** The manager checked understanding by using _____ (Step 4).

　　　　a. direct questions　　　　　*c.* both

　　　　b. paraphrasing　　　　　　*d.* neither

_____ **9.** The amount of checking was:

      a. too frequent   *b.* too infrequent   *c.* about right

_____ **10.** The manager got a commitment and followed up (Step 5).

      a. true   *b.* false

_____ **11.** The manager and/or employee got emotional.

      a. true   *b.* false

_____ **12.** The primary response style used by the manager was:

      a. advising   *c.* probing   *e.* reflecting

      b. diverting   *d.* reassuring

_____ **13.** The primary response style used by the employee was:

      a. advising   *c.* probing   *e.* reflecting

      b. diverting   *d.* reassuring

_____ **14.** The manager used the _____ supervisory style.

      a. autocratic   *c.* participative

      b. consultative   *d.* laissez-faire

_____ **15.** The appropriate style was:

      a. autocratic   *c.* participative

      b. consultative   *d.* laissez-faire

16. Were the objects drawn to approximate scale? If not, why not?

17. Did you follow the rules? If not, why not?

18. If you could do this exercise over again, what would you do differently?

Conclusion: The instructor leads a class discussion and/or makes concluding remarks.

Application (2–4 minutes):   What did I learn from this experience? How will I use this knowledge in the future?

Sharing: Volunteers give their answers to the application section.

EMPLOYEE DRAWING

Listening Skills

Preparation

In-Class Exercise

Recall a time when you did something really good that you shared with a friend. It should take around 5 minutes to describe. Write a brief description. _____

_____

Objective: To experience and/or observe and assess listening skills.

AACSB: The primary AACSB learning standard skill developed through this exercise is communication abilities.

Procedure 1
(2–3 minutes)

Select an option and set up for the role play.

Options: A. One person tells his or her good news to one other person as the class observes.

B. Break into groups of 6 to 8. One person tells his or her good news to one other person as the other group members observe.

Procedure 2
(5–7 minutes)

Tell the other person your good news as though it just happened.

Procedure 3
(8–12 minutes)

Assess the listening skills below by giving specific examples of how the person did or did not do a good job of listening.

- What level of listening did he or she use (marginal, evaluative, or projective)? Explain.

- Was the person an empathic listener? Explain.

Assess the listener on the 13 active projective listening tips:

Turn to the tips on pages 162–163 and assess the person on each of the 13 tips, with examples of what was done well and what could be improved.

- Which response styles did the listener use (advising, diverting, probing, reassuring, or reflecting)?

Conclusion: The instructor leads a class discussion and/or makes concluding remarks.

Application: (2–4 minutes):   What did I learn from this experience? How will I use this knowledge in the future?

Sharing: Volunteers give their answers to the application section.

ANSWERS TO TRUE/FALSE QUESTIONS

1. T.
2. F. High-context cultures rely heavily on nonverbal communication and subtle situational cues during the communication process.
3. F. Asking direct questions and paraphrasing are two techniques used to check understanding.
4. F. Empathic listening is not about feeling sorry, it's about understanding and relating to another's situation and feelings.
5. T.
6. T.
7. T.

Organizational Structure and Communication

After completing this chapter, you should be able to:

1. Explain five principles of organization.

2. Explain six types of departmentalization.

3. Identify contemporary organization trends.

4. Describe how communication flows through organizations.

5. Explain the advantage the all-channel communication network has over the other networks.

6. List the three primary message transmission channels.

7. Describe how to deal with an emotional employee.

8. Explain how to give effective criticism.

9. Define the following 14 key terms (in order of appearance in the chapter):

organizational structure
departmentalization
cross-functional teams
reengineering
virtual organizations
boundaryless organizations
organizational communication

vertical communication
horizontal communication
grapevine
communication networks
channels
5-15-1 writing rule
nonverbal communication

How Organizational Structure and Communication Affect Behavior, Human Relations, and Performance

Organizational Structure

   Principles of Organization

   Departmentalization

   Contemporary Organization

Organizational Communication

   Vertical Communication

   Horizontal Communication

   Grapevine Communication

   Communication Networks

Message Transmission Channels

   Oral Communication

   Written Communication

   Writing Skills

   Nonverbal Communication

   Combining Channels

Emotions

   Emotional Labor

   Dealing with Emotional Employees

Criticism

   Getting Criticism

   Giving Criticism

The former Digital Equipment Corporation held a "state of the company" meeting for top managers. Senior Vice President Jack Shields was not present at the meeting. Mr. Shields was sometimes mentioned as the likely successor to President Kenneth Olsen. However, a new organization chart of U.S. field operations presented at the meeting did not include Mr. Shields. During the meeting, when one of the vice presidents asked Mr. Olsen where Mr. Shields was, Mr. Olsen responded vaguely. The managers present still did not know where Mr. Shields was or why he was not at the meeting.

Rumors that Mr. Shields had resigned or had been fired by Mr. Olsen started moving through the sales force and outside of Digital. The gossip hit Wall Street, raising questions about executive succession at Digital. The price of Digital stock fell more than a point.

Then the media got wind of the rumor and called Digital to get the story. The company denied the resignation rumors. However, a television show misread a wire story of the denial and reported that Mr. Shields had resigned. Then an electronic bulletin board on Digital's inhouse computer network repeated the TV report.

When Mr. Shields heard the news, he invited a reporter to an interview in his office at Digital. Mr. Shields stated that he had no plans to resign or indication he was expected to. He missed the meeting because he was attending the annual meeting of another company for which he was a board member. The organization chart did not show him because it did not go up to the level of the executive committee where he sat. Mr. Olsen could not be reached for comment.

HOW ORGANIZATIONAL STRUCTURE AND COMMUNICATION AFFECT BEHAVIOR, HUMAN RELATIONS, AND PERFORMANCE

In the last chapter we discussed the effect of interpersonal communications that also affect organizational structure and communication, because it is employees who run organizations. In this chapter, we are expanding our study of communications to the organizational level.

The *organization structure* determines who works together, and *organizational communication* flows through this structure, affecting behavior, human relations, and performance.[1] The transition from an economy based on materials to an economy based on flows of information has created considerable challenges for organizational structure and communication.[2] Today corporate strategy and survival can depend heavily on the firm's ability to innovate rapidly.[3] As a result, new organizational structures are being developed in search of alternatives to conventional bureaucracy.[4]

As organizations struggle to enhance competitive performance, downsizing continues as a restructuring strategy.[5] Job insecurity directly influences behavior; it increases stress, which often hurts human relations, and it decreases performance,[6] which in turn leads to more *emotional* employees,[7] and a more *criticizing* environment.[8]

The opening case is based on an actual company, Digital Equipment Corporation. The communication problem described in the case did occur and was reported in major newspapers. Digital was slow to change its strategy and organizational structure in a rapidly changing computer environment. It had communication problems, downsized through a series of layoffs, and eventually went out of business when the company was purchased. Clearly, organizational structure and communications do affect behavior, human relations, and performance.

ORGANIZATIONAL STRUCTURE

Organizational structure *refers to the way managers design their firms to achieve their organization's mission and goals.* In the development of an organizational structure, there are important questions to be answered,[9] and the answers affect behavior, human relations, and performance.[10] In this section, we begin with principles of organization, followed by details of departmentalization and contemporary organizational designs.

Principles of Organization

Managers need to answer at least five questions when designing organizational structures. The five questions appear in Exhibit 6.1, along with the principles to be used to find the answers. The five principles of organization are discussed next.

Division of Labor and Departmentalization   Division of labor, or work specialization, refers to the degree to which tasks are subdivided into separate jobs.[11] Although specialization can lead to efficiency and increased performance, if jobs become too specialized and boring, performance can decrease.[12] Some people like highly specialized jobs and others don't. Which do you prefer? The important thing is to have a good person–job fit.[13] However, with the importance of knowledge and the use of teams, the trend is to have less specialized jobs.[14] **Departmentalization** *is the grouping of related activities into units.* We'll discuss this in more detail later in this section. In Exhibit 6.2, labor is divided into production, finance, and marketing departments, with multiple jobs within each department.

Chain of Command   The chain of command is the line of authority from the top to the bottom of the organization, which is shown in an organization chart. The chain of command tells you who your boss is and who to go to for help. Today the rigid structure of reporting and communicating only through the chain of command is less common.[15] To work quickly, employees at all levels need to communicate directly, and who the boss is can change according to the task to be performed.[16] The common organizational hierarchy chain of command was illustrated in Exhibit 1.1, and it is illustrated in this chapter in Exhibit 6.2. The organization chart shows the president, vice presidents, and managers; the workers, who are below the managers, are not commonly shown on an organization chart.

Span of Management   The span of management refers to the number of employees reporting to a manager. In Exhibit 6.2, within the formal structure, the president has three vice presidents, and the vice presidents have a span of management of five, three, and four. How many employees should report to one manager is an important consideration in structure because it affects the number of levels of managers.[17] Exhibit 6.2 has three levels (president, vice president, and manager). With downsizing, the trend has clearly been to increase the span of management.[18] Layers of management have been cut from some companies, creating flatter organizational structures.[19]

EXHIBIT 6.1 | Designing Organizational Structure

Question	Principle Used to Find the Answer
1. How should we subdivide the work?	Division of labor and departmentalization
2. To whom should departments and individuals report?	Chain of command
3. How many individuals should report to each manager?	Span of management
4. At what level should decisions be made?	Centralized and decentralized authority
5. How do we get everyone to work together as a system?	Coordination

EXHIBIT 6.2 | Organization Chart

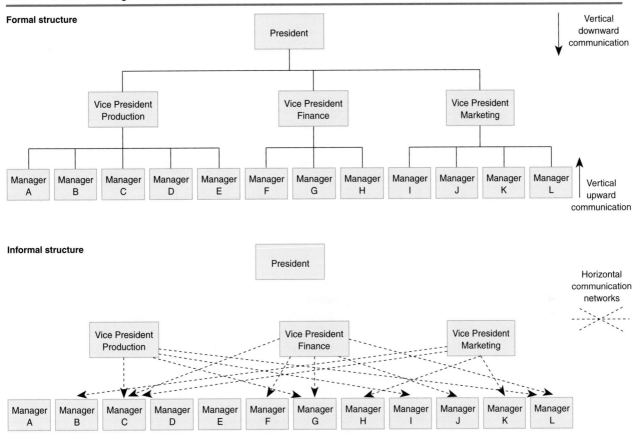

Centralized and Decentralized Authority   With centralized authority, top managers make important decisions. With decentralized authority, middle and first-line managers make important decisions where the action is. The trend today at firms, including Microsoft, is toward decentralization so that decisions can be made quickly to take advantage of opportunities and to solve problems.[20] Decentralization allows more input into decision making and greater employee commitment to carrying out the decisions.[21] Centralization cannot be seen on an organization chart; however, it is common for organizations—including GM—with many levels of management to be centralized. Part of the reason for cutting layers of management is to facilitate decentralization.[22]

Coordination   With the division of labor and departmentalization comes the need to coordinate the work of all departments.[23] Coordination is even more difficult with wider spans of management and decentralization.[24] The production people make the product, the marketing people sell it, and the finance people collect the money. Through the systems effect, if any department is ineffective, it will influence the performance of the other departments and the organization as a whole.[25] Coordination cannot be directly seen on most organization charts.

WORK APPLICATIONS

1. Select an organization for which you work or have worked. Is the division of labor specialized? Identify the chain of command from your job to the top of the organization. How many people are in your boss's span of management? Is authority centralized or decentralized? How is work coordinated?

Learning Outcome

2. Explain six types of departmentalization.

Departmentalization

Following are six common types of departmentalization.

Functional Departmentalization   Functional departmentalization involves organizing departments around essential input activities, such as production and operations, finance and accounting, marketing and sales, and human resources. Exhibit 6.2 is a functional departmentalization organization chart. Most small businesses are functionally organized. An offshoot of functional departmentalization is process departmentalization, in which specific phases in production are separated into departments.

Product (Service) Departmentalization   Product departmentalization involves organizing departments around goods and services provided. For example, Procter & Gamble has many major product lines, including Charmin, Pampers, Pringles, and Tide. Chrysler in the United States could be organized this way:

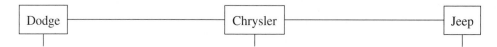

Customer Departmentalization   Customer departmentalization involves organizing departments around the needs of different types of customers. Unique customer needs may call for different sales staffs and products, sometimes only by quantity. For example, Motorola restructured to merge about six business units into two huge divisions—one geared to consumers and the other to industrial customers. An office supply company could be organized this way:

Divisional Departmentalization (M-Form)   When a firm develops independent lines of business that operate as separate companies, all contributing to the corporation profitability, the design is called divisional departmentalization (or M-Form). The Limited, Inc., has these divisions: The Limited, Express, Lerner New York, Lane Bryant, Structure, Limited Too, and Mast Industries. PepsiCo has these five major divisions:

Territory (Geographic) Departmentalization   Territory, also called geographic, departmentalization involves organizing departments in each area in which the enterprise does business. Many retail chains, such as Sears, and the federal government are organized by territory. Possible territories could include:

Matrix Departmentalization   Matrix departmentalization combines the functional and product departmentalization structures. The employee works for a functional department and is also assigned to one or more products as part of a project team.[26] The major advantage of the matrix is its flexibility.[27] It allows the firm to temporarily organize for a project, and projects can change fairly quickly. It is commonly used by advertising agencies, construction companies, research and development laboratories, hospitals, government agencies, universities, and management consulting firms. Rand, Xerox, Boeing, and Google use a formal matrix structure.[28] See the following simple example for a construction company. If you were a carpenter, you would work on multiple houses, usually simultaneously.

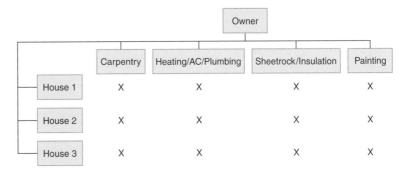

Combination   Many large companies have more than one form of departmentalization. For example, IBM uses customer departmentalization, in addition to divisional and territory departmentalization.

WORK APPLICATIONS

2. Draw an organization chart illustrating the type of departmentalization in the organization for which you work or have worked.

APPLICATION SITUATIONS

Departmentalization

AS 6–1

Identify the five organization charts below as being departmentalized by one of the following methods:

A. Functional   C. Customer   E. Matrix

B. Product (service)   D. Territory   F. Divisional

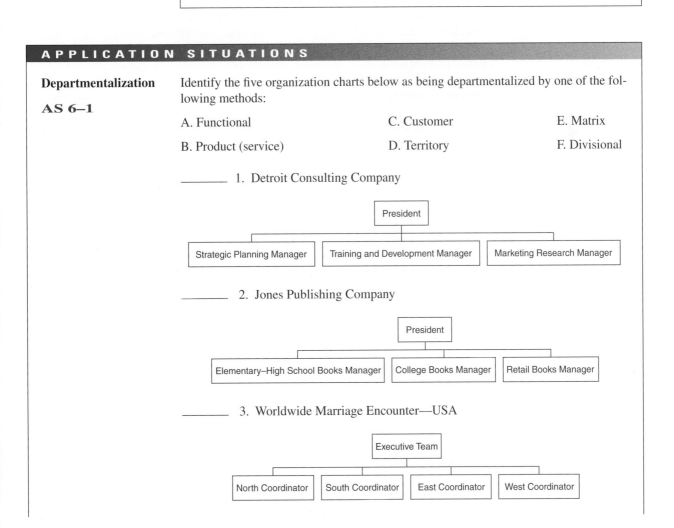

_____ 1. Detroit Consulting Company

_____ 2. Jones Publishing Company

_____ 3. Worldwide Marriage Encounter—USA

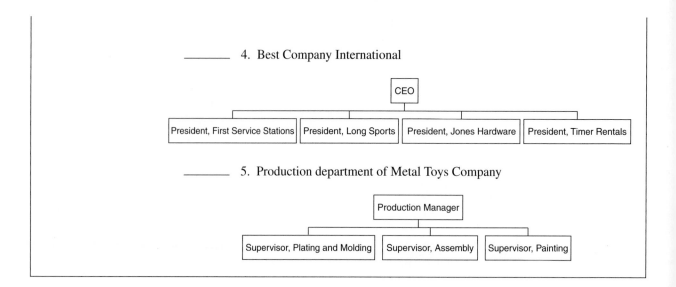

_____ 4. Best Company International

_____ 5. Production department of Metal Toys Company

Learning Outcome

3. Identify contemporary organization trends.

Contemporary Organization

Let's discuss some of the contemporary trends in organizational design based on the organizational principles we've talked about. The focus here is not so much on departmentalization, but rather on how to make any form of departmentalization work effectively. We'll discuss learning, team, virtual network, boundaryless, and e-organizations. As you read, keep in mind they are not actual departmentalization designs and that a firm may have characteristics of one, some, or all of these organizations. All of these organization forms use the current trends discussed with the principles of organization.

Learning Organizations   As discussed in Chapter 2, knowledge and continuous improvement are important. Organizations are transferring learning within and between firms, which is leading to new organizational structures.[29] Although there is no actual departmentalization of a learning organization, the concept is used more as a means of coordinating the sharing of knowledge for innovation throughout the entire organization.[30] The terms *knowledge-based organization* and *learning organization* are being used to identify these structures.

Team Organizations and Reengineering   Contemporary organizations are using teams as a central coordinating organizational principle.[31] The coordinating focus is horizontal rather than vertical; thus these organizations have also been called horizontal organizations. Cross-functional teams are commonly being used for coordination.[32] **Cross-functional teams** *have members from different departments to coordinate tasks between departments.* For example, in previous structures, the engineers designed a product, then it went to production to be manufactured, and then marketing sold it. Today team members representing each of these departments work on the product from conception to service after the sale. These teams break down functional departmental barriers and decentralize decision making down to the work team level.[33] You will learn about teams in Chapters 12 and 13.

Teams are used to streamline structures through reengineering. **Reengineering** *is the redesign of work to combine fragmented tasks into streamlined processes that save time and money.* One of the objectives is to speed up the processes used to make products.[34] Reengineering assumes there are no current jobs. W. L. Gore & Associates has 8,000 employees, and every employee is part of at least one team.[35] All engineers at Google work on one or more teams.[36]

Virtual Organizations   **Virtual organizations** *outsource major business functions and focus on core competencies. Core competencies* are the functions an organization does well.

Many organizations are outsourcing functions that are not core competencies. Thousands of companies, including Nike, Reebok, and Liz Claiborne, outsource the manufacturing of their products. Virtual organizations are also called network organizations because of the need for a good network of vertical interorganizational relationships.[37] Thus, human relations skills are important to virtual organizations.

Ben Greenfield developed a virtual organization to sell potato chips. First Ben convinced Mystic Seaport Maritime Museum in Connecticut to allow him to use its brand name for a royalty fee. He got a Maine processing company to make the potato chips, and a Boston food broker placed the chips in about 300 stores for a fee.

Boundaryless Organizations   **Boundaryless organizations** *seek to break down vertical and horizontal barriers within the firm and between the firm and its suppliers and customers.* Jack Welch, former CEO of General Electric, coined the term *boundaryless organization* to describe his vision of what he wanted GE to become.

There is some overlap between the virtual organization and the boundaryless organization because they both use an outsourcing network. However, while the virtual organization is here now, the boundaryless organization is yet to come, as GE, AT&T, Hewlett-Packard, Motorola, and others continue to work toward achieving it. You should realize that boundaryless organizations also include the characteristics of learning organizations, team organizations, and e-organizations—our next topic.

E-organizations   In this information-intense age, electronic technology is changing organizational forms.[38] *E-commerce* (the sales side of electronic business), *b2b* (business connected to business, such as suppliers), and *e-business* (a full range of activities using the Internet) are common elements of business terminology. An *e-organization* uses e-business. E-organizations communicate over the Internet (a worldwide network of interconnected computers), intranets (organizations' private networks), and extranets (intranets extended to authorized outsiders).

With e-business over the Internet, all employees can quickly and easily get information from sources both inside and outside the organization to break down boundary barriers.[39] For example, teams can include members from all over the globe sharing information, knowledge, and learning. Team members can work in the office or telecommute from home or on the road. Firms have instant access to customers and suppliers. Team meetings include virtual organizational outsource members.[40]

Contemporary Organizations Affect Human Relations   With the increasing use of teams and virtual outsource suppliers, the need for good human relations skills is increasing in importance, but at the same time, human relations are changing in the global economy with contemporary organizations.[41] Face-to-face team meetings are not common in international business. *Virtual meetings* are being held regularly over the Internet with e-written communications. It's now easier for employees in Boston and Brazil to gossip about the company via e-mail. Many virtual team members never meet and rarely talk.

You need to be ready for a new form of human relations based more on written communications to convey warmth, trust, and leadership. In the next section, you will learn how to improve your writing skills, and in other chapters we discuss how the e-organization affects decision making, motivation, leadership, politics, and networking.

WORK APPLICATIONS

3. Identify contemporary organization trends that are used where you work or have worked.

Learning Outcome

4. Describe how
    communication flows
    through organizations.

ORGANIZATIONAL COMMUNICATION

Employees often complain about the quality and quantity of communication in their organization.[42] Managers have the responsibility to tell employees what is going on within the organization.[43] An important management issue is what information should be given to employees and which employees should be given access to what information.[44] Effective organizational communication helps improve human relations and performance and is therefore critical to meeting the goal of human relations.[45]

In general, **organizational communication** *is the compounded interpersonal communication process across an organization.* The interpersonal communication building blocks affect the organization's performance. Communication within an organization flows in a vertical, horizontal, or lateral way throughout the firm.[46] It may also be conveyed through the grapevine, which goes in all directions.

Vertical Communication

One type of communication is **vertical communication,** *the flow of information both up and down the chain of command.* It is often called *formal communication* because it follows the chain of command and is recognized as official. It flows both upward and downward. Interorganizational communication is considered vertical.[47]

Downward Communication   When top-level managers make decisions, they are often communicated down the chain of command. It is the process of higher-level management telling those below them what to do. Organizational structures tend to facilitate the downward flow of communication, so this type of communication generally occurs easily and successfully.

When communicating down the chain of command, management should give careful thought to the possible consequences of messages, as illustrated in the opening case.

Upward Communication   When employees send a message to their manager, they are using upward communication. Hierarchical systems do not facilitate an upward flow of information, and this tends to result in communication failure.[48] To help facilitate upward communications, some organizations, such as Caterpillar, use an open-door policy. Other techniques (which have already been discussed or will be in future chapters) include attitude surveys, suggestion systems, and employee meetings.

The Digital Equipment Corporation's "state of the company" meeting, in which one of the vice presidents asked the president why Mr. Shields was absent, is an example of upward communication, while Mr. Olsen's response is an example of downward communication. Both are examples of vertical communication. For an illustration of downward and upward vertical communication, see Exhibit 6.2.

> **WORK APPLICATIONS**
>
> **4.** Give a specific example of when you used vertical communication. Identify it as upward or downward.

Horizontal Communication

Another type of communication, **horizontal communication,** *is the flow of information between colleagues and peers.* It is often called *informal communication* because it does not follow the chain of command and is often not recognized as official. All communication outside the chain of command is horizontal. It is also called *lateral communication.* Most messages processed by an organization are carried via informal channels. Coordination of departments and employees requires communication between colleagues and peers.[49] As an employee, you will often find it necessary to communicate with other department members and members of different departments in order to meet your objectives.

The Digital meeting for top managers was a form of both vertical and horizontal communications. Mr. Olsen got the chance to talk to his subordinates, subordinates got to talk to Mr. Olsen, and the vice presidents got to talk to each other.

> ## WORK APPLICATIONS
>
> **5.** Give a specific example of when you used horizontal communication.

Grapevine Communication

The **grapevine** *is the informal vehicle through which messages flow throughout the organization.* The grapevine is a useful organizational reality that will always exist. It should be considered as much a communication vehicle as the company newsletter or employee meetings. When the grapevine allows employees to know about a management decision almost before it is made, management is doing something right. Unfortunately, 46 percent of employees say they first hear about major changes at work through the grapevine, whereas only 17 percent of managers think employees hear about change through the grapevine.[50]

Reports on the accuracy of the grapevine vary. Rumors tend to spread out of fear of the unknown; people typically believe what supports their fears.[51] Rumors often start when management disastrously tries to hide things from employees.

At the Digital meeting, when the vice president asked Mr. Olsen where Mr. Shields was, Mr. Olsen responded vaguely. Because Mr. Olsen did not respond to reports, we cannot be sure that he was trying to hide the reason for Mr. Shields's absence. The vagueness could have been because of other reasons, such as poor communication skills. In any case, the major reasons for the rumor were that Mr. Olsen did not clearly state why Mr. Shields was not at the meeting and that it was not clear that the new organization chart was incomplete. If Mr. Olsen had clearly stated why Mr. Shields was not at the meeting and that the new organization chart didn't go to his level, employees would not have assumed that Mr. Shields had resigned or had been fired by Mr. Olsen.

Rather than ignore or try to repress the grapevine, tune into it. Identify the key people in the organization's grapevine and feed them information. To help prevent incorrect rumors, keep the information flowing through the grapevine as accurate and rumor-free as possible. Share all nonconfidential information with employees; tell them of changes as far in advance as possible. Encourage employees to ask questions about rumors they hear.

> ## WORK APPLICATIONS
>
> **6.** Give a specific example of a message you heard through the grapevine. How accurate was it? Was it the exact same message management sent?

Gossiping about people can really hurt your human relations with them when they find out what you said about them. In a diverse workplace, it is even more important to be careful about what you say about those who are different from yourself.[52] The adage "If you can't say anything good about someone, don't say anything at all" is a good human relations rule to follow.

APPLICATION SITUATIONS

Communication Flow

AS 6–2

Identify the communication flow as:

A. Vertical—downward   C. Horizontal

B. Vertical—upward   D. Grapevine

_____ 6. "Hey, Jim, have you heard that Mr. Smith and Cindy went out on a date last night? They went to the . . ."

_____ 7. "Pete, will you come here and hold this so I can get the plate on straight—the way I do it for you all the time?"

_____ 8. "Karen, here is the letter you asked me to type. Proofread it and I'll make any necessary changes."

_____ 9. "Ronald, I have a new customer here who wants to set up a charge account. Please do the credit check and make the decision soon. I can sell them lots of our merchandise, and you can bill them for it."

_____ 10. "Ed, take this over to Carl for me."

Learning Outcome

5. Explain the advantage the all-channel communication network has over the other networks.

Communication Networks

Within organizations, **communication networks** *are sets of employees who have stable contact through which information is generated and transmitted.* Two major types of communication networks are those within organizations and those within departments and small groups, and both can be within the e-organization and include people outside the firm.[53]

Networks in Organizations   The formal chain of command illustrates the vertical flow of communications. See Exhibit 6.2. As the top of Exhibit 6.2 illustrates, the vertical lines represent the formal reporting relationship and flow of vertical communication, both upward and downward. However, the organization chart does not show the networks within the organization. The vice presidents are responsible for the three major functions within any organization. These functions of production, finance, and marketing must be coordinated. Yet within the formal organization structure, you cannot tell who talks to whom to get the job done. The vice president of production may be in an informal horizontal communication network (see the informal structure in Exhibit 6.2). The possible networks are endless. In addition, the organization chart does not show the many social grapevines within an organization that could start and end with anyone in the organization.[54]

The person in the communications hub tends to have considerable power, regardless of his or her formal position in the organization's structure. In Exhibit 6.2, it appears that managers C and G are in the communications hub, tied into all three communication networks.

Networks in Departments and Small Groups   As within organizations, networks are formed within departments. To get the marketing jobs done, managers I, J, K, and L in Exhibit 6.2 may all be involved in a network, while in production the managers may be producing different products that do not require them to work together as a network. Yet in the finance area, managers F and H may form a network, with G being excluded.

Within departments, smaller groups tend to form networks as well.[55] Within the production area, all the managers could constitute a network. Managers A, C, and D and managers B and E could form small group networks.

Within the organization and the department, small group communication networks can be developed in a variety of structures. Exhibit 6.3 is an example of the five common network designs, each including five members. The number in the network could be increased or decreased without changing the structure. Notice that the wheel, chain, and Y networks all include a central person, A, through whom much of the communication must pass. The all-channel pattern involves all members equally in exchanges of information.

EXHIBIT 6.3 |
Small Group
Communication
Networks

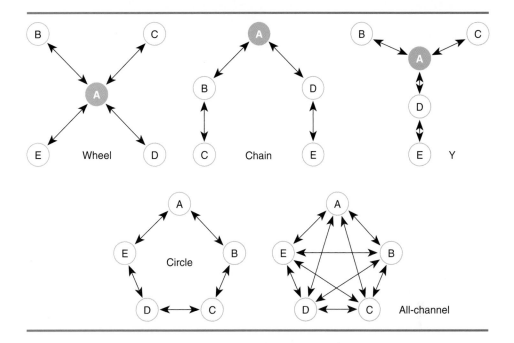

When small groups work together, they can use any network pattern. However, different patterns work best for different tasks. For simple, routine tasks, the wheel, chain, and Y work fast and accurately; for complex, nonroutine tasks, the circle and all-channel patterns, in which the free flow of communication exists, tend to work best, even though communication tends to be slower.

WORK APPLICATIONS

7. Identify a communication network in which you participate or have participated. List the other members and their positions within the organization or department.

Networks in College   Researchers have found that students who network with their professors (vertical) and with fellow students (horizontal, such as study groups) have higher grades. The positive impact of networking on grade performance also has global implications because the students were from three different countries.[56] Networks developed in college also often provide career assistance after graduation. Thus, if you are not networking in college, regardless of your home country, you may want to start. You will learn how to network in Chapter 11.

Learning Outcome

6. List the three primary message transmission channels.

MESSAGE TRANSMISSION CHANNELS

Recall that when encoding the message, you should give careful consideration to selection of the channel. **Channels** *are the forms of the transmitted message.* In this section, you will learn the three primary channels you can use when transmitting messages: oral, written, and nonverbal.

Oral Communication

Four common media for oral communication are face-to-face, telephone, meetings, and presentations. Below you will learn the appropriate use of each.

Face-to-Face   Much of our communication time is spent one-on-one, or face-to-face.[57] The late Sam Walton, founder of Wal-Mart Stores, the largest discount store chain in the world, relied on face-to-face communication to keep the firm growing. Top executives visit 6 to 12 stores each week.

This form of oral communication is the appropriate medium for delegating tasks, coaching, disciplining, instructing, sharing information, answering questions, checking progress toward objectives, developing and maintaining human relations, and interviewing.

Telephone   The amount of time spent on the telephone varies greatly with one's job.[58] No matter how much time you spend on the phone, before making a call, set an objective and write down what you plan to discuss.[59] Use the paper to write notes during the call.

The telephone is the appropriate medium for quick exchanges of information and checking up on things.[60] It is especially useful for saving travel time.[61] However, it is inappropriate for personal matters such as discipline.

Meetings   There are a variety of types of meetings, which will be discussed in Chapter 12. The manager's most common meeting is the brief, informal get-together with two or more employees.[62] It is appropriate for coordinating employee activities, delegating a task to a group, and resolving employee conflicts. (Conflict resolution is covered in Chapter 7.)

Presentations   Public speaking skills are considered an important part of communication skills. On occasion, you may be required to make a formal presentation. Prepare your presentations, and be sure they have the following three parts: beginning, middle, end.[63] For example, Jamal is making a sales presentation to his superiors requesting the addition of another employee for his department. Jamal begins by stating that his department needs a new employee. He then moves to the middle of his presentation by explaining all the reasons for needing the employee and how the company will benefit. Jamal ends with a quick summary and a request that his superiors grant his request for a new employee.

Written Communication

Recall that with the increasing use of e-mail in e-orgs, the need for writing skills has increased as managers substitute face-to-face communication with e-mail.[64] However, writing skills have deteriorated over the years to the point where they are a major skill problem.[65] Thus, in this subsection we are going to review grammar to help you improve your writing skills.

Do you like writing, receiving, and reading written communications? The higher up in the organization you plan to go, the more important writing skills are to get there. Probably nothing else can reveal your weaknesses more clearly than poor writing. People judge you on your ability to write your thoughts effectively and correctly.[66] When you put your ideas on paper, solutions become more apparent. Writing helps you become more systematic in your thinking.

Written communication is appropriate for sending general information; messages requiring future action; and formal, official, or long-term messages. It is also appropriate when the message affects several people in a related way.

Communication Objective Guidelines   With all communication, you should start with a clear objective.[67] In written communications, the first paragraph should clearly state why you are writing. Tell the reader the reason for reading.[68] If you don't answer the receiver's "What's in it for me?" question fast, your message may not be read at all or it may be just glanced over.

Common written communication channels include the following:

- *Memos.* They are commonly used for intraorganizational communications and commonly have a heading that includes *Date, To, From,* and *Subject* lines.

- *Letters.* They are commonly used for interorganizational communications, are usually more formal than memos, and are written on the firm's letterhead.

- *Reports.* They don't need to be long and specially formatted to be called reports. A report means you are reporting on performance of some type. Start reports with a single statement telling what the report is about, followed by two or three main points, each highlighted with statistics, brief examples, or a one-sentence explanation.

- *Computers/e-mail.* Memos, letters, and reports can be sent via e-mail with or without a computer.[69] The use of the Internet is growing globally.[70]

- *Fax.* Memos, letters, and reports can be sent via fax machine.

- *Bulletin board notices.* They are commonly used for more informal, often less business-oriented, communication, such as sign-ups for a sports team.

- *Posters.* They are typically signs, with messages such as "Keep the work area clean" or, as at Ford, "Quality Is Job One."

APPLICATION SITUATIONS

Channel Selection

Select the most appropriate channel for each message.

AS 6–3

A. Face-to-Face	C. Meeting	E. Memo	G. Report
B. Telephone	D. Presentation	F. Letter	H. Poster

_____ 11. The supervisor has to assign a new customer order to Karen and Ralph.

_____ 12. The supervisor is expecting needed material for production this afternoon. She wants to know if it will arrive on time.

———— 13. Employees have been leaving the lights on when no one is in the stock-room. The manager wants this practice to stop.

———— 14. The boss asked for the production figures for the month.

———— 15. An employee has broken a rule and needs to be discouraged from doing it again.

Writing Skills

I first wrote these basics on 3 × 5 cards about 10 years ago, to improve my own writing. I wrote this subsection to help you improve your writing skills. It covers grammar, syntax, rhetoric, editing, and punctuation using commas. When writing, use this review as I do.

Grammar refers to the rules for use of the eight parts of speech, which are defined as follows:

1. *Nouns* are the names of people, places, or things. Nouns often answer the *who* question in a sentence.

2. *Pronouns* take the place of nouns. Starting sentences with nouns and using pronouns within sentences is a good practice; you can avoid repeating the noun, and the reader knows what the pronoun means.

3. *Verbs* are the action words in a sentence. Verbs have tenses (past, present, future) and number (singular or plural) that must agree with the subject or with the noun or pronoun, and voice (active or passive). There are also linking and auxiliary verbs (e.g., *be, have, do*).

4. *Adjectives* tell us something about the noun. Adjectives often answer the *which, what kind of,* and *how many* questions in a sentence.

5. *Adverbs* tell us something about a verb, an adjective, or another adverb. Adverbs often answer the *how, why, when,* and *where* questions in a sentence.

6. *Prepositions* tell us how a noun or pronoun is related to another part of the sentence (e.g., *to, of, if, for, at, by, as, on, in, before, after, when*). Avoid using more than three prepositions in a sentence; most sentences of more than three lines have more than three prepositions.

7. *Conjunctions* connect two words or parts of a sentence (e.g., *and, but, or, for, so, yet, because*). Conjunctions often follow commas when connecting two sentences.

8. *Interjections* are words used to express feelings (e.g., surprise—*wow*, pain—*ouch*); they are not commonly used in business and technical writing.

To simplify grammar, we use subjects, predicates, modifiers, and connectives.

1. *Subjects* are *nouns* or *pronouns* about which something is said.

2. *Predicates* express what is said about the subject; they include *verbs*.

3. *Modifiers* include both *adjectives* and *adverbs*.

4. *Connectives* include both *prepositions* and *conjunctions*.

Syntax is the grammatical functioning of words, phrases, and clauses to form sentence structure.

1. A *sentence* needs a subject (noun or pronoun) and predicate (verb), and it often has modifiers (adjectives and adverbs) and connectives (prepositions and conjunctions) to convey meaning.

2. A *phrase* is a group of words that do not form a complete sentence.

3. A *clause* is a part of a sentence that has a subject and a predicate. A phrase may be connected to a clause with punctuation to form a complete sentence.

Rhetoric refers to the effective writing of sentences, paragraphs, and entire papers, memos, letters, and reports.

1. *Paragraphs* should have only one main idea. Start with a topic sentence to introduce the idea; follow with sentences to give more details about the idea. Generally, paragraphs should have a minimum of three sentences, an average of five sentences, and a maximum of eight sentences.

2. *Sentences* should include only one idea, and that idea should relate to the main idea of the paragraph. Vary sentence length, but sentences should average 15 words.

The **5-15-1 writing rule** *states that paragraphs should average 5 sentences with 15 words expressing 1 idea.*

Editing improves the quality of your writing.

1. Edit after writing, not during. Get your ideas out first.

2. Run spelling and grammar checks on the computer, and then edit your work onscreen.

3. Run spelling and grammar checks again, and then print your work.

4. Edit the printed draft. Does each paragraph have only one idea, with all sentences related to that one idea? Does each paragraph have at least three sentences and a maximum of eight? Edit each sentence for punctuation using the writing guide.

5. Edit a classmate's or coworker's paper or letter, and have that person edit yours.

6. Make the changes on the computer, run spelling and grammar checks, and print out the final copy.

Punctuation is the use of special marks (e.g., commas, semicolons, colons, dashes, parentheses, brackets) to group words, phrases, and clauses. We'll discuss *commas,* which are the most important mark of internal punctuation that is used or not used in error more frequently than the others. Below are three major uses of commas and ways to test if their use is correct.

1. *Commas separate items in a series.* A series needing commas has three or more consecutive words, phrases, or clauses in one sentence. Do not use a comma with a series of two; this is explained below.

2. *Commas precede coordinating conjunctions that join clauses.* Conjunctions put closely related ideas together. In essence, you are putting two sentences into one. Conjunctions help you avoid having several short, choppy sentences. The primary coordinating conjunctions are *and, but, or,* and *nor. Yet, for,* and *so* are also used to connect phrases and clauses.

   - To test if the comma with a conjunction is used correctly, *replace the conjunction with a period.* If you have two complete sentences, the comma is used correctly. If you do not have two sentences, omit the comma because the conjunction is most likely connecting words or phrases rather than clauses (a series of two). Conjunctions commonly connect items in a series of two items that do not require a comma, as illustrated below.

Conjunction Comma Errors

Wrong: Smith studied the age of participants, *and* the length of time they were sick. (series of two)

Correct: Smith studied the age of participants *and* the length of time they were sick.

Wrong: Smith studied age *and* he also studied length of sickness. (two sentences)

Correct: Smith studied age, *and* he also studied length of sickness.

---

3. *Commas set off nonrestrictive words and phrases at the beginning, middle, and end of the sentence.* Another way of thinking of commas is that they separate less important information (*nonrestrictive*) from more important information (*restrictive*). The comma is used to separate the nonrestrictive modifying words and phrases (the portion that can be eliminated from the sentence) that provide details from the restrictive clause (the portion that cannot be eliminated). Nonrestrictive words and phrases could be eliminated and you would still have a complete sentence. The word *which* is nonrestrictive; thus, it commonly has a comma before it. The word *that* is restrictive; thus, it does not have a comma before it.

- *Beginning.* When you start a sentence with a preposition (e.g., *to, of, if, for, at, by, as, on, in, before, after, when*), you usually have an *introductory prepositional phrase.* As just shown, you need a comma after this type of phrase. To test if you have a nonrestrictive introductory word or phrase:

  (1) Check to see if you *started the sentence with a preposition.* If you did, and you don't have a comma, add one to make sure there is no error. (Technically, it is not an error *not* to use the comma with a phrase with less than four words that is not dependent on the clause. However, it is never wrong to use the comma, so use it to ensure correct punctuation.)

      Avoiding starting sentences with prepositions eliminates the need to check for commas. Starting sentences with subjects is not only effective writing but also avoids introductory prepositional phrases.

  (2) *Replace the comma with a period.* If you do not have two complete sentences, one part is a word or phrase and the other is a clause, so the comma is correctly used. If you do have two complete sentences, replace the comma with a semicolon or a period or use a conjunction.

- *Middle.* To test if you have a nonrestrictive word or phrase in the middle of a sentence (parenthetical element), *cross out the information between the commas.* If you have a sentence, the commas are correct.

- *End.* The word *which* is commonly used to start an ending phrase. Microsoft Word grammar check will catch this error for you. To test if you have an ending phrase, *cross out the phrase at the end of the sentence.* If you still have a sentence, the comma is correct.

Nonrestrictive and Restrictive Comma Errors

Wrong: To improve my conflict team skill I will confront others using the conflict model XYZ statement.

Correct: *To improve my conflict team skill,* I will confront others using the conflict model XYZ statement.

Wrong: To improve my conflict team skill my weakest area I will confront others.

Correct: To improve my conflict team skill, *my weakest area,* I will confront others.

Wrong: Smith controlled for age which makes the study more robust.

Correct: Smith controlled for age, *which makes the study more robust.*

APPLICATION SITUATIONS

Correct the Punctuation

AS 6–4

16. If, I stop speaking without thinking I will improve my team skills.

17. My score was a 92 percent which is good.

18. I scored 6 for planning, and 5 for conflict.

19. After reviewing the survey I will improve my team skills.

20. To improve my score I will confront others in conflict.

21. I will improve my conflict team skills and I really want to by letting others participate more.

22. When planning with the group I will give my ideas.

23. I scored 8 on conflict and I scored 7 for listening.

24. William Shakespeare the great English author wrote *Hamlet*.

25. José is a great guy, I like him a lot.

Nonverbal Communication

Every time you use oral communication, you also use nonverbal communication. **Nonverbal communication** *is the facial expressions, vocal quality, gestures, and posture used while transmitting messages.* Nonverbal communication can be anything that sends a message. The adage "Actions speak louder than words" is true.

WORK APPLICATIONS

8. Give a specific example of when someone's nonverbal communication did not support the verbal message.

Nonverbal communication is important in sending and understanding others' messages.[71] In fact, people communicate mainly in nonverbal language and only secondarily in verbal language. Studies have shown that although people may not realize it, they pay much more attention to a person's nonverbal communication than verbal when interpreting (decoding) the message being sent. In fact, saying nothing at all often sends a message. Therefore, it is important to pay attention to nonverbal communication.

Below you will learn about common interpretations of nonverbal communication techniques. However, even though they are generally accepted, be careful because there are always exceptions to the rule. By reading others' nonverbal communication, you can often find out how they feel about you. You should change your communication style if you can read that it is interpreted to be negative by others, or if others tell you it is.[72]

To really improve human relations, you can read others' verbal and nonverbal communication, understand their preferred means of communicating, and use it when communicating with them. If you work at it, you can improve your ability to use and interpret nonverbal communications.

Facial Expressions   It is commonly thought that a person with a smile is happy and friendly, while a frown conveys unhappiness and displeasure. Raised eyebrows are interpreted as disbelief or amazement. Pursed lips are interpreted as a sign of anger. The use of eye contact shows interest; not using eye contact shows disinterest. When people lie, they tend to avoid eye contact. Biting one's lips is considered a sign of nervousness.

Sometimes people communicate using only facial expressions. Have you ever done something wrong and had a parent, teacher, or boss give you a dirty look, or a look of disapproval? Or have you ever made an error and gotten a look of disappointment?

Vocal Quality   The proper use of voice is important for effective communication. You need to monitor the sound of your voice to make sure it isn't too high pitched, whiny, breathy, cute, or mumbly. Your vocal quality enables others to recognize your voice. It is made up of (1) tone, the attitude in your voice (warm, friendly, upset, etc.); (2) pitch, highness or lowness of sound; (3) volume, loud to soft; (4) pace, fast or slow; and (5) pauses, how you manage silence. Adjusting any of these components changes vocal quality. Without any changes in voice, your speech is monotonous. Try to avoid annoying vocal repetition of junk words such as "y'know," "all right," "man," "um," "ah," and "etcetera."

To determine your vocal quality, tape (preferably videotape so you can see your other nonverbal communication techniques as well) conversations or speeches and ask others about your voice quality and how to improve it.

Gestures   To a large extent the adage "You speak with your hands" is true. Putting a hand over your mouth and placing your head in your hands while seated are generally interpreted as signs of objection or boredom. Placing hands on hips is considered a sign of anger or defensiveness. Hands uplifted outward show disbelief, puzzlement, or uncertainty. Folding your arms is interpreted as being closed to communication and change, or preparing to speak. Keeping your arms by your side is considered being open to communication and suggestions and being relaxed. Pointing your finger shows authority, displeasure, or lecturing. Try to avoid the overuse of any gesture; it becomes annoying and distracting to others. We are often unaware of our gestures and their effects. Ask your friends whether you have any annoying gestures.

Posture   Sitting on the edge of a chair and leaning slightly forward is a sign of interest. Slouching in a chair is a sign of boredom or lack of interest. Fidgeting and doodling are signs of boredom. Shrugging your shoulders is considered a sign of indifference. Shifting and jiggling money are interpreted as nervousness.

Another important part of posture is the use of space. How close we get while communicating affects the results. If you get too close to people, you can make them uncomfortable. On the other hand, being too far away can be interpreted as not caring. In the United States, close friends and loved ones tend to communicate from actually touching to about 1½ feet apart. People who are friends or who are conducting personal business tend to communicate from a distance of 1½ to 4 feet. When conducting impersonal business, such as shopping for clothes or meeting a new client, people communicate from 4 to 12 feet apart.

Notice whether people are moving toward you because you are too far away or backing away because you are too close. If you continue to move, you can end up dancing around. When working in a global environment, you will be dealing with people from other cultures. Be aware that Eastern Europeans, Latin Americans, and Arabs all prefer a close distance for communications. Therefore, they may tend to move closer to you. Refer to Chapter 2 for a review of how one's eye contact and handshake can affect one's image.

Nonverbal communication techniques are used together and may send different messages. For example, a person may be smiling (a sign of openness to communication) while having his or her arms and legs crossed (a sign of being closed to communication).

It is important for you to be aware of your nonverbal communication techniques and to make sure they are consistent with your oral and/or written communication. You can use nonverbal communication, such as a nod of the head, to facilitate face-to-face communication. Be aware of other people's nonverbal communication techniques. They tell you their feelings and attitudes toward the communication and toward you as a person or as a manager.

Combining Channels

As stated above, nonverbal communication is always combined with oral communication. The manager can also combine oral and written communication. Repetition is often needed

EXHIBIT 6.4 | Message Transmission Channels

Oral Communication	Written Communication	Nonverbal Communication
1. Face-to-face	1. Memos	1. Facial expressions
2. Telephone	2. Letters	2. Vocal quality
3. Meetings	3. Reports	3. Gestures
4. Presentations	4. Computers/e-mail	4. Posture
	5. Fax	
	6. Bulletin board notices	
	7. Posters	

to ensure that the message has been conveyed with mutual understanding. It is common for a manager to give an oral message followed by a written message to reinforce it. For example, the manager could conduct a safety program orally with the support of a written manual. Posters could also be placed in the work area to remind employees to follow the safety rules.

Oral communication followed by written communication is appropriate for the development of objectives and plans; to communicate new or changed standing plans; when praising employees; when delegating complex tasks; to communicate safety, quality, and good housekeeping; and when reporting progress toward departmental objectives.

Before you send a message, be sure to select the best channel. Exhibit 6.4 lists the major channels from which to select.

WORK APPLICATIONS

9. Which message transmission channel is your strongest? Your weakest? How will you improve your ability to communicate with your weakest channel?

In the opening case, Mr. Olsen handled the oral and nonverbal, face-to-face communications with employees poorly. The employees spread rumors orally and in writing. The media also made errors in oral and written communications; in turn, Digital's in-house computer network repeated the incorrect TV report. Mr. Shields called the media in to Digital for an oral, face-to-face interview to correct the communication errors.

EMOTIONS

Recall that the total person approach realizes that an organization employs the whole person. Our emotions, often just called feelings, are an important part of us.[73] Our feelings affect our behavior, human relations, and performance at work.[74] Emotions in the workplace, which includes emotional intelligence but is broader, is a hot topic in management research and practice today.[75] Our discussion of emotions will be in two subsections. First, you will learn about emotions at work, or emotional labor; then you will learn how to deal with emotional employees.

Emotional Labor

Emotional labor requires the expression of desired emotions during interpersonal relations. For example, employees are expected to be cheerful with customers, to be pleasant with coworkers, and to avoid violence at work.[76] Managers give speeches to emotionally charge employees and motivate them to increase performance. Our discussion of emotional labor includes understanding feelings, as well as gender and global differences with regard to expressing feelings.

Understanding Feelings   There are six universal emotions. We can feel *happiness* when we get a raise, *surprise* when we don't expect the raise, *fear* that we will lose our jobs, *sadness* if our coworkers get laid off, *anger* if we get laid off, and *disgust* with management for taking large raises while laying off employees. You should realize that:

1. Feelings are subjective; they tell you people's attitudes and needs.

2. Feelings are usually disguised as factual statements. For example, when people are hot, they tend to say, "It's hot in here," rather than "I feel hot."

3. Most importantly, feelings are neither right nor wrong, but behavior is.

We cannot choose our feelings or control them. However, we can control how we express our feelings, which is what management wants through emotional labor.[77] For example, if Vern, an employee, says "You _____" (mentally fill in the blank with a word that would make you angry) to Bonnie, his supervisor, she will feel its impact. Bonnie can express her feelings in a calm manner, or she can yell at, hit, or give Vern a dirty look, and so on. Supervisors should encourage employees to express their feelings in a positive way.[78] However, they shouldn't allow employees to go around yelling, swearing, or hitting others. And they should not get caught up in others' emotions. Although we may not like some of our coworkers, we should treat them with respect.

Gender Differences   Research supports that women are more emotional than men. Women show greater emotional expression; experience emotions more intensely; express both positive and negative feelings, except anger, more often; are more comfortable expressing feelings; and are better at reading nonverbal clues than men. There may be three reasons for these differences. First, many boys are socialized to be tough and brave and to not show emotions, whereas girls are socialized to be nurturing and to show emotions. Second, women may be genetically better at dealing with emotions. Third, women may have a greater need for social approval, so they may be more willing to share emotions than men.[79]

Global Differences   As we have discussed in preceding chapters, what is acceptable in one culture may not be acceptable in another. Some cultures lack words to express feelings such as anxiety, depression, sadness, and guilt, and they interpret the same emotions differently. Emotional labor expectations vary culturally. For example, in the United States, employees are generally expected to be friendly and to smile in their human relations with customers. However, in Muslim cultures, smiling is commonly taken as a sign of sexual attraction, so women are discouraged from smiling at men. In Israel, smiling by supermarket cashiers is commonly taken as a sign of inexperience, so they are not expected to smile.

Learning Outcome

7. Describe how to deal with an emotional employee.

Dealing with Emotional Employees

Recall that emotions can be a barrier to communications.[80] You will have better communications and human relations if you can deal with emotional employees effectively.[81] Following are some guidelines.

Calming the Emotional Person   When an emotional employee comes to you, *never* make put-down statements like these: "You shouldn't be angry," "Don't be upset," "Don't be a baby," "Just sit down and be quiet," or "I know how you feel." (No one knows how anyone else feels. Even people who experience the same thing at the same time don't feel the same.) Don't try to make the person feel guilty or bad[82] with statements like, "I'm ashamed of you," "I'm disappointed in you," or "You should be ashamed of yourself." These types of statements only make the feelings stronger. While you may get the employee to be quiet, communication will not take place. The problem will still exist, and your human relations with the employee will suffer because of it, as will your relations with others who see or hear about what you said and did. When the employee complains to peers, they will tend to feel you were too hard or too easy on the person. You lose either way.

Use Reflecting Responses   To calm emotional employees, don't argue with them. Encourage them to express their feelings in a positive way.[83] Use *empathic listening* to try to put yourself in their place. Do not agree or disagree with the feelings; simply identify them verbally with reflecting responses, paraphrasing the feeling to the employee. Use statements like these: "You were *hurt* when you didn't get the assignment." "You *resent* Bill for not doing his share of the work. Is that what you mean?" "You are *doubtful* that the job will be done on time. Is that what you're saying?"

After you deal with emotions, you can go on to work on content (solving problems).[84] It may be wise to wait until a later time when emotions cool down. You will find that understanding the reasons for someone's feelings is often the solution. Throughout the next chapter you will learn how to deal with your emotions and those of others in an effective way to enhance behavior, human relations, and performance.

At Digital, some of the employees who spread the rumor about Jack Shields were emotional and others reacted to the rumor emotionally because some of them liked him and wanted him to stay, while others disliked him and were glad he was gone—so they thought. In either case, people got emotional for no reason other than miscommunications.

WORK APPLICATIONS

10. Give an example of emotions at work. What was the emotional labor expectation and the actual behavior? How did the emotions affect behavior, human relations, and performance?

CRITICISM

In this section we discuss criticism. We begin with getting criticized, which is difficult for most people. Then we focus on giving criticism, with guidelines to help you do it well.

Getting Criticism

You should realize that criticism from your boss, peers, or employees is painful.[85] People do not enjoy being criticized, even when it is constructive. Keep the saying "no pain, no gain" in mind when it comes to criticism. If you want to improve your performance and your chances of having a successful career, seek honest feedback about how you can improve your performance.[86]

You will most likely run into people who are very critical and perhaps sarcastic. If that's the case, focus on the issue and try not to overreact.[87] Even if the criticizer is a jerk, do a self-evaluation seeking opportunity for improvement.[88] Assume the person is trying to help you do a better job.[89]

If you're asking for personal feedback, remember that you are asking to hear things that may surprise, upset, or insult you, or that may hurt your feelings. If you become defensive and emotional (and it is hard not to when you feel you are being attacked), the person will stop giving feedback.[90] The criticizer will probably tell others what happened, and others will not give you truthful feedback either.

When you get criticism, whether you ask for it or not, view it as an opportunity to improve, stay calm (even when the other person is emotional), and don't get defensive. Use the feedback to improve your performance.[91] If you cannot take criticism, you may not be perceived as a credible source to give criticism.

Learning Outcome

8. Explain how to give effective criticism.

Giving Criticism

Some people don't like to use the word *criticizing* and prefer the word *critiquing*. Regardless of the word used, the objectives are the same. Part of the job of a manager, teacher, and parent is to criticize others to improve their performance. How criticism is given makes a difference in how—or whether—it is accepted. The goal of criticism should be to improve performance while maintaining human relations, not to get even or to show superiority. When criticizing others, follow these guidelines:

1. *Give more praise than criticism.* As a manager, try to praise 80 percent of the time and give criticism 20 percent. When employees receive above-average amounts of negative criticism, it generally harms, rather than improves, performance. Praise produces better results. For example, a manager praised an employee for setting up the display nice and straight, rather than criticizing the employee for being too slow. The praise resulted in improved performance. Criticism probably would not have worked. Rewarding employees for meeting expectations encourages them to repeat the behavior. (This is reinforcement theory, discussed in Chapter 9.)

2. *Criticize immediately.* Criticism should be given as soon after the performance as is feasible. Criticism loses its impact with time. Give feedback immediately, unless people are emotional.[92] When people are emotional, following the other criticism guidelines becomes difficult.

3. *Keep criticism performance-oriented.* Focus on the task, not the person. Distinguish between the employee and his or her performance. For example, do not say, "You are lazy," which is an attack on the person. It would be more useful to the employee to hear, "Your rate of production is 10 percent slower than the standard," or "You are letting our group down by doing only five, while the rest of us do seven."

4. *Give specific and accurate criticism.* Generalities are of little use to employees. Avoid saying "always" and "never." The more descriptive the feedback, the more useful it is to the receiver.[93] For example, do not say things like, "You always make mistakes." It would be more useful to the employee to hear, "Your work has three errors; they are …" Giving inaccurate information can cause problems and embarrassment.

5. *Open on a positive note and close by repeating what action is needed.* People remember longest what was said first and last. The opening statement should set the stage for the criticism, and the conclusion should reinforce it. Try to let the employee realize that you care about and value him or her as a person and that it is some small aspect of behavior that needs to be changed.

WORK APPLICATIONS

11. Give a specific example of an occasion when a manager should give an employee criticism (do not simply say for poor performance).

Generally, employees are open to criticism. Employees prefer to be told when they are not performing adequately, rather than to receive no criticism at all. They cannot improve performance without the necessary praise or criticism. However, employees do not like to be criticized in a negative way. Chastising, using sarcasm, and joking should not take place when giving criticism. This type of behavior generally makes things worse.

Praise and criticism are the keys to high levels of performance.[94] Following these guidelines will help you do a better job of giving criticism, and it will help employees do a better job. This creates a win–win situation.

Exhibit 6.5 lists the guidelines for giving effective criticism.

EXHIBIT 6.5 | Guidelines for Giving Effective Criticism

- Give more praise than criticism.
- Criticize immediately.
- Keep criticism performance-oriented.
- Give specific and accurate criticism.
- Open on a positive note and close by repeating what action is needed.

12. Give an example of criticism you received from a manager. List all five guidelines from the text, stating whether or not each was followed. If you can't think of an example, interview someone and report another person's example.

As we bring the chapter to a close, complete Self-Assessment Exercise 6–1 to determine how your personality affects your behavior, human relations, and performance.

Self-Assessment Exercise 6–1

Your Personality Traits and Structure, Communication, Emotions, and Criticism

Let's tie personality traits from Chapter 2 together with what we've covered in this chapter. We are going to present some general statements about how your personality may affect your behavior, human relations, and performance. For each area, determine how the information relates to you. This will help you better understand your behavioral strengths and weakness and the areas you may want to improve.

If you have a high *surgency* personality, you most likely are an extrovert and have no difficulty initiating conversations and communicating with others orally. However, you may be dominating during communication and prefer vertical communications following the chain of command with centralized authority. You may try to control communication networks using the wheel, chain, or Y networks. Be a team player. Surgency types are often not good at dealing with emotions. You may need to be more attentive to nonverbal communication and emotions. You may be better at giving than getting feedback, so you may need to work at being receptive to feedback. You may also need to work at giving more praise and less criticism.

If you are high in *agreeableness* personality traits, you are most likely a good listener and communicator, preferring oral horizontal communications with decentralized authority using the circle and all-channel communication networks as a team player. You are probably connected to the grapevine, so be careful not to spread false rumors. You are probably in tune with emotions and nonverbal communication cues. You may be reluctant to give criticism even though it will help others improve.

Your *adjustment* level affects the emotional tone of your communications. If you tend to get emotional, and it is a barrier to communications, you may want to work to keep your emotions under control. Watch your nonverbal communication because it tells people how you feel about them and it can hurt your human relations. We cannot control our feelings, but we can control our behavior. Try not to be sensitive to criticism and not to become defensive.

If you are high in *conscientiousness,* you tend to have reliable communications. If you are not conscientious, you may want to work at returning messages quickly. You may be so concerned with your own success that you don't pay attention to emotions and nonverbal communication. Criticism may be painful to you, because you try hard to do a good job. But remember that it can lead to more conscientiousness and greater success.

People who are *open to new experience* often initiate communications, because communicating is often part of the new experience. If you are not open to new experience, you may be reluctant to change organizational structure and flows of communication, and you may not like the e-org.

Action plan: Based on your personality, what specific things will you do to improve?

_____

_____

_____

_____

Videos

Manager's Hot Seat and Behavior Model Videos are available for this chapter.

Online Learning Center Resources

Go to the Internet (http://mhhe.com/lussier8e) where you will find a broad array of resources to help maximize your learning.

- Review the vocabulary.
- Try a quiz.

R E V I E W

The chapter review is organized to help you master the 9 learning outcomes for Chapter 6. First provide your own response to each learning outcome, and then check the summary provided to see how well you understand the material. Next, identify the final statement in each section as either true or false (T/F). Correct each false statement. Answers are given at the end of the chapter.

1. **Explain five principles of organization.**

   With the division of labor, employees have specialized jobs within departments. The chain of command is the line of authority from the top to the bottom of the organization. The span of management refers to the number of employees reporting to a manager. With centralized authority, top managers make important decisions; with decentralized authority, middle and first-line managers make important decisions. There is a need to coordinate the work of all departments.

   The current trends are toward more specialized jobs, less following of the chain of command, greater spans of management, and decentralized decision making. T F

2. **Explain six types of departmentalization.**

   Functional departmentalization involves organizing departments around essential input activities. Product departmentalization involves organizing departments around goods and services provided. Customer departmentalization involves organizing departments around the needs of different types of customers. When the firm develops independent lines of business, which operate as separate companies all contributing to the corporation's profitability, the design is called divisional departmentalization (or M-form). Territory, or geographic, departmentalization involves organizing departments in each area in which the enterprise does business. Matrix departmentalization combines the functional and product departmentalization structures. The employee works for a functional department and is also assigned to one or more products or projects.

   Functional departmentalization is outdated and no longer commonly used. T F

3. **Identify contemporary organization trends.**

   The hierarchy chain of command is getting flatter, which has increased the span of management. Organizations are reengineering their structures into team-based forms, in which authority is decentralized to empower lower-level employees. Contemporary organizations include the learning, team, virtual, boundaryless, and e-organization.

   Contemporary organizations are using teams as a central coordinating organizational principle. T F

4. **Describe how communication flows through organizations.**

   Formal communication flows through communication networks in vertical and horizontal directions. The grapevine is also a major source of informal communication flowing in all directions.

   When an employee goes to talk to the boss, the employee is using vertical upward communication. T F

5. **Explain the advantage the all-channel communication network has over the other networks.**

   The all-channel communication network allows communication to flow in all directions, making it the most effective communication network.

   For simple, routine tasks, the wheel, chain, Y, and circle networks work fast and accurately. T F

6. **List the three primary message transmission channels.**

   The three primary message transmission channels are: (1) oral communication (face-to-face, telephone, meetings, presentations), (2) written communication (memos, letters, reports, computers, fax, bulletin boards, posters), and (3) nonverbal communication (facial expressions, vocal quality, gestures, posture).

   Nonverbal communication is more important than verbal communication when interpreting messages. T F

7. **Describe how to deal with an emotional employee.**

   Do not make put-down statements or try to make the person feel guilty or bad. Listen empathically and use reflective responses to paraphrase the feeling.

   Making logical statements is the important factor in calming emotional employees. T F

8. **Explain how to give effective criticism.**

   Tips for giving effective criticism include: (1) give more praise than criticism; (2) criticize immediately; (3) keep criticism performance-oriented; (4) give specific and accurate criticism; and (5) open on a positive note and close by repeating what action is needed.

   Joking while giving criticism is an effective way to get people to improve performance. T F

Learning Outcome

9. Define the following 14 key terms.

9. **Define the following 14 key terms.**

   Select one or more methods: (1) Fill in the missing key terms from memory; (2) match the key terms from the end of the review with their definitions below; or (3) copy the key terms in order from the key terms at the beginning of the chapter.

   _____ refers to the way managers design their firms to achieve their organization's mission and goals.

   _____ is the grouping of related activities into units.

   _____ have members from different departments to coordinate tasks between departments.

   _____ is the redesign of work to combine fragmented tasks into streamlined processes that save time and money.

   _____ outsource major business functions and focus on core competencies.

   _____ seek to break down vertical and horizontal barriers within the firm and between the firm and its suppliers and customers.

   _____ is the compounded interpersonal communications process across an organization.

   _____ is the flow of information both up and down the chain of command.

   _____ is the flow of information between colleagues and peers.

   The _____ is the informal vehicle through which messages flow throughout the organization.

   _____ are sets of employees who have stable contact through which information is generated and transmitted.

   _____ are the forms of the transmitted message.

The _____ states that paragraphs should average 5 sentences with 15 words expressing 1 idea.

_____ is the facial expressions, vocal quality, gestures, and posture used while transmitting messages.

K E Y   T E R M S

boundaryless
   organizations   189
channels   193
communication
   networks   192
cross-functional
   teams   188
departmentalization   184

5-15-1 writing rule   197
grapevine   191
horizontal
   communication   190
nonverbal
   communication   199
organizational
   communication   190

organizational
   structure   184
reengineering   188
vertical
   communication   190
virtual organizations   188

C O M M U N I C A T I O N   S K I L L S

The following critical thinking questions can be used for class discussion and/or as written assignments to develop communication skills. Be sure to give complete explanations for all questions.

1. Would you rather: Have a specialized or general/variety job? Have a manager with a wide or narrow span of management? Work under centralized or decentralized authority?

2. In which type of departmentalization would you prefer to work?

3. Many employees, including managers, complain about organizational communications. What are some of the complaints and how can communications be improved?

4. E-mail continues to be preferred over oral communication at work. What are the pros and cons of oral versus e-mail communication? Which form of communication do you use more often? Which one do you prefer?

5. Are writing skills really that important to career success? State how to test if you have a series of two (no comma needed) or two sentences (need a comma). Write an example of each similar to the "Conjunction Comma Errors" feature on page 197. State how to test if you have a nonrestrictive word or phrase at the beginning, middle, or end of a sentence. Write an example similar to the "Nonrestrictive and Restrictive Comma Errors" feature on page 198.

6. How do you rate your ability to read nonverbal communications (e.g., facial expressions, vocal quality, gestures, and posture)? What can you do to improve your ability to understand nonverbal communications?

7. Do you agree that women are more emotional than men? Do they show greater emotional expression, experience emotions more intensely, express both positive and negative feelings (except anger) more often, feel more comfortable expressing feelings, and read nonverbal clues better than men?

8. Do you actively seek criticism? How do you rate your ability to accept criticism? Do you get emotional and defensive? How can you improve your ability to accept criticism? After getting criticized, do you change to improve? What advice would you give others to help them accept criticism and change to improve performance?

Hewlett-Packard: Smart Growth or Chaos?

While Hewlett-Packard may be known for product innovation, the company's corporate development is a tale of reinvention. . . . HP, which already boasts an IT service organization that is among the world's largest, acquired Electronic Data Systems (EDS) for about $13.9 billion in cash in 2008. HP expects the purchase to more than double its revenue from services. It plans to use the EDS brand for the combined services business, which will provide IT and business process outsourcing, application development and management, consulting, systems integration, and other technology services to customers in more than 80 countries.

Years after its acquisition of Compaq Computer—a deal valued at approximately $19 billion—HP continues to integrate its operations. Debate over the wisdom of the merger and speculation about the possibility of spinning off certain divisions of HP also continues, but CEO Mark Hurd has so far opted to keep HP intact. Since taking over in 2005, Hurd has been charged with streamlining operations, and soon after his appointment, he split the printer and personal systems units that his predecessor, Carly Fiorina, had combined only months earlier. Other restructuring measures include the dissolution of its Customer Solutions Group, and a workforce reduction of roughly 10 percent. The company is now made up of seven business segments, most of which fall under three broad units: Technology Solutions Group, Personal Systems Group, and Imaging and Printing Group.[95]

HP manages this widely decentralized organization with a central council to coordinate activity and eliminate duplication. With more than 140,000 employees on six continents, HP is by necessity a highly decentralized organization and its internal communication function mirrors the company's geographical and business line matrix. In essence, it is the typical system of devolved communication—a group of over 150 communication professionals worldwide performing a variety of roles in different markets, business groups, and reporting relationships. Internal communication reports to the company's senior vice president for corporate marketing and the executive vice president for human resources. This dual reporting structure enables internal communication to help coordinate myriad internal messages within a framework consistent with HP's external messaging and branding.

There are challenges to such a decentralized structure, explains Robin Andrews, global internal communication manager at HP. "I've been in decentralized and centralized structures and I can see that it is an issue that has to be managed," Andrews says. On the one hand, if you're working in a division in a small region and all that you do is driven by the needs of that part of the business, why should you report in to corporate? On the other hand, I do see the benefits it brings to have greater consistency, and a greater resource base from which to implement programs more easily across the whole company."

This is the guiding ethos at the heart of the new structure HP created: If both centralization and decentralization offer benefits to the organization, is there a way you can take the best of both models? The idea led to the roll-out of the team Andrews now manages—the Program Management Office (PMO). The PMO is a standing internal communication committee that acts, at a base level, as an air traffic controller for internal communication. Its purpose is to unify messaging across regions, businesses, and functions. According to Andrews, "If you've got a strong enough PMO structure, you can resolve some of those typical issues that trouble us and other large, global organizations. It's a way to enable individual market-driven communication without being uncoordinated."[96]

Go to the Internet: For more information on HP and to update the information provided in this case, do a name search on the Internet and visit www.hp.com.

Support your answers to the following questions with specific information from the case and text, or other information you get from the Web or other sources.

Chapters 5 and 6

1. Describe the overall organizational structure of HP. Which type of departmentalization seems to best describe HP?

2. Is authority in this structure centralized or decentralized? Why does HP use that type of authority system?

3. What are the challenges with HP's dual centralized/decentralized authority system? How does HP address that challenge? Be sure to identify the flow of organizational communications.

4. In this case, what types of organizational communication flow has HP not addressed with its new structure? Be sure to identify how contemporary organizational designs and communication networks can be used at HP.

5. Given the complexity and size of HP, what communication skills would you emphasize with employees if you worked in the PMO?

6. Given HP's global operation, what global differences should the PMO be aware of when coordinating internal communications?

Cumulative Questions

7. What 21st century challenges has HP addressed through its new structure and communication system (Chapter 1)?

8. What seems to be HP management's attitude toward employees given the firm's decentralized structure and coordination system (Chapter 3)?

OBJECTIVE CASE   ## I've Got a Complaint

The following monologue takes place when Lowell storms into the office of his boss, Liza.

LOWELL: (*Speaking in a loud voice, talking fast without stopping.*) Liza, you told me you were giving me a $1-an-hour raise, effective the first of the month. My friend in payroll tells me that you only put through for a half-dollar-an-hour raise. How can you stab me in the back like that? I thought we were friends. You told me I was getting a $1-an-hour raise and I need it. I just went out and bought a new motorcycle, counting on the money to make my payment. My brother is a lawyer and he told me that this is a breach of contract. I'll sue the company for it if you don't give it to me. Am I going to get my $1-an-hour raise the easy way or hard way?

Answer the following questions. Then in the space between questions, state why you selected that answer.

_____ 1. The monologue was a _____ flow of communication.
   a. vertical–downward   *c.* horizontal
   b. vertical–upward   *d.* grapevine

_____ 2. Lowell's statements are based on information he got through _____ communication flow.
   a. vertical–downward   *c.* horizontal
   b. vertical–upward   *d.* grapevine

_____ 3. Lowell and Liza are members of a communication network.
   a. true   *b.* false

_____ 4. Lowell began his monologue with a(n) _____ barrier to communication.
   a. perception   *c.* emotional
   b. noise   *d.* filtering

_____ 5. Lowell's third statement indicates a(n) _____ barrier to communication.
   a. perception   *c.* trust
   b. emotional   *d.* information overload

_____ 6. The place Lowell selected _____ appropriate for the message.
   a. was   *b.* was not

_____ 7. Lowell's selection of a one-on-one, face-to-face channel _____ appropriate for the message.

   a. was   b. was not

_____ 8. Lowell used the _____ communication style.

   a. autocratic   b. laissez-faire   c. participative

_____ 9. Liza's decision to wait until Lowell finished before she began to speak shows her selection of the _____ communication style.

   a. autocratic   b. laissez-faire   c. participative

_____ 10. So far, Lowell has handled this situation in an _____ manner.

   a. effective   b. ineffective

11. If you were in Lowell's situation, what would you do or say?

12. Assume you are in Liza's position and that you thought you authorized a $1-an-hour raise. A change or error could have been made somewhere. But at the moment you don't know how it was changed, if it in fact was changed. You have only Lowell's word that it was. Lowell is standing in front of you. What do you do and say to him?

Note: This situation, with possible responses by Liza, can be role-played in class.

The Grapevine

In-Class Exercise
(Group)

Objective: To better understand organizational communication flow of rumors.

AACSB: The primary AACSB learning standard skill developed through this exercise is communication abilities.

Preparation: No preparation is necessary for this exercise.

Experience: You will observe a rumor being spread and determine its accuracy.

Procedure 1
(2–3 minutes)

Six students volunteer or are selected to spread a rumor. Each student has a number 1 through 6. Number 1 remains in the classroom while numbers 2 through 6 leave the room so they cannot overhear the discussion. They may stand in the hall with the door closed. All students should spread the rumor as accurately as possible.

Procedure 2
(2–5 minutes)

Student 1 and the class read the rumor below. When student number 1 is ready, he or she goes to the front of the room.

Rumor has it that Chris Wilson, the president of Wilson Company, a 55-year-old married man with four children, is having an affair with a 16-year-old girl, Betty Harris. Jean Fleaming saw Chris with Betty in a bar and told Rick Jones about it. Rick told her that he saw them in a hotel on Fifth Street. Carlos Veldas, the chairperson of the board of directors, is investigating and may ask Chris to resign, or he may fire him. If this happens, Vice President Kathy Likert will probably be named president.

Procedure 3
(1–3 minutes)

Student 2 returns to the classroom. Student 1 tells student 2 the rumor loud enough for the class to hear. The rest of the class observe and take notes in the spaces provided on the next page. The instructor may record the rumor spreading.

Procedure 4
(5–10 minutes)

Student 2 spreads the rumor to student 3; 3 to 4; 4 to 5; 5 to 6. Student 6 writes the rumor on the board. After spreading the rumor, students return to their seats, read the rumor, and become observers.

Discussion Questions:

1. How accurately was the rumor spread? Is the rumor verified? Was it distorted as it spread? If so, how was it distorted? Was it longer and more complex, or was it shortened?
2. What could be done to improve the accuracy of the rumor?
3. Does spreading rumors like this help the organization?
4. If Chris Wilson hears about the rumor, what should he do? Would the answer be different if the rumor were true or false?

Conclusion: The instructor may make concluding remarks.

Application (2– 4 minutes):   What have I learned through this exercise? How will I use this knowledge in the future?

Sharing: Volunteers give their answers to the application section.

RUMOR OBSERVATION SHEET

Students	Accuracy: Correct Statements	Errors: Distortions, Additions, Deletions
1–2		
2–3		
3–4		
4–5		
5–6		

SKILL-BUILDING EXERCISE 6–2

Communication Networks

In-Class Exercise (Group)

Objective: To better understand how communication networks affect performance.

AACSB: The primary AACSB learning standard skill developed through this exercise is communication abilities.

Preparation: No preparation is necessary for this exercise.

Experience: Fifteen of the class members will form three teams that will try to put a puzzle together using different communication networks.

Procedure 1
(2–3 minutes)

Set up three teams of five members. The members should be seated in the network positions shown below. All other class members should form a circle around the three groups and observe them work.

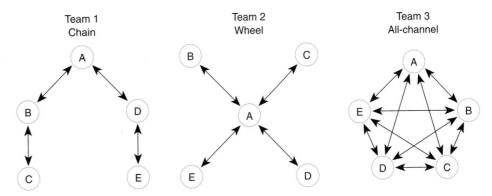

The arrows represent the communication flow. In team 1, A can talk only to B or D; B can talk only to A or C; C can talk only to B; D can talk only to A or E; and E can talk only to D. In team 2, A can talk to B, C, D, or E individually but not as a group. B, C, D, and E cannot talk to each other, only to A. In team 3, anyone can talk to anyone.

The instructor gives each team member one of the 5" × 5" square puzzle pieces. Wait until told to start before making the puzzle.

Procedure 2
(5 minutes)

Each team has up to five minutes to finish the puzzle following its communication network.

Procedure 3
(2–3 minutes)

The instructor gives each team a copy of the completed puzzle to check accuracy, or to show them how to do it.

Questions:

1. Each team tells the class how they felt about following their communication network.
2. Did any team finish? Which was first?
3. How did the communication network affect the performance of the team?
4. Which structure was most appropriate for this task?

Conclusion: The instructor leads a class discussion and/or makes concluding remarks.

Application (2–4 minutes):   What did I learn from this experience? How will I use this knowledge in the future?

Sharing: Volunteers give their answers to the application section.

**Nonverbal
Communication
and Listening**

Preparation (Group)

During class you will be given the opportunity to practice using effective nonverbal communication and listening skills. This will be done while you are getting acquainted with someone whom you do not know, or do not know well.

In preparation, make sure you have read Chapters 5 and 6 and have completed Self-Assessment Exercise 5–1. Review the feedback sheet below, which you will be using during the exercise to analyze how well you used the text material.

Feedback on Nonverbal
Communication and
Listening Skills

You and your partner will discuss the feedback areas below. After the discussion, using feedback from your partner, rate yourself by putting an X in the blank next to the word(s) that best describes the communication you used during the discussion.

Nonverbal Communication:

Facial expressions

1. I _____ smiled _____ frowned.

2. I _____ did _____ did not use eye contact effectively. It was _____ too frequent _____ about right _____ not frequent enough.

3. My facial expressions conveyed:

Vocal quality

4. My pitch was _____ high _____ about right _____ low.

5. My volume was _____ loud _____ about right _____ soft.

6. My pace was _____ fast _____ about right _____ slow.

7. My pauses and silence were _____ too frequent _____ about right _____ too infrequent.

8. I _____ did _____ did not use repetitive words like "y'know."

9. Tone, the attitude in my voice, was:

10. I _____ did _____ did not vary my vocal qualities enough.

Gestures

11. List gestures that you used and indicate whether they were used too frequently.

12. My gestures conveyed:

Posture

13. I sat in my chair _____ leaning slightly forward _____ slouched.

14. Our distance was _____ 0–1½ feet _____ 1½–4 feet _____ 4–7 feet apart.

15. I _____ did _____ did not make my partner comfortable with the distance between us.

Combined

16. My nonverbal and verbal communications _____ were _____ were not consistent.

Self-Evaluations: Evaluate your listening ability without your partner's feedback. However, you may ask each other questions if you want to.

Listening Skills: Mark the following statements true or false by placing the letter T or F on the line before each statement.

_____ **1.** I liked listening to my partner talk. I encouraged him or her to talk by showing interest, by smiling and nodding, and the like.

_____ **2.** I paid close attention to my partner. I did not stereotype him or her. If the person were more interesting or similar to me, I would not have listened differently.

_____ **3.** I did not evaluate my partner's words and/or nonverbal communication ability as he or she talked.

_____ **4.** I avoided the distractions in the class.

_____ **5.** I gave my partner my complete attention. I put everything else out of sight and mind.

_____ **6.** I allowed my partner time to finish talking. I did not interrupt, anticipate what he or she was going to say, or jump to conclusions.

_____ **7.** I did not tune out my partner because he or she did not agree with my views.

_____ **8.** While my partner talked, my mind did not wander to other personal topics.

_____ **9.** While my partner talked, I paid close attention to the nonverbal communication cues to help me fully understand what he or she was trying to get across.

_____ **10.** I did not tune out and pretend I understood when the topic was difficult or not interesting.

_____ **11.** When my partner was talking, I did not think about what I was going to say in reply.

_____ **12.** When I felt there was something missing or contradictory, I asked direct questions to get my partner to explain the idea more fully.

_____ **13.** When I didn't understand something, I let my partner know it in an effective way.

_____ **14.** When listening to my partner, I tried to put myself in his or her position and see things from his or her perspective.

_____ 15. During the conversation, I repeated back to my partner what had been said in my own words to be sure I understood correctly what had been said so far (paraphrase). I paraphrased _____ too often _____ about right _____ not enough.

If all 15 statements were answered T (true), you used the listening skills effectively. If you answered F (false) to any statements, you may want to work on improving these areas. Overall, how can you improve your listening skills?

In-Class Exercise	*Objectives:* To increase your awareness of the effects of nonverbal communication on conversations. To practice and develop listening skills.
	AACSB: The primary AACSB learning standard skill developed through this exercise is communication abilities.
	Preparation: You should have completed the preparation on the preceding pages.
	Experience: You will have a personal discussion while trying to be aware of nonverbal communication and listening actively. After the conversation, you will analyze the nonverbal communication and listening skills you and your team member used.
Procedure 1 *(2–4 minutes)*	Pair off with someone you don't know or don't know well. If there is an odd number in the class, have one group of three people, or have an observer.
Procedure 2 *(5–10 minutes)*	Group members have a conversation to get to know one another better. Possible topics include school activities, present/summer jobs, career goals, and nonacademic interests. Or members can share how they are feeling.
Procedure 3 *(5–10 minutes)*	Turn to the preparation feedback sheet and give each other feedback on your use of nonverbal communication and listening skills. To be useful, the feedback must be honest, specific, and accurate.
	Conclusion: The instructor leads a class discussion and/or makes concluding remarks.
	Application (2–4 minutes): What did I learn from this experience? How will I use this knowledge in the future?
	Sharing: Volunteers give their answers to the application section.

SKILL-BUILDING EXERCISE 6–4

Giving Criticism

Preparation (Group)

In class, you will be given the opportunity to role-play giving criticism. Think of a job situation in which you or another employee should have been criticized to improve performance. If you prefer, you can act as criticizer in a nonjob situation in which criticism is warranted. Below, you will be asked to briefly state the situation. Write some notes on what you will say when giving the criticism. Be sure to follow the five guidelines for giving effective criticism in Exhibit 6.5. Remember to maintain good human relations while criticizing.

You will get more from the exercise if you think of your own situation. However, if you cannot think of your own situation after making a serious effort, you may use this situation: The employee is a waiter or waitress in an ice cream shop. He or she knows that the tables should be cleaned up quickly after customers leave so that the new customers do not have to sit at a dirty table. It is a busy night. You as the manager notice customers seated at two dirty tables. The employee responsible for clearing the tables is socializing with some friends at one of the tables. Employees are supposed to be friendly. When criticized, the employee may use this fact as an excuse for the dirty tables.

In-Class Exercise	*Objective:* To develop your skill at improving performance through giving criticism while maintaining good human relations.

AACSB: The primary AACSB learning standard skills developed through this exercise are analytic skills and communication abilities.

Preparation: You should have developed criticism to role-play in class.

Experience: You will give criticism, be criticized, and observe criticism following the guidelines for giving effective criticism.

Procedure 1
(2–4 minutes)

Break into groups of three. Make one or two groups of two if necessary. It is recommended that only one person per group use the example given in the preparation. The other two should have their own situations.

Each member selects a number from 1 to 3 to determine the order of giving, receiving, and observing criticism.

Procedure 2
(5–8 minutes)

Number 1 will give the criticism to number 2, and number 3 will be the observer. Number 1 explains the situation to numbers 2 and 3. If the person criticized would most likely make some comment in response, tell number 2 what it is so that he or she can make it. When numbers 2 and 3 understand the situation, number 1 role-plays giving the criticism while number 3 observes and takes notes on the observer sheet. When the role play is finished, the observer leads a discussion on how well number 1 criticized number 2 using the observer sheet.

Do not go on to the next criticism until asked to do so. If you finish early, wait for the others to finish.

Observer Sheet

For each question, think of what was done well and how the criticizer could improve. Telling others how to improve is criticism. The person criticized and the observer now criticize the criticizer.

1. Was criticism given immediately (if appropriate)?

2. Was the criticism performance-oriented?

3. Was the criticism specific and accurate?

4. Did the criticizer open on a positive note?

5. Did the criticizer close by repeating what action was needed (if appropriate)?

6. Do you think the person criticized will change her or his behavior? Why or why not?

7. Was criticism given in a way that will maintain human relations? Explain your answer.

Procedure 3
(5–8 minutes)

Number 2 will give the criticism to number 3, and number 1 will be the observer. Number 2 explains the situation to numbers 1 and 3. If the person criticized would most likely make some comment, tell number 3 what it is so that he or she can make it. When numbers 1 and 3 understand the situation, number 2 role-plays giving the criticism while number 1 observes and takes notes on the observer sheet. When the role play is finished, the observer leads a discussion on how well number 2 criticized number 3 using the observer sheet.

Do not go on to the next criticism until asked to do so. If you finish early, wait for the others to finish.

Procedure 4
(5–8 minutes)

Each person plays the role not yet played, following the same procedures as above.

Conclusion: The instructor leads a class discussion and/or makes concluding remarks.

Application (2–4 minutes):   What did I learn from this experience? How will I use this knowledge in the future to give effective criticism while maintaining human relations?

Sharing: Volunteers give their answers to the application section.

SKILL-BUILDING EXERCISE 6–5

Situational Communication

Preparation (Individual and Group)

BMV–6
Self-Assessment
Exercise 6–2

Begin this exercise by determining your preferred communication style in Self-Assessment Exercise 6–2.

Determining Your Preferred Communication Style

To determine your preferred communication style, select the *one* alternative that most closely describes what you would do in each of the 12 situations below. Do not be concerned with trying to pick the correct answer; select the alternative that best describes what *you* would actually do. Circle the letter *a, b, c,* or *d.* Ignore the _____ time _____ information _____ acceptance _____ capability/ _____ style and S _____ lines. They will be explained later.

_____ 1. Wendy, a knowledgeable person from another department, comes to you, the engineering supervisor, and requests that you design a special product to her specifications. You would: _____ time _____ information _____ acceptance _____ capability/ _____ style

a. Control the conversation and tell Wendy what you will do for her. S _____
b. Ask Wendy to describe the product. Once you understand it, you would present your ideas. Let her realize that you are concerned and want to help with your ideas. S _____

    c. Respond to Wendy's request by conveying understanding and support. Help clarify what is to be done by you. Offer ideas, but do it her way. S _____

    d. Find out what you need to know. Let Wendy know you will do it her way. S _____

_____ 2. Your department has designed a product that is to be fabricated by Saul's department. Saul has been with the company longer than you have; he knows his department. Saul comes to you to change the product design. You decide to:
_____ time _____ information _____ acceptance _____ capability/ _____ style

    a. Listen to the change and why it would be beneficial. If you believe Saul's way is better, change it; if not, explain why the original design is superior. If necessary, insist that it be done your way. S _____

    b. Tell Saul to fabricate it any way he wants to. S _____

    c. You are busy; tell Saul to do it your way. You don't have time to listen and argue with him. S _____

    d. Be supportive; make changes together as a team. S _____

_____ 3. Upper management has a decision to make. They call you to a meeting and tell you they need some information to solve a problem they describe to you. You:
_____ time _____ information _____ acceptance _____ capability/ _____ style

    a. Respond in a manner that conveys personal support and offer alternative ways to solve the problem. S _____

    b. Respond to their questions. S _____

    c. Explain how to solve the problem. S _____

    d. Show your concern by explaining how to solve the problem and why your solution is an effective one. S _____

_____ 4. You have a routine work order. The work order is to be placed verbally and completed in three days. Sue, the receiver, is very experienced and willing to be of service to you. You decide to: _____ time _____ information _____ acceptance _____ capability/ _____ style

    a. Explain your needs, but let Sue make the order decision. S _____

    b. Tell Sue what you want and why you need it. S _____

    c. Decide together what to order. S _____

    d. Simply give Sue the order. S _____

_____ 5. Work orders from the staff department normally take three days; however, you have an emergency and need the order today. Your colleague, Jim, the department supervisor, is knowledgeable and somewhat cooperative. You decide to:
_____ time _____ information _____ acceptance _____ capability/ _____ style

    a. Tell Jim that you need the work order by three o'clock and will return at that time to pick it up. S _____

    b. Explain the situation and how the organization will benefit by expediting the order. Volunteer to help in any way you can. S _____

    c. Explain the situation and ask Jim when the order will be ready. S _____

    d. Explain the situation and together come to a solution to your problem. S _____

_____ 6. Danielle, a peer with a record of high performance, has recently had a drop in productivity. Her problem is affecting your performance. You know Danielle has a family problem. You: _____ time _____ information _____ acceptance _____ capability/ _____ style

    a. Discuss the problem; help Danielle realize the problem is affecting her work and yours. Supportively discuss ways to improve the situation. S _____

    b. Tell the boss about it and let him decide what to do about it. S _____

    c. Tell Danielle to get back on the job. S _____

    d. Discuss the problem and tell Danielle how to solve the work situation; be supportive. S _____

_____ 7. You are a knowledgeable supervisor. You buy supplies from Peter regularly. He is an excellent salesperson and very knowledgeable about your situation. You are placing your weekly order. You decide to: _____ time _____ information _____ acceptance _____ capability/ _____ style

    a. Explain what you want and why. Develop a supportive relationship. S _____

    b. Explain what you want and ask Peter to recommend products. S _____

    c. Give Peter the order. S _____

    d. Explain your situation and allow Peter to make the order. S _____

_____ 8. Jean, a knowledgeable person from another department, has asked you to perform a routine staff function to her specifications. You decide to: _____ time _____ information _____ acceptance _____ capability/ _____ style

    a. Perform the task to her specifications without questioning her. S _____

    b. Tell her that you will do it the usual way. S _____

    c. Explain what you will do and why. S _____

    d. Show your willingness to help; offer alternative ways to do it. S _____

_____ 9. Tom, a salesperson, has requested an order for your department's services with a short delivery date. As usual, Tom claims it is a take-it-or-leave-it offer. He wants your decision now, or within a few minutes, because he is in the customer's office. Your action is to: _____ time _____ information _____ acceptance _____ capability/ _____ style

    a. Convince Tom to work together to come up with a later date. S _____

    b. Give Tom a yes or no answer. S _____

    c. Explain your situation and let Tom decide if you should take the order. S _____

    d. Offer an alternative delivery date. Work on your relationship; show your support. S _____

_____ 10. As a time-and-motion expert, you have been called in regard to a complaint about the standard time it takes to perform a job. As you analyze the entire job, you realize the one element of complaint should take longer, but other elements should take less time. The end result is a shorter total standard time for the job. You decide to: _____ time _____ information _____ acceptance _____ capability/ _____ style

    a. Tell the operator and foreman that the total time must be decreased and why. S _____

    b. Agree with the operator and increase the standard time. S _____

    c. Explain your findings. Deal with the operator and/or foreman's concerns, but ensure compliance with your new standard. S _____

    d. Together with the operator, develop a standard time. S _____

_____ 11. You approve budget allocations for projects. Marie, who is very competent in developing budgets, has come to you. You: _____ time _____ information _____ acceptance _____ capability/ _____ style

    a. Review the budget, make revisions, and explain them in a supportive way. Deal with concerns, but insist on your changes. S _____

    b. Review the proposal and suggest areas where changes may be needed. Make changes together, if needed. S _____

    c. Review the proposed budget, make revisions, and explain them. S _____

    d. Answer any questions or concerns Marie has and approve the budget as is. S _____

_____ 12. You are a sales manager. A customer has offered you a contract for your product with a short delivery date. The offer is open for two days. The contract would be profitable for you and the organization. The cooperation of the production department is essential to meet the deadline. Tim, the production manager, and you do not get along very well because of your repeated requests for quick delivery. Your action is to: _____ time _____ information _____ acceptance _____ capability/ _____ style

a. Contact Tim and try to work together to complete the contract. S _____

b. Accept the contract and convince Tim in a supportive way to meet the obligation. S _____

c. Contact Tim and explain the situation. Ask him if you and he should accept the contract, but let him decide. S _____

d. Accept the contract. Contact Tim and tell him to meet the obligation. If he resists, tell him you will go to his boss. S _____

To determine your preferred communication style, in the table below, circle the letter corresponding to the alternative you chose in situations 1 to 12. The column headings indicate the style you selected.

	Autocratic (S-A)	Consultative (S-C)	Participative (S-P)	Laissez-Faire (S-L)
1.	*a*	*b*	*c*	*d*
2.	*c*	*a*	*d*	*b*
3.	*c*	*d*	*a*	*b*
4.	*d*	*b*	*c*	*a*
5.	*a*	*b*	*d*	*c*
6.	*c*	*d*	*a*	*b*
7.	*c*	*a*	*b*	*d*
8.	*b*	*c*	*d*	*a*
9.	*b*	*d*	*a*	*c*
10.	*a*	*c*	*d*	*b*
11.	*c*	*a*	*b*	*d*
12.	*d*	*b*	*a*	*c*
Total				

Add the number of circled items per column. Adding the numbers in the Total row should equal 12. The column with the highest number represents your preferred communication style. There is no one best style in all situations. The more evenly distributed the numbers are between the four styles, the more flexible your communication style is. A total of 0 or 1 in any column may indicate a reluctance to use that style. You could have problems in situations calling for the use of that style.

Situational Communication Styles

Following is the process used with each of the four situational supervisory styles. Notice that behavior can be characterized as a combination of two dimensions—task and relationship. In task behavior, the sender tells the receiver what to do and how to do it; performance is closely supervised. In relationship behavior, the sender listens to the other person in an effort to develop support, trust, and respect; performance is not closely supervised. Both task and relationship can be described as high or low depending on the amount of emphasis placed on each of the two dimensions during communication.

One style, **autocratic communication style (S-A),** *demonstrates high task–low relationship behavior (HT–LR), initiating a closed presentation.* The other party has little, if any, information and is low in capability.

- *Initiation/Response.* You initiate and control the communication with minimal, if any, response.

- *Presentation/Elicitation.* You make a presentation letting the other parties know they are expected to comply with your message; there is little, if any, elicitation.
- *Closed/Open.* You use a closed presentation; you will not consider the receiver's input.

The **consultative communication style (S-C)** *demonstrates high task–high relationship behavior (HT–HR), using a closed presentation for the task with an open elicitation for the relationship.* The other party has moderate information and capability.

- *Initiation/Response.* You initiate the communication by letting the other party know that you want him or her to buy into your influence. You desire some response.
- *Presentation/Elicitation.* Both are used. You use elicitation to determine the goal of the communication. For example, you may ask questions to determine the situation and follow up with a presentation. When the communication goal is known, little task elicitation is needed. Relationship communication is elicited to determine the interest of the other party and acceptance of the message. The open elicitation should show your concern for the other party's point of view and motivate him or her to follow your influence.
- *Closed/Open.* You are closed to having the message accepted (task), but open to the person's feelings (relationship). Be empathetic.

The **participative communication style (S-P)** *demonstrates low task–high relationship behavior (LT–HR), responding with open elicitation, some initiation, and little presentation.* The other party is high in information and capability.

- *Initiation/Response.* You respond with some initiation. You want to help the other party solve a problem or get him or her to help you solve one. You are helpful and convey personal support.
- *Presentation/Elicitation.* Elicitation can occur with little presentation. Your role is to elicit the other party's ideas on how to reach objectives.
- *Closed/Open.* Open communication is used. If you participate well, the other party will come to a solution you can accept. If not, you may have to reject the other party's message.

Another style, **laissez-faire communication style (S-L),** *demonstrates low task–low relationship behavior (LT–LR), responding with the necessary open presentation.* The other party is outstanding in information and capability.

- *Initiation/Response.* You respond to the other party with little, if any, initiation.
- *Presentation/Elicitation.* You present the other party with the information, structure, and so forth, that the sender wants.
- *Closed/Open.* Open communication is used. You convey that the other party is in charge; you will accept the message.

Situational Variables

When selecting the appropriate communication style, you should consider four variables: time, information, acceptance, and capability. Answering the questions related to each variable below can help you select the appropriate style for the situation.

Time   Do I have enough time to use two-way communication? When there is no time, the other three variables are not considered; the autocratic style is appropriate. When time is available, any of the other styles may be appropriate, depending on the other variables. Time is a relative term; in one situation a few minutes may be considered a short time period, while in another a month may be a short period of time.

Information   Do I have the necessary information to communicate my message, make a decision, or take action? When you have all the information you need, the autocratic style may be appropriate. When you have some of the information, the consultative style may be appropriate. When you have little information, the participative or laissez-faire style may be appropriate.

Acceptance   Will the other party accept my message without any input? If the receiver will accept the message, the autocratic style may be appropriate. If the receiver will be reluctant to accept it, the consultative style may be appropriate. If the receiver will reject the message, the participative or laissez-faire style may be appropriate to gain acceptance. There are situations where acceptance is critical to success, such as in the area of implementing changes.

Capability   Capability has two parts:

Ability   Does the other party have the experience or knowledge to participate in two-way communication? Will the receiver put the organization's goals ahead of personal needs or goals?

Motivation   Does the other party want to participate?
When the other party is low in capability, the autocratic style may be appropriate; moderate in capability, the consultative style may be appropriate; high in capability, the participative style may be appropriate; outstanding in capability, the laissez-faire style may be appropriate.

Capability levels can change from one task to another. For example, a professor may have outstanding capability in classroom teaching, but be low in capability for advising students.

Selecting Communication Styles

Successful managers understand different styles of communication and select communication styles based on the situation. There are three steps to follow when selecting the appropriate communication style in a given situation.

Step 1: Diagnose the situation.   Answer the questions for each of the four situation variables. In Self-Assessment Exercise 6–2 you were asked to select one alternative situation. You were told to ignore the _____ time _____ information _____ acceptance _____ capability/ _____ style and S _____ lines. Now you will complete this part in the In-Class Skill-Building Exercise 6–5 by placing the style letters (S-A, S-C, S-P, S-L) on the lines provided for each of the 12 situations.

Step 2: Select the appropriate style for the situation.   After analyzing the four variables, select the appropriate style for the situation. In some situations, where variables support conflicting styles, select the style of the most important variable for the situation. For example, capability may be outstanding (C-4), but you have all the information needed (S-A). If the information is more important, use the autocratic style even though the capability is outstanding. When doing In-Class Skill-Building Exercise 6–5, place the letters (S-A, S-C, S-P, S-L) for the appropriate styles on the _____ style lines.

Step 3: Implement the appropriate communication style.   During In-Class Skill-Building Exercise 6–5, you will identify one of the four communication styles for each alternative action; place the S-A, S-C, S-P, or S-L on the S _____ lines. Select the alternative *a, b, c,* or *d* that represents the appropriate communication for each of the 12 situations.

The table below summarizes the material in this section. Use it to determine the appropriate communication style in situation 1 below and during In-Class Skill-Building Exercise 6–5.

Situational Communications Model

Step 1: Diagnose the Situation

Resource	Use of Communication Style
Time	No S-A
	Yes S-A, S-C, S-P, or S-L
Information	All S-A
	Some S-C
	Little S-P or S-L
Acceptance	Accept S-A
	Reluctance S-C
	Reject S-P or S-L
Capability	Low S-A
	Moderate S-C
	High S-P
	Outstanding S-L

Step 2: Select the Appropriate Style for the Situation

Autocratic (S-A)
High task–low relationship
Initiate a closed presentation.
Consultative (S-C)
High task–high relationship
Initiate a closed presentation for the task. Use open elicitation for feelings and relationship.
Participative (S-P)
Low task–high relationship
Respond with open elicitation, some initiation, and little presentation.
Laissez-faire (S-L)
Low task–low relationship
Respond with the necessary open presentation.

Step 3. Implement the Appropriate Communication Style

During In-Class Skill-Building Exercise 6–5, you will identify each communication style and select the alternative (*a, b, c,* or *d*) that represents the appropriate style.

Determining the Appropriate Communication Style for Situation 1
Step 1: Diagnose the situation.   Answer the four variable questions from the model, and place the letters on the four variable lines below.

1. Wendy, a knowledgeable person from another department, comes to you, the engineering supervisor, and requests that you design a special product to her specifications. You would:

   time _____ information _____ acceptance _____ capability/ _____ style

   a. Control the conversation and tell Wendy what you will do for her. S _____

   b. Ask Wendy to describe the product. Once you understand it, you would present your ideas. Let her realize that you are concerned and want to help with your ideas. S _____

   c. Respond to Wendy's request by conveying understanding and support. Help clarify what is to be done by you. Offer ideas, but do it her way. S _____

   d. Find out what you need to know. Let Wendy know you will do it her way. S _____

Step 2: Select the appropriate style for the situation. Review the four variables. If they are all consistent, select one style. If they are conflicting, select the most important variable as the style to use. Place its letters (S-A, S-C, S-P, or S-L) on the style line.

Step 3: Select the appropriate action. Review the four alternative actions. Identify the communication style for each, placing its letters on the S _____ line then check the appropriate match alternative.

Let's see how you did.

1. *Time* is available; it can be either S-C, S-P, or S-L. *Information:* You have little information, so you need to use a participative or laissez-faire style to find out what Wendy wants done: S-P or S-L. *Acceptance:* If you try to do it your way rather than Wendy's way, she will most likely reject it. You need to use a participative or laissez-faire style: S-P or S-L. *Capability:* Wendy is knowledgeable and is highly capable: S-P.

2. Reviewing the four variables, you see that there is a mixture of S-P and S-L. Since you are an engineer, it is appropriate to participate with Wendy to give her what she needs. Therefore, the choice is S-P.

3. *Alternative a* is S-A; this is the autocratic style, high task–low relationship. *Alternative b* is S-C; this is the consultative style, high task–high relationship. *Alternative c* is S-P; this is the participative style, low task–high relationship. *Alternative d* is S-L; this is laissez-faire, low task–low relationship behavior.

If you selected *c* as your action, you chose the most appropriate action for the situation. This was a three-point answer. If you selected *d* as your answer, this is also a good alternative; it scores two points. If you selected *b,* you get one point for overdirecting. If you selected *a,* you get zero points; this is too much directing and will most likely hurt communication.

The better you match your communication style to the situation, the more effective you will be at communicating.

In-Class Exercise	*Objectives:* To develop your ability to communicate using the appropriate style for the situation.

Objectives: To develop your ability to communicate using the appropriate style for the situation.

AACSB: The primary AACSB learning standard skills developed through this exercise are analytic skills and communication abilities.

Preparation: You should have completed the 12 situations in Self-Assessment Exercise 6–2. In the self-assessment, you were selecting the alternative that *you* would choose in the situation. In this part of the skill-building exercise, you are trying to select the *most appropriate* alternative that will result in the most effective communication. Thus, you may be selecting different answers.

Experience: You will work at selecting the appropriate style for the 12 situations in Self-Assessment Exercise 6–2. On the time, information, acceptance, and capability lines, place the letters S-A, S-C, S-P, or S-L, whichever is appropriate for the situation. Based on your diagnoses, select the one style you would use. Place the letters S-A, S-C, S-P, or S-L on the style line. On the four S lines write the letters S-A, S-C, S-P, or S-L to identify each style being used.

Procedure 1
(3–8 minutes)

The instructor reviews the Situational Communications Model and explains how to apply it to determine the appropriate style for situation 1.

Procedure 2
(6–8 minutes)

Turn to situation 2. Using the model, select the appropriate style. If you have time, identify each alternative style (3–4 minutes). The instructor goes over the recommended answers (3–4 minutes).

Procedure 3
(20–50 minutes)

A. Break into groups of two or three. As a team, apply the model to situations 3 through 7 (15–20 minutes). The instructor will go over the appropriate answers when all teams are done or the time is up (4–6 minutes).

B. (Optional) Break into new groups of two or three and do situations 8 through 12 (15–20 minutes). The instructor will go over the appropriate answers (4–6 minutes).

Conclusion: The instructor leads a class discussion and/or makes concluding remarks.

Application (2–4 minutes):   What did I learn from this experience? How will I use this knowledge in the future?

Sharing: Volunteers give their answers to the application section.

A N S W E R S   T O   T R U E / F A L S E Q U E S T I O N S

1. F. The current trends are toward *LESS* specialized jobs, *less* following of the chain of command, *greater* spans of management, and *decentralized* decision making.
2. F. Small companies commonly use functional departmentalization.
3. T.
4. T.
5. F. For simple, routine tasks, the wheel, chain, and Y work fast and accurately. The circle and all-channel networks are best for complex, nonroutine tasks.
6. T.
7. F. Emotional employees don't think logically until they are calm again. After you deal with the emotion, you can logically deal with the content (solve the problem).
8. F. Chastising, using sarcasm, and joking should not take place when giving criticism.

Dealing with Conflict

After completing this chapter, you should be able to:

1. Describe the three ego states of transactional analysis.

2. Explain the three types of transactions.

3. Identify the differences between passive, aggressive, and assertive behavior.

4. List the four steps of assertive behavior.

5. Explain when a conflict exists.

6. State when and how to use five conflict management styles.

7. List the steps of initiating, responding to, and mediating conflict resolutions.

8. Define the following 14 key terms (in order of appearance in the chapter):

transactional analysis	**accommodating conflict style**
ego states	**compromising conflict style**
types of transactions	**collaborating conflict style**
assertiveness	**initiating conflict resolution steps**
conflict	**XYZ model**
forcing conflict style	**responding to conflict resolution steps**
avoiding conflict style	**mediating conflict resolution steps**

How Interpersonal Dynamics Affect Behavior, Human Relations, and Performance

Transactional Analysis

    Ego States

    Types of Transactions

    Life Positions and Stroking

Assertiveness

    Passive Behavior

    Aggressive Behavior

    Passive-Aggressive Behavior

    Assertive Behavior

    Dealing with Anger and Preventing Workplace Violence

Conflict Management Styles

    Reasons for Conflict and Avoiding Conflicts

    Forcing Conflict Style

    Avoiding Conflict Style

    Accommodating Conflict Style

    Compromising Conflict Style

    Collaborating Conflict Style

Resolving Conflicts with the Collaborating Conflict Style

    Initiating Conflict Resolution

    Responding to Conflict Resolution

    Mediating Conflict Resolution

Putting It All Together

Larry and Helen work together doing the same job at Harvey's, a department store in Springfield. They share a special calculator because it is expensive and it is used for only part of their job. The calculator is generally kept in one person's possession until the other person requests it. Recently, the amount of time each needs to use the calculator has increased.

When Larry wants the calculator, he says, "I need the calculator now" (in a bold, intimidating voice), and Helen gives it to him, even when she is using it. When Helen needs the calculator, she says, "I don't like to bother you, but I need the calculator." If Larry is using it, he tells Helen that he will give it to her when he is finished with it, and Helen says, "OK." Helen doesn't think this arrangement is fair and is getting upset with Larry. But she hasn't said anything to Larry yet. Larry comes over to Helen's desk, and this conversation takes place:

LARRY: I need the calculator right now.

HELEN: I'm sick and tired of your pushing me around. Go back to your desk, and I'll bring it to you when I'm good and ready.

LARRY: What's wrong with you? You've never acted like this before.

HELEN: Just take the calculator and go back to your desk and leave me alone.

LARRY: *(Says nothing; just takes the calculator and leaves.)*

HELEN: *(Watches Larry walk back to his desk with the calculator, feels a bit guilty, and thinks to herself)* Why do I let little annoyances build up until I explode and end up yelling at people? It's rather childish behavior to let people walk all over me, then to reverse and be tough and rude. I wish I could stand up for my rights in a positive way without hurting my relations.

HOW INTERPERSONAL DYNAMICS AFFECT BEHAVIOR, HUMAN RELATIONS, AND PERFORMANCE

This is the third and last chapter on developing interpersonal skills. Interpersonal dynamics are the give-and-take behavior between people during human relations,[1] and interpersonal dynamics grow increasing complex as more people interact.[2] The three topics of this chapter—transactional analysis, assertiveness, and conflict management—all involve interpersonal dynamics through communication. All three topics focus on dealing with your *emotions* and those of others in an effective way to enhance behavior, human relations, and performance. Dealing with emotions, your own and others', is part of emotional intelligence.[3]

Transactional analysis is a method for determining how people interact. When we interact, behavior can be passive, aggressive, or assertive. During human relations, transactions can go poorly, people can be aggressive, and it is common for people to disagree and be in *conflict.* Behavior used when people agree and when they are in conflict differs, and those differences affect human relations.[4] How teams manage conflict is a crucial factor in their success.[5]

When you interact with people, you respond (transactional analysis). You can try to push people around, you can let people push you around, or you can stand up for your rights (assertiveness).[6] When you are in disagreement with others (conflict), you can decide to ignore or to resolve your differences.[7] Dealing with your emotions and transacting with people on the appropriate level, assertively standing up for your rights, and resolving your conflicts without hurting human relations will improve your effectiveness in organizations and in your personal life. That's what this chapter is about.

TRANSACTIONAL ANALYSIS

Before we begin, complete Self-Assessment Exercise 7–1 to determine your preferred transactional analysis (TA) style.

Your Preferred Transactional Analysis Style

Turn to Skill-Building Exercise 7–1, Transactional Analysis, on page 262. Ignore the directions, steps 1 to 4. Go directly to the 10 situations. Put yourself in the responder's position (1—Sue, 2—Saul, . . . 10—Mike), and place a check mark after the letter (*not* on the line) of the one response that best describes what you would say in each situation. Be honest; don't try to pick the response you think is correct. After selecting your 10 responses, circle the letter of your response for each situation in the table below.

Situation	Critical Parent	Sympathetic Parent	Natural Child	Adapted Child	Adult
1.	a	b	d	c	e
2.	d	c	e	a	b
3.	b	d	a	c	e
4.	c	e	b	d	a
5.	e	b	d	a	c
6.	a	b	e	d	c
7.	e	a	b	c	d
8.	b	c	e	d	a
9.	a	c	d	b	e
10.	a	e	d	c	b
Total					

Scoring: Add the number of letters circled in each column. The number in each column should be between 0 and 10, and the total of all columns should equal 10. The column with your highest total is your preferred TA style. If it's not adult, or even if it is, you may want to improve your TA behavior.

Transactional analysis (TA) *is a method of understanding behavior in interpersonal dynamics.* In fact, there is an International Transactional Analysis Association (www.itaa-net.org) that publishes the *Transactional Analysis Journal.* Eric Berne developed TA in 1960 in the field of psychology,[8] and TA is being used today for healthy development[9] in psychiatry[10] and social psychology.[11] A few years after its development, Berne applied TA to business in his bestselling book, *Games People Play.*[12] Today, TA is being used in business to improve relationships,[13] communications,[14] handling emotions,[15] professional development,[16] understanding of self,[17] empathy for others,[18] resolving conflict,[19] building trust,[20] supervisory success,[21] and consulting results,[22] as well as to reduce stress,[23] and improve education.[24] Clearly then, studying TA can improve your ability to deal with emotions and develop better human relations.[25]

In this section you will learn about your preferred TA style (called ego state in TA jargon), the types of human relations transactions you have, and your attitude toward yourself and others (called life positions). You will also learn about giving positive and negative feedback (called stroking) during human relations.

Learning Outcome

1. Describe the three ego
   states of transactional
   analysis.

Ego States

According to Berne, we all have three major ego states that affect our behavior or the way we transact through communication. The three **ego states** *are the parent, child, and adult.* We change ego states throughout the day; even during a single discussion, a series of transactions can take place between different ego states. Your parent, child, and adult ego states interact with other people's parent, child, and adult ego states. Understanding the ego state of the person you are interacting with can help you understand his or her behavior and how to transact in an effective way.[26]

Parent Ego State   When the parent ego state is in control, people behave from one of two perspectives:

1. *Critical parent.* When you behave and respond with advising responses (Chapter 5) that are critical, judgmental, opinionated, demanding, disapproving, disciplining, and so on, you are in the critical parent ego state. People in the critical parent ego state use a lot of do's and don'ts and control the conversation.[27] Managers using the autocratic style tend to be in the critical parent ego state because they use high task-directive behavior.

2. *Sympathetic parent.* On the other hand, you can be a different type of parent. When you behave and respond with reassuring responses (Chapter 5) that are protecting, permitting, consoling, caring, nurturing, and so on, you are in the sympathetic parent ego state. Managers using the consultative and participative styles tend to be in the sympathetic parent state because they are using high supportive-relationship behavior.

Child Ego State   When the child ego state is in control, people behave from one of two perspectives:

1. *Natural child.* When you behave and respond with probing responses (Chapter 5) that show curiosity, intimacy, fun, joyfulness, fantasy, impulsiveness, and so on, you are in the natural child ego state. Successful managers tend not to operate continually from the natural child ego state.

2. *Adapted child.* When you behave and respond with confronting, advising responses (Chapter 5) that express rebelliousness, pouting, anger, fear, anxiety, inadequacy, procrastination, finger-pointing and so on, you are in the aggressive, adapted child ego state.[28] Managers should avoid behaving from the adapted child ego state because this type of behavior often leads to the employee becoming emotional and behaving in a similar manner. When managers are transacting with an employee in this ego state, they should not react with similar behavior, but should be in the adult ego state.[29]

Adult Ego State   When the adult ego state is in control, people behave in a thinking, rational, calculating, factual, unemotional manner. The adult gathers information, reasons things out, estimates probabilities, and makes decisions with cool and calm behavior. When communicating in the adult ego state, you avoid becoming the victim of the other person by controlling your response to the situation.[30]

Generally, the most effective behavior, human relations, and performance come from the adult ego state. When interacting with others, you should be aware of their ego state. Are they acting like a parent, a child, or an adult? Identifying their ego state will help you understand why they are behaving the way they are and help you determine which ego state you should use during the interaction. For example, if the person is acting like an adult, you most likely should too. If the person is acting like a child, it may be appropriate for you to act like a parent rather than an adult. And there are times when it is appropriate to act out of the child ego state and have a good time.

Learning Outcome

2. Explain the three types of transactions.

Types of Transactions

Within ego states there are three different **types of transactions:** *complementary, crossed, and ulterior.*

Complementary Transactions   A complementary transaction occurs when the sender of the message gets the intended response from the receiver. For example, an employee makes a mistake and, wanting some sympathy, apologizes to the boss. Employee: "I just dropped the thing when I was almost done. Now I have to do it all over again." Supervisor: "It happens to all of us; don't worry about it." This complementary transaction is illustrated below.

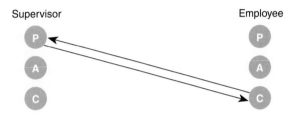

Another example of a complementary transaction is a supervisor who wants a job done and delegates it, expecting the employee to do it. The supervisor behaves on an adult-to-adult level. Supervisor: "Please get this order ready for me by two o'clock." Employee: "I'll have it done before two o'clock, no problem."

Generally, complementary transactions result in more effective communication with fewer hurt feelings and arguments. In other words, they help human relations and performance.[31] Exceptions are if an employee uses an adapted child or critical parent ego state and the supervisor does too. These complementary transactions can lead to problems.

WORK APPLICATIONS

1. Give an example of a complementary transaction you experienced. Be sure to identify the ego states involved.

Crossed Transactions   Crossed transactions occur when the sender of a message does not get the expected response from the receiver. Let's return to our first example. Employee: "I just dropped the thing when I was almost done. Now I have to do it all over again." Supervisor: "You are so clumsy." This crossed transaction is illustrated below.

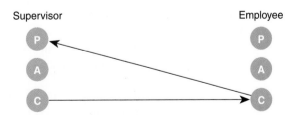

Back to our second example. Supervisor: "Please get this order ready for me by two o'clock." Employee: "Why do I have to do it? Why don't you do it yourself? I'm busy." This crossed transaction is an adult-to-adapted-child response.

Generally, crossed transactions result in surprise, disappointment, and hurt feelings for the sender of the message. The unexpected response often gets the person emotional, which often results in his or her changing to the adapted child ego state, which causes the communication to deteriorate further. Crossed transactions often end in arguments and hurt human relations.[32]

Crossed transactions can be helpful when the negative parent or child ego response is crossed with an adult response. This crossover may result in the preferred adult-to-adult conversation.

WORK APPLICATIONS

2. Give an example of a crossed transaction you experienced. Be sure to identify the ego states involved.

Ulterior Transactions   Ulterior, or hidden, transactions occur when the words seem to be coming from one ego state, but in reality the words or behaviors are coming from another. For example, after a training program, one of the participants came up to a consultant and asked for advice in an adult ego state. When the consultant gave advice, the participant twice had quick responses as to why the advice would not work (child rather than adult behavior). The consultant realized that what the participant actually wanted was sympathetic understanding for his situation, not advice. The consultant stopped making suggestions and listened actively, using reflecting responses (Chapter 5). The consultant changed from the adult to the sympathetic parent ego state in order to have a complementary transaction.

Sometimes people don't know what they want or how to ask for it in a direct way, so they use ulterior transactions. When possible, it is best to avoid ulterior transactions because they tend to waste time. Avoid making people search for your hidden meaning. Plan your message (Chapter 5) before you send it. When receiving messages, look for ulterior transactions and turn them into complementary transactions.

WORK APPLICATIONS

3. Give an example of an ulterior transaction you experienced. Be sure to identify the ego states involved.

APPLICATION SITUATIONS

Transactional Analysis

AS 7–1

Identify each transaction as being:

A. Complementary   B. Crossed   C. Ulterior

_____ 1. "Would you help me move this package over there?" "Sure thing."

_____ 2. "Will you serve on my committee?" "Yes, I think the experience will be helpful to me" (thinking—I want to get to know you, you're cute).

_____ 3. "Will you help me fill out this report?" "You have done several of them. Do it on your own; then I will check it for you."

_____ 4. "How much will you pay me to do the job?" "$10." "What! You're either joking or trying to take advantage of me."

_____ 5. "You're lying." "No, I'm not! You're the one who is lying."

EXHIBIT 7.1 | Life
Positions

EXHIBIT 7.1 | Life Positions

Life Positions and Stroking

Life Positions   As stated in Chapter 3, attitudes affect your behavior and human relations. Within the transactional analysis framework, you have attitudes toward yourself and toward others. Positive attitudes are described as "OK," and negative attitudes are described as "not OK." The four life positions are illustrated in Exhibit 7.1.

The most desirable life position is shown in the upper right-hand box: "I'm OK—You're OK." With a positive attitude toward yourself and others, you have a greater chance for having adult-to-adult ego state communication. You can change your attitudes (Chapter 3), and you should if they are not positive, to create win–win situations. People with positive self-concepts (Chapter 3) tend to have positive attitudes.

Stroking   Stroking is any behavior that implies recognition of another's presence. Strokes can be positive and make people feel good about themselves, or they can be negative and hurt people in some way.[33]

We all want praise and recognition. Giving praise (positive strokes) is a powerful motivation technique that is easy to use and costs nothing.[34] We should all give positive strokes and avoid giving negative strokes.

Through work and effort, you can learn to control your emotional behavior and transact on an adult-to-adult level in most situations.[35] Skill-Building Exercise 7–1 presents 10 situations in which you are required to identify the ego states being used to help you communicate on an adult-to-adult level.

In the opening case, Larry was behaving out of the critical parent ego state. He showed disapproval of Helen by asking, "What's wrong with you? You never acted like this before." Helen responded to Larry's request for the calculator from the adapted child ego state. Helen was rebellious and showed her anger by saying, "I'm sick and tired of your pushing me around. Go back to your desk and I'll bring it to you when I'm good and ready." They had a crossed transaction because Larry opened in his usual manner but was surprised when Helen did not respond in her typical manner. Larry was in the "I'm OK—You're not OK" life position, while Helen was in the "I'm not OK—You're not OK" life position. Both used negative strokes.

WORK APPLICATIONS

4. Identify your present or past boss's life position and use of stroking.

Learning Outcome

3. Identify the differences between passive, aggressive, and assertive behavior.

ASSERTIVENESS

Begin this section by completing Self-Assessment Exercise 7–2 to determine your use of the assertiveness style, which is sometimes included with the situational communication styles discussed in Chapter 6.

Your Use of the Assertiveness Style

Turn to Skill-Building Exercise 7–2, Assertiveness, on page 265. Ignore the directions. Go directly to the 10 situations. Put yourself in the situation, and place a check mark after the letter (*not* on the line) of the one response that best describes what you would say or do in each situation. Be honest; don't try to pick the response you think is correct. After selecting your 10 responses, circle the letter of your response for each situation in the table below.

Situation	Passive		Assertive	Aggressive	
1.	b	d	c	a	e
2.	d	e	c	a	b
3.	c	e	a	b	d
4.	b	d	c	a	e
5.	a	e	b	c	d
6.	a	d	b	c	e
7.	b	d	a	c	e
8.	b	c	d	a	e
9.	a	c	d	b	e
10.	b	c	a	d	e
Total					

Scoring: Add the number of letters circled in each column. The number in each column should be between 0 and 10, and the total of all three columns should equal 10. The column with your highest total is your preferred style. If it's not assertive, or even if it is, you may want to improve your assertiveness behavior.

Arnold Lazarus popularized what is known as assertiveness in the 1970s,[36] and others have since adapted his work.[37] Hundreds of organizations have trained their employees to be assertive, including HSBC, Mazda, Ford Motor Co., and the U.S. government. Walt Disney Productions trains all its managers in assertiveness. Through assertiveness training, people learn how to deal with anxiety-producing situations in productive ways.[38] Participants learn to express feelings, ask for favors, give and receive compliments, request behavior changes, and refuse unreasonable requests.[39] Trainees learn to ask for what they want in a direct, straightforward, deliberate, and honest way that conveys self-confidence without being obnoxious or abusive. When people stand up for their rights without violating the rights of others, they are using assertive behavior.[40]

Assertiveness *is the process of expressing thoughts and feelings while asking for what one wants in an appropriate way.* You need to present your message without falling into stereotypical "too pushy" (aggressive) or "not tough enough" (nonassertive–passive) traps.[41]

Assertiveness Is Becoming More Global   For example, the employees in Thailand are becoming more assertive, and the Japanese now include more strategies of assertiveness.

Being assertive is generally the most productive behavior. However, there are situations in which passive or aggressive behavior is appropriate. These situations are discussed in the section on conflict resolution. Next we discuss passive, aggressive, passive–aggressive, and assertive behavior. We end with guidelines on how to deal with anger and prevent workplace violence.

Passive Behavior

Passive or nonassertive behavior comes primarily through the obedient child or supportive parent ego state. Passive people are in an "I'm not OK" life position. Passive behavior is an avoidance of behavior or an accommodation of the other party's wishes without standing up for one's own rights.[42] It involves self-denial and sacrifice.

Nonverbal communication of the passive person includes downcast eyes, soft voice, helpless gestures, and slouched posture. Passive people tend to deny the importance of things. They rationalize things—"It doesn't matter to me"—and take an attitude of "It's not my responsibility, let someone else do it." Passive people are often internally distressed and in pain. Becoming assertive decreases stress.[43]

When people know someone is passive, they tend to take advantage of the person. They make unreasonable requests, knowing the person cannot say no, and refuse to meet the passive person's rare mild request. When the passive person does speak, others tend not to listen and tend to interrupt. In fact, men freely interrupt women and dismiss women's ideas—and many women tolerate this![44]

Passive people often have a poor self-concept and are unhappy. Passivity is often based on fear: fear of failure, fear of rejection, fear of displeasing others, fear of retaliation, fear of hurting others, fear of being hurt, fear of getting into trouble, and so on. Some women are passive as a result of a lifetime of conditioning in which they were taught to please others and to give way to men. Many men are also passive; you may know some.

Continued passive behavior is usually unproductive for both the individual and the organization.[45] If you are always passive, determine what really is important, and stand up for your rights in an assertive way.

Aggressive Behavior

Aggressive behavior comes primarily through the adapted child and the critical parent ego states. Aggressive people are demanding, tough, rude, and pushy.[46] They insist on getting their own way and use force to gain control. They are very competitive, hate to lose to the point of cheating, and tend to violate the rights of others to get what they want.[47]

Nonverbal communication used by aggressive people includes glaring and frowning to convey coldness. Aggressive people tend to speak loudly and quickly with threatening gestures and an intimidating posture.[48]

When faced with aggressive behavior, the other party often retaliates with aggressive behavior (fights back) or withdraws and gives in (takes flight). People often avoid contact with the aggressive person or prepare themselves for a fight when transacting.[49]

Aggressive people seem to be self-confident, but their behavior is more often the result of a poor self-concept. They are in an "I'm not OK" life position, but consistently try to prove they are OK by beating and controlling others. They must win to prove their self-worth, and because they violate others' rights, they are often unhappy and feel guilty. They seem to have a complaint about everything. Some women become aggressive because they feel it is necessary to compete in the business world. No one should feel as though he or she has to be aggressive to be taken seriously; assertiveness is more effective.[50]

Continuous use of aggressive behavior is usually destructive to the individual and the organization.[51] If you are continually aggressive, work at becoming more sensitive to the needs of others. Learn to replace aggressive behavior with assertive behavior.

Violence is clearly aggressive behavior at the extreme level. Violence is an increasing danger in the workplace as workloads and stress levels rise.[52] Workplace violence remains a security concern today. Because anger and workplace violence are so important, we will discuss these issues separately later in this section.

Passive–Aggressive Behavior

Passive–aggressive behavior is displayed in three major ways:

1. The person uses both types of behavior sporadically. For example, a manager may be very aggressive with subordinates, yet passive with superiors. Or the person may be passive one day or moment and aggressive the next. This type of person is difficult to work with because no one knows what to expect.[53]

2. The person uses passive behavior during the situation, then shortly after uses aggressive behavior. For example, an employee may agree to do something, then leave and slam the door, yell at the next person he or she sees, or sabotage the task.

3. The person uses passive behavior but inside is building up hostility. After the repeated behavior happens often enough, the passive person becomes aggressive. Too often the person who was attacked really doesn't understand the full situation and blames everything on the exploder, rather than examining his or her self-behavior, and changing. The person who becomes aggressive often feels guilty. The end result is usually hurt human relations and no change in the situation.[54] For example, during a meeting, Carl interrupted June three times when she was speaking. June said nothing each time, but was building up hostility. The fourth time Carl interrupted June, she attacked him by yelling at him for being so inconsiderate of her. He simply said, "What's wrong with you?" It would have been better for June to assertively tell Carl not to interrupt her the first time he did it.

If you use passive–aggressive behavior, try to learn to be assertive on a consistent basis and you will be easier to work with. You will also get the results you want more often.

WORK APPLICATIONS

5. Recall an example of when you used or observed passive–aggressive behavior. How did it affect human relations?

Assertive Behavior

Assertive behavior comes through the adult ego state, with an "I'm OK—You're OK" life position. As stated earlier, the assertive person expresses feelings and thoughts and asks for things without aggressive behavior. The person stands up for his or her rights without violating the rights of others.[55]

The nonverbal communication of the assertive person includes positive facial expressions such as smiling and eye contact, pleasant voice qualities, firm gestures, and erect posture.

People who use assertive behavior tend to have a positive self-concept. They are not threatened by others, and they do not let others control their behavior. When others are out of the adult ego state, people using assertive behavior continue to transact in an adult ego state. Assertive people project a positive image (Chapter 3) of being confident, friendly, and honest. Using assertive behavior wins the respect of others.[56] Use it on a consistent basis.

Being Assertive Assertive behavior is generally the most effective method of getting what you want while not taking advantage of others.[57] Being assertive can create a win–win situation.[58] Note that assertive behavior is different from aggressive behavior and that the terms are not interchangeable.[59] To better understand the differences between passive, aggressive, and assertive behavior, see Exhibit 7.2. The phrases can be thought of as do's and don'ts. Do make assertive phrases and don't make passive and aggressive phrases. But remember, there are times when passive and aggressive behavior are appropriate. You will learn when later in this chapter.

Below is an example that puts it all together. When a person who is talking is interrupted, he or she can behave in one of three ways:

1. Passively. The person can say and do nothing.

2. Aggressively. The person can say, "I'm talking; mind your manners and wait your turn," in a loud voice, while pointing to the interrupter.

3. Assertively. The person can say, "Excuse me; I haven't finished making my point," with a smile and in a friendly but firm voice.

EXHIBIT 7.2 | Passive, Assertive, and Aggressive Phrases

Passive Phrases

Passive speakers use self-limiting, qualifying expressions without stating their position or needs.

- I don't know/care (when I do).
- It doesn't matter (when it does).
- Either one/way is fine with me (when I have a preference).
- I'm sorry (when I don't mean it).
- It's just my opinion . . .
- I don't want to bother you, but . . .
- It's not really important, but . . .

Assertive Phrases

Assertive speakers state their position or needs without violating the rights of others.

- I don't understand . . .
- I need/want/prefer . . .
- I would like . . .
- No, I won't be able to . . .
- I'd prefer that you don't tell me these jokes anymore.
- My opinion is . . .
- I need some of your time to . . .
- I thought that you would like to know . . .

Aggressive Phrases

Aggressive speakers state their position or needs while violating the rights of others using "you-messages" and absolutes.

- You don't need/want . . .
- Your opinion is wrong.
- You don't know what you're talking about.
- You're doing it wrong.
- That won't work!
- You have to . . .
- You need to know . . .

The passive behavior will most likely lead to the person's being cut off and not listened to on a regular basis. The aggressive behavior will most likely lead to hurt human relations and may lead to an argument, while the assertive response will most likely lead to the interrupted person's getting to finish now and in the future, without hurting human relations.

We will further explain how to be assertive in the next section, which deals with conflict management.

In the opening case introduction, before the conversation took place, Helen used passive behavior, while Larry used aggressive behavior. During the confrontation Helen used aggressive behavior, but when Larry responded with aggressive behavior, she returned to passive behavior, giving him the calculator. In other words, Helen used passive–aggressive–passive behavior with Larry.

WORK APPLICATIONS

6. Recall an actual conflict you faced. Identify passive, aggressive, and assertive responses to the situation.

Learning Outcome

4. List the four steps of assertive behavior.

Assertiveness Steps   Below are the four assertive steps that Helen, in the opening case, could have used. These steps are summarized in Exhibit 7.3.

EXHIBIT 7.3 | Assertiveness Steps

Step 1: Set an objective.
Step 2: Determine how to create a win–win situation.
Step 3: Develop assertive phrase(s).
Step 4: Implement your plan persistently.

Step 1: Set an objective.   Specify what you want to accomplish. Helen's objective could have been "to tell Larry that I will give him the calculator after I'm finished with it."

Step 2: Determine how to create a win–win situation.   Assess the situation in terms of meeting your needs and the other person's needs. Larry's needs are already being met by Helen's giving him the calculator any time he wants it. Presently, there is a win–lose situation. Helen needs to be assertive to meet her own needs to get her work done. Equitably sharing the use of the calculator will create a win–win situation. The present system of giving it to each other when done may work fine if Helen finishes using it before giving it to Larry.

Step 3: Develop assertive phrase(s):   Before confronting Larry, Helen could have developed a statement such as, "I'm using it now, and I'll give it to you as soon as I'm finished with it."

Step 4: Implement your plan persistently.   Helen could have used the above statement. If Larry continued to use aggressive behavior to get the calculator, Helen could persistently repeat the phrase until it sinks in, until Larry leaves without the calculator. It is not necessary, but Helen could explain why she feels the situation is not fair and repeat that she will give the calculator to Larry when she is done with it.

APPLICATION SITUATIONS

Assertiveness

AS 7–2

Identify each response to a supervisor's request for an employee to make a personal purchase for him on company time:

A. Passive   B. Aggressive   C. Assertive

_____ 6. "I'm not doing that, and I'll report you to the union if you ask again."

_____ 7. "Is that a part of my job description?"

_____ 8. "I'll get on it just as soon as I finish this."

_____ 9. "You know I'm not going to do a stupid thing like that. Do your own shopping."

_____ 10. "Your request is unreasonable because it is not part of my job. I will not do it because we could both get in trouble."

Dealing with Anger and Preventing Workplace Violence

Now that we know the difference between passive, aggressive, and assertive behavior, let's focus on aggressive behavior with anger that can lead to violence, and how to prevent it. Human resource managers have reported increased incivility and violence between employees, stating it can happen anywhere. Women commit nearly a quarter of all threats or attacks. There has also been an increase in violence between outsiders and employees, such as customers shooting employees and other customers at fast-food restaurants. One million workers are assaulted each year, and in some years more than 1,000 workers have been killed. The key to preventing workplace violence is to recognize and handle suspicious behavior before it becomes violent.[60]

Causes of Anger and Violence   Anger can lead to violence. You have most likely heard of road rage. In business we have *desk rage,* which can take the form of yelling, verbal abuse, and physical violence.[61] People low on the personality adjustment dimension, using aggressive behavior, are more apt to become angry and violent. Frustration, stress, and fear bring out anger. Interpersonal unresolved conflicts make people angry. In fact, violence is almost always prompted by unresolved conflict, and the violence is often a form of sabotage on other employees (back stabbing, spreading false rumors) or on the organization (property damage) to get even.[62]

The physical work environment, such as work space, noise, odors, temperature (hot), ventilation, and color, can contribute to making people angry. A hostile work environment, called toxicity, leads to violence. People tend to copy, or model, others' behavior. For example, children who have been abused (emotionally and/or physically) are more likely, as parents, to abuse their children. If employees see others being violent, especially managers, and nothing is done about it, they are more apt to also use violent behavior at work.[63] Violence in the community, which includes family violence, surrounding an organization is brought into the workplace. Some, but not all, experts report that drugs contribute to violence.

Dealing with Anger   Anger can be tough to deal with, especially in an organizational setting.

Your Anger and Emotional Control   A secondary feeling of anger follows many of our feelings. Your boss may surprise you with extra work, which makes you angry. Disappointment often leads to anger. Your coworker doesn't do his share of the work, so you get mad at him. Buddha said, "You will not be punished *for* your anger; you will be punished *by* your anger." Anger can lead to perception problems, poor decisions, and hostility, which is stressful and can harm your health.[64] On the positive side, anger can lead to assertive behavior to resolve problems.[65]

Recall our discussion of emotions in Chapter 6. It is natural to get angry sometimes.[66] Although we cannot control the feeling of anger, we can control our behavior; we can learn to deal with anger in more positive ways to get rid of it.[67] Letting anger build up often leads to passive–aggressive behavior. Here are some tips for effectively getting rid of your anger:

- Use rational thinking. For example, when dealing with customers, tell yourself their anger is to be expected; it's part of your job to stay calm.
- Look for positives. In many bad situations, there is some good.
- Look for the humor in the situation to help defuse the anger. Finding appropriate humor can help keep you from moping and getting angry.
- A key factor in controlling your anger is using assertive behavior. If you tend to be passive or aggressive, work at being assertive.
- Develop a positive attitude about how you deal with anger. Use the techniques from Chapter 3 for changing your attitudes and building a positive self-concept. Review Skill-Building Exercise 3–2. Develop positive affirmations, such as "I stay calm when in traffic" (not "I must stop getting mad in traffic"); "I get along well with Joe" (not "I must stop letting Joe make me angry").
- Use an anger journal. A first step to emotional control of anger is self-awareness. Answer these questions: How often do you get irritated or angry each day? What makes you irritated or angry? How upset do you get? What feelings do you have when you are angry? What behavior (yell, say specific words, pound desk, or do and say nothing, accommodate) do you use when you are angry? Are you good at dealing with your irritations or anger? One good way to improve your ability to control your anger is to write the answers to these questions in an anger journal. It is a method of letting out the anger in an effective way. People who use a journal change their behavior without even trying.

Anger of Others and Emotional Control   Below are some tips from the Crisis Prevention Institute and the National Institute for Occupational Safety and Health (NIOSH) to help you deal with the anger of others through your emotional control and to prevent violence. We start this discussion with a review.

- Our tips in Chapter 6 for dealing with emotional employees apply here. Again, never make any type of put-down statement; that type of response can make the person angrier. As stated above, you may use appropriate humor to cut the tension, but be careful that the humor is not viewed as being sarcastic. Such behavior can lead to violence.

- Don't respond to anger and threats with the same behavior. Angry people are rarely in the adult ego state, and they are often aggressive (although they may be passive). The key to success in maintaining your emotional control is to stay in the adult ego state.

- Don't give orders or ultimatums. This approach can increase anger and push the person to violence.

- Watch your nonverbal communication; show concern and avoid appearing aggressive. Use eye contact to show concern, but be aware that staring or glaring can make you appear aggressive. Maintain a calm, soothing tone to defuse anger and frustration. Talking loud and with frustration, anger, or annoyance in your tone of voice will convey aggression. Don't move rapidly, point at the person, get too close (stay 2 to 5 feet apart), or touch the person.

- Realize that anger is natural, and encourage people to vent in appropriate ways. With the aggressor, the problem is usually to keep the behavior acceptable. With the passive person, you may need to ask probing questions to get her or him to vent, such as "What is making you angry? What did I do to make you mad?"

- Acknowledge the person's feelings. Using reflecting responses by paraphrasing the way the person is feeling shows that you care and helps calm the person so that he or she can get back in the adult ego state.

- Get away from the person if necessary. If possible, call in a third party (security) to deal with the person; then leave.

Signs of Potential Violence   Workplace violence is rarely spontaneous; it's more commonly passive–aggressive behavior in rising steps, related to an unresolved conflict. Employees do give warning signs that violence is possible, so it can be prevented if you look for these signs and take action to defuse the anger before it becomes violent.[68]

- Take verbal threats seriously. Most violent people do make a threat of some kind before they act. If you hear a threat, or hear about a threat from someone, talk to the person who made the threat and try to resolve the issue.

- Watch nonverbal communication. Gestures or other body language that convey anger can indicate a threat of violence just as much as behavior such as yelling can. Talk to the person to find out what's going on.

- Watch for stalking and harassment. It usually starts small but can lead to violence. Put a stop to it.

- Watch for damage to property. If an employee kicks a desk, punches a wall, or the like, talk to the person to get to the reason for the behavior. People who damage property can become violent to coworkers.

- Watch for indications of alcohol and drug use. People can become violent under the influence of these substances. Get them out of the workplace and get them professional help if it's a recurring problem.

- Include the isolated employee. It is common for violent people to be employees who don't fit in, especially if they are picked on or harassed by coworkers. Reach out to such employees and help them fit in, or get them to a place where they do.

- Look for the presence of weapons or objects that might be used as weapons. You may trying talking to the person if you feel safe, but get security personnel involved.

Organizational Prevention of Violence   The number one preventive method is to train all employees to deal with anger and prevent violence,[69] which is what you are learning now. However, the starting place is with a written policy addressing workplace violence, and a zero-tolerance policy is the best preventive policy. From the manager's perspective, it is very important to take quick disciplinary action against employees who are violent at work. Otherwise, aggression will spread in the organization and it will become more difficult to stop. Managers especially need to avoid using aggression at work, because employees more readily copy managers' behavior than that of other employees. The organization should have a system for dealing with grievances and should track incidents of violence as part of its policy.

Organizations can also screen job applicants for past or potential violence so that they are not hired. Organizations should also develop a good work environment that addresses the issues listed above as causes of violence. Demotions, firings, and layoffs should be handled in a humane way, following the guidelines for dealing with anger. Outplacement services to help employees find new jobs can help cut down on violence.

Individual Prevention of Violence   One thing you should realize is that the police department will not help you prevent personal or workplace violence. Police get involved only after violence takes place. Here are a few more tips for preventing violence.[70] Keep in mind that there is always the potential for violence; look for escalating frustration and anger so that you can defuse the situation before it becomes violent. Never be alone with a potentially violent person or stand between the person and the exit. Know when to get away from the person. Be aware of the organization's policy for calling in security help. Report any troubling incidents to security staff.

WORK APPLICATIONS

7. Recall a situation in which someone was angry with you, preferably your boss. What was the cause of the anger? Did the person display any signs of potential violence? If so, what were they? How well did the person deal with his or her anger? Give the specific tips the person did and did not follow.

8. Recall a situation in which you were angry with someone. What was the cause of your anger? Did you display any signs of potential violence? If so, what were they? How well did you deal with your anger? Give the specific tips you did and did not follow.

CONFLICT MANAGEMENT STYLES

Learning Outcome

5. Explain when a conflict exists.

Some people think that a conflict exists only in serious issues with anger. However, in human relations, a **conflict** *exists whenever two or more parties are in disagreement.* Conflict is inherent in a team or organizational system,[71] and as the workforce becomes more diverse, conflict can increase.[72] Do you agree with everything people do and say in your human relations at work? If not, you are in conflict, most likely every day. Dealing with conflict is part of emotional intelligence,[73] and your ability to manage conflict is critical to your success.[74] In this section, we discuss reasons for conflict and avoiding conflicts as well as the five conflict management styles you can use when you are in conflict.

Reasons for Conflict and Avoiding Conflicts

All human relations rely on unwritten, implicit expectations by each party, called the psychological contract.[75] Often we are not aware of our expectations until they have not been met. Communication problems or conflicts arise for three primary reasons: (1) we fail to make our expectations known to other parties; (2) we fail to find out the expectations of other parties; (3) we assume that the other parties have the same expectations that we have.

In any relationship, to avoid conflict, share information and assertively discuss expectations early, before the conflict escalates. Unfortunately, avoiding conflict is easier said than done.[76]

In the opening case, Larry expected Helen to give him the calculator when he wanted it, which he made explicit to Helen. Larry failed to find out Helen's expectations (probably did not care), and may have assumed that she did not mind giving him the calculator whenever he wanted it. Helen's expectation was that Larry would share the calculator, and she found out his expectations were not the same as hers. However, she did not assertively tell Larry this early. Thus, they are in conflict and need to talk about their expectations. Also, there are times when the other party (Larry) is not being reasonable, making conflict more common and more difficult to resolve. Helen is going to need to be assertive with Larry.

Conflict Has Benefits   People often think of conflict as fighting and view it as disruptive. Conflict, however, can be beneficial. The question today is not whether conflict is good or bad but rather how to manage conflict to benefit the organization.[77] A balance of conflict is essential to all organizations.[78] Too little or too much conflict is usually a sign of management's unwillingness or inability to adapt to a diversified environment. Challenging present methods and presenting innovative change causes conflict, but can lead to improved performance.

WORK APPLICATIONS

9. Describe a conflict you observed in an organization, preferably an organization with which you are or were associated. Explain the conflict by the people involved and the reasons for the conflict.

Before learning the five conflict management styles, complete Self-Assessment Exercise 7–3 to determine your preferred style.

Self-Assessment Exercise 7–3

Determining Your Preferred Conflict Management Style

Below are four situations. Rank all five alternative actions from 1, the first approach you would use (most desirable), to 5, the last approach you would use (least desirable). Don't try to pick a best answer. Select the alternative that best describes what you would actually do in the situation based on your past experiences.

1. You are the general manager of a manufacturing plant. The purchasing department has found a source of material at a lower cost than the one being used. However, the production manager says the current material is superior, and he doesn't want to change. The quality control manager says that both will pass inspection with similar results. You would:

   _____ *a.* Do nothing; let the purchasing and production managers work it out between themselves.

   _____ *b.* Suggest having the purchasing manager find an alternative material that is cheaper but acceptable to the production manager.

   _____ *c.* Have the purchasing and production managers compromise.

   _____ *d.* Decide who is right and make the other comply.

   _____ *e.* Get the purchasing and production managers together and work out an agreement acceptable to both parties.

Self-Assessment
Exercise 7–3 (*continued*)

2. You are a professor at a college. You have started a consulting organization and have the title of director of consulting services, which the dean has approved. You run the organization through the business department, using other faculty and yourself to consult. It has been going well. Randy, the director of continuing education, says that your consulting services should come under his department and not be a separate department. You would:

_____ a. Suggest that some services be under continuing education, but that others, like your consulting service, remain with you in the business department.

_____ b. Do what you can to stop the move. Go to the dean and request that the consulting services stay under your direction in the business department, as originally approved by the dean.

_____ c. Do nothing. The dean will surely see through this "power grab" and turn Randy down.

_____ d. Go and talk to Randy. Try to come up with an agreement you are both satisfied with.

_____ e. Go along with Randy's request. It's not worth fighting about; you can still consult.

3. You are a branch manager for a bank. One of your colleagues cut you off twice during a managers' meeting that just ended. You would:

_____ a. Do nothing; it's no big deal.

_____ b. Discuss it in a friendly manner, but try to get the colleague to stop this behavior.

_____ c. Don't do or say anything because it might hurt your relations, even if you're a little upset about it.

_____ d. Forcefully tell the colleague that you put up with being cut off, but will not tolerate it in the future.

_____ e. Tell the colleague that you will listen without interrupting if he or she does the same for you.

4. You are the human resources/personnel manager. You have decided to have visitors sign in and wear guest passes. However, only about half of the employees sign their guests in before taking them to their offices to do business. You would:

_____ a. Go talk to the general manager about why employees are not signing in visitors.

_____ b. Try to find a method that will please most employees.

_____ c. Go to the general manager and request that she require employees to follow your procedures. If the general manager says to do it, employees will comply.

_____ d. Do not require visitors to sign in; require them only to wear guest passes.

_____ e. Let employees do things the way they want to.

To determine your preferred conflict management style, place your numbers 1 to 5 on the lines below.

	Situation 1		**Situation 2**
_____	a. Forcing	_____	a. Compromising
_____	b. Avoiding	_____	b. Forcing
_____	c. Accommodating	_____	c. Avoiding
_____	d. Compromising	_____	d. Collaborating
_____	e. Collaborating	_____	e. Accommodating

	Situation 3		**Situation 4**
_____	a. Avoiding	_____	a. Collaborating
_____	b. Collaborating	_____	b. Accommodating
_____	c. Accommodating	_____	c. Forcing
_____	d. Forcing	_____	d. Compromising
_____	e. Compromising	_____	e. Avoiding

Self-Assessment Exercise 7–3 (*continued*)

Now place your ranking numbers 1 to 5 that correspond to the styles from the four situations in order; then add the four numbers.

Situation 1	Situation 2	Situation 3	Situation 4	
_____ a.	_____ b.	_____ d.	_____ c.	= _____ total, Forcing style
_____ b.	_____ c.	_____ a.	_____ e.	= _____ total, Avoiding style
_____ c.	_____ e.	_____ c.	_____ b.	= _____ total, Accommodating style
_____ d.	_____ a.	_____ e.	_____ d.	= _____ total, Compromising style
_____ e.	_____ d.	_____ b.	_____ a.	= _____ total, Collaborating style

The total with the lowest score is your preferred conflict management style. There is no one best conflict style in all situations. The more even the totals are, the more flexible you are at changing conflict management styles. Very high and very low totals indicate less flexibility.

It is also helpful to identify others' preferred styles so that you can plan how to resolve conflicts with them.

Learning Outcome

6. State when and how to use five conflict management styles.

The five conflict management styles—forcing, avoiding, accommodating, compromising, and collaborating—are presented next. See Exhibit 7.4 for an overview of the five styles integrated with TA and assertiveness.

Forcing Conflict Style

The **forcing conflict style** *user attempts to resolve the conflict by using aggressive behavior.* The forcer uses the critical parent or adapted child ego state, with aggressive behavior. The forcing approach uses an uncooperative, autocratic attempt to satisfy one's own needs at the expense of others, if necessary.[79] A win–lose situation is created. Forcers use authority, threaten, intimidate,[80] and call for majority rule when they know they will win. For example, a manager tells an employee, "If you don't do it now, you're fired!"

Advantages and Disadvantages of the Forcing Conflict Style   The advantage of the forcing style is that better organizational decisions will be made (assuming the forcer is correct)

EXHIBIT 7.4 |
Conflict Management Styles

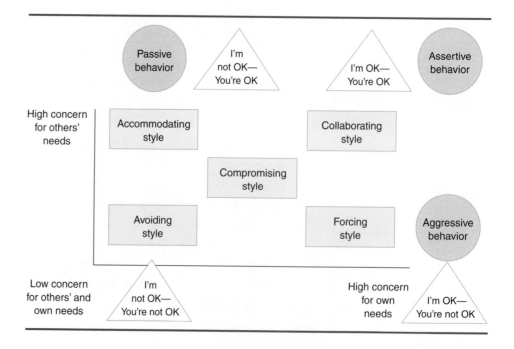

rather than less effective, compromised decisions. The disadvantage is that overuse of this style leads to hostility and resentment toward its user.[81]

Appropriate Use of the Forcing Conflict Style   The forcing style is appropriate to use when (1) the conflict is about personal differences (particularly values that are hard to change); (2) maintaining close, supportive relationships is not critical; and (3) conflict resolution is urgent.

Avoiding Conflict Style

The **avoiding conflict style** *user attempts to passively ignore the conflict rather than resolve it.* The avoider uses the obedient child or sympathetic parent ego state, with passive behavior.[82] Its user is unassertive and uncooperative, and wants to avoid or postpone confrontation. A lose–lose situation is created because the conflict is not resolved.[83] People avoid the conflict by refusing to take a stance, physically leaving it, or escaping the conflict by mentally leaving the conflict.

Advantages and Disadvantages of the Avoiding Conflict Style   The advantage of the avoiding style is that it may maintain relationships that would be hurt through conflict resolution. The disadvantage of this style is the fact that conflicts do not get resolved. An overuse of this style leads to conflict within the individual. People tend to walk all over the avoider. Supervisors use this style when they allow employees to break rules without confronting them. Avoiding problems usually does not make them go away; the problems usually get worse. Being afraid to be assertive is not a problem; it's not being assertive when you are afraid that's the problem.

Appropriate Use of the Avoiding Conflict Style   The avoiding style is appropriate to use when (1) one's stake in the issue is not high; (2) confrontation will damage a critical working relationship; and (3) a time constraint necessitates avoidance. Some people use the avoiding style out of fear that they will handle the confrontation poorly, making the situation worse rather than better. After studying this chapter and following its guidelines, you should be able to handle confrontations effectively.

Accommodating Conflict Style

The **accommodating conflict style** *user attempts to resolve the conflict by passively giving in to the other party.* The user is in the obedient child or sympathetic parent ego state, using passive behavior. The accommodating approach is unassertive and cooperative.[84] It attempts to satisfy the other party while neglecting one's own needs.[85] A win–lose situation is created, with the other party being the winner.

Advantages and Disadvantages of the Accommodating Conflict Style   The advantage of the accommodating style is that relationships are maintained. The disadvantage is that giving in to the other party may be counterproductive. The accommodating person may have a better solution. An overuse of this style leads to people's taking advantage of the accommodator, and the relationship the accommodator tries to maintain is often lost.

Appropriate Use of the Accommodating Conflict Style   The accommodating style is appropriate when (1) maintaining the relationship outweighs all other considerations; (2) the changes agreed to are not important to the accommodator, but are to the other party; and (3) the time to resolve the conflict is limited. This is often the only style one can use with an autocratic boss.

The Difference between Avoiding and Accommodating   With the avoiding style, you can simply say or do nothing. However, with the accommodating style, you have to do or say something you don't want to. For example, if your boss says something you disagree with, you can avoid by saying nothing. However, if your boss asks you to take a letter to the mailroom, and you don't want to but do it anyway, you have accommodated the boss.

Compromising Conflict Style

The **compromising conflict style** *user attempts to resolve the conflict through assertive give-and-take concessions.* Its user is in the adult ego state, using assertive behavior. This approach attempts to meet one's need for harmonious relationships.[86] An I-win-part–I-lose-part situation is created through compromise, making the compromising style intermediate in assertiveness and cooperation. It is used in negotiations.

Advantages and Disadvantages of the Compromising Conflict Style   The advantage of the compromising style is that the conflict is resolved quickly and relationships are maintained. The disadvantage is that the compromise often leads to counterproductive results (suboptimum decisions). An overuse of this style leads to people's playing games, such as asking for twice as much as they need in order to get what they want. It is commonly used during management and labor collective bargaining.

Appropriate Use of the Compromising Conflict Style   The compromising style is appropriate to use when (1) the issues are complex and critical, and there is no simple and clear solution; (2) all parties have a strong interest in different solutions; and (3) time is short.

Collaborating Conflict Style

The **collaborating conflict style** *user assertively attempts to resolve the conflict with the best solution agreeable to all parties.* It is also called the *problem-solving style.* Its user is in the adult ego state, using assertive behavior.[87] The collaborating approach is assertive and cooperative. The collaborator attempts to fully address the concerns of all. The focus is on finding the best solution to the problem that is satisfactory to all parties.[88] Unlike the forcer, the collaborator is willing to change if a better solution is presented. This is the only style that creates a true win–win situation.

Advantages and Disadvantages of the Collaborating Conflict Style   The advantage of the collaborating style is that it tends to lead to the best solution to the conflict using assertive behavior. One great disadvantage is that the time and effort it takes to resolve the conflict is usually greater and longer than with the other styles.

Appropriate Use of the Collaborating Conflict Style   The collaborating style is appropriate when (1) maintaining relationships is important; (2) time is available; and (3) it is a peer conflict. To be successful, one must confront conflict. The collaborating conflict style is generally considered the best style because it confronts the conflict assertively, rather than passively ignoring it or aggressively fighting one's way through it.

The Difference between Compromising and Collaborating   Let's explain with an example. With the compromising style, when you and a coworker are delivering furniture, you take turns listening to the radio station you like; thus, each of you wins and loses some. With collaborating, you would agree on a station you both like to listen to—you both win. Unfortunately, collaboration is not always possible.

The situational perspective states that there is no one best style for resolving all conflicts. A person's preferred style tends to meet his or her needs. Some people enjoy forcing, others prefer to avoid conflict, and so forth. Success lies in one's ability to use the appropriate style to meet the situation. Of the five styles, the most difficult to implement successfully (and probably the most underutilized when appropriate) is the collaborative style.

Therefore, the collaborative style is the only one that will be given detailed coverage in the next section of this chapter.

In the opening case, Larry consistently used the forcing conflict resolution style, while Helen began by using the accommodating style, changed to the forcing style, and returned to the accommodating style. To create a true win–win situation for all parties, Helen could have used the collaborating conflict management style.

WORK APPLICATIONS

10. Give an example of a conflict situation you face or have faced. Identify and explain the appropriate conflict management style to use.

APPLICATION SITUATIONS

Selecting Conflict Management Styles

AS 7–3

Identify the most appropriate conflict management style as:

A. Forcing   C. Compromising   E. Collaborating

B. Avoiding   D. Accommodating

_____ 11. You are in a class that uses small groups for the entire semester. Under normal class conditions the most appropriate style is _____.

_____ 12. You have joined a committee so that you can meet people. Your interest in its function itself is low. While serving on the committee, you make a recommendation that is opposed by another member. You realize that you have the better idea. The other party is using a forcing style.

_____ 13. You are the supervisor of a production department. An important order is behind schedule. Two of your employees are in conflict, as usual, over how to meet the deadline.

_____ 14. You are on a committee that has to select a new computer. The four alternatives will all do the job. It's the brand, price, and service that people disagree on.

_____ 15. You are a sales manager. One of your competent salespersons is trying to close a big sale. The two of you are discussing the next sales call she will make. You disagree on strategy.

_____ 16. You are on your way to an important meeting. You're late. As you turn a corner, at the end of the shop you see one of your employees goofing off instead of working.

_____ 17. You have a department crisis. Your boss calls you and tells you, in a stern voice, "Get up here right away."

_____ 18. You are in a special one-hour budget meeting with your boss and fellow supervisors. You have to finalize the total budget for each department.

_____ 19. You and a fellow supervisor are working on a report. You disagree on the format to use.

_____ 20. You're over budget for labor this month. It's slow today so you asked a part-time employee to go home early. He tells you he doesn't want to go because he needs the money.

RESOLVING CONFLICTS WITH THE COLLABORATING CONFLICT STYLE

Learning Outcome

7. List the steps of initiating, responding to, and mediating conflict resolutions.

When a conflict exists, determine the appropriate style to use. Collaboration is not always appropriate in supervisor–employee conflicts. However, it is generally the appropriate style for conflict between colleagues and peers.

The objective of this section is to develop your ability to assertively confront (or be confronted by) people you are in conflict with, in a manner that resolves the conflict without damaging interpersonal relationships. We examine the roles of initiator, responder, and mediator in conflict resolution.

Initiating Conflict Resolution

An initiator is a person who confronts another person (or other people) about a conflict. The initiator's attitude will have a major effect on the outcome of the confrontation. We tend to get what we are looking for. If you go into a confrontation expecting to argue and fight, you probably will. If you expect a successful resolution, you will probably get it.[89] (See our discussion of the self-fulfilling prophecy in Chapter 3.)

To resolve conflicts, you should develop a plan of action. When you initiate a conflict resolution using the collaborating style, follow the **initiating conflict resolution steps:** *step (1) plan to maintain ownership of the problem using the XYZ model; step (2) implement your plan persistently; and step (3) make an agreement for change.* (See Exhibit 7.5.)

Step 1: Plan to Maintain Ownership of the Problem Using the XYZ Model   Part of the reason confronters are not successful at resolving conflict is that they wait too long before confronting the other party, and they do it in an emotional state without planning (passive–aggressive behavior). People end up saying things they don't mean because they haven't given thought to what it is they want to say and accomplish through confrontation.[90] You should realize that when you are upset and frustrated, the problem is yours, not the other party's. For example, you don't smoke and someone visits you who does smoke. The smoke bothers you, not the smoker. It's your problem. Open the confrontation with a request for the respondent to help you solve your problem. This approach reduces defensiveness and establishes an atmosphere of problem solving.

Know what you want to accomplish and what your expectations are, and state them ahead of time. Be descriptive, not evaluative. Avoid trying to determine who is to blame. Both parties are usually partly to blame. Fixing blame only gets people defensive, which is counterproductive to conflict resolution. Keep the opening statement short. The longer the statement, the longer it will take to resolve the conflict. People get defensive when kept waiting for their turn to talk. Use the XYZ model. The **XYZ model** *describes a problem in terms of behavior, consequences, and feelings.* For example: When you do X (behavior), Y (consequences) happens, and I feel Z (feelings). For example, when you smoke in my room (behavior), I have trouble breathing and become nauseated (consequence), and I feel uncomfortable and irritated (feeling). You can vary the sequence and start with a feeling or consequence to fit the situation.

Notice that in the XYZ statement, the word *advice* is not included. You don't give advice to start. You let the other person respond; the person may have a good solution. If the person does not offer a solution, or offers one you can't agree with, then you can try giving advice. In the smoking example above, don't tell the person that smoking is bad and give advice to quit smoking.

Timing is also important. Don't confront people when they are involved in something else. If the other party is busy, set an appointment to discuss the conflict. In addition, don't confront a person on several unrelated issues at once.

WORK APPLICATIONS

11. Use the XYZ model to describe a conflict problem you face or have faced.

Step 2: Implement Your Plan Persistently   After making your short, planned XYZ statement, let the other party respond. If the confronted party acknowledges the problem and says he or she will change, you may have succeeded. Often people do not realize there is a conflict and when approached properly, they are willing to change. However, if the other party does not understand or avoids acknowledgment of the problem, persist. You cannot resolve a conflict if the other party will not even acknowledge its existence. Repeat your planned statement several times, and/or explain it in different terms, until you get an acknowledgment or realize that the situation is hopeless. But don't give up too easily,[91] and be sure to listen to the other party and watch for nonverbal clues.

When the other party acknowledges the problem, but is not responsive to resolving it, appeal to common goals. Make the other party realize the benefits to him or her and the organization as well.

Step 3: Make an Agreement for Change   Try to agree on a specific action you both will take to resolve the conflict. Remember that you are collaborating, not forcing. If possible, get a commitment statement describing the change.

Below is an example of conflict resolution:

PAM: Hi, Bill! Got a few minutes to talk?

BILL: Sure, what's up?

PAM: Something's been bothering me lately, and I wanted you to know about it. When you come to class without doing your homework [*behavior*], I get irritated [*feeling*], and our group has to wait for you to read the material, or make a decision without your input [*consequences*].

BILL: Hey, I'm busy!

PAM: Do you think the rest of the group isn't?

BILL: No.

PAM: Are grades important to you?

BILL: Yeah. If I don't get good grades, I can't play on the football team.

PAM: You get a grade for doing your homework, and we all get the same group grade. Your input helps us all get a better grade.

BILL: You're right; sometimes I forget about that. Well, sometimes I don't do it because I don't understand the assignment.

PAM: I'll tell you what; when you don't understand it, call me, or come over, and I'll explain it. You know my number and address.

BILL: I'd appreciate that.

PAM: So you agree to do your homework before class, and I agree to help you when you need it.

BILL: OK, I'll do it from now on.

Responding to Conflict Resolution

A responder is a person confronted by an initiator. Most initiators do not follow the model above. Therefore, the responder must take responsibility for successful conflict resolution by following the conflict resolution model. The **responding to conflict resolution steps** *are as follows: step (1) listen to and paraphrase the problem using the XYZ model; step (2) agree with some aspect of the complaint; step (3) ask for, and/or give, alternative solutions; and step (4) make an agreement for change.* (See Exhibit 7.5.)

Mediating Conflict Resolution

Frequently, conflicting employees cannot resolve their dispute. In these cases, the manager,[92] or an outside mediator[93] should mediate to help them resolve their differences.

Before bringing the conflicting parties together, the manager should decide whether to start with a joint meeting or individual meetings. If one employee comes to complain, but has not confronted the other party, or if there is a serious discrepancy in employee perceptions, the manager should meet one-on-one with each party before bringing them together. On the other hand, when both parties have a similar awareness of the problem and are motivated to solve it, the manager can begin with a joint meeting when all parties are calm. The manager should be a mediator, not a judge. Make employees realize it's their problem, not yours, and that they are responsible for solving it. Get the employees to resolve the conflict, if possible. Remain impartial, unless one party is violating company policies. Don't belittle the parties in conflict. Don't make comments like, "I'm disappointed in you two; you're acting like babies."

When bringing conflicting parties together, follow the mediating conflict model. The **mediating conflict resolution steps** *are as follows: step (1) have each party state his or her complaint using the XYZ model; step (2) agree on the problem(s); step (3) develop alternative solutions; and step (4) make an agreement for change, and follow up.* The steps for initiating, responding to, and mediating conflict resolution are summarized in Exhibit 7.5.

EXHIBIT 7.5 | Conflict Resolution

Initiating Conflict Resolution

Step 1: Plan to maintain ownership of the problem using the XYZ model.
Step 2: Implement your plan persistently.
Step 3: Make an agreement for change.

Responding to Conflict Resolution

Step 1: Listen to and paraphrase the problem using the XYZ model.
Step 2: Agree with some aspect of the complaint.
Step 3: Ask for, and/or give, alternative solutions.
Step 4: Make an agreement for change.

Mediating Conflict Resolution

Step 1: Have each party state his or her complaint using the XYZ model.
Step 2: Agree on the problem(s).
Step 3: Develop alternative solutions.
Step 4: Make an agreement for change, and follow up.

Westin Hotels & Resorts Tries to Clear the Air about Smoking

Westin Hotels & Resorts is owned by Starwood Hotels & Resorts Worldwide. Back in 2006, Westin made a strategic move as all Westin hotels and resorts implemented a 100 percent smoke-free policy, including all guest rooms and public areas. Becoming smoke-free was a bold move as it was the first hotel to do so. The decision was based on industry and company research confirming a clear consumer demand for a clean, smoke-free hotel environment.

Yet this decision has not been without controversy. Smokinglobby.com notes that "if you have a reservation with this hotel . . . you might want to change your reservation." Smokers United claims that "smokers in America today are treated like second-class citizens" while Angry Smokers Against Hypocrisy state that they "would like to see all the smokers boycotting those establishments that are a party to removing one step at a time, OUR FREEDOM [to smoke]. Sure, today it's the smoker, but who will it be next? These people do not realize that taking our rights away makes it easier to take theirs. Stupid is as Stupid does."

Questions

Assume that you are current CEO Frits van Paasschen at an annual stockholders' meeting and are confronted by an angry group of patrons who are smokers.

1. Would you avoid a conflict with this group? Why or why not?

2. What style of conflict would you employ? Why? What are the pros and cons to that style?

3. What steps would you take to resolve this conflict?

4. What about the rights of smokers? Do you agree with Westin's decision to become smoke-free?

Sources: http://come.to/SmokersInfo; http://sev.prnewswire.com; http://www.angrysmoker.com; http://www.hospitalitynet.org; http://www.smokinglobby.com; www.starwoodhotels.com, retrieved August 12, 2008.

In the discussion of assertiveness, there was an example of how Helen could have been assertive with Larry in the opening case. In addition to being assertive with Larry, Helen could have used the collaborating conflict style to resolve the calculator problem. Helen could have suggested to Larry that the two of them go to the boss and ask for another calculator so that they could each have their own. A second calculator could create a win–win situation for all parties. Helen and Larry would both win because they would not have to wait for the calculator. The department would win because productivity would increase; there would be less time wasted getting and waiting for the calculator. The organization would win because the department would perform more efficiently. Obtaining a second calculator is a good conflict resolution. However, the department or organization may not have the money in the budget to buy a new calculator, or the idle time may actually be cheaper. If this is the case, Helen can be assertive and keep the calculator until she is finished—this is a win–win situation; or she and Larry could work out some other collaborative agreement, such as each having the calculator during specific hours. If Larry is not willing to collaborate, their boss will have to mediate the conflict resolution.

WORK APPLICATIONS

12. Describe an actual situation in which the initiating, responding, and/or mediating conflict resolution model would be appropriate.

PUTTING IT ALL TOGETHER

To see the relationship between TA, assertiveness, and conflict management, see Exhibit 7.6. Notice that the first two columns come from conflict management, the third from assertiveness, and the fourth and fifth from TA. The last column relates to the goal of human relations. The last column shows the order of priority of which interpersonal behavior to use to meet the goal of human relations. However, remember that this is general advice. As stated in the chapter, at times other behavior is appropriate. In the majority of your human relations, you should strive to have a high concern for meeting your needs while

EXHIBIT 7.6 | Interpersonal Dynamics Styles

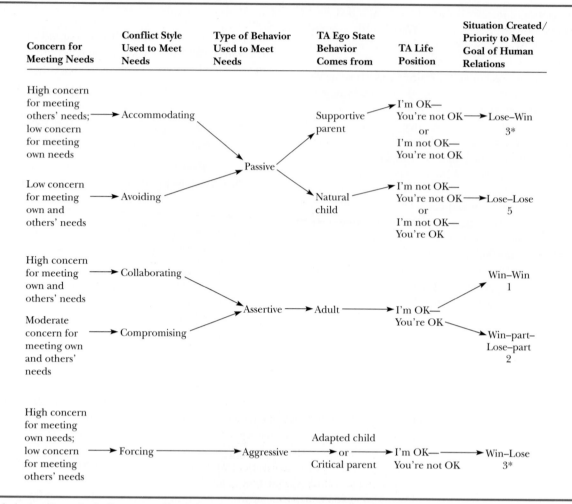

*The win–lose and lose–win situations are equal in priority to the group or organization because both an individual and the group or organization lose. The individual's loss is more important to the loser than to the group.

meeting the needs of others. You should use an assertive, adult, collaborating style to create a win–win situation for all parties.

In reviewing Exhibit 7.6, you should see that the behavior of people using the passive, accommodating, avoiding conflict styles is the opposite of the behavior of people who use the aggressive, forcing conflict styles. Assertive people use the collaborating, compromising conflict styles, and their behavior is between the other two extremes.

You should also understand that people using the passive, accommodating, avoiding conflict styles tend to have human relations that are the opposite of people using the aggressive, forcing conflict styles. The passive person tends to shy away from making friends and being actively involved, while the aggressive person tries to take over and is offensive to the group. Assertive people use the collaborating style and tend to be friendly and outgoing as they work to create win–win situations for all parties. Generally, people who are passive don't get their needs met; they get walked over by the aggressive people. Aggressive people are disliked because they violate the rights of others. Assertive people tend to have the best human relations.

No clear relationship exists between individual performance and the interpersonal dynamic style used. Many passive people work well alone, and so do aggressive people. Aggressive people are sometimes more productive than passive people because they can take advantage of passive people. This happened in the opening case. When it comes to group and organizational performance, the assertive person is generally the most responsible for the group effort. Passive people may have great ideas on doing a good group job, but they don't say how. Aggressive people look out only for themselves. If someone offers an idea different from theirs, they are not willing to collaborate for the good of all. The assertive group member collaboratively shares ideas but is willing to change to a better alternative to create a win–win situation for all. By following the guidelines in this chapter, you can develop assertive collaborating skills.

As we bring this chapter to a close, let's discuss how your personality affects your ego state, assertiveness, and preferred conflict style in Self-Assessment Exercise 7–4.

Self-Assessment Exercise 7–4

Your Personality and Interpersonal Dynamics

People with the same personality type (Chapter 2) tend to get along better and have less conflict than those with different personality types. So be careful during human relations with people different from you.

If you have a high *surgency* personality, watch your use of the critical parent ego state and be sure to give lots of positive strokes to help human relations. You may be in the "I'm OK" life position, but make sure that you treat others as "You're OK." As a surgency, you also need to be careful not to use aggressive behavior to get what you want. You most likely have no problem confronting others when in conflict. However, be careful not to use the forcing style with others.

If you have a high *agreeableness* personality, you tend to get along well with others. But be careful not to use the sympathetic parent ego state, and watch the appropriate use of the child ego state. Don't let others take advantage of you so that you put them in the "You're not OK" life position, and so that you can stay in the "I'm OK" position. Be careful not to be passive and not to use the avoiding and accommodating conflict styles to get out of confronting others; you need to satisfy your needs too.

How well you deal with your emotions, especially anger, is what *adjustment* is about. If you are not high on adjustment personality traits, you will tend to use the parent or child ego states. You may be in the "I'm not OK" position, and others will be in the "You're not OK" position. Based on your adjustment personality, you can be passive (let people take advantage of you) or aggressive (try to take advantage of others), and poor adjustment can lead to violence. Low adjustment people are usually poor at dealing with conflict, because they tend to avoid and accommodate or to force in conflict situations. Try not to be low in adjustment and get too emotional. Use the tips on dealing with emotions, especially anger.

There is a relationship between adjustment and *openness to experience*. If you are not well adjusted, you are probably not open to experience. If you are low on openness, you may not handle conflicts well since their resolution often requires change. So try to be open to new experiences.

If you are a high *conscientious* personality, you can still transact from the parent or child ego state. You may be in the "I'm OK" life position, but be sure not to put others in the "You're not OK" position. Watch your use of aggressive behavior to achieve your objectives. You may be good at conflict resolution, but be careful to meet others' needs too.

Action plan: Based on your personality, what specific things will you do to improve your TA, assertiveness, and conflict management skills?

_____

_____

_____

_____

Videos

Manager's Hot Seat and Behavior Model Videos are available for this chapter.

Online Learning Center Resources
Go to the Internet (http://mhhe.com/lussier8e) where you will find a broad array of resources to help maximize your learning.

• Review the vocabulary.

• Try a quiz.

R E V I E W

The chapter review is organized to help you master the 8 learning outcomes for Chapter 7. First provide your own response to each learning outcome, and then check the summary provided to see how well you understand the material. Next, identify the final statement in each section as either true or false (T/F). Correct each false statement. Answers are given at the end of the chapter.

1. **Describe the three ego states of transactional analysis.**
   The three ego states of transactional analysis are: (1) *parent:* the critical parent is evaluative, while the sympathetic parent is supportive; (2) *child:* the natural child is curious, while the adapted child is rebellious; and (3) *adult:* the adult is a thinking, unemotional state of ego.
   Transactional analysis was first developed for the field of psychology and later applied to business. T F

2. **Explain the three types of transactions.**
   The three types of transactions are: (1) *complementary:* the sender of the message gets the intended response from the receiver; (2) *crossed:* the sender does not get the expected response; and (3) *ulterior:* the person appears to be in one ego state, but his or her behavior comes from a different ego state.
   Complementary transactions always come from the same ego state. T F

3. **Identify the differences between passive, aggressive, and assertive behavior.**
   Passive behavior is nonassertive. The passive person gives in to the other party without standing up for his or her rights.
   Aggressive behavior includes the use of force to get one's own way, often at the expense of violating others' rights.
   Assertive behavior involves standing up for one's rights without violating the rights of others.
   Passive–aggressive behavior occurs when a person says nothing when irritated, lets anger build up, and then blows up. T F

4. **List the four steps of assertive behavior.**
   The four steps of assertive behavior are: (1) set an objective; (2) determine how to create a win–win situation; (3) develop an assertive phrase; and (4) implement your plan persistently.
   Assertive behavior should be used to get what you want, while the other party loses. T F

5. **Explain when a conflict exists.**
   A conflict exists whenever two or more parties are in disagreement.
   The primary reason conflicts happen is that expectations are not met. T F

6. **State when and how to use five conflict management styles.**
   The five conflict management styles are: (1) *forcing,* when the user attempts to resolve the conflict by using aggressive behavior. It should be used when the conflict is one involving personal differences; (2) *avoiding,* when the user attempts to passively ignore the conflict rather than resolve it. It should be used when one's stake in the issue is not high; (3) *accommodating,* when the user attempts to resolve the conflict by passively giving in to the other party. It should be used when maintaining relations outweighs all

other considerations; (4) *compromising,* when the user attempts to resolve the conflict through assertive give-and-take concessions. It should be used when the issues are complex and critical, and when there is no simple and clear solution; and (5) *collaborating,* when the user assertively attempts to jointly resolve the conflict with the best solution agreeable to all parties. It should be used for peer conflicts.

When an employee doesn't do what the supervisor requests, the forcing conflict style is appropriate. T F

7. **List the steps of initiating, responding to, and mediating conflict resolutions.**

The initiating conflict resolution steps are: (1) plan to maintain ownership of the problem using the XYZ model; (2) implement your plan persistently; and (3) make an agreement for change. The responding to conflict resolution steps are: (1) listen to and paraphrase the problem using the XYZ model; (2) agree with some aspect of the complaint; (3) ask for, and/or give, alternative solutions; and (4) make an agreement for change. The mediating conflict resolution steps are: (1) have each party state his or her complaint using the XYZ model; (2) agree on the problem(s); (3) develop alternative solutions; and (4) make an agreement for change, and follow up.

Initiating, responding to, and mediating a conflict all take the same level of skill. T F

Learning Outcome

8.   Define the following 14 key terms.

8. **Define the following 14 key terms.**

Select one or more methods: (1) fill in the missing key terms from memory; (2) match the key terms from the end of the review with their definitions below; and/or (3) copy the key terms in order from the key terms at the beginning of the chapter.

_____ is a method of understanding behavior in interpersonal dynamics.

_____ are the parent, child, and adult.

_____ are complementary, crossed, and ulterior.

_____ is the process of expressing thoughts and feelings while asking for what one wants in an appropriate way.

_____ exists whenever two or more parties are in disagreement.

The _____ user attempts to resolve the conflict by using aggressive behavior.

The _____ user attempts to passively ignore the conflict rather than resolve it.

The _____ user attempts to resolve the conflict by passively giving in to the other party.

The _____ user attempts to resolve the conflict through assertive give-and-take concessions.

The _____ user assertively attempts to resolve the conflict with the best solution agreeable to all parties.

The _____ are these: step (1) plan to maintain ownership of the problem using the XYZ model; step (2) implement your plan persistently; and step (3) make an agreement for change.

The _____ describes a problem in terms of behavior, consequences, and feelings.

The _____ are as follows: step (1) listen to and paraphrase the problem using the XYZ model; step (2) agree with some aspect of the complaint; step (3) ask for, and/or give, alternative solutions; and step (4) make an agreement for change.

The _____ are these: step (1) have each party state his or her complaint using the XYZ model; step (2) agree on the problem(s); step (3) develop alternative solutions; and step (4) make an agreement for change, and follow up.

KEY TERMS

accommodating conflict style   247
assertiveness   236
avoiding conflict style   247
collaborating conflict style   248

compromising conflict style   248
conflict   243
ego states   232
forcing conflict style   246
initiating conflict resolution steps   250

mediating conflict resolution steps   252
responding to conflict resolution steps   252
transactional analysis   231
types of transactions   233
XYZ model   250

COMMUNICATION SKILLS

The following critical thinking questions can be used for class discussion and/or as written assignments to develop communication skills. Be sure to give complete explanations for all questions.

1. Some people say that because transactional analysis was developed in the 1960s, it is outdated. Do you agree, or do you believe that TA can help us to understand behavior and improve human relations?

2. Some people intentionally use ulterior transactions to get what they want without others knowing it. Are ulterior transactions ethical?

3. Some people have negative attitudes and use negative strokes that hurt others. Is giving negative strokes unethical behavior?

4. Select a person you know who is consistently passive. Do people take advantage of this person, such as getting them to do more work? Do you? Is it ethical to take advantage of passive people?

5. Select a person you know who is consistently aggressive. Do people let this person get his or her way? Do you? What is the best way to deal with an aggressive person? What is the best way to deal with a passive–aggressive person?

6. Select a person you know who is consistently assertive. Do people tend to respect this person, and does this person have effective human relations? Do you have effective human relations? What will you do to improve your assertiveness?

7. Recall an occasion of violence at school or work. Describe the situation. Were there signs that violence was coming? What can you do to help prevent violence?

8. Which conflict management style do you use most often? Why do you tend to use this conflict style? How can you become more collaborative?

9. How do you feel about the use of the forcing conflict style? Do you use it often? Is using the forcing style ethical?

CASE

William D. Perez and Phillip H. Knight: Nike, Inc.

Nike is the world's number one shoemaker. With total revenues in 2008 of over $18 billion, it controls more than 20 percent of the U.S. athletic shoe market. Nike does more dominating than assisting, to capture a hefty share of the U.S. athletic shoe market. It designs and sells shoes for a variety of sports, including baseball, cheerleading, golf, volleyball, hiking, tennis, and football. Nike also sells Cole Haan dress and casual shoes, as well as athletic apparel and equipment. In addition, Nike operates Niketown shoe and sportswear stores, Nike factory outlets, and Nike Women shops. Nike sells its products throughout the U.S. and in more than 180 other countries. The firm has increased its net profit margin in the last three years from 9.3 to 10.1 percent while simultaneously increasing its dividends per share from 56 cents to 83 cents.

Given the company's historically positive financial performance, one would think that the firm would be operating as one big happy family; unfortunately, in 2005 that was anything but the case. The newly appointed CEO William D. Perez realized that Nike's founder and chairman, Phillip H. Knight, was battling him on everything from where Nike could sell its sneakers to how much time executives should be spending attending meetings. Mr. Knight claimed that the fallout was due to Mr. Perez's inability to acclimate to the Nike culture, while Mr. Perez felt that Mr. Knight, a former CEO of the firm, was overbearing and overcontrolling as chair of the board.

"Phil didn't back off," said Mr. Perez. "He hired me to replace him and he never left. His level of interaction with employees was the same as the day before I got there. As Phil often says, he is not the greatest communicator. I would hear that he had a different position from mine—not from him but from another person I talked to at Nike. That leads to confused employees and a very frustrated CEO."

Mr. Knight, on the other hand, said that "Nike was operating at 80 percent efficiency under Mr. Perez—an awkward position to be in when its biggest rivals are ganging up on it. I did not see that getting any better." Adidas and Reebok account for nearly 30 percent of the world's market share, slightly less than Nike's 31 percent market share. However, in the U.S. market Nike controls over 36 percent of the market compared to 21 percent of Adidas and Reebok combined. Outside of the U.S., Adidas has overtaken Nike in Japan and has been very active in both China and India, two emerging markets that Nike has been less active in.

Mr. Perez, however, saw the problem dealing more with a disagreement over the firm's basic strategy and management philosophy. "The lower-price-point segment was the fastest growing segment of the footwear market. Where you sell your products is all about the selling environment. Apple is for sale in Apple, Best Buy, and Wal-Mart. If you can sell a brand as powerful and important in Wal-Mart points of distribution, you can sell any brand."

These dissimilarities filtered down into operational and style issues. Knight was more in the meeting mold. Perez would get things done and move on to the next subject. People were spending lots of time in frustrating meetings where decisions were not being made. Perez, a data man, wants to know what the facts are. Nike is very different because feel is very important. Feel can't be replaced with facts, but data can be used as a guide. Perez wanted Knight to be involved, but wanted him to be inspiring and energizing, not running the business. Perez didn't expect him to get involved to the extent that he did.

As a result, Nike veteran Mark Parker succeeded William Perez as president and CEO. He has been employed by Nike since 1979 with primary responsibilities in product research, design and development, marketing, and brand management. Mr. Parker was appointed divisional vice president in charge of development in 1987, corporate vice president in 1989, general manager in 1993, vice president of global footwear in 1998, and president of the Nike brand in 2001.[94]

Go to the Internet: For more information on Nike and to update the information provided in this case, do a name search on the Internet and visit www.nike.com.

Support your answers to the following questions with specific information from the case and text, or with other information you get from the Web or other sources.

1. Using transactional analysis, describe the implied nature of the interaction between Mr. Perez and Mr. Knight. What do you believe led to these crossed transactions?

2. Using the terms *assertive, passive,* and *aggressive,* describe the implied behaviors of Mr. Knight and Mr. Perez in their interactions.

3. What conflict management style is being exhibited in this case?

4. How was the conflict resolved between Mr. Knight and Mr. Perez? How would you have resolved the conflict between Mr. Knight and Mr. Perez?

Cumulative Questions

5. What roles do perception (Chapter 2), attitudes, and values (Chapter 3) play in this case?

6. How might active listening (Chapter 5) have assisted Mr. Knight and Mr. Perez in understanding each others' positions?

7. How is Mr. Knight, as chair of the board of Nike, bypassing the traditional chain of command (Chapter 6) at Nike?

OBJECTIVE CASE   **Bill and Saul's Conflict**

The following conversation takes place over the telephone between Bill, the salesperson, and Saul, the production manager.

BILL: Listen, Saul, I just got an order for 1,000 units and promised delivery in two days. You'll get them out on time, won't you?

SAUL: Bill, you know the normal delivery time is five days.

BILL: I know, but I had to say two days to get the order, so fill it.

SAUL: We don't have the capability to do it. You should have checked with me before taking the order. The best I can do is four days.

BILL: What are you—my mother, or the production manager?

SAUL: I cannot have 1,000 units ready in two days. We have other orders that need to be filled before yours. Four days is the best I can do on short notice.

BILL: Come on, Saul, you cannot do this to me, I want to keep this account. It can mean a lot of business.

SAUL: I know, Bill; you've told me this on three other orders you had.

BILL: But this is a big one. Don't you care about sales?

SAUL: Yes, I do, but I cannot produce the product as fast as you sales reps are selling it lately.

BILL: If I don't meet my sales quota, are you going to take the blame?

SAUL: Bill, we are going in circles here. I'm sorry, but I cannot fill your request. The order will be ready in four days.

BILL: I was hoping you would be reasonable. But you've forced me to go to Mr. Carlson. You know he'll be telling you to fill my order. Why don't you just do it and save time and aggravation?

SAUL: I'll wait to hear from Mr. Carlson. In the meantime, have a good day, Bill.

Answer the following questions. Then in the space between the questions, state why you selected that answer.

_____ 1. Bill was transacting from the _____ ego state.

     a. critical parent   *c.* adult   *e.* adapted child

     b. sympathetic parent   *d.* natural child

_____ 2. Saul was transacting from the _____ ego state.

     a. critical parent   *c.* adult   *e.* adapted child

     b. sympathetic parent   *d.* natural child

_____ 3. The telephone discussion was a(n) _____ transaction.

     a. complementary   *b.* crossed   *c.* ulterior

_____ 4. Bill's life position seems to be:

     a. I'm OK—   *c.* I'm not OK—

        You're not OK   You're not OK

     b. I'm OK—   *d.* I'm not OK—

        You're OK   You're OK

_____ 5. Bill's behavior was:

     a. passive   *b.* aggressive   *c.* assertive

_____ 6. Saul's behavior was:

     a. passive   *b.* aggressive   *c.* assertive

_____ 7. Bill and Saul have an _____ conflict.

     a. individual   *c.* individual/group

     b. interpersonal   *d.* intragroup

_____ 8. Their source of conflict is:

     a. personal differences   *c.* objectives

     b. information   *d.* environment

_____ 9. Bill used the _____ conflict style.

     a. forcing   *c.* accommodating   *e.* collaborating

     b. avoiding   *d.* compromising

_____ 10. Saul used the _____ conflict style.

     a. forcing   *c.* accommodating   *e.* collaborating

     b. avoiding   *d.* compromising

11. What would you have done if you were Bill?

12. Assume you are Mr. Carlson, the boss. How will you respond when Bill calls?

Note: The conversation between Bill and Saul and/or their meeting with Mr. Carlson can be role-played in class.

Transactional Analysis

Preparation (Individual and Group)

Below are 10 situations. For each situation:

1. Identify the sender's communication ego state as:

   CP—Critical Parent

   SP—Sympathetic Parent

   NC—Natural Child

   AC—Adapted Child

   A—Adult

2. Place the letters CP, SP, NC, AC, or A on the S _____ to the left of each numbered situation.

3. Identify each of the five alternative receiver's ego states as in instruction 1 above. Place the letters CP, SP, NC, AC, or A on the R _____.

4. Select the best alternative to achieve effective communication and human relations. Circle the letter *a, b, c, d,* or *e.*

S _____ 1. Ted delegates a task, saying, "It's not much fun, but someone has to do it. Will you please do it for me?" Sue, the delegatee, says:

    a. "A good boss wouldn't make me do it."   R _____

    b. "I'm always willing to help you out, Ted."   R _____

    c. "I'm not cleaning that up."   R _____

    d. "You're not being serious, are you?"   R _____

    e. "I'll get right on it."   R _____

S _____ 2. Helen, a customer, brought a dress to the cleaners, and later she picked it up, paid, and went home. At home she opened the package and found that the dress was not clean. Helen returned to the cleaners and said, "What's wrong with this place? Don't you know how to clean a dress?" The cleaning person, Saul, responds:

    a. "It's not my fault. I didn't clean it personally."   R _____

    b. "I'm sorry this happened. We'll do it again right now."   R _____

    c. "I can understand your disappointment. Were you planning on wearing it today? What can I do to make this up to you?"   R _____ *d.* "These are stains caused by your carelessness, not ours."   R _____

   e. "Gee whiz, this is the first time this has happened."   R _____

S _____ 3. In an office, Bill drops a tray of papers on the floor. Mary, the manager, comes over and says, "This happens once in awhile to all of us. Let me help you pick them up." Bill responds:

   a. "Guess I slipped, ha ha ha."   R _____

   b. "This wouldn't have happened if people didn't stack the papers so high."   R _____

   c. "It's not my fault; I'm not picking up the papers."   R _____

   d. "Thanks for helping me pick them up, Mary."   R _____

   e. "It will not take long to pick them up."   R _____

S _____ 4. Karl and Kelly were talking about the merit raise given in their branch of the bank. Karl says: "I heard you did not get a merit raise." Kelly responds:

   a. "It's true; how much did you get?"   R _____

   b. "I really don't need a raise anyway."   R _____

   c. "The branch manager is unfair."   R _____

   d. "The branch manager didn't give me a raise because he is prejudiced. The men got bigger raises than the women."   R _____

   e. "It's nice of you to show your concern. Is there anything I can do to help you out?"   R _____

S _____ 5. Beckie, the store manager, says to an employee: "Ed, there is no gum on the counter; please restock it." Ed responds:

   a. "Why do I always get stuck doing it?"   R _____

   b. "I'd be glad to do it. I know how important it is to keep the shelves stocked for our customers."   R _____

   c. "I'll do it just as soon as I finish this row."   R _____

   d. "I'll do it if I can have a free pack."   R _____

   e. "Why don't we buy bigger boxes so I don't have to do it so often?"   R _____

S _____ 6. Carol, the manager, asked Tim, an employee, to file some forms. A while later Carol returned and asked Tim why he hadn't filed the forms. Tim said: "Oh, oh! I forgot about it." Carol responds:

   a. "I've told you before; write things down so you don't forget to do them."   R _____

   b. "It's OK. I know you're busy and will do it when you can."   R _____

   c. "Please do it now."   R _____

   d. "What's wrong with you?"   R _____

   e. "You daydreaming or what?"   R _____

S _____ 7. Joan just finished making a budget presentation to the controller, Wayne. He says: "This budget is padded." Joan responds:

   a. "I'm sorry you feel that way. What is a fair budget amount?"   R _____

   b. (*laughing*) "I don't pad any more than the others."   R _____

   c. "You don't know what you're talking about. It's not padded."   R _____

   d. "What items do you believe are padded?"   R _____

   e. "You can't expect me to run my department without some padding for emergencies, can you?"   R _____

S _____ 8. Jill, a computer repair technician, says to the customer: "What did you do to this computer to make it malfunction like this?" The customer responds:

a. "Can you fix it?"   R ____

b. "I take good care of this machine. You better fix it fast."   R ____

c. "I'm sorry to upset you. Are you having a rough day?"   R ____

d. "I'm going to tell your boss what you just said."   R ____

e. "I threw it down the stairs, ha ha."   R ____

S _____ 9. Pete is waiting for his friend, Will, whom he hasn't seen for some time. When Will arrives, Pete says, "It's good to see you," and gives Will a hug, spinning him around. Will responds:

a. "Don't hug me on the street; people can see us."   R ____

b. "I'm not late; you got here early."   R ____

c. "Sorry I'm late. Is there anything I can do to make it up to you? Just name it."   R ____

d. "Let's go party, party, party."   R ____

e. "Sorry I'm late; I got held up in traffic."   R ____

S _____ 10. Sally gives her secretary, Mike, a note saying: "Please type this when you get a chance." About an hour later, Sally returns from a meeting and asks: "Mike, is the letter I gave you done yet?" Mike responds:

a. "If you wanted it done by 11, why didn't you say so?"   R ____

b. "I'm working on it now. It will be done in about 10 minutes."   R ____

c. "You said to do it when I got a chance. I've been too busy doing more important things."   R ____

d. "Sure thing, boss lady, I'll get right on it."   R ____

e. "I'm sorry, I didn't realize how important it was. Can I type it right now and get it to you in about 15 minutes?"   R ____

In-Class Exercise

Objective: To improve your ability to use transactional analysis.

AACSB: The primary AACSB learning standard skills developed through this exercise are analytic skills and communication abilities.

Preparation: You should have completed the preparation (10 situations) for this exercise.

**Procedure
(5–50 minutes)**

Select one option:

1. The instructor goes over the recommended answers to the 10 situations.

2. The instructor asks students for their answers to the situations, followed by giving the recommended answers.

3. Break into groups of two or three and together follow the three-step approach for two to three situations at a time, followed by the instructor's going over the recommended answers. Discuss the possible consequences of each alternative response in the situation. Would it help or hurt human relations and performance? How?

Conclusion: The instructor leads a class discussion and/or makes concluding remarks.

Application: What have I learned from this experience? How will I use this knowledge in the future?

Sharing: Volunteers give their answers to the application section.

Assertiveness

Preparation (Individual and Group)

In this exercise there are 10 situations with 5 alternative statements or actions. Identify each as assertive (A), aggressive (G), or passive (P). Place the letter A, G, or P on the line before each of the five alternatives. Circle the letter (*a* to *e*) of the response that is the most appropriate in the situation.

1. In class, you are in small groups discussing this exercise; however, two of the members are talking about personal matters instead. You are interested in this exercise.

   _____ *a.* "Don't you want to learn anything in this class?"

   _____ *b.* Forget the exercise, join the conversation.

   _____ *c.* "This is a valuable exercise. I'd really appreciate your input."

   _____ *d.* "This exercise is boring, isn't it?"

   _____ *e.* "Stop discussing personal matters, or leave the class!"

2. You and your roommate do not smoke. Smoke really bothers you. However, your roommate has friends over who smoke in your room regularly.

   _____ *a.* Throw them out of your room.

   _____ *b.* Purposely cough, repeatedly saying, "I cannot breathe."

   _____ *c.* Ask your roommate to have his guests refrain from smoking, or meet at a different place.

   _____ *d.* Complain to your favorite professor.

   _____ *e.* Do and say nothing.

3. Your boss has repeatedly asked you to go get coffee for the members of the department. It is not part of your job responsibility.

   _____ *a.* "It is not part of my job. Why don't we set up a rotating schedule so that everyone has a turn?"

   _____ *b.* "Go get it yourself."

   _____ *c.* Continue to get the coffee.

   _____ *d.* File a complaint with the personnel department or the union.

   _____ *e.* "Why don't we skip coffee today?"

4. You are riding in a car with a friend. You are nervous because your friend is speeding, changing lanes frequently, and passing in no-passing zones.

   _____ *a.* "Are you trying to kill me?"

   _____ *b.* "What did you think of Professor Lussier's class today?"

   _____ *c.* "Please slow down and stay in one lane."

   _____ *d.* Try not to look where you are going.

   _____ *e.* "Stop driving like this or let me out right here."

5. You are in a department meeting to decide on the new budget. However, some of the members are going off on tangents and wasting time. Your boss hasn't said anything about it.

   _____ *a.* Don't say anything. After all, it's your boss's meeting.

   _____ *b.* "So far we agree on XYZ, and we still need to decide on ABC. Does anyone have any ideas on these line items?"

   _____ *c.* "Let's stop wasting time and stay on the subject."

   _____ *d.* "Let's just vote so we can get out of here."

   _____ *e.* "Excuse me, I have to go to the bathroom."

6. One of your coworkers repeatedly tries to get you to do her work with all kinds of excuses.

    _____ *a.* Do the work.

    _____ *b.* "I have no intention of doing your work, so please stop asking me to do it."

    _____ *c.* "Buzz off. Do it yourself, freeloader."

    _____ *d.* "I'd like to do it for you, but I'm tied up right now."

    _____ *e.* "Get away from me and don't bother me again."

7. You bought a watch. It doesn't work, so you return to the store with the receipt. The salesclerk says you cannot exchange it.

    _____ *a.* Insist on the exchange. Talk to the person's boss and his or her boss if necessary.

    _____ *b.* Leave with the watch.

    _____ *c.* Drop the watch on the counter and pick up a new watch and walk out.

    _____ *d.* Come back when a different salesclerk is there.

    _____ *e.* Create a scene, yell, and get other customers on your side. Disrupt business until you get the new watch.

8. You are about to leave work and go to see your child perform in a play. Your boss comes to you and asks you to stay late to do a report she needs in the morning.

    _____ *a.* "Sorry, I'm on my way to see a play."

    _____ *b.* "I'd be happy to stay and do it."

    _____ *c.* "Are you sure I cannot do it tomorrow?"

    _____ *d.* "I'm on my way to see a play. Can I take it home and do it later tonight?"

    _____ *e.* "Why should I get stuck here? Why don't you do it yourself?"

9. You believe that cheating is wrong. Your roommate just asked you if he could copy the homework you spent hours preparing.

    _____ *a.* "Here you go."

    _____ *b.* "I don't help cheaters."

    _____ *c.* "OK, if you don't copy it word for word."

    _____ *d.* "I'd like to help you. You're my friend, but in good conscience I cannot let you copy my homework."

    _____ *e.* "You go out and have a good time, then you expect me to be a fool and get you off the hook? No way."

10. Some people you know stop by your dorm room. One of them pulls out some drugs, takes some, and passes them along. You don't take drugs.

    _____ *a.* "I don't approve of taking drugs. You can get me into trouble. Please put them away or leave."

    _____ *b.* Grab them and get rid of them.

    _____ *c.* Take some drugs because you don't want to look bad.

    _____ *d.* Pass them along without taking any.

    _____ *e.* "Are you trying to kill yourselves? Get out of here with that stuff."

In-Class Exercise

Objective: To improve your ability to be assertive.

AACSB: The primary AACSB learning standard skills developed through this exercise are analytic skills and communication abilities.

Preparation: You should have completed the preparation (the 10 situations) for this exercise.

Procedure
(5–30 minutes)

Select one option:

1. The instructor goes over the recommended answers to the 10 situations.

2. The instructor asks students for their answers to the situations, followed by giving the recommended answers.

3. Break into groups of two or three and together follow the three-step approach for two or three situations at a time, followed by the instructor's going over the recommended answers. Discuss the possible consequences of each alternative response in the situation. Would it help or hurt human relations and performance? How?

Conclusion: The instructor leads a class discussion and/or makes concluding remarks.

Application: What have I learned from this experience? How will I use this knowledge in the future?

Sharing: Volunteers give their answers to the application section.

Using the XYZ Conflict Model

Preparation (Individual and Group)

Below are five conflict situations. Write the XYZ statement you would use to resolve the conflict. Remember the goal of resolving the conflict while maintaining human relations.

1. A coworker has asked you to go out after work for the second time. The first time you gave an excuse for not being able to go, but you really don't want to go out with this person. What would you say?

   X _____

   Y _____

   Z _____

2. A coworker keeps coming to your work area to socialize. You have been talking as long as the person wants to. But it is affecting getting your work done, and you have had to stay late. What would you say?

   X _____

   Y _____

   Z _____

3. A coworker has been taking it easy and not doing his share of the work on your two-person assignment. You have had to do more than your share, and you don't want it to continue. What would you say?

   X _____

   Y _____

   Z _____

4. A coworker has continued to interrupt another coworker friend of yours as she speaks. It is upsetting you, and you have decided to talk to the interrupter privately about it. What would you say?

   X _____

   Y _____

   Z _____

5. A coworker is playing music loud for the third time. You don't like the music, and it affects your ability to concentrate. You haven't said anything, but you plan to now. What would you say?

X _____

Y _____

Z _____

In-Class Exercise	*Objective:* To improve your ability to initiate conflict resolution with positive statements.

AACSB: The primary AACSB learning standard skills developed through this exercise are analytic skills and communication abilities.

Preparation: You should have completed the preparation (the five situations) for this exercise.

Procedure
(5–30 minutes)

Select one option:

1. The instructor goes over possible answers to the five situations.
2. The instructor asks students for their XYZ statements to the situations, followed by giving possible answers.
3. Break into groups of two or three, and together come up with an XYZ statement, followed by the instructor's going over the recommended answers. Discuss the possible consequences of each alternative response in the situation. Would it help or hurt human relations and performance? How?

Conclusion: The instructor leads a class discussion and/or makes concluding remarks.

Application: What have I learned from this experience? How will I use this knowledge in the future?

Sharing: Volunteers give their answers to the application section.

Initiating Conflict Resolution

Preparation (Group)

During class you will be given the opportunity to role-play a conflict you face, or have faced, in order to develop your conflict skills. Fill in the information below, and also record your answers on a separate sheet of paper.

Other party (or parties) (You may use fictitious names) _____

Define the situation:

1. List pertinent information about the other party (e.g., relationship with you, knowledge of the situation, age, background).
2. State what you wish to accomplish (objective) as a result of the conflict confrontation or discussion.
3. Identify the other party's possible reaction to your confrontation (resistance to change: intensity, source, focus).

How will you overcome this resistance to change?

Using the three steps in initiating conflict resolution, on a separate sheet of paper write out your plan to initiate the conflict resolution. Bring your written plan to class.

In-Class Exercise

Objective: To experience and develop skills in resolving a conflict.

AACSB: The primary AACSB learning standard skills developed through this exercise are analytic skills and communication abilities.

Preparation: You should have completed the information and written plan in preparation for this exercise.

BMV 7–1

Experience: You will initiate, respond to, and observe a conflict role play, and then evaluate the effectiveness of its resolution.

Procedure 1
(2–3 minutes)

Break into as many groups of three as possible. If there are any people not in a triad, make one or two groups of two. Each member selects the number 1, 2, or 3. Number 1 will be the first to initiate a conflict role play, then 2, followed by 3.

Procedure 2
(8–15 minutes)

1. Initiator number 1 gives his or her information from the preparation to number 2 (the responder) to read. Once number 2 understands, role-play (see number 2 below). Number 3 is the observer.

2. Role-play the conflict resolution. Number 3, the observer, writes his or her observations on the feedback sheet (see following page).

3. Integration: When the role play is over, the observer leads a discussion on the effectiveness of the conflict resolution. All three should discuss the effectiveness. Number 3 is not a lecturer. Do not go on until told to do so.

Procedure 3
(8–15 minutes)

Follow procedure 2; this time number 2 is the initiator, number 3 is the responder, and number 1 is the observer.

Procedure 4
(8–15 minutes)

Follow procedure 2; this time number 3 is the initiator, number 1 is the responder, and number 2 is the observer.

Conclusion: The instructor leads a class discussion and/or makes concluding remarks.

Application (2–4 minutes):   What did I learn from this experience? How will I use this knowledge in the future?

BMV 7–2
Mediating Conflict
Resolution *may be
shown.*

Sharing: Volunteers give their answers to the application section.

Feedback for _____

Try to have positive improvement comments for each step in initiating conflict resolution. Remember to be descriptive and specific, and for all improvements have an alternative positive behavior (APB) (i.e., if you would have said/done . . . , it would have improved the conflict resolution by . . .).

Step 1: Did the initiator *maintain ownership* of the problem?

Did he or she have and implement a well-thought-out *XYZ plan?*

Step 2: Did he or she *persist* until the confrontee acknowledged the problem?

Step 3: Did the initiator get the confrontee to *agree to a change* or solution?

ANSWERS TO TRUE/FALSE QUESTIONS

1. T.
2. F. Complementary transactions can come from *any* ego state, such as parent to child.
3. T.
4. F. Assertive behavior is used to create a win–win situation, not a win–lose situation as stated.
5. T.
6. T.
7. F. It is more difficult to mediate a conflict.

PART **3**

Leading and Trust

After completing this chapter, you should be able to:

1. Explain what leadership is and how it affects behavior, human relations, and performance.

2. Describe leadership trait theory.

3. List and describe four behavioral leadership theories.

4. List and describe four contingency leadership theories.

5. Explain four situational supervisory styles.

6. Identify three characteristics that substitute for management.

7. Briefly describe the five dimensions of trust.

8. Define the following 14 key terms (in order of appearance in the chapter):

leadership	**normative leadership theory**
leadership trait theory	**situational leadership**
behavioral leadership theories	**autocratic style**
Leadership Grid	**consultative style**
contingency leadership theories	**participative style**
contingency leadership theory	**laissez-faire style**
leadership continuum	**trust**

How Leadership Affects Behavior, Human Relations, and Performance

Leadership Trait Theory

The Ghiselli Study

Current Studies

Behavioral Leadership Theories

Basic Leadership Styles

Two-Dimensional Leadership Styles

The Leadership Grid

Transformational Leadership

Contingency Leadership Theories

Contingency Leadership Theory

Leadership Continuum

Normative Leadership Theory

Situational Leadership

Situational Supervision

Defining the Situation

Using the Appropriate Supervisory Style

Applying the Situational Supervision Model

Putting the Leadership Theories Together

Substitutes for Leadership?

Diversity and Global Leadership

Trust

Types of Trust

Developing Trust

Mike Templeton is a branch manager at the Northwest Bank in Davenport, Iowa. Mike has authority over subordinates to make decisions regarding hiring and firing, raises, and promotions. Mike gets along well with his subordinates. The branch atmosphere is friendly. His boss has asked for a special report about the loans the branch has made so far this year. Mike could have done the report himself, but he thought it would be better to delegate the task to one of the three loan officers. After thinking about the qualifications of the three loan officers, Mike selected Jean. He called her into his office to talk about the assignment.

MIKE: Hi, Jean, I've called you in here to tell you that I've selected you to do a year-to-date loan report for the branch. It's not mandatory; I can assign the report to someone else. Are you interested?

JEAN: I don't know; I've never done a report before.

MIKE: I realize that, but I'm sure you can handle it. I selected you because of my faith in your ability.

JEAN: Will you help me?

MIKE: Sure. There is more than one way to do the report. I can give you the details on what must be included in the report, but you can use any format you want, as long as I approve it. We can discuss the report now; then as you work on it, you can come to me for input. I'm confident you'll do a great job. Do you want the assignment?

JEAN: Okay, I'll do it.

Together, Mike and Jean discuss how she will do the report.

What leadership style would you use to get the report done? This chapter explains 10 leadership theories. Each will be applied to the loan report.

In Part 1 (Chapters 1 to 4) we focused on developing intrapersonal skills, and in Part 2 (Chapters 5 to 7) we built on those skills to develop interpersonal skills. We are now in Part 3, so we turn to developing leadership skills, which are clearly based on intrapersonal and interpersonal skills. These three skills form a natural, overlapping developmental sequence.[1] Leadership is both a skill and a behavior that exhibits that skill.[2]

HOW LEADERSHIP AFFECTS BEHAVIOR, HUMAN RELATIONS, AND PERFORMANCE

Leadership *is the process of influencing employees to work toward the achievement of objectives.* Leadership is one of the most talked-about, researched, and written-about management topics.[3] However, even though leadership skills can be taught,[4] recruiters say they often see a lack of interpersonal and leadership skills in job applicants.[5] Strong leadership is needed.[6] With today's focus on teamwork, leadership ability is important to everyone in the organization, not just managers.[7]

There are various styles of leadership.[8] The leader's style affects the leader's behavior.[9] In other words, the leader's behavior actually makes the leader's style. An autocratic leader displays behavior different from that of a democratic leader. The human relations between leader and follower will differ according to the leadership style.[10] This will be explained in more detail throughout the chapter.

Leadership can make a difference in performance.[11] The success of individual careers and the fate of organizations are determined by how effectively leaders behave.[12] In most cases, effective leadership leads to better performance.[13] Transformational leadership has been shown to have a positive relationship with performance.[14] Truly outstanding leaders tend to elicit commitment and high performance from others through trust relationships.[15]

Leadership and Management Are Not the Same   People tend to use the terms *manager* and *leader* interchangeably. However, that usage is not correct. Management and leadership are related but different concepts. Leadership is one of the five management functions (planning, organizing, staffing, leading, and controlling). Someone can be a manager without being a true leader.[16] There are managers—you may know of some—who are not leaders because they do not have the ability to influence others. There are also good leaders who are not managers.[17] The informal leader, an employee group member, is a case in point. You may have worked in a situation where one of your peers had more influence in the department than the manager.

Our definition of leadership does not suggest that influencing employees is the task of the manager alone; employees do influence other employees.[18] Anyone can be a leader within any group or department, and everyone in a team is expected to be a leader.[19] Thus, regardless of your position, you are expected to share leadership, because leadership is a shared activity.[20]

WORK APPLICATIONS

1. Give detailed reasons why leadership skills are important to a specific organization.

For years researchers have been trying to answer these questions: "What does it take to be an effective leader?" and "What is the most effective leadership style?" There is no universal agreement about the answers to these questions.[21] We will now turn to a chronological review of how researchers have tried to answer these questions. After studying the major leadership theories, you can select the one you like best, combine some, or develop your own.

LEADERSHIP TRAIT THEORY

Learning Outcome

2. Describe leadership trait theory.

In the early 1900s, an organized approach to studying leadership began. The early studies were based on the assumption that leaders are born, not made. This concept was later called the "great man" theory of leadership.[22] Researchers wanted to identify a set of characteristics, or traits, that distinguished leaders from followers or effective from ineffective leaders. **Leadership trait theory** *assumes that there are distinctive physical and psychological characteristics accounting for leadership effectiveness.* In fact, personality traits do affect leadership style.[23] Researchers analyzed traits, or qualities, such as appearance, aggressiveness, self-reliance, persuasiveness, and dominance in an effort to identify a set of traits that all successful leaders possess.[24] The list of traits was to be used as a prerequisite for the promotion of candidates to leadership positions. Only candidates possessing all the identified traits were to be given leadership positions.

Inconclusive Findings: In 70 years, more than 300 trait studies were conducted.[25] However, no one has come up with a universal list of traits that all successful leaders possess.[26] In all cases, there were exceptions. For example, several lists identified successful leaders as being tall. However, Napoleon was short. In addition, some people were successful in one leadership position but not in another.

People also questioned whether traits such as assertiveness and self-confidence were developed before or after one became a leader. It is practically impossible to uncover a universal set of traits. Indeed, if leaders were simply born and not made (in other words, if leadership skills could not be developed), there would be no need for courses in management and human relations.[27]

The Ghiselli Study

Probably the most widely publicized trait theory study was conducted by Edwin Ghiselli.[28] His study concluded that there are traits important to effective leadership, though not all are necessary for success. Ghiselli identified the following six traits, in order of importance, as being significant traits for effective leadership:

1. *Supervisory ability.* Getting the job done through others. Basically, the ability to perform the five functions of management. You will develop these skills in this course.
2. *Need for occupational achievement.* Seeking responsibility. The motivation to work hard to succeed (Chapter 9).
3. *Intelligence.* The ability to use good judgment, reasoning, and thinking capacity commonly called cognitive capabilities[29] (Chapter 2).
4. *Decisiveness.* The ability to solve problems and make decisions competently (Chapter 13).
5. *Self-assurance.* Viewing oneself as capable of coping with problems. Behaving in a manner that shows others that you have self-confidence (Chapter 3).
6. *Initiative.* Self-starting in getting the job done with a minimum of supervision from one's boss (Chapter 9).

In the opening case, Mike appears to have supervisory ability. He is getting the job done through Jean, using the supervisory process. Based on the case, one cannot determine if Mike has the other five traits.

Current Studies

Even though it is generally agreed that there is no universal set of leadership traits or qualities, people continue to study and write about leadership traits.[30] Current research supports the hypothesis that traits do play a role in predicting leadership qualities.[31] One study found that the Big Five personality does have a preferred leadership profile, with high surgency and conscientiousness being positively related to successful leadership and high agreeableness and low adjustment being negatively related to leadership success.[32] Also, neuroscientists are finding that leaders actually may think differently.[33] In a survey conducted by *The Wall Street Journal*/Gallup, 782 top executives in 282 large corporations were asked, "What are the most important traits for success as a supervisor?"[34] Before the results are revealed, complete Self-Assessment Exercise 8–1 to determine if you have the qualities necessary to be a successful leader.

Self-Assessment Exercise 8–1

Your Leadership Traits

Select the response that best describes the frequency of your actual behavior. Place the number 1 to 5 on the line before each statement.

Almost always	Usually	Frequently	Occasionally	Seldom
5	4	3	2	1

_____ 1. I am trustworthy. If I say I will do something by a set time, I do it.

_____ 2. I am loyal. I do not do or say things that hurt my friends, relatives, coworkers, boss, or others.

_____ 3. I can take criticism. If people tell me negative things about myself, I give them serious thought and change when appropriate.

_____ 4. I am honest. I do not lie, steal, cheat, or the like.

_____ 5. I am fair. I treat people equally. I don't take advantage of others.

Self-Assessment
Exercise 8–1 (*continued*)

_____ 6. I want to be successful. I do things to the best of my ability.

_____ 7. I am a self-starter. I get things done without having to be told to do them.

_____ 8. I am a problem solver. If things aren't going the way I want them to, I take corrective action to meet my objectives. I don't give up easily.

_____ 9. I am self-reliant. I don't need the help of others.

_____ 10. I am hardworking. I enjoy working and getting the job done.

_____ 11. I enjoy working with people. I prefer to work with others rather than work alone.

_____ 12. I can motivate others. I can get people to do things they may not really want to do.

_____ 13. I am respected. People enjoy working with me.

_____ 14. I am cooperative. I strive to help the team do well, rather than to be the star.

_____ 15. I am a leader. I enjoy teaching, coaching, and instructing people.

To determine your score, transfer the numbers 1 to 5 that represent your responses below. The column headings represent the trait or quality listed in each statement. Total each column; then add those numbers to determine the grand total.

Integrity	Industriousness	Ability to Get Along with People	
_____ 1.	_____ 6.	_____ 11.	
_____ 2.	_____ 7.	_____ 12.	
_____ 3.	_____ 8.	_____ 13.	
_____ 4.	_____ 9.	_____ 14.	
_____ 5.	_____ 10.	_____ 15.	
_____ Total	_____ Total	_____ Total	_____ Grand Total

Your total for each column will range from 5 to 25, and your grand total will range from 15 to 75. In general, the higher your score, the better your chances of being a successful manager. If you are interested in being (or are) a manager, you can work on improving your integrity, industriousness, and ability to get along with others. As a start, review the list of traits. In which were you strongest? Weakest? Set objectives and develop plans to improve.

Answers to *The Wall Street Journal*/Gallup survey revealed integrity, industriousness, and the ability to get along with people as the three most important traits for success. The survey also identified traits that lead to failure in a manager: having a limited viewpoint, not being able to understand others, not being able to work with others, being indecisive, lacking initiative, not assuming responsibility, lacking integrity, lacking the ability to change, being reluctant to think independently, being unable to solve problems, and wanting to be popular.

WORK APPLICATIONS

2. What are your views on leadership trait theory? Recall a manager you have now or have had in the past. Which of Ghiselli's six traits does or did the person have? Which traits does or did the person lack?

Learning Outcome

3. List and describe four behavioral leadership theories.

BEHAVIORAL LEADERSHIP THEORIES

By the late 1940s, most of the leadership research had switched from trait theory to a focus on the leader's behavior. In the continuing quest to find the one best leadership style in all situations, studies attempted to identify the differences in the behavior of effective leaders versus ineffective leaders.[35] **Behavioral leadership theories** *assume that there are distinctive styles that effective leaders use consistently, that is, that good leadership is rooted in behavior.*[36]

In this section, you will learn the basic leadership styles, two-dimensional leadership styles, the Leadership Grid, and transformational leadership.

Basic Leadership Styles

In the 1930s, before behavioral theory became popular, studies at the University of Iowa concentrated on the manner or style (behavior) of the leader. The studies identified three basic leadership styles:

Autocratic. The leader makes the decisions and closely supervises employees.

Democratic. The leader allows participation in decisions and does not closely supervise employees.

Laissez-faire. The leader takes a leave-the-employees-alone approach.

The Iowa studies contributed to the human relations movement and ushered in an era in which attention was focused on behavior rather than trait research. Leadership style was also found to affect employee behavior.[37]

In the opening case, Mike is using the democratic style because he is allowing Jean to participate in the format of the report.

Two-Dimensional Leadership Styles

Structuring and Consideration Styles   In 1945, Ohio State University began a study to determine effective leadership styles. In their attempt to measure leadership styles, the researchers developed an instrument known as the Leader Behavior Description Questionnaire (LBDQ). Respondents to the questionnaire perceived their leaders' behavior toward them on two distinct dimensions:[38]

* *Initiating structure.* The extent to which the leader takes charge to plan, organize, direct, and control as the employee performs the task.
* *Consideration.* The extent to which the leader communicates to develop trust, friendship, support, and respect.

Job-Centered and Employee-Centered Styles   At approximately the same time the Ohio State studies began, the University of Michigan's Survey Research Center began leadership studies. Researchers at Michigan identified the same two dimensions, or styles, of leadership behavior. However, they called the two styles by different names:[39]

* *Job-centered.* This is the same as initiating structure. The Managerial Grid (to be discussed next) refers to this dimension as concern for production.
* *Employee-centered.* This is the same as consideration. The Managerial Grid refers to this dimension as concern for people.

Leadership Styles   Different combinations of the two dimensions of leadership result in four leadership styles, illustrated in Exhibit 8.1. Today, managers still understand the importance of good relationships,[40] and academics are still studying task and relationship behavior.[41]

In the opening case, Mike is using the high-consideration (employee-centered) and low-structure (job-centered) style, box 3, because he is telling Jean what needs to be in the report, but how she does the report is up to her. Mike also offers supportive statements.

EXHIBIT 8.1 | Two-Dimensional Leadership Models

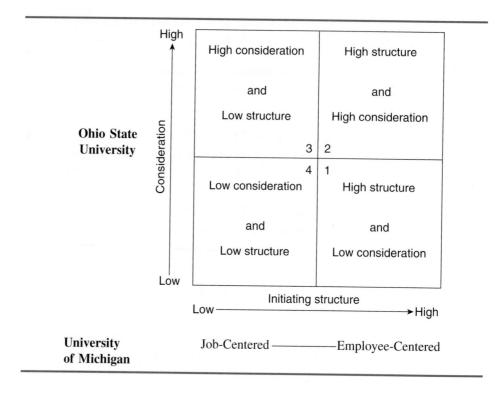

The Leadership Grid

Robert Blake and Jane Mouton developed the Managerial Grid. They published it in 1964[42] and updated it in 1978[43] and 1985.[44] In 1991 it became the Leadership Grid, with Anne Adams McCanse replacing Mouton.[45]

APPLICATION SITUATIONS

Two-Dimensional Leadership Styles

AS 8–1

Using Exhibit 8.1, identify the behavior by its quadrant:

A. 1   B. 2   C. 3   D. 4.

_____ 1. "Bill, I want you to take the mail out. It's your turn; you haven't done it for quite a while."

_____ 2. "I don't care; do whatever you want to do."

_____ 3. "Put out that butt; there is no smoking allowed."

_____ 4. "You're not doing a very good job because you're new. I'll work with you until you get it right. Do it like this."

_____ 5. "I know you can do the task. You're just not too sure of yourself because you never did it before. Try it; if you have a problem, come and get me."

The Leadership Grid is based on the two leadership dimensions called *concern for production* and *concern for people*. The **Leadership Grid** *is Blake and Mouton's model identifying the ideal leadership style as having a high concern for both production and people.* Although the grid has 81 possible combinations of concern for production and people, the model identifies five major styles:

EXHIBIT 8.2 | The Leadership Grid

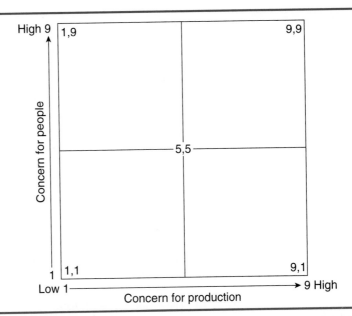

Source: The Leadership Grid Figure (adapted from *Leadership Dilemmas—Grid Solutions* by Robert R. Blake and Anne Adams McCanse. Houston: Gulf Publishing Company, p. 29. Copyright © 1991, by Scientific Methods, Inc.

The impoverished manager (1,1). This leader has low concern for both production and people. The leader does the minimum required to remain employed in the position.

The sweatshop manager (9,1). This leader has a high concern for production and a low concern for people. The leader uses position power to coerce employees to do the work. People are treated like machines.

The country club manager (1,9). This leader has a high concern for people and a low concern for production. The leader strives to maintain good relations and a friendly atmosphere.

The organized-person manager (5,5). This leader has balanced, medium concern for both production and people. The leader strives to maintain satisfactory middle-of-the-road performance and morale.

The team manager (9,9). This leader has a high concern for both production and people. This leader strives for maximum performance and employee satisfaction. Participation, commitment, and conflict resolution are emphasized.

The horizontal axis of the grid (see Exhibit 8.2) represents the concern for production, and the vertical axis represents the concern for people. Each axis is on a point scale of 1 to 9. The 1 indicates low concern, while the 9 indicates high concern.

Through grid training, which is still being used today, managers fill in an instrument that indicates what they would do in certain situations. The results are scored to indicate where they are on the Leadership Grid, one of the 81 combinations of concern for production and people. They go through training designed to help them become ideal 9,9 managers, having a high concern for both production and people.

In the opening case, Mike has a high concern for getting the report done and a high concern for Jean. If you had to select one of the five major styles, you would probably choose the 9,9 team manager. However, Mike is giving more support to Jean than direction for doing the report. Mike is actually using closer to a 9,7 leadership style.

WORK APPLICATIONS

3. What are your views on the Leadership Grid? Recall a manager you have now or have had. Which of the five styles does or did the manager use?

APPLICATION SITUATIONS

The Leadership Grid

AS 8–2

Match the five situations with the leader's probable style. (Refer to Exhibit 8.2.)

A. 1,1 (impoverished)   C. 9,1 (sweatshop)   E. 9,9 (team manager)

B. 1,9 (country club)   D. 5,5 (organized person)

_____ 6. The group has very high morale; the members enjoy their work. Productivity in the department is one of the lowest in the company.

_____ 7. The group has adequate morale. Members have an average productivity level.

_____ 8. The group is one of the top performers. Members have high morale.

_____ 9. The group has one of the lowest levels of morale. It is one of the top performers.

_____ 10. The group is one of the lowest producers. It has a low level of morale.

Transformational Leadership

Transformational leadership, a contemporary view of leadership, is a behavioral theory because it focuses on the behavior of successful leaders.[46] Studies examine successful leaders to determine the behavior they use to make their organizations successful.[47] The focus of transformational leadership is on top-level managers, primarily chief executive officers of large organizations.[48]

Transformational leadership is about change, innovation, and entrepreneurship. Transformational leaders perform, or take the organization through, three acts, on an ongoing basis:

Act 1: Recognizing the need for revitalization. The transformational leader recognizes the need to change the organization in order to keep up with the rapid changes in the environment and to keep ahead of the global competition, which is becoming more competitive all the time.

Act 2: Creating a new vision. The transformational leader visualizes the changed organization and motivates people to make it become a reality. They are visionary leaders.

Act 3: Institutionalizing change. The transformational leader guides people as they make the vision become a reality.

Some of the characteristics, or traits, of transformational leaders are the following: (1) they see themselves as change agents; (2) they are courageous individuals who take risks; (3) they believe in people and motivate them; (4) they are value-driven; (5) they are lifelong learners; (6) they have the ability to deal with complexity, ambiguity, and uncertainty; and (7) they are visionaries. These traits are evident during leader–member exchanges.[49]

Martin Luther King, Jr.'s "I Have a Dream" speech can be considered an example of transformational leadership.

Charismatic Leadership   Transformational leaders also can be charismatic leaders. There is a theory of charismatic leadership. Charismatic leaders inspire loyalty, enthusiasm, and high levels of performance.[50] However, they may not take the organization through the three acts. Not too many leaders are truly charismatic.[51] Although charisma is not needed to lead, it can help.

Transactional Leadership   Transformational leadership has been contrasted with transactional leadership.[52] The transaction is based on the principle of "you do this work for me and I'll give this reward to you." Transactional leadership focuses more on middle and first-line managers who help the transformational leader take their unit through the three acts.

In the opening case, Mike is not a transformational leader because he is not a top-level manager capable of changing the entire bank. Mike is a middle-level branch manager, and he is a transactional leader.

CONTINGENCY LEADERSHIP THEORIES

Learning Outcome

4. List and describe four contingency leadership theories.

Both the trait and behavioral leadership theories were attempts to find the one best leadership style in all situations. In the late 1960s, it became apparent that there is no one best leadership style in all situations.[53] Both the Ohio State and University of Michigan studies revealed that no set of leader behaviors is effective in all situations. **Contingency leadership theories** *assume that the appropriate leadership style varies from situation to situation.* Contingency theory is still being researched today.[54]

In this section, we discuss some of the most popular contingency leadership theories, including contingency leadership theory, leadership continuum, normative leadership theory, and situational leadership.

Contingency Leadership Theory

In 1951, Fred E. Fiedler began to develop the first situational leadership theory. He called the theory "Contingency Theory of Leader Effectiveness."[55] Fiedler believed that one's leadership style is a reflection of one's personality (trait theory–oriented) and is basically constant. Leaders do not change styles. **Contingency leadership theory** *developed by Fiedler, is used to determine if a person's leadership style is task- or relationship-oriented and if the situation matches the leader's style.* If there is no match, Fiedler recommends that the leader change the situation, rather than the leadership style.

Leadership Style   The first major factor is to determine whether one's leadership style is task- or relationship-oriented. To do so, the leader fills in the Least Preferred Coworker (LPC) scales. This is followed by determining the favorableness of the leader's situation.

Situational Favorableness   Situational favorableness refers to the degree to which a situation enables the leader to exert influence over the followers. The three variables, in order of importance, are:

1. *Leader–member relations.* Is the relationship good or poor? Do the followers trust, respect, accept, and have confidence in the leader? Is it a friendly, tension-free situation? Leaders with good relations have more influence. The better the relations, the more favorable the situation.

2. *Task structure.* Is the task structured or unstructured? Do employees perform routine, unambiguous, standard tasks that are easily understood? Leaders in a structured situation have more influence. The more structured the jobs are, the more favorable the situation.

3. *Position power.* Is position power strong or weak? Does the leader have the power to assign work, reward and punish, hire and fire, and give raises and promotions? The leader with position power has more influence. The more power, the more favorable the situation.

Determining the Appropriate Leadership Style   To determine whether task or relationship leadership is appropriate, the user answers the three questions pertaining to situational favorableness, using the Fiedler contingency theory model. See Exhibit 8.3 for an adapted model. The user starts with question 1 and follows the decision tree to determine the situation (1 to 8) and appropriate leadership style (task or relationship).

EXHIBIT 8.3 |

Fiedler's Contingency
Leadership Theory Model

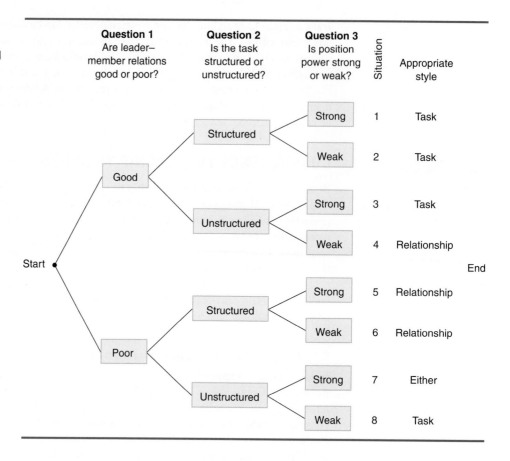

One of the criticisms of Fiedler's model comes from those who believe that the leader should change his or her style rather than the situation. The other contingency writers in this chapter take this position. Fiedler has thus helped contribute to the other contingency theories.

In the opening case, Mike has good relations with Jean, the task is unstructured, and Mike's position power is strong. This is situation 3, in which the appropriate leadership style is task (Exhibit 8.3). However, Mike is using a relationship style. Fiedler would suggest that Mike change the situation to meet his preferred relationship style.

WORK APPLICATIONS

4. What are your views on contingency leadership theory? Do you agree with Fiedler's recommendation to change the situation rather than the leader's style?

APPLICATION SITUATIONS

**Contingency
Leadership Theory**

Using Exhibit 8.3, match the situation with its corresponding appropriate leadership style. Select two answers for each situation.

AS 8–3

A. 1   B. 2   C. 3   D. 4   E. 5   F. 6   G. 7   H. 8

a. Task-oriented   b. Relationship-oriented

_____ 11. Ben, the supervisor, oversees the assembly of mass-produced containers. He has the power to reward and punish. Ben is viewed as a hard-nosed supervisor.

_____ 12. Jean, the manager, is from the corporate planning staff. She helps the other departments plan. Jean is viewed as being a dreamer; she doesn't understand the departments. People tend to be rude in their dealings with Jean.

_____ 13. Ron, the supervisor, oversees the processing of canceled checks for the bank. He is well liked by the employees. Ron's boss enjoys hiring and evaluating his employees' performance.

_____ 14. Connie, the principal of a school, assigns teachers to classes and various other duties. She hires teachers and decides on tenure appointments. The school atmosphere is tense.

_____ 15. Len, the chairperson of the committee, is highly regarded by its volunteer members from a variety of departments. They are charged with recommending ways to increase organizational performance.

Leadership Continuum

Robert Tannenbaum and Warren Schmidt state that leadership behavior is on a continuum from boss-centered to employee-centered leadership. Their model focuses on who makes the decisions. They identify seven major styles the leader can choose from. Exhibit 8.4 is an adaptation of their model, which lists the seven styles.[56] The **Leadership continuum,** _developed by Tannenbaum and Schmidt, identifies seven leadership styles based on the use of boss-centered versus employee-centered leadership._

Before selecting one of the seven leadership styles, the user must consider the following three factors, or variables:

The manager. What is the leader's preferred style, based on experience, expectation, values, background, knowledge, feeling of security, and confidence in the subordinates?

The subordinates. What is the subordinates' preferred style for the leader, based on experience, expectation, and so on? Generally, the more willing and able the subordinates are to participate, the more freedom to participate should be given.

EXHIBIT 8.4 | Continuum of Leadership Behavior

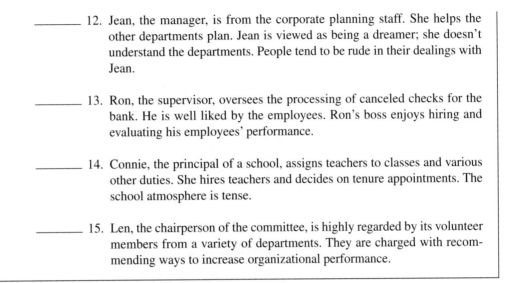

Autocratic style						Participative style
Leader makes decision and announces it	Leader sells decision	Leader presents ideas and invites questions	Leader presents tentative decision subject to change	Leader presents problem, gets suggestions, and makes decision	Leader defines limits and asks group to make decision	Leader permits subordinates to function within limits defined by leader
1	2	3	4	5	6	7

The situation. What are the environmental considerations, such as the organization's size, structure, climate, goals, and technology? Upper-level managers also influence leadership styles.

As you read about the situational variables, you will realize that they are descriptive; the model does not state which style to use in a situation. The leadership styles discussed in the next two sections have models that tell the leader which style to use in a given situation.

In the opening case, Mike began the discussion using style 4, in which the leader presents a tentative decision subject to change. Jean did not have to do the report. Mike would have given it to another employee if she did not want to do it. Mike also used style 5, leader presents problem—the need for the report and what must be included in the report—and told Jean he would allow her to select the form, subject to his final approval.

WORK APPLICATIONS

5. What are your views on the leadership continuum? Recall a manager you have now or have had. Which of the seven styles does or did the manager use?

APPLICATION SITUATIONS

Leadership Continuum

AS 8–4

Using Exhibit 8.4, identify the statements by their leadership style:

A. 1   B. 2   C. 3   D. 4   E. 5   F. 6   G. 7

_____ 16. "Samantha, I selected you to be transferred to the new department, but you don't have to go if you don't want to."

_____ 17. "Sally, go clean off the tables right away."

_____ 18. "From now on, this is the way it will be done. Does anyone have any question about the procedure?"

_____ 19. "These are the two weeks we can go on vacation. You select one."

_____ 20. "I'd like your ideas on how to stop the bottleneck on the line. But I have the final say on the solution we implement."

Normative Leadership Theory

Based on empirical research into managerial decision making, Victor Vroom and Philip Yetton attempted to bridge the gap between leadership theory and managerial practice. To do so, they developed a model that tells the manager which leadership style to use in a given situation.[57] **Normative leadership theory,** *developed by Vroom and Yetton, is a decision-tree model that enables the user to select from five leadership styles the one that is appropriate for the situation.*

Leadership Styles In 2000 Victor Vroom published a revised version of this normative leadership model with the title *Leadership and the Decision Making Process.*[58] In it, he changed the names of the leadership styles. Vroom identified five leadership styles based on the level of participation in the decision by the followers. Vroom adapted the model from Tannenbaum and Schmidt's leadership continuum model (Exhibit 8.4), which ranges from autocratic to participative styles. Here is Vroom's latest version of the five leadership styles:

1. *Decide.* Leader makes decision alone.
2. *Consult individually.* Talk to employees individually to get information and suggestions; then leader makes decision.
3. *Consult group.* Talk to group of employees to get information and suggestions; then leader makes decision.
4. *Facilitate.* Have group meeting for employee participation with leader in making decision.
5. *Delegate.* Group makes the decision.

Although the normative leadership model is primarily a leadership model, it is also used to determine the level of participation in decision making. So we'll discuss the model again in Chapter 13, which deals with teams, creative problem solving, and decision making.

In the opening case, Mike used the consult individually style. Mike told Jean that she could select the style subject to his approval. Mike makes the final decision based on Jean's input.

WORK APPLICATIONS

6. What are your views on normative leadership theory? Recall a manager you have now or have had. Which of the five styles does or did the manager use?

Situational Leadership

Situational leadership, *developed by Paul Hersey and Kenneth Blanchard, is a model for selecting from four leadership styles the one that matches the employees' maturity level in a given situation.* For the most part, situational leadership[59] takes the two-dimensional leadership styles and the four quadrants (see Exhibit 8.1), and develops four leadership styles, which Hersey and Blanchard call *telling* (lower-right quadrant—high task, low relationship); *selling* (upper-right quadrant—high task, high relationship); *participating* (upper-left quadrant—high relationship, low task); and *delegating* (lower-left quadrant—low relationship, low task).

Hersey and Blanchard went beyond the behavioral theory by developing a model that tells the leader which style to use in a given situation. To determine the leadership style, one determines the followers' maturity level. If it is low, the leader uses a telling style; if it is moderate to low, the leader uses a selling style; if it is moderate to high, the leader uses the participating style; and if it is high, the leader uses a delegating style.

In the opening case, Mike used the participating style with Jean. Since Mike had a higher concern for Jean than for the task, he gave Jean more support than directions. Mike gave her the specifics of what had to be included, but he let her decide on the format, subject to his approval.

In general, contingency leadership theories attempt to create a win–win situation by giving the followers the support and direction they need.[60] Overdirecting can frustrate the employee with a need for esteem, growth, or power.[61] Not providing enough support can frustrate the employee with a need for social relatedness or affiliation-achievement.[62]

See Exhibit 8.5 for a review of the major theories of leadership.

SITUATIONAL SUPERVISION

Situational supervision is similar to the situational communications model in Chapter 6. It begins with Self-Assessment Exercise 8–2, which identifies your preferred supervisory style. Next follows a presentation of the situational supervision theory. Application of this model produces situational supervisors who change leadership styles to meet the capability level of their followers.[63] Using a variety of leadership styles with a diverse workforce is often necessary.[64]

EXHIBIT 8.5 | Leadership Theories

Assumes that there are distinctive physical and psychological characteristics accounting for leadership effectiveness.

Assume that there are distinctive styles that effective leaders use consistently.

Basic Leadership Styles

Autocratic, democratic, laissez-faire.

Two-Dimensional Leadership Styles

Initiating structure/job-centered and consideration/employee-centered.

Leadership Grid

Blake and Mouton's model identifies the ideal leadership style as having high concern for both production and people.

Transformational Leadership

Takes the organization through three acts on an ongoing basis.

Major Theories of Leadership

Assume that the appropriate leadership style varies from situation to situation.

Contingency Leadership Theory

Fiedler's model is used to determine if a person's leadership style is task- or relationship-oriented and if the situation matches the leader's style.

Leadership Continuum

Tannenbaum and Schmidt's model identifies seven leadership styles based on the use of boss-centered versus employee-centered leadership.

Normative Leadership Theory

Vroom and Yetton's decision-tree model enables the user to select from five leadership styles the one that is appropriate for the situation.

Situational Leadership

Hersey and Blanchard's model enables the user to select from four leadership styles the one that matches the employee's maturity level in a given situation.

Situational Supervision

Lussier's model enables the user to select from four leadership styles the one that matches the employee's capability level in a given situation.

Self-Assessment
Exercise 8–2

Determining Your Preferred Supervisory Style

This exercise is designed to determine your preferred supervisory style. Below are 12 situations. Select the one alternative that most closely describes what you would do in each situation. Don't be concerned with trying to pick the right answer; select the alternative you would really use. Circle the letter *a, b, c,* or *d.* Ignore the C _____ and S _____ lines, which will be explained later in this chapter and used in class in Skill-Building Exercise 8–1.

C _____   1. Your rookie crew seems to be developing well. Their need for direction and close supervision is diminishing. You would:
　　　　　a. Stop directing and overseeing performance unless there is a problem.
　　　　　　 S _____
　　　　　b. Spend time getting to know them personally, but make sure they maintain performance levels. S _____
　　　　　c. Make sure things keep going well; continue to direct and oversee closely.
　　　　　　 S _____
　　　　　d. Begin to discuss new tasks of interest to them. S _____

C _____   2. You assigned Joe a task, specifying exactly how you wanted it done. Joe deliberately ignored your directions and did it his way. The job will not meet the customer's standards. This is not the first problem you've had with Joe. You decide to:
　　　　　a. Listen to Joe's side, but be sure the job gets done right away. S _____
　　　　　b. Tell Joe to do it again the right way and closely supervise the job. S _____

Self-Assessment
Exercise 8–2 (*continued*)

       c. Tell him the customer will not accept the job and let Joe handle it his way.
         S _____

       d. Discuss the problem and what can be done about it. S _____

C _____   3. Your employees work well together. The department is a real team. It's the top performer in the organization. Because of traffic problems, the president okayed staggered hours for departments. As a result, you can change your department's hours. Several of your workers have suggested changing. The action you take is to:

       a. Allow the group to decide the hours. S _____

       b. Decide on new hours, explain why you chose them, and invite questions.
         S _____

       c. Conduct a meeting to get the group members' ideas. Select new hours together, with your approval. S _____

       d. Send around a memo stating the hours you want. S _____

C _____   4. You hired Bill, a new employee. He is not performing at the level expected after one month's training. Bill is trying, but he seems to be a slow learner. You decide to:

       a. Clearly explain what needs to be done and oversee his work. Discuss why the procedures are important; support and encourage him. S _____

       b. Tell Bill that his training is over and it's time to pull his own weight.
         S _____

       c. Review task procedures and supervise his work closely. S _____

       d. Inform Bill that although his training is over, he can feel free to come to you if he has any problems. S _____

C _____   5. Helen has had an excellent performance record for the past five years. Recently you have noticed a drop in the quality and quantity of her work. She has a family problem. You would:

       a. Tell her to get back on track and closely supervise her. S _____

       b. Discuss the problem with Helen. Help her realize her personal problem is affecting her work. Discuss ways to improve the situation. Be supportive and encourage her. S _____

       c. Tell Helen you're aware of her productivity slip and that you're sure she'll work it out soon. S _____

       d. Discuss the problem and solution with Helen and supervise her closely.
         S _____

C _____   6. Your organization does not allow smoking in certain areas. You just walked by a restricted area and saw Joan smoking. She has been with the organization for 10 years and is a very productive worker. Joan has never been caught smoking before. The action you take is to:

       a. Ask her to put it out, then leave. S _____

       b. Discuss why she is smoking and what she intends to do about it. S _____

       c. Encourage Joan not to smoke in this area again, and check up on her in the future. S _____

       d. Tell her to put it out, watch her do it, and tell her you will check on her in the future. S _____

C _____   7. Your department usually works well together with little direction. Recently a conflict between Sue and Tom has caused problems. As a result, you:

       a. Call Sue and Tom together and make them realize how this conflict is affecting the department. Discuss how to resolve it and how you will check to make sure the problem is solved. S _____

       b. Let the group resolve the conflict. S _____

       c. Have Sue and Tom sit down and discuss their conflict and how to resolve it. Support their efforts to implement a solution. S _____

       d. Tell Sue and Tom how to resolve their conflict and closely supervise them.
         S _____

C _____   8. Jim usually does his share of the work with some encouragement and direction. However, he has migraine headaches occasionally and doesn't pull his weight when they occur. The others resent doing Jim's work. You decide to:

a. Discuss his problem and help him come up with ideas for maintaining his work; be supportive. S _____

b. Tell Jim to do his share of the work and closely watch his output. S _____

c. Inform Jim that he is creating a hardship for the others and should resolve the problem by himself. S _____

d. Be supportive, but set minimum performance levels and ensure compliance. S _____

C _____   9. Bob, your most experienced and productive worker, came to you with a detailed idea that could increase your department's productivity at a very low cost. He can do his present job plus this new assignment. You think it's an excellent idea and you:

a. Set some goals together. Encourage and support his efforts. S _____

b. Set up goals for Bob. Be sure he agrees with them and sees you as being supportive of his efforts. S _____

c. Tell Bob to keep you informed and to come to you if he needs any help. S _____

d. Have Bob check in with you frequently so that you can direct and supervise his activities. S _____

C _____   10. Your boss asked you for a special report. Fran, a very capable worker who usually needs no direction or support, has all the necessary skills to do the job. However, Fran is reluctant because she has never done a report. You:

a. Tell Fran she has to do it. Give her direction and supervise her closely. S _____

b. Describe the project to Fran and let her do it her own way. S _____

c. Describe the benefits to Fran. Get her ideas on how to do it and check her progress. S _____

d. Discuss possible ways of doing the job. Be supportive; encourage Fran. S _____

C _____   11. Jean is the top producer in your department. However, her monthly reports are constantly late and contain errors. You are puzzled because she does everything else with no direction or support. You decide to:

a. Go over past reports, explaining exactly what is expected of her. Schedule a meeting so that you can review the next report with her. S _____

b. Discuss the problem with Jean and ask her what can be done about it; be supportive. S _____

c. Explain the importance of the report. Ask her what the problem is. Tell her that you expect the next report to be on time and free of errors. S _____

d. Remind Jean to get the next report in on time and without errors. S _____

C _____   12. Your workers are very effective and like to participate in decision making. A consultant was hired to develop a new method for your department using the latest technology in the field. You:

a. Explain the consultant's method and let the group decide how to implement it. S _____

b. Teach them the new method and closely supervise them. S _____

c. Explain the new method and why it is important. Teach them the method and make sure the procedure is followed. Answer questions. S _____

d. Explain the new method and get the group's input on ways to improve and implement it. S _____

To determine your supervisory style:

1. In the table below, circle the letter you selected for each situation. The column headings represent the supervisory style you selected.

Situation	S-A	S-C	S-P	S-L
1.	*c*	*b*	*d*	*a*
2.	*b*	*a*	*d*	*c*
3.	*d*	*b*	*c*	*a*
4.	*c*	*a*	*d*	*b*
5.	*a*	*d*	*b*	*c*
6.	*d*	*c*	*b*	*a*
7.	*d*	*a*	*c*	*b*
8.	*b*	*d*	*a*	*c*
9.	*d*	*b*	*a*	*c*
10.	*a*	*c*	*d*	*b*
11.	*a*	*c*	*b*	*d*
12.	*b*	*c*	*d*	*a*
Total				

S-A Autocratic
S-C Consultative
S-P Participative
S-L Laissez-faire

2. Add the number of circled items per column. The highest number is your preferred supervisory style. Is this the style you tend to use most often?

The more evenly distributed the numbers are, the more flexible your style is. A score of 1 or 0 in any column may indicate a reluctance to use the style.

Note that there is no "right" leadership style. This part of the exercise is designed to enable you to better understand the style you tend to use or prefer to use.

Defining the Situation

Having determined a preferred supervisory style, it is time to learn about the four supervisory styles and when to use each. As mentioned, no one best supervisory style exists for all situations.[65] Instead, the effective supervisor adapts his or her style to meet the capabilities of the individual or group.[66] Supervisor–employee interactions fall into two distinct categories: directive and supportive.

- *Directive behavior*. The supervisor focuses on directing and controlling behavior to ensure that the task gets done. The supervisor tells employees what the task is and when, where, and how to do it, and oversees performance.

- *Supportive behavior*. The supervisor focuses on encouraging and motivating behavior. He or she explains things and listens to employee views, helping employees make their own decisions.

In other words, when a supervisor interacts with employees, the focus can be on directing (getting the task done), supporting (developing relationships), or both.

These definitions lead us to the question, What style should I use and why? The answer is, It depends on the situation. And the situation is determined by the capability of the employee(s). There are two distinct aspects of capability:

- *Ability*. Do the employees have the experience, education, skills, and so on, to do the task without direction from the supervisor?

- *Motivation*. Do the employees want to do the task? Will they perform the task without a supervisor's encouragement and support?

Employee capability can be located on a continuum from low to outstanding, which the supervisor will determine by selecting the one capability level that best describes the employee's ability and motivation for the specific task. These levels are as follows:

- *Low (C-1).* The employees can't do the task without detailed directions and close supervision. Employees in this category may have the ability to do the task, but they lack the motivation to perform without close supervision.

- *Moderate (C-2).* The employees have moderate ability and need specific direction and support to get the job done properly. The employees may be highly motivated but still need direction, support, and encouragement.

- *High (C-3).* The employees are high in ability but may lack the confidence to do the job. What they need most is support and encouragement to motivate them to get the task done.

- *Outstanding (C-4).* The employees are capable of doing the task without direction or support.

Most people perform a variety of tasks on the job. It is important to realize that their capability may vary depending on the specific task.[67] For example, a bank teller may be a C-4 for routine transactions, but a C-1 for opening new or special accounts. Employees tend to start working with a C-1 capability, needing close direction. As their ability to do the job increases, supervisors can begin to be supportive and stop supervising closely. A supervisor must gradually develop employees from C-1 to C-3 or C-4 levels over time.

Using the Appropriate Supervisory Style

Learning Outcome

5. Explain four situational supervisory styles.

As mentioned, the "correct" supervisory style depends on the situation. And the situation, in turn, is a function of employee capability. Each of the supervisory styles, discussed in greater detail below, also involves varying degrees of supportive and directive behavior.

The four supervisory styles—autocratic, consultative, participative, and laissez-faire— are summarized in Exhibit 8.6 in relation to the different levels of employee capability.

The **autocratic style (S-A)** *involves high-directive–low-supportive behavior (HD–LS) and is appropriate when interacting with low-capability employees (C-1).* When interacting with employees, the supervisor gives very detailed instructions, describing exactly what the task is and when, where, and how to perform it. He or she also closely oversees performance. The supportive style is largely absent. The supervisor makes decisions without input from the employees.

The **consultative style (S-C)** *involves high-directive–high-supportive behavior (HD–HS) and is appropriate when interacting with moderate-capability employees (C-2).* Here, the supervisor would give specific instructions, telling employees what the task is and when, where, and how to perform it, as well as overseeing performance at all major stages through completion. At the same time, the supervisor would support the employees by explaining why the task should be performed as requested and answering their questions. Supervisors should work on relationships as they sell the benefits of completing the task their way. When making decisions, they may consult employees, but they have the final say. Once a supervisor makes the decision, which can incorporate employees' ideas, he or she directs and oversees the employees' performance.

The **participative style (S-P)** *is characterized by low-directive–high-supportive behavior (LD–HS) and is appropriate when interacting with employees with high capability (C-3).* When interacting with employees, the supervisor gives general directions and spends limited time overseeing performance, letting employees do the task their way and focusing on the end result. The supervisor should support the employees by encouraging them and building up their self-confidence. If a task needs to be done, the supervisor should not tell them how to do it, but ask them how they will accomplish it. The supervisor should make decisions together with employees or allow employees to make the decision subject to the supervisor's limitations and approval.

EXHIBIT 8.6 |
Situational Supervision
Model

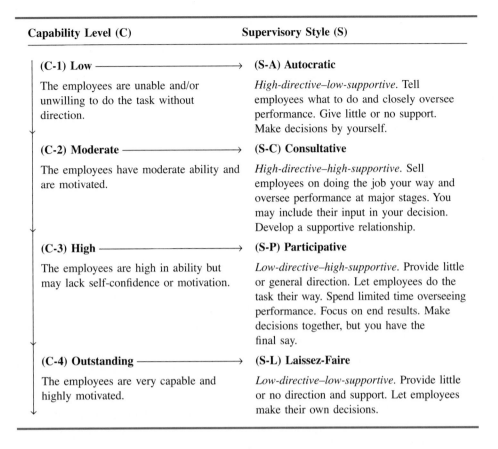

Capability Level (C)	Supervisory Style (S)
(C-1) Low ————→	**(S-A) Autocratic**
The employees are unable and/or unwilling to do the task without direction.	*High-directive–low-supportive*. Tell employees what to do and closely oversee performance. Give little or no support. Make decisions by yourself.
(C-2) Moderate ————→	**(S-C) Consultative**
The employees have moderate ability and are motivated.	*High-directive–high-supportive*. Sell employees on doing the job your way and oversee performance at major stages. You may include their input in your decision. Develop a supportive relationship.
(C-3) High ————→	**(S-P) Participative**
The employees are high in ability but may lack self-confidence or motivation.	*Low-directive–high-supportive*. Provide little or general direction. Let employees do the task their way. Spend limited time overseeing performance. Focus on end results. Make decisions together, but you have the final say.
(C-4) Outstanding ————→	**(S-L) Laissez-Faire**
The employees are very capable and highly motivated.	*Low-directive–low-supportive*. Provide little or no direction and support. Let employees make their own decisions.

The **laissez-faire style (S-L)** *entails low-directive–low-supportive behavior (LD–LS) and is appropriate when interacting with outstanding employees (C-4)*. When interacting with these employees, supervisors should merely inform employees about what needs to be done. The supervisor answers their questions, but provides little, if any, direction. It is not necessary to oversee performance. These employees are highly motivated and need little, if any, support. The supervisor allows these employees to make their own decisions subject to the supervisor's limitations, although approval by the supervisor will not be necessary.

Applying the Situational Supervision Model

The situation below comes from Self-Assessment Exercise 8–2. Now the information in Exhibit 8.6 will be applied to this situation.

To begin, identify the employee capability level described. The levels are listed in the left-hand column of the exhibit. Indicate the capability level (1 through 4) on the line marked "C" to the left of the situation. Next, determine the management style that each response (*a, b, c,* or *d*) represents. Indicate that style (A, C, P, or L) on the line marked "S" at the end of each response. Finally, identify the most appropriate response by placing a check mark (✓) next to it.

C _____ 1. Your rookie crew seems to be developing well. Their need for direction and close supervision is diminishing. You would:
  a. Stop directing and overseeing performance, unless there is a problem. S _____
  b. Spend time getting to know them personally, but make sure they maintain performance levels. S _____
  c. Make sure things keep going well; continue to direct and oversee closely. S _____
  d. Begin to discuss new tasks of interest to them. S _____

Let's see how well you did.

1. The capability was C-1, but they have now developed to the C-2 level. If you put the number 2 on the C line, you were correct.

2. Alternative *a* is S-<u>L</u>, the laissez-faire style. There is no direction or support. Alternative *b* is S-<u>C</u>, the consultative style. There is both direction and support. Alternative *c* is S-<u>A</u>, the autocratic style. There is direction but no support. Alternative *d* is S-<u>P</u>, the participative style. There is low direction and high support (in discussing employee interests).

3. If you selected *b* as the appropriate response, you were correct. However, in the business world, there is seldom only one way to handle a problem successfully. Therefore, in this exercise, you receive points based on how successful your behavior would be in each situation. In this situation, *b* is the most successful alternative because it involves developing the employees gradually; it's a three-point answer. Alternative *c* is the next best alternative, followed by *d*. It is better to keep things the way they are now than try to rush employee development, which would probably cause problems. So *c* is a two-point answer, and *d* is a one-point answer. Alternative *a* is the least effective because you are going from one extreme of supervision to the other. This is a zero-point answer because the odds are great that this style will cause problems that will affect supervisory success.

The better a supervisor is at matching his or her supervisory style to employees' capabilities, the greater the chances of being a successful supervisor.

In completing Skill-Building Exercise 8–1, Situational Supervision, you will apply the model to the remaining situations and be given feedback on your success at applying the model as you develop your situational supervision skills.

WORK APPLICATIONS

7. What are your views on situational supervision? Recall a manager you have now or have had. Which of the four styles does or did the manager use? Would you use the model on the job?

8. Which of the four supervisory styles would you like your boss to use with you? Why would you prefer this particular style?

PUTTING THE LEADERSHIP THEORIES TOGETHER

This chapter has presented 10 different leadership theories. Exhibit 8.7 puts the 10 leadership theories together, converting them into four leadership style categories. A review of this exhibit should lead to a better understanding of the similarities and differences between these leadership theories.

WORK APPLICATIONS

9. Which leadership theory or model do you prefer? Why?

10. Describe the type of leader you want to be.

EXHIBIT 8.7 | Leadership Styles

Behavioral Leadership Theories

Basic Leadership Styles	Leadership Style Categories			
	Autocratic	**Democratic**		**Laissez-Faire**
Two-dimensional leadership styles	High structure/job-centered Low consideration/ employee-centered	High structure/job-centered High consideration/ employee-centered	High consideration/ employee-centered Low structure/job-centered	Low consideration/ employee-centered Low structure/job-centered
Leadership Grid	High concern for production; low concern for people (9,1 sweatshop manager)	High concern for both production and people (9,9 team manager)	High concern for people; low concern for production (1,9 country club manager)	Low to moderate concern for both people and production (1,1 impoverished and 5,5 organized managers)
Transformational leadership	Three acts; no actual style			

Contingency Leadership Theories

Contingency Leadership Theory	Task Orientation		Relationship Orientation	
Leadership continuum	1. Make decision and announce it	2. Sell decision 3. Present ideas and invite questions	4. Present tentative decision subject to change 5. Present problem, get suggestions, and make decision	6. Define limits and ask group to make decision 7. Permit subordinates to function within limits defined by leader
Normative leadership theory	Make decision alone using available information (Decide)	Meet individually or as a group with subordinates, explain the situation, get information and ideas on how to solve the problem, make final decision alone (Consult individual and group)	Have group meeting for employee participation with leader in decision making (Facilitate)	Meet with subordinates as a group, explain the situation, and allow the group to make decision (Delegate)
Situational leadership	High task, low relationship (Telling)	High task, high relationship (Selling)	High relationship, low task (Participating)	Low relationship, low task (Delegating)
Situational supervision	High directive, low support (Autocratic)	High directive, high support (Consultative)	High support, low directive (Participative)	Low support, low directive (Laissez-faire)

Leadership Trait Theory

Based on traits of leader; no actual style

SUBSTITUTES FOR LEADERSHIP?

Learning Outcome

6. Identify three characteristics that substitute for leadership.

The leadership theories presented assume that some leadership style will be effective in each situation. Steven Kerr and John Jermier[68] argue that certain individual, task, and organizational variables prevent managers from affecting subordinates' attitudes and behaviors.

Substitutes for managers, or characteristics that negate or replace managers' influence, are those that structure tasks (directive) for followers or give them positive strokes (support) for their action. Rather than having the managers provide the necessary direction and support, the subordinates, task, or organization may provide them.

Thus, because leadership is a shared process between the group members, there is no substitute for leadership. However, there are substitutes for managers.[69]

The following characteristics may substitute for management by providing direction and/or support:

1. *Characteristics of subordinates.* Ability, knowledge, experience, training; need for independence; professional orientation; indifference toward organizational rewards.

2. *Characteristics of task.* Clarity and routine; invariant methodology; provision of own feedback concerning accomplishment; intrinsic satisfaction.

3. *Characteristics of the organization.* Formalization (explicit plans, goals, and areas of responsibility); inflexibility (rigid, unbending rules and procedures); highly specified and active advisory and staff functions; closely knit, cohesive work groups; organizational rewards not within the leader's control; spatial distance between superior and subordinates.

WORK APPLICATIONS

11. Do you agree that characteristics of subordinates, task, and the organization can substitute for leadership direction and support? Explain your answer.

DIVERSITY AND GLOBAL LEADERSHIP

Thinking globally and having global leadership skills are essential to effective organizations.[70] Europeans travel between countries the way Americans travel between states. Most large companies conduct business in many parts of the world. This makes cultural awareness and diversity in leadership necessary for business success in the increasingly global business environment.[71]

Most leadership theories were developed in the United States, so they do have an American bias. Theories assume employee responsibility, rather than employee rights; self-gratification, rather than employee commitment to duty or altruistic motivation; democratic values, rather than autocratic values; rationality, rather than spirituality, religion, or superstition. Thus, the theories may not be as effective in cultures based on different assumptions.[72]

In the 1970s, Japan's productivity rate was increasing faster than that of the United States. Research was conducted to determine why the Japanese were more productive, and it became apparent that Japanese firms were managed and led differently than U.S. organizations. Over the years, many U.S. companies have adopted more collective decision making and responsibilities, and have taken a more holistic view of employees (recall the total person approach from Chapter 1). Furthermore, the number of firms using total quality management (TQM) techniques from Japan and self-directed virtual work teams has increased.[73]

Within Europe there are diverse management models, which raise a range of management education issues. European managers deal more with cultural than technical issues in the context of diverse value systems and religious backgrounds. Management is organized more as a language than as a set of techniques.

American, European, and Japanese executives realize that they must manage and lead their business units in other countries differently than they do at home.[74] Toyota and Honda run their plants in the United States somewhat differently from those in Japan. Similarly, IBM's management style in Japan differs from its style in the United States.

Here are a few examples of differences in leadership styles based on national culture. Korean leaders are expected to be paternalistic toward employees. Arab leaders are viewed as weak if they show kindness or generosity without being asked to do so. Japanese leaders are expected to be humble and speak infrequently. Scandinavian and Dutch leaders embarrass, rather than motivate, employees with public, individual praise. Autocratic leadership styles tend to be appropriate in high-context cultures (Chapter 5), such as those in Arab, Far Eastern, and Latin American countries, whereas participative leadership styles tend to be appropriate in low-context cultures, such as those in the United States, Norway, Finland, Denmark, and Sweden.[75]

Leadership is also different in e-organizations, which are often global companies. According to executives who have worked in e-org and traditional organizations, e-org leaders focus more on speed in decision making, flexibility, and a vision of the future. Online leadership, managing people from all over the world in virtual and boundaryless organizations, calls for much less face-to-face communication and more written communication to get the job done. You may lead or be part of a virtual team, working interdependently with shared purpose across space, time, and organization boundaries, using technology to communicate and collaborate.[76]

Although cultural differences will continue to affect leadership, the instant communication, individualism, and material acquisition of global products in our society today threaten traditional family, religious, and social structures, as the trend toward the development of a more global culture continues.[77] For example, Chinese workers are more like Americans than people realize. China is moving away from its collectivist roots and becoming a more individualist society, caused in part by the one-child rule and the resulting smaller families. Also, the power distance (wanting to be told what to do versus participating in management) is now the same in both countries.[78] But don't look for a one-size-fits-all solution[79] or leadership style.[80]

TRUST

In business, as in life, trust is an essential building block in developing human relations with customers, suppliers, coworkers, and management.[81] Before reading about trust, complete Self-Assessment Exercise 8–3, Your Trustworthiness.

Self-Assessment Exercise 8–3

Your Trustworthiness

For each statement, select the frequency with which you use, or would use, the behavior at work. Be honest; that's part of trustworthiness.

Almost always				Almost never
1	2	3	4	5

_____ 1. I tell the truth; I tell it like it is.

_____ 2. When I make a commitment to do something, I do it.

_____ 3. I strive to be fair by creating a win–win situation for all parties.

_____ 4. I do the task to the best of my ability.

_____ 5. I volunteer to help others when I can, and I seek help when I need it.

_____ 6. I am humble; I don't brag about my accomplishments.

_____ 7. When I make a mistake, I admit it rather than try to cover it up or downplay it.

_____ 8. I don't overcommit to the point of breaking commitments.

_____ 9. I practice what I preach and walk the talk; I don't say one thing and do another.

_____ 10. I treat coworkers—both friends and others—fairly.

_____ 11. I stand by, protect, and save face for coworkers.

_____ 12. When someone tells me something in confidence, I don't tell anyone else.

_____ 13. I say only positive things, or nothing, about coworkers; I don't gossip.

_____ 14. I am viewed by coworkers as being collaborative rather than competitive.

_____ 15. I let coworkers know the real me—what I stand for and what I value. I share my feelings.

_____ 16. When coworkers tell me something private about themselves, I offer acceptance and support and share something about myself.

_____ 17. I deal effectively with diverse opinions, people, and types of conflict.

Place the numbers (1 to 5) you recorded for the situations on the lines below. Total each by column; then add the totals of the five columns and place the grand total on the continuum (17–85) below the totals.

Integrity	Competence	Consistency	Loyalty	Openness
_____ 1.	_____ 4.	_____ 8.	_____ 11.	_____ 15.
_____ 2.	_____ 5.	_____ 9.	_____ 12.	_____ 16.
_____ 3.	_____ 6.	_____ 10.	_____ 13.	_____ 17.
	_____ 7.		_____ 14.	
_____	_____	_____	_____	_____ Totals

Trustworthy 17 - - - 20 - - - 30 - - - 40 - - - 50 - - - 60 - - - 70 - - - 80 - - - 85 Untrustworthy

The lower your score, the more trustworthy you are. Note your strongest (lowest-score column) and weakest (highest-score column) dimensions of developing trust. You will learn how to develop trust in all five dimensions in the following section.

The traditional hierarchical organizational structure is now being replaced with trust-bound entities and flexible networks.[82] Trust is especially important in teams.[83] However, it is often difficult to develop trust and cooperation across teams.[84] Recall that trust and credibility are potential barriers to communication (Chapter 5). People will not follow a leader that they do not trust.[85] Your ability to develop human relations is built on trust.[86] Your intrapersonal skills affect your willingness to trust, which in turn affects your human relations and leadership skills. If you're going to influence people, they have to trust you.[87] Are you trustworthy? In this section, we discuss types of trust and how to develop trust.

Types of Trust

Trust *is the positive expectation that another will not take advantage of you.* Trust is not simply given; it is earned.[88] Positive expectations, based on knowledge, familiarity, and experience with the other person, take time to develop.[89] Being taken advantage of is always a risk in human relations; thus, trust makes us vulnerable to being hurt.[90]

The three types of trust in organizational human relations are deterrence-, knowledge-, and identification-based trust.[91] They can also be called levels of trust, because they form a building block of trust. Organizational trust is based on these assumptions: Two people are entering a new relationship with no previous experiences, they are uncertain about each other, they believe they are vulnerable if they disclose too much too quickly, and they are uncertain how long the relationship will last.

Deterrence-Based Trust   Most new human relations begin with deterrence-based trust because we lack experience dealing with the other person. Deterrence-based trust is the most fragile since one violation or inconsistency can destroy the human relations.[92] The relationship is based on fear of reprisal if the trust is violated. People do what they say they will because they fear the consequences from not following through.[93] When we start a new job, we tend to fear messing up and getting into trouble with our coworkers and boss, so we try to do a good job. Customer–sales employee relationships are commonly based on deterrence.

Knowledge-Based Trust   Knowledge-based trust is the most common organizational trust. Trust is based on experience dealing with the other person.[94] Based on our knowledge, we can predict the other person's behavior. Predictability is also relevant for people we don't trust, because we do know how they will behave. The better we know people, the better we can predict their behavior—and trust them.[95]

Unlike fragile deterrence-based trust, knowledge-based trust is not broken by inconsistent behavior. If we incorrectly predict behavior and are disappointed or taken advantage of in some way, often we can understand the violation, accept it, forgive the person, and move on with the relationship. To maintain good human relations, we must acknowledge mistakes, apologize, and learn from them.

Identification-Based Trust   Identification-based trust occurs when there is an emotional connection—friend rather than just coworker.[96] It is the highest level of trust. Employees look out for each other's best interest and act for the other. Team managers strive for this level of trust because members are so comfortable and trusting of each other that they can anticipate each other and freely act in each other's absence.[97]

One gender difference in personal relations, off and often on the job, is that generally men are more willing than women to say directly what is important to them and state their expectations.[98] Women generally trust that the other person will anticipate what's important to them without having to state expectations and ask for desired behavior. But women do drop hints, so men may want to pay closer attention. There are more exceptions with younger generations as women have become more assertive and aggressive. See Exhibit 8.8 for a list of trust levels and dimensions.

WORK APPLICATIONS

12. Give an example of each of the three levels of trust you have experienced on the job.

Developing Trust

Learning Outcome

7. Briefly describe the five dimensions of trust.

Now let's discuss how to develop trust so that you can achieve the identification-based level of trust. As shown in Exhibit 8.8, there are five dimensions of trust. Note that integrity is in the center, holding the other four dimensions of competence, consistency, loyalty, and openness together, because without integrity, trust breaks apart.[99] The five also bring you the necessary respect and confidence you need to lead.

The five columns in Self-Assessment Exercise 8–3, Your Trustworthiness, are the five dimensions of trust. Although they are all important, you may want to pay particular attention to your weaker areas.

EXHIBIT 8.8 |
Three Levels and Five
Dimensions of Trust

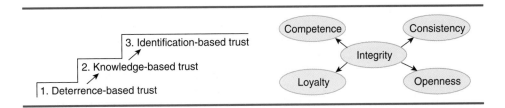

Integrity   People who have *integrity* are honest, truthful, and sincere. Integrity is the most important dimension when people assess another's trustworthiness. Without integrity, the other dimensions are meaningless, because it is the first and perhaps the most important characteristic of leadership.[100]

Tips to develop your integrity include:

- *Tell the truth.* Do you trust people who lie to you? Don't lie or mislead people.[101] Say what you mean and mean what you say. Tell it like it is. You can trust people who aren't afraid to tell it like it is. But be careful how you say it so that you don't hurt human relations; following the guidelines in previous chapters will help. To be truthful, follow the guidelines for ethical behavior (Chapter 3).

- *Keep your commitments.* Do you trust people who don't keep their commitments? To trust you, people must believe that you are dependable. Promises made must be promises kept. You're only as good as your word and commitments, so if you say you will do something, follow through.

- *Be fair.* Do you trust people who treat you unfairly? Fairness establishes your credibility.[102] According to Joe Lee (CEO of Darden Restaurants, the largest casual-dining restaurant company in the world, operating Red Lobster, Olive Garden, Bahama Breeze, and Smokey Bones BBQ Sports Bar), integrity and fairness are the important core values to business. Perceived unfairness causes distrust and a desire for revenge and restitution.

Competence   People who are *competent* have technical and interpersonal knowledge, ability, and skills. To trust, respect, and have confidence in you, people need to believe that you have the skills and abilities to carry out your commitments.

Tips to develop your competence include:

- *Be conscientious.* Do you trust people who don't do a good job? Do the job to the best of your ability. Before finishing a task, ask yourself if the other party will be satisfied. Seek feedback (see the guidelines in Chapter 5) on how you can continually improve your performance.[103]

- *Know your strengths and limitations.* Do you trust people who can't do what they say they will do? Volunteer to help others when you can, and seek assistance when you need it. Don't commit to doing something that you cannot deliver on.

- *Don't brag.* Do you trust braggers? Let your accomplishments speak for themselves. Humility helps build trust. People don't want to hear how good you are, especially when you are comparing yourself with them.

- *Admit your mistakes.* Do you trust know-it-alls? By admitting doubt and acknowledging mistakes, you are seen as competent, not incompetent. Others will think, "I can trust you." People don't trust those who insist on being right all the time.

Consistency   *Consistent* people use the same behavior in similar situations; they are predictable.

Tips to develop your consistency include:

- *Keep your commitments.* Yes, this tip is a repeat because consistent people do what they say they will do. Don't overcommit to the point of breaking commitments.

- *Practice what you preach.* Walk the talk, because actions speak louder than words. Do you trust people who say one thing and do something else? Managers who say one thing and do another lack credibility. Others won't follow their advice, and they don't inspire trust.

- *Be impartial.* Do you trust managers who give special treatment to their favorite employees? Be sure you treat diverse people the same way.[104] Be fair; don't discriminate against those who are different from you or in favor of your friends.

Loyalty   People who are *loyal* look out for others' interests (they don't take advantage of others). Loyalty requires identification-based trust.
Tips to develop your loyalty include:

- *Invest heavily in loyalty.* If others know that you're always looking out for them, they'll give you the same consideration in return. Do you trust people who look out only for themselves? Be willing to stand by, protect, and save face for others.

- *Maintain confidences.* Do you trust people who stab you in the back? When someone tells you something in confidence, that person is being vulnerable in trusting you, so don't tell others. One time could be your last because it's hard to repair a breach of trust.[105]

- *Don't gossip negatively about individuals.* Do you trust people who say bad things about you and others? If people hear you gossip about others, they may assume you do the same behind their backs. Follow this rule: If you don't have anything nice to say, don't say anything.

- *Be viewed as a collaborator, not a competitor.* Can you fully trust someone who is trying to beat you? Be a team player and help others do well.[106]

Openness   People who are *open* accept new ideas and change. They give the full truth.
Tips to develop your openness include:

- *Self-disclose.* Do you trust people who don't let you know who they really are? Sharing your knowledge builds loyalty and trust.[107] Mistrust comes as much from what people don't know as from what they do know. Tell people what you think in a positive, assertive way, and share your feelings with others. Follow the guidelines on emotions and dealing with anger (Chapters 6 and 7). See more self-disclosure tips below.

- *Accept others' self-disclosure.* Do you trust people who put you down? When others self-disclose to you, be encouraging and offer acceptance and support, as opposed to judgment and ridicule. Use reflecting, reassuring, and probing responses, rather than advising and diverting responses (Chapter 5). And self-disclose back.

- *Accept diversity and conflict.* Do you trust people who don't like people different from them? Accept disagreements, differences of opinion, and conflict.[108] Follow the guidelines for resolving conflicts (Chapter 7). We will discuss diversity again in Chapter 15.

Self-Disclosure and the Johari Window   Self-disclosure enhances human relations and is what takes the level of trust to the identification level. The Johari Window was developed by Joseph Luft and Harry Ingram, who called it by a combination of their first names.[109] As shown in Exhibit 8.9, the window has four regions representing the intersection of two axes: (1) the degree to which information about you (values, attitudes, beliefs) is known to or understood by you, and (2) the degree to which information about you is known by others.
Based on our understanding of self, we select those aspects of self that are appropriate to share with others; we *open* the *hidden* self areas of the window. As we self-disclose, we also find out things about ourselves that others know, such as irritating things we do; we open the *blind* area. The *unknown* area cannot be open until we experience a new situation, such as getting laid off, because we don't know how we will behave until it happens. Thus,

EXHIBIT 8.9 | The Johari Window

	Known to Self	Unknown to Self
Known to Others	Open	Blind
Unknown to Others	Hidden	Unknown

Scott Adams is the creator of the cartoon character Dilbert. Adams makes fun of managers in part because he distrusts top-level managers, saying that leadership is really a crock. According to Adams, leadership is about manipulating people to get them to do something they don't want to do, and there may not be anything in it for them. CEOs basically run the same scam as fortune-tellers, who make up a bunch of guesses and when by chance one is correct, they hope you forget the other errors. First, CEOs blame their predecessors for anything that is bad, then they shuffle everything around, start a new strategic program, and wait. When things go well, despite the CEO, the CEO takes the credit and moves on to the next job. Adams says we may be hung up on leadership as part of our DNA. It seems we have always sought to put somebody above everybody else.

Questions

1. Do you agree with Scott Adams that leadership is a crock?

2. Do we really need to have someone in the leadership role?

3. Do you trust top-level managers?

to develop trust and improve human relations, we gradually share self-disclosure to *open* the *hidden* and *blind* areas of the Johari Window.

Risk and Destroying Trust   Developing trust through self-disclosure does include the risk of being hurt, disappointed, and taken advantage of. Although people often fear the risk of self-disclosure, the rewards of improved human relations and personal friendship are worth the risk. If you follow the guidelines above, you can minimize your risk. When it comes to gender differences, women are generally more willing to self-disclose than men are, and they are more supportive of others' self-disclosure. So men who want to increase self-disclosure might want to start with empathetic women to help develop confidence.

Trust is earned and builds over time. It is much easier to destroy trust than to build it. Years of trust can be hurt or destroyed with one bad act of distrust. For example, if you are inconsistent and get caught in a lie, miss a deadline or do a poor job, or are disloyal, you may hurt your relationship and you might not be trusted again. With knowledge- and identification-based trust levels you may be forgiven, but you may not. Your relationship may never be the same again, or it could end. So be sure to always be trustworthy.[110]

WORK APPLICATIONS

13. What are your strongest and weakest dimensions of trust at work? How will you improve your trustworthiness? What tips will you implement?

As we bring this chapter to a close, complete Self-Assessment Exercise 8–4 to determine how your personality affects your leadership style and ability to develop trust.

Self-Assessment
Exercise 8–4

Your Personality and Leadership and Trust

Recall that your personality is based on traits. So your personality does affect your leadership behavior and your use of contingency leadership styles. What was your preferred situational leadership style? Are you flexible? Can you change styles to meet the situation?

If you have a high *surgency* personality, you most likely have a higher task-oriented leadership style than people-oriented, so you may want to work on the people side. Watch your use of autocratic leadership behavior. Use participation (participative and laissez-faire styles) when appropriate. You may be competent and consistent, but because getting the job done is more important to you than developing human relations, you may need to work on integrity, loyalty, and openness to develop greater *trust*.

If you have a high *agreeableness* personality, you most likely have a high people-oriented leadership style, but you need to make sure the job gets done. You may be reluctant to use the

**Self-Assessment
Exercise 8–4 (continued)**

autocratic leadership style when it is appropriate. You are most likely high on openness and are loyal on *trust* dimensions and you may have integrity, but you may need to work on competence and consistency, because getting the job done is less important to you than developing human relations.

How well you deal with your emotions is what *adjustment* is about. If you are not high on adjustment personality traits, you may tend to be reluctant to be a leader. Low adjustment personalities are usually not open to disclosure, so you may have trouble being *trusted* for competence, consistency, and integrity.

If you are a high *conscientious* personality, you may push others to be conscientious too. Are you more task- or people-oriented? That orientation will affect your leadership style more than your conscientiousness. Conscientiousness tends to lead to competence and consistency *trust* dimensions. However, you may need to work on integrity, loyalty, and openness, based on your task or people orientation.

If you have a high *openness to experience,* you may use participative leadership styles to bring about change. You will use openness to develop *trust,* but you may need to work on other dimensions of trust.

Action plan: Based on your personality, what specific things will you do to improve your leadership style and develop trust?

_____

_____

_____

_____

Videos

Manager's Hot Seat and Behavior Model Videos are available for this chapter.

Online Learning Center Resources
Go to the Internet (http://mhhe.com/lussier8e) where you will find a broad array of resources to help maximize your learning.

• Review the vocabulary.

• Try a quiz.

R E V I E W

The chapter review is organized to help you master the 8 learning outcomes for Chapter 8. First provide your own response to each learning outcome, and then check the summary provided to see how well you understand the material. Next, identify the final statement in each section as either true or false (T/F). Correct each false statement. Answers are given at the end of the chapter.

1. **Explain what leadership is and how it affects behavior, human relations, and performance.**
   Leadership is the process of influencing employees to work toward the achievement of objectives. A leader using one style will behave differently than another leader using a different style. The leader's style also affects the type of human relations between the leader and followers. Leaders can affect followers' performance, but not always.
   The terms *leadership* and *management* mean the same thing. T F

2. **Describe leadership trait theory.**
   Leadership trait theory assumes that distinct physical and psychological characteristics account for effective leadership. According to Ghiselli, the major leadership traits needed for success are supervisory ability, the need for occupational achievement, intelligence, decisiveness, self-assurance, and initiative.
   Leadership trait theory is outdated and no longer studied. T F

3. **List and describe four behavioral leadership theories.**

Behavioral leadership theories assume that there are distinctive styles which effective leaders use consistently. The four theories are: (1) basic leadership style—autocratic, democratic, laissez-faire; (2) two-dimensional leadership styles—initiating structure and consideration styles (Ohio State) and job-centered and employee-centered styles (University of Michigan); (3) the Leadership Grid—Blake and Mouton's model identifying the ideal leadership style as having a high concern for both production and people; and (4) transformational leadership—leaders bring about change, innovation, and entrepreneurship by taking the organization through three acts.

Charismatic leadership is a behavioral leadership theory. T F

4. **List and describe four contingency leadership theories.**

Contingency leadership theories assume that the appropriate leadership style varies from situation to situation. The four theories are: (1) contingency leadership theory—Fiedler's model used to determine whether leadership style is task- or relationship-oriented, and whether the situation matches the style; (2) leadership continuum—Tannenbaum and Schmidt's identified boss-centered and employee-centered leadership at the extremes; (3) normative leadership theory—Vroom and Yetton's decision-tree model that enables the user to select from five leadership styles the one that is appropriate for the situation; and (4) situational leadership—Hersey and Blanchard's model for selecting from four leadership styles the one that fits the employees' maturity level in a given situation.

Contingency leadership theory is the only one that recommends changing the situation, rather than your leadership style. T F

5. **Explain four situational supervisory styles.**

The four situational supervisory styles are: (1) autocratic—high-directive–low-support; (2) consultative—high-directive–high-support; (3) participative—low-directive–high-support; and (4) laissez-faire—low-directive–low-support.

When the employee's capability level is high (C-3), the consultative leadership style is appropriate. T F

6. **Identify three characteristics that substitute for management.**

Characteristics of subordinates, task, and the organization can substitute for management by providing direction and/or support.

Subordinates, task, and the organization are substitutes for management, but they can't substitute for leadership. T F

7. **Briefly describe the five dimensions of trust.**

The five dimensions of trust are: (1) integrity—being honest, truthful, and sincere; (2) competence—having technical and interpersonal knowledge, ability, and skill; (3) consistency—using the same behavior in similar situations; (4) loyalty—looking out for the interests of others; and (5) openness—accepting new ideas and change.

The Johari Window is a measure of openness. T F

Learning Outcome

8. Define the following 14 key terms.

8. **Define the following 14 key terms.**

Select one or more methods: (1) Fill in the missing key terms from memory; (2) match the key terms from the end of the review with their definitions below; and/or (3) copy the key terms in order from the key terms at the beginning of the chapter.

_____ is the process of influencing employees to work toward the achievement of objectives.

_____ assumes that there are distinctive physical and psychological characteristics accounting for leadership effectiveness.

_____ assume that there are distinctive styles that effective leaders use consistently.

The _____ is Blake and Mouton's model identifying the ideal leadership style as having a high concern for both production and people.

_____ assume that the appropriate leadership style varies from situation to situation.

_____ is Fiedler's model, which is used to determine if a person's leadership style is task- or relationship-oriented, and if the situation matches the leader's style.

The _____ is Tannenbaum and Schmidt's model, which identifies seven leadership styles based on the use of boss-centered versus employee-centered leadership.

_____ is Vroom and Yetton's decision-tree model, which enables the user to select from five leadership styles the one that is appropriate for the situation.

_____ is Hersey and Blanchard's model for selecting from four leadership styles the one that matches the employees' maturity level in a given situation.

The four situational supervision styles are _____, which involves high-directive–low supportive behavior and is appropriate when interacting with low-capability employees; _____, which involves high-directive–high-supportive behavior and is appropriate when interacting with moderate-capability employees; _____, which is characterized by low-directive–high-supportive behavior and is appropriate when interacting with employees with high capability; and _____, which entails low-directive–low-supportive behavior and is appropriate when interacting with outstanding employees.

_____ is the positive expectation that another will not take advantage of you.

K E Y   T E R M S

autocratic style   290
behavioral leadership
   theories   277
consultative style   290
contingency leadership
   theories   281

contingency leadership
   theory   281
laissez-faire style   291
leadership   273
leadership continuum   283
Leadership Grid   278

leadership trait theory   274
normative leadership
   theory   284
participative style   290
situational leadership   285
trust   296

C O M M U N I C A T I O N   S K I L L S

The following critical thinking questions can be used for class discussion and/or as written assignments to develop communication skills. Be sure to give complete explanations for all questions.

1. There are many traits that are said to be important to leadership success. Which three traits do you believe are the most important? List in order of priority.

2. The two-dimensional leadership styles developed at Ohio State University and the University of Michigan back in the 1940s still serve as the bases for the current contingency leadership theories. Are the task and relationship dimensions outdated?

3. The Leadership Grid states that the one best style to use in all situations is the 9,9 team manager style, with a high concern for both people and production. Do you agree with this statement?

4. Fiedler's contingency leadership theory states that managers can't change their leadership style; they are either task- or relationship-oriented. Do you agree with this statement?

5. Which of the five contingency leadership theories (Exhibit 8.5) do you prefer?

6. Do you agree with the statement that you can substitute for management but you can't substitute for leadership, or is this just semantics?

7. Give some examples of global cultural diversity that you have experienced.

8. Do you agree that integrity is at the center of trust, holding the other four dimensions together? Can competence, consistency, loyalty, and/or openness lead to trusting relationships if there is no integrity?

9. Based on your life and work experience, what percentage of people would you say really have integrity (that is, are honest—don't lie, steal, or cheat—and sincere)? Give some examples of how certain people damaged your trust in them.

CASE

Howard Schultz

Starbucks is a large multinational chain of coffee shops headquartered in Seattle, Washington, with more than 15,000 stores serving 50 million customers a week. Starbucks sells more than just coffee. Other product categories include fresh food, handcrafted beverages, merchandise, Starbucks Entertainment, Global Consumer Products, the Starbucks Card, and a brand portfolio. Starbucks has 7,087 company-operated stores and 4,081 licensed stores in the United States. It also does business in 43 other countries, with 1,796 company-operated stores in Australia, Canada, Chile, China (Northern China, Southern China), Germany, Ireland, Puerto Rico, Singapore, Thailand, and the United Kingdom. Starbucks also has 2,792 joint venture and licensed stores in Austria, the Bahamas, Bahrain, Brazil, Canada, China (Shanghai/Eastern China), Cyprus, the Czech Republic, Denmark, Egypt, France, Greece, Hong Kong, Indonesia, Ireland, Japan, Jordan, Kuwait, Lebanon, Macau S.A.R., Malaysia, Mexico, the Netherlands, New Zealand, Oman, Peru, the Philippines, Qatar, Romania, Russia, Saudi Arabia, South Korea, Spain, Switzerland, Taiwan, Turkey, the United Arab Emirates, and the United Kingdom.[111]

Sitting in his office, Dr. Sherman, professor of management at Long Island University, stared at a man wearing blue jeans, a T-shirt, and a black leather jacket. It was hard for Dr. Sherman to fathom that the driving force behind Starbucks was a Brooklyn-born man, who went to Northern Michigan University on a football scholarship, and who traveled to Seattle to fall in love not only with a city but also with a way of doing business—the Starbucks way. Howard Schultz's method included the shop owners' dedication to coffee connoisseurship and caring for employees.

His entrepreneurial drive was inspired by what he saw in Italy. That country's plethora of coffeehouses were part of the national social structure, a place for discourse and, of course, for fashionable display. The original Starbucks founders were reluctant to expand into the restaurant business, but Schultz eventually bought the company for $3.8 million.

Sherman found Schultz surprisingly humble for a gentleman who expanded a small firm selling drip coffeemakers into a worldwide, multibillion-dollar business. Schultz's main goal was to serve a great cup of coffee but attached to this goal was a principle: Schultz wanted to build a company with soul. This led to a series of practices that were unprecedented in retail. Schultz insisted that all employees working at least 20 hours a week get comprehensive health coverage—including coverage for unmarried spouses. Then he introduced an employee stock-option plan. These moves boosted loyalty and led to extremely low worker turnover, even though employee salaries were fairly low.

"You have to understand," Schultz said, "that employees are the cornerstone of my firm. Without happy employees we cannot have happy customers, and without happy customers we cannot have happy stockholders. So, if you take care of your employees, everything else falls into place." Starbuck's guiding principles include providing a great work environment and treating each other with respect and dignity; embracing diversity as an essential component in the way it does business; applying the highest standards of excellence to the purchasing, roasting, and fresh delivery of its coffee; developing enthusiastic, satisfied customers all of the time; contributing positively to its communities and the environment, and recognizing that profitability is essential to its future success. With Starbucks, Schultz wanted to create "the kind of company that my father never got a chance to work for, in which people were respected."

Asked the secret of his success, Schultz recounts four principles: Don't be threatened by people smarter than you. Compromise anything but your core values. Seek to renew yourself even when you are hitting home runs. And everything matters.

Howard Schultz created Starbucks and served as CEO and chairman of the board for several years. Schultz eventually stepped down from his CEO position, letting Jim Donald take over the day-to-day operations as CEO. However, Starbucks ran into problems and its stock price plunged, so Schultz took back the CEO position. Schultz's turnaround strategy included improving the current state of its U.S. stores by giving store partners better training and tools, launching new products (some of which will have an impact as significant as its Frappuccino products and the Starbucks Card), and introducing new concepts in store design, among other enhancements to the *Starbucks Experience*. At the same time, Starbucks slowed the pace of its U.S. store openings and closed a number of underperforming locations. Starbucks also is focusing on growth outside the U.S.[112] However, with the downturn of the economy in 2008, penny-pinching customers, and competition from Dunkin' Donuts and McDonald's, some question whether Howard Schultz can keep his company from getting creamed (pun intended).

Go to the Internet: For more information on Howard Schultz and Starbucks and to update the information provided in this case, do a name search on the Internet and visit www.starbucks.com.

Support your answers to the following questions with specific information from the case and text, or with other information you get from the Web or other sources.

1. Which traits has Howard Schultz exhibited that would indicate he is an effective leader?

2. Describe Howard Schultz's basic leadership style. How would you rate his leadership using the Leadership Grid?

3. Which factors might lead Dr. Sherman to conclude that Howard Schultz is a transformational and charismatic leader?

4. What actions does Howard Schultz take to build employee trust in his firm? Would you trust him?

5. Which leadership challenges might going international pose to Howard Schultz? In which countries might his style of leadership work or not work?

Cumulative Questions

6. Personality (Chapter 2) is best associated with which leadership theory?

7. What is the role of communication (Chapters 5 and 6) in leadership?

8. In implementing the turnaround strategy, which assertiveness (passive, aggressive, assertive) and conflict management styles (Chapter 7) would be most appropriate for Schultz?

OBJECTIVE CASE   ## The Cleanup Job

Brenda is the head meat cutter in the Big K Supermarket. Brenda hires and has fired meat cutters; she also determines raises. Although it has never been said, she speculates that the all-male meat-cutting crew isn't friendly toward her because they resent having a female boss. They are all highly skilled.

Once a month the meat and frozen foods cases are supposed to be cleaned by a meat cutter; they are all equally capable of doing it. It is not any one person's job, and no one likes to do it. It's that time of month again, and Brenda has to select someone to clean up. She just happens to see Rif first, so she approaches him.

BRENDA: Rif, I want you to clean the cases this month.

RIF: Why me? I just did it two months ago. Give someone else a turn.

BRENDA: I didn't ask you to tell me when you did it last. I asked you to do it.

RIF: I know, but I'm a meat cutter, not a janitor. Why can't the janitor do it? Or something more fair?

BRENDA: Do I have to take action against you for not following an order?

RIF: OK, I'll do it.

Answer the following questions. Then in the space between questions, state why you selected that answer.

_____ 1. The basic leadership style Brenda used with Rif was:

   a. autocratic   *b.* democratic   *c.* laissez-faire

_____ 2. With Rif, Brenda used the _____ quadrant leadership style in Exhibit 8.1.

   a. 1   *b.* 2   *c.* 3   *d.* 4

_____ 3. With Rif, Brenda should have used the _____ quadrant leadership style in Exhibit 8.1.

   a. 1   *b.* 2   *c.* 3   *d.* 4

_____ 4. The Leadership Grid style Brenda used with Rif was _____ (see Exhibit 8.2).

   a. 1,1   *b.* 9,1   *c.* 1,9   *d.* 5,5   *e.* 9,9

_____ 5. According to Leadership Grid theory, Brenda used the appropriate leadership style.

     a. true   *b.* false

_____ 6. According to Fiedler's contingency theory model (see Exhibit 8.3), Brenda is in a _____ situation, and _____ -oriented behavior is appropriate.

     a. task   *b.* relationship

_____ 7. Brenda used the _____ leadership continuum style (see Exhibit 8.4).

     a. 1   *b.* 2   *c.* 3   *d.* 4   *e.* 5   *f.* 6   *g.* 7

_____ 8. The appropriate normative leadership style to resolve the monthly cleanup job is:

     a. decide   *c.* consult group   *e.* delegate

     b. consult individually   *d.* facilitate

_____ 9. The situational supervision style Brenda used with Rif was _____ (see Exhibit 8.6).

     a. autocratic   *c.* participative

     b. consultative   *d.* laissez-faire

_____ 10. The situational supervision style Brenda should use to resolve the monthly cleanup job is _____ (see Exhibit 8.6).

     a. autocratic   *c.* participative

     b. consultative   *d.* laissez-faire

_____ 11. In Brenda's situation, how would you get the cases cleaned each month?

Note: Different leadership styles can be role-played in class.

SKILL-BUILDING EXERCISE 8–1

Situational Supervision

In-Class Exercise
(Individual and Group)

BMV 8–1

Objectives: To learn to use the situational supervision model. To develop your ability to supervise employees using the appropriate situational supervisory style for their capability level.

AACSB: The primary AACSB learning standard skills developed through this exercise are reflective thinking, analytic, and leadership skills.

Experience: In groups of two, you will apply the Situational Supervision Model in Exhibit 8.6 to situations 2 through 12 in Self-Assessment Exercise 8–2. After you have finished, your instructor will give you the recommended answers, enabling you to determine your level of success at selecting the appropriate style.

For each situation, use the left-hand column in Exhibit 8.6 to identify the employee capability level the situation describes. Write the level (1 through 4) on the line marked "C" to the left of each situation in Self-Assessment Exercise 8–2. Now identify the supervisory style that each response (*a* through *d*) represents. (These are listed in the right-hand column of the exhibit.) Indicate the style (A, C, P, or L) on the line marked "S" at the end of each response. Finally, choose the management style you think is best for each situation by placing a check mark (✓) next to the appropriate response (*a, b, c,* or *d*).

Procedure 1
(3–8 minutes)

The instructor reviews the Situational Supervision Model, Exhibit 8.6, and explains how to use the model for situation 1.

Procedure 2
(29–43 minutes)

1. Turn to situation 2 in Self-Assessment Exercise 8–2, page 286, and to Exhibit 8.6, page 291, Situational Supervision Model. (You may tear the exhibit out of your book.) Apply the model to the situation in an attempt to select the best course of action (3–4 minutes). The instructor will go over the answers and scoring (3–4 minutes).

2. Divide into teams of two; you may have one group of three if there is an odd number in the class. Apply the model as a team to situations 3 through 6. Team members may select different answers if they don't agree (8–12 minutes). Do not do situations 7 through 12 until you are told to do so. Your instructor will go over the answers and scoring for situations 3 through 6 (2–4 minutes).

3. As a team, select your answers to situations 7 through 12 (11–15 minutes). Your instructor will go over the answers and scoring to situations 7 through 12 (2–4 minutes).

Caution: There is no proven relationship between how a person performs on a pencil-and-paper test and how he or she actually performs on the job. People have a tendency to choose the answer they think is correct, rather than what they would actually do. The objective of this exercise is to help you better understand your supervisory style and how to improve it.

Conclusion: The instructor leads a class discussion and/or makes concluding remarks.

Application (2–4 minutes): What have I learned from this experience? How will I use this knowledge in the future?

Sharing: Volunteers give their answers to the application section.

SKILL-BUILDING EXERCISE 8–2

**A Leadership
Style Role Play**

In-Class Exercise
(Group)

Objectives: To experience leadership in action. To identify the leadership style, and how using the appropriate versus inappropriate leadership style affects the organization.

AACSB: The primary AACSB learning standard skills developed through this exercise are analytic and leadership skills.

Preparation: All necessary material is below; no preparation is necessary.

Procedure 1
(5–10 minutes)

Break into groups and select the style (autocratic, consultative, participative, or laissez-faire) your group would use to make the following decision:

You are an office manager with four subordinates who all do typing on outdated computers. You will be receiving a new computer to replace one of the outdated ones. (Everyone knows about it because several salespeople have been in the office.) You must decide who gets the new computer. Below is some information about each subordinate.

- Pat—He or she has been with the organization for 20 years, is 50 years old, and presently has a two-year-old computer.
- Chris—He or she has been with the organization for 10 years, is 31 years old, and presently has a one-year-old computer.
- Fran—He or she has been with the organization for five years, is 40 years old, and presently has a three-year-old computer.
- Sandy—He or she has been with the organization for two years, is 23 years old, and presently has a five-year-old computer.

Possible Leadership Styles

Instructor selects one option:

Option A: Continuum of Leadership Behavior Styles 1 through 7. See Exhibit 8.4 for definitions of these seven styles.

Option B: Situational Supervisory Styles

S-A Autocratic	*a.* Make the decision alone; then tell each subordinate individually your decision and how and why you made it.
	b. Make the decision alone; then have a group meeting to announce the decision and how and why you made it. No discussion is allowed.
S-C Consultative	*a.* Before deciding, talk to the subordinates individually to find out if they want the word processor, and why they think they should get it. Then make the decision and announce it to the group or to each person individually.
	b. Before deciding, have a group meeting to listen to why all the subordinates want it, and why they think they should get it. Have no discussion among subordinates. Then make the decision and announce it to the group or to each person individually.
S-P Participative	*a.* Tentatively decide to whom you want to give it. Then hold a meeting to tell the group your plans, followed with a discussion that can lead to your changing your mind. After the open discussion, you make the decision and announce it, explaining the rationale for selection.
	b. Call a group meeting and explain the problem. Lead an open discussion about who should get the word processor. After the discussion, make your decision and explain the rationale for it.
S-L Laissez-faire	*a.* Call a meeting and explain the situation. Tell the group that they have *X* amount of time (5–7 minutes for the exercise) to make the decision. You do not become a group member; you may or may not stay for the decision. However, if you do stay, you cannot participate.

Procedure 2 (5–10 minutes)

1. Four volunteers from different groups go to the front of the class. Take out a sheet of 8½-by-11-inch paper and write the name of the person you are role-playing (in big, dark letters), fold it in half, and place it in view of the manager and class. While the managers are planning, turn to the end of this exercise and read your role and the roles of your colleagues. Try to put yourself in the person's position, and do and say what he or she actually would during the role play. No one but the typist should read this additional subordinate role information.

2. The instructor will tell each group which leadership style their manager will role-play; it may or may not be the one selected.

3. The group selects a manager to do the actual role play of making the decision; and the group plans "who, what, when, where, how." The manager will perform the role play. No one should read the additional subordinate role information.

Procedure 3
(1–10 minutes)

One manager goes to the front of the class and conducts the leadership role play.

Procedure 4
(1–5 minutes)

The class members (other than the group being represented) vote for the style (1 to 7 or Tell *a. b.*; Sell *a. b.*; Participate *a. b.*; Delegate *a.*) they think the manager portrayed. Then the manager reveals the style. If several class members didn't vote for the style portrayed, a discussion can take place.

Procedures 3 and 4
continued
(25–40 minutes)

Repeat procedures 3 and 4 until all managers have their turn or the time runs out.

Procedure 5
(2–3 minutes)

The class members individually determine the style they would use when making the decision. The class votes for the style the class would use in this situation. The instructor gives his or her recommendation and/or the author's.

Conclusion: The instructor leads a class discussion and/or makes concluding remarks.

Application (2–4 minutes): What did I learn from this experience? How will I apply this knowledge in the future?

Sharing: Volunteers give their answers to the application section.

Subordinate Roles

Additional information (for subordinates' role playing only):

Pat
    You are happy with the way things are now. You do not want the new computer. Be firm and assertive in your stance.

Chris
    You are bored with your present job. You really want the new computer. Being second in seniority, you plan to be aggressive in trying to get it. You are afraid that the others will complain because you got the last new computer. So you have a good idea: You will take the new one, and Sandy can have your old one.

Fran
    You are interested in having the new computer. You spend more time each day typing than any of the other employees. Therefore, you believe you should get the new computer.

Sandy
    You want the new computer. You believe you should get it because you are by far the fastest typist, and you have the oldest computer. You do not want a hand-me-down computer.

SKILL-BUILDING EXERCISE 8–3

Self-Disclosure and Trust (Johari Window)

In-Class Exercise
(Group)

Objective: To develop trust by self-disclosing to open your Johari Window.

AACSB: The primary AACSB learning standard skill developed through this exercise is communication abilities.

Experience: You will self-disclose by asking and answering questions to develop trust.

Rules:

1. Take turns asking questions.
2. You may refuse to answer a question as long as you did not ask it (or plan to).
3. You don't have to ask the questions in order.
4. You can add your own questions to ask anytime during the exercise.

Procedure 1
(7–15 minutes)

Break into groups of two or three. Take a minute to read the questions. Check questions you want to ask, and add your own questions. Follow the rules above.

1. What is your name and major?
2. Why did you select your major?

3. What career plans do you have?

4. How do you feel about doing this exercise?

5. What do you do in your spare time?

6. What is your Big Five Personality profile, or what do you think my profile is?

7. In Self-Assessment Exercise 8–3 what was your trustworthiness score and your strongest and weakest dimensions, or what do you think my score was, and which are my strongest and weakest dimensions?

8. What was your first impression of me?

9. How do you and/or others view me?

10. _____

11. _____

12. _____

Procedure 2
(5–15 minutes)

Review the tips for developing trust. How well did I follow the tips, or did I not follow any of the tips?

Answer the following questions in the same group. Then you may ask the questions from the list above and/or your own questions to further self-disclose.

1. Have I/you taken any risk during this self-disclosure?

2. What level of trust have we developed (deterrence-, knowledge-, identification-based)?

3. Did I/you not follow any of the tips for developing trust?

4. With regard to the Johari Window, have I/you simply focused on opening the unknown to others (hidden), or have I/you opened the unknown to self (blind)?

5. Have I/you learned anything unknown to self?

Conclusion: The instructor may lead a class discussion and/or make concluding remarks.

Application (2–4 minutes):   What did I learn from this experience? How will I apply this knowledge in the future?

Sharing: Volunteers give their answers to the application section.

A N S W E R S   T O   T R U E / F A L S E   Q U E S T I O N S

1. F. Leadership and management are not the same thing.

2. F. As stated in the text, although there is no universal list of leadership traits, leadership trait theory is still being studied today.

3. T.

4. T.

5. F. In Exhibit 8.6, with C-3 employees the participative leadership style is appropriate.

6. T.

7. T.

Motivating Performance

Latoia Henderson was recently promoted to a management position at Ford Motor Company. She is enthusiastic about her work. Generally, things are going well, but Latoia is having a problem with Hank. Hank is often late for work, and even though he can do a good job, he does not regularly perform to expectations. Latoia had a talk with Hank to find out what the problem was. Hank said the money and benefits were great, and the people in the department were nice, but the job was boring. He complained that he didn't have any say about how to do his job and that Latoia was always checking up on him. Hank believes he is treated fairly because of the union, which gives him job protection. But because everyone is paid the same, working hard is a waste of time. If you were in Latoia's position, how would you motivate Hank? This chapter examines specific motivation theories and techniques that can be used to motivate not only Hank but employees in all organizations.

Learning Outcome

1. Explain the motivation process and the three factors affecting performance.

THE IMPORTANCE OF MOTIVATION

In this section, we discuss what motivation is and why it is important and how motivation affects behavior, human relations, and performance.

What Is Motivation and Why Is It Important?

Motivation *is the internal process leading to behavior to satisfy needs.* Have you ever wondered why people do the things they do? The primary reason people do what they do is to meet their needs or wants.[1] The process people go through to meet their needs is

$$\text{Need} \rightarrow \text{Motive} \rightarrow \text{Behavior} \rightarrow \text{Satisfaction or Dissatisfaction}$$

For example, you are thirsty (need) and have a drive (motive) to get a drink. You get a drink (behavior) that quenches (satisfaction) your thirst. However, if you could not get a drink, or a drink of what you really wanted, you would be dissatisfied. Satisfaction is usually short-lived. Getting that drink satisfied you, but soon you will need another drink.

Managers often view motivation as an employee's willingness to put forth effort and commitment to achieve organizational objectives.[2] Latoia is concerned because Hank is not motivated to work hard.

WORK APPLICATIONS

1. Give an example of how you have gone through the motivation process. Identify the need, motive, behavior, and satisfaction or dissatisfaction.

Why Knowing How to Motivate Employees Is Important   The topic of motivation plays a central role in the field of management.[3] Understandably, it is one of the most popular management topics.[4] Motivation derives from the Latin word for *movement,* and it has been widely acknowledged as a critical determinant of our behavior.[5] Motivation affects how and to what extent we utilize our skills and abilities.[6] Unmotivated employees are less willing to be cooperative and supportive, and they may decrease work effort, time on the job, productivity, and performance.[7] Thus, we need to motivate employees to boost productivity.[8] Jeff Taylor, founder of Monster.com, said that to be successful, you have to be able to motivate others. To this end, researchers are studying the factors that energize, direct, and sustain work-related behavior,[9] and you will learn about their motivation theories in this chapter.

Because they can't simply buy motivation,[10] organizations are designing incentive systems to motivate employees.[11] Self-motivation is one of the most important skills companies look for when hiring.[12] Thus, your ability to motivate yourself and others is critical to your career success, and the goal of this chapter is to increase your ability to do both.

How Motivation Affects Behavior, Human Relations, and Performance

All behavior is motivated by some need. However, needs and motives are complex; we don't always know what our needs are or why we do the things we do.[13] Have you ever done something and not known why you did it? Understanding needs will help you understand behavior.[14]

We cannot observe motives; however, we can observe behavior and infer what the person's motive is.[15] We call this attribution (Chapter 3). However, it is not easy to know why a person behaved the way he or she did because people do the same thing for different reasons. And people often attempt to satisfy several needs at once.

People with Theory X and Theory Y attitudes have different motives and human relations. Personality also affects a person's motivation to have effective human relations. Generally, people with a Big Five agreeableness personality are highly motivated to work at having effective human relations to satisfy their need for affiliation.

Generally, an employee who is motivated will try harder to do a good job than one who is not motivated.[16] However, performance is not based simply on motivation. The level of performance attained is determined by three interdependent factors: ability, motivation, and resources. This relationship can be stated as a **performance formula:** *Performance = Ability × Motivation × Resources.* Ability and motivation are driving forces of behavior that result in a specific level of performance.[17]

For performance levels to be high, all three factors must be high. If any one factor is low or missing, the performance level will be adversely affected. For example, Mary Lou, a very intelligent student, has the books, but because she does not care about grades, she does not study (low motivation) and does not get an A.

As an employee and manager, if you want to attain high levels of performance, you must be sure that you and your employees have the ability, motivation, and resources to meet objectives. When performance is not at the standard level or above, you must determine which performance factor needs to be improved, and improve it. In the opening case, Hank has the ability and resources, but he lacks motivation.

APPLICATION SITUATIONS

The Performance Formula

AS 9–1

Identify the factor contributing to low performance in the five situations below.

A. Ability   B. Motivation   C. Resources

_____ 1. In recent years, the U.S. steel industry has not been as productive as the foreign competition.

_____ 2. I don't think you produce as much as the other department members because you're lazy.

_____ 3. I practice longer and harder than my track teammates Heather and Linda. I don't understand why they beat me in the races.

_____ 4. I could get all A's if I wanted to. But I'd rather relax and have a good time in college.

_____ 5. The government would be more efficient if it cut down on waste.

When employee needs are not met through the organization, employees are dissatisfied and are generally lower performers.[18] This is the case with Hank; he finds the job boring and is not performing to expectations. To increase Hank's performance, Latoia must meet the goal of human relations. She must create a win–win situation so that Hank's needs are met to motivate him to perform to her expectations. As each motivation theory and technique is presented, you will learn how Latoia can apply it to motivate Hank or others.

There is no single universally accepted theory of how to motivate people.[19] In this chapter you will learn seven major motivation theories and how you can use them to motivate yourself and others. After studying all the theories, you can select one theory to use, take from several to make your own theory, or apply the theory that best fits the specific situation.

CONTENT MOTIVATION THEORIES

A satisfied employee is usually productive because job satisfaction is a motivator.[20] If an organization wants to increase performance, it must meet employees' needs.[21] Each year hundreds of millions of dollars are spent on employee needs satisfaction programs to increase productivity. To increase performance, managers must know their own needs and their employees' needs, and they must satisfy them.[22] This is the goal of human relations.

The **content motivation theories** *focus on identifying people's needs in order to understand what motivates them.* In this section, you will learn four content motivation theories: (1) needs hierarchy, (2) ERG theory, (3) two-factor theory, and (4) manifest needs theory. You will also learn how organizations use these theories to motivate employees.

Needs Hierarchy

The **needs hierarchy** *is Maslow's theory of motivation, which is based on five needs.* In the 1940s, Abraham Maslow developed one of the most popular and widely known motivation theories.[23] His theory is based on three major assumptions:

- People's needs are arranged in order of importance (hierarchy), going from basic needs (physiological) to more complex needs (self-actualization).

- People will not be motivated to satisfy a higher-level need unless the lower-level need(s) has been at least minimally satisfied.

- There are five classifications of needs. Listed below are these five classes of needs in order of importance to the individual.

Physiological Needs   These are people's primary or basic needs. They include air, food, shelter, sex, and relief or avoidance of pain. In an organizational setting, these needs include adequate salary, breaks, and working conditions.

Safety Needs   Once the physiological needs are met, the individual is concerned with safety and security. In the organizational setting, these needs include safe working conditions, salary increases to meet inflation, job security, and fringe benefits that protect the physiological needs. However, jobs are less secure today, and fewer benefits are given.[24]

Social Needs   After establishing safety, people look for love, friendship, acceptance, and affection. In the organizational setting, these needs include the opportunity to interact with others, be accepted, and have friends.[25]

Esteem Needs   After the social needs are met, the individual focuses on ego, status, self-respect, recognition for accomplishments, and a feeling of self-confidence and prestige. In the organizational setting, these needs include titles, the satisfaction of completing the job itself, merit pay raises, recognition, challenging tasks, participation in decision making, and the chance for advancement.[26]

EXHIBIT 9.1 |

Needs Hierarchy and
ERG Theory

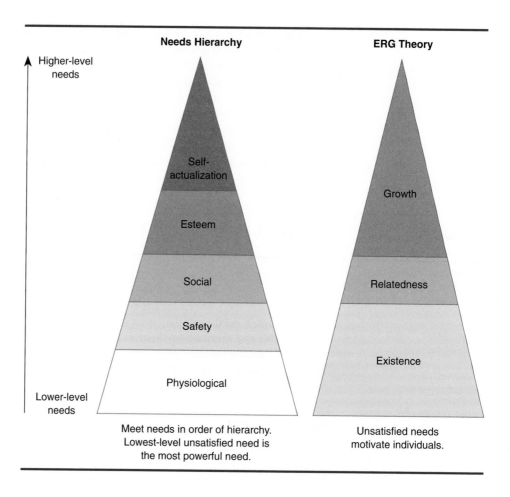

Self-Actualization   The highest level of need is to develop one's full potential. To do so, one seeks growth, achievement, and advancement. In the organizational setting, these needs include the development of one's skills; the chance to be creative; achievement and promotions; and the ability to have complete control over one's job.[27]

Many research studies do not support Maslow's hierarchy theory. However, it has a sound foundation and is still used today. In fact, Maslow's work serves as a basis for several other theories. Today, organizations still strive to meet self-actualization needs.[28]

See Exhibit 9.1 for an illustration of Maslow's five needs.

ERG Theory

The classification of needs has been long debated. Some say there are only two needs, while others claim there are seven. Several researchers have combined categories to simplify the theory. ERG is a well-known simplification. As Exhibit 9.1 illustrates, Clayton Alderfer reorganizes Maslow's needs hierarchy into three levels of needs: existence (physiological and safety needs), relatedness (social), and growth (esteem and self-actualization). Alderfer maintains the higher- and lower-order needs. He agrees with Maslow that unsatisfied needs motivate individuals. In the opening case, Hank's performance was poor, but he can be motivated to meet Latoia's expectations if his performance results in satisfying his needs.

Motivating with Needs Hierarchy and ERG Theory   Based on Maslow's work, we conclude that the major recommendation to managers is to meet employees' lower-level needs so that they will not dominate the employees' motivational process. Managers should get to know and understand people's needs and strive to meet them as a means of increasing performance.[29] How organizations meet needs is discussed in a later section.

To use ERG theory, answer six questions: (1) What need does the individual have? (2) What needs have been satisfied? (3) Which unsatisfied need is the lowest in the hierarchy?

(4) Have some higher-order needs been frustrated? If so, how? (5) Has the person refocused on a lower-level need? (6) How can the unsatisfied needs be satisfied? Latoia observed Hank and took the time to talk to him to determine his needs. Hank's need for existence and relatedness have been met. However, his need for growth has been frustrated. To motivate Hank, Latoia must meet his need for growth. In this chapter, you will learn ways to satisfy growth needs.

Two-Factor Theory

The **two-factor theory** *is Herzberg's classification of needs as hygienes and motivators.* Before learning Herzberg's theory, complete Self-Assessment Exercise 9–1 to learn what motivates you.

In the 1950s, Frederick Herzberg and associates interviewed 200 accountants and engineers.[30] They were asked to describe situations in which they were satisfied or motivated and dissatisfied or unmotivated. Their findings disagreed with the traditional view that satisfaction and dissatisfaction were at opposite ends of a continuum.

Self-Assessment
Exercise 9–1

Your Motivators and Hygienes

Below are 12 job factors that contribute to job satisfaction. Rate each according to how important it is to you. Place the number 1 to 5 on the line before each factor.

Very important		Somewhat important		Not important
5	4	3	2	1

_____ 1. An interesting job I enjoy doing.

_____ 2. A good boss who treats everyone the same, regardless of circumstances.

_____ 3. Recognition and appreciation for the work I do.

_____ 4. The opportunity for advancement.

_____ 5. A job that is routine, without much change from day to day.

_____ 6. A prestigious job title regardless of pay.

_____ 7. Job responsibility that gives me the freedom to do the job my way.

_____ 8. Good working conditions (nice office).

_____ 9. A focus on following company rules, regulations, procedures, and policies.

_____ 10. The opportunity to grow through learning new things.

_____ 11. A job I can do well and succeed at.

_____ 12. Job security.

To determine if hygienes or motivators are important to you, on the lines below place the numbers (1 to 5) that represent your answers for the statements.

Hygienes Score	Motivators Score
2. _____	1. _____
5. _____	3. _____
6. _____	4. _____
8. _____	7. _____
9. _____	10. _____
12. _____	11. _____
Total _____	Total _____

Add each column. Did you select hygienes or motivators as being more important to you? Now we'll find out their significance.

EXHIBIT 9.2 | Two-Factor Theory

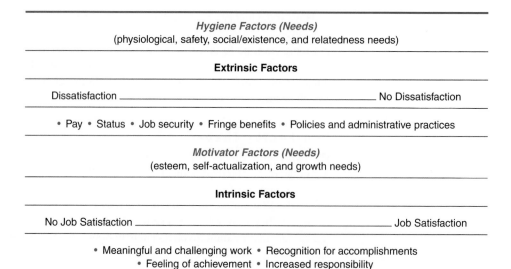

Hygiene Factors (Needs)
(physiological, safety, social/existence, and relatedness needs)

Extrinsic Factors

Dissatisfaction ——————————————————————— No Dissatisfaction

• Pay • Status • Job security • Fringe benefits • Policies and administrative practices

Motivator Factors (Needs)
(esteem, self-actualization, and growth needs)

Intrinsic Factors

No Job Satisfaction ——————————————————————— Job Satisfaction

• Meaningful and challenging work • Recognition for accomplishments
• Feeling of achievement • Increased responsibility
• Opportunity for growth • Opportunity for advancement

While Maslow classifies five needs and Alderfer classifies three needs, Herzberg classifies two needs that he calls *factors.* Herzberg combines lower-level needs (physiological, safety, social/existence, and relatedness) into one classification he calls *hygienes;* and he combines higher-level needs (esteem, self-actualization, growth) into one classification he calls *motivators.* Hygienes are also called *extrinsic factors* because attempts to motivate come from outside the job itself, such as pay, job security, and job title; working conditions; fringe benefits; and relationships. Motivators are called *intrinsic factors* because motivation comes from the job itself, such as achievement, recognition, challenge, and advancement. See Exhibit 9.2 for an illustration of Herzberg's theory.

Herzberg contends that providing hygiene factors keeps people from being dissatisfied, but it does not motivate people. For example, if people are dissatisfied with their pay and they get a raise, they will no longer be dissatisfied. They may even be satisfied for a short period of time. However, before long they get accustomed to the new standard of living and will no longer be satisfied. They need another raise to be satisfied again. The vicious cycle goes on.[31] If you got a pay raise, would you be motivated and be more productive? How many people do you know who increased their level of productivity and maintained it until the next pay raise?

To motivate, Herzberg says that you must first ensure that hygiene factors are adequate. Once employees are satisfied with their environment, they can be motivated through their jobs.[32] Today, many people are striving to find meaning in their work.[33]

Review Self-Assessment Exercise 9–1. According to Herzberg, if you seek and attain hygiene job factors, you may not be dissatisfied, but you may not be satisfied either. Do not expect external rewards for everything you are asked to do. To be satisfied, you must seek and attain internal rewards.

WORK APPLICATIONS

2. In Self-Assessment Exercise 9–1, did you select motivators or hygienes as being important to you? Explain.

Using Two-Factor Theory to Motivate Employees   In the opening case, Hank said he was not dissatisfied with hygiene factors. He lacked job satisfaction. If Latoia is going to motivate him, she will have to focus on intrinsic motivation, not hygiene. Hank says the job is boring. Will a pay raise or better working conditions make the job more interesting and challenging? Motivation and happiness come from doing what you like and enjoy doing.[34] According to Herzberg, the best way to motivate employees is to build challenge and

EXHIBIT 9.3 |

Classification of Needs
by Four Theories of
Motivation

Maslow's Needs Hierarchy Theory	Alderfer's ERG Theory	Herzberg's Two-Factor Theory	McClelland's Manifest Needs Theory
Self-actualization	Growth	Motivators	Achievement
Esteem			Power
Social	Relatedness	Hygienes	Affiliation
Safety	Existence		
Physiological			

opportunity for achievement into the job itself.[35] Herzberg has developed a method for increasing motivation, which he calls *job enrichment*. In a later section of this chapter, you will learn about job enrichment and how Latoia could use it to motivate Hank.

Manifest Needs Theory

Like Maslow, Alderfer, and Herzberg, manifest needs theorists believe people are motivated by their needs. However, they classify needs differently. The **manifest needs theory** *of motivation is primarily McClelland's classification of needs as achievement, power, and affiliation.* It is a personality-based approach to motivation. McClelland does not have a classification for lower-level needs. His affiliation needs are the same as social and relatedness needs, and power and achievement are related to esteem and self-actualization and growth. See Exhibit 9.3 for a comparison of the need classifications of the four theories of motivation.

Manifest needs theory was originally developed by Henry Murry,[36] and then adapted by John Atkinson[37] and David McClelland.[38] Unlike Maslow, they believe that needs are based on personality and are developed as people interact with the environment. All people possess the need for achievement, power, and affiliation, but to varying degrees. One of these three needs tends to be dominant in each one of us and motivate our behavior. Before getting into the details of each need, complete Self-Assessment Exercise 9–2 to determine your dominant or primary need. After you have a better understanding of your needs, you will learn more about all three needs.

Self-Assessment
Exercise 9–2

Your Manifest Needs

Identify each of the following 15 statements according to how accurately it describes you. Place the number 1 to 5 on the line before each statement.

Like me		Somewhat like me		Not like me
5	4	3	2	1

_____ 1. I enjoy working hard.

_____ 2. I enjoy competition and winning.

_____ 3. I want/have lots of friends.

_____ 4. I enjoy a difficult challenge.

_____ 5. I enjoy leading and being in charge.

_____ 6. I want to be liked by others.

_____ 7. I want to know how I am progressing as I complete tasks.

_____ 8. I confront people who do things I disagree with.

_____ 9. I enjoy frequent parties.

_____ 10. I enjoy setting and achieving realistic goals.

_____ 11. I enjoy influencing other people to get my way.

_____ 12. I enjoy belonging to lots of groups or organizations.

_____ 13. I enjoy the satisfaction of completing a difficult task.

_____ 14. In a leaderless situation I tend to take charge.

_____ 15. I enjoy working with others more than working alone.

To determine your primary need, on the lines below, place the numbers (1 to 5) that represent your scores for the statements.

Achievement	Power	Affiliation
1. _____	2. _____	3. _____
4. _____	5. _____	6. _____
7. _____	8. _____	9. _____
10. _____	11. _____	12. _____
13. _____	14. _____	15. _____
Total _____	Total _____	Total _____

Add the numbers in each column. Each column total should be between 5 and 25. The column with the highest score is your dominant or primary need.

The Need for Achievement (*n*-Ach)   People with a high *n*-Ach tend to be characterized as follows: wanting to take personal responsibility for solving problems; goal-oriented (they set moderate, realistic, attainable goals); seeking challenge, excellence, and individuality; taking calculated, moderate risks; desiring concrete feedback on their performance; willing to work hard.

People with a high *n*-Ach think about ways to do a better job, how to accomplish something unusual or important, and career progression.[39] They perform well in nonroutine, challenging, and competitive situations, while people with a low *n*-Ach do not perform well in these situations.

McClelland's research shows that only about 10 percent of the U.S. population has a high dominant need for achievement. There is evidence of a correlation between high achievement need and high performance. People with a high *n*-Ach tend to enjoy sales and entrepreneurial-type positions. Managers tend to have a high, but not a dominant, *n*-Ach.[40]

Motivating Employees with a High n-Ach   Give them nonroutine, challenging tasks in which there are clear, attainable objectives. Give them fast and frequent feedback on their performance. Continually give them increased responsibility for doing new things.[41]

The Need for Power (*n*-Pow)   People with a high need for power tend to be characterized as follows: wanting to control the situation; wanting influence or control over others; enjoying competition in which they can win (they do not like to lose); willing to confront others.

People with high *n*-Pow think about controlling situations and controlling others while seeking positions of authority and status. People with high *n*-Pow tend to have a low need for affiliation. Managers tend to have a dominant need for power. Power is essential for successful supervision.[42] Today employees want more power to control their jobs.

Motivating Employees with a High n-Pow   Let them plan and control their jobs as much as possible. Try to include them in decision making, especially when they are affected by the decision. They tend to perform best alone rather than as team members. Try to assign them to a whole task rather than just part of a task.

People are motivated to gain power because having it meets their needs. In the opening case, Hank's primary need seems to be power. Hank wants more say in how to do his job, and he wants Latoia to do less checking up on him. If Latoia empowers Hank by giving him more job-related responsibility, it may satisfy Hank's needs and create a win–win situation, resulting in higher performance.

The Need for Affiliation (*n*-Aff) People with a high *n*-Aff tend to be characterized as follows: seeking close relationships with others; wanting to be liked by others; enjoying lots of social activities; seeking to belong (they join groups and organizations).

People with a high *n*-Aff think about friends and relationships. They tend to enjoy developing, helping, and teaching others. They tend to have a low *n*-Pow. People with high *n*-Aff seek jobs as teachers and personnel managers, as well as positions in other helping professions. They tend to avoid supervision because they like to be one of the group rather than its leader.[43]

Motivating High n-Aff Employees Be sure to let them work as part of a team. They derive satisfaction from the people they work with rather than the task itself. Give them lots of praise and recognition. Delegate responsibility for orienting and training new employees to them. They make great buddies and mentors.

WORK APPLICATIONS

3. Explain how your personal *n*-Ach, *n*-Pow, and *n*-Aff affect your motivation, behavior, and performance. How can you use manifest needs theory to motivate employees?

How Organizations Meet Employee Needs

See Exhibit 9.4 for a list of methods used by organizations to meet employee needs. Note that pay is important and can meet both higher- and lower-level needs.[44] Motivating employees

EXHIBIT 9.4 | How Organizations Meet Employee Needs

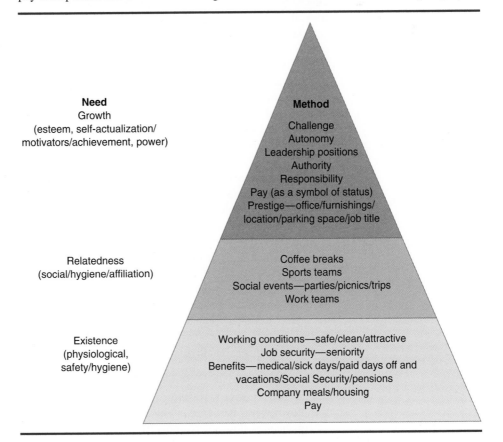

Need
Growth
(esteem, self-actualization/
motivators/achievement, power)

Method
Challenge
Autonomy
Leadership positions
Authority
Responsibility
Pay (as a symbol of status)
Prestige—office/furnishings/
location/parking space/job title

Relatedness
(social/hygiene/affiliation)

Coffee breaks
Sports teams
Social events—parties/picnics/trips
Work teams

Existence
(physiological,
safety/hygiene)

Working conditions—safe/clean/attractive
Job security—seniority
Benefits—medical/sick days/paid days off and
vacations/Social Security/pensions
Company meals/housing
Pay

and paying them well affect performance.[45] Managers in many organizations pay employees based on their performance.[46]

PROCESS MOTIVATION THEORIES

Content motivation theories attempt to understand what motivates people, whereas **process motivation theories** *attempt to understand how and why people are motivated.* Their focus is more on behavior than needs.[47] Why do people select certain goals to work toward?[48] Why do people select particular behavior to meet their needs?[49] How do people evaluate need satisfaction?[50] Expectancy and equity theories attempt to answer these questions.

Expectancy Theory

The **expectancy theory,** *which is Vroom's formula, states that Motivation = Expectancy $\times$ Valence.* Under Victor Vroom's theory,[51] motivation depends on how much people want something and how likely they are to get it. The theory is based on the following assumptions:

- Both internal (needs) and external (environment) factors affect behavior.
- Behavior is the individual's decision.
- People have different needs, desires, and goals.
- People make behavior decisions based on their perception of the outcome.

Expectancy and valence are two important variables in Vroom's formula that must be met for motivation to take place.

Expectancy   Expectancy refers to the person's perception of his or her ability (probability) to accomplish an objective.[52] Generally, the higher one's expectancy, the better the chance for motivation.[53] When employees do not believe that they can accomplish objectives, they will not be motivated to try.

Also important is the perception of the relationship between performance and the outcome or reward.[54] Generally, the higher one's expectancy of the outcome or reward, the better the chance for motivation. This is called *instrumentality.* If employees are certain to get a reward or to be successful, they probably will be motivated. When not sure, employees may not be motivated. For example, Dan believes he would be a good supervisor and wants to get promoted. However, Dan has an external locus of control and believes that working hard will not result in a promotion anyway. Therefore, he will not be motivated to work for the promotion.

Valence   Valence refers to the value a person places on the outcome or reward. Generally, the higher the value (importance) of the outcome or reward, the better the chance of motivation.[55] For example, the supervisor, Jean, wants an employee, Sim, to work harder. Jean talks to Sim and tells him that working hard will result in a promotion. If Sim wants a promotion, he will probably be motivated. However, if a promotion is not of importance to Sim, it will not motivate him.

Motivating with Expectancy Theory   Prior research supports that expectancy theory can accurately predict a person's work effort, satisfaction level, and performance, but only if the correct values are plugged into the formula. Therefore, this theory makes accurate predictions in certain contexts but not in others. The following conditions should be implemented to motivate employees:

1. Clearly define objectives and the necessary performance needed to achieve them.[56]
2. Tie performance to rewards. High performance should be rewarded.[57] When one employee works harder to produce more than other employees and is not rewarded, he or she may slow down productivity.

3. Be sure rewards are of value to the employee. The supervisor should get to know his or her employees as individuals.[58] Develop good human relations.

4. Make sure your employees believe you will do as you promise. For example, they must believe you will promote them if they do work hard—instrumentality. And you must do as you promise, so employees will believe you—trust (Chapter 8).

Expectancy theory also works best with employees who have an internal locus of control because if they believe they control their destiny, their efforts will result in success. Expectancy theory does not work well with employees who have an external locus of control because they do not believe their efforts will result in success. Since success is due to fate or to chance, why should they be motivated to work hard?

In the opening case, Hank says that because of the union, everyone is paid the same, so working hard is a waste of time. In the expectancy formula, since expectancy is low, there is no motivation. Paying more for higher performance motivates many employees. However, in a union organization, Latoia has no control over giving Hank a raise if he does a better job. However, the chance for advancement to a higher-level job that pays more may motivate him to work harder. Organizations generally do not promote people to a higher-level job unless they are good performers at the present job. Assuming Hank is interested in advancement, Latoia can explain to Hank that if he does a good job, she will recommend him for a promotion when an opportunity arises, provided he does a good job. If a promotion is not important to Hank, Latoia may find some other need to help him meet. If Latoia can find a need with expectancy and valence, Hank will be motivated to perform to expectations, creating a win–win situation for all parties.

WORK APPLICATIONS

4. Give an example of how expectancy theory has affected your motivation. How can you use expectancy theory to motivate employees?

Equity Theory

The **equity theory** *is primarily Adams's motivation theory, which is based on the comparison of perceived inputs and outputs.* J. Stacy Adams popularized equity theory with his contention that people seek social equity in the rewards they receive (output) for their performance (input).[59] Based on the knowledge of equity, one can predict behavior.[60]

According to equity theory, people compare their inputs (effort, experience, seniority, status, intelligence, and so forth) and outputs (praise, recognition, pay promotions, increased status, supervisor's approval, and the like) with those of relevant others. A relevant other could be a coworker or a group of employees from the same or from different organizations or even from a hypothetical situation. Notice that our definition mentions *perceived,* not *actual* inputs and outputs. Equity may actually exist. However, if employees believe there is inequity, they will change their behavior to create equity.[61] Employees must perceive that they are being treated fairly relative to others.[62]

Most employees tend to inflate their own efforts or performance when comparing themselves with others. They also overestimate what others earn. Employees may be very satisfied and motivated until they find out that a relevant other is earning more for the same job or earning the same for doing less work. When inequity is perceived, employees attempt to reduce it by reducing input or increasing output.

A comparison with relevant others leads to three conclusions:

1. *Equitably rewarded.*   Inputs and outputs are perceived as being equal; motivation may exist. Employees may believe that relevant others should have greater outputs when they have more experience, education, and so on.

2. *Underrewarded.*   When employees perceive that they are underrewarded, they may reduce the inequity by trying to increase outputs (getting a raise); reducing inputs (doing less work, being absent, taking long breaks); rationalizing (finding a logical

explanation for the inequity); changing others' inputs or outputs (getting them to do more or get less); leaving the situation (getting transferred or leaving for a better job); or changing the object of comparison (they make or get less than I do).

3. *Overrewarded.*   Being overrewarded is not too disturbing to most employees. However, research suggests that employees may reduce perceived inequity by increasing inputs (working harder or longer); reducing output (taking a pay cut); rationalizing (I'm worth it); or trying to increase others' output (giving them the same as me).

Motivating with Equity Theory   Using equity theory in practice can be difficult because you don't know (1) who the employee's reference group is, and (2) what his or her view of inputs and outcomes is.[63] However, it does offer some useful general recommendations:

- The supervisor should be aware that equity is based on perception, which may not be correct. It is possible for the supervisor to create equity or inequity. Some managers have favorite subordinates who get special treatment; others don't.

- Rewards should be equitable.[64] When employees perceive that they are not treated fairly, morale and performance problems occur; resentment and retaliation are common.[65]

- High performance should be rewarded, but employees must understand the inputs needed to attain certain outputs.[66]

In the opening case, Hank said that he was equitably treated because of the union. Therefore, Latoia does not need to be concerned about equity theory with Hank. However, it could be an issue with another employee.

WORK APPLICATIONS

5. Give an example of how equity theory has affected your motivation. How can you use equity theory to motivate employees?

Learning Outcome

4. State how reinforcement is used to increase performance.

REINFORCEMENT THEORY

Research supports the effect of reinforcement theory on task performance.[67] Several organizations, including 3M, Frito-Lay, and B. F. Goodrich, have used reinforcement to increase productivity. Michigan Bell had a 50 percent improvement in attendance and above-standard productivity and efficiency levels. Emery Air Freight went from 30 percent of employees meeting productivity standards to 90 percent after using reinforcement. Emery estimates that its reinforcement program has resulted in a $650,000 yearly savings.

As you have seen, content motivation theories focus on what motivates people and process motivation theories focus on how and why people are motivated; reinforcement theory focuses on getting people to do what you want them to do.[68] **Reinforcement theory** *is primarily Skinner's motivation theory: Behavior can be controlled through the use of rewards.* It is also called *behavior modification* and *operant conditioning.*

B. F. Skinner contends that people's behavior is learned through experiences of positive and negative consequences. He believes that rewarded behavior tends to be repeated, while unrewarded behavior tends not to be repeated. The three components of Skinner's framework are[69]

$$\text{Stimulus} \longrightarrow \underset{\substack{\text{(Behavior/} \\ \text{Performance)}}}{\text{Response}} \longrightarrow \underset{\substack{\text{(Reinforcement/} \\ \text{Positive or Negative)}}}{\text{Consequences}}$$

An employee learns what is, and is not, desired behavior as a result of the consequences for specific behavior.

Reinforcement theory is concerned with maintaining desired behavior (motivation) over time. In other words, people behave in ways that are reinforced.[70] For example, if

Beth, a student, wants to get an A on an exam, she will study for the outcome. If Beth gets the A (reward), she will probably study in the same way for the next exam. However, if Beth does not get the A, she will probably change her method of study for the next exam. We tend to learn to get what we want through trial and error. What gets measured and reinforced gets done.[71]

Skinner states that supervisors can control and shape employees' behavior while at the same time making them feel free. The two important concepts used to control behavior are the types of reinforcement and the schedule of reinforcement.

Types of Reinforcement

The four types of reinforcement are as follows:

Positive Reinforcement   A method of encouraging continued behavior is to offer attractive consequences (rewards) for desirable performance.[72] For example, an employee is on time for a meeting and is rewarded by the supervisor's thanking him or her. The praise is used to reinforce punctuality. Other reinforcers are pay, promotions, time off, and increased status.[73] Positive reinforcement is the best motivator for increasing productivity.

Avoidance Reinforcement   Avoidance is also called *negative reinforcement.* As with positive reinforcement, avoidance reinforcement encourages continued desirable behavior. The employee avoids the negative consequence. For example, an employee is punctual for a meeting to avoid negative reinforcement, such as a reprimand. Standing plans, especially rules, are designed to get employees to avoid certain behavior.[74]

Extinction   Rather than encouraging desirable behavior, extinction (and punishment) attempts to reduce or eliminate undesirable behavior by withholding reinforcement when the behavior occurs. For example, an employee who is late for the meeting is not rewarded with praise. Or a pay raise is withheld until the employee performs to set standards. Supervisors who do not reward good performance can cause its extinction.[75]

Punishment   Punishment is used to provide an undesirable consequence for undesirable behavior. For example, an employee who is late for a meeting is reprimanded. Notice that with avoidance there is no actual punishment; it's the threat of the punishment that controls behavior. Other methods of punishment include harassing, taking away privileges, probation, fining, and demoting. Using punishment may reduce the undesirable behavior, but it may cause other undesirable behavior, such as poor morale, lower productivity, and acts of theft or sabotage. Punishment is the most controversial method and the least effective at motivating employees.

Schedules of Reinforcement

The second reinforcement consideration in controlling behavior is when to reinforce performance. The frequency and magnitude of the reinforcement may be as important as the reinforcement itself. The two major classifications are continuous and intermittent:

Continuous Reinforcement   With a continuous method, each desired behavior is reinforced. Examples of this method would be a machine with an automatic counter that lets the employee know, at any given moment, exactly how many units have been produced, at a piece rate of $1 for each unit produced, or a supervisor who comments on every customer report.

Intermittent Reinforcement   With intermittent reinforcement, the reward is given based on the passage of time or output. When the reward is based on the passage of time, it is called an *interval schedule.* When it is based on output, it is called a *ratio schedule.* When electing to use intermittent reinforcement, there are four alternatives:

1. *Fixed interval schedule* (giving a salary paycheck every week, breaks and meals at the same time every day).

2. *Variable interval schedule* (giving praise only now and then, a surprise inspection, a pop quiz).

3. *Fixed ratio schedule* (giving a piece rate or bonus after producing a standard rate).

4. *Variable ratio schedule* (giving praise for excellent work, a lottery for employees who have not been absent for a set time).

Ratios are generally better motivators than intervals. The variable ratio tends to be the most powerful schedule for sustaining behavior.

Motivating with Reinforcement   Generally, positive reinforcement is the best motivator. Continuous reinforcement is better at sustaining desired behavior; however, it is not always possible or practical. Following are some general guidelines:

- Make sure employees know exactly what is expected of them. Set clear objectives.[76]

- Select appropriate rewards.[77] A reward to one person could be considered a punishment by another. Know your employees' needs.[78]

- Select the appropriate reinforcement schedule.

- Do not reward mediocre or poor performance.[79]

- Look for the positive and give praise, rather than focusing on the negative and criticizing.[80] Make people feel good about themselves (Pygmalion effect).

- Never go a day without giving praise.

- Do things *for* your employees, instead of *to* them, and you will see productivity increases that are off the scales.

In the opening case, Hank has been coming to work late and performing below expectations. If Latoia offers Hank the possible promotion (expectancy theory), she has used a positive reinforcement with a variable interval schedule. There is no set time before an opening comes up, and Hank doesn't get it after completing a specific amount of work. If the recommendation for a promotion does not change Hank's behavior, Latoia should try some other positive reinforcement such as job enrichment. If positive reinforcement doesn't change Hank's behavior, Latoia can use avoidance reinforcement. Based on her authority, she could tell Hank that the next time he is late or performs below a specific level, he will receive a specific punishment, such as having part of his pay withheld. If Hank does not avoid this behavior, Latoia must follow up and give the punishment. As a manager, try the positive first. Positive reinforcement is a true motivator because it creates a win–win situation by meeting both the employee's and the manager's or organization's needs. From the employees' perspective, avoidance and punishment create a lose–win situation. The organization or manager wins by forcing them to do something they really don't want to do.

Organizational Reinforcement for Getting Employees to Come to Work and to Be on Time

The traditional attempt to get employees to come to work and to be on time has been avoidance and punishment. If employees miss a specific number of days, they don't get paid. If an employee is late, the time card indicates this, and the employee receives punishment.

Many organizations today are using positive reinforcement by offering employees rewards for coming to work and being on time. For example, ADV Marketing Group, a Stamford, Connecticut, company, uses continuous reinforcement by offering prizes simply for showing up and being on time: a $100 dinner certificate after 13 on-time weeks and an $800 vacation plus two days off after a year of on-time performance. Mediatech, a Chicago company, uses a variable ratio schedule by holding a lottery for the employees who have attended on time that week. The lottery winner gets $250.

APPLICATION SITUATIONS

Motivation Theories

AS 9–2

Identify each supervisor's statement of how to motivate employees by the theory underlying the statement.

A. Expectancy	C. Needs hierarchy	E. Two-factor
B. Equity	D. Manifest needs	F. Reinforcement

_____ 6. "I motivate employees by making their jobs interesting."

_____ 7. "I make sure I treat everyone fairly."

_____ 8. "I know Wendy likes people, so I give her jobs in which she works with other employees."

_____ 9. "Paul would yell in the shop because he knew it got to me. So I decided to ignore his yelling, and he stopped."

_____ 10. "I got to know all of my employees' values fairly well. Now I can offer rewards that will motivate them."

_____ 11. "We offer good working conditions, salaries, and benefits, so I'm working at developing more teamwork."

_____ 12. "When my employees do something outstanding, I write them a thank-you note."

_____ 13. "I used to try to improve working conditions to motivate employees. But I stopped and now focus on giving employees more responsibility so they can grow and develop new skills."

_____ 14. "I set clear objectives that are attainable. And I offer rewards that employees like when they achieve their objectives."

_____ 15. "I now realize that I tend to be an autocratic supervisor because it helps fill my needs. I will work at giving some of my employees more autonomy."

A popular technique used by many organizations, which virtually eliminates the problem of being late for work, is flextime.[81] *Flextime* allows employees to determine when they start and end work, provided they work their full number of hours, with certain restrictions on working hours. Some companies are removing incentives to lie about being sick to get a paid day off by having only one category, paid time off; there are no categories for vacation time, holidays, personal days, sick days, or volunteer leave. Every employee gets a set number of paid days off per year to be taken when wanted, with approval.

WORK APPLICATIONS

6. What reinforcement type(s) and schedule(s) does/did your present/past supervisor use to motivate you? Explain each. How can you use reinforcement to motivate employees?

Poison Pill Hard to Swallow for a Healthy Bally's Total Fitness

Bally Total Fitness is the largest and only nationwide commercial operator of fitness centers, with approximately 400 clubs in the U.S., the Caribbean, Mexico, South Korea, and China. Bally uses the franchise business model. It has more than 40 years of experience and approximately 3.5 million members, more than the next 10 fitness center operators combined. Its employees include 23,500 on-site staff members, 6,700 group exercise instructors, and 3,500 personal trainers. Bally is committed to building upon its position and brand as the leading provider of fitness services, as it is helping its members achieve their fitness goals by providing the highest quality service, facilities, and products in a fun, friendly, safe, and welcoming environment.

Bally states that it operates in a manner designed to ensure its long-term success and maximize returns to shareholders. To this end, its CEO thought that the company should sell off some of its high-end gym brands in order to focus on its mid-sized clubs, and it was announced that he was exploring a possible sale or merger of the company. To the CEO's surprise, two investors were unhappy with this divestiture strategy and demanded for new management, an action that might trigger the firm's poison pill shareholders' rights plan.

The poison pill, which is triggered when investors join together and acquire 15 percent or more of the firm, allows the company to issue discounted shares to all stockholders except the acquirers, thereby diluting the acquirers' stake and voting rights. Bally said it had evidence that the two shareholders (whose combined holdings exceed 15 percent) were acting together; this could trigger the plan. The shareholders in question denied the charges and stated that they had no agreements, arrangements, or understandings with respect to the voting of Bally shares and that management had no reasonable basis to claim otherwise.

Questions

1. What might have motivated the two stockholders to demand for new management? Support your answer by referring to specific theories of motivation.

2. Using expectancy or reinforcement theory, describe why the CEO was surprised at the negative reactions of the stockholders to his divestiture strategy.

3. Using equity theory, describe how the poison pill plan might be perceived to maintain fairness among stockholders.

4. Is it ethical of the two stockholders to try to get rid of the CEO and stop any sale or merger?

Source: Bally Total Fitness Web site (www.ballyfitness.com), retrieved September 12, 2008.

MOTIVATION TECHNIQUES

The previous sections discussed the major motivation theories. Now we examine specific on-the-job techniques to motivate employees: giving praise, MBO, job enrichment, and job design. Organizations that use effective motivation techniques are able to recruit and retain good employees.[82]

Giving Praise

In the 1940s, a survey revealed that what employees want most from a job is full appreciation for work done. Similar studies have been performed over the years with little change in results.[83] Giving recognition to employees motivates them.[84] Workers say they rarely or never get praise from the boss. When was the last time your boss gave you a thank-you or some praise for a job well done? When was the last time your boss complained about your work? If you are a manager, when was the last time you praised or criticized your employees? What is the ratio of praise to criticism?

Giving praise develops a positive self-concept in employees and leads to better performance[85] through the Pygmalion effect. Praise is a motivator (not a hygiene) because it meets employees' needs for esteem/self-actualization, growth, and achievement.[86] Praise works physically, too, because when we receive praise it actually boosts the levels of dopamine (a chemical linked to joy) in the brain.[87] Giving praise creates a win–win situation. It is probably the most powerful, least expensive, simplest, and yet most underused motivational technique.

Ken Blanchard and Spencer Johnson popularized giving praise through their best-selling book, *The One-Minute Manager*.[88] They developed a technique that involves giving one minute of praise. Exhibit 9.5 is an adaptation. The steps in **giving praise** are as

EXHIBIT 9.5 | Model for Giving Praise

Step 1:   Tell the person exactly what was done correctly.
Step 2:   Tell the person why the behavior is important.
Step 3:   Stop for a moment of silence.
Step 4:   Encourage repeat performance.

follows: *step (1) tell the person exactly what was done correctly; step (2) tell the person why the behavior is important; step (3) stop for a moment of silence; and step (4) encourage repeat performance.* Blanchard calls it one-minute praise because it should not take more than one minute to give the praise. It is not necessary for the employee to say anything. The four steps are illustrated below.

Step 1: Tell the person exactly what was done correctly. When giving praise, look the person in the eye. Eye contact shows sincerity and concern. It is important to be very specific and descriptive. General statements like "You're a good worker" are not as effective. On the other hand, don't talk too long or the praise loses its effectiveness.

SUPERVISOR: Julio, I just overheard you deal with that customer's complaint. You did an excellent job of keeping your cool; you were polite. That person came in angry and left happy.

Step 2: Tell the person why the behavior is important. Briefly state how the organization and/or person benefits from the action. It is also helpful to tell the employee how you feel about the behavior. Be specific and descriptive.

SUPERVISOR: Without customers we don't have a business. One customer bad-mouthing us can cause hundreds of dollars in lost sales. It really made me proud to see you handle that tough situation the way you did.

Step 3: Stop for a moment of silence. This is a tough one. Most supervisors the author trains have trouble being silent. The rationale for the silence is to give the employee the chance to feel the impact of the praise. It's like "the pause that refreshes."

SUPERVISOR: (*Silently counts to five.*)

Step 4: Encourage repeat performance. This is the reinforcement that motivates the employee to keep up performance. Blanchard recommends touching the employee. Touching has a powerful impact. However, he recommends it only if both parties feel comfortable. Others say not to touch employees; touching could lead to a sexual harassment charge.

SUPERVISOR: Thanks, Julio, keep up the good work (*while touching him on the shoulder or shaking hands*).

As you can see, giving praise is easy, and it doesn't cost a penny. Bob Iger, CEO of Walt Disney, also likes to send a personal handwritten note of praise to people he spends little time with. He thinks it goes a long way with people.[89] Several managers trained to give praise say it works wonders. It's a much better motivator than giving a raise or other monetary reward. One manager stated that an employee was taking his time stacking cans on a display. He gave the employee praise for stacking the cans so straight. The employee was so pleased with the praise that the display went up with about a 100 percent increase in productivity. Notice that the manager looked for the positive and used positive reinforcement, rather than punishment. The manager could have made a comment such as, "Quit goofing off and get the display up faster." That statement would not have motivated the employee to increase productivity. All it would have done was hurt human relations, and it could have ended in an argument. Notice that in the above example the cans were straight. The employee was not praised for the slow work pace. However, if the praise had not worked, the manager should have used another reinforcement method.

In the opening case, if Hank is interested in changing behavior to get a promotion, Latoia should give him praise for coming in on time and increasing his performance to encourage him to continue this behavior. Praise is a reinforcement that is very effective when used with a variable interval schedule.

Learning Outcome

6. List the criteria for setting objectives.

Objectives and MBO

For many years, writers have been saying that setting difficult objectives leads to higher levels of motivation and performance, and research supports this statement.[90] In fact, goal setting theory was rated number 1 in importance among 73 management theories.[91]

The **objectives** *state what is to be accomplished within a given period of time.* Objectives are end results; they do not state how the objective will be accomplished. How to achieve the objective is the plan. Some writers define goals and objectives differently; we do not. In this section, you will learn the five criteria objectives should meet, how to write objectives, and how to use management by objectives (MBO).

Criteria for Setting Objectives   To motivate people to high levels of performance, objectives should be:

- *Difficult but achievable.*[92] Individuals perform better when assigned difficult objectives, as opposed to being assigned easy ones, or having no goals, or simply being told to "do your best." If they are going to motivate people to high levels of performance, objectives must be challenging.[93] However, if people do not believe that the objectives are achievable (expectancy theory), they will not be motivated to work for their accomplishment.

- *Observable and measurable.* If people are to achieve objectives, they must be able to observe and measure their progress regularly.[94] Individuals perform better when their performance is measured and evaluated.[95]

- *Specific, with a target date.* To be motivated, employees must know exactly what is expected of them and when they are expected to have the task completed. Employees should have specific objectives with deadlines.[96] However, some objectives do not require or lend themselves to target dates. For example, the objectives in the skill-building exercises do not list a target date.

- *Participatively set when possible.* Groups that participate in setting their objectives generally outperform groups with assigned objectives.[97] Managers should use the appropriate level of participation for the employees' capabilities. The higher the capabilities, the higher the level of participation.

EXHIBIT 9.6 | Model for Writing Objectives

Objectives Model
To + Action verb + Specific, measurable, and singular behavior + Target date

Example Objectives for a Student:
To + receive + a B as my final grade in human relations + in December/May 20___.   To increase my cumulative grade point average to 3.0 by May 20___.

Example Objectives for a Manager:
To produce 1,000 units per day.   To keep absences to three or fewer per month.   To decrease accidents by 5 percent during 20___.

Example Objectives for an Organization:
Domino's: To deliver pizza within 30 minutes starting December 2007.[98]   Toyota: To sell 10.4 million vehicles worldwide by year-end 2009.[99]   BMW: To increase sales worldwide by more than 40 percent by 2020.[100]

• *Accepted.* For objectives to be met, employees must accept them. Without acceptance, even meeting the above four criteria can lead to failure. If employees are not committed to strive for the objective, they may not meet it.[101] Using participation helps get employees to accept objectives.

APPLICATION SITUATIONS

Objectives

AS 9–3

For each objective, state which criterion is *not* met.

A. Difficult but achievable

B. Observable and measurable

C. Specific, with a target date

_____ 16. To increase production of widgets during the fiscal year 20__.

_____ 17. To increase total sales by 40 percent during 20__.

_____ 18. To increase the company's image by June 20__.

_____ 19. To write objectives within two weeks.

_____ 20. To pass this human relations course this semester.

Learning Outcome

7. Identify the four parts of the model for writing objectives.

Writing Objectives   Objectives should be written. To help write objectives that meet the five criteria above, use Max E. Douglas's model, shown in Exhibit 9.6.

Management by Objectives (MBO)   Pointing workers to a common goal is what managers need to do.[102] This is what the MBO process attempts to do. **Management by objectives (MBO)** *is the process in which managers and their employees jointly set objectives for the employees, periodically evaluate the performance, and reward according to the results.*

For a program to truly be MBO, it should be organizationwide. Management by objectives starts at the top of the management hierarchy and works its way down to the workers. Each level of management's objectives must contribute to the next level's objectives. To be successful, the MBO process takes a lot of commitment, time, and participation. You can use the MBO process successfully with subordinates if you are truly committed and willing to involve employees.

The three steps of an MBO program are as follows:

Step 1. Set Individual Objectives and Plans.   Each subordinate jointly sets objectives with the manager. The objectives are the heart of the MBO program and should meet the five criteria discussed earlier.[103]

Step 2. Give Feedback and Evaluate Performance.   Xerox Learning Systems states that giving feedback is the most important management skill. Employees must know how they are progressing toward their objectives.[104] Thus, the manager and employee must meet frequently to review the latter's progress. The frequency of evaluations depends on the individual and the job performed. However, most managers probably do not conduct enough review sessions.

Step 3. Reward According to Performance.   Employees' performance should be measured against their objectives. Employees who meet their objectives should be rewarded through recognition, praise, pay raises, promotions, and so on. Many organizations now link pay to meeting goals.[105]

An MBO program is a motivator (not a hygiene) because it meets employees' needs for esteem/self-actualization, growth, and power/achievement. An MBO program empowers employees to increase responsibility with an opportunity for creating meaningful, challenging work to help them grow and accomplish what *they* and the manager want to accomplish.[106] An MBO program creates a win–win situation.

In a union situation, such as the opening case, using an MBO program may not be possible without union consent and input.

Job Enrichment

Learning Outcome

8. State ways to enrich, design, and simplify jobs.

Job enrichment *is the process of building motivators into the job itself by making it more interesting and challenging.* It differs from job rotation, in which employees learn to perform other employees' jobs, and job enlargement, in which the employee is assigned more tasks of a similar nature.

Job enrichment is an effective motivation tool. Many organizations, including IBM, AT&T, Polaroid, Monsanto, General Motors, Motorola, Maytag, and The Traveler's Insurance Company, have used job enrichment successfully.

Before implementing job enrichment, the manager should be sure that the job is of low motivation potential and that the employees want their jobs enriched. Some people with an external locus of control are happy with the jobs the way they are. Hygiene factors must also be adequate before using job enrichment.

Here are some simple ways managers can enrich jobs:

*   *Delegate more variety and responsibility.* Give employees challenging assignments that help them grow and develop new skills. Managers can delegate some of the responsibility and tasks they perform themselves.

*   *Form natural work groups.* Allow the team of employees to work together. The work group can also perform its own identifiable work with increased responsibility.

*   *Make employees responsible for their own identifiable work.* Let employees make the entire product rather than one part of it. Units not meeting quality control can be returned to the person for repair, rather than repaired randomly by assemblers.

*   *Give employees more autonomy.* Allow employees to plan, schedule, organize, and control their own jobs. Making employees responsible for checking their own work eliminates the need for checkers.

WORK APPLICATIONS

7. Describe how to enrich a present or past job of yours.

Job Design

Poorly designed jobs cause more performance problems than managers realize.[107] **Job design** *is the employee's system for transforming inputs into outputs.* The more effective and efficient the method, the more productive the employee.[108] The current trend is to have teams design their own jobs, or at least change them to their specifications, which motivates employees to perform at higher levels through continuous learning.[109]

A common approach to job design is work simplification. The idea behind work simplification is to work smarter, not harder. **Job simplification** *is the process of eliminating, combining, and/or changing the work sequence to increase performance.* To motivate employees, have them break the job down into steps and see if they can:

*   *Eliminate.* Does the task have to be done at all? If not, don't waste time doing it. At Intel, management decided it was not necessary to fill out a voucher for expenses amounting to less than $100. Work volume went down by 14 percent in 30 days.

*   *Combine.* Doing more than one thing at a time often saves time. Make one trip to the mail room at the end of the day instead of several throughout the day.

*   *Change sequence.* Often a change in the order of doing things results in a lower total time.

When used appropriately, work simplification can be effective at motivating employees. However, the danger lies in making a job too simple and boring rather than making it more interesting and challenging, as with job enrichment.

WORK APPLICATIONS

> **8.** Describe how to simplify a present or past job of yours. Does an elimination, combination, or change in sequence help to simplify the job?

Accordingto Herzberg, job enrichment and job design are motivators (not hygienes) because they meet employees' needs for esteem, self-actualization, growth, power, and achievement. They empower employees to increase responsibility with an opportunity for creating meaningful, challenging work to help them grow and accomplish what *they* and the manager want to accomplish, creating a win–win situation. Thus, job design and job enrichment are processes used to motivate employees.[110]

In a union situation like that in the opening case, job enrichment and/or job design may not be possible without union consent and input. Assuming Latoia can use these techniques, she and Hank could work together to transform Hank's present boring job into a challenging and interesting one. This is the most appropriate motivation technique to use with Hank because it directly addresses the boring job. Hopes of a promotion in the unknown future will not change the present situation; however, if job enrichment is not possible, it may at least make the job tolerable until the promotion comes. If Hank finds his job interesting, he will most likely come to work on time and perform to expectation, creating a win–win situation.

Putting the Motivation Theories Together

Researchers suggest an integration of motivation theories.[111] To this end, review the major motivation theories in Exhibit 9.7. For a review of the four steps in the motivation process, see Exhibit 9.8.

WORK APPLICATIONS

> **9.** Which motivation theory is the best? Explain why.
>
> **10.** What is your motivation theory? What are the major methods, techniques, and so on you plan to use on the job as a manager to increase motivation and performance?

EXHIBIT 9.7 | Motivation Theories

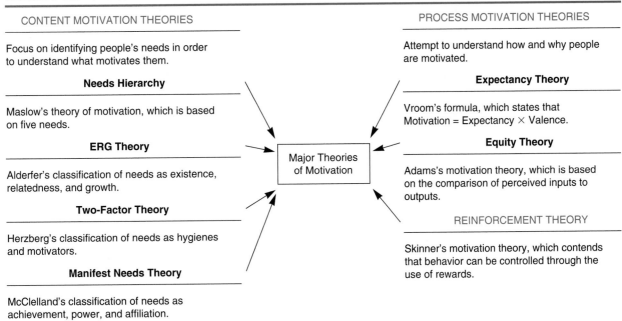

CONTENT MOTIVATION THEORIES

Focus on identifying people's needs in order to understand what motivates them.

Needs Hierarchy

Maslow's theory of motivation, which is based on five needs.

ERG Theory

Alderfer's classification of needs as existence, relatedness, and growth.

Two-Factor Theory

Herzberg's classification of needs as hygienes and motivators.

Manifest Needs Theory

McClelland's classification of needs as achievement, power, and affiliation.

PROCESS MOTIVATION THEORIES

Attempt to understand how and why people are motivated.

Expectancy Theory

Vroom's formula, which states that Motivation = Expectancy × Valence.

Equity Theory

Adams's motivation theory, which is based on the comparison of perceived inputs to outputs.

REINFORCEMENT THEORY

Skinner's motivation theory, which contends that behavior can be controlled through the use of rewards.

Major Theories of Motivation

EXHIBIT 9.8 |
The Motivation Process

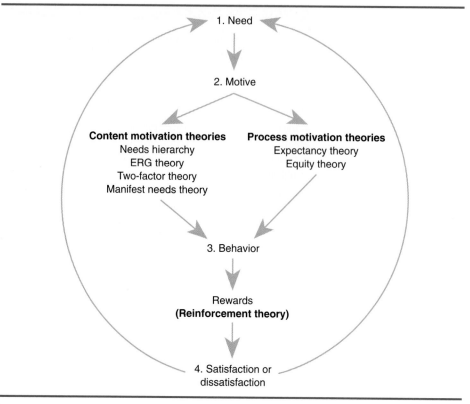

Notice that the motivation process is circular, or ongoing, because meeting needs is a never-ending process.

9. Explain possible limitations of using motivation theories outside North America.

DO MOTIVATION THEORIES APPLY GLOBALLY?

The motivation theories you have learned were developed in North America. As firms become increasingly global, they must be aware of the cultural limitations of theories. There is support for the idea that motivational concerns vary across nations.[112] Successful global companies, including Sodexho Alliance, which does business in 74 countries, are managed by local teams in each nation to incorporate local motivation issues.

Cross-Cultural Differences in Motivation

Let's discuss how the specific motivation theories differ across cultures.

Hierarchy of Needs, ERG, and Two-Factor Theory   Cultural differences suggest that the order of hierarchy may vary across cultures. In risk-averse countries such as Japan, Greece, and Mexico, security needs would be at the top of the needs hierarchy. In countries such as Denmark, Sweden, Norway, the Netherlands, and Finland, which prefer quality of life (relationships) over quantity of life (possessions), social needs would be at the top. A U.S. firm in Mexico learned this difference the hard way. It gave workers a raise to motivate them to work more hours, but the raise actually motivated the employees to work fewer hours. Because they could now make enough money to live and enjoy life (one of their primary values) in less time, why should they work more hours? As related to two-factor theory, the intrinsic motivation of higher-level needs can be more relevant to wealthy societies than to poor societies.

Manifest Needs Theory   Cultures also differ in the extent to which they value need for achievement. The concern for high performance is common in high quantity-of-life countries, including the United States, Canada, and Great Britain; it is almost absent in high quality-of-life countries, including Chile and Portugal.

One major cultural difference is in the focus on individualistic versus group approaches to business. Individualistic societies (the United States, Canada, Great Britain, Australia) tend to value self-accomplishment. Collective societies (Japan, Mexico, Singapore, Pakistan) tend to value group accomplishment and loyalty. So individual versus group incentives tend to vary by country, with the United States moving toward more group pay-for-performance plans in addition to individual pay.[113]

Equity Theory   Equity theory as it relates to fairness tends to be a value upheld in most cultures. However, equity can call for higher producers to be paid more. This tends to be more of a motivator in individualistic countries than it is in collective countries, where people tend to prefer equality and all are paid the same regardless of output. On the other hand, U.S. unions, including teachers, also tend to prefer equal pay to merit pay. But pay for performance in the United States is clearly increasing in nonunion organizations.[114]

Expectancy Theory   Expectancy theory holds up fairly well cross-culturally because it is flexible. It allows for the possibility that there may be differences in expectations and valences across cultures. For example, societal acceptance may be of higher value than individual recognition in collective societies. So managers in different countries can offer rewards that are of value to their employees—unlike the U.S. company in Mexico that mistakenly used the reward of more money to try to motivate employees to work more hours.

Reinforcement Theory   Reinforcement theory also holds up well cross-culturally. People everywhere tend to use behavior that is reinforced. We all can be told or can figure out what behavior is rewarded and use the behavior to our benefit. Management everywhere tends to set up rules and penalties for breaking them. So people tend to avoid the behavior that leads to punishment. However, how well the punishment fits the offense can vary. In the United States it is much easier to fire employees than it is in Europe.

Goal Setting   An eight-country study found that goal setting is effective for any task in which people have control over their performance.[115] Motivational goal setting relies on a need for achievement and high levels of performance, and it is based on quantity-of-life issues. Thus, the United States sets challenging objectives and achieves them. However, goal setting is less motivational to cultures in which achievement is not important and quality of life is important, such as Portugal and Chile.

Motivation in e-Organizations   As discussed in Chapter 6, most global companies are e-organizations. E-orgs have unique motivation issues to deal with. A major motivational problem in all organizations is distractions that lower productivity. But with the Internet, we now have employees surfing the Net, playing games, trading stocks, shopping at work, engaging in "cyberaffairs," and searching for another job online. This "cyberloafing" is costing employers billions a year. To try to stop cyberloafing, employers have installed Web-monitoring software. Although employers can catch cyberloafing, the software undermines trust and hurts employee morale, causing a catch-22 situation.

It is difficult for global e-orgs to recruit and retain experienced technical and professional employees. These e-org employees want to be higher on the needs hierarchy than traditional employees. They have a higher need for achievement, set and meet challenging goals, and want motivational rewards. They have higher expectations and don't want equity with traditional employees. They demand higher rewards through compensation packages, including stock options, which cause equity problems. Being in high demand, these technical and professional employees will leave if they are treated like traditional employees. Many foreign-born U.S. e-org employees came to the United States for tech jobs.

As we bring the chapter to a close, complete Self-Assessment Exercise 9–3 to determine how your personality affects your motivation.

Self-Assessment Exercise 9–3

Your Personality and Motivation

If you have a high *surgency* personality, you most likely have a high need for power. You are probably realistic in your expectations, tend to know what you want and set reasonable objectives, and work to achieve your objectives. You may be concerned about being treated equitably but not too concerned if others are. You may like positive reinforcement for yourself, but you have no problem using punishment to get what you want. You like praise, but may not give much praise to others. You tend to like jobs in which you are in control of what you do and how you do it.

If you have a high *agreeableness* personality, you most likely have a high need for affiliation. Your expectations are most likely related more to relationships than to setting task objectives and working to achieve them. You may be concerned about your being treated equitably, and you tend to help others get equal treatment. You may like positive reinforcement for yourself, but you may need to be careful not to use extinction (do nothing and the problem will solve itself) if you are not being treated fairly—be assertive. You need acceptance and like praise, and you tend to give both to others. You tend to like jobs in which you work with others.

If you have a high *conscientious* personality, you most likely have a high need for achievement. You are most likely realistic in your expectations, tend to know what you want and set reasonable objectives, and work to achieve your objectives. You may be concerned about being treated equitably but not too concerned if others are. You like positive reinforcement of your accomplishments and tend to avoid punishment. You like praise, but may not give much praise to others. You tend to like jobs in which you can measure your accomplishments and succeed.

The *adjustment* personality dimension is not a need in the manifest needs motivation theory. However, it clearly affects behavior in a positive or negative way. If you are low in adjustment, you most likely have unrealistic expectations, don't really know what you want, and don't set goals and work to achieve them. You are probably being treated fairly, but you perceive that you are not being treated equitably. You probably get more punishment than rewards. You may not like your job, but changing jobs may not make you happy or more adjusted. A new job will not change your personality; you need to change.

The *openness to experience* personality dimension is not a need in the manifest needs motivation theory. However, it clearly affects behavior in a positive or negative way. If you are open to experience, you are more of a risk taker and tend to set more challenging, realistic objectives than people who are closed to new experiences.

Action plan: Based on your personality, what specific things will you do to improve how you motivate yourself and others?

_____

_____

_____

_____

Videos

Manager's Hot Seat and Behavior Model Videos are available for this chapter.

Online Learning Center Resources
Go to the Internet (http://mhhe.com/lussier8e) where you will find a broad array of resources to help maximize your learning.

•   Review the vocabulary.

•   Try a quiz.

R E V I E W

The chapter review is organized to help you master the 10 learning outcomes for Chapter 9. First provide your own response to each learning outcome, and then check the summary provided to see how well you understand the material. Next, identify the final statement in each section as either true or false (T/F). Correct each false statement. Answers are given at the end of the chapter.

1. **Explain the motivation process and the three factors affecting performance.**
   The motivation process steps are: need → motive → behavior → satisfaction or dissatisfaction. The three factors affecting performance are Ability × Motivation × Resources.
   Motivation is the most important factor in the performance formula. T F

2. **Describe four content motivation theories.**
   Content motivation theories focus on identifying people's needs in order to understand what motivates them. *Needs hierarchy* is Maslow's theory of motivation based on five categories of needs. Alderfer's *ERG theory* classifies existence, relatedness, and growth needs. *Two-factor theory* is Herzberg's classification of needs as hygienes and motivators. The *manifest needs theory* of motivation is primarily McClelland's classification of needs as achievement, power, and affiliation.
   Motivating factors are primarily extrinsic factors. T F

3. **Describe two process motivation theories.**
   Process motivation theories attempt to explain how and why people are motivated. *Expectancy theory* is Vroom's formula, which states that Motivation = Expectancy × Valence. *Equity theory* is primarily Adams's motivation theory, which is based on the comparison of perceived inputs to outputs.
   Valence refers to one's need for perceived inputs to match outputs. T F

4. **State how reinforcement is used to increase performance.**
   Reinforcement theory is primarily Skinner's motivation theory, which contends that behavior can be controlled through the use of rewards. Through the use of four types of reinforcement—positive, avoidance, extinction, and punishment—and two schedules of reinforcement—continuous and intermittent—employees can learn which behavior is and is not appropriate. Appropriate behavior that is productive is encouraged, while nonproductive behavior is discouraged.
   The two variables of intermittent reinforcement are passage of time (fixed or variable interval) and output (fixed or variable ratio), resulting in four alternative schedules. T F

5. **List the four steps in the model for giving praise.**
   The four steps for giving praise are: (1) tell the person exactly what was done correctly; (2) tell the person why the behavior is important; (3) stop for a moment of silence; and (4) encourage repeat performance.
   Praise works best when it is not used very often. T F

6. **List the criteria for setting objectives.**
   In setting objectives, they should be: difficult but achievable; observable and measurable; specific, with a target date; participatively set when possible; and accepted.
   Letting employees set their own objectives generally leads to their acceptance and achievement. T F

7. **Identify the four parts of the model for writing objectives.**
   The formula for writing objectives is as follows: To + Action verb + Specific, measurable, and singular behavior + Target date.
   "To make a profit this year" is a well-written objective. T F

8. State ways to enrich, design, and simplify jobs.

Job enrichment is the process of building motivators into the job itself by making it more interesting and challenging. *Job design* is the employee's system for transforming inputs into outputs. *Job simplification* is the process of eliminating, combining, and/or changing the work sequence to increase performance.

The objective of all three methods is the same—to make the job more interesting and challenging and to motivate employees to higher levels of performance. T F

9. Explain possible limitations of using motivation theories outside North America.

People of different cultures have different needs and values. What works well in one country may not be effective in a different one.

Hierarchy of needs, ERG, two-factor, and manifest needs theories don't tend to work well across cultures, but equity, expectancy, reinforcement, and goal setting theories do. T F

Learning Outcome

10. Define the following 16 key terms.

10. Define the following 16 key terms.

Select one or more methods: (1) fill in the missing key terms from memory; (2) match the key terms from the end of the review with their definitions below; and/or (3) copy the key terms in order from the key terms at the beginning of the chapter.

_____ is the internal process leading to behavior to satisfy needs.

The _____ is: Performance = Ability × Motivation × Resources.

_____ focus on identifying people's needs in order to understand what motivates them.

_____ is Maslow's theory of motivation, which is based on five needs.

_____ is Herzberg's classification of needs as hygienes and motivators.

The _____ of motivation is primarily McClelland's classification of needs as achievement, power, and affiliation.

_____ attempt to understand how and why people are motivated.

_____ is Vroom's formula, which states that Motivation = Expectancy × Valence.

_____ is primarily Adams's motivation theory, which is based on the comparison of perceived inputs and outputs.

_____ is primarily Skinner's motivation theory: Behavior can be controlled through the use of rewards.

The steps in _____ are as follows: step (1) tell the person exactly what was done correctly; step (2) tell the person why the behavior is important; step (3) stop for a moment of silence; and step (4) encourage repeat performance.

_____ state what is to be accomplished within a given period of time.

_____ is the process by which managers and their employees jointly set objectives for the employees, periodically evaluate the performance, and reward according to results.

_____ is the process of building motivators into the job itself by making it more interesting and challenging.

_____ is the employee's system for transforming inputs into outputs.

_____ is the process of eliminating, combining, and/or changing the work sequence to increase performance.

K E Y   T E R M S

content motivation
    theories   315
equity theory   323
expectancy theory   322
giving praise   328
job design   332
job enrichment   332

job simplification   332
management by objectives
    (MBO)   331
manifest needs
    theory   319
motivation   313
needs hierarchy   315

objectives   330
performance formula   314
process motivation
    theories   322
reinforcement theory   324
two-factor theory   317

C O M M U N I C A T I O N   S K I L L S

The following critical thinking questions can be used for class discussion and/or as written assignments to develop communication skills. Be sure to give complete explanations for all questions.

1. Some people have stated that the performance formula is oversimplified. Do you agree? Can it really be used to increase performance?
2. Give examples of how all five of your needs in Maslow's hierarchy of needs have been or are being met.
3. Herzberg says that pay is a hygiene factor, whereas others say it is a motivator. What do you say?
4. Which do you believe are more useful in motivating employees: content or process motivation theories?
5. Some people say that reinforcement theory is a means of manipulating employees to do what the company wants them to do. Do you agree? Is the use of reinforcement theory ethical?
6. Does giving praise really motivate employees, or do they view it as a means of getting them to do more work?
7. Some managers say that what gets measured gets done. Do you agree? What does this have to do with setting objectives?
8. What are the advantages and disadvantages of an MBO program?
9. Which of the motivational theories do you prefer? Why?

CASE

Michael Parks, Todd Miller, and The Revere Group

Michael Parks and Todd Miller observed that the business goals of forward-thinking enterprises weren't being met by the conventional approaches of the traditional, much larger consulting firms. So in 1992, they founded The Revere Group to meet this need. Revere's vision since its inception has remained steadfast—to build an organization that clients rely upon as their trusted advisor. This vision of both Parks and Miller was implemented through a refined approach to people, processes, and technology. In an industry marked by innovation and relentless change, organizations can look to Revere for its senior consulting model, strong business and technology expertise, client-focused project management methodology, and partner relationships. Revere offers services in five core areas: operational efficiency, interactive, analytics and collaboration, enterprise platforms, and managed services.

The Revere Group was originally started in the Chicagoland area but moved its headquarters to Chicago, Illinois. Expansion continued to include offices in Boston, Charlotte, Denver, Los Angeles, Milwaukee, Orlando, Raleigh, San Francisco, Tampa, and Bangalore, India. In 2005, Revere became a wholly owned subsidiary of NTT DATA, a multinational organization, further extending its reach and capabilities. Although they have since sold their company, the founders still run the business, as Michael Parks remains CEO and Todd Miller remains president and COO.

The Revere Group practices what it preaches and attributes its longevity to its core values, one of which is teamwork. "We hire people who work well with their coworkers and clients. We encourage a high level of respect for others' opinions—while still driving for the right solution. This collaborative approach has served us well," comments Todd Miller. "The Revere Group is always looking for qualified, dedicated people to join our team. We hire individuals who have depth and breadth of experience and a functional, technical, or industry specialty. Our employees are grounded in teamwork, integrity, service, and accountability."

Michael Parks knows it's hard to grow a company if your employees don't grow too, and he believes in investing in his human capital. "The simple fact is that an organization's most valuable function is strategizing the ever-changing and unique [human resource] opportunities provided by today's business environment. As a result, the ability to adapt quickly and effectively to new challenges, corporate strategies and employee demands may be your most valuable asset."

To take advantage of his employees' potentials, Parks has had in place what he calls a "career-pathing" program almost since he started the business. At the beginning of the year, each Revere employee sits down with a company-assigned mentor to develop an individual annual growth plan. That plan typically details how the employee will spend his or her required two weeks of training, as well as what progress he or she needs to make to receive a promotion or change jobs. Employees receive quarterly updates on their progress and have periodic check-ins with their mentors.

Parks says the program is great for retention. He selects mentors not by titles or tenure but by their people skills and their knowledge of both the company and the industry. After a bit of experimentation, Parks learned that assigning a manager to mentor the employees who report to him or her didn't work. "It's a natural conflict," he says. "If I'm your manager and you want to make a change, how do you tell me that you really don't want to work in my area?"[116]

Go to the Internet: For more information on The Revere Group and to update the information provided in this case, do a name search on the Internet and visit http://www.reveregroup.com.

Support your answers to the following questions with specific information from the case and text, or with other information you get from the Web or other sources.

1. Referring to the needs hierarchy, ERG, and manifest needs theories, describe what motivators The Revere Group concentrates on.

2. How might expectancy theory explain The Revere Group's success in hiring and retaining productive employees?

3. Compare and contrast The Revere Group's career-pathing program with MBO programs. What are the similarities and differences?

4. How does the career-pathing program motivate Revere employees?

Cumulative Questions

5. What is the role of attitudes and values (Chapter 3) in this case?

6. What steps should the career-pathing program include to facilitate career planning and development (Chapter 4)?

7. Describe why Michael Parks and Todd Miller might be described as charismatic or transformational leaders (Chapter 8).

OBJECTIVE CASE   ## Friedman's Motivation Technique

The following conversation takes place between Art Friedman and Bob Lussier. In 1970, Art Friedman implemented a new business technique. At that time the business was called Friedman's Appliances. It employed 15 workers in Oakland, California. Friedman's is an actual business that uses the technique you will read about.

BOB: What is the reason for your success in business?

ART: My business technique.

BOB: What is it? How did you implement it?

ART: I called my 15 employees together and told them, "From now on I want you to feel as though the company is ours, not mine. We are all bosses. From now on you decide what you're worth and tell the accountant to put it in your pay envelope. You decide which days and hours you work and when to take time off. We will have an open petty cash system that will allow anyone to go into the box and borrow money when they need it."

BOB: You're kidding, right?

ART: No, it's true. I really do these things.

BOB: Did anyone ask for a raise?

ART: Yes, several people did. Charlie asked for and received a $100-a-week raise.

BOB: Did he and the others increase their productivity to earn their raises?

ART: Yes, they all did.

BOB: How could you run an appliance store with employees coming and going as they pleased?

ART: The employees made up schedules that were satisfactory to everyone. We had no problems of under- or overstaffing.

BOB: Did anyone steal from the petty cash box?

ART: No.

BOB: Would this technique work in any business?

ART: It did work, it still works, and it will always work!

In 1976, Art Friedman changed his business to Friedman's Microwave Ovens. He developed a franchise operation to use his motivation technique of making everyone a boss.

Answer the following questions. Then in the space between questions, state why you selected that answer.

_____ 1. Art's business technique increased performance.

        a. true   *b.* false

_____ 2. Art focused on the _____ factor in the performance formula.

        a. ability   *b.* motivation   *c.* resources

_____ 3. Art's employees seem to be on the _____ needs level.

        a. physiological   *c.* social   *e.* self-actualization

        b. safety   *d.* esteem

_____ 4. Art's technique has less emphasis on meeting _____ needs.

        a. achievement   *b.* power   *c.* affiliation

_____ 5. Frederick Herzberg would say Art is using:

        a. hygienes   *b.* motivators

_____ 6. Victor Vroom would say that Art uses expectancy motivation theory.

        a. true   *b.* false

_____ 7. J. Stacy Adams would say Art:

        a. has equitable rewards   *b.* underrewards   *c.* overrewards

_____ 8. Art uses _____ reinforcement.

        a. positive   *c.* extinction

        b. avoidance   *d.* punishment

_____ 9. Art's technique is most closely associated with:

        a. giving praise   *c.* job enrichment

        b. MBO   *d.* job design

_____ 10. Art's technique focuses most on:

        a. delegating variety   *c.* making work identifiable

        b. forming natural work groups   *d.* giving autonomy

    11. Do you know of any organizations that use any of Art's or other unusual techniques? If yes, what is the organization's name? What does it do?

12. Could Art's technique work in all organizations? Explain your answer.

13. In a position of authority, would you use Art's technique? Explain your answer.

What Do You Want from a Job?

In-Class Exercise
(Individual and Group)

Objectives: To help you better understand how job factors affect motivation. To help you realize that people are motivated by different factors. What motivates you may turn someone else off.

AACSB: The primary AACSB learning standard skills developed through this exercise are reflective thinking and self-management.

Preparation: You should have completed Self-Assessment Exercise 9–1.

Experience: You will discuss the importance of job factors.

Procedure 1
(8–20 minutes)

Break into groups of five or six, and discuss job factors selected by group members in Self-Assessment Exercise 9–1. Come to a consensus on the three factors that are most important to the group. They can be either motivators or hygienes. If the group mentions other job factors not listed, such as pay, you may add them.

Procedure 2
(3–6 minutes)

A representative from each group goes to the board and writes its group's three most important job factors.

Conclusion: The instructor leads a class discussion and/or makes concluding remarks.

Application (2–4 minutes): What did I learn from this experience? How will I use this knowledge in the future?

Sharing: Volunteers give their answers to the application section.

Giving Praise

Preparation (Group)

BMV 9–1

Think of a job situation in which you did something well, deserving of praise and recognition. You may have saved the company some money, you may have turned a dissatisfied customer into a happy one, and so on. If you have never worked or done something well, interview someone who has. Put yourself in a supervisory position and write out the praise you would give to an employee for doing what you did.

Briefly describe the situation:

Step 1. Tell the employee exactly what was done correctly.

Step 2. Tell the employee why the behavior is important.

Step 3. Stop for a moment of silence. (Count to five silently.)

Step 4. Encourage repeat performance.

In-Class Exercise

Objective: To develop your skill at giving praise.

AACSB: The primary AACSB learning standard skills developed through this exercise are communication abilities and leadership.

Preparation: You will need your prepared praise.

Experience: You will give and receive praise.

Procedure
(12–17 minutes)

Break into groups of five or six. One at a time, give the praise.

1. Explain the situation.
2. Select a group member to receive the praise.
3. Give the praise. (Talk; don't read it off the paper.) Try to select the position you would use if you were actually giving the praise on the job (for example, both standing, both sitting).
4. Integration. The group gives the giver of praise feedback on how he or she did:
   - Step 1. Was the praise very specific and descriptive? Did the giver look the employee in the eye?
   - Step 2. Was the importance of the behavior clearly stated?
   - Step 3. Did the giver stop for a moment of silence?
   - Step 4. Did the giver encourage repeat performance? Did the giver of praise touch the receiver [optional]?
   - Did the praise take less than one minute? Was the praise sincere?

Conclusion: The instructor leads a class discussion and/or makes concluding remarks.

Application (2–4 minutes): What did I learn from this experience? How will I use this knowledge in the future?

Sharing: Volunteers give their answers to the application section.

Setting Objectives

Preparation (Individual)

In Chapter 1, you were asked to write five course objectives. Rewrite the five objectives, or new ones, using the Douglas model below:

To + Action verb + Specific, measurable, and singular behavior + Target date

1.

2.

3.

4.

5.

Also write two personal objectives and two career objectives using Douglas's model:

Personal

1.

2.

Career

1.

2.

In-Class Exercise

Objective: To gain skill at setting objectives.

AACSB: The primary AACSB learning standard skills developed through this exercise are analytic skills and strategic management.

Preparation: You should have written nine objectives in preparation for this exercise.

Procedure
(2–12 minutes)

Break into groups of five or six people and share your objectives. One person states one objective and the others give input to be sure it meets the criteria of effective objectives.

A second person states one objective, followed by feedback. Continue until all group members have stated all their objectives or the time runs out.

Conclusion: The instructor may lead a discussion and/or make concluding remarks.

Application (2–4 minutes):   What did I learn from this experience? How will I use this knowledge in the future?

Sharing: Volunteers give their answers to the application section.

A N S W E R S   T O   T R U E / F A L S E   Q U E S T I O N S

1. F. They are all important because if any of the factors are missing, performance will be lower.
2. F. Motivating factors are primarily "intrinsic" factors.
3. F. Valence refers to the value a person places on the outcome or reward in expectancy theory—not equity theory.
4. T.
5. F. We should praise good behavior often.
6. T.
7. F. Because it is not specific, it is not a well-written objective. How much profit? Also, stating the month and year, rather than simply "this year," would provide a better target date.
8. T.
9. T.

Ethical Power and Politics

LEARNING OUTCOMES

After completing this chapter, you should be able to:

1. State how power, politics, and ethics affect behavior, human relations, and performance.

2. Describe seven bases of power.

3. List techniques to increase your power bases.

4. Describe five influencing tactics.

5. Discuss the necessity of organizational politics and three political behaviors.

6. State the difference between ethical and unethical politics.

7. Identify techniques to develop effective human relations with superiors, subordinates, peers, and members of other departments.

8. Define the following 15 key terms (in order of appearance in the chapter):

power	**politics**
coercive power	**reciprocity**
connection power	**Type I ethics**
reward power	**Type II ethics**
legitimate power	**ethical politics**
referent power	**unethical politics**
information power	**open-door policy**
expert power	

CHAPTER OUTLINE

How Power, Politics, and Ethics Affect Behavior, Human Relations, and Performance

Power

  Organizational Power

  Bases of Power and How to Increase Your Power

  Influencing Tactics

Organizational Politics

  The Nature of Organizational Politics

  Political Behavior

  Developing Political Skills

Business Ethics and Etiquette

  Type I and Type II Ethics

  Ethical and Unethical Politics

  Codes of Ethics

  Etiquette

Vertical Politics

  Relations with Your Boss

  Relations with Subordinates

Horizontal Politics

  Relations with Peers

  Relations with Members of Other Departments

Do Power, Politics, and Etiquette Apply Globally?

Bob and Sally are at the water fountain, talking. They both are employed at Scitor Corporation, which is headquartered in Sunnyvale, California.

BOB: I'm sorry the Peterson account was not assigned to you. You deserved it. Roger's claim of being more qualified to handle the job is not true. I'm really surprised that our boss, Ted, believed Roger's claim.

SALLY: I agree. Nobody likes Roger because he always has to get his own way. I can't stand the way Roger puts down coworkers and members of other departments to force them to give him his own way. Roger has pulled the old emergency routine so many times now that purchasing and maintenance ignore his requests. This hurts our department.

BOB: You're right. Roger only thinks of himself; he never considers other people or what's best for the company. I've overheard Ted telling him he has to be a team player if he wants to get ahead.

SALLY: The way he tries to beat everyone out all the time is sickening. He'll do anything to get ahead. But the way he behaves, he will never climb the corporate ladder.

Besides good work, what does it take to get ahead in an organization? In most cases, getting ahead involves gaining power and using ethical political skills with superiors, subordinates, peers, and members of other departments. That's what this chapter is all about.

HOW POWER, POLITICS, AND ETHICS AFFECT BEHAVIOR, HUMAN RELATIONS, AND PERFORMANCE

Learning Outcome

1. State how power, politics, and ethics affect behavior, human relations, and performance.

Some people want and seek power,[1] while others wouldn't take it if you offered it to them. You discovered the reason for this difference in Chapter 9, where you learned about the need for power in McClelland's manifest needs theory. Do you have a need for power?

Power is needed to reach objectives in all organizations, and power affects performance.[2] Your boss has a direct influence over your behavior. The way managers use power also affects human relations and performance.[3] For example, in the opening case, Ted gave the Peterson account to Roger, which will affect both Roger's and Sally's behavior and human relations. Roger may not perform as well as Sally and may hurt department performance.

Managers who abuse power tend to have difficulties in working with others and can markedly impair an organization's morale and performance. They can drive away even the most talented employees, doing significant damage.[4] When organizations use excessive power to get employees to do things such as take on more work or take a pay cut, workers may give in, but they also may get even by lowering performance.

Like power, *politics* is important to organizational performance.[5] People who use organizational politics tend to use different behavior than those who do not use politics.[6] People who are *ethical* behave differently than those who are not ethical.[7] Roger behaves differently than Bob and Sally. Think about the highly ethical and unethical people you have worked with. How do their behavior and human relations differ?

People using unethical politics tend to lie, cheat, and break the rules. In time, people recognize unethical people and distrust them.[8] Bob and Sally don't have effective human relations with Roger because of his political behavior. The purchasing and maintenance department members ignore Roger's requests because of his behavior, while Bob and Sally have good relations with these departments. As a result of Roger's behavior, his performance, his peers' performance, his boss Ted's performance, other departments' performance, and the performance of the organization as a whole are affected negatively.

POWER

To be effective in an organization, you must understand how power is used. In this section, we discuss the importance of power in organizations, bases of power and how to increase your power, and influencing tactics. Begin by completing Self-Assessment Exercise 10–1, Your Power Base, to determine your preferred use of power.

Your Power Base

When you want to get something and need others' consent or help, which approach do you use most often? Think of a recent specific situation in which you tried to get something. If you cannot develop your own example, assume you and a coworker both want the same job assignment for the day. How would you get it? Rank all seven approaches below from 1, the first approach you would most commonly use, to 7, the last approach you would most commonly use. Be honest.

_____   I did/would somehow use a form of *coercive power*—pressure, blackmail, force, threat, retaliation, and so forth—to get what I want.

_____   I did/would use the influential *connection power* I have. I'd refer to my friend, or actually have my friend tell the person with authority (such as my boss) to let me get (or do) what I want.

_____   I did/would use *reward power* by offering the coworker something of value to him or her as part of the process or in return for compliance.

_____   I did/would convince the coworker to give me what I want by making a *legitimate* request (such as referring to my seniority over the coworker).

_____   I did/would convince the coworker by using *referent power*—relying on our relationship. Others would comply because they like me or are my friends.

_____   I did/would convince my coworker to give me what I want with *information power*. The facts support the reason why he or she should do what I want. I have information my coworker needs.

_____   I did/would convince my coworker to give me what I want by making him or her realize that I have the skill and knowledge. Since I'm the *expert,* it should be done my way.

Your selection rank (1 to 7) prioritizes your preferred use of power. Each power base is a key term and will be explained in this chapter.

Organizational Power

Some people view power as the ability to make people do what they want them to do, or the ability to do something to people or for people. These definitions may be true, but they tend to give power a manipulative, negative connotation, as does the adage "Power corrupts and absolute power corrupts absolutely." Within an organization, power should be viewed in a positive sense.[9] Without power, managers could not achieve organizational objectives.[10] Employees are not influenced without a reason, and the reason is often related to the power a manager wields over them.[11] However, people do not actually have to use power to influence others. Often it is the perception of power, rather than the actual power, that influences employees. Leadership and power go hand in hand. For our purposes, **power** *is a person's ability to influence others to do something they would not otherwise do.* Leaders get others to willingly go over and above what they would normally do.[12]

Bases of Power and How to Increase Your Power

There are two sources of power—position power and personal power. Position power is derived from top-level management and is delegated down the chain of command. Personal power is derived from the follower.[13] Everyone has personal power to varying degrees.

Personal power is largely attributed to one's personality and interpersonal skills.[14] Leaders with personal power get it from followers because they meet their needs through effective relationships.[15]

John French and Bertram Raven proposed five bases of power—coercive, reward, legitimate, referent, and expert—which are commonly used today.[16] Below, we will examine seven bases of power and how to increase each. You do not have to take power away from others to increase your power base. Generally, power is given to those who get results. High-level performers are given increased power as they take on more responsibility.

Coercive Power   The use of **coercive power** *involves threats and/or punishment to influence compliance.* Out of fear that noncompliance will lead to reprimands, probation, suspension, or dismissal, employees often do as the supervisor or coworker requests.[17] Other examples of coercive power include verbal abuse, humiliation, and ostracism. In the opening case, when Roger puts down coworkers and members of other departments to force them to give him his own way, he is using coercive power.

Coercive power is appropriate to use in maintaining discipline when enforcing rules. When an employee is not willing to do as the manager requests, the manager may use coercive power to gain compliance. However, it is advisable to keep the use of coercive power to a minimum because it hurts human relations and often productivity as well.[18]

Increasing Coercive Power   To have strong coercive position power, you need to have a management job that enables you to gain and maintain the ability to hire, discipline, and fire your employees. However, some people can pressure others to do what they want without management authority.

Connection Power   **Connection power** *is based on the user's relationship with influential people.* It relies on the use of contacts or friends who can influence the person you are dealing with.[19] The right connections can give you the perception of having power, and they can give you actual power. If people know you are friendly with people in power, they are more apt to do as you request. The Objective Case, Politicking, at the end of the chapter illustrates how people use networking connection power to get ahead.

Increasing Connection Power   To increase your connection power, expand your network of contacts with important managers who have power.[20] Join the "in crowd" and the "right" clubs. Sports like golf may help you meet influential people. When you want something, identify the people who can help you attain it, make alliances, and win them over to your side. Get people to know your name. Get all the publicity you can. Have your accomplishments known by the people in power.

Reward Power   **Reward power** *is based on the user's ability to influence others with something of value to them.* In a management position, use positive reinforcement with incentives such as praise, recognition, pay raises, and promotions to ensure compliance. With peers, you can exchange favors as a reward or give something of value to the other party.[21]

When appropriate, let people know what's in it for them. If you have something attractive to others, use it. For example, when Professor Smith is recruiting student aides, he tells candidates that if they are selected and do a good job, he will recommend them for an MBA fellowship at Suffolk University, where he has connection power. As a result, he gets good, qualified help for minimum wages, while helping both his student aide and his alma mater. Professor Smith meets the goal of human relations by creating a win–win situation for himself, the student, and the university.

Increasing Reward Power   Get a management position, and gain and maintain control over resources. Have the power to evaluate your employees' performance and determine their raises and promotions. Find out what others value, and try to reward them in that way. Using praise can help increase your power. Employees who feel they are appreciated rather than being used will give the manager more power.

Legitimate Power   **Legitimate power** *is based on the user's position power,* which is given by the organization.[22] Employees tend to feel that they ought to do what the supervisor says within the scope of the job. For example, the supervisor asks an employee to take out the trash. The employee does not want to do it, but thinks, "The boss made a legitimate request and I ought to do it," and takes it out. If the employee was hesitant to take out the trash, the supervisor could refer to his or her position power as well.

The use of legitimate power is appropriate when asking people to do something that is within the scope of their jobs. Most day-to-day interactions are based on legitimate power.

Increasing Legitimate Power   Let people know the power you possess, and work at gaining people's perception that you do have power. Remember—people's perception that you have power gives you power.

Referent Power   **Referent power** *is based on the user's personal power.* A person using referent power relies on personality and the relationship with employees to gain compliance. For example, say, "Will you please do it for me?" not "This is an order." Identification stems primarily from the employee's attractiveness to the person using power and is manifested in personal feelings of liking someone.[23] Since Roger is not well liked in the organization, he has weak referent power.

The use of referent power is particularly appropriate for people with weak, or no, position power. Today managers are sharing power, or empowering employees.[24] Roger has no position power, so he should increase his referent power.

Increasing Referent Power   To gain referent power, develop your relationship with others; stand up for them. Using the guidelines in this book can help you win referent power. Remember that your boss's success depends on you. Gain his or her confidence in order to get more power; work at your relationship with the boss.[25] We will discuss this in more detail later in the chapter.

Information Power   **Information power** *is based on the user's information being desired by others.* Managers rely on the other person's need for the information they possess. However, with central computer networks, individual managers today have less of this type of power. Some administrative assistants have more information than the managers they work for. The information is usually, but not always, related to the job.

Increasing Information Power   Have information flow through you. Know what is going on in the organization. Provide service and information to other departments. Serve on committees; it gives you both information and a chance to increase connection power. Attend seminars and other meetings.

Expert Power   **Expert power** *is based on the user's skill and knowledge.* Being an expert makes other people dependent on you. The fewer the people who possess the skill or knowledge, the more power the individual who does possess it has. People often respect an expert. For example, because there are so few people possessing the ability to become top athletes and executives, they command multimillion-dollar contracts.

Expert power is essential to people who have to work with people from other departments and organizations.[26] They have no direct position power to use, so being seen as an expert gives credibility and power. Roger, rather than Sally, got the Peterson account because he convinced Ted of his expertise.

EXHIBIT 10.1 |

Sources and Bases of
Power with Situational
Supervision and
Communication Styles

Personal power					Position power
Expert		Referent		Reward	Coercive
	Information		Legitimate		Connection
	Laissez-faire		*Participative*		*Consultative*	*Autocratic*

Increasing Expert Power   To become an expert, take all the training and educational programs your organization provides. Stay away from routine tasks, in favor of more complex,
hard-to-evaluate tasks. Project a positive image.

Remember to use the appropriate type of power in a given situation. Exhibit 10.1
matches the two sources of power and the seven bases of power with the four situational
supervision and communication styles (from Exhibit 8.6). As shown, coercive, connection,
and reward power come from position power, while referent, information, and expert
power come from personal power.

WORK APPLICATIONS

1. Of the many suggestions for increasing your power bases, which two are your
   highest priority for using on the job? Explain.

2. Give two examples, preferably from an organization for which you work or
   worked, of people using power. Identify the power base and describe the
   behavior and how it affected human relations and performance.

APPLICATION SITUATIONS

Using Power   Identify the appropriate power base to use in each situation.

AS 10–1

A. Coercive   C. Reward or legitimate   E. Information or expert

B. Connection   D. Referent

_____ 1. Carl is one of the best workers you supervise. He needs little direction, but
he has slowed down his production level. You know he has a personal
problem, but the work needs to get done.

_____ 2. You want a new personal computer to help you do a better job.

_____ 3. José, one of your best workers, wants a promotion. He has asked you to
help prepare him for when the opportunity comes.

_____ 4. Your worst employee has ignored one of your directives again.

_____ 5. Wanda, who needs some direction and encouragement to maintain production, is not working to standard today. Wanda claims to be ill, as she does
occasionally.

Learning Outcome

4. Describe five
   influencing tactics.

Influencing Tactics

Your power is your ability to influence others to do something they would not otherwise do
to help you meet your objectives. So along with power sources and bases, you need to have
persuasion skills.[27] Persuasion takes careful preparation and proper presentation of arguments and supporting evidence in an appropriate and compelling way; it is not coercive
power or manipulation. Are you more willing to do something for a person (not your boss)

who tells you what to do (or pressures you) or are you more willing to do it because you are persuaded that you want to?

To help persuade people you don't supervise, you can use influencing tactics that focus primarily on personal power. Five influencing tactics are ingratiation (praise), rational persuasion, inspirational appeal, personal appeal, and legitimization. Before we discuss each tactic, let's discuss reading people and creating and presenting a win–win situation so you know which influencing tactic may work best in a given situation.

Reading People   Reasons for or an argument presenting your view may sound good to you, but they may seem irrelevant to the other person. If you are going to influence someone, you have to understand the person's values, attitudes, beliefs, and motivation. Reading people is a key interpersonal skill; it has four parts:

1. Put yourself in the place of the person you want to persuade (your boss, coworker, a person in another department). Anticipate how the person sees the world and what his or her expectations are during your persuasion interaction.

2. Get the other person's expectations right. If you don't, you most likely will not influence the person.

3. Incorporate the information about the other person's expectations into your persuasive presentation. In other words, use the influencing tactic that will work best with the person. For example, if you know the person likes to be praised, use ingratiation. If the person likes or expects a rational persuasion with facts and figures, use that tactic. If the person doesn't care much about facts and figures and is more emotional, use an inspirational appeal.

4. Keep the focus on the other person's expectations when trying to persuade. This ties in with achieving win–win situations.

Creating and Presenting a Win–Win Situation   When you want someone to do something to help you, it is easy to focus just on yourself. But recall that the key to human relations success is to develop a win–win situation for all relevant parties. So spend time reading the other person, as suggested above, and answer the other person's often unasked question, What's in it for me? Remember that most people are concerned about themselves, not about you. So spending time telling them how you will benefit will be boring to many. What they want to hear is how they will benefit, so, as it says in step 4 above, keep the focus on the other person's expectations.

Ingratiation (Praise)   With the *ingratiation tactic,* you are friendly and give praise to get the person in a good mood before making your request.[28] You learned the importance of, and how to give, praise in Chapter 9. Never go a day without giving praise.

Appropriate Use of Ingratiation   Ingratiation works best as a long-term influencing strategy to improve relationships. The ingratiation must also be sincere to be effective. If you usually don't compliment a person and all of a sudden you compliment him or her and then ask for a favor, the person will think you are manipulating. Thus, this technique can backfire on you.

Using Ingratiation   When using ingratiation, follow these guidelines:

1. Be sensitive to the follower's moods. Ingratiation works well with people who are moody, so asking them at the wrong time can lead to resistance to the change. With moody followers, start out with some compliments to determine their mood. If it's good, make the request; if not, wait for a more opportune time, if possible.

2. Compliment the follower's past related achievements. Begin by talking about how well the follower handled some prior task. Be specific about what she or he did well;

use the model for giving praise in Chapter 9. Then move into the request. If you start with the request first, but find resistance, and then proceed to give compliments, the compliments may be seen as insincere manipulation to get what you want.

3. State why the follower was selected for the task. Compliment followers by saying how uniquely qualified they are to do the task. When followers believe the task is important and they are well qualified, they will find it tough to refuse an assignment.

4. Acknowledge inconvenience posed by your request. Apologize for adding to a busy workload and any inconvenience that will result from doing the task. Praise the follower as you show your appreciation for the follower's willingness to be inconvenienced with your request.

Rational Persuasion The *rational persuasion tactic* includes logical arguments with factual evidence to persuade the person that the behavior will result in meeting the objective. Use facts and figures to build a persuasive case; visuals are also helpful. When you use rational persuasion, read the other person.

Appropriate Use of Rational Persuasion Logical arguments generally work well with people whose behavior is more influenced by thinking than by emotions. It works well when you share the same objective and create a true win–win situation.

Using Rational Persuasion When you develop rational persuasion, follow these guidelines:

1. Explain the reason your objective needs to be met. To get a commitment to meet your objective, you want people to know why it needs to be met and why it is important.

2. Explain how the other person will benefit by meeting your objective, again based on reading the other person and your win–win situation.

3. Provide evidence that your objective can be met. Remember the importance of expectancy motivation theory (Chapter 9). Offer a detailed, step-by-step plan.

4. Explain how potential problems and concerns will be handled. Know the potential problems and concerns, and deal with them in the rational persuasion. If others bring up problems that you have not anticipated when reading the person, which is likely, be sure to address them. Do not ignore people's concerns or make simple statements like, "That will not happen" or "We don't have to worry about that." Get the person's input on how to resolve any possible problems as they come up. This will help gain commitment.

5. If there are competing plans to meet the objective, explain why your proposal is better than the competing ones. Again, do your homework. You need to be well versed about the competition. To simply say, "My idea is better than theirs," won't cut it. Be sure to state how your plan is superior to the others and to identify the weaknesses and problems within the other plans.

Inspirational Appeal The *inspirational appeal tactic* attempts to arouse follower enthusiasm through internalization to meet the objective. You appeal to the other person's values, ideals, and aspirations or increase his or her self-confidence by displaying feelings that appeal to the person's emotions and enthusiasm.[29]

Appropriate Use of Inspirational Appeals Inspirational appeals generally work well with people whose behavior is more influenced by emotions than by logical thinking. To be inspirational, you need to understand the values, hopes, fears, and goals of others; having charisma helps. Great sports coaches, such as Vince Lombardi, are well respected for their inspirational appeals to get the team to win the game. Have you heard the saying from Notre Dame, "Win one for the Gipper"?

Using Inspirational Appeals   When you develop an inspirational appeal, follow these guidelines:

1. When you use inspirational appeals, you need to develop emotions and enthusiasm based on the followers' values. When dealing with multiple followers, different inspirational appeals may be made to meet individual values.

2. Link the appeal to the person's self-concept. Appeal to his or her self-image as a professional or a member of a team, department, or organization. Accomplishing objectives should help people feel good about themselves, which enhances self-concept.

3. Link the request to a clear, appealing vision. Create a vision of how things will be when your objective is achieved.

4. Be positive and optimistic. Make your confidence and optimism that the objective can be met contagious. For example, talk about when, not if, the objective will be accomplished.

5. Use nonverbal communication to bring emotions to the verbal message. Raise and lower your voice tone, and pause to intensify key points. Maintain eye contact. Using facial expressions, body movement, and gestures such as pounding a table can effectively reinforce verbal messages with emotions.

Personal Appeal   With the *personal appeal tactic,* you request the person to meet your objective based on loyalty and friendship.[30] Present your request as a favor to you: "Please do it for me," not "This is an order."

Appropriate Use of Personal Appeals   Personal appeals are especially important when you have weak power. Thus, personal appeals are more commonly used with peers and outsiders than with subordinates or bosses. It is also important to have a good relationship with the person. If you ask a personal favor of a person who doesn't like you, the request may end in resistance.

Using Personal Appeals   When using personal appeals, follow these guidelines:

1. Begin by stating that you need a favor and why it is important. Then ask for the favor. In effect, you are hoping for a positive commitment before giving the details. When a person understands why it is important to you and agrees to do you the favor, it is tough to say no after finding out what is required. But be sure not to be viewed as manipulative and hurt the relationship.

2. Appeal to your friendship. When you have a relationship, a friendship appeal is usually not needed, and it will generally not work with people you don't know. When you use a personal appeal, you might say, "We have been friends for a long time and I've asked very little of you, would you please . . . ?"

3. Tell the person that you are counting on him or her. This helps the person realize the importance to you and your friendship. This statement lets the person know that you don't want the request ignored and that failure to help you could hurt your relationship. Again, friendship is needed for full effect.

Legitimization   With the *legitimization tactic,* you rely on organizational authority that a reasonable request is being made and that the person should meet your objective.[31] Yes, legitimization is closely tied to legitimate power, but the tactic is used when you don't have position power, such as with people at higher levels in the organization.[32]

Appropriate Use of Legitimization   Legitimization is an appropriate tactic to use when you have legitimate authority or the right to make a particular type of request.

Using Legitimization   When using legitimization, follow these guidelines:

1. Refer to organizational policies, procedures, rules, and other documentation. Explain how the request is verified within the organization structure.
2. Refer to written documents. If the person doesn't believe your reference to documents, show the policy manual, contract, letter of agreement, blueprint, work order, or the like that makes your request legitimate.
3. Refer to precedent. If some other person has made the same request, refer to it for equity in support of your request.

You should realize that the five influencing tactics can be used together to help you influence others. For example, praise usually needs to be backed up with another tactic. When one tactic does not work, you may need to change to another.

WORK APPLICATIONS

3. Give an example of when you or someone else in an organization for which you work or have worked used one of the five influencing tactics to achieve an objective. Be sure to state the tactic used.

APPLICATION SITUATIONS

Influencing Tactics

AS 10–2

Select the most appropriate individual tactic for each situation.

A. Rational persuasion   C. Legitimization   E. Personal appeal

B. Inspirational appeal   D. Ingratiation

_____ 6. You are in sales and want some information about a new product that has not been produced yet, nor publicly stated internally or externally. You know a person in the production department who has been working on the new product, so you decide to contact this person.

_____ 7. Two of your five crew workers did not come in to work today. You have a large order that should be shipped out at the end of the day. It will be tough for the small crew to meet the deadline.

_____ 8. This situation relates to number 7. Although the crew members have agreed to push to meet the deadline, you would like to give them some help. You have an employee whose job is to perform routine maintenance and cleaning. He is not one of your five crew workers. However, you realize that he could be of help filling in for the two missing workers. You decide to talk to this nonunion employee about working with the crew for two hours today.

_____ 9. The nonunion employee in situation 8 is resisting helping the other workers. He is basically asking, "What's in it for me?"

_____ 10. You believe you deserve a pay raise, so you decide to talk to your boss about it.

ORGANIZATIONAL POLITICS

In this section, you will learn the nature of politics and how to develop political skills. Begin by determining your use of political behavior by completing Self-Assessment Exercise 10–2.

Your Political Behavior

Select the response that best describes your actual or planned use of the following behavior on the job. Place the number 1 to 5 on the line before each statement.

(5) Usually   (4) Frequently   (3) Occasionally   (2) Seldom   (1) Rarely

_____ 1. I get along with everyone, even those recognized as difficult. I avoid or delay giving my opinion on controversial issues.

_____ 2. I try to make people feel important and compliment them.

_____ 3. I compromise when working with others and avoid telling people they are wrong; instead, I suggest alternatives that may be more effective.

_____ 4. I try to get to know the managers and what is going on in as many of the other departments as possible.

_____ 5. I take on the same interests as those in power (watch or play sports, join the same clubs, and the like).

_____ 6. I purposely seek contacts and network with higher-level managers so they will know who I am by name and face.

_____ 7. I seek recognition and visibility for my accomplishments.

_____ 8. I form alliances with others to increase my ability to get what I want.

_____ 9. I do favors for others and use their favors in return.

_____ 10. I say I will do things when I am not sure I can deliver; if I cannot meet the obligation, I explain why it was out of my control.

To determine your political behavior, add the 10 numbers you selected as your answers. The number will range from 10 to 50. The higher your score, the more political behavior you use. Place your score here _____ and mark the point that represents your score on the continuum below.

Nonpolitical   10 - - - - 20 - - - - 30 - - - - 40 - - - - 50   Political

Learning Outcome

5. Discuss the necessity of organizational politics and three political behaviors.

The Nature of Organizational Politics

Politics is critical to your career success.[33] You cannot keep out of politics and be successful.[34] Politics is a fact of organizational life.[35] In our economy, money is the medium of exchange; in an organization, politics is the medium of exchange. Managers cannot meet their objectives without the help of other people and departments over which they have no authority or position power.[36] Politics is the network of interactions by which power is acquired, transferred, and exercised upon others. **Politics** *is the process of gaining and using power.* As you can see from the definition, power and politics go hand in hand.

Like power, politics often has a negative connotation due to people who abuse political power.[37] Mahatma Gandhi called politics without principle a sin. However, ethical politics helps the organization by meeting the goal of human relations without negative consequences. The amount and importance of politics varies from organization to organization. However, larger organizations tend to be more political; and the higher the level of management, the more important politics becomes.[38]

As you can see, organizational politics is an integral part of everyday corporate life. You should develop your political behavior to take advantage of political realities that can help you and the organization and to avoid being hurt by politics.

Political Behavior

Political behavior is used to develop relationships that are necessary to get the job done. Three primary political behaviors commonly used in organizations are: networking, reciprocity, and coalition building. As you will learn below, these three behaviors are interrelated.

Networking   Networking is the process of developing relationship alliances with key people for the purpose of politicking. Your network of people helps you get your job done, and, in turn, you help the people in your network get their jobs done.[39] Successful managers spend more time networking than do average managers, and networking may be the most important contributor to their success. Networking is such an important topic that we discuss it in detail in the next chapter.

Reciprocity   Politics is about reciprocal exchanges.[40] **Reciprocity** *involves creating obligations and debts, developing alliances, and using them to accomplish objectives.* Have you ever heard the expression, "You owe me one"? When others do something for you, you incur an obligation that they may expect to be repaid. When you do something for others, you create a debt that you may be able to collect at a later date when you need a favor.[41] Researchers have found that the mere mention of the word "favor" increases the odds of getting help.[42] So use statements such as, Will you please do me a favor? And be ready to return the favor when asked.[43]

WORK APPLICATIONS

4. Give an example of reciprocity, preferably from an organization for which you work or have worked. Explain the trade-off.

Coalition Building   A coalition is a network of alliances that helps you achieve a specific objective. Reciprocity is primarily used to achieve ongoing objectives, whereas coalitions are developed for achieving a specific objective. Many organizational decisions that are supposed to be made during a meeting or vote are actually decided through coalition building. For example, let's say that the selection of the department chair at your college is by election at a department meeting.

Professor Smith would like to replace the current chair. Rather than just put her name on the ballot for the department election at the next meeting, she goes around to several people in the department telling them she wants to be chair. Smith may agree to do things in exchange for votes. Members of her coalition may also get votes for Smith, and someone may have asked her to run. She gets a majority of the department members saying they will vote for her, so Smith puts her name on the ballot. If she did not get the coalition, she would not run. So going into the meeting, the coalition has really already made the decision to elect Smith.

Putting the Political Behaviors Together   So to put the three political behaviors together, political success is about developing networks of alliances and coalitions in reciprocal exchanges. When the exchanges create a win–win situation for all members of the alliance and the organization, the goal of human relations is met.

Developing Political Skills

Yes, you can be good at politics without being a jerk. Human relations skills are also political skills in organizations. Following the human relations guidelines throughout this book can help you develop political skills. More specifically, review the 10 statements in Self-Assessment Exercise 10–2 and consciously increase your use of these behaviors. Successfully implementing these behaviors results in increased political skills. However, if you don't agree with a political behavior, don't use it. You may not need to use all the political behaviors to be successful. Learn what it takes in the organization where you work. Use number 10, saying you will do something when you are not sure you can, sparingly and don't use the word *promise*. You don't want to be viewed as a person who doesn't keep his or her word. Developing trust is very important.[44] And being honest builds trust (Chapter 8).

5. Of the 10 political behaviors in Self-Assessment Exercise 10–2, which two need the most effort on your part? Which two need the least? Explain your answers.

BUSINESS ETHICS AND ETIQUETTE

Learning Outcome

6. State the difference between ethical and unethical politics.

In Chapter 3, we discussed ethics as an intrapersonal skill from the individual level of analysis. Now we focus on ethics as a leadership skill from the organizational level. When seeking power and using politics to meet your objectives, you need to be ethical.[45] Recall from Chapter 1 that under the systems effect, all people in the organization are affected by at least one other person, and each person affects the whole group or organization. Remembering that the goal of human relations is to create a win–win situation for all relevant parties will help keep you ethical. In this section, we discuss Type I and Type II ethics, ethical and unethical politics, codes of ethics, and etiquette.

Type I and Type II Ethics

Behavior known as **Type I ethics** *refers to behavior that is considered wrong by authorities, yet is not accepted by others as unethical.* The number of people who do not accept authorities' decisions regarding wrong behavior affects people's decision to behave in unethical ways. In Self-Assessment Exercise 3–4 (Chapter 3), these behaviors are considered unethical by most organizations, yet many employees do not agree and perform them anyway. Generally, the more people disagree with specific behavior as being unethical, the more people will perform the behavior. People tend to rationalize; they think that because everyone else does it, it's okay for them to do it. People also tend to exaggerate the numbers. Often "everyone" is actually a small percentage of the population.

A person who knowingly conducts unethical behavior because he or she does not agree with authorities' views on ethical behavior is guilty of Type I ethics. For example, the company rules say there shall be no smoking in a specific area, yet the employee does not believe smoking is dangerous and smokes in that area anyway.

Type II ethics *refers to behavior that is considered wrong by authorities and the individual, yet is conducted anyway.* A person who agrees that the behavior is unethical yet conducts the behavior anyway is guilty of Type II ethics. Continuing the smoking example above: The employee knows smoking is not allowed and agrees that it is dangerous, yet smokes anyway. See Exhibit 10.2 for an illustration of Type I and II behavior.

6. Give an example of Type I and Type II ethics behavior, preferably from an organization for which you work or have worked.

EXHIBIT 10.2 | Type I and Type II Ethics

Type I	Type II
Ethical and Legal	Unethical and Legal
Type I	*Type II*
Ethical and Illegal	Unethical and Illegal

Source: Based on comments from Robert Losik, Southern New Hampshire University, February 1, 2006.

Type I and Type II Ethics

AS 10–3

Identify the type of ethical behavior represented in each statement.

A. Type I ethics   B. Type II ethics

_____ 11. "Bill just let another toy go as acceptable quality, when it's not. He agrees that it's wrong to do this, so why does he do it?"

_____ 12. "Carla told me it's OK to take home company pens and things; everyone does it."

_____ 13. "Wayne is spreading stories about coworkers again. Why doesn't he agree that this is unethical?"

_____ 14. "Danielle is using the department's copier to make copies of directions to the party she is having. I told her it was wrong, and she agreed with me, but she did it anyway."

_____ 15. "Mike just left work early again. He says he is underpaid, so it's OK."

Ethical and Unethical Politics

Politics can be helpful or harmful to an organization depending on the behavior. We classify political behavior into two categories: ethical and unethical. **Ethical politics** *includes behavior that benefits both the individual and the organization.* Behavior that helps the individual but does not hurt the organization is also considered ethical. Ethical politics creates a win–win situation, meeting the goal of human relations. On the other hand, **unethical politics** *includes behavior that benefits the individual and hurts the organization.* Unethical politics creates a win–lose situation. Unethical politics also includes behavior that helps the organization, but hurts the individual and other stakeholders.[46] The term *organization* includes people inside the firm, because if employees are hurt, so is the organization. When dealing with people outside the firm, use the *stakeholders'* approach to ethics. By creating a win–win situation for all relevant parties, it increases the firm's financial performance.

The 10 political behavior statements in Self-Assessment Exercise 10–2 are generally ethical. Another example of ethical political behavior involves Tom, the computer manager, who wants a new computer. He talks to several of the powerful managers and sells them on the benefits to them. They form an alliance and attain the funds to purchase the computer. Tom benefits because he now has a new and more powerful computer. He also looks good in the eyes of the other managers, who will also benefit through the use of the new computer. Overall, the organization's performance increases.

Examples of unethical behavior that hurt the organization include the following: (1) Karl, a production manager, wants to be promoted to the general manager's position. To increase his chances, he spreads untrue gossip about his main competitor. (2) There is a vacant office, which is large and well furnished. Sam, a sales manager who spends most of his time on the road, sees the office as prestigious, so he requests it, even though he knows that Cindy, a public relations manager, wants it and will get better use from it. Sam speaks to his friends in high-level management positions and he gets the office. (3) A person lies on his or her resume. (4) A manager asks an employee to lie. Although goal setting increases performance, high goals can also lead to unethical behavior to achieve the goal, including cooked books and false sales reports.

At first, one may appear to be richly rewarded for knifing people in the back, but retaliation follows, trust is lost, and productivity declines. This is illustrated in the opening case. Roger uses unethical politics in hopes of getting ahead. But according to his peers, he will not climb the corporate ladder. It is difficult to get ahead when people don't like you and you make a lot of enemies. Exercising good human relations skills is exercising good ethics.

WORK APPLICATIONS

7. Give an example of ethical and unethical politics, preferably from an organization for which you work or have worked. Describe the behavior and the consequences for all parties involved.

APPLICATION SITUATIONS

Ethical and Unethical Politics

AS 10–4

Identify the type of politics represented in each statement.

A. Ethical politics   B. Unethical politics

_____ 16. Pete goes around telling everyone about any little mistake his peer Sue makes.

_____ 17. Tony is taking tennis lessons so he can challenge his boss.

_____ 18. Carol delivers her daily figures at 10:00 each day because she knows she will run into Ms. Big Power on the way.

_____ 19. Carlos goes around asking about what is happening in other departments during his work time.

_____ 20. Frank sent a copy of his department's performance record to three high-level managers to whom he does not report.

Codes of Ethics

Although we all live by our own personal codes of ethics, to improve ethical behavior, organizations also develop codes of ethics.[47] A good code of ethics establishes guidelines that clearly describe ethical and unethical behavior. Most organizations consider ethics codes important, and most large firms have developed codes of ethics. Exhibit 10.3 is an example of an organization's code of ethics as it relates to its employees.

To be ethically successful, firms must not justify unethical behavior. Organizations must audit the ethical behavior of their employees and confront and discipline employees who are unethical. Top managers need to lead by ethical example, they need to be honest with employees, and they need to build trust. Ethical behavior by leaders contributes to building trust, respect, and confidence.[48]

Etiquette

Etiquette is the socially accepted standard of right and wrong behavior. It includes manners beyond simply saying "please" and "thank you." Notice the similarity in our definitions of ethics and etiquette. Etiquette is very important to your career success. However, unlike ethics, organizations don't usually have codes or any formal training dealing with etiquette.

EXHIBIT 10.3 | Code of Ethics*

- We will treat our employees fairly with regard to wages, benefits, and working conditions.
- We will never violate the legal or moral rights of employees in any way.
- We will never employ children in our facilities, nor will we do business with any company that makes use of child labor.
- We are committed to an ongoing program of monitoring all our facilities and those of companies with whom we do business.

*Excerpts from the Phillips-Van Heusen statement of Corporate Responsibility.

Are They Striking It Rich or Striking Out?

In September 2008, the International Association of Machinists rejected Boeing's final contract offer and went on strike. The stakes were high for the company, its customers, and its suppliers—and also for the union leadership and rank-and-file workers. But the Machinists' strike effects would ripple out around the world, and the longer the strike, the more it cost all types of stakeholders: Boeing would miss hundreds of millions of dollars in profits in 2008, and the 787 Dreamliner program would slip again. Machinists and their families would have to make do without paychecks. Suppliers would stop making more parts, resulting in layoffs. Airlines desperate for fuel-efficient 737s and 777s would be frustrated, contributing to higher airfares.

Along with improvements in compensation and benefits, the union is fighting for job protection. At the heart of the scrimmage is the growing use of contract workers at factories doing the same jobs as full-time union employees. Indeed, the contingency workforce—including independent contractors, part-timers, and temporary workers—tends to be paid less, have little or no health insurance or retirement plans, and few if any protections under existing labor laws. There are about 42 million contingent workers, or about 30 percent of the overall workforce. Boeing says it needs to cut costs to compete with Airbus and other competitors, whereas the union says it needs good-paying full-time jobs. Boeing's striking workers are on the front line of a battle for job security that's playing out in workplaces across the country, unionized or not. Yet, the strike could mean more outsourcing in the future.

Questions

1. Union strikes involve which bases of power?

2. How might unions use influencing tactics to win public support? Which influencing tactic might work best?

3. Is it ethical for Boeing and other companies to use contingency workers?

4. Knowing that the strike would cause a ripple effect, thereby hurting many other stakeholders, was it ethical to strike?

5. Using Exhibit 10.2, which one of the four types of ethics is illustrated in this ethical dilemma by both Boeing management and the union?

Sources: D. Gates, "A Strike's Financial Hit to Boeing," *Seattle Times* (September 2, 2008). Retrieved online September 17, 2008, http://seattletimes.nwsource.com/html/nationworld/2008149181_boeing31.html; and E. Tahmincioglu, "Union Says Boeing Strike Is about Contractors," MSNBC.com (September 10, 2008). Retrieved online September 17, 2008, http://www.msnbc.msn.com/id/26647110/.

Many organizations weigh etiquette during the job interview as part of the selection criteria. In fact, some managers will take the job candidate out to eat and observe etiquette, including table manners. Candidates with poor etiquette are not offered the job. You may be thinking that it is unfair to judge job candidates by their etiquette, and you may be right. However, the reality of the business world is that firms do not want employees representing their organization who do not project a favorable image for the organization. Recall that customers, suppliers, and everyone else the organization comes into contact with judge the organization based on individual behavior. Organizations do not want employees who will embarrass them.

Organizations assume that people are taught etiquette at home or that it is learned through experience or observation. However, this is not always the case. Etiquette skills can be improved. If you haven't been concerned with business etiquette, start now. We'll give you some tips.

Job Interview Etiquette   The career service department at your college may offer job interview training. Take advantage of its services. Here are some do's and don'ts of job interviewing:

- Do research the organization before the interview so that you can talk intelligently about it. For example, what products or services does it offer? How many employees and locations does it have? What is the company's financial status, such as revenues and net profit last year? What are its strategic plans? Much of this information can be found in the company's annual report or on its Web site.

- Do go to the job interview properly dressed (see the discussion in Chapter 2 regarding first impressions).

- Do be sure to get there a little early. Allow plenty of time for traffic and parking. If you are more than 10 minutes early, you can relax and wait before going to the receptionist.

- Do bring extra copies of your resume and other material you may need in a briefcase or nice folder.

- Do get the last name and proper pronunciation of the person who will be interviewing you, and greet the interviewer by using her or his last name. For example, "How do you do, Mr. Smith?"

- Don't call the interviewer by first name unless told to do so by the interviewer.

- Do firmly shake hands and make eye contact if the interviewer extends his or her hand to you, but don't make the first move.

- Do state the interviewer's name a few times during the job interview. For example, "That is a good question, Mr. Smith."

- Don't sit down until the interviewer invites you to sit, and wait for the interviewer to sit first.

- Do be careful of your nonverbal communication (Chapter 5). Don't sit back and slouch. Sit up straight, leaning a bit forward in the seat, and maintain adequate eye contact to show your interest. You may cross your legs, but crossed arms are a sign of defensiveness or being closed.

- Don't be the first one to bring up salary and benefits. If asked what you expect for a salary, give a range below and above the actual figure you expect. Part of your research prior to the interview should be to find out the salary range for the job you are interviewing for.

- Do take a little time to think about your answers. Talk clearly and loud enough while watching your vocabulary to include proper English; avoid street talk or jargon.

- Do thank the interviewer for his or her time at the close of the interview. If the interviewer does not tell you how long it will take to make a decision, ask when you can expect an answer.

- Do send a short follow-up, written thank-you letter with another copy of your resume the same day or the next, if you want the job. Include any other information in the letter that you thought about after the interview and state that you look forward to the selection decision date given by the interviewer.

- Do call back if you do not hear whether you got the job by the decision date given by the interviewer.

Table Manners   Following are a few simple tips in case you are taken out to eat during the job interview. If you get the job and take others out to eat, you are in the interviewer role even if it's not a job interview. Many of the tips also apply to eating with others during your lunch breaks.

- Don't be starving when you go out to eat. Pigging out is not appropriate behavior and will not make a good impression on the interviewer.

- Do follow the lead of the interviewer; don't take charge.

- Do let the interviewer sit first.

- Do place your napkin on your lap after the interviewer does.

- If the server asks if you want a drink, do wait for the interviewer to respond. Don't ask for alcohol if you are underage.

- Don't order alcohol unless asked if you want a drink by the interviewer. If asked, ask the interviewer if he or she will be having a drink. If the interviewer say yes, have one; if the answer is no, don't have a drink. However, don't have a drink if you will feel its effects. You want to be in top form for the interview questions and discussion, and you want to maintain your proper etiquette.

- Do expect to order an appetizer, main course, and dessert. However, you don't have to order them all, especially if the interviewer does not. For example, if the interviewer asks if you would like an appetizer or a dessert, ask the interviewer if he or she is having one. If the server asks, wait for the interviewer to answer.
- Don't begin to eat any serving until everyone at the table has been served and the interviewer has begun to eat.
- Do try to eat at the same pace as the interviewer so that you are not eating each serving much faster or slower than the interviewer.
- Don't talk with food in your mouth. Take small bites to help avoid this problem.
- Don't take the last of anything that you are sharing. It is also polite to leave a little food on your plate, even if you are still hungry.
- Do start using the silverware from the outside in. Follow the interviewer's lead when in doubt.
- Do not offer to pay part or all of the bill. The general rule is that whoever invites the other out to eat pays the bill, unless otherwise agreed before going to eat.
- Do thank the interviewer for the meal. Also, be polite (say "please" and "thank you") to the server.

Telephone Etiquette   After you get the job, you likely will use the telephone as part of your job. These tips assume you are not a telephone operator, a position which should get proper training. The following are some etiquette tips for when you call others:

- Do have a written outline or plan of the topics you want to discuss. Do write notes on the plan sheet as you talk. Don't use a small piece of scrap paper; a notebook works well to keep track of your calls.
- Do leave a brief message if the person does not answer. Do state (1) your name, (2) the reason for the call and message, (3) the telephone number to call back, and (4) the best time for the return call. Do speak loudly and clearly enough and speak slowly, especially when leaving your number. Don't use voice mail for bad news, sensitive or confidential information, and complicated information and instructions. Do control your emotions; don't leave emotional messages that can be played back for the entertainment of others or against you in any way, such as a complaint against you to a boss.
- Do ask if the person has time to talk. If he or she is busy, set up a time to call back.
- Do call the person back if you get disconnected; it's the caller's responsibility to call back.
- Don't eat while on the phone.
- Don't talk to others while you or they are on the phone.
- Do be the first to hang up, and do hang up gently.

Etiquette tips for when others call you include the following:

- Do try to answer the phone within three rings.
- Do say "hello" followed by your name (not a nickname) and department or organization.
- If people are calling you at a bad time and did not ask if you have time to talk, do tell them you do not have time to talk now. Do give them a time when you will call them back, and be sure to call back on time.
- If you have to put people on hold for more than a minute, for example, if you have to look up information, do offer to call them back.
- Don't take multiple calls at one time, keeping people on hold. Do let voice mail take a message and call the person back.

- Do keep paper (telephone notebook) and pencil ready. Do write down the person's name immediately when you don't know the person, and call her or him by name during the conversation as you jot down notes.

- Don't give out personal information about others over the phone.

- Do be the last one to hang up.

- Do leave a brief message on your voice mail for callers. Do include (1) your name, (2) your organization, (3) an invitation for the caller to leave a message, and (4) a suggestion for a good time to call. Do remember to send calls directly into your voice mail when you are not in so people don't have to wait to leave their message.

- Do call people back within 24 hours.

Etiquette tips for calls involving pagers and cellular phones include:

- Don't interrupt others with your messages. Do use the vibrating function on your pager or cell phone rather than the audio. But even with a vibrating pager, don't interrupt meetings and other activities unless the message is a true emergency.

- Don't disrupt others with your cellular phone conversations, such as by talking in meetings and public places (while walking down the street or in a theater, restaurant, or classroom). Do go to a private place.

- Do be extra careful when talking on the phone while driving, for your own safety and that of others; many accidents are phone-related. Be aware that it's now against the law in some states to use a handheld cell phone while driving.

E-mail Etiquette   In most workplaces today, e-mail has become a dominant method of communication. Some tips for good e-mail etiquette include:

- Do use e-mail for short messages; stick to a two-page maximum. Do get to the point quickly and clearly; don't ramble.

- Do use attachments for sending messages of three or more pages. Do send the attachment so that it is readable to the receiver.

- Do use the spelling and grammar checkers, and do proofread your message. People place more value on what you say when it is said correctly.

- Do avoid Internet and other jargon that others may not know.

- Don't say anything in an e-mail that you don't want others to know about. It is possible for organizations to read your e-mail; even the ones you delete can be read by some systems.

- Don't send emotional messages, for the same reasons as leaving emotional phone messages.

- Do avoid junk e-mail. Don't send needless messages. Don't send copies to people who don't need to know your message.

Meeting Etiquette   If you are running a meeting, follow the guidelines in Chapter 12 on skills for managing meetings. Below is etiquette for attendees of meetings:

- Do arrive on time.

- Do come to the meeting properly prepared. Do any reading and assignments before the meeting.

- If you are late, do apologize. But do not give a reason for being late. Excuses only take up meeting time and are often not believed anyway.

- Don't be a problem member. Problem members are discussed along with meeting skills in Chapter 12.

Hoteling Etiquette   *Hoteling* is the sharing of workspace and equipment, such as desks, computers, phones, fax machines, copiers, eating areas, refrigerators, coffee machines, water coolers, and so on.

- Do follow the general rule to do unto others as you would have them do unto you.
- Do clean up after yourself and make sure the equipment is ready for the next person to use when you are done, even if you find the area cluttered or dirty, the machine without paper, the coffee pot without coffee, and so on. Do assertively confront others who do not clean up or ready the equipment.
- Do pay your fair share of any expenses, such as coffee or water money, splitting the bill for lunch, chipping in for employee presents, and so on. Don't take other people's food and drinks without permission. And if they give food or drinks to you, return the favor.
- Do respect others' privacy. Don't read anything on anyone's desk, computer screen, messages, or fax. Doing so is like opening and reading their mail, which is a don't.
- Don't monopolize shared workspace and equipment; share it equitably.

WORK APPLICATIONS

8. Give a job example of when a coworker behaved with improper etiquette.

VERTICAL POLITICS

Vertical human relations are important to your career success.[49] Vertical politics are relations with superiors and subordinates. Your boss and the employees you supervise and who report to you are the most important persons with whom to develop effective relations.[50]

Relations with Your Boss

Your relationship with your boss will affect your job satisfaction and can mean the difference between success or failure on the job.[51] Not getting along with your boss can make life miserable for you.[52] Needless to say, you should develop a good working relationship with your boss.[53] Doing so is also called *managing* your boss.

Don't try to change your boss. Analyze your boss's style and preferences, and if necessary, change your style to match his or hers. For example, if your boss is very businesslike and you are very informal and talkative, be businesslike when you are with your boss. If your boss likes you and your work to be early, not just on time, be early.[54] Remember, people generally like people who behave like themselves, and being liked can lead to career advancement.

Knowing your boss can lead to better human relations between the two of you.[55] It is helpful to know your boss's primary responsibility, what your boss regards as good performance, how your performance will be evaluated, and what your boss expects of you. So get feedback from your boss to make sure you are on the same page.[56] As discussed in Chapter 8, your boss must trust you. It's your job to help your boss be successful and to offset his or her weaknesses.

Common Expectations of Bosses   Your boss will expect loyalty, cooperation, initiative, information, and openness to criticism.

Loyalty   Recall that loyalty is an important part of trust. You need to be loyal and have a proper attitude. You should not talk negatively about your boss behind his or her back, even if others are doing so. Regardless of how careful you are, or how trustworthy the other person is, gossip seems to get back to the boss. When it does, it can seriously hurt your relationship. Your boss may never forget it or forgive you for doing it. The benefits, if any, don't outweigh the cost of not being loyal.

Continuing to listen to, and especially agreeing with, negative statements only encourages others to continue this behavior. The discussion between Bob and Sally is an example of negative talk about others. If people are talking negatively about others, encourage them to stop in a nice way, change the subject, or leave them. For example, "Complaining about Roger really doesn't change anything. Why don't we talk about the things we can change, such as . . ." or "Did anyone see the movie on TV last night?"

Cooperation   Your boss expects you to be cooperative with him or her and with everyone else you must work with. If you cannot get along with others, you can be an embarrassment to your boss. And bosses don't like to be embarrassed. Roger is not cooperative; his boss Ted has told him that if he wants to get ahead, he will have to be a team player.

Initiative   Your boss will expect you to know your responsibility and authority and to act without having to be told to do so. Jack Welch says that if you only do what your boss tells you to do, you haven't done enough—overdeliver. Volunteer for assignments.[57] If there is a problem, the boss may expect you to solve it rather than bring it to him or her to solve. If it is appropriate to include the boss in solving a problem, at least analyze the situation and have a recommended solution to present.

Information   Your boss expects you to keep him or her informed about what your objectives are and how you are progressing. If there are problems, your boss expects you to tell him or her about them. You should not cover up your mistakes, your employees' mistakes, or your boss's mistakes. You can cause your boss embarrassment if he has to learn from others what's going on in his department. Bosses don't like to be surprised.

Openness to Criticism   We all make mistakes; part of your boss's job is to help you avoid repeating them. When your boss criticizes you, try not to become defensive and argumentative. Remember that criticism is a means of improving your skills; be open to it even though it hurts (Chapter 6).

If you use the guidelines to effective human relations, get to know your boss, and meet and exceed his or her expectations, you should develop a good relationship. If you meet your boss's expectations, he or she will most likely be willing to help you meet your needs. Meeting and exceeding your boss's expectations can help you meet the goal of human relations by creating a win–win situation for both of you.

If you don't get along with your boss, your chances of promotion may be hurt, and you could stay in or be transferred to a dead-end job. Also, be careful about going over his or her head (to your boss's boss) because you may be viewed as a betrayer of loyalty and as unethical. Going to complain about your boss can create more problems for you than solutions. Before you do, think, "What are the chances that my boss's boss will take my side against my boss?" It is especially doubtful if you don't have a good relationship with the higher-level manager and your boss does. Going over the boss's head is an issue in the first case at the end of this chapter.

Regaining Your Boss's Trust   If you have done something that makes your boss look bad or in some way hurt your relationship, such as breaking any of the above expectations, you need to earn back his or her trust to reestablish your good working relationship. Not being willing to apologize and regain trust can be dangerous to your career. Your boss can give you poor evaluations and make your life miserable by trying to get you to quit or to fire you. To regain trust, follow this process:

- Apologize immediately, face-to-face, speaking slowly to sound truly remorseful.
- Accept responsibility for what you did or said.
- Empathize with the discomfort you caused.

- Offer a credible explanation for the deed.

- Vow not to repeat this mistake again, stating your plan to prevent it, or ask your boss for suggestions on avoiding it again.

Although the focus here is on rebuilding trust with your boss, the same process should be used to maintain human relations when you make your subordinates, peers, and members of other departments or organizations look bad or in some way hurt your relationship. You may also apply this process to your personal relationships.

WORK APPLICATIONS

9. Of the five common expectations of bosses, which is your strongest area? Your weakest area? Explain your answers.

Relations with Subordinates

If the goal of human relations—to satisfy employee needs while achieving organizational objectives—is easy, why are poor human relations common? One reason is the fact that the manager must consider the work to be accomplished as ultimately more important than the needs and desires of those doing the work, including the manager's own needs. Managers get so busy getting the job done that they forget about the needs of the employees doing the work. Employees tend to start a job enthusiastically, but the manager often does not take the time to develop the human relations necessary to maintain that enthusiasm. As a manager, you must take the time to develop effective human relations.

Developing Manager–Employee Relations   In developing manager–employee relations, you should follow the guidelines to human relations throughout this book. Perfect human relations probably don't exist. The manager should strive for harmonious relations where differences of opinion are encouraged and settled in a peaceful manner. Morale should be kept at high levels, but the manager shouldn't try to please all the people all the time. As a manager, you may face resentment from an employee who resents you for *what* you are (the manager) rather than for *who* you are. Others may not like you for any number of reasons. A manager can have good human relations without being well liked personally or popular. Leader–follower relations should be reciprocal exchanges, so both parties win.[58]

Friendship   The relationship between manager and employee cannot be one of real friendship. The nature of supervision excludes true friendship because the manager must evaluate the employee's performance; true friends don't evaluate or judge each other in any formal way. The manager must also give employees directions; friends don't order each other around. The manager must also get the employee to change; friends usually don't try to change each other.

Trying to be friends may cause problems for you, the employee, and the department. Will your friend try to take advantage of your friendship to get special favors? Will you be able to treat your friend like the other members of the department? The other employees may say you play favorites. They may resent your friend and ostracize him or her. Your friendship could adversely affect department morale.

Not being true friends to employees does not mean that managers should not be friendly. If the manager takes an "I'm the boss" attitude, employees may resent him or her and morale problems could result. As in most cases, there are exceptions to the rule. Some managers are friends with employees and are still very effective managers.

WORK APPLICATIONS

10. Assume you are hired for or promoted to a management position. Will you develop a relationship with your employees based on friendship? Describe the relationship you plan to develop.

The Open-Door Policy   The **open-door policy** *is the practice of being available to employees.* Your management ability is directly proportional to the amount of time your door is open, both literally and figuratively. For effective human relations, you must be available to employees to give them the help they need, when they need it. If employees view the manager as too busy or not willing to help them, poor human relations and low morale can result. An open-door policy does not mean that you must stop everything whenever an employee wants to see you. For nonemergencies the employee should make an appointment. You should prioritize spending time with an employee along with other responsibilities. Managers are also using an open e-mail policy.

Use your power wisely. Remember, your success as a manager depends on your subordinates. If you want employees to meet your expectations, create a win–win situation. Help your subordinates meet their needs while attaining the high performance that will make you a success. When you ask subordinates to do something, answer their unasked question, "What's in it for me?" The Professor Smith–student aide example in the section on reward power is a superior–subordinate win–win situation example.

HORIZONTAL POLITICS

Horizontal politics are your relations with your peers and with members of other departments and organizations. Your peers are the people who are on the same level in the organizational hierarchy as you. Your direct peers also report to your boss. You will now learn how to develop effective horizontal politics.

Relations with Peers

To be successful, you must cooperate, compete with, and sometimes even criticize your peers.

Cooperating with Peers   Your success as an employee is linked to other employees in the organization.[59] If you are cooperative and help them, they should have a positive attitude toward you and be willing to help you meet your objectives.[60] Innovations are created by employees sharing ideas and collaborating.[61] If you don't cooperate with your peers, your boss will know it.

Competing with Peers   Even though you are cooperative with your peers, you are still in competition with them. Your boss will compare you with them when evaluating your performance, giving raises, and granting promotions. Like a great athlete, you must learn to be a team player and help your peers be successful, but at the same time, you have to look good as well.

Criticizing Peers   Do not go looking for faults in your peers. But if your peers do something they shouldn't, you owe it to them to try to correct the situation or prevent it from recurring. Tactfully and sincerely telling a peer of a shortcoming is often appreciated. Sometimes peers are not aware of the situation. But there are people who don't appreciate criticism or unsolicited advice. Chapter 7 provides details on how to approach peers, and others, to resolve conflicts, and Chapter 6 offers suggestions for giving criticism.

Do not go to the boss unless the offense is serious, such as disregarding safety rules, which will endanger the welfare of employees. Unless your own safety is in danger, tell the boss only after discussing the offense with the peer and warning him or her of the consequences of continuing the behavior. Do not cover for a peer in trouble—you will only make things worse for everyone involved. And don't expect or ask others to cover for you.

Roger violates peer relations. He always has to get his own way. Roger is uncooperative and too competitive; he criticizes coworkers and members of other departments to force them to give him his own way.

WORK APPLICATIONS

12. Give an example, preferably from an organization for which you work or have worked, of a situation in which you had good human relations with your peers. Describe how you cooperated with, competed with, and/or criticized your peers.

Relations with Members of Other Departments

As an employee, you will most likely need the help of other departments and organizations to succeed. You will need the human resources department to hire new employees, accounting to approve budgets, purchasing to get materials and supplies, maintenance to keep the department's equipment running efficiently, payroll to approve overtime pay, and so forth.

Some of these departments have procedures you should follow. Develop good human relations through being cooperative and following the guidelines set by the organization. It is also advisable to develop good relations with people in other organizations.[62]

Roger's pulling "the old emergency routine" so many times has resulted in purchasing and maintenance ignoring him. This is an embarrassment for Ted and the department, and it is hurting performance.

Putting It All Together   See Exhibit 10.4 for an illustration that puts the concepts of power, politics, and ethics together. Starting in the center, with the goal of human relations, you create a win–win situation through horizontal politics with your peers and people in other departments and through vertical politics with your superiors and subordinates. You also use appropriate power with your politics.

Learning Outcome

7. Identify techniques to develop effective human relations with superiors, subordinates, peers, and members of other departments.

WORK APPLICATIONS

13. Give an example, preferably from an organization you work(ed) for, of a situation in which you had good human relations with members of other departments. Describe how your relations affected your performance, the other departments, and the organization as a whole.

APPLICATION SITUATIONS

Relations with Others

AS 10–5

Identify the other party being mentioned in each statement.

A. Subordinate   C. Peers

B. Superior   D. Other departments

_____ 21. "As a supervisor, I report to a middle manager named Kim."

_____ 22. "The guys in sales are always trying to rush us to ship the product."

_____ 23. "Willy is reluctant to accept the task I delegated to him."

_____ 24. "That's the owner of the company."

_____ 25. "The supervisors are getting together for lunch. Will you join us?"

EXHIBIT 10.4 |
Human Relations Guide
to Ethical Decision
Making

If you are proud to tell all relevant parties your decision, it is probably ethical.

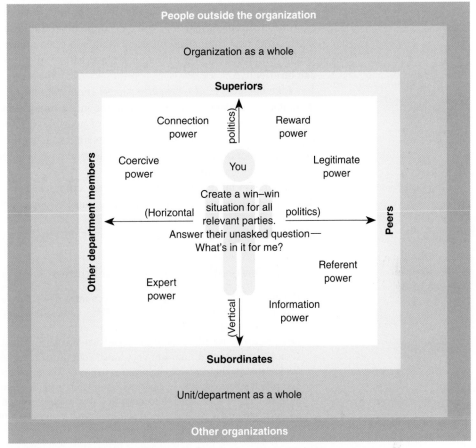

If you are embarrassed to tell all relevant parties your decision or if you keep rationalizing,
the decision is probably unethical.

DO POWER, POLITICS, AND ETIQUETTE APPLY GLOBALLY?

If you said no, you are correct. Based on cultural values and history, *power* is perceived
and exercised differently around the globe. A method of understanding global differences
is called *power distance*.[63] Power distance centers on the extent to which employees feel
comfortable interacting across hierarchical levels; it reflects expectations of centralized or
decentralized decision making. In high power distance, employees believe management
should have the power and make the decisions, whereas in low power distance, employees
want power and want to be involved with management in decision making.

In high power distance cultures (for example, in Mexico, Venezuela, the Philippines,
Yugoslavia, and France), using strong power and politics is acceptable, because leaders are
expected to behave differently from people in low ranks, and differences in rank are more
apparent. In low power distance cultures (for example, in the United States, Ireland, Australia,
New Zealand, Denmark, Israel, and the Netherlands), using strong power and politics is not
acceptable, because power is expected to be shared with employees through empowerment.[64]
In low power distance cultures, people are less comfortable with differences in power and
there is less emphasis on social class distinction and hierarchical rank. Thus, when U.S. companies try to empower their business units in high power distance cultures, they need to integrate and change the culture within the business unit slowly to be effective.

Power and politics in the *e-organization* are different from those in traditional organizations. E-orgs lend themselves to less power distances, since direct observation of

employees by managers is less frequent and is from a distance. Visible political behavior, such as having face-to-face meetings and going to places to meet influential managers, is often not easy for e-org employees. E-org politics uses more online cyberschmoozing over the electronic grapevine. You can supplement traditional face-to-face politics by using Internet chat rooms and message boards to open opportunities to meet and talk with people who can help you with your job and career advancement. E-mail networking also can be effective.[65]

Like business ethics, proper business *etiquette* in one culture may not be appropriate in another. For example, pointing with the index finger is considered rude in most Asian and Middle Eastern countries. Be aware of possible differences in etiquette, such as gift giving, dining, and drinking alcoholic beverages, as well as when and where to discuss business. Other differences in business etiquette have been presented in other chapter discussions on global differences.

Before we bring this chapter to a close, complete Self-Assessment Exercise 10–3 to determine how your personality affects your use of power and politics.

Self-Assessment
Exercise 10–3

Your Personality and Power and Politics

If you have a high *surgency* personality, you most likely have a high need for power. Watch your use of coercive power and the use of the autocratic leadership style with subordinates. The way to get power is through politics, so you may be inclined to use political behavior; just make sure you use ethical politics to get what you want. Although you may not be too concerned with what others think of you, watch your use of proper etiquette so that you don't offend others. Being liked does help you gain power. You also need the help of peers and members of other departments, so create win–win situations for all parties. Don't expect your boss to agree with all your ideas. Remember that your relationship with your boss is critical to your advancement. So if you want to advance, do what your boss wants, the way the boss wants it done, no matter how much you disagree.

If you have a high *agreeableness* personality, you most likely have a high need for affiliation. You most likely have a low need for power. However, you may be political to gain relationships. Being concerned about what others think of you, you may be good at etiquette and have good relations with your boss, peers, and others. Watch out for others using power to take advantage of you; be assertive.

If you have a high *conscientious* personality, you most likely have a high need for achievement. You may not care for politics, but you most likely try to gain power to achieve your specific objectives. You most likely use good, rational persuasion; however, you may not be good at reading people and may need to develop this skill to help you get what you want. To maintain a good relationship with your boss, you may need to make sure what you want to accomplish is what your boss wants you to accomplish. Watch the tendency to seek individual objectives unrelated to those of your peers and others if you want to advance.

How high your *adjustment* is affects how you use power and politics. People low on adjustment (and some can fake it) generally don't use power and politics ethically; they seek to get what they want and to take advantage of others. If you are not high on adjustment personality traits, you may want to stop being self-centered and work on creating win–win situations. You will be surprised at how much more you can get when you give. There is a lot of truth in the adage, "The more you give, the more you receive." Have you ever noticed that the givers are usually happier than the takers? Have you ever done something for someone figuring there is nothing in it for you, only to find out that you got more than you expected?

Your *openness to experience* will have a direct affect on how much power you have. To maintain expert power, you have to keep up with the latest developments in your field. Be the first to get the latest training; volunteer for assignments. Read the appropriate journals to keep up in your field. Go to trade or professional meetings, and network with others outside your organization to stay current. Be a part of the learning organization's quest for continual improvement; try to bring new developments into your department or organization.

**Self-Assessment
Exercise 10–3 (*continued*)**

Action plan: Based on your personality, what specific things will you do to improve your power, ethical political skills (vertical and horizontal), and etiquette?

_____

_____

_____

_____

Videos

Manager's Hot Seat and Behavior Model Videos are available for this chapter.

Online Learning Center Resources

Go to the Internet (http://mhhe.com/lussier8e) where you will find a broad array of resources to help maximize your learning.

*   Review the vocabulary.
*   Try a quiz.

R E V I E W

The chapter review is organized to help you master the 8 learning outcomes for Chapter 10. First provide your own response to each learning outcome, and then check the summary provided to see how well you understand the material. Next, identify the final statement in each section as either true or false (T/F). Correct each false statement. Answers are given at the end of the chapter.

1. **State how power, politics, and ethics affect behavior, human relations, and performance.**

    The use of power and politics are needed in organizations to perform successfully to meet goals. People who use abusive power and politics tend to use unethical behavior and hurt human relations and performance. In the long run, people using ethical power and political behavior with integrity have more positive human relations and outperform people who use unethical behavior.

    Power is the ability to influence others to do something they would not otherwise do, and politics is the process of gaining and using power. T F

2. **Describe seven bases of power.**

    The seven bases of power are: (1) *coercive power,* which is based on threats and/or punishment to influence compliance; (2) *connection power,* which is based on relationships with influential people; (3) *reward power,* which is based on the ability to influence others with something of value to them; (4) *legitimate power,* which is based on position power; (5) *referent power,* which is based on personal power; (6) *information power,* which is based on information desired by others; and (7) *expert power,* which is based on skill and knowledge.

    The bases of position power include coercive, connection, reward, and legitimate; whereas referent, information, and expert power are bases of human relations power. T F

3. **List techniques to increase your power bases.**

    Techniques to increase your power bases include: (1) To have *coercive power,* you need to gain and maintain the ability to hire, discipline, and fire employees. (2) To increase your *connection power,* you need to expand your network of contacts with important managers who have power and to get in with the "in crowd." (3) *Reward power* can be gained by evaluating employees' performance and determining their raises and promotions. Using praise can help increase your power. (4) *Legitimate power* can be increased by letting people know the power you do possess, and by working at gaining people's perception that you do have power. (5) To gain *referent power,* you need to develop your relationships with others. Show a sincere interest in others. (6) To increase *information power,* have information flow through you. Know what is going on in the organization. Provide services and information to other departments. Serve on committees; it gives you both information and a chance to increase connection power. (7) To increase your *expert power,* take all the training and educational programs your organization provides. Stay away from routine tasks, in favor of more complex, hard-to-evaluate tasks.

People don't actually have to use power to influence others. T F

4. Describe five influencing tactics.

Five influencing tactics include: (1) ingratiation, giving praise; (2) rational persuasion, giving logical arguments with factual evidence; (3) inspirational appeal, arousing follower enthusiasm; (4) personal appeal, focusing on loyalty and friendship; and (5) legitimization, using organizational authority.

Rational persuasion is the most effective influencing tactic. T F

5. Discuss the necessity of organizational politics and three political behaviors.

In our economy, money is the medium of exchange; in an organization, politics is the medium of exchange. Political behavior is used to develop relationships that are necessary to get your job done. Three political behaviors that people use include: (1) networking, the process of developing relationship alliances with key people for the purpose of politicking; (2) reciprocity, which involves creating obligations and debts, developing alliances, and using them to accomplish objectives; and (3) coalition building, which involves creating a network of alliances to help you achieve a specific objective.

Power and politics are interrelated, as they are often used together. T F

6. State the difference between ethical and unethical politics.

Ethical politics benefits both the individual and the organization, whereas unethical politics benefits the individual and hurts the organization. Unethical politics also includes behavior that helps the organization, but hurts the individual and other stakeholders.

A way of classifying behavior is Type A and Type B ethics. T F

7. Identify techniques to develop effective human relations with superiors, subordinates, peers, and members of other departments.

To develop effective human relations with superiors, meet the common expectations of your boss: be loyal, be cooperative, use initiative, keep your boss informed, and be open to criticism. With subordinates, be friendly, but remember that you cannot be real friends with employees. Use an open-door policy. With peers, be cooperative while competing with them and help them to do an effective job. In your relations with other departments, be cooperative, and follow the requirements they set.

Your relations with your boss and peers are called vertical politics, and your relations with subordinates and other departments are called horizontal politics. T F

Learning Outcome

8. Define the following 15 key terms.

8. Define the following 15 key terms.

Select one or more methods: (1) fill in the missing key terms from memory; (2) match the key terms from the end of the review with their definitions below; and/or (3) copy the key terms in order from the key terms at the beginning of the chapter.

_____ is a person's ability to influence others to do something they would not otherwise do.

The seven bases of power are:

_____, based on threats and/or punishment to influence compliance.

_____, based on the user's relationship with influential people.

_____, based on the user's ability to influence others with something of value to them.

_____, based on the user's position power.

_____, based on the user's personal power.

_____, based on the user's information being desired by others.

_____, based on the user's skill and knowledge.

_____, the process of gaining and using power, is an important part of meeting organizational objectives.

_____ involves creating obligations and debts, developing alliances, and using them to accomplish objectives.

_____ refers to behavior that is considered wrong by authorities, yet is not accepted by others as being unethical.

_____ refers to behavior that is considered wrong by authorities and the individual, yet is conducted anyway.

_____ includes behavior that benefits both the individual and the organization.

_____ includes behavior that benefits the individual and hurts the organization.

A(n) _____ is the practice of being available to employees.

K E Y   T E R M S

coercive power   350
connection power   350
ethical politics   360
expert power   351
information power   351

legitimate power   351
open-door policy   369
politics   357
power   349
reciprocity   358

referent power   351
reward power   350
Type I ethics   359
Type II ethics   359
unethical politics   360

C O M M U N I C A T I O N   S K I L L S

The following critical thinking questions can be used for class discussion and/or as written assignments to develop communication skills. Be sure to give complete explanations for all questions.

1. Some people say that power and politics can't be used ethically. Do you agree?

2. Do you agree with the saying, "It's not what you know, it's who you know that is important"? Is it ethical to use connection power to get jobs and other things?

3. When someone tries to influence you, which influencing tactic works best and why? Why doesn't this same tactic work best for everyone?

4. How would you assess your political skill at using networking, reciprocity, and coalition building to help you get what you want? What can you do to improve?

5. Review the list of etiquette tips. Which three tips that you don't use often now might help you in the future? How will you change your etiquette?

6. Describe your relationship with your current or past boss. Did you meet the five common expectations of bosses? How can you improve your relationship with your current and/or future boss?

7. Describe your relationship with your current peers and members from other departments. How do you cooperate with them, compete with them, and criticize them? How can you improve your relationship with your current peers and members of other departments?

Chris Walker: Department of Business

Chris Walker is a tenured professor of business at a small teaching college in the Midwest. The Department of Business (DB) has nine faculty members; it is one of 10 departments in the School of Arts and Sciences (SAS). The business department chair is Judi Jackson, who is in her first year as chair. Six faculty members, including Chris, have been in the department for longer than Judi. She likes to have policies so that faculty members have guides for their behavior. On the collegewide level, there is no policy about the job of graduate assistants. Judi asked the dean of the SAS what the policy was. The dean stated that there is no policy, and he had spoken to the vice president for academic affairs. The vice president and the dean suggested letting the individual departments develop their own policy regarding what graduate assistants can and cannot do. So Judi put "use of graduate assistants" on the department meeting agenda.

During the DB meeting, Judi asked for members' views on what graduate assistants should and should not be allowed to do. Judi was hoping that the department would come to a consensus on a policy. Chris Walker was the only faculty member who was using graduate assistants to grade exams. All but one of the other faculty members spoke out against the use of having graduate assistants grade exams. Other faculty members believed it was the job of the professor to grade the exams. Chris made a few statements in hopes of not having to correct his own exams. He stated that his exams were objective; thus, because there was a correct answer for each item on the exams, it was not necessary for him to personally correct the exams. He also pointed out that across the campus, and across the country, other faculty members were using graduate assistants to teach entire courses and to correct subjective papers and exams. Chris stated that he did not think it would be fair to tell him that he could not use graduate assistants to grade objective exams when others could do so. He also stated that the department did not need to have a policy, and requested that the department not set a policy. However, Judi stated that she wanted a policy. He held a single minority view during the meeting. However, after the meeting, one other member of the department, Ted Brown, who had said nothing during the meeting, told Chris that he agreed that it was not fair to deny him the use of a graduate assistant.

There was no department consensus, as Judi hoped there would be. Judi said that she would draft a department policy, which would be discussed at a future DB meeting. The next day, Chris sent a memo to department members asking if it was ethical and legal to deny him the use of the same resources as others across the campus. He also stated that if the department set a policy stating that he could no longer use graduate assistants to correct objective exams, he would appeal the policy decision to the dean, the vice president, and the president.

Go to the Internet: This case actually did happen. However, the names have been changed for confidentiality. Thus, you cannot go to the college Web site where the case really happened. Therefore, go to your own college Web site and get information that you did not know about your college.

Support your answer to the following questions with specific information from the case and text, or with other information you get from the Web or other sources.

1. What source of power does Judi have, and what type of power is she using during the meeting?

2. (a) What source of power does Chris have, and what type of power is he using during the meeting? (b) Is the memo a wise political move for Chris? What may be gained/ lost by sending it?

3. What would you do if you were Judi? (a) Would you talk to the dean, letting him know that Chris said he would appeal the policy decision? (b) Which political behavior would that discussion represent? (c) Would you draft a policy directly stating that graduate assistants cannot be used to grade objective exams? (d) Would your answer to (c) be influenced by your answer to (a)?

4. If you were Chris, (a) knowing you had no verbal supporters during the meeting, would you have continued to defend your position or agreed to stop using a graduate assistant? (b) What do you think of Chris's sending the memo? (c) As a tenured full professor, Chris is secure in his job. Would your answer change if you had not received tenure or promotion to the top rank?

5. If you were Chris, and Judi drafted a policy and department members agreed with it, what would you do? (a) Would you appeal the decision to the dean? (b) Again, would your answer change if you had not received tenure or promotion to the top rank?

6. If you were the dean of the SAS, knowing that the vice president does not want to set a collegewide policy, and Chris appealed to you, what would you do? Would you develop a schoolwide policy for the SAS?

7. At what level (collegewide, by schools, or by departments within each school) should a graduate assistant policy be set?

8. (a) Should Ted Brown have spoken up in defense of Chris during the meeting? (b) If you were Ted, would you have taken Chris's side against the seven other members? (c) Would your answer change if you were or were not friends with Chris, and if you were or were not a tenured full professor?

Cumulative Questions

9. What is the role of perception (Chapter 2) and attitudes and values (Chapter 3) in this case?

10. What type of communications (Chapters 5 and 6) were used in this case? What was the major barrier to communications?

11. Which conflict management style (Chapter 7) did Judi and Chris use in setting the policy? Which conflict management style would you have used if you were in Chris's situation?

12. Which situational supervisory business style (Chapter 8) was Judi using to set the policy?

13. Which motivation theory (Chapter 9) was Chris using to defend his position to use graduate assistants?

OBJECTIVE CASE   ## Politicking

Karen Whitmore is going to be promoted in two months. She will be replaced by one of her subordinates, Jim Green or Lisa Fesco. Both Jim and Lisa know they are competing for the promotion. Their years of experience and quality and quantity of work are about the same. Below is some of the political behavior each used to help get the promotion.

Lisa has been going to night classes and company training programs in management to prepare herself for the promotion. Lisa is very upbeat; she goes out of her way to be nice to people and compliment them. She gets along well with everyone. Knowing that Karen was an officer in a local businesswomen's networking organization, Lisa joined the club six months ago and now serves on a committee. At work Lisa talks regularly to Karen about the women's organization. Lisa makes an effort to know what is going on in the organization. One thing Karen doesn't like about Lisa is the fact that when she points out Lisa's errors, Lisa always has an answer for everything.

Jim is good at sports and has been playing golf and tennis with upper-level managers for over a year now. In the department, especially with Karen, Jim refers to conversations with managers all the time. When Jim does something for someone, he expects that person to do a favor in return. Jim really wants this promotion, but he fears that with more women being promoted to management positions, Lisa will get the job just because she is a woman.

To increase his chances of getting the job, Jim stayed late and made a few changes—errors—in the report Lisa was working on. Jim sees nothing wrong with making the changes to get ahead. When Lisa passed in the report, without checking prior work, Karen found the errors. The one thing Karen doesn't like about Jim is the fact that, on occasion, she has to tell him what to do before he acts.

Answer the following questions. Then in the space between the questions, state why you selected that answer.

_____ 1. We know that Karen has _____ power.

a. position   *b.* personal

_____ 2. To be promoted, Lisa is stressing _____ power. Refer to the opening statement about Lisa.

a. coercive   *c.* reward   *e.* referent   *g.* expert
b. connection   *d.* legitimate   *f.* information

_____ 3. To be promoted, Jim is stressing _____ power. Refer to the opening statement about Jim.

a. coercive   *c.* reward   *e.* referent   *g.* expert
b. connection   *d.* legitimate   *f.* information

_____ 4. _____ appears to use reciprocity the most.

a. Lisa   *b.* Jim

_____ 5. Lisa _____ conducted unethical political behavior.

a. has   *b.* has not

_____ 6. Jim _____ conducted unethical political behavior.

a. has   *b.* has not

_____ 7. Jim has committed _____ behavior in changing the report.

a. Type I   *b.* Type II

_____ 8. Who was *not* affected by Jim's changing the report?

a. supervisors   *c.* peers   *e.* other departments
b. subordinates   *d.* Karen's department *f.* the organization

_____ 9. Lisa does not meet Karen's expectation of:

a. loyalty   *c.* initiative   *e.* openness to criticism
b. cooperation   *d.* information

_____ 10. Jim does not meet Karen's expectation of:

a. loyalty   *c.* initiative   *e.* openness to criticism
b. cooperation   *d.* information

11. In Lisa's situation, she suspects Jim made the changes in the report, but she has no proof. What would you do?

12. In Karen's situation, she suspects Jim made the changes in the report, but she has no proof. What would you do?

Note: Meetings between Lisa and Jim, Karen and Jim, or all three may be role-played in class.

Who Has the Power?
In-Class Exercise
(Group)

Note: This exercise is designed for permanent groups that have worked together at least twice.

Objective: To better understand power and how people gain power.

AACSB: The primary AACSB learning standard skills developed through this exercise are reflective thinking and leadership.

Preparation: You should have read and understood the text chapter.

Experience: Your group will discuss power within the group.

Procedure 1
(5–10 minutes)

Permanent teams get together and decide which member has the most power at this time (greatest ability to influence group members' behavior). Power can change with time. Before discussion, all members select the member they believe has the most power. You may select yourself. Write the most powerful person's name here: _____.
After everyone has made their selection, each member should state who was selected and explain why. Record the names of those selected below.

Procedure 2
(7–12 minutes)

Come to an agreement on the one person with the most power. Write the group's choice here: _____.

Was there a struggle for power?

Why is this person the most powerful in the group? To help you answer this question, as a group, answer the following questions about your most powerful person:

1. Which of the nine human relations guidelines (discussed in Chapter 1) does he or she follow: (1) be optimistic, (2) be positive, (3) be genuinely interested in other people, (4) smile and develop a sense of humor, (5) call people by name, (6) listen to people, (7) help others, (8) think before you act, and (9) create win–win situations?

2. How does this person project a positive image? What type of image does his or her appearance project? What nonverbal communication does this person project that sends a positive image? What behavior does this person use that gains him or her power?

3. What is the primary source of this person's power (position, personal)?

4. What is the primary base for this person's power in the group (coercive, connection, reward, legitimate, referent, information, expert)?

5. Which political behaviors does this person use (gets along with everyone, makes people feel important and compliments them, compromises and avoids telling people they are wrong)?

6. Does this person use ethical or unethical politics?

7. Does this person cooperate with, compete with, or criticize group members?

   Overall, why is this person the most powerful? (Agree and write the reason below.) Share the feeling you experienced doing this exercise. How did you feel about not being, or being, selected as the most powerful group member? Who wanted power and who didn't? Is it wrong or bad to want and seek power?

Optional:

1. A spokesperson from each group tells the class which member was selected as the most powerful, and the overall reason why the person is considered to be the most powerful.

2. A spokesperson from each group does not tell the class which member was selected as the most powerful, but does state the overall reason why the person is considered to be the most powerful.

Conclusion: The instructor leads a class discussion and/or makes concluding remarks.

Application (2–4 minutes):   What did I learn from this exercise? How will I use this knowledge in the future?

Sharing: Volunteers give their answers to the application section.

Influencing Tactics

Preparation
(Individual and Group)

Below are three situations. For each situation, select the most appropriate influencing tactic(s) to use. Write the tactics on the lines following the situations. At this time, don't write out how you would behave (what you would say and do).

1. You are doing a college internship, which is going well. You would like to become a full-time employee a few weeks after you graduate.

Which influencing tactic(s) would you use?

_____

Who would you try to influence? How would you do so (behavior)?

_____

_____

2. You have been working for six months. As you are approaching the elevator, you see a powerful person, one who could potentially help you advance in your career, waiting for the elevator. You have never met her, but you do know that her committee has recently completed a new five-year strategic plan for the company and that she plays

tennis and is active in the same religious organization as you. Although you have only a couple of minutes, you decide to try to develop a connection.

Which influencing tactic(s) would you use?

_____

How would you strike up a conversation? What topic(s) would you raise?

_____

_____

3. You are the manager of the production department. Some of the sales staff has been scheduling delivery dates for your product that your department can't meet. Customers are blaming you for late delivery. This situation is not good for the company, so you decide to talk to the sales staff manager about it over lunch.

Which influencing tactic(s) would you use?

_____

How would you handle the situation (behavior)?

_____

_____

Select one situation that seems real to you, that is, one you can imagine yourself in. Or write in a real-life situation that you can quickly explain to a small group. Now, briefly write out the behavior (what you would do and say) that you would use in the situation to influence the person to do what you want.

Situation # _____ or my situation:

_____

_____

Influencing tactic(s) to use:

_____

Behavior:

_____

_____

_____

_____

_____

In-Class Exercise

Objective: To develop your persuasion skills by using influencing tactics.

AACSB: The primary AACSB learning standard skills developed through this exercise are analytic skills, leadership, and strategic management.

Preparation: You should understand the five influencing tactics and have completed the preparation.

Experience: You will discuss which influencing tactics are most appropriate for the preparation situations. You may also be given the opportunity to role-play how you would handle the one situation you selected; you will also play the role of the person to be influenced and the observer.

SB 10–2
Procedure 1
(10–20 minutes)

Break up into groups of three, with one or two groups of two if needed. Try not to have in the group two members that selected the same situation; use people who selected their own situation. First, try to agree quickly on which influencing tactics are most appropriate in each situation. Select a spokesperson to give group answers to the class. In preparation for role playing, have each person state the behavior to handle the situation selected. The others give feedback to improve how to handle the situation—by avoiding, changing, and/or adding to the behavior (for example, "I would not say _____; I'd say _____; I'd add _____ to what you have now).

Procedure 2
(5–10 minutes)

SB 10−3
Preparation
(1–2 minutes)

One situation at a time, each group spokesperson tells the class which influencing styles it would use, followed by brief remarks from the instructor. The instructor may also ask people who selected their own situation to tell the class the situation.

During the three role plays, you will be the influencer, influencee, and observer. In preparation, determine who will be the first to role-play the selected situation, who will play the role of the person being influenced, and who will be the observer. Do the same for each of the other two role plays, giving each person a chance to play all three roles.

Role play 1
(7–15 minutes)

The influencer role-plays influencing the influencee while the observer takes notes on what was done well and how the influencing could be improved. After the role play, both the influencee and observer give the influencer feedback for future improvement. Do not start the next role play until told to do so.

Role play 2
(7–15 minutes)

The second influencer role-plays influencing the influencee while the observer takes notes on what was done well and how the influencing could be improved. After the role play, both the influencee and observer give the influencer feedback for future improvement. Do not start the next role play until told to do so.

Role play 3
(7–15 minutes)

The third influencer role-plays influencing the influencee while the observer takes notes on what was done well and how the influencing could be improved. After the role play, both the influencee and observer give the influencer feedback for future improvement.

Conclusion: The instructor may lead a class discussion and/or make concluding remarks.

Application (2–4 minutes):   What did I learn from this exercise? How will I use this knowledge in the future?

Sharing: Volunteers give their answers to the application section.

A N S W E R S   T O   T R U E / F A L S E   Q U E S T I O N S

1. T.
2. F. "Human relations" is not a source of power—personal power is the power source.
3. T.
4. F. There is no most effective influencing tactic; it depends on the situation.
5. T.
6. F. A way of classifying behavior is Type I and Type II ethics. Recall that Type A and B are personality types (Chapter 2).
7. F. Relations with bosses and subordinates are called vertical politics; relations with peers and others are called horizontal politics.

CHAPTER 11

Networking and Negotiating

LEARNING OUTCOMES

After completing this chapter, you should be able to:

1. List and explain the steps in the networking process.

2. Describe what a one-minute self-sell is and what it contains.

3. Briefly describe how to conduct a networking interview.

4. List and explain the steps in the negotiating process.

5. Briefly describe how to plan for negotiations.

6. Briefly describe how to bargain.

7. Explain the influencing process.

8. Define the following 13 key terms (in order of appearance in the chapter):

networking	distributive bargaining
networks	integrative bargaining
networking process	negotiating process
one-minute self-sell	negotiating planning
networking interview process	bargaining
coalition	influencing process
negotiating	

Toyota started as a family business, and the Toyoda family still has power over the company. Hiroski Okuda was the first nonfamily member in over 30 years to head Toyota as president. Toyota had become lethargic and overly bureaucratic and had lost market share in Japan to both Mitsubishi and

Honda. Hiroski was not the typical Japanese president, that is, one who would make changes slowly and with consensus.

President Hiroski Okuda moved quickly and powerfully to change Toyota, going against Japanese cultural traditions to embrace a more global (primarily American) perspective of managing. Even though lifetime employment is common in Japan, Hiroski replaced almost one-third of the highest-ranking executives. He changed the long-standing Japanese promotion system based on seniority by adding performance as a factor. Some outstanding performers moved up several management levels at one time—a practice unheard of in the history of Toyota.

Hiroski Okuda turned Toyota around; in a few short years, the company better understood the Japanese customer, and market share and sales were growing. Toyota plans to take GM's number one position as the world's leading auto maker. However, it has been speculated that although Hiroski did a great job, at the same time he offended Toyoda family members. Thus, he was promoted to chairman of the board to keep him out of day-to-day management and then replaced as chairman by Fujio Cho.[1] For more information about Toyota and to update the information provided, visit Toyota's Web site at www.toyota.com.

HOW NETWORKING AND NEGOTIATING AFFECT BEHAVIOR, HUMAN RELATIONS, AND PERFORMANCE

Recall that *networking* is a form of political behavior. People who are good at networking tend to use outgoing, extroverted behavior and have better human relations than those who are not proficient at networking.[2] You can't be an expert at everything and perform at high levels alone; you need some help and you need to help others through networking reciprocity (Chapter 10).[3] Getting others to implement innovation takes networking.[4] Interpersonal skills are part of initiating, building, and maintaining relationships through networking.[5] Recall that learning organization performance is based on knowledge sharing; it is through networking effort that you gain access to new knowledge.[6] Your networking relationships will affect your learning and integration within an organization.[7]

Negotiation is about coming to an agreement to do something, such as reaching an agreement on compensation with an employer who is offering you a job. Your ability to negotiate will affect your compensation throughout your professional career.[8] People who are good at negotiating tend to use influencing tactics successfully and develop good human relations.[9] Have you ever noticed that some people consistently get what they want and others don't? A big part of day-to-day success is negotiation skills.[10] There is often a big difference in the performance of good negotiators and poor negotiators.[11] Successful organizations, such as Wal-Mart, use their strong bargaining power to keep costs and prices down and profits high.

WORK APPLICATIONS

1. Explain how networking and/or negotiating have affected behavior, human relations, and performance where you work or have worked.

NETWORKING

Before we get into the details of networking, complete Self-Assessment Exercise 11–1 to determine your networking skill.

Self-Assessment
Exercise 11–1

Your Networking Skill

Identify each of the 16 statements according to how accurately they describe your behavior. Place the number (1 to 5) on the line before each statement.

Describes me   Does not describe me

5	4	3	2	1

_____ 1. When I take on a task (a new project, a career move, a major purchase), I seek help from people I know and from new contacts.

_____ 2. I view networking as a way to create win–win situations.

_____ 3. I like to meet new people; I can easily strike up a conversation with people I don't know.

_____ 4. I can quickly state two or three of my most important accomplishments.

_____ 5. When I contact businesspeople who can help me (such as with career information), I have goals for the communication.

_____ 6. When I contact businesspeople who can help me, I have a planned, short opening statement.

_____ 7. When I contact businesspeople who can help me, I praise their accomplishments.

_____ 8. When I contact people who can help me, I have a set of questions to ask.

_____ 9. I know contact information for at least 100 people who can potentially help me.

_____ 10. I have a file or database with contact information of people who can help me in my career, and I keep it updated and continue to add new names.

_____ 11. During communications with people who can help me, I ask them for names of others I can contact for more information.

_____ 12. When seeking help from others, I ask how I might help them.

_____ 13. When people help me, I thank them at the time and for big favors, I write a follow-up thank-you note.

_____ 14. I keep in touch with people who have helped or can potentially help me in my career at least once a year, and I update them on my career progress.

_____ 15. I have regular communications with people in my industry who work for different organizations, such as members of trade or professional organizations.

_____ 16. I attend trade, professional, and career meetings to maintain relationships and to make new contacts.

Add up your score and place it here _____. Then on the continuum below, mark the point that represents your score.

Effective networking   80- - -70- - -60- - -50- - -40- - -30- - -20- - -10   Ineffective networking

If you are a full-time student, you may not score high on networking effectiveness, but that's OK. You can develop networking skills by following the steps and guidelines in this chapter.

Networking is not about asking everyone you know for help.[12] How would you react if someone directly said, "I sell cars and I have a good deal for you," or "Can you give me a job?" Networking implies helping others and giving advice, industry information, contacts, or assistance.[13] **Networking** *is the ongoing process of building interconnected relationships for the purpose of politicking and socializing.* Networking is about building professional relationships and friendships through effective communications.[14] **Networks** *are clusters of people joined by a variety of links,*[15] as illustrated in Exhibit 11.1. Notice that the lines are the links, or the interconnected relationships, between people in the networks. Your primary connections give you access to their networks, which are secondary connections for you.[16] Write in some names of people who can help you in your career.

EXHIBIT 11.1 |
Networks

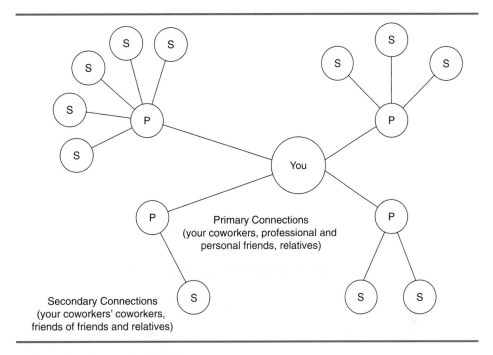

Networking is about marketing yourself and thinking of yourself as the CEO of You, Inc.; in other words, *you* are responsible for your career and the exposure of your talents and skills.[17] You will find that a secondary connection (the friend of a friend) is often where you will get the help you need. Whenever you start something—working on a new project, planning a career move, buying a car or a house—use networking.

The Why and Reality of Networking

Why should you network? Consider this statement: It's not what you know, it's who you know, that's important.[18] Is the statement true? If it is, is it fair? Let's begin to find answers to these questions by stating some of the objectives of networking.

Networking Objectives   Here are some of the many reasons to develop your networking skills:

- *To get a job or a better position.* Network to get feedback on your resume and career preparation as well as the hiring patterns and growth potential and opportunities in your field, and to learn about posted job openings that you haven't heard of and about jobs that have not been posted or advertised. Many jobs being filled today are not posted, and many that are posted are unofficially filled before they are posted. Without networking, you will never know about these job opportunities.[19] If you have a job and want a better position, do not quit your current job until you find a new one; it is easier to get a job when you already have one.

- *To perform better at your current job.* Network to help you do your job, especially new assignments.[20] Don't reinvent the wheel; find someone who has "been there and done that" for help. Learn more about your current organization and its culture, and gain support and recognition from colleagues with networking.[21] Some jobs, such as sales, require networking to acquire new business.

- *To advance within an organization.* Networking is how you develop connection power. Network to get to know the power players and their management styles, to gain support and recognition from higher-level managers, and to find a mentor to help you advance.[22] You also need to network with people in other departments or units, not just within your department, to know what is going on throughout the firm and to find out about job openings.

- *To stay current in your field.* Network through trade and professional organization meetings with people outside your organization to understand the latest developments in your field.[23] Give and collect business cards at meetings and conferences and everywhere you go. If your firm is not on the cutting edge, you may be able to bring innovations to your organization through expert power.

- *To maintain mobility.* If you think that once you have a job, you don't have to network or stay current in your field, you may be in for a big surprise. Thousands of Americans have been laid off in recent years. If you got laid off today, what would you do? People without a network take much longer to get another job than do those who maintain networks, and the longer it takes to get another job, the harder it is to get one. Networking, like working out, must be continued or you lose what you have already gained. Think of networking as career insurance—you need it.

- *To develop relationships.* We all want to have both professional and personal friends. Networking is especially important if you take a job in a new location.

WORK APPLICATIONS

2. Explain how you have used or will use networking to help your career.

It's Not What You Know, It's Who You Know, That's Important   To a large extent, this statement is true, but there are exceptions. Here is a general job-related illustration. Sending out resumes and posting them on the Web (Monster.com, Headhunter.net, CareerBuilder.com, and HotJobs.com) are not how most people are getting jobs today. Of the many ways to secure a job, networking is by far the most successful way to discover employment opportunities. According to the U.S. Department of Labor, two-thirds of all jobs are located through word of mouth, informal referrals, relatives, friends, and acquaintances. Networking results in more job opportunities than all the other job search methods combined.[24] However, many people looking for jobs don't use networking to find a job.

Fairness is often perceived differently depending on who benefits. If you get a job through networking, is that fair? Being fair is really not the issue—reality is. Networking is really about human nature in action. As you know, people are subjective, at times irrational, and sometimes unfair. The reason networking is so powerful and useful is because people want to help others and to be helped by others.[25] So networking is about reciprocity.[26] You have two choices: complain about how unfair networking is, or develop your networking skills.

Learning Outcome

1. List and explain the steps in the networking process.

When you need any type of help, do you have a network of people ready to turn to or do you know how to develop a network to assist you? Networking sounds easy and we tend to think it should come naturally. However, the reality is that networking is a learned skill that just about everyone struggles with at some time or another. The next five subsections provide a how-to network process that will enhance your career development.[27] The networking process is summarized in Exhibit 11.2. The **networking process** *includes these tasks: (1) perform a self-assessment and set objectives, (2) create a one-minute self-sell, (3) develop a network, (4) conduct networking interviews, and (5) maintain the network.*

Although the same networking process applies to broad career development, as discussed under networking objectives, we'll focus more on the job search.

EXHIBIT 11.2 | The Networking Process

1. Perform a self-assessment and set objectives.
2. Create a one-minute self-sell.
3. Develop a network.
4. Conduct networking interviews.
5. Maintain the network.

Perform a Self-Assessment and Set Objectives

The task of self-assessment can help clarify your skills, competencies, and knowledge. Self-assessment can also give you insight into your transferable skills and the criteria that are important to you in a new job. Listing the criteria that are most important to you in a new job and prioritizing them can help clarify your ideal next position. If you completed Career Planning Skill-Building Exercise 4–2, you have done a self-assessment. If not, go back to Chapter 4 and do so now.

Accomplishments   After completing a self-assessment, you are ready to translate your talents into accomplishments. The results you achieved in your jobs and/or college are the best evidence of your skills. Your future employer knows that your past behavior predicts your future behavior and that if you achieved results in the past, you will likely produce similar results again. Accomplishments are what set you apart and provide evidence of your skills and abilities. To be an effective networker, you must articulate what you have accomplished in your past in a way that is clear, concise, and compelling. Write down your accomplishments (at least two or three), and include them in your resume.[28] Whether you are looking for a job or not, you should always have an updated resume handy.

Tying Your Accomplishments to the Job Interview   You want to be sure to state those accomplishments that are based on your skills during the job interview. Many interviews begin with a broad question such as, "Tell me about yourself." Oftentimes candidates do not reveal anything compelling. The second step after listing key results you achieved is to elaborate on the problem that was solved or the opportunity that was taken and how you solved or achieved it using your skills. These simple results statements should also appear in your resume. Thus, if you are asked a broad general question, such as, "Tell me about yourself," you can use the accomplishment statements in your resume as your answer.

Set Networking Objectives   After your self-assessment that focuses on your accomplishments, you need to clearly state your goal,[29] for example, to get a mentor; to determine the expertise, skills, and requirements needed for . . .; to get feedback on my resume and job and/or career preparation for a career move into . . .; to attain a job as . . .; and so on.

WORK APPLICATIONS

3. Write a networking objective.

Learning Outcome

2. Describe what a one-minute self-sell is and what it contains.

Create Your One-Minute Self-Sell

Based on your goal, your next step is to create a one-minute self-sell to help you accomplish your goal. The **one-minute self-sell** *is an opening statement used in networking that quickly summarizes your history and career plan and asks a question.* To take 60 seconds or less, your message must be concise, but it also needs to be clear and compelling. It gives the listener a sense of who you are and your background, identifies your career field and a key result you've achieved, plus provides the direction of your next job. It tells the listener what you plan to do next and why. It also stimulates conversation by asking your network for help in the area of support, coaching, contacts, knowledge of the industry, and the like.[30]

History   Start with a summary of the highlights of your career to date. Include your most recent career and/or school history and a description of the type of work or internship performed and/or the courses you have taken. Be sure to include the industry and type of organization.

Plans   Next, state the target career you are seeking, the industry you prefer, and a specific function or role. You can also mention names of organizations you are targeting as well as letting the acquaintance know why you are looking for work.

Question   Last, ask a question to encourage two-way communication. The question will vary depending on the contact person and your goal or the reason you are using the one-minute self-sell. Following are some sample questions:

- In what areas might there be opportunities for a person with my experience?
- In what other fields can I use these skills or this degree?
- In what other positions in your organization could my skills be used?
- How does my targeted future career sound to you? Is it a match with my education and skills?
- Do you know of any job openings in my field?

Write and Practice Your One-Minute Self-Sell   Write out your one-minute self-sell. Be sure to clearly separate your history, plans, and help question, and customize your question based on the contact you are talking to. Here's a sample self-sell: "Hello, my name is Will Smith. I am a senior at Springfield College, graduating in May with a major in marketing, and I have completed an internship in the marketing department at the Big Y supermarket. I'm seeking a job in sales in the food industry. Can you give me some ideas on the types of sales positions available in the food industry?" Practice delivering your self-sell with family and friends, and get feedback to improve it. The more opportunities you find to use this brief introduction, the easier it becomes. Skill-Building Exercise 11–1, Networking Skills, will give you the opportunity to develop and practice a one-minute self-sell.

WORK APPLICATIONS

4. Write a one-minute self-sell to achieve your networking objective from Work Application (3).

Develop Your Network

Begin with people you know—your primary contacts. Everyone can create a network list of about 200 people consisting of professional and personal contacts. Address books (paper and e-mail) and phone lists are written network listings that you need to continually update and develop. A simple way to start is to set up a separate e-mail for network contacts. Professional contacts include colleagues (past and present), trade and professional organizations, alumni associations, vendors, suppliers, managers, mentors, and many other professional acquaintances. On a personal level, your network includes family, neighbors, friends, religious groups, and personal service providers (doctor, dentist, insurance agent, stock broker, accountant, hairstylist, politician).

Ask your primary contacts for secondary contacts with whom you can network. Compose a list of your network contacts using the categories noted above, and continually update and add to your list with referrals from others.[31] You will discover that your network grows exponentially and can get you closer to the decision makers in a hiring position.

Next, expand your list to include people you don't know. Where should you go to develop your network? Anywhere people gather. Get more involved with professional associations;[32] many have special student memberships and some even have college chapters. If you really want to develop your career reputation, become a leader in your associations, not just a member. Volunteer to be on committees and boards, give presentations, and so on. Other places to go to network with people you don't know include the Chamber of Commerce; college alumni clubs and reunions; civic organizations (Rotary, Lions, Kiwanis, Elks, Moose); trade shows and career fairs; charity, community, and religious

EXHIBIT 11.3 | Job Search Network Form

Primary Contact: Bill Smith, fraternity brother

Secondary Contact: John Smith

Smith Brothers Corporation

225 Westwood Street

Anytown, WI 59025

643-986-1182

john_smith@smith.com

Contacts with person:

6/2/09 Bill called his dad from our fraternity house and I spoke with John and set up an appointment to meet him at his office on 6/5.

6/5/09 Talked for 20 minutes about Smith Brothers and career opportunities. No openings.

6/6/09 Mailed thank-you note for meeting and career info and advice, with copy of business card and resume.

6/18/09 Sent e-mail telling Smith I met with Peter Clark.

Secondary Contacts Received [Make separate page for each.]

Peter Clark, The Ranch Golf Club

Tom Broadhurst, Lobow Mercedes Dealer

Carol Shine, Consultant

---

groups (Goodwill, American Cancer Society, your local church); and social clubs (exercise, boating, golf, tennis). E-groups and chat rooms are available for all types of interests. Taking courses of any type exposes you to networking opportunities.

Another important point is to work at developing your ability to remember people by name. If you want to impress people you have never met or hardly know, call them by their name. Ask others who they are; then call them by name and introduce yourself with your one-minute sell. When you are introduced to people, call them by name two or three times during the conversation. If you think they can help you, don't stop with casual conversation; make an appointment at a later time for a phone conversation, personal meeting, coffee, or lunch. Get their business cards to add to your network list, and give them your card and/or resume when appropriate.

Computer software is available to help you. Using any word processor, database, or e-mail account, you can easily create a network system with one contact per page or file. See Exhibit 11.3 for an example. Of course, you can customize your system to suit your needs.

Conduct Networking Interviews

Based on your goals, use your network list of people to set up a networking interview to meet your objective. It may take many interviews to meet a goal, such as the goal of getting a job. An informational interview is a phone call or, preferably, a face-to-face meeting that you initiate to meet objectives, such as to gain information from a contact with hands-on experience in your field of interest. You are the interviewer (in contrast to your position in a job interview), so you need to be prepared with specific questions to ask the contact regarding your targeted career or industry based on your self-assessment and goal.[33]

Ask for a 15- to 20-Minute Meeting   Ask for a 15- to 20-minute meeting and many people will talk to you. Such a meeting can be most helpful when you have accessed someone within an organization you'd like to join or have a contact in an industry you are targeting. Having a face-to-face meeting of 15 to 20 minutes can have many benefits. Be sure not to linger beyond the time you have been offered, unless you are invited to stay. Leave a business card and resume so the person can contact you in case something comes up. If you are a full-time student or between jobs, you can have professional business cards made up for a relatively low cost. Leaving a card could make the difference between getting a job and losing out on the opportunity. Some college career centers will help you develop business cards and have them printed.

Learning Outcome

3.   Briefly describe how to conduct a networking interview.

The **networking interview process** *includes these steps: (1) establish rapport—praise and read the person, (2) deliver the one-minute self-sell, (3) ask prepared questions, (4) get additional contacts for your network, (5) ask your contacts how you might help them, and (6) follow up with a thank-you note and status report.* Let's discuss each step.

Establish Rapport—Praise and Read the Person   Provide a brief introduction (your name and title—which can be "student at . . . college"), and thank the contact for his or her time. Give the person a copy of your business card and resume. Clearly state the purpose of the meeting; be clear that you are not asking for a job. Don't start selling yourself; project an interest in the other person. Do some research,[34] and impress the person by stating an accomplishment, such as "I enjoyed your presentation at the CLMA meeting on . . ." As we discussed in Chapter 10, you should read the person and try to match his or her style.

Deliver Your One-Minute Self-Sell   Even if the person has already heard it, say it again. This enables you to quickly summarize your background and career direction and start your questions.

Ask Prepared Questions   Ask questions.[35] As stated above, do your homework before the meeting and compose a series of questions to ask during the interview. Your questions should vary depending on your objective, the contact, and how the person may be able to help you with your job search. Sample questions include:

- What do you think of my qualifications for this field?
- With your knowledge of the industry, what career opportunities do you see in the future?
- What advice do you have for me as I begin/advance in my career?
- If you were exploring this field, with whom would you talk?

During the interview, if the interviewee mentions anything that could hinder your search, ask how such obstacles could be overcome.

Get Additional Contacts for Your Network   The last question above is an example of how to ask for additional contacts. Always ask for names of others you should speak with.[36] Even if the contact was no help at all, you may get a lead that is helpful. Most people can give you three names, so if you are offered only one, ask for others. Add the new contact to your network list. Note that this is done in the job search network form in Exhibit 11.3. When contacting new people, be sure to refer to your primary network person's name as an introduction.

Ask Your Contacts How You Might Help Them   Offer a copy of a recent journal article, or any additional information that came up in your conversation. Remember, it's all about building relationships and reciprocity. So do favors for others.[37]

Follow up with a Thank-You Note and Status Report   Your contacts will remember you after a personal meeting, and the likelihood of getting a job lead increases. Keeping them posted on your job search progress as well as sending a thank-you note (or e-mail) after the meeting also solidifies the relationship.[38] By sending a thank-you note (or e-mail) with another business card and/or resume and following up with your progress, you are continuing the networking relationship and maintaining a contact for the future. Note that this is noted in the job search network form in Exhibit 11.3.

Be sure to assess the effectiveness of your networking meetings using the steps as your criteria. It is always helpful to create a log of calls, meetings, and contacts in order to maintain your network as it expands. See Exhibit 11.4 for a review of the networking interview steps.

EXHIBIT 11.4 | Networking Interview Process

Step 1: Establish rapport—praise and read the person.

Step 2: Deliver your one-minute self-sell.

Step 3: Ask prepared questions.

Step 4: Get additional contacts for your network.

Step 5: Ask your contacts how you might help them.

Step 6: Follow up with a thank-you note and status report.

Maintain Your Network

To keep your network informed of your career progress, send e-mails. If an individual was helpful in finding your new job, be sure to let that person know the outcome. Saying thank-you to those who have helped in your transition will encourage the business relationship; providing this information will increase the likelihood of getting help in the future. It is also a good idea to notify everyone in your network that you are in a new position and to provide contact information. Networking doesn't stop once you've made a career change. Make a personal commitment to continue networking in order to be in charge of your career development. Continue to update, correct, and add to your network list. Always thank others for their time.

Networking is also about helping others,[39] especially those in your network. As you have been helped, you should help others. Besides, you will be amazed at how helping others comes back to you. Try to contact everyone on your network list at least once a year (call, send an e-mail or a card), and find out what you can do for each person. Send congratulations on recent achievements.

Coalitions

Like networking, building coalitions is an influencing tactic of political behavior. Recall our discussion of coalitions in Chapter 10. A **coalition** *is a short-term network used to meet an objective.* Try to get powerful people on your side, and they can help you get other people in your coalition either directly (they can ask others) or indirectly (you can use their name as connection power to get others to join you).

When developing a coalition, don't simply ask for help. Follow the influencing tactics from Chapter 10. Read the person and create a win–win situation so that the person gains something by helping you get what you want.

In general, the Japanese conduct business using networking, and social skills are important. They will not transact business until a relationship has been established. This can be frustrating for Americans who want to rush right into conducting business, rather than start slowly and develop a relationship based on networking. Hiroski Okuda was good at networking within Toyota and with its family owners. If he hadn't been a good networker, he never would have been the first nonfamily member in over 30 years to head the company. It was through networking that Hiroski climbed the corporate ladder. A coalition of family members got him promoted to chairman of the board to remove him from day-to-day management.

WORK APPLICATIONS

5. Give a job example of how a coalition was used to achieve an objective.

6. What are your strongest and weakest areas of networking? How will you improve your networking skills? Include two or three of the most important tips you learned that you will use.

Networking Do's and Don'ts

AS 11–1

State if you should or should not do each item.

A. Do   B. Don't

_____ 1. Start networking with secondary contacts.

_____ 2. Network to know the latest developments in your field.

_____ 3. Network to get help with your current job.

_____ 4. View networking as being unfair.

_____ 5. To keep networking flexible, stay away from having specific goals.

_____ 6. Focus on your weakness during the networking self-assessment.

_____ 7. Develop a self-sell with your history, plans, and question.

_____ 8. During the networking interview, be sure to ask directly for what you want, especially if you are asking for a job.

_____ 9. Ask for a 30-minute networking interview.

_____ 10. Begin the networking interview with your one-minute self-sell.

_____ 11. Be sure to ask for additional contacts during the networking interview; try for three.

_____ 12. When a networking interview is helpful, send a thank-you note and status report.

_____ 13. Contact the people in your network at least once a month.

NEGOTIATING

Campus officials say that the skill college freshman need most, and often lack, is asking and negotiating for what they need.[40] In this section, we focus on getting what you want through negotiating. **Negotiating** *is a process in which two or more parties have something the other wants and attempt to come to an exchange agreement.* Negotiation is also called *bargaining*. Networking can lead to negotiating.[41] For example, when you search for a job, you can negotiate the compensation.[42] Sales reps network to negotiate sales.[43]

As with networking, when negotiating, you should be building relationships.[44] Power, influence tactics, and politics can all be used during the negotiation process.[45] In this section, we discuss negotiating and the negotiating process. Before we begin, complete Self-Assessment Exercise 11–2 to determine the behavior you use during negotiating.

Your Negotiating Skills

Identify each of the 16 statements according to how accurately they describe your behavior. Place the number (1 to 5) on the line before each statement.

Describes me   Does not describe me

5	4	3	2	1

_____ 1. Before I negotiate, if possible, I find out about the person I will negotiate with to determine what she or he wants and will be willing to give up.

_____ 2. Before I negotiate, I set objectives.

_____ 3. When planning my negotiating presentation, I focus on how the other party will benefit.

_____ 4. Before I negotiate, I have a target price I want to pay, a lowest price I will pay, and an opening offer.

_____ 5. Before I negotiate, I think through options and trade-offs in case I don't get my target price.

_____ 6. Before I negotiate, I think of the questions and objections the other party might have, and I prepare answers.

_____ 7. At the beginning of negotiations, I develop rapport and read the person.

_____ 8. I let the other party make the first offer.

_____ 9. I listen to what the other parties are saying and focus on helping them get what they want, rather than focusing on what I want.

_____ 10. I don't give in too quickly to others' offers.

_____ 11. When I compromise and give up something, I ask for something in return.

_____ 12. If the other party tries to postpone the negotiation, I try to create urgency and tell the other party what he or she might lose.

_____ 13. If I want to postpone the negotiation, I don't let the other party pressure me into making a decision.

_____ 14. When I make a deal, I don't second-guess my decision.

_____ 15. If I can't make an agreement, I ask for advice to help me with future negotiations.

_____ 16. During the entire business negotiating process, I'm trying to develop a relationship, not just a one-time deal.

Add up your score and place it here _____. Then on the continuum below, mark the point that represents your score.

Effective negotiating   80- - -70- - -60- - -50- - -40- - -30- - -20- - -10   Ineffective negotiating

If you did not score high on negotiating effectiveness, that's OK. You can develop negotiating skills by following the steps and guidelines in this chapter.

Negotiating Strategies

Negotiating involves shared interests (parties want to agree and exchange) and opposing interests (parties want different things and don't agree on everything), resulting in a conflict of interests (thus, negotiating is a conflict situation).[46] There are times when negotiations are appropriate, such as management–union collective bargaining, buying and selling goods and services, accepting a new job, getting a raise—all without a fixed price or deal. If there is a set take-it-or-leave-it deal, there is no negotiation. For example, in almost all U.S. retail stores, you either buy the product for the price listed or you don't buy it; you don't negotiate price. Most car dealers negotiate. Let's discuss two bargaining strategies.

Distributive Bargaining Strategy   **Distributive bargaining** *is negotiating over shares of a fixed pie; it creates a win–lose situation.* It's also called a zero–sum game or condition, because any gain you make is at the other party's expense. Every dollar you save on the price is your gain and the seller's loss, or it's labor's gain and management's loss, or vice versa. So it is more of a win–lose situation than a win–win situation. Parties work out a compromise through give and take.

Integrative Bargaining Strategy   **Integrative bargaining** *is negotiating to give everyone a good deal; it creates a win–win situation.* Let's say you and a friend want to go see a movie. A distributive solution would be to state what movie you want to see and state that you will not go to see any others. Under integrative bargaining, you both list movies you are interested in seeing and find one that you both like. The key is being open to options rather than taking a take-it-or-leave-it approach.[47]

Today the view of distributive bargaining has changed; the fixed pie is considered a mythical fixed pie. Successful firms use integrative strategies to work together to increase the size of the pie for all to share, such as in union–management negotiations.

Why Isn't Integrative Bargaining Used More Often?   A major problem is trust.[48] To use integrative bargaining, you have to have open, honest communications and be flexible to agree on creative solutions. Unfortunately, in many organizations, labor does not trust management, so neither party communicates in an open and honest way. Thus, they fight over a fixed pie, rather than making it larger and sharing it. To be a good integrative negotiator, develop trust by following the guidelines in Chapter 8.

All Parties Should Believe They Got a Good Deal   Negotiating is about getting what you want but at the same time developing and maintaining good relationships.[49] To be a successful negotiator, work at the goal of human relations by developing a win–win situation for all parties.[50] How many times would you go to the movies with the person who has a take-it-or-leave-it approach? How many times would you buy from a person that you thought gave you a poor deal?

Negotiating Skills Can Be Developed   Negotiating is an important leadership skill; thus, you should develop your negotiating style.[51] Not everyone is born being a great negotiator. Following the steps in the negotiating process can help you develop your negotiation skills, and as with everything else, practice makes perfect. Skill-Building Exercise 11–2 will give you the opportunity to practice negotiating.

WORK APPLICATIONS

7. Give a job example of distributive and integrative bargaining.

Learning Outcome

4. List and explain the steps in the negotiating process.

The Negotiating Process

The **negotiating process** *has three, and possibly four, steps: (1) planning, (2) bargaining, (3) possibly a postponement, and (4) an agreement or no agreement.* These steps, which are summarized in Exhibit 11.5, are discussed in separate subsections. Like other model exhibits in this book, Exhibit 11.5 is meant to give you step-by-step guidelines to follow. However, in applying it to multiple types of negotiations, you may have to make slight adjustments.

Learning Outcome

5. Briefly describe how to plan for negotiations.

Negotiating Planning

Success or failure in negotiating is often based on preparation.[52] Be clear about what it is you are negotiating over.[53] Is it price, options, delivery time, sales quantity, or all four? **Negotiating planning** *includes researching the other parties, setting objectives,*

EXHIBIT 11.5 | The Negotiating Process

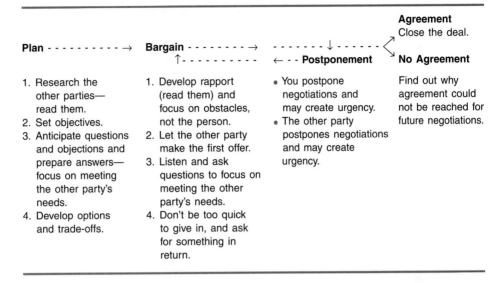

anticipating questions and objections and preparing answers, and developing options and trade-offs. It is helpful to write out your plan; doing so forces you to develop a detailed plan.[54] Exhibit 11.6 is a sample negotiating plan sheet, with a professional job offer compensation that is not simply a take-it-or-leave-it offer.[55] You can use the headings and write in your own plan by answering the types of questions that relate to the situation as shown in Exhibit 11.6 and discussed below. As you read about each part of the plan, you can return to the exhibit for a job-related sample plan.

Step 1: Research the Other Parties—Read Them   Researching the other party doesn't mean only the person; it includes the person's situation.[56] For example, if you are buying or selling something, find out about competing brands, quality, prices, and so on. Try to

EXHIBIT 11.6 | Sample Negotiating Plan

Negotiating Situation

Job offer from the X Company

(1) Research the other parties—read them.

What is the cost of living in the job area? What is the going pay for this job in other organizations? What does this company pay others in this job? What is the job market like? Are there lots of others with my qualifications seeking this job—expert power? What is the negotiation style of the person who will make me the offer? What can I expect to be offered for compensation?

(2) Set objectives.

Based on my research, what is the lowest compensation I will accept? What is my target compensation? What is my opening "asking" compensation, if I make the first offer? What is my best alternative to a negotiated agreement [BATNA]? If I don't get my minimum limit, I'll continue to work part-time/keep my current job/get a job with a temporary agency.

(3) Anticipate questions and objections and prepare answers.

I may be asked why I should be paid my target compensation or told that it is too high. If so, I'll say that the competitors pay . . . and your company pays . . . and I have this to offer to earn my compensation. I'll say that I have other possible jobs or that I really need . . . to make it worth moving.

(4) Develop options and trade-offs.

If I can't get the pay I want, I'll ask for more days off, more in my retirement account, a nice office, an assistant, or the like.

read the other party;[57] follow the guidelines from Chapter 10 before you even meet to negotiate. Be careful in reading the other party; it is not unusual for people to misread the other party's interests or to rely on flawed judgment.

Know the key power players. When negotiating with one person, find out to whom that person reports and who really makes the decision. Try to meet with the decision maker to negotiate. Try to find out what the other parties want and what they will and will not be willing to give up *before* you meet to negotiate.[58] Find out their personality traits and negotiation style through networking with people who have negotiated with the person you will negotiate with. The more you know about the other party, the better your chances of reaching an agreement. If possible, establish a personal relationship before the negotiation. If you have worked with the other party, such as your boss or a potential customer, recall what worked and did not work in the past. Figure out how you can use the past experience in your negotiation, such as to get a raise or make a sale.

Step 2: Set Objectives   Based on your research, what can you expect?[59] You have to identify the one thing you must come away with. Set limit, target, and opening objectives, and a best alternative to a negotiated agreement (BATNA).

- Set a specific *limit* objective, and be willing to walk away (not come to an agreement) unless you get it. The limit can be considered an upper (most you will pay) or lower (least you will sell for) limit. You need to be willing to walk away from a bad deal.[60]

- Set a *target* objective of what you really want.[61]

- Set an *opening* objective offer that is higher than you expect; you might get it.

- Plan your best alternative to a negotiated agreement (BATNA). Know in advance what you will do if you don't get your limit objective.[62] A BATNA helps you walk away from a bad deal. For example, "If I can't sell my house for my limit by June 10, I'll rent it for six months and then try again." See Exhibit 11.6 for job BATNAs.

Remember that the other party is probably also setting three objectives with a BATNA. So don't view the opening offer as final. Most successful negotiations result in all parties' reaching an agreement that is between their limit and target objectives. This creates a good deal for all, a win–win situation.[63]

As you know, most people don't come right out and identify their objective range and BATNA. These objectives and alternatives come out through negotiations. We'll discuss objectives again later in this section (see "Agreement or No Agreement").

WORK APPLICATIONS

8. Write negotiating objectives that include limit, target, and opening objectives and a BATNA.

Step 3: Anticipate Questions and Objections and Prepare Answers   Focus on meeting the other party's needs.[64] The other party may want to know why you are selling something, why you are looking for a job, how the product or service works, what the features and benefits are. You need to be prepared to answer the unasked question—"What's in it for me?" Don't focus on what you want, but on how your deal will benefit the other party.[65] Talk in "you" and "we," not "I," terms, unless you are telling others what you will do for them.

There is a good chance that you will be given objections—reasons why the negotiations will not result in an agreement or a sale.[66] When a union asks for a raise, management typically says the organization can't afford it. However, the union has done its research and quotes the specific profits for a set period of time to overcome the objection. Unfortunately, not everyone will come out and directly tell you their real objections. Thus, you need to listen and ask questions to find out what is preventing an agreement.[67] Make things sound positive so that the person believes he or she is getting a good deal.[68] For example, don't say, "I will give you half of what you asked for" (a \$2 raise instead of \$4); instead, say, "I'll give you \$2 more than you make now" (not \$2 less than you asked for).

You need to fully understand your product or deal and project positive self-esteem that shows enthusiasm and confidence. If the other party does not trust you and believes the deal is not a good one, you will not reach an agreement.[69] Thus, during the job selection process, for example, you must convince the manager that you can do the job. During the sales presentation, you must show how your product will benefit the customer. When you are in sales, you should have some closing statements prepared,[70] such as, "Will you take the white one or the blue one?"

Step 4: Develop Options and Trade-Offs   In purchasing or in looking for a job, if you have multiple sellers or job offers, you are in a stronger power position to get your target price.[71] It is common practice to quote other offers and to ask if the other party can beat them. Let other parties know not only what they have to gain, but also what they have to lose. Options should focus on "giving" the other parties what they want while getting what you want so that you all get a good deal.[72]

If you have to give up something, or cannot get exactly what you want, be prepared to ask for something in return. When an airline was having financial difficulty, it asked employees to take a pay cut. Rather than simply accept a cut, the union asked for a trade-off and got company stock. Based on your research, determine the trade-offs you expect from the other party. If the other party asks for a lower price, ask for a concession, such as a large-volume sale, or a longer delivery time, or a less popular color.

Learning Outcome

6. Briefly describe how to bargain.

Bargaining

After you have planned, you are ready to bargain. Whether you realize it or not, whether you like it or not, we are all negotiators.[73] Be willing to negotiate in good faith. Face-to-face negotiations are generally preferred because you can see (read) the other person's nonverbal behavior (Chapter 5) and better understand objections. However, telephone and written negotiations work too. Again, know the other party's preference.[74] **Bargaining** *includes (1) developing rapport and focusing on obstacles, not on the person, (2) letting the other party make the first offer, (3) listening and asking questions to focus on meeting the other party's needs, (4) not being too quick to give in, and (5) asking for something in return.* As we go through the bargaining steps, you will realize that you have already planned for each step of bargaining.

Step 1: Develop Rapport (Read the Person) and Focus on Obstacles, Not on the Person
Smile and call other parties by name as you greet them. A smile tells people you like them, are interested in them, and enjoy them. Open with some small talk.[75] Start developing trust and a cooperative relationship.[76] How much time you should wait until you get down to business depends on the other party's style. Some people like to get right down to business, while others want to get to know you before discussing business. You need to be able to negotiate successfully with people with diverse styles.[77] So read their style and try to match it.[78] Is it what you had anticipated through your researching the other party in step 1 of planning the negotiation? Adjust your style as needed. However, remember that the more you are like the other person, the better your chances of getting a good deal. Think about the salespeople who you liked and who got you to buy from them. Were they more like you, or were they the opposite?

Focusing on the obstacle, not on the person, means never attacking the other's personality or putting someone down with negative statements, such as, "You are being unfair to ask for such a price cut."[79] If you do so, the other party will become defensive, you may end up arguing, and it will be harder to reach an agreement. So even if the other person starts it, refuse to fight on this name-calling level. Make statements such as, "You think my price is too high?" Not saying negative things about others includes competitors; just state your competitive advantage in a positive way.

People look for four things: inclusion, control, safety, and respect. If people perceive that you are trying to push them into something, threaten them in some way, or belittle them, they will not trust you and may not make the agreement.[80]

Step 2: Let the Other Party Make the First Offer   Without setting objectives in preparation for bargaining, how do you know if an offer is any good? With objectives in mind, you have the advantage because if the other party offers you more than your opening and target objective, you can close the agreement. Let's assume you are expecting to be paid $30,000 a year (your target objective), your minimum limit is $27,000, and your opening offer to the employer is $33,000. If the employer offers you $35,000, are you going to say "That's too high; give me $30,000"?

Use the opening offer as a starting point. Remember that the other party probably is starting with an opening offer that can be negotiated up. So start the negotiations from this offer to get to your target objective when you need to. In the job negotiation above, if you are offered $26,000, which is below your limit, you realize that the offer may be low and you can work the compensation up toward your target. Often, the key to a large raise or beginning salary is bargaining; you must be willing to ask for it and not back down too easily (bargaining step 4). Women tend to be less assertive in negotiating salary, which contributes to their lower pay.[81]

If the other party seems to be waiting for you to make the first offer, get the other party to make the first offer with questions like these: "What is the salary range?" "What do you expect to pay for such a fine product?" To illustrate the importance of letting the other party make the first offer, Bob Lussier was selling a used car and went to seven used-car dealers stating that he would go to several places and take the best offer. How many offers do you think Bob got? The answer is zero. Not one of them would make an offer. They all asked, "How much do you want for it"?[82]

Try to avoid negotiating simply on price. When others pressure you to make the first offer with a comment like, "Give us your best price, and we'll tell you whether we'll take it," try asking them a question such as, "What do you expect to pay?" or "What is a reasonable price?" When this does not work, say something like, "Our usual [or list] price is . . . However, if you make me a proposal, I'll see what I can do for you."

If things go well during steps 1 and 2 and you get or exceed your opening offer or target objective, you may skip steps 3 and 4 and go to closing the agreement. If you are not ready to agree, proceed to the next step.

Step 3: Listen and Ask Questions to Focus on Meeting the Other Party's Needs   Recall that people want inclusion, control, safety, and respect. When you listen, you give the person all four. So listen with empathy during bargaining, especially when you are in conflict. This is your chance to find out if your preparation in anticipating questions and objections was accurate. And it's your opportunity to give your prepared answers to the objections while focusing on the other party's needs.

Create opportunities for the other party to disclose reservations and objections. When you speak, you give out information, but when you ask questions and listen, you receive information that will help you overcome the other party's objections.[83] If you go on and on about the features you have to offer, without finding out what features the other party is really interested in, you may be killing the deal. Ask questions like these: "Is the price out of the ballpark?" "Is it fast enough for you?" "Is any feature you wanted missing?" If the objection is a "want" criterion, such as two years' work experience and you have only one, play up the features the other party wants that you do have and you may get an agreement. If the objection is something you cannot meet, at least you find out and don't waste time chasing a deal that will not happen. However, be sure the objection is really a "must" criterion. What if the employer gets no applicants with two years' experience and you apply? You may be offered the job.

Steps 4 and 5: Don't Be Too Quick to Give in, and Ask for Something in Return   Those who ask for more get more. If you've planned, you have developed options (at least a BATNA) and you have trade-offs ready. After bargaining, you won't have to say, "I should have asked for . . ." Don't simply give up whatever it takes to get the agreement. If your competitive advantage is service and you quickly give in during negotiation for a lower price, you blow all the value in a minute. You want to satisfy the other party without giving up too much during the negotiation. Remember not to go below your limit objective; if that limit is realistic, be prepared to walk away.[84] When you are not getting what you want, having other planned options can help give you bargaining power.[85] If you do walk away, you may be called back, and if not, you may be able to come back for the same low price.

Avoid Desperation and Being Intimidated   If others know you are desperate, or just weak, and will accept a low agreement, they will likely take advantage of you.[86] Have you ever seen someone's sign on a product saying, "Must sell, need cash bad"? What type of price do you think such a person gets? You also need to avoid being intimidated by comments such as, in a loud voice, "Are you kidding me? That's too much." Many people will quickly drop the price, but don't be intimidated by such tactics.

Make the First Concession   When you are involved with a complex deal, such as a management–union contract negotiation with trade-offs, be willing to be the first to make a concession. Concessions tend to be reciprocated and to lead to agreements. The other party tends to feel obligated, and then you can come back with a counter trade-off that is larger than the one you gave up.

Avoid Giving Unilateral Concessions   Recall your planned trade-offs. If the other party asks for a lower price, ask for a concession such as a large-volume sale to get it, or a longer delivery time, or a less popular color. You need to send the message that you don't just give things away, that you are not a pushover.[87]

Postponement

When there doesn't seem to be any progress, it may be wise to postpone the negotiations.

When the Other Party Is Postponing, You May Create Urgency   The other party says, "I'll get back to you." Let other parties know not only what they have to gain, but also what they have to lose. When you are not getting what you want, you may try to create urgency, for example, by saying, "This is on sale and it ends today," "It's our last one," or "They are going fast and it may not be here when you come back." But to create long-term relations, you need to be sure you are giving the other party a good deal.[88] Honesty is the best policy. The primary reason people will negotiate with you is that they trust and respect you.[89] Establishing a relationship of trust is the necessary first step in closing a deal. Honesty and integrity are the most important assets a negotiator can possess. If you do have other options, you can use them to create urgency.[90] For example, you might say, "I have another job offer pending; when will you let me know if you want to offer me the job?"

If urgency does not apply or does not work, and the other party says, "I'll think about it," say, "That's a good idea." Then at least review the major features the other party liked about your proposed deal and ask if your offer meets their needs. The other party may decide to come to an agreement. If not, and they don't tell you when they will get back to you, ask, "When can I expect to hear if I got the job?" Try to pin the other party down for a specific time, and tell the person that if you don't hear anything by then, you will call. If you are really interested, follow up with a letter (mail, e-mail, or fax) of thanks for their time and again highlight your features they liked.[91] If you forgot to include any features during the negotiation, add them in the letter.

One thing to remember when the other party resists making the agreement is that the hard sell will not work. Take off the pressure. For example, ask a client, "Where do you want to go from here?" If you press for an answer, it may be no. If you wait, however, you may have a better chance. You might say to a boss, "Why don't we think about it and discuss it some more later?" Then pick an advantageous time to meet with your boss.

You also need to learn to read between the lines, watching for nonverbal communications, especially when working with people from different cultures. Some people will not come right out and tell you "no deal." For example, it is common for the Japanese to say something like, "It will be difficult to do business." Americans tend to perceive this to mean they should keep trying to close the deal, while the Japanese businessperson means stop trying, but will not say so directly because doing so would be impolite.

When You Want to Postpone, the Other Party May Create Urgency   If you are not satisfied with the deal, or want to shop around, tell the other party you want to think about it. You may also need to check with your boss, or someone else, which simply may be for advice, before you can finalize the deal. If the other party is creating urgency, be sure it really is urgent. In any case, you may get the same deal at a later date; don't be pressured into making a deal you are not satisfied with or may regret later. If you do want to postpone, give the other party a specific time that you will get back to them, and then do so—whether it is with more prepared negotiations or to simply say you cannot make an agreement.

Agreement or No Agreement

Agreement   You may sometimes get your opening offer, or better, if the other party offers more before you open with an offer. But if you do your research, you'll find that it is not likely you'll get an exceptional deal too often. If your target and the other party's target are the same, you could both get that target and have a great deal. So when you get your opening offer and both parties get their target objective, there is no real bargaining compromise.

However, it is common for targets to be in opposition. The *bargaining range* is the range between your limit and the other party's limit, which falls between each party's target and limit. Within that range, there is a good deal for both parties. See Exhibit 11.7 for an illustration of the bargaining range; we continue the job example from page 400, using its objectives. Note that the negotiated pay will most likely be between $27,000 and $30,000. In reality, most people don't tell the other parties their objectives and settle between those objectives; it just happens through bargaining.

Once the agreement has been made, restate it and/or put it in writing when appropriate. It is common to follow up an agreement with a letter of thanks and a restatement of the agreement to ensure the other parties have not changed their minds as to what they agreed to.

After the deal is made, stop selling it. Change the subject to a personal one and/or leave, depending on the other person's preferred negotiation style. If the other person wants to work on the relationship, stick around; if not, leave.

Avoid the so-called winner's curse. Be happy that you got a good deal. Don't start second-guessing your decision. Don't ask yourself, "Could I have bought (or sold) it for less (or more) than I did?" After you make the deal, it's usually too late to change anything,

EXHIBIT 11.7 | The Bargaining Range

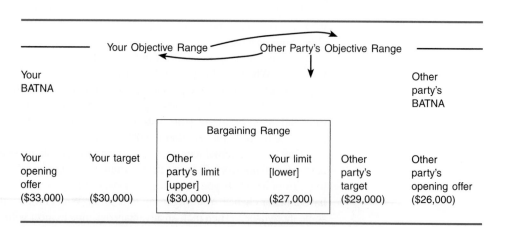

		Bargaining Range			
Your opening offer ($33,000)	Your target ($30,000)	Other party's limit [upper] ($30,000)	Your limit [lower] ($27,000)	Other party's target ($29,000)	Other party's opening offer ($26,000)

so why worry about it? By planning (researching the negotiation and setting effective objectives), you can reduce your chances of experiencing the winner's curse and be more confident that you did get a good deal.[92]

No Agreement   Rejection, refusal, and failure happen to us all, even the superstars. The difference between the also-rans and the superstars lies in how they respond to the failure. The successful people keep trying and learn from their mistakes and continue to work hard; failures usually don't persevere. Remember that success is the ability to go from failure to failure without losing your enthusiasm, and happiness is nothing more than a poor memory for the bad things (failures) that happen to us. Peter Lowe puts on seminars with big-name speakers. Peter wanted former president Ronald Reagan to be one of his speakers. He called every week for over a year until Reagan agreed to speak at a seminar for Peter. However, no one wins them all, so you need to know when to give up and cut your losses.[93]

If you cannot come to an agreement, analyze the situation and try to determine where you went wrong so you can improve in the future. You may also ask the other party for advice. For instance, you could say, "I realize I did not get the job, but thanks for your time. Can you offer me any ideas for improving my resume or my interview skills? Do you have any other ideas to help me get a job in this field?"

Former Toyota chairman Hiroski Okuda was viewed as a tough negotiator who used his power to get what he wanted. He had to negotiate to become president and to take the position of chairman. Toyota is also known to be a tough company to negotiate with. It negotiates with hundreds of suppliers to provide top quality at low prices. At the same time, Toyota uses its network and develops long-term relationships with its suppliers. It is agreed that Hiroski Okuda was a successful businessperson. However, you don't have to try to be like he or anyone else. You need to be you, and to be the best that you can be. Skill Building Exercise 11–2 gives you the opportunity to develop your negotiating skills.

WORK APPLICATIONS

9. What are your strongest and weakest areas of negotiating? How will you improve your negotiating skills? Include two or three of the most important tips you learned that you will use.

APPLICATION SITUATIONS

Negotiating Do's and Don'ts

AS 11–2

State if you should or should not do each item.

A. Do   B. Don't

_____ 14. Strive to develop distributive bargaining.

_____ 15. Make sure you get the best deal.

_____ 16. Research the other parties before you meet with them.

_____ 17. Set one objective.

_____ 18. Keep your focus on helping the other person meet his or her objective.

_____ 19. Get down to business quickly.

_____ 20. Make the first offer.

———— 21. Present a take-it-or-leave-it offer.

———— 22. Spend most of your negotiating time telling the other parties how great a deal they are getting.

———— 23. Don't be too quick to give in, and ask for something in return.

———— 24. Try to postpone bargaining.

———— 25. If you can't come to an agreement, ask for suggestions that can help you in future negotiations.

DO NETWORKING AND NEGOTIATING APPLY GLOBALLY?

Let's begin by getting back to the *e-organization*. The Internet makes networking even easier, since the network potential is limitless. Think about the potential the Internet has to help you develop your network. You can communicate with people from all over the world through e-mail and by joining online lists, chat rooms, blogs, and Web boards. The Web also makes it even easier to research parties you will negotiate with. As an alternative to traveling around the world, you can negotiate online too. So get online and do some cyber-schmoozing.

Yes there are cultural differences in networking, and you need to appreciate and embrace the host culture.[94] Networking is part of politicking and socializing, which we discussed in the last chapter, so we'll keep it brief here. The need to *network* to develop relationships to get business does vary culturally. We'll discuss networking within the context of negotiating.

With increased globalization, there is an increase in cross-cultural *negotiating*. There is strong support for the existence of negotiating style differences among national cultures.[95] For example, the Israelis like to argue, so a heated emotional negotiation (even yelling) is common behavior, but that is not the case for the Japanese. The amount of time you need to spend researching the other party and the type of information you will need will vary based on the culture, but in general, you need to spend more time when you don't know the customs, practices, and expectations of a particular culture.

There are many implications for negotiating globally. Throughout this section, we refer to classic studies comparing cultural differences regarding the following issues:[96]

- *Time to reach an agreement and deadlines.* The French like conflict and tend to take a long time in negotiating agreements, and they are not too concerned about being liked by the other parties. The Chinese like to drag out negotiations. Just when you think you are about to close the deal, the executive might smile and start the negotiations all over again. Americans are different in that they are known globally to be impatient and eager for quick agreement, and they want to be liked. So good negotiators often drag out the negotiations with Americans and make relationships conditional on the final settlement. One study found negotiating deadlines to be viewed as important by North Americans, treated casually by Arabs, and ignored by Russians. So is the deadline really the deadline?

- *The focus on task versus relationship.* In Japan and many South American countries, without a relationship there will be no task accomplishment of an agreement, or the task will be to develop the relationship. Like the Japanese, the Chinese tie close networking relationships and negotiating together in conducting business, and gift giving is expected. But give an appropriate gift; for example, don't give clocks to the

Busted: Delta Tries to Break Pilots' Union Contract

After the September 11 attacks, which led to the decline of the airline industry in the U.S., many of the major carriers in the industry went bankrupt. Delta was one of the few major carriers that managed to stay afloat. However, due to issues like the high cost of pilots, increasing operational expenses and legacy costs, falling yields, and severe competition from low-cost airlines, Delta was losing money. The airline announced that it might have to file for bankruptcy protection if it failed to obtain pay cuts of $1 billion from its pilots, who were the only unionized employees at the airline. It went through hard negotiations with pilots and other employees to cut their compensation, and Delta ended up in Chapter 11 bankruptcy protection.

Through the negotiations, employees did take large pay cuts, but in return they received a substantial financial stake in the company's future through stock ownership. Delta did emerge from Chapter 11, and on September 25, 2008, Delta Air Lines and Northwest Airlines announced that their respective stockholders overwhelmingly approved the pending merger between the two companies.

Questions

1. Describe the type of negotiating strategy of Delta Airlines and Delta's pilots.

2. How is Delta using its Chapter 11 status as a negotiating tactic?

3. Does this tactic represent good faith (ethical) bargaining on the part of Delta Air Lines?

4. According to your textbook, how should bargaining occur between Delta and its pilots?

Source: Delta Air Lines Web site (www.delta.com), retrieved September 29, 2008.

Chinese, because they symbolize death. North Americans tend to have shorter-term relationships than the Japanese and the Arabs, and Russians are often not concerned about ongoing relationships.

- *The use of power and influencing tactics* (plus concessions with reciprocity). The power base to use also varies, based on the power distance of the culture. Influencing tactics (Chapter 10) used during negotiating also vary across cultures. To counter arguments or obstacles to closing the deal, Americans tend to use the rational persuasion tactic, using logical arguments with facts and figures. Arabs tend to use the inspirational tactic, using emotional appeal with feelings. Russians tend to assert their ideas with power, more than with influencing tactics. Concessions are made and reciprocated by both Americans and Arabs, but not often by Russians, because they view concessions as a sign of weakness. In summary, the Russians tend to use distributive bargaining more so than the North Americans and Arabs, who use more integrative bargaining.

- *Communications—both verbal and nonverbal.* In some cultures (the United States, Germany, England, Switzerland) negotiators use direct verbal messages, whereas in other cultures (Japan, China, Egypt, France, and Saudi Arabia) they rely more on nonverbal communications, so you have to read between the lines. Here are the results of another classic study comparing North Americans, Japanese, and Brazilians during half-hour bargaining sessions. When it comes to touching, Americans and Japanese tend only to shake hands, whereas the Brazilians touch around five times every half hour. Brazilians also say no much more frequently than the Americans and Japanese (83, 9, and 5 times per half hour, respectively). Brazilians don't like silence, Japanese are more comfortable with it, and Americans are in between, as measured by the number of periods of silence that last longer than 10 seconds (0, 5, and 3½, respectively). The Brazilians also interrupt the other party 2½ to 3 times more often than both the North Americans and Japanese. Also, Americans tend to like to talk about one issue at a time (linear progression), whereas the French often talk about multiple issues at once.

- *Where the negotiations should take place and the use of alcohol and choice of food.* These are important considerations. You should know the proper place and when (time of day can vary) to talk business. For example, the CEO of Saber Enterprises says that when Japanese executives come to the United States and when American executives go to Japan, it is almost expected that you will go out to dinner and have several drinks and some sake while talking business. If a client orders a glass of wine, are you going to order a cola? And you certainly don't want to offer and order a drink with a Mormon client. Whether alcohol is available or not expected through the negotiation, you need to be careful not to offend the other party. You don't want to let alcohol impair your professional performance or cause you to make bad decisions because you were under its influence. Also remember that people of different religions and cultures don't eat certain foods. For example, the pig is considered unclean to many Jewish people and the cow is sacred to many Indians, so Jewish people don't eat pork and Indians don't eat beef. In India, the Big Mac is made from lamb.

- *Name, rank or title, dress, greetings, and rituals.* Note that these issues also apply to same-culture negotiations. During your research or, when with the other party, find out how the person prefers to be addressed (is it Christine/Chris, Ms. Smith, President Smith?). Also find out what he or she will wear (a suit, a casual outfit). Note that special or sacred articles may be worn. Know if there are certain greetings (such as bowing) or rituals (such as praying before eating) that you may be expected to participate in.

THE INFLUENCING PROCESS

Learning Outcome

7. Explain the influencing process.

Recall that Part 3 of this book is entitled "Leadership Skills: Influencing Others." In Chapters 8 through 11, we have covered many factors that can help you influence others to get what you want by developing trust and motivating others with power, influencing tactics, politics, networking, and negotiating. We have focused on getting what we want by being ethical and giving others what they want; thus, we meet the goal of human relations by creating a win–win situation for all parties. Here, we put all the influencing concepts together and create the influencing process.

Review of Influencing Key Terms   Let's discuss the interrelationship of these concepts by reviewing their definitions. *Leadership* is the process of influencing employees to work toward the achievement of objectives. So leadership is about getting people to do what the organization wants. *Motivation* is the internal process leading to behavior to satisfy needs. *Power* is a person's ability to influence others to do something they would not otherwise do. *Politics* is the process of getting and using power. *Networking* is the ongoing process of building interconnected relationships for the purpose of politicking and socializing. *Negotiating* is a process in which two or more parties have something the other wants and attempt to come to an exchange agreement. *Trust* is the positive expectation that another will not take advantage of you.

The Influencing Process   The **influencing process** *begins with an objective; ethical leadership, power, politics, networking, and negotiating are used to motivate others to help reach the objective; and through trust and creating a win–win situation for all parties, the objective is met.* See Exhibit 11.8 for an illustration of this influencing process, which shows the interrelationships among our influencing key terms.

We can view leadership skills from the personal level within and outside organizations as they relate to your behavior, human relations, and performance. You begin with a need or something you want, so you set an objective. (Referring to "setting an objective" rather than to "getting what you want" is using politically correct language; after all, we don't want to appear selfish or to offend anyone.) Often, you need other people to help you get what you want, so you have to motivate them to help you. You use power, politics, and networking behavior to get others to help you meet your objective, and you, in turn, do favors for others in your network. When others have something you want and you have something they want, you negotiate so you both meet your objectives—creating a win–win

EXHIBIT 11.8 | The Influencing Process

Motivation	Behavior	Human Relations	Performance
You begin with a need or something you want, so you set an objective. You need to motivate others to get them to help you meet the objective.	You use power, politics, and networking to motivate others to help you meet the objective. When others have something you want and you have something they want, you negotiate so you both can meet your objectives.	Effective human relations are based on good intrapersonal and interpersonal skills (Chapters 1 to 7) and on using ethical behavior to develop trust.	Using good human relations based on trust leads to a win–win situation for all parties, which results in meeting the objective.

situation. But to get people to help you, you need to develop trust by using ethical behavior to get what you want.

Let's bring this chapter to a close by discussing how your personality affects your networking and negotiating style, in Self-Assessment Exercise 11–3.

Self-Assessment
Exercise 11–3

Your Personality and Networking and Negotiating

You should realize that personality can be used more accurately to predict networking behavior than negotiating style. This is why in bargaining, you should focus on obstacles, not on the person. When you research the other party, you do so to find out negotiating style, not personality. Thus, in this exercise, when we discuss negotiating and how it may affect your behavior, the generalities noted may not be accurate in all cases. But keep in mind that there are always exceptions to the generalities presented regarding personality and behavior.

If you have a high *surgency* personality, you most likely have a high need for power and try to network with people who can help you. Remember, however, that even people who you don't think can help you might be the key to something you want down the road. So network with people of all levels. Often the secretary to an important person can get the key person to help you. Watch your use of coercive power during negotiations. Remember that being the first to make a concession usually results in the other person's reciprocating. At that point you can come back with a counter trade-off that is larger than the one you gave up.

If you have a high *agreeableness* personality, you most likely have a high need for affiliation and you enjoy networking at all levels to gain relationships. Watch out for others who might use power during negotiating to take advantage of you. Be assertive, don't give in too easily, and ask for something in return.

If you have a high *conscientious* personality, you most likely have a high need for achievement and don't care too much about having a large network. But you enjoy reciprocity with friends. You may need to work on developing your networking skills, such as making small talk and meeting new people. You probably develop good rational reasons to get what you want in negotiations, but remember to read the other parties and focus on giving them what they want so that you get what you want.

How high your *adjustment* is affects how you network and negotiate. People low on adjustment, and some can fake it, generally don't use networking and negotiating ethically; they seek to get what they want and to take advantage of others through distributive bargaining. If you are not high on adjustment personality traits, you may want to stop being self-centered and work on creating win–win situations. You will be surprised at how much more you can

Self-Assessment
Exercise 11–3 (continued)

receive in your network when you learn to give in return. There is truth in the adage, "The more you give, the more you receive." Have you ever done something for someone figuring there was nothing in it for you, only to find out that you got more than you expected?

Your *openness to experience* will have a direct effect on your networking skills. People who are open to new experiences are generally outgoing and enjoy meeting new people. Introverts tend not to enjoy meeting new people and thus are not good at networking, so they may need to work harder at it than others. Openness often leads to compromise and integrative bargaining, which is needed in negotiating successfully.

Action plan: Based on your personality, what specific things will you do to improve your networking and negotiating skills?

_____

_____

_____

_____

Where We've Been and Where We are Going   To sum up Parts 2 and 3, Chapters 5 through 11, interpersonal and leadership skills are all about how you interact with people and your relationships in your personal and professional lives. It's *not* about what you know or technical skills; it's about how you behave (what you say and do) in teams and organizations, which is the topic of Part 4, Leadership Skills: Team and Organizational Behavior, Human Relations, and Performance.

Videos

Manager's Hot Seat Videos are available for this chapter.

Online Learning Center Resources

Go to the Internet (http://mhhe.com/lussier8e) where you will find a broad array of resources to help maximize your learning.

• Review the vocabulary.

• Try a quiz.

R E V I E W

The chapter review is organized to help you master the 8 learning outcomes for Chapter 11. First provide your own response to each learning outcome, and then check the summary provided to see how well you understand the material. Next, identify the final statement in each section as either true or false (T/F). Correct each false statement. Answers are given at the end of the chapter.

1. **List and explain the steps in the networking process.**
   The first step in the networking process is to perform a self-assessment to determine your accomplishments and to set objectives. Second, create a one-minute self-sell that quickly summarizes your history and career plan and asks a question. Next, develop a written network list. Fourth, conduct networking interviews to meet your objective. Finally, maintain your network for meeting future objectives.
   People in the workforce use networking primarily to get a job. T F

2. **Describe what a one-minute self-sell is and what it contains.**
   The one-minute self-sell is an opening statement used in networking to begin developing a relationship with another person. It briefly summarizes one's career/educational history, states one's career plans, and asks a question.
   A good one-minute self-sell question to ask is, "Can you give me a job?" T F

3. **Briefly describe how to conduct a networking interview.**

   The steps for conducting a networking interview are as follows: (1) establish rapport—praise and read the person; (2) deliver the one-minute self-sell; (3) ask prepared questions; (4) get additional contacts for your network; (5) ask your contacts how you might help them; and (6) follow up with a thank-you note and status report.

   When establishing rapport, it is a good idea to praise the person and to "read" the person. T F

4. **List and explain the steps in the negotiating process.**

   The negotiating process has three, and possibly four, steps: (1) planning, (2) bargaining, (3) possibly a postponement, and (4) an agreement or no agreement.

   The best negotiating strategy to use is distributive bargaining. T F

5. **Briefly describe how to plan for negotiations.**

   Negotiating planning includes: (1) researching the other parties, (2) setting objectives, (3) anticipating questions and objections and preparing answers, and (4) developing options and trade-offs.

   Planning for the negotiation should include three objectives: a limit, a target, and an opening objective. T F

6. **Briefly describe how to bargain.**

   Steps for bargaining include: (1) develop rapport and focus on obstacles, not the person; (2) let the other party make the first offer; (3) listen and ask questions to focus on meeting the other party's needs; (4) don't be too quick to give in; and (5) ask for something in return.

   If you don't get your limit objective, you should not come to an agreement. T F

7. **Explain the influencing process.**

   The influencing process begins with an objective. To achieve it, ethical leadership, power, politics, networking, and negotiating are used to motivate others to help reach the objective. Through trust and creating a win–win situation for all parties, the objective is met.

   If people actually followed the influencing process—were ethical and tried to meet the goal of human relations—performance in organizations would increase. T F

Learning Outcome

8. Define the following 13 key terms.

8. **Define the following 13 key terms.**

   Select one or more methods: (1) Fill in the missing key terms from memory; (2) match the key terms from the end of the review with their definitions below; and/or (3) copy the key terms in order from the key terms at the beginning of the chapter.

   _____ is the ongoing process of building interconnected relationships for the purpose of politicking and socializing.

   _____ are clusters of people joined by a variety of links.

   The _____ includes these tasks: perform a self-assessment and set objectives, create a one-minute self-sell, develop a network, conduct networking interviews, and maintain the network.

   The _____ is an opening statement used in networking that quickly summarizes your history and career plan and asks a question.

   The _____ includes these steps: establish rapport—praise and read the person; deliver your one-minute self-sell; ask prepared questions; get additional contacts for your network; ask your contacts how you might help them; and follow up with a thank-you note and status report.

A(n) _____ is a short-term network used to meet an objective.

_____ is a process in which two or more parties have something the other wants and attempt to come to an exchange agreement.

_____ is negotiating over shares of a fixed pie; it creates a win–lose situation.

_____ is negotiating to give everyone a good deal; it creates a win–win situation.

The _____ has three, and possibly four, steps: (1) planning, (2) bargaining, (3) possibly a postponement, and (4) an agreement or no agreement.

_____ includes researching the other parties, setting objectives, anticipating questions and objections and preparing answers, and developing options and trade-offs.

_____ includes developing rapport and focusing on obstacles, not on the person; letting the other party make the first offer; listening and asking questions to focus on meeting the other party's needs; and not being too quick to give in, and asking for something in return.

The _____ begins with an objective. Ethical leadership, power, politics, networking, and negotiating are used to motivate others to help reach the objective. Through trust and creating a win–win situation for all parties, the objective is met.

K E Y   T E R M S

bargaining   399
coalition   393
distributive
    bargaining   396
influencing process   406
integrative
    bargaining   396

negotiating   394
negotiating
    planning   396
negotiating process   396
networking   386
networking interview
    process   392

networking process   388
networks   386
one-minute self-sell   389

C O M M U N I C A T I O N   S K I L L S

The following critical thinking questions can be used for class discussion and/or as written assignments to develop communication skills. Be sure to give complete explanations for all questions.

1. This chapter lists six networking objectives (see page 387). For which of these reasons (or for what other reasons) do you have to network?

2. You have heard the expression, "It's not what you know, it's who you know, that's important." Do you agree? If it is true, is it fair?

3. The first step of the networking process is to perform a self-assessment. What are your three most important accomplishments?

4. If you didn't write out a one-minute self-sell for Work Application (4), do so now.

5. College students are poor at negotiating. Do you agree with this statement?

6. The text states that the distributive bargaining strategy of fighting over a fixed pie is being replaced by the integrative bargaining strategy, in which the size of the pie is increased, for all to share. Give examples of negotiation situations in which a seemingly fixed pie can be increased and shared.

7. The next time you negotiate, will you actually set three—limit, target, and opening—objectives? Why or why not?

8. In bargaining, does it really matter who makes the first offer?

9. Think of a past, present, or future negotiation situation. Describe the situation and state what you can ask for in return if you don't get your target.

10. Can the influencing process really be conducted ethically and in a way that meets the goal of human relations, or is it just manipulation?

CASE

Andrea Jung

Avon, the company for women, is a leading global beauty company, with over $10 billion in annual revenue. As the world's largest direct seller, Avon markets to women in more than 100 countries through over 5.4 million independent Avon sales representatives and more than 42,000 employees. Avon's product line includes beauty products, fashion jewelry and apparel, and features such as the well-recognized brand names *Avon Color, Anew, Skin-So-Soft, Advance Techniques, Avon Naturals,* and *Mark.* Andrea Jung became CEO in 1999.

Avon's vision is to be the company that best understands and satisfies the product, service, and self-fulfillment needs of women globally. Its dedication to supporting women touches not only beauty, but also health, fitness, self-empowerment, and financial independence.

According to Andrea Jung, Avon's more-than-a-century-old heritage of changing people's lives for the better is the cornerstone of the company's corporate mission. Andrea Jung has directed the successful transformation of the company by reiterating Avon's vision as a company for women. Her main objective was to revitalize Avon's reputation as the world's foremost direct seller of beauty products while leading the company into attractive new lines of business, launching a series of bold and image-enhancing products, and expanding career opportunities for women around the world.

Andrea Jung and her management team have been very aggressive at capitalizing on new opportunities to accelerate the company's long-term growth. Some of Avon's initiatives since Andrea Jung assumed the role of strategic leader include the following:

- Launched new product lines.
- Targeted the growing Hispanic market in the United States to meet the lifestyle needs of Latina women and their families.
- Continued global expansion with a new organizational structure with six geographic regions: North America; Latin America; Central and Eastern Europe (CEE); Western Europe, Middle East, and Africa (WEMEA); China; and Asia Pacific.
- Introduced the sale of Avon online, with the help of a representative.
- Restructured manufacturing operations to more fully leverage the benefits of a unified supply chain.

There is ample evidence to show that Andrea Jung's strategic initiatives at Avon have paid off for the 122-year-old company. Andrea Jung and her chief operating officer, Susan Kropf, were named among the best managers of the year by *BusinessWeek,* which commended the pair for achieving strong business growth for Avon in both domestic and international markets despite a challenging global economic environment. Two key accomplishments since Jung took the helm are consecutive years of double-digit earnings growth and a steady increase in the number of active Avon sales representatives worldwide.

Avon has been named among the top 10 companies in *Business Ethics* magazine's annual "100 Best Corporate Citizens" listing and by *Fortune* magazine as one of "America's Most Admired Companies." Avon has also received recognition for its philanthropic work. Through the Avon Worldwide Fund for Women's Health, which includes the Avon Breast Cancer Crusade, Avon has raised more than $350 million toward the cure for cancer.

Avon has a strong cohesive culture that emphasizes social responsibility, participation, diversity, and empowerment. According to Andrea Jung, "around the world, the name 'Avon' stands for aspiration and empowerment." Having a strong culture like Avon has, which guides and sustains everyone's behavior, does not happen by chance. Andrea Jung's leadership in embedding and reinforcing Avon's people-centered culture has helped advance the company's purpose. Avon's employee policies, ethics, and values all derive from its culture. Today, Andrea Jung sits on top of this unique Fortune 500 company with more women in management positions than any other. Almost half (4 of 10) of Avon's board of directors are women.[97]

Go to the Internet: For more information on Andrea Jung and Avon and to update the information provided in this case, do a name search on the Internet and visit Avon's Web site at www.avon.com.

Support your answers to the following questions with specific information from the case and text, or with other information you get from the Web or other sources. When answering the questions, keep in mind that most of Avon's sales come through 3.9 million independent sales representatives.

1. What is the role of networking at Avon?

2. Is networking more important for Avon than for other sellers of similar products through retail stores?

3. What are some of the types of deals Avon negotiates?

4. How do cross-cultural differences affect the way Avon does business?

5. How has the Internet affected Avon?

Cumulative Questions   6. Why is customer perception (Chapter 2) important to Avon?

7. Is customer trust (Chapter 8) more important for Avon than for other companies?

8. Does Avon have to motivate (Chapter 9) its sales reps differently than other companies do?

OBJECTIVE CASE   ## John Stanton: Amway

Charley Roys wanted to get more consulting jobs, so he went to a Rotary International meeting to make more contacts that could lead to consulting jobs. During the meeting he was talking to different people and giving out his business card.

This one guy, John Stanton, said to Charley, "Hi, my name is John Stanton, and I have an interesting part-time business. I'm looking for people to share this business opportunity with. Would you be interested in making an additional $50,000 a year part-time?" Charley said yes, and he tried to get some ideas of what the business was all about, but all John would say was, "Let's meet for a half hour or so and I will tell you about it." So they agreed to meet the next day at Charley's house.

Charley asked John what the business name was, and John said, "Let me explain the opportunity first." John started drawing layers of people, stating how much Charley would earn from each layer of people selling products for him. All Charley would have to do is sign people up like John was doing and the money would come in. The figures were showing that Charley could make $50,000 a year from a part-time business.

Before John finished, Charley asked, "Is this Amway?" John said, "Yes, it is." Charley said, "I've seen this type of presentation before, and I'm not interested in being an Amway distributor." Charley told him that he did not want to sell products. John replied, "That's not where the money is. You don't have to actually sell the Amway products yourself. You just sign people up and get them to sell the products."

Charley said, "How can I expect others to sell the products if I don't sell any? The whole pyramid is based on selling products." Charley asked John why he did not tell him it was Amway when he asked him at the Rotary Club meeting. John said, "Many people have the wrong impression of Amway, and you really have to have time to see the presentation."

Charley said that he knew that there were some Amway distributors who were really making a lot of money, but that it was not the type of business he would be successful in. Amway was not for him. Before John left, he asked Charley if he knew of anyone who would be interested in making a lot of money part-time. But Charley said no, so John left.

Answer the following questions. Then in the space between questions, state why you selected that answer.

_____ 1. This case is mainly about:

    _a._ networking   _b._ negotiating

_____ **2.** Was John successful at networking at the Rotary Club meeting?

         a. yes   *b.* no

_____ **3.** To sell Amway products, salespeople need to start with _____ connections.

         a. primary   *b.* secondary

_____ **4.** John's networking objective was to:

         a. get a job or a better one   *d.* stay current in his field

         b. perform better at his current job   *e.* maintain mobility

         c. advance within Amway   *f.* develop relationships

_____ **5.** Did John have a good one-minute self-sell?

         a. yes   *b.* no

_____ **6.** Which part of the networking interview did John clearly try to do?

         a. develop rapport   *d.* get additional contacts

         b. deliver one-minute self-sell   *e.* offer help

         c. ask questions   *f.* follow up

_____ **7.** Are coalitions needed for John to be successful at Amway?

         a. yes   *b.* no

_____ **8.** Did John and Charley bargain?

         a. yes   *b.* no

_____ **9.** Amway's business is based mainly on _____ bargaining.

         a. distributive   *b.* integrative

_____ **10.** Is Amway, and other similar businesses, trying to give all parties a good deal?

         a. yes   *b.* no

11. Why wasn't John successful in using the influencing process with Charley?

12. Was it unethical for John not to tell Charley the business was Amway at the Rotary Club meeting?

Networking Skills

Preparation
(Group)

Complete the following steps:

1. Perform a self-assessment and set objectives. List two or three of your accomplishments. Clearly state your goal, which can be to learn more about career opportunities in your major; to get an internship; to get a part-time, summer, or full-time job; and so on.

2. Create your one-minute self-sell. Write it out. See page 390 for an example.

History:

Plan:

Question:

3. Develop your network. List at least five people to be included in your network, preferably people who can help you achieve your objective.

4. Conduct networking interviews. To help meet your objective, select one person to interview by phone if it is difficult to meet in person for a personal 20-minute interview. List the person and write questions to ask during the interview. This person can be someone in your college career center or a professor in your major.

In-Class Exercise	*Objective:* To develop networking skills by implementing the steps in the networking process.
	AACSB: The primary AACSB learning standard skills developed through this exercise are reflective thinking and communication abilities.
	Experience: You will deliver your one-minute self-sell from the preparation and get feedback for improvement. You will also share your network list and interview questions and get feedback for improvement.
Procedure 1 *(7–10 minutes)*	A. Break into groups of two. Show each other your written one-minute self-sell. Is the history, plan, and question clear (do you understand it?), concise (does it take 60 seconds or less to say?), and compelling (does it generate interest in helping?)? Offer suggestions for improvement.
	B. After the self-sell is perfected, each person states (no reading) the one-minute self-sell. Was it stated clearly, concisely, and with confidence? Offer improvements. State it a second and third time, or until told to go on to the next procedure.
Procedure 2 *(7–10 minutes)*	Break into groups of three with people you did not work with during procedure 1. Follow steps A and B above in your triad. Repeating your self-sell should improve your delivery and confidence.
Procedure 3 *(10–20 minutes)*	Break into groups of four with people you did not work with during procedures 1 and 2, if possible. Share your answers to preparation steps 3 (your network list) and 4 (your interview questions). Offer each other improvements to the list and the questions.
	Application (outside of class): Expand your written network list to at least 25 names. Conduct the networking interview using the questions developed through this exercise.
	Conclusion: The instructor leads a class discussion and/or makes concluding remarks. Written network lists and/or interview questions and answers may be passed in.
	Sharing: Volunteers may share what they have learned about networking.

Source: This exercise was developed by Andra Gumbus, assistant professor, College of Business, Sacred Heart University. © Andra Gumbus, 2002. It is used with Dr. Gumbus's permission.

Car Dealer Negotiation	*Objective:* To develop negotiation skills.
In-Class Exercise (Group)	*AACSB:* The primary AACSB learning standard skills developed through this exercise are reflective thinking and communication abilities.
	Experience: You will be the buyer or seller of a used car.
	Preparation: You should have read and should understand the negotiation process.
Procedure 1 *(1–2 minutes)*	Break into groups of two and sit facing each other so that you cannot read each other's confidential sheet. Each group should be as far away from other groups as possible so that they cannot overhear each other's conversations. If there is an odd number of students in the class, one student will be an observer or work with the instructor. Select who will be the buyer and who will be the seller of the used car.

Procedure 2
(1–2 minutes)

The instructor goes to each group and gives the buyer and seller their confidential sheets.

Procedure 3
(5–6 minutes)

Buyers and sellers read their confidential sheets and in the space below write some plans (what your basic approach will be, what you will say) for the lunch meeting.

Procedure 4
(3–7 minutes)

Negotiate the sale of the car. Try not to overhear your classmates' conversations. You do not have to buy or sell the car. After you make the sale or agree not to sell, read the confidential sheet of your partner in this exercise and discuss the experience.

Integration
(3–7 minutes)

Answer the following questions:

1. Which of the seven bases of power (Chapter 10) did you use during the negotiations? Did both parties believe that they got a good deal?

2. Which of the influencing tactics (Chapter 10) did you use during the negotiations?

3. During your planning, did you (1) research the other party, (2) set an objective— (limit, target, open—price to pay or accept), (3) anticipate questions and objections and prepare answers, and (4) develop options and trade-offs?

4. During the negotiations, did you (1) develop a rapport and focus on obstacles, not on the person, (2) let the other party make the first offer, (3) listen and ask questions to focus on meeting the other party's needs, (4) avoid being too quick to give in, and (5) ask for something in return?

5. Did you reach an agreement on the price of the car? If you were the seller, did you get your target price? Or did you get more or less than your target?

6. When you are negotiating, is it a good practice to open high, that is, to ask for more than you expect to receive?

7. When you are negotiating, is it better to be the one to give or to receive the initial offer?

8. When you are negotiating, is it better to appear to be dealing with strong or weak power? In other words, should you try to portray that you have other options and don't really need to make a deal with this person? Or should you appear to be in need of a deal?

9. Can having the power to intimidate others be helpful in negotiations?

Conclusion: The instructor leads a class discussion or simply gives the answers to the integration questions and makes concluding remarks.

Application: What did I learn from this experience? How will I use this knowledge in the future?

Sharing: Volunteers give their answers to the application section.

Source: The car dealer negotiation confidential information is from Arch G. Woodside, Tulane University. The car dealer game is part of a paper, "Bargaining Behavior in Personal Selling and Buying Exchanges," that was presented at the 1980 Eighth Annual Conference of the Association for Business Simulation and Experiential Learning (ABSEL). It is used with Dr. Woodside's permission.

ANSWERS TO TRUE/FALSE QUESTIONS

1. F. Most people in the workforce have jobs, so they network primarily for other reasons. Networking is not all about getting a job: it's about developing relationships to help you meet your personal and professional goals.
2. F. In a one-minute self-sell, you should not directly ask for a job.
3. T.
4. F. Distributive bargaining creates a win–lose situation, whereas integrative bargaining creates a win–win situation.
5. T.
6. T.
7. T.

Leadership Skills: Team and Organizational Behavior, Human Relations, and Performance

Team Dynamics and Leadership

Bonnie Sue Swinaski is a machine operator for the Western Pacific Manufacturing Company in Jackson, Mississippi. In the past, she has recommended ways to increase performance, which management used. As a result, management appointed Bonnie Sue to lead an ad hoc committee charged with recommending ways to increase performance in her work area. Her group has six members, all from her department, who volunteered to serve on the committee. The committee has been meeting biweekly now for three weeks for one- to two-hour sessions. The members have grown quite close over the weeks, and participation has been fairly equal.

Bonnie Sue, however, has not been very pleased with the group's performance. Only three weeks remain before the group's report is to be presented to management. She has been thinking about some of the problems and wondering how to handle them. At first, the members came to the meetings really enthusiastic and came up with crazy ideas. But over time, they lost some of the enthusiasm, even though they were developing better ideas for improving the performance of the department. During meetings, members have been suggesting the need for work to be done outside the meeting, but no one seems to do it. Three of the members cause different kinds of problems in the group. Kirt is destructive—he is constantly putting other people's ideas down, and others have followed his lead. Kirt always thinks his way is better, and he never gives an inch, even when he knows he is wrong. Kirt ends up fighting with members over whose idea is better. Shelby is very pleasant—she tries to keep peace in the group. The problem with Shelby is that she is consistently getting the group off the topic at hand. Carl is the opposite of Shelby—he puts the group back on the topic. He doesn't believe in wasting any time, but he's a motor mouth. Carl dominates the airtime at meetings.

What are the issues? If you were in Bonnie Sue's situation, how would you turn the group into a top performer?

HOW TEAMS AFFECT BEHAVIOR, HUMAN RELATIONS, AND PERFORMANCE

Teams have evolved into mainstream management practice.[1] Much of the work in organizations is completed through teamwork.[2] **Teamwork** *involves working together to achieve something beyond the capabilities of individuals working alone.* Effective team members behave differently from ineffective members.[3] One form of ineffective team behavior is social loafing, not doing one's share of the work, which spreads among team members.[4] Some members of groups are not team players; they look out for their own self-interest at the expense of team performance.[5] Their destructive behavior diverts other members' energies away from the real work.[6]

How the team members interact (human relations), called *group dynamics* and *process,* also affects individual and team behavior and performance.[7] Understanding group process can improve your team behavior and performance.[8] The foundation of team performance is interpersonal skills.[9] Organizations are continually expecting teams to achieve higher levels of performance in less time with fewer resources.[10] Therefore, group process plays a pivotal role in team performance.[11]

EXHIBIT 12.1 | The Team Performance Model

Team Performance	(f)*	Team Structure	+	Team Dynamics	+	Team Development Stage

*(f) = is a function of.

The Team Performance Model

The **team performance model** *states that a team's performance is based on its structure, dynamics, and stage of development.* The performance model can be stated as a formula. *Team performance* is a function of team structure[12] + team dynamics + team development stage.[13] The three components of the model are shown in Exhibit 12.1. You should realize that, to have high levels of performance, the team must have an effective structure for working together as a team, have good dynamic human relations, and develop its ability to work as a team.[14] Teams face the systems effect; if any one of the components is weak, performance suffers. In this chapter, we discuss each component in sequence in separate sections.

Types of Teams

We use the terms *groups* and *teams* interchangeably. There are *formal groups,* which are sanctioned by the organization, and *informal groups,* which develop spontaneously when members get together voluntarily because of similar interests. Groups can also be *ongoing,* without ending, or *temporary,* discontinuing after the objective is met. In this section, we discuss formal groups. Two of the major types of formal groups are functional and task.

Functional Groups   *Functional groups* are formal, ongoing teams that consist of managers and their employees. Each work unit or department makes up a functional group. As we noted in Chapter 6, the marketing, production, and operations departments are each a functional group with multiple other functional groups. There are also cross-functional groups, which can be ongoing or temporary.[15] Some functional groups are called *self-directed* groups or *self-managed* teams because team leadership is shared.[16]

Task Groups   *Task groups* consist of functional team members who work together on a specific task, usually with members of other functional teams; they are commonly cross-functional.[17] However, task groups are also created with a selected number of functional task team members. Being a member of a task group is in addition to your job in a functional group, so you can have two bosses. Task groups are often called committees. Managers facing decisions often create task groups to assist in the decision-making process.[18] There are two common types of task groups or committees.

The *ad hoc committee,* or *task force,* is a formal, temporary team that discontinues when its purpose is accomplished. For example, a task force can be created to select a new computer. The task force is no longer needed once it has selected the computer, so it disbands.

The *standing committee* is a formal, ongoing team that often has rotating members. For example, labor and management commonly have standing committees who work together to negotiate the ongoing collective bargaining agreements that result in a new contract.

Higher-level managers commonly serve on multiple task force and standing committees and spend a good part of their day in committee meetings.[19] Throughout this chapter we will be discussing functional and task groups, and you will learn how to conduct meetings.

Before we get into the details of the components of the team performance model, complete Self-Assessment Exercise 12–1 to determine your use of team behavior.

Your Team Behavior

For each statement, identify how accurately it describes your behavior. Place the number (1 to 5) on the line before each statement.

Describes me				Does not describe me
5	4	3	2	1

_____ 1. I influence the team members to do a good job of meeting organizational objectives.

_____ 2. I try to include the ideas and perspectives of all team members.

_____ 3. I offer creative ways to solve problems that help my team get the job done well.

_____ 4. I offer input in the decisions my team makes.

_____ 5. When there are team conflicts, I help members resolve the differences.

_____ 6. I make sure the team develops clear objectives.

_____ 7. When completing a task, I consider how many members are needed to accomplish the task and include the best team members for the task.

_____ 8. I use behavior that will help meet the organization's or team's objectives, and I encourage others to develop and enforce positive norms.

_____ 9. I try to include every member of the team so that they all feel like full, active members of the team. I don't exclude others in any way.

_____ 10. I'm comfortable with my place on the team; I can be a star or just one of the team's members. I try to help others be comfortable with their status.

_____ 11. I do and say things that directly help the team get the job done.

_____ 12. I do and say things that directly help the team develop and maintain good human relations.

_____ 13. I don't do and say things that benefit me at the expense of the team.

_____ 14. When I join a team that is just starting, such as a new committee, I help the team clarify and set objectives.

_____ 15. If members are dissatisfied with the team, I try to help resolve the issues so that everyone is satisfied with the team.

_____ 16. If a team member has a drop in commitment to the team, such as having personal problems or a bad day, I try to help that person get through the situation and keep his or her commitment to the team.

_____ 17. When the team is doing a good job, I don't interfere with the team's getting along or its performance.

Add your score and place the total here: _____. Then on the continuum below, mark the point that represents your score.

Effective team behavior	85 - - - 75 - - - 65 - - - 55 - - - 45 - - - 35 - - - 25 - - - 17	Ineffective team behavior

You don't need to do all these things for the team to be effective as long as someone else on the team does them. An important part of team skills is knowing the behavior that is needed to have a successful team and providing the needed behavior to help the team continue to develop.

Questions 1 to 5 refer to team structure, 6 to 13 to team dynamics, and 14 to 17 to team development. As you read about each of the three components, you may want to turn back and review your answers.

TEAM STRUCTURE

As shown in Exhibit 12.2, there are four team structure components that, along with team dynamics and development, affect team performance. All four components are discussed in detail in other chapters; therefore, we will be brief here. Refer to the other chapters for more details.

EXHIBIT 12.2 |
Team Structure
Components

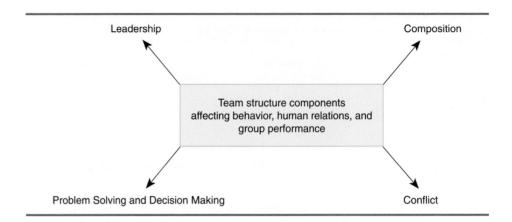

Leadership

We discussed leadership in Chapter 8. In this chapter we expand the coverage to leading teams as a situational supervisor, based on team development stages. We also cover how to run a meeting using leadership skills. Teams with effective leadership—and it should be shared by all[20]—clearly outperform teams lacking leadership skills.[21] Chapters 8 through 15 focus on developing your leadership skills.

Composition

Composition refers to the diversity of team members. Team mix, or diversity, involves more than gender and race. Functional technical skills are important. Recall the importance of using cross-functional teams (Chapter 6) to provide diversity.[22] Organizations expect to generate important benefits through diversity. However, diversity does not always increase performance; it must be effectively managed.[23] Managing diverse groups is one of the most difficult and pressing challenges in modern organizations.[24] However, effective diverse teams are more innovative,[25] make better decisions,[26] and are better with managing change[27] than homogeneous teams. We will discuss diversity in Chapter 15.

Problem Solving and Decision Making

All teams encounter problems in getting the job done. How the members work together to solve the problems affects team performance.[28] How decisions are made, whether the teams are centralized or decentralized (Chapter 6), and the decisions themselves also affect performance.[29] Effective use of employee participation in team decision making results in higher levels of performance.[30] Teams and creative problem solving and decision making are topics discussed in Chapter 13.

Conflict

Recall that conflict can be functional or dysfunctional; it can help or hurt team performance.[31] Diversity is a double-edged sword; it brings differences of opinion and perspective, which can increase performance, but it can also increase conflict, which can compromise performance.[32] How teams manage internal conflict is a critical factor in their success.[33] See Chapter 7 for a review of how to handle conflict.

TEAM DYNAMICS

Learning Outcome

1. Explain the six components of team dynamics and how they affect team performance.

Team dynamics *refers to the patterns of interactions that emerge as groups develop.* These interactions are also called *group process*.[34] Team success depends on the process team members use to interact with each other to accomplish the work.[35] So to be a good team player, you have to understand group dynamics.[36] Bill Gates, CEO of Microsoft, recommends doing projects in college to learn about group dynamics. Job recruiters are looking for applicants with leadership and team dynamics skills.[37] However, most team members have not been trained to work in a group. You will get training in this section, and with practice, you will become more effective, because team skills can be developed.[38] Next we discuss the six components of group dynamics: objectives, team size, team norms, group cohesiveness, status within the team, and group roles.

Objectives

To be effective, teams must agree on clear objectives and be committed to achieving them.[39] The leader should allow the group to have input in setting objectives, based on its capability to participate.[40]

Implications for Managers   Managers should be certain that their functional groups have measurable objectives and know the priorities. As an aid in setting objectives, you should follow the guidelines in Chapter 9 and use the model for writing objectives. The team objectives should be coordinated with organizational goals.[41]

When you are a member or follower, rather than the leader, try to get the group to set clear objectives that its members agree to and are committed to.[42] As a member of a team, you have an obligation to help the team be successful. If the team starts out without proper objectives, it probably will not be successful.[43]

WORK APPLICATIONS

For Work Applications (1) through (8), recall a specific group to which you belong or have belonged. If you will be doing Skill-Building Exercise 12–1, do not use your class group for this specific group now.

1. Does the group agree on, and are members committed to, clear objectives? Explain your answer.

Team Size

What is the ideal team size? The number varies, depending on the team's purpose. For functional groups to work well as self-directed teams, some companies use teams of 12 to 18, but most believe the ideal size is 14 or 15. Task groups are often smaller than functional groups. Fact-finding groups can be larger than problem-solving groups. There is no consensus on the ideal size for groups; some say three to nine, others say five, while still others say six to eight. If the group is too small, it tends to be too cautious; if it is too large, it tends to be too slow. But larger groups tend to generate more alternatives and higher-quality ideas because they benefit from diverse participation.[44]

How Size Affects Group Dynamics   Team size affects leadership, members, and the process of getting the job done. The larger the team size, the more formal or autocratic the leadership needs to be to provide direction. Managers tend to be more informal and participative when they have smaller functional groups. Group members are more tolerant of autocratic leadership in large groups. Larger groups tend to inhibit equal participation. Generally, participation is more equal in groups of around five members (and the greater need there is for formal plans, policies, procedures, and rules). Groups of 20 or more tend to be too large to reach consensus on decisions, and they tend to form subgroups.

Implications for Managers   Usually managers have no say in the size of their functional groups. However, the appropriate leadership style may vary with team size. Managers who chair a committee may be able to select the team size. In doing so, the chairperson should be sure to get the right people on the committee, while trying to keep the group size appropriate for the task.

Team Norms

Functional groups generally have standing plans to help provide the necessary guidelines for behavior, while task groups do not. However, standing plans cannot be complete enough to cover all situations. All groups tend to form their own unwritten rules about how things are done.[45] **Norms** *are the group's shared expectations of its members' behavior.* Norms determine what should, ought to, or must be done for the group to maintain consistent and desirable behavior.

How Norms Develop   Norms are developed spontaneously as the group members interact through the routine of the team. Each member brings cultural values and past experience to the group. The group's beliefs, attitudes, and knowledge influence the type of norms developed.[46] For example, a group produces 100 units per day. Thus 100 units becomes the norm if the group members develop a shared expectation that this behavior is desirable, and they produce it. Norms can change over time to meet the needs of the group.

How Teams Enforce Norms   If a team member does not follow the norm, the other members may try to enforce compliance.[47] The common ways teams enforce norms include ridicule, ostracism, sabotage, and physical abuse. Following the above example, if a member, Sal, produces more than 100 units per day, other members may kid or ridicule him. If Sal continues to break the norm, members could use physical abuse or ostracize him to enforce compliance with the norm. Members could also damage his units or take his tools or supplies to slow down his production.

Implications for Managers   Team norms can be positive, helping the team meet its objective(s), or they can be negative, hindering the group from meeting its objective(s).[48] Continuing the above example, if the company's production standard is 110 units per day, the team's norm of 100 is a negative norm; however, if the standard is 90, it would be a positive norm. Managers should be aware of their group's norms. They should work toward maintaining and developing positive norms, while trying to eliminate negative norms. Managers should confront groups with negative norms and try to work out agreeable solutions to both parties' satisfaction.

Group Cohesiveness

The extent to which a group will abide by and enforce its norms depends on its degree of cohesiveness. **Group cohesiveness** *is the attractiveness and closeness group members have for one another and for the group.* The more cohesive the group, the more it sticks together as a team. The more desirable group membership is, the more willing the members are to behave according to the team's norms. For example, if some team members take drugs, the team may develop a norm of taking drugs. This peer pressure to take drugs often wins out. To be accepted by the team, members will behave in ways they really don't agree with.

Factors Influencing Cohesiveness   Six factors affecting group cohesiveness are:

Objectives   The stronger the agreement and commitment made to the achievement of the group's objective(s), the greater the cohesiveness of the group.[49]

Size   Generally, the smaller the group, the greater the cohesiveness. The larger the group, the more difficulty there is in gaining consensus on objectives and norms. Three to nine members seems to be a good group size for cohesiveness.

Homogeneity   Generally, the more similar the group members are, the greater the cohesiveness. People tend to be attracted to people who are similar to themselves. However, homogeneity is on the decline as the workforce continues to diversify.[50]

Participation   Generally, the more equal the level of participation among group members, the greater the group's cohesiveness.[51] Groups dominated by one or a few members tend to be less cohesive since other members are excluded.

Competition   The focus of the competition affects cohesiveness. If the group focuses on intragroup competition and everyone tries to outdo one another, low cohesiveness results. If the group's focus is intergroup, the members tend to pull together as a team to beat the rivals. It is surprising how much a group can accomplish when no one cares who gets the credit.

Success   The more successful a group is at achieving its objectives, the more cohesive it tends to become. Success tends to breed cohesiveness, which in turn breeds more success. People want to be on a winning team. Have you ever noticed that losing teams tend to argue more than winning teams and complain that other members are messing up?

How Cohesiveness Affects Team Performance   Many research studies have compared cohesive and noncohesive teams and concluded that cohesive teams tend to have a higher level of success at achieving their objectives, with greater job satisfaction. Cohesive team members tend to miss work less often, are more trusting and cooperative, and exhibit less tension and hostility. S. E. Seashore has conducted one of the most highly recognized studies on this subject. Seashore found that:

- Groups with the highest levels of productivity were highly cohesive and accepted management's level of productivity.

- Groups with the lowest levels of productivity were also highly cohesive, but rejected management's level of productivity; they set and enforced their own level below that of management.

- Groups with intermediate levels of productivity were low cohesive groups, irrespective of their acceptance of management's level of productivity. The widest variance of individual group members' performance was among the groups with the lower levels of cohesiveness. They tended to be more tolerant of nonconformity with group norms.

Implications for Managers   Managers should strive to develop cohesive groups that accept their level of productivity. The use of participation helps the group develop cohesiveness while it builds agreement and commitment toward its objective(s).[52] While some intragroup competition may be helpful, managers should focus primarily on intergroup competition. This helps to develop a cohesive winning team, which in turn motivates the group to higher levels of success. Gaining team cohesiveness becomes an increasingly challenging task as the environment becomes more globally diversified.[53]

WORK APPLICATIONS

4. Is the group cohesive? How do the six factors listed above influence the group's cohesiveness? How does the level of cohesiveness affect the group's performance? Explain your answers.

Status within the Team

As team members interact, they develop respect for one another on numerous dimensions. The more respect, prestige, influence, and power a group member has, the higher his or her status within the team.[54] **Status** *is the perceived ranking of one member relative to other members of the group.*

The Development of Status   Status is based on several factors: a member's job title, wage or salary, seniority, knowledge or expertise, interpersonal skills, appearance, education, race, age, sex, and so on. Group status depends on the group's objectives, norms, and cohesiveness. Members who conform to the group's norms tend to have higher status than members who do not. A group is more willing to overlook a high-status member's breaking the norms. High-status members also have more influence on the development of the group's norms.[55] Lower-level members tend to copy high-status members' behavior and standards.

How Status Affects Team Performance   The high-status members have a major impact on the group's performance. In a functional group, the manager is usually the member with highest status. The manager's ability to manage affects group performance. In addition to the manager, high-status employees of the functional group also affect performance.[56] If high-status members support positive norms and high productivity, chances are the group will, too. The informal leader can have a lot of influence on the group.

Another important factor influencing group performance is status congruence. Status congruence is the acceptance and satisfaction members receive from their group status. Members who are not satisfied with their status may feel excluded from the team, and they may not be active team participants.[57] They may physically or mentally escape from the team and not perform to their full potential. Or they may cause team conflict as they fight for a higher status level.[58] Leadership struggles often go on for a long period or are never resolved. The group member who is dissatisfied with his or her status and decides on flight or fight leads the group to the same end result: lower performance levels for the group.

Implications for Managers   To be effective, the manager needs to have high status within the functional group.[59] To do so, the manager must perform the five functions of management—planning, organizing, staffing, leading, and controlling—well and have the necessary skills. The manager should maintain good human relations with the group, particularly with the high-status informal leader(s), to be sure they endorse positive norms and objectives. In addition, managers should be aware of conflicts that may be the result of lack of status congruence.[60] Managers should use the conflict management techniques discussed in Chapter 7.

WORK APPLICATIONS

5. List each team member in order by status in the team, including yourself. What are some of the characteristics that lead to high or low status on the team?

Group Roles

As a group works toward achieving its objective(s), it has to perform certain functions. As functions are performed, people develop roles.[61] **Roles** *are shared expectations of how group members will fulfill the requirements of their position.*

How Roles Develop   People develop their roles based on their own expectations, the organization's expectations, and the group's expectations.[62] Individuals come to the organization with expectations about how they should fulfill their positions or roles. When they join the organization, they learn about the organization's expectations through orientations, job descriptions, and managerial supervision. When interacting with the team, they learn the team's expectations of them—its norms. As employees internalize the expectations of these three sources, they develop their roles.

People often have multiple roles within the same position.[63] For example, a professor may have the roles of teacher, researcher, writer, consultant, advisor, and committee member. Our roles also expand outside the workplace. The professor may also be a family member, belong to professional and civic organizations, and have different circles of friends, all of which may have very different expectations.

Classifying Group Roles   Chapter 8 stated that when managers interact with employees, they can use directive behavior (structuring, job-centered, production- and task-oriented), supportive behavior (consideration, employee-centered, people's- and relationship-oriented), or both. These same two dimensions can also be performed by group members as they interact. When used to relate to group interactions, they are commonly called *task roles* and *maintenance roles.* A third category, called *self-interest roles,* is often added. Below we will discuss each type of role in more detail.

The group's **task roles** *are the things group members do and say that directly aid in the accomplishment of its objective(s).* Task roles can be subclassified as follows:

- Objective clarifiers—their role is to be sure everyone understands the objective.
- Planners—their role is to determine how the objective will be met.
- Organizers—their role is to assign and coordinate the resources.
- Leaders—their role is to influence members through direction as the task is performed.
- Controllers—their role is to take corrective action to ensure the objective is achieved.

The group's **maintenance roles** *are the things group members do and say to develop and sustain group dynamics.* Maintenance roles can be subclassified as follows:

- Formers—their role is to get the members involved and committed to the group.
- Consensus seekers—their role is to get members' input and agreement on group decisions.
- Harmonizers—their role is to help group members resolve their conflicts so that they do not interfere with group performance.
- Gatekeepers—their role is to see that appropriate norms are developed and enforced.
- Encouragers—their role is to be supportive, friendly, and responsive to the needs of the members.
- Compromisers—their role is to modify or to get others to modify their positions in the interest of cohesiveness.

In contrast to these two types of roles, **self-interest roles** *are the things members do and say to meet their own needs or objectives at the expense of the team.* Notice that this definition is similar to unethical politicking (Chapter 10) and the forcing conflict style (Chapter 7). When team members use self-interest roles, it is often in association with a *hidden agenda.*[64] These self-interest seekers often tell the team members how the team and the organization will benefit without coming out and saying what's in it for them personally. They may use unethical politics and the forcing conflict style to push others to get what they want. In other words, they often give the impression that they are concerned about others and the organization when in reality such behavior is a cover to get what they want, and they may do whatever it takes to get it.

As a team member, watch for self-interest roles and hidden agendas as you distinguish between a self-interest that benefits both the individual and the organization (a win–win situation) versus one that benefits the individual and hurts the organization (a win–lose situation). People using self-interest roles are problem team members. You will learn how to handle problem teammates later in the chapter.

Self-interest roles can be subclassified as follows:

- Aggressors—they deflate others' status through negative criticism or putting members and their ideas down.

- Blockers—they resist the group's efforts and prevent it from achieving its objectives.
- Recognition seekers—they try to take credit for the group's accomplishments.
- Withdrawers—they are physically or mentally involved in personal matters rather than those of the group.

How Roles Affect Team Performance   To be effective, a team must have members who play task roles and maintenance roles, while minimizing self-interest roles. Teams that have only task performers will suffer performance problems because the team does not deal effectively with conflict. Its group process will hurt performance. On the other hand, teams that do not have members playing task roles will not get the job done. Any team that has members playing self-interest roles will not produce to its fullest potential.

Implications for Managers   Managers should make the group aware of the need to play these roles. When in a group, you should be aware of the roles its members play. If the members are not playing the task and/or maintenance role required at a given time, you should play the role.[65] The next section discusses group development and the manager's use of task and maintenance roles as the group develops.

In the opening case, the objective is fairly clear, group size is adequate, and cohesiveness, status, and roles are not major problems. Kirt has been discrediting others' ideas, and others have followed his lead. A negative norm has developed that needs to be addressed by Bonnie Sue as the leader to ensure success of the group. Bonnie Sue can begin the next meeting by stating that the norm has developed and explain how it is destructive to the group. She can interrupt when Kirt and others put ideas down by reminding the group to be positive. The group can also discuss whether there are other negative norms that should be stopped. In addition, they can discuss the development of positive norms that can help the group do a better job. In terms of group roles, Carl is playing a task role for the group. Shelby is playing a maintenance role for the group. And Kirt is playing a self-interest role. How to handle Kirt, Shelby, and Carl as problem individuals will be discussed near the end of the chapter.

> ### WORK APPLICATIONS
>
> **6.** Using your list from Work Application (5), identify the major roles played by each group member, including yourself.

In summary, effective groups should have clear objectives with agreement and commitment to those objectives by its members, appropriate group size to achieve its objectives, positive norms, cohesiveness, status congruence, and members who play task and maintenance roles while minimizing self-interest roles. Developing effective group dynamics that meet the needs of the individuals and the group or organization creates a win–win situation for all parties. See Exhibit 12.3 for a review of the six components of team dynamics.

EXHIBIT 12.3 |
Team Dynamics
Components

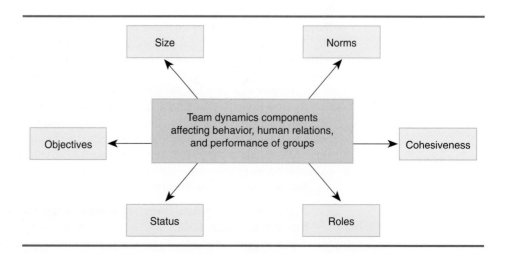

APPLICATION SITUATIONS

Group Dynamics

AS 12–1

Match each statement with the group dynamics issue it represents.

A. Objectives   C. Norms   E. Status

B. Size   D. Cohesiveness   F. Roles

_____ 1. "I'm a union man. If it wasn't for the union, we would not be getting the pay we do. Collective bargaining really works."

_____ 2. "I could use another employee, but there is no workplace available."

_____ 3. "I wish the administration would make up its mind. One month we produce one product, and the next month we change to another."

_____ 4. "When you need advice, go see Sharon; she knows the ropes around here better than anyone."

_____ 5. "Conrad, you're late for the meeting. Everyone else was on time, so we started without you."

APPLICATION SITUATIONS

Roles

AS 12–2

Match each statement with the role it fulfills.

A. Task   B. Maintenance   C. Self-interest

_____ 6. "Wait, we have not heard Kim's idea yet."

_____ 7. "Could you explain why we are doing this again?"

_____ 8. "We tried that before you came here; it does not work. My idea is much better."

_____ 9. "What does this have to do with the problem? We are getting sidetracked."

_____ 10. "I like that idea better than mine. Let's go with it."

Learning Outcome

2. Describe the five stages of a team's development.

TEAM DEVELOPMENT STAGES

Team development affects team dynamics, satisfaction, effort, and performance.[66] All teams are unique, with dynamics that change over a period of time.[67] However, it is generally agreed that all groups go through the same stages as they grow from a collection of individuals to a smoothly operating and effective team, department, or unit. R. B. Lacoursiere reviewed more than 200 articles and studies of group dynamics and developed a five-stage model that synthesizes most of what is known about group development.[68] The five stages are orientation, dissatisfaction, resolution, production, and termination. Although these five stages are described as separate and distinct, some elements of most group development stages (GDS) can be found in every other stage. Below we will describe each GDS.

Stage 1: Orientation

This *forming* stage is characterized by low development level (D1), high commitment, and low competence. When people first form a group, they tend to come to the group with a moderate to high commitment to the group. However, because they have not worked together, they do not have the competence to achieve the task. When first interacting, members tend to have anxiety over how they will fit in, what will be required of them, what the group will be like, what the purpose of the group is, and so forth.[69] When task groups are started, this stage is very apparent because the group is new. Traditional functional groups, on the other hand, are rarely started with all new members. Some functional groups never go beyond this forming stage. They never resolve these anxiety issues to progress to the next stage of development.[70] If roles and group objectives are never clearly stated and understood by members, it is difficult to develop as a group.[71]

Stage 2: Dissatisfaction

This *storming* stage is characterized by moderate development level (D2), lower commitment, and some competence. As members work together for some time, they tend to become dissatisfied with the group.[72] Members start to question: Why am I a member? Is the group going to accomplish anything? Why don't other group members do what is expected? and so forth. Often the task is more complex and difficult than anticipated; members become frustrated and have feelings of incompetence. However, the group does develop some competence to perform the task. Team members need to learn more about each other and build trust to develop as a group.[73] Groups stuck in this storming stage of development are characterized by demoralization, low motivation, and low productivity. They never progress to being satisfied with the group and learning to perform as a team as long as they are in stage 2.

Stage 3: Resolution

This *norming* stage is characterized by high development level (D3), variable commitment, and high competence. With time, members often resolve the differences between initial expectations and realities in relation to the objectives, tasks, skills, and so forth. As members develop competence, they often become more satisfied with the group and committed to it. Relationships develop that satisfy group members' affiliation needs. They learn to work together as they develop a group structure with acceptable norms and cohesiveness.[74] Commitment can vary from time to time as the group interacts. During periods of conflict or change, the group needs to resolve these issues.[75] If the group does not deal effectively with group dynamics issues, the group may regress to stage 2, or the group may plateau, fluctuating in commitment and competence. If the group successfully develops a positive group structure and dynamics, it will move to the next stage.

Stage 4: Production

This *performing* stage is characterized by outstanding development level (D4), high commitment, and high competence. At this stage, commitment and competence do not fluctuate much. This high commitment enhances productivity and performance, as does the high competence skill level.[76] The group works as a team and there is a high level of satisfaction of members' affiliation needs. The group maintains a positive group structure and dynamics. The fact that members are very productive helps lead to positive feelings.[77] The group dynamics may change with time, but the conflict issues are resolved quickly and easily; members are open with each other and their relationship is based on trust.[78]

Stage 5: Termination

In functional groups, the *adjourning* stage is not reached unless there is some drastic reorganization; however, it does occur in task groups. During this stage, members experience feelings about leaving the group. In groups that have progressed through all four stages of group development, the members usually feel sad that the group is ending. However, for groups that did not progress through the stages of development, a feeling of relief is often experienced. The group may talk about its termination over a period of time or only at the last

EXHIBIT 12.4 |

Team Development
Stages 1 through 4

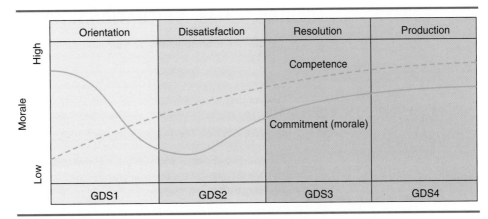

Note: If a team is at stage 5, it terminates and has no competence and commitment. There is no development.

meeting. Feelings about adjourning tend to vary with the meaningfulness of the relationship, and whether the members will be seeing each other at all after the group terminates.

The two key variables identified through each stage of group development are work on the task (competence) and the socioemotional tone or morale (commitment). The two variables do not progress in the same manner. Competence tends to continue to increase through each of the first four stages, while commitment tends to start high in stage 1, drop in stage 2, and then rise through stages 3 and 4. This pattern is illustrated in Exhibit 12.4.

In the opening case, Bonnie Sue's committee is in stage 2—dissatisfaction. The group has had a decrease in commitment and an increase in competence. The group needs to resolve the dissatisfaction to progress to stages 3 and 4 of development. Being an ad hoc committee, the group will go through stage 5—termination—in three weeks. The next section discusses how Bonnie Sue can help the group develop to stages 3 and 4 as a situational supervisor.

WORK APPLICATIONS

7. Identify the group's stage of development and the leader's situational supervisory style. Does the leader use the appropriate style?

8. What can be done to improve the group's dynamics? Explain.

APPLICATION SITUATIONS

Group Development Stages

AS 12–3

Identify the group's development stage as:

A. GDS1   B. GDS2   C. GDS3   D. GDS4   E. GDS5

_____ 11. Members have come to realize that their initial expectations are not a reality and they accept the situation.

_____ 12. The ad hoc committee has presented its recommendations to management.

_____ 13. Group members are trying to get to know one another.

_____ 14. The group set a new record level of production.

_____ 15. Members are sitting around and complaining.

LEADING TEAMS: A SITUATIONAL APPROACH

Before we discuss leading teams as a situational supervisor, complete Self-Assessment Exercise 12–2.

Determining Your Preferred Group Leadership Style

In the 12 situations below, select the response that represents what you would actually do as the group's leader. Ignore the D _____ and S _____ lines; they will be used as part of Skill-Building Exercise 12–2.

1. Your group works well together; members are cohesive, with positive norms. They maintain a fairly consistent level of production that is above the organizational average, as long as you continue to provide maintenance behavior. You have a new assignment for them. To accomplish it, you would: D _____
   a. Explain what needs to be done and tell them how to do it. Oversee them while they perform the task. S _____
   b. Tell the group how pleased you are with their past performance. Explain the new assignment, but let them decide how to accomplish it. Be available if they need help. S _____
   c. Tell the group what needs to be done. Encourage them to give input on how to do the job. Oversee task performance. S _____
   d. Explain to the group what needs to be done. S _____

2. You have been promoted to a new supervisory position. The group appears to have little talent to do the job, but members do seem to care about the quality of the work they do. The last supervisor was terminated because of the department's low productivity level. To increase productivity, you would: D _____
   a. Let the group know you are aware of its low production level, but let them decide how to improve it. S _____
   b. Spend most of your time overseeing group members as they perform their jobs. Train them as needed. S _____
   c. Explain to the group that you would like to work together to improve productivity. Work together as a team. S _____
   d. Tell the group some ways productivity can be improved. With their ideas, develop methods, and make sure they are implemented. S _____

3. Your department continues to be one of the top performers in the organization. It works well as a team. In the past, you generally let members take care of the work on their own. You decide to: D _____
   a. Go around encouraging group members on a regular basis. S _____
   b. Define members' roles, and spend more time overseeing performance. S _____
   c. Continue things the way they are; let them alone. S _____
   d. Hold a meeting. Recommend ways to improve and get members' ideas as well. After agreeing on changes, oversee the group to make sure it implements the new ideas and does improve. S _____

4. You have spent much of the past year training your employees. However, they do not need as much of your time to oversee production as they used to. Several group members no longer get along as well as they did in the past. You've played referee lately. You: D _____
   a. Have a group meeting to discuss ways to increase performance. Let the group decide what changes to make. Be supportive. S _____
   b. Continue things the way they are now. Supervise them closely and be the referee when needed. S _____
   c. Let the members alone to work things out for themselves. S _____
   d. Continue to supervise closely as needed, but spend more time playing maintenance roles; develop a team spirit. S _____

5. Your department has been doing such a great job that it has grown in numbers. You are surprised at how fast the new members were integrated. The team continues to come up with ways to improve performance on its own. As a result of the growth, your department will be moving to a new, larger location. You decide to: D _____
   a. Design the new layout and present it to the group to see if they can improve it. S _____
   b. In essence, become a group member and allow the group to design the new layout. S _____
   c. Design the new layout and put a copy on the bulletin board so employees know where to report for work after the move. S _____
   d. Hold a meeting to get employee ideas on the layout of the new location. After the meeting, think about it and finalize the layout. S _____

6. You are appointed to head a task group. Because of the death of a relative, you had to miss the first meeting. At the second meeting, the group seems to have developed objectives and some ground rules. Members have volunteered for assignments that have to be accomplished. You: D _____
   a. Take over as a strong leader. Change some ground rules and assignments. S _____
   b. Review what has been done so far, and keep things as is. However, take charge and provide clear direction from now on. S _____
   c. Take over the leadership but allow the group to make the decisions. Be supportive and encourage them. S _____
   d. Seeing that the group is doing so well, leave and do not attend any more meetings. S _____

7. Your group was working at, or just below, standard. However, there has been a conflict within the group. As a result, production is behind schedule. You: D _____
   a. Tell the group how to resolve the conflict. Then closely supervise to make sure your plan is followed and production increases. S _____
   b. Let the group work it out. S _____
   c. Hold a meeting to work as a team to come up with a solution. Encourage the group to work together. S _____
   d. Hold a meeting to present a way to resolve the conflict. Sell the members on its merits, include their input, and follow up. S _____

8. The organization has allowed flextime. Two of your employees have asked if they could change work hours. You are concerned because all busy work hours need adequate coverage. The department is very cohesive, with positive norms. You decide to: D _____
   a. Tell them things are going well; keep things as they are now. S _____
   b. Hold a department meeting to get everyone's input; then reschedule members' hours. S _____
   c. Hold a department meeting to get everyone's input; then reschedule members' hours on a trial basis. Tell the group that if there is any drop in productivity, you will go back to the old schedule. S _____
   d. Tell them to hold a department meeting. If the department agrees to have at least three people on the job during the busy hours, they can make changes, giving you a copy of the new schedule. S _____

9. You have arrived 10 minutes late for a department meeting. Your employees are discussing the latest assignment. This surprises you because, in the past, you had to provide clear direction and employees rarely would say anything. You: D _____
   a. Take control immediately and provide your usual direction. S _____
   b. Say nothing and just sit back. S _____
   c. Encourage the group to continue, but also provide direction. S _____
   d. Thank the group for starting without you, and encourage them to continue. Support their efforts. S _____

10. Your department is consistently very productive. However, occasionally, the members fool around and someone has an accident. There has never been a serious injury. You hear a noise and go to see what it was. From a distance you can see Sue

sitting on the floor, laughing, with a ball made from company material in her
hand. You: D _____

a. Say and do nothing. After all, she's OK, and the department is very productive; you
   don't want to make waves. S _____

b. Call the group together and ask for suggestions on how to keep accidents from recurring. Tell them you will be checking up on them to make sure the fooling around does
   not continue. S _____

c. Call the group together and discuss the situation. Encourage them to be more careful
   in the future. S _____

d. Tell the group that from now on, you will be checking up on them regularly. Bring
   Sue to your office and discipline her. S _____

11. You are at the first meeting of an ad hoc committee you are leading. Most of the mem-
    bers are second- and third-level managers from marketing and financial areas; you are a
    supervisor from production. You decide to start by: D _____

    a. Working on developing relationships. Get everyone to feel as though they know each
       other before you talk about business. S _____

    b. Going over the group's purpose and the authority it has. Provide clear directives.
       S _____

    c. Asking the group to define its purpose. Because most of the members are higher-level
       managers, let them provide the leadership. S _____

    d. Start by providing both direction and encouragement. Give directives and thank peo-
       ple for their cooperation. S _____

12. Your department has done a great job in the past. It is now getting a new computer,
    somewhat different from the old one. You have been trained to operate the computer, and
    you are expected to train your employees to operate it. To train them, you: D _____

    a. Give the group instructions, work with them individually, providing direction and en-
       couragement. S _____

    b. Get the group together to decide how they want to be instructed. Be very supportive
       of their efforts to learn. S _____

    c. Tell them it's a simple system. Give them a copy of the manual and have them study it
       on their own. S _____

    d. Give the group instructions. Then go around and supervise their work closely, giving
       additional instructions as needed. S _____

To determine your preferred group leadership style, in the table below, circle the letter you
selected in situations 1 through 12. The column headings indicate the style you selected.

	Autocratic (S-A)	Consultative (S-C)	Participative (S-P)	Laissez-faire (S-L)
1.	a	c	b	d
2.	b	d	c	a
3.	b	d	a	c
4.	b	d	a	c
5.	c	a	d	b
6.	a	b	c	d
7.	a	d	c	b
8.	a	c	b	d
9.	a	c	d	b
10.	d	b	a	c
11.	b	d	a	c
12.	d	a	b	c
Total				

**Self-Assessment
Exercise 12–2 (*continued*)**

Add the number of circled items per column. The total for all four columns should equal 12. The column with the highest number represents your preferred group leadership style. There is no one best style in all situations.

The more evenly distributed the numbers are among the four styles, the more flexible you are at leading groups. A total of 0 or 1 in any column may indicate a reluctance to use that style. You could have problems in situations calling for that style.

Is your preferred group leadership style the same as your preferred situational supervision style (Chapter 8) and situational communication style (Chapter 6)?

Learning Outcome

3. Explain the four situational supervisory styles to use with a group, based on its stage of development.

Situational Supervision and Group Development Stages

Situational supervision can be applied to the stages of group development. Chapter 8 presented the situational supervision model. In that chapter, the major focus was on supervising individual employees. Below you will find changes, with the focus on applying the model to the stages of group development. With each stage of group development, a different supervisory style is needed to help the group perform effectively at that stage and to develop to the next level.

As stated, when managers interact with their groups, they can perform task roles, maintenance roles, or both. You will learn which role(s) the manager should play during the different stages of group development.

The **group development stage 1,** *orientation—low development D1 (high commitment/ low competence), uses the autocratic supervisory style (high task/low maintenance), S-A.* When a task group first comes together, the manager needs to help the group clarify its objectives to provide the direction to be sure the group gets off to a good start. Because the members are committed to joining the group, the manager needs to help the group develop its competence with task behavior.[79]

When managers work with their functional groups, they must be sure that the group has clear objectives and that members know their roles.[80] If the group does not, or when there are complex changes, the manager must play the appropriate task role.

The **group development stage 2,** *dissatisfaction—moderate development D2 (lower commitment/some competence), uses the consultative supervisory style (high task/high maintenance), S-C.* Even though task and functional groups know their objectives and their roles are clear, the members become dissatisfied for a variety of reasons, such as not getting along with one or more members or not being happy with the amount of influence they have in the group.[81] When morale drops, the manager needs to focus on maintenance roles to encourage members to resolve issues.[82] The manager should help the members meet their needs as they develop the appropriate group structure. At the same time, the manager needs to continue to play the task role necessary to help the group develop its level of competence.

The **group development stage 3,** *resolution—high development D3 (variable commitment/high competence), uses the participative supervisory style (low task/high maintenance), S-P.* When task and functional group members know their objectives and their roles are clear, there is little need to provide task leadership; the members know how to do the job.[83]

When commitment varies, it is usually due to some problem in the group's dynamics, such as a conflict or a loss of interest.[84] What the manager needs to do is focus on the maintenance behavior to get the group through the issue(s) it faces. If the manager continues to provide task directives that are not needed, the group can become dissatisfied and regress or plateau at this level.

Managers who can develop the type of group structure and dynamics discussed will develop groups to the third or fourth levels. The managers who cannot will have groups that plateau on the second level of group development. Motivating employees and developing and maintaining human relations is an ongoing process. Using the participative style helps the members develop their commitment, which, in turn, affects their competence.[85]

EXHIBIT 12.5 | Group Situational Supervision

Group Development Stage (D)	Supervisory Styles/Roles (S)
D1 Low Development ⟶ *High commitment/low competence →*	**S-A Autocratic** *High task/low maintenance*
Members come to the group committed, but they cannot perform with competence.	Provide direction so that the group has clear objectives and members know their roles. Make the decisions for the group.
D2 Moderate Development ⟶ *Low commitment/some competence →*	**S-C Consultative** *High task/high maintenance*
Members have become dissatisfied with the group. They have started to develop competence but are frustrated with results.	Continue to direct the group so it develops task ability. Provide maintenance to regain commitment as the group structure takes place. Include members' input in decisions.
D3 High Development ⟶ *Variable commitment/high competence →*	**S-P Participative** *Low task/high maintenance*
Commitment changes over time while production remains relatively constant.	Provide little direction. Focus on developing an effective group structure. Have the group participate in decision making.
D4 Outstanding Development ⟶ *High commitment/high competence →*	**S-L Laissez-faire** *Low task/low maintenance*
Commitment remains constantly high and so does production.	Members provide their own task and maintenance roles. The supervisor is a group member. Allow the group to make its own decisions.

The **group development stage 4,** *production—outstanding development D4 (high commitment/high competence), uses the laissez-faire supervisory style (low task/low maintenance), S-L.* Groups that develop to this stage have members who play the appropriate task and maintenance roles; the manager does not need to play either role unless there is a problem.

As a manager, you should determine your group's current level of development and strive to bring it to the next stage of development.

In the opening case, Bonnie Sue's committee is in stage 2—dissatisfaction. Bonnie Sue needs to play both task and maintenance roles to help the group progress to stages 3 and 4. Focusing on solving the negative norm of putting each other's ideas down works on both task and maintenance levels. Bonnie Sue also needs to provide stronger leadership in the areas of completing meeting assignments and making Kirt, Shelby, and Carl more productive. You will learn how in the next section.

The four stages of group development, along with their appropriate situational supervisory styles, are summarized in Exhibit 12.5.

LEADERSHIP SKILLS IN MEETINGS

Meeting skills are necessary to create an environment of trust, respect, and confidence.[86] Managers spend a lot of hours per week in meetings.[87]

With the trend toward self-directed teams, meetings in the workplace are taking up an increasing amount of time. Since time spent in meetings is increasing for all levels of employees, the need for meeting management skills is stronger than ever.[88] The most common complaints about meetings are these: There are too many meetings, they are too long, and they are unproductive.[89] Even so, meetings are very important to career success. Careers may be made or broken in the power arenas of meetings. The success or failure of meetings rests primarily with the leader and interpersonal communications.[90] In this section, we discuss planning meetings, conducting meetings, and handling problem team members.

Ganging Up on Management: Storming Shareholders Form Activist Groups

CEOs of public corporations have been put on notice by a new type of shareholder—shareholders who do not accept the company line and create activist groups. Shareholders could always participate in the overall direction of these firms through the election of members of the board and through their ability to have shareholder propositions placed on the ballots, yet several have recently felt that these rights were not enough to have any real effect on these firms. The formation of stockholder activist groups or teams represents a splintering of stockholders' interests from the general group of firm investors.

What is driving all this activity? Displeasure on the part of a growing number of antsy investors with how executives at many companies are managing their businesses and allocating capital. The investors aren't bashful about telling the companies how to get shares higher. Companies continue to grant executives excessive pay packages, or engage in wasteful spending. A lot of companies in our country are poorly managed and bloated, with too many layers at the top.

Although management cannot disregard these activist groups and their plans for the firm, activist behavior has been questioned by management because these vocal investors are looking for short-term gains and paybacks, potentially leaving firms in less healthy condition for the long term.

Also, these groups do not represent the majority of the shareholders of the firm; therefore, they are creating what might be called minority tyranny. It has been argued that if these shareholder groups want to have their voices heard they should go through the normal processes of nominating members to the board of directors and then conducting an election campaign for their representatives.

Questions

1. In general, how might firm performance (structure + dynamics + development stage) factor into the formation of these stockholder interest groups?

2. Specifically, how might firm leadership and management–stockholder conflicts apply as well?

3. What norms are driving these stockholders to form these new groups and what factors may lead to high or low group cohesion?

4. Corporations, like democratic governments, are formed with the underlying philosophy of majority rule; those who own the most shares have the most voice. How equitable to managers and regular stockholders are the changed firm dynamics being caused by these activist groups (even if these firms are underperforming and/or their executives are overpaid)?

5. Are activist groups who represent a minority of stockholders' interests being ethical in pressing management for change?

6. Are managers who ignore or fight activist groups being ethical?

Learning Outcome

4. Explain how to plan for and conduct effective meetings.

Planning Meetings

There are at least five areas in which meeting planning is needed: the objectives, the participants and assignments, the agenda, the time and place for the meeting, and leadership. A written copy of the plan should be sent to members prior to the meeting.[91]

Objectives Before getting a group started, determine what is wanted from the team.[92] The single greatest mistake made by those who call meetings is that they often have no clear idea and purpose for the meeting. Leaders should state what they want to happen as a result of the meeting. Before calling a meeting, you should clearly define its purpose and objective.[93]

Participants and Assignments Before calling the meeting, the leader should decide who is qualified to attend the meeting. The more people who attend a meeting, the less chance there is that any work will get done. Does the full group or department need to attend? Should some nongroup specialist be invited to provide input? On controversial issues, the leader may find it wiser to meet with the key members before the meeting to discuss and/or vote on an issue. Recall the discussion of coalitions in Chapter 11.

Participants should know in advance what is expected of them at the meeting. If any preparation is expected (reading material, doing some research, preparing a report, and the like), they should have adequate advance notice.

Agenda   Before calling the meeting, the leader should identify the activities that will take place during the meeting to achieve the objective of the meeting.[94] The agenda tells the members what is expected and how the meeting will progress. Having a set time limit for each agenda item helps keep the group on target; getting off the subject is common in meetings.

Place agenda items in order of priority. Then if the group does not have time to cover every item, the least important items carry forward. At too many meetings, a leader puts all the so-called quick items first. The group gets bogged down and either rushes through the important items or puts them off until later.

Members who are to give reports should do so early in the meeting. The reason for this procedure is that people get anxious and tend to be preoccupied with their report. Once it's over, they are more relaxed and can become more actively involved in the meeting. It is frustrating to prepare to give a report, only to be told "we'll get to it next time." This sends a message that the member and the report are not important.

Date, Time, and Place   In determining which day(s) and time(s) of the week are best for meetings, get members' input. Members tend to be more alert early in the day. Clearly specify the beginning and ending time. Be sure to select an adequate place for the meeting and plan for the physical comfort of the group. Be sure seating provides eye contact for small discussion groups, and plan enough time so that the members do not have to rush. If reservations are needed for the meeting place, make them far enough in advance to get a proper meeting room.

With advances in technology, telephone conferences and meetings are becoming quite common. Videoconferences are also gaining popularity. These techniques have saved travel costs and time, and they have resulted in better and quicker decisions. Some of the companies using videoconferencing include Arco, Boeing, Aetna, Ford, IBM, TRW, and Xerox. The personal computer has been said to be the most useful tool for running meetings since *Robert's Rules of Order*. The personal computer can be turned into a large-screen "intelligent chalkboard" that can dramatically change meeting results. Minutes (notes on what took place during the meeting) can be taken on the personal computer and a hard copy distributed at the end of the meeting.

Leadership   The leader should determine the group's level of development and plan to provide the appropriate task and/or maintenance behavior. Each agenda item may need to be handled differently.[95] For example, some items may simply call for disseminating information, while others may require a discussion or a vote to be taken; some items may require a report from a member.

An effective way to develop group members' abilities is to rotate the role of the group moderator or leader for each meeting, with groups that are capable of doing so.

The Written Plan   After leaders have planned the above five items, they should put them in writing and make copies to be distributed to each member who will attend the meeting. Exhibit 12.6 provides the recommended contents, in sequence, of a meeting plan.

Conducting Meetings

Below, you will learn about the group's first meeting, the three parts of each meeting, and leadership, group structure and dynamics, and emotions.

EXHIBIT 12.6 | Written Meeting Plan

Time: Date, day, place, beginning and ending times.

Objectives: A statement of the purpose and/or objective of the meeting.

Participants and Assignments: List each participant's name and assignment, if any. If all members have the same assignment, make one assignment statement.

Agenda: List each item to be covered in priority order with its approximate time limit.

The First Meeting   At the first meeting, the group is in the orientation stage. The leader should use the high task role; however, the members should be given the opportunity to spend some time getting to know one another. Introductions set the stage for subsequent interactions. If members find that their social needs will not be met, dissatisfaction may occur quickly. A simple technique is to start with introductions, then move on to the group's purpose, objectives, and members' roles. Sometime during or following this procedure, have a break that enables members to interact informally.

The Three Parts of Each Meeting   Each meeting should cover the following:

1. *Objectives.* Begin the meetings on time; waiting for late members penalizes the members who are on time and develops a norm for coming late. Begin by reviewing progress to date, the group's objectives, and the purpose or objective for the specific meeting. If minutes are recorded, they are usually approved at the beginning of the next meeting. For most meetings, it is recommended that a secretary be appointed to take minutes.

2. *Agenda.* Cover the agenda items. Try to keep to the approximate times, but be flexible. If the discussion is constructive and members need more time, give it to them; however, if the discussion is more of a distractive argument, move ahead.

3. *Summarize and review assignments.* End the meeting on time. The leader should summarize what took place during the meeting. Were the meeting's objectives achieved? Review all of the assignments given during the meeting. Get a commitment to the task that each member should perform for the next or a specific future meeting. The secretary and/or leader should record all assignments. If there is no accountability and follow-up on assignments, members may not complete them.

Leadership, Group Structure and Dynamics, and Emotions   As stated in the last section, leadership needs to change with the group's level of development.[96] The leader must be sure to provide the appropriate task and/or maintenance behavior when it is needed.

The leader is responsible for helping the team develop an effective group structure. The leader must focus on the group's dynamics as it performs the task and make the team aware of how its process affects its performance and members' commitment. The team needs to create and maintain positive emotions that promote working together effectively. Negative emotions should not be ignored; they should be refocused in a positive direction. Individual members, subgroups, or the entire team may get emotional. Feelings can be caused by the meeting content, the members' perception of the group structure, and the group dynamics. As a member of a team, you need to focus on both verbal and nonverbal communications (see Chapter 5) to help the team understand how its group dynamics are affecting its behavior, human relations, and performance. Do not look only at the speaker; watch others as they listen. When team members show signs of being upset, bring it to the team's attention and discuss it using active listening and conflict resolution skills.[97] Team building (Chapter 14) is a productive technique to help the group develop an effective group structure and dynamics.

WORK APPLICATIONS

9. Recall a specific meeting you attended. Did the group leader plan for the meeting by stating meeting objectives, identifying participants and their assignments, making an agenda, and stating the date, time, and place of the meeting? Did the leader provide a written meeting plan to the members prior to the meeting? Explain your answers and state what you would do differently if you were the leader.

Learning Outcome

5. Identify five problem
    members and explain
    how to handle them so
    they do not have a
    negative effect on your
    meetings.

Handling Problem Team Members

As team members work together, personality types tend to emerge. Certain personality types can cause the group to be less efficient than possible.[98] Some of the problem members you may have in your team are the following: the silent member, the talker, the wanderer, the bored member, and the arguer. Below we will discuss how to handle each type to make the member and the group more effective.

The Silent Member   For a team to be fully effective, all group members should participate. If members are silent, the team does not get the benefit of their input.

It is the leader's responsibility to encourage the silent member to participate, without being obvious or overbearing. A technique the leader can use is the simple rotation method, in which all members take turns giving their input. These methods are generally less threatening than directly calling on members. However, these methods are not appropriate all the time. To build up the silent members' confidence, call on them with questions they can easily answer. When you believe they have convictions, ask them to express them. Watch their nonverbal communications.

If you are a silent type, try to participate more often. Know when to stand up for your views and be assertive. Silent types generally do not make good leaders.

The Talker   Talkers have something to say about everything. They like to dominate the discussion. However, if they do dominate, the other members do not get to participate. The talker can cause intragroup problems.

It is the leader's responsibility to slow talkers down, not to shut them up. Do not let them dominate the group. The simple rotation method is effective with talkers, helping them learn that they have to wait their turn. When not using a rotation method, gently interrupt the talker and present your own ideas or call on other members to present their ideas. Prefacing questions with statements like, "Let's give those who have not answered yet a chance" can also slow the talker down.

The penny technique can also be used to slow down the talker and encourage the silent to participate. At the start of the meeting, give each participant five pennies and ask for one back every time a person speaks. When a participant's pennies run out, deny further input. At the end of the meeting, collect the remaining pennies to see who did not participate, and encourage them to do so in future meetings. This is admittedly a rather clumsy technique, but it works.

If you tend to be a talker, try to slow down. Give others a chance to talk and do things for themselves. Good leaders develop employees' abilities in these areas.

The Wanderer   Wanderers distract the team from the agenda items and often like to complain and criticize.

The leader is responsible for keeping the group on track. If the wanderer wants to socialize, cut off the conversation. Be kind, thank the member for the contribution, and then throw a question out to the group to get it back on track. However, if the wanderer has a complaint that is legitimate and solvable, allow the group to discuss it. Group structure issues should be addressed and resolved; however, if it is not resolvable, get the group back on track. Griping without resolving anything tends to reduce morale and commitment to task accomplishment. If the wanderer complains about unresolvable issues, the leader should make statements like, "We may be underpaid, but we have no control over our pay. Complaining will not get us a raise; let's get back to the issue at hand."

If you tend to be a wanderer, try to be aware of your behavior and stay on the subject at hand.

The Bored Member   Your team may have one or more members who are not interested in the task. The bored person may be preoccupied with other issues and not pay attention or participate in the group meeting. The bored member may be a know-it-all, who feels superior and wonders why the group is spending so much time on the obvious.

The leader is responsible for keeping members motivated. Assign the bored member a task such as recording ideas on the board or recording the minutes. Call on bored members; bring them into the group. If you allow them to sit back, things may get worse and others may decide not to participate either. Negative feelings can easily be carried to other team members.

If you tend to be bored, try to find ways to help motivate yourself. Work at becoming more patient and in control of behavior that can have negative effects on other members.

The Arguer   Like the talker, the arguer likes to be the center of attention. This behavior can occur when you use the devil's advocate approach, which is helpful in developing and selecting alternative courses of action. However, arguers enjoy arguing for the sake of arguing, rather than helping the group. They turn things into a win–lose situation, and they cannot stand losing.

The leader should resolve conflict but not in an argumentative way. Do not get into an argument with arguers; that is exactly what they want to happen. If an argument starts, bring others into the discussion. If it is personal, cut it off. Personal attacks only hurt the group. Keep the discussion moving on target. Try to minimize arguers' opportunities for confrontation.

If you tend to be an arguer, strive to convey your views in an assertive debate format, not as an aggressive argument. Listen to others' views and be willing to change if they have better ideas.

Conclusion   Whenever you work in a team, do not embarrass, intimidate, or argue with any members, no matter how much they provoke you. If you do, the result will make martyrs of them and a bully of you to the team. If you have serious problem members who do not respond to the above techniques, confront them individually outside the team meeting. Get them to agree to work in a cooperative way.

In the opening case, Bonnie Sue's meetings lacked specific assignments. She needs to use more directive leadership and assign tasks to specific members to complete outside the meetings. Recall that the problem members in Bonnie Sue's group were Carl, a talker; Shelby, a wanderer; and Kirt, an arguer. Bonnie Sue needs to use her leadership skills to slow Carl down, keep Shelby on topic, keep Kirt from fighting with others, and resolve conflicts quickly.

WORK APPLICATIONS

10. Identify group problem members at a meeting you attended. Was the leader effective in handling them? What would you have done to make them more productive members? Explain in detail.

APPLICATION SITUATIONS

Problem Team Members

AS 12–4

Identify the problem member as:

A. Silent member   C. Wanderer   E. Arguer

B. Talker   D. Bored member

_____ 16. Jesse is always first or second to give his ideas. He is always elaborating on ideas. Because Jesse is so quick to respond, others sometimes make comments to him about it.

_____ 17. Two of the group members are sitting back quietly today for the first time. The other members are doing all the discussing and volunteering for assignments.

_____ 18. As the group is discussing a problem, a member asks the group if anyone heard about the vice president and the sales clerk.

_____ 19. Eunice is usually last to give her ideas. When asked to explain her position, Eunice often changes her answers to agree with the group.

_____ 20. Hank enjoys challenging members' ideas. He likes to have the group do things his way. When a group member does not agree with Hank, he makes wise comments about the member's past mistakes.

PUTTING IT ALL TOGETHER

Organizations use groups to meet performance objectives. As the people in a team interact, they develop group dynamics. The group structure—leadership and ability to solve problems and make decisions—is a major determinant of the group's stage of development. The more effective the group structure and dynamics, the higher the stage of development. And the higher the stage of development, the greater the level of performance of the group. The group's performance, in turn, affects its behavior and human relations. Have you ever noticed that the behavior and human relations of a group or team varies, depending on whether it meets its objectives (wins) or doesn't (loses)?

When you lead groups in a manner that meets the needs of the individuals while attaining the performance objective of the group, you create a win–win situation.

See Exhibit 12.7 for an illustration of how the factors discussed in this chapter influence teams.

Reading Exhibit 12.7, do you understand that the group's behavior and human relations are influenced by the group's structure and dynamics, as it progresses through stages of development? These, in turn, affect the group's performance. The group's performance also influences group behavior and human relations because the process is an ongoing one, rather than one having a clear starting and ending point.

Global Team Differences

At major global multinational corporations (MNCs), teamwork has been a buzzword in management for years.[99] However, the level of teamwork does vary. In general, in Asian countries, including Japan, teamwork is considered very important and leadership and decision making are participative, the group composition is not very diversified, with shared norms and cohesiveness, and there is less conflict than within the United States and many European countries. Unlike in the United States and many European countries, there are fewer status differences, as Asians don't want to stand out as being the stars—they just want to be part of the team.[100]

U.S. team behavior that is offensive in most other countries (especially Asian and Latin American countries and Mexico) includes getting down to business too quickly. Taking time to develop human relations is important. Also, being aggressive or impatient

EXHIBIT 12.7 | Team Performance Model Components

Team Performance (f)*	Team Structure	Team Dynamics	Team Development Stage
High ↔ Low	• Leadership • Composition • Problem solving and decision making • Conflict	• Objectives • Size • Norms • Cohesiveness • Status • Roles	1. Orientation 2. Dissatisfaction 3. Resolution 4. Production 5. Termination

*(f) = is a function of.

and making frequent interruptions to get your point across are signs of a poor team player.[101] Many MNCs are screening out nonteam players before they hire, rather than firing them later. So if you are part of a team with people from other countries, be careful of your behavior so that it develops, not hurts, human relations.

Learning to develop group dynamics, group leadership, and group problem-solving and decision-making skills will help you become a more effective group member.

As we bring this chapter to a close, complete Self-Assessment Exercise 12–3 to better understand how your personality affects your team behavior.

**Self-Assessment
Exercise 12–3**

Personality Traits and Teams

Read the two statements below:

I enjoy being part of a team and working with others more than working alone.

Strongly agree   7   6   5   4   3   2   1   Strongly disagree

I enjoy achieving team goals more than individual accomplishments.

Strongly agree   7   6   5   4   3   2   1   Strongly disagree

The stronger you agree with these two statements, the higher the probability that you will be a good team player. [However, not agreeing strongly does not mean that you are not a good team player.] Below is some information on how the Big Five personality dimensions and their related motive needs can affect your teamwork.

If you have a high *surgency* personality, you probably have a high need for power. Whether you are the team leader or not, you have to be careful not to dominate the group. Seek others' input, and know when to lead and when to follow. Even when you have great ideas, be sensitive to others so they don't feel that you are bullying them, and stay calm as you influence them. Be aware of your motives to make sure you benefit the team. You have the potential to make a positive contribution to the team with your influencing leadership skills. If you have a low need for power, try to be assertive so that others don't take advantage of you, and speak up when you have good ideas.

If you are high in *agreeableness* personality traits, with a high need for affiliation, you will tend to be a good team player. However, don't let the fear of hurting relationships get in your way of influencing the team when you have good ideas. Don't be too quick to give in to others. It doesn't help the performance of the team when you have a better idea that is not implemented. You have the potential to be a valuable asset to the team as you contribute your skills of working well with others and making them feel important. If you have a low need for affiliation, be careful to be sensitive to others.

If you are high in *conscientiousness,* with a high need for achievement, you have to watch your natural tendency to be more of an individualist than a team player. It's good to have your own goals, but if the team and organization fail, so do you. Remember that there is usually more than one good way to do anything; your way is not always the best. Don't be a perfectionist because you can cause problems with team members. Being conscientious, you have the potential to help the team do a good job and reach its full potential. If you have a low need for achievement, push yourself to be a valuable contributor to the group; pull your own weight.

Being high on *adjustment,* in control of your emotions, helps the team. If you have a tendency to get emotional, make an effort to stay calm and help the team.

If you are *open to new experiences,* you will try new things that may help the team improve. When you have ideas that can help the team improve, share them with the team; use your influencing skills. If you are reluctant to change, strive to be more open-minded and to try new things.

Action plan: Based on your personality, what specific things will you do to improve your team skills?

_____

_____

_____

_____

Online Learning Center Resources

Go to the Internet (http://mhhe.com/lussier8e) where you will find a broad array of
resources to help maximize your learning.

- Review the vocabulary.

- Try a quiz.

R E V I E W

The chapter review is organized to help you master the 6 learning outcomes for Chapter 12.
First provide your own response to each learning outcome, and then check the summary
provided to see how well you understand the material. Next, identify the final statement in
each section as either true or false (T/F). Correct each false statement. Answers are given
at the end of the chapter.

1. **Explain the six components of team dynamics and how they affect team
   performance.**

   Team dynamics refers to the patterns of interactions that emerge as groups develop.
   The six components of team dynamics are: (1) *objectives*—without clear objectives,
   groups will not be effective; (2) *group size*—if the group is too large or small, it will
   not be effective; (3) *group norms*—the group's shared expectations concerning members' behavior. With norms that do not support high-level performance the group will
   not be effective; (4) *group cohesiveness*—the attractiveness and closeness of the group
   members. Generally, noncohesive groups are not as effective as cohesive groups;
   (5) *status within the group*—a member's rank within the group. When members are
   not satisfied with their status they tend to hold back group performance; and (6) *group
   roles*—shared expectations of how group members will fulfill the requirements of their
   position. When members do not understand or do not play their roles as expected, the
   group's performance suffers.

   The best size for teams is five members. T F

2. **Describe the five stages of a team's development.**

   There are five stages of team development. In stage 1, *orientation* (low development
   level D1), members have a high commitment but low competence to perform the task.
   In stage 2, *dissatisfaction* (moderate development level D2), members have a lower
   commitment but have developed some competence. In stage 3, *resolution* (high development level D3), members' commitment varies and the competence is high. In stage
   4, *production* (outstanding development level D4), members have a high commitment
   and high competence. In stage 5, *termination,* the group no longer exists.

   Functional groups and standing committees don't usually go through a termination stage of development. T F

3. **Explain the four situational supervisory styles to use with a group, based on its
   stage of development.**

   In stage 1, *orientation* (low development level D1), the supervisor should use the autocratic style, S-A, which is high task/low maintenance. In stage 2, *dissatisfaction*
   (moderate development level D2), the supervisor should use the consultative style,
   S-C, which is high task/high maintenance. In stage 3, *resolution* (high development
   level D3), the supervisor should use the participative style, S-P, which is low task/high
   maintenance. In stage 4, *production* (outstanding development level D4), the supervisor should use the laissez-faire style, S-L, which is low task/low maintenance.

   At group stage 4, the leader lets the group make its own decisions. T F

4. **Explain how to plan for and conduct effective meetings.**

   Areas in which meeting planning is needed include: (1) setting objectives; (2) determining who will participate and their assignments; (3) developing an agenda;

(4) setting a time and place for the meeting; and (5) determining the appropriate leadership style. In conducting the meeting, the leader should go over objectives, cover agenda items, and summarize and review assignments.

The way the manager runs the meeting should be based on the group's level of development. T F

5. **Identify five problem members and explain how to handle them so they do not have a negative effect on your meetings.**

Problem group members include: (1) the silent member—bring them into the discussion without pushing them. The rotation method is helpful; (2) the talker—slow them down, gently interrupt and call on other members for their input. The rotation method is helpful; (3) the wanderer—keep them on the subject, gently remind the group of its objective, and ask a question that will get the group back on track; (4) the bored member—keep them interested. Keep them involved by asking for their input. Assign them tasks that will hold their attention; and (5) the arguer—don't argue with them. Keep the discussion moving, and call on other members to diffuse arguments.

Managers should embarrass, intimidate, or argue with members who provoke them during meetings. T F

6. **Define the following 14 key terms.**

Select one or more methods: (1) fill in the missing key terms from memory; (2) match the key terms from the end of the review with their definitions below; and/or (3) copy the key terms in order from the key terms at the beginning of the chapter.

_____ involves working together to achieve something beyond the capabilities of individuals working alone.

The _____ states that a team's performance is based on its structure, dynamics, and stage of development.

_____ refers to the patterns of interactions that emerge as groups develop.

_____ are the group's shared expectations of its members' behavior.

_____ is the attractiveness and closeness group members have for one another and for the group.

_____ is the perceived ranking of one member relative to other members of the group.

_____ are shared expectations of how group members will fulfill the requirements of their position.

_____ are the things group members do and say that directly aid in the accomplishment of the group's objective(s).

_____ are the things group members do and say to develop and sustain group dynamics.

_____ are the things members do and say to meet their own needs or objectives at the expense of the group.

The four stages of group development, with their appropriate situational supervisory styles are:

_____, orientation—low development D1 (high commitment/low competence), which uses the autocratic supervisory style (high task/low maintenance), S-A.

_____, dissatisfaction—moderate development D2 (lower commitment/some competence), which uses the consultative supervisory style (high task/high maintenance), S-C.

_____, resolution—high development D3 (variable commitment/high competence), which uses the participative supervisory style (low task/high maintenance), S-P.

_____, production—outstanding development D4 (high commitment/high competence), which uses the laissez-faire supervisory style (low task/low maintenance), S-L.

For a brief summary of topics in Chapter 12, see Exhibit 12.7.

K E Y   T E R M S

group cohesiveness   426
group development
  stage 1   437
group development
  stage 2   437
group development
  stage 3   437

group development
  stage 4   438
maintenance roles   429
norms   426
roles   428
self-interest roles   429
status   428

task roles   429
team dynamics   424
team performance
  model   422
teamwork   421

C O M M U N I C A T I O N   S K I L L S

The following critical thinking questions can be used for class discussion and/or as written assignments to develop communication skills. Be sure to give complete explanations for all questions.

1. Many of the TV reality shows have an element of teamwork. However, they often have members of the teams doing negative things to each other to get ahead. Do you believe that these negative examples of poor teamwork influence peoples' behavior in real-life groups? Can you give any examples of TV shows that give *positive* examples of good teamwork?

2. It has been said that the team performance model is too simplistic; group performance is much more complex. Do you agree with this statement? How can the model be used?

3. What is the difference between a rule and a norm? Do norms help or hurt groups? Is it ethical to make group members comply with group norms? Can groups stop having norms?

4. It has been said that success breeds cohesiveness, which in turn leads to more success. What does this mean? How is it supposed to work? Do you agree with the statement?

5. Select a work or sports team to which you belong/have belonged. Which team member (not the manager or coach) had the highest level of status? Identify the factors that contributed to that person's high status.

6. The younger generations have been called the "me generation" because they only care about themselves. Do you agree with this statement? How does putting oneself

as number one affect group performance? Which group role is illustrated through the "me generation" statement?

7. Team development stages state that most people coming to a new group are enthusiastic, but that with time they lose some of their morale. What types of things happen in most groups to cause this decline in morale? Be sure to focus on the components of team structure and team dynamics.

8. Many people complain about meetings. Recall a meeting that you have attended. Do you have any complaints about it? State whether or not the meeting had each of the four parts of a written meeting plan (Exhibit 12.6) and whether the meeting included (1) reviewing objectives, (2) covering agenda items, and (3) summarizing and reviewing assignments. How could the meeting have been improved?

9. Identity the types of problem team members you have encountered. Did the team leader effectively handle these problem members? How could the leader have done a better job of managing these members?

10. With virtual team members from all over the world, how does the global economy affect team performance?

CASE

The Semco Group

The Semco Group, of São Paulo, Brazil, provides a diverse array of products and services, from air-conditioning components for the workplace to environmental projects for local parks. In 2000, Semco Ventures, a part of the group specializing in prospecting and developing new businesses, was created. In 2001, Semco Manutenção Volante was created to provide electrical and civil maintenance and other services. In 2002, the Semco Group became one of the founding shareholders in Tarpon Investimentos. In 2005, Semco formed a partnership with Pitney Bowes, a worldwide leading company in document and postal management solutions. In 2006, the Bioenergy project was created, later giving rise to BRENCO (Brazilian Renewable Energy Company). In 2007, Tarpon Investimentos went public and listed its shares on the Luxembourg stock market and on Bovespa, making it one of the first asset managers in Brazil to access the capital market.

Looking at the outside of its plant, this entrepreneurial firm looks like any other manufacturing operation; however, it is what is on the inside that makes this firm so extraordinary. There are no job titles and no personal assistants. Employees set their own salaries and everyone shares in the profits. That sounds like a recipe for disaster, or at least for chaos, but Semco has grown consistently for the last 20 years despite being located in one of the most volatile economies in the world. Many credit this revolutionary management approach to the CEO and son of the founder of Semco, Ricardo Semler. He is the leading proponent and most tireless evangelist of what has variously been called participative management, corporate democracy, and "the company as village." What makes Ricardo Semler all the more notable is the way he has put theory into practice. Many people have talked the talk of corporate democracy; his company actually walks the walk.

Semco's 3,000 employees set their own work hours and pay levels. Subordinates hire and review their supervisors. Hammocks are scattered about the grounds for afternoon naps, and employees are encouraged to spend Monday morning at the beach if they spent Saturday afternoon at the office. There are no organization charts, no five-year plans, no corporate values statements, no dress code, and no written rules or policy statements beyond a brief "Survival Manual," in comic-book form, that introduces new hires to Semco's unusual ways. The employees elect the corporate leadership and initiate most of Semco's moves into new businesses and out of old ones. Of the 3,000 votes at the company, Ricardo Semler has just one. Employees are invited to attend board meetings and actively participate in the firm's management.

The firm's overall structure could be described as a set of concentric circles. At the center are the Counselors, including Ricardo Semler. There are six of them and a different one takes the CEO job every six months. They deal with general policy and strategy and overall financial results, and they work to inspire the Partners who make up the second circle. Partners are six or seven leaders from each Semco group. Everyone else is an Associate. Some Associates also work as team leaders. In the plants, workers handle multiple job duties and use their knowledge of how the factory works to come up with new procedures that will save time and money. Any time a procedure saves the firm some operating expenses, the "profits" are shared with the employees who implemented the new process.

The key to Semco's success seems to be in its use and development of self-managed work groups or teams. The team approach started at one factory when the workers elected to divide themselves into three manufacturing units of about 150 people each. Each unit was given complete responsibility for manufacturing, sales, and financial management. With the success of these units, the autonomous team idea was adopted throughout the company. As the teams evolved, they began hiring and firing both workers and supervisors by democratic vote. Policy manuals disappeared, to be replaced by a policy of common sense. There is an actual manual, though. It runs about 20 pages and is filled with cartoons and brief statements of principle. Each team operates entirely on its own, making its own decisions, though within the same culture as Semco. Its performance is reviewed every six months and members take a percentage of sales as compensation.

The company is now comprised solely of autonomous, democratically run units or groups of 150–200 people. Having a small group makes it easy to spot a threat or opportunity, figure out what to do, and swing into action. Above this size you need formal processes to get this done; below this size it becomes a natural function. This structure provides excellent flexibility—new groups can be formed in order to take advantage of new prospects while underperforming groups can be eliminated without dramatically impacting the rest of the operation of the firm.[102]

Go to the Internet: For more information on the Semco Group and to update the information provided in this case, do a name search on the Internet and visit www.semco.com.br.

Support your answers to the following questions with specific information from the case and text, or with other information you get from the Web or other sources.

1. Describe Semco's team structure relative to team leadership and decision making.

2. At Semco, how does size affect the performance of these teams? Are these teams too large?

3. What factors positively affect the cohesiveness of each of these teams?

4. Since Semco does not have work rules, how do norms impact team performance?

5. Given the democratic operation of the firm and its teams, how do status and roles impact team performance?

Cumulative Questions

6. How do employee and owner attitudes, values, and ethics (Chapter 3) affect the Semco Group?

7. How would you describe the firm's organizational structure (Chapter 6)?

8. Describe Ricardo Semler, Semco's CEO, style of leadership (Chapter 8).

9. Apply one motivational theory (Chapter 9) to explain how Semco meets its employees' needs to increase their work performance.

10. What forms of power (Chapter 10) is CEO Semler employing to influence his employees?

11. Explain why networking (Chapter 11) would be critical in an organization like Semco, which has no organizational chart and therefore no formal channels of communication (Chapter 6).

OBJECTIVE CASE   # Group Performance

Through reorganization, Christen has been assigned three additional departments that produce the same product. Ted, Jean, and Paul are the supervisors of these departments. Christen would like to increase productivity, so she set up a group to analyze the present situation and recommend ways to increase productivity. The group consists of Christen, the three supervisors, an industrial engineer, and an expert on group dynamics from personnel. The group analyzed the present situation in each department as follows:

Group 1: Ted's department produces at or above standard on a regular basis. It averages between 102 and 104 percent of standard on a monthly basis. (Standard is 100 percent.) Members work well together; they often go to lunch together. Members' productivity levels are all about the same.

Group 2: Jean's department produces between 95 and 105 percent on a monthly basis. However, it usually produces 100 percent. The members do not seem to interact too often. Part of the reason for the standard production level is two employees who consistently produce at 115 percent of standard. Jean will be retiring in six months, and they both want to fill her position. There are three members who consistently produce at 80 to 90 percent of standard.

Group 3: Paul's department achieves between 90 and 92 percent of standard on a monthly basis. Betty is a strong informal leader who oversees the productivity level. She lets members know if they produce too much or too little. John is the only member in the department who reaches production standards. The rest of the department members do not talk to John. At times they intentionally keep his level of production down. All other department members produce at about 90 percent of standard.

Answer the following questions. Then in the space between the questions, state why you selected that answer.

_____ 1. Christen, Ted, Jean, and Paul make up a _____ group.

           a. functional   *b.* task   *c.* informal

_____ 2. To increase productivity, Christen set up a _____ group.

           a. functional   *b.* ad hoc committee   *c.* standing committee

_____ 3. Which group(s) has high agreement and commitment to its own objectives?

           a. 1   *d.* 1 and 2   *g.* 1, 2, and 3

           b. 2   *e.* 1 and 3

           c. 3   *f.* 2 and 3

_____ 4. Which group(s) has objectives (positive norms) in agreement with those of management?

           a. 1   *d.* 1 and 2   *g.* 1, 2, and 3

           b. 2   *e.* 1 and 3

           c. 3   *f.* 2 and 3

_____ 5. Which group(s) is cohesive?

           a. 1   *d.* 1 and 2   *g.* 1, 2, and 3

           b. 2   *e.* 1 and 3

           c. 3   *f.* 2 and 3

_____ 6. Which group most clearly plays self-interest roles?

           a. 1   *b.* 2   *c.* 3

_____ 7. Betty primarily plays a _____ role for her group.

           a. task   *b.* maintenance   *c.* self-interest

_____ 8. Group 1 appears to be in stage _____ of group development.

           a. 1   *c.* 3   *e.* 5

           b. 2   *d.* 4

_____ 9. Group 2 appears to be in stage _____ of group development.

           a. 1   *c.* 3   *e.* 5

           b. 2   *d.* 4

_____ 10. Group 3 appears to be in stage _____ of group development.

           a. 1   *c.* 3   *e.* 5

           b. 2   *d.* 4

11. What would you recommend doing to increase productivity in each of the three groups?

Team Dynamics

Preparation (Group)

Note: This exercise is designed for class groups that have worked together for some time. (Five or more hours are recommended.)

Answer the following questions as they apply to your class group.

1. Based on attendance, preparation, and class involvement, identify each group member's level of commitment to the group, including yourself. (Write each member's name on the appropriate line.)

   High commitment _____

   Medium commitment _____

   Low commitment _____

2. Our group size is:

   _____ too large   _____ too small   _____ OK

   Explain why.

3. List at least five norms your group has developed. Identify each as positive or negative.

   1.

   2.

   3.

   4.

   5.

   What positive norms could the group develop to help it function?

4. Based on the group's commitment, size, homogeneity, equality of participation, intragroup competition, and success, identify its cohesiveness level as:

   _____ high   _____ medium   _____ low

   How does cohesiveness affect performance? What can be done to increase cohesiveness?

5. Identify each group member's status, including your own. (Write each group member's name on the appropriate line.)

   High _____

   Medium _____

   Low _____

   Does the group have status congruence? How can the group improve it?

6. Identify the roles members play. Write the name of each group member who plays each role on the appropriate line. You will most likely use each name several times and have more than one name on each role line, but rank them by dominance.

   Task roles

   Objective clarifier _____

   Planner _____

Organizer _____

Leader _____

Controller _____

Maintenance roles

Former _____

Consensus seeker _____

Harmonizer _____

Gatekeeper _____

Encourager _____

Compromiser _____

Self-interest roles (if appropriate)

Aggressor _____

Blocker _____

Recognition seeker _____

Withdrawer _____

Which roles should be played more, and which less, to increase effectiveness? Who should and should not play them?

7. Our group is in stage _____ of group development.

    1. Orientation
    2. Dissatisfaction
    3. Resolution
    4. Production

    What can be done to increase the group's level of development?

8. Identify problem people, if any, by placing their names on the appropriate line(s).

    Silent member _____

    Talker _____

    Wanderer _____

    Bored member _____

    Arguer _____

    What should be done to help eliminate the problems caused by these people? Specifically, who should do what?

9. Review the answers to questions 1 through 8. In order of priority, what will the group do to improve its group structure? Specify what each group member will do to help the group's structure.

In-Class Exercise

Note: This exercise is designed for groups that have met for some time. (Five or more hours are recommended.)

Objectives: To gain a better understanding of the group structure components and how they affect group performance, and to improve group structure.

AACSB: The primary AACSB learning standard skills developed through this exercise are teamwork and leadership; in addition, communication, reflective thinking, self-management, and analytic skills are developed.

Preparation: You should have answered the preparation questions.

Experience: You will discuss your group's structure and develop plans to improve it.

Procedure 1
(10–20 minutes)

Groups get together to discuss their answers to the nine preparation questions. Be sure to fully explain and discuss your answers. Try to come up with some specific ideas on how to improve your group's process and dynamics.

Conclusion: The instructor leads a class discussion and/or makes concluding remarks.

Application (2–4 minutes): What did I learn from this experience? How will I use this knowledge in the future?

Sharing: Volunteers give their answers to the application section.

Team Situational Supervision

In-Class Exercise (Individual and Group)

Objectives: To help you understand the stages of group development, and to use the appropriate situational supervision style.

AACSB: The primary AACSB learning standard skills developed through this exercise are teamwork and leadership; in addition, analytic skills are developed.

Preparation: You should have completed Self-Assessment Exercise 12–2.

Experience: You will discuss your selected supervisory styles for the 12 preparation situations, and you will be given feedback on your accuracy in selecting the appropriate style to meet the situation.

Procedure 1
(3–10 minutes)

The instructor reviews the group situational supervision model, Exhibit 12.5, and explains how to apply it to situation 1 in Self-Assessment Exercise 12–2. The instructor states the group's developmental stage, the supervisory style of each of the four alternative actions, and the scoring for each alternative. Follow the three steps below as you try to select the most appropriate alternative action for each of the 12 situations in Self-Assessment Exercise 12–2.

Step 1. For each situation, determine the team's level of development. Place the number 1, 2, 3, or 4 on the D _____ lines.

Step 2. Identify the supervisory style of all four alternatives *a* through *d.* Place the letters A, C, P, or L on the S _____ lines.

Step 3. Select the appropriate supervisory style for the team's level of development. Circle its letter, either *a, b, c,* or *d.*

Procedure 2

Option A (3–5 minutes):   The instructor gives the class the recommended answers to situations 2 through 12, as in procedure 1, without any explanation.

Option B (10–30 minutes):   Break into teams of two or three, and go over the situations chosen by the instructor. The instructor will go over the recommended answers.

Conclusion: The instructor leads a class discussion and/or makes concluding remarks.

Application (2–4 minutes):   What did I learn from this experience? How will I use this knowledge in the future?

Sharing: Volunteers give their answers to the application section.

ANSWERS TO TRUE/FALSE QUESTIONS

1. F. There is no one best size for all teams. Size is based on the team's purpose.
2. T.
3. T.
4. T.
5. F. Managers should not embarrass, intimidate or argue with any team members.

Teams and Creative Problem Solving and Decision Making

After completing this chapter, you should be able to:

1. Describe the three decision-making styles and know which style is preferred.

2. List the five steps in the decision-making model.

3. Describe five techniques for generating creative alternatives.

4. Explain the advantages and disadvantages of group decision making.

5. Describe the normative leadership model.

6. Define the following 14 key terms (in order of appearance in the chapter):

problem	**brainstorming**
problem solving	**synetics**
decision making	**nominal grouping**
decision-making model	**consensus mapping**
cost–benefit analysis	**Delphi technique**
creativity	**devil's advocate technique**
stages in the creative process	**normative leadership model**

How Decision Making Affects Behavior, Human Relations, and Performance

Ted Williams was asked to serve on the budget committee of the Windy Company, in Chicago, Illinois. Ted looks forward to the change because it will give him a chance to get away from his regular job for a few hours a day over several weeks. But more importantly, Ted knows that the chair of the budget committee is Sonia Windy, president of the company. Ted hopes to do well on the committee so he can impress her in hopes of future advancement. Ted has never served on a committee before and wonders what it will be like.

The budget committee was formed 10 years ago, and its members come from a variety of departments. Membership changes from year to year, except that the president remains as chair. The budget committee has the authority to make the actual allocation decision of the budget, but Ted wonders how much participation Sonia will allow from the committee and what supervisory style she will use.

After serving his one-year term on the budget committee, Ted thought about his experience. Sonia had allowed the group members to give their suggestions on how much each department should be given, but no one could speak against the numbers being allocated. After everyone had presented his or her suggested allocation, everyone debated about the figures. After all the debating was over, Sonia made the final decision on how much each department would get. She clearly explained her decision regarding the allocation of funds for each department.

HOW DECISION MAKING AFFECTS BEHAVIOR, HUMAN RELATIONS, AND PERFORMANCE

One of the major reasons managers are hired is to solve problems and make decisions.[1] Decisions managers make can affect the health, safety, and well-being of consumers, employees, and the community.[2] Making bad decisions can destroy companies and careers.[3] For example, many entrepreneurs who make the decision to start a business end in failure, and business failure is both frequent and potentially damaging to the efficient operation of a market economy.[4] On the positive side, effective decisions are consistently related to higher individual performance, organizational productivity, and solid financial performance.[5]

Today's employees enjoy the human relations of shared decision making,[6] as they take on responsibility for problem solving and decision making.[7] We will talk more about this later when we discuss the advantages of group decision making.

Another reason for failed decisions is ignoring *ethics;* unethical decisions are usually bad decisions.[8] Recall the unethical chain of decisions that led Enron to its demise. Ethical decision making is becoming more important as rapid change continues in the diverse global environment.[9] We have already discussed ethics, so we stop here. But as you study this chapter, remember that ethical decisions do pay.[10]

You should realize that problem-solving and decision-making skills will affect your performance.[11] You can develop problem-solving and decision-making skills;[12] that's what this chapter is all about. The decision-making styles and models in this chapter apply to individuals and teams, but the focus here is primarily on teams.

WORK APPLICATIONS

1. Give reasons not listed in the text why problem-solving and decision-making skills are important.
2. Give an example of how a decision affected behavior, human relations, and performance where you work or have worked.

THE RELATIONSHIP BETWEEN PROBLEM SOLVING AND DECISION MAKING

In short, decisions are made to solve problems and take advantage of opportunities, which can occur at the same time.[13] For example, you produce your product slower than your competitors, so your prices are higher. So you develop a faster production process, which gives you the opportunity to have the cost advantage over your competitors. Below is further explanation of the relationship between problem solving and decision making. Keep in mind that, throughout the chapter, when we discuss problems, we also include opportunities, and when we discuss decision making, we are also including problem solving.

A **problem** *exists whenever there is a difference between what is actually happening and what the individual or group wants to be happening.* If your objective is to produce 500 units per day, but only 475 units are produced, there is a problem. A major cause of problems is change. A change in material, tools, and so forth may be the cause of producing 475 rather than 500 units. **Problem solving** *is the process of taking corrective action in order to meet objectives.*

Decision making *is the process of selecting an alternative course of action that will solve a problem.* Decisions must be made when you are faced with a problem.[14] The first decision is whether or not to take action to solve the problem. For example, one can simply change objectives and eliminate the problem. In the above example, you can change the objective to 475 units per day.

Some problems cannot be solved, while other problems are not worth the time and effort to solve. But they do need to be managed, particularly those that defy resolution. Since part of a manager's job is to achieve objectives, you will have to attempt to manage and solve most of your problems if you want to be successful.[15] Following the suggestions in this chapter can help you develop your problem-solving and decision-making skills.

In the opening case, the problem is that there is not enough money to give all departments as much in their budgets as they want. The decision to be made is how much money each department will get.

WORK APPLICATIONS

3. Give an example of a problem you face now.

Learning Outcome

1. Describe the three decision-making styles and know which style is preferred.

Self-Assessment Exercise 13–1

DECISION-MAKING STYLES

There are various decision-making styles,[16] including reflexive, consistent, and reflective. To determine your decision-making style, answer the questions in Self-Assessment Exercise 13–1.

Decision-Making Styles

Select the answer (1 to 3) that best describes how you make decisions.

A. Overall I'm _____ to act.

   1. quick   2. moderate   3. slow

B. I spend _____ amount of time making important decisions as/than I do making less important decisions.

   1. about the same   2. a greater   3. a much greater

C. When making decisions, I _____ go with my first thought.

   1. usually   2. occasionally   3. rarely

D. When making decisions, I'm _____ concerned about making errors.

   1. rarely   2. occasionally   3. often

**Self-Assessment
Exercise 13–1 (*continued*)**

E. When making decisions, I _____ recheck my work.

    1. rarely   2. occasionally   3. usually

F. When making decisions, I gather _____ information.

    1. little   2. some   3. lots of

G. When making decisions, I consider _____ alternative actions.

    1. few   2. some   3. lots of

H. When making a decision, I usually make it _____ before the deadline.

    1. long   2. somewhat   3. just

I. After making a decision, I _____ look for other alternatives, wishing I had waited.

    1. rarely   2. occasionally   3. usually

J. I _____ regret having made a decision.

    1. rarely   2. occasionally   3. often

    To determine your style, add the numbers that represent your answers to the 10 questions. The total will be between 10 and 30. Place an X on the continuum at the point that represents your score.

            Reflexive   Consistent   Reflective

10 – – – – – – – – – – – – – 16 – – – – – – – – – – – – – 23 – – – – – – – – – – – – 30

A score of 10 to 16 indicates a reflexive style; 17 to 23 indicates a consistent style; and 24 to 30 indicates a reflective style. You have determined your preferred personal decision-making style. Groups also have a preferred decision-making style, based on how their members make decisions. Changing the *I* to *we,* you could answer the 10 questions to refer to a group rather than to yourself.

Reflexive Style

A reflexive decision maker likes to make quick decisions ("to shoot from the hip"), without taking the time to get all the information that may be needed and without considering all alternatives.[17] On the positive side, reflexive decision makers are decisive; they do not procrastinate. On the negative side, making quick decisions can lead to waste and duplication when a decision is not the best possible alternative.[18] The reflexive decision maker may be viewed by employees as a poor manager if he or she is consistently making bad decisions. If you use a reflexive style, you may want to slow down and spend more time gathering information and analyzing alternatives. Following the steps in the decision-making model can help you develop your skills.

Reflective Style

A reflective decision maker likes to take plenty of time to make decisions, taking into account considerable information and an analysis of several alternatives.[19] On the positive side, the reflective type does not make decisions that are rushed. On the negative side, he or she may procrastinate and waste valuable time and other resources. The reflective decision maker may be viewed as wishy-washy and indecisive. If you use a reflective style, you may want to speed up your decision making. As Andrew Jackson once said, "Take time to deliberate; but when the time for action arrives, stop thinking and go on."

Consistent Style

A consistent decision maker makes decisions without rushing or wasting time. Consistent decision makers know when they have enough information and alternatives to make a sound decision.[20] They have the most consistent record of good decisions.[21] Consistent decision makers tend to follow the decision-making steps below.

Learning Outcome

2. List the five steps in the
   decision-making model.

THE DECISION-MAKING MODEL

This model is also called the rational model,[22] and it is appropriate to use for important nonrecurring decisions.[23] It is not necessary to follow all five steps in the model when making unimportant recurring decisions. In some situations, such as with very limited information, intuitive decisions are appropriate. Intuition can also be used within the steps of the model.[24]

Following the steps in the model will not guarantee success; however, following the model increases the probability of successful decision making.[25] Consult others for advice as you progress through the steps. Consciously use the model in your daily life, and you will improve your ability to make decisions.

The **decision-making model** *steps are as follows: step (1) define the problem; step (2) set objectives and criteria; step (3) generate alternatives; step (4) analyze alternatives and select one; and step (5) plan, implement the decision, and control.* Let's examine each step.

Step 1: Define the Problem

As a result of time pressure, managers and employees are often in a hurry to solve problems.[26] In haste, they often neglect the first step in problem solving—define the problem. To fully define the problem, the employee or group must determine the cause of the problem. "What caused us to produce 475 units rather than 500?" In determining the cause(s) of the problem, people need time to think, preferably quietly, apart from others, reflectively, and with focus. Determining the causes of a problem involves looking back to understand the past, and then forward to predict the future. You must get the necessary information and facts to determine the problem.[27] However, problems are not solved by putting blame on others.[28]

In analyzing a problem, first distinguish the symptoms from the cause of the problem. To do so, list the observable and describable occurrences (symptoms) that indicate a problem exists. Once this is done, you can determine the cause of the problem. After you eliminate the cause, the effects should disappear. For example, Wayne, an employee with five years' tenure, has been an excellent producer on the job. However, in the last month, Wayne has been out sick and tardy more times than in the past two years. What is the problem? If you say absenteeism or tardiness, you are confusing symptoms and causes. They are symptoms of the problem. If the supervisor simply disciplines Wayne, he may decrease the tardiness and absenteeism, but the problem will not be solved. It would be wiser for the supervisor to talk to the employee and find out the reason (cause) for the problem. The real problem may be a personal problem at home or on the job. The key issue is that the decision maker must define the problem correctly in order to solve it.

Step 2: Set Objectives and Criteria

After the problem has been defined, you are now ready to set an objective and develop the criteria for the decision. The manager should have an objective for solving the problem.[29] Managers with specific objectives generate better operational plans and decisions.[30] Unfortunately, identifying the decision to be made is not as simple as it sounds: the objective must state exactly what is to be accomplished.[31] Refer to Chapter 9 for a discussion of how to set objectives.

In addition to setting objectives, you should identify the criteria the decision must meet to achieve the objective. It is helpful to specify "must" and "want" criteria. Must criteria should be met, while want criteria are desirable but not necessary. An example of an objective and criteria for a personnel department hiring a manager is as follows: Objective: "To hire a store manager by June 30, 20__." The must criteria are a college degree and a minimum of five years' experience as a store manager. The want criterion is that the hiree should be a minority group member. The organization wants to hire a minority but will not hire one who does not meet the must criteria.

Continuing the example with Wayne: The objective is to improve Wayne's attendance record. The criterion is his prior good record of attendance.

Step 3: Generate Alternatives

After the problem has been defined and the objectives and criteria set, you are ready to generate possible methods, or alternatives, for solving the problem. There are usually many ways to solve a problem;[32] in fact, if you don't have two or more alternatives, you don't have to make a decision. When making routine decisions, the alternatives are fairly straightforward. However, when making nonroutine decisions, new, creative solutions are needed.[33] When gathering the information needed to generate alternatives, you should consider the time, energy, action, and cost involved. You can neither expect nor afford complete information. However, you must get enough information to enable you to make good decisions.[34] When generating alternatives, be creative. Continuing the example with Wayne: Some alternatives are giving Wayne a warning, punishing him in some way, or talking to him to determine the reason for the change in his behavior.

Step 4: Analyze Alternatives and Select One

After generating alternative solutions to the problem, you must evaluate each in terms of the objectives and criteria.[35] You should not always try to select the optimum alternative. In many cases a satisfactory decision (*satisficing*) will do the job.[36] Think forward and try to predict the outcome of each alternative.[37] One method you can use to analyze alternatives is cost–benefit analysis. **Cost–benefit analysis** *is a technique for comparing the cost and benefit of each alternative course of action.* Each alternative has its positive and its negative aspects, or its costs and benefits. Costs are more than monetary. They may include a sacrifice of time, money, and so forth. To make the best choice, you need to use some intuition, feelings, and judgment when doing a cost–benefit analysis.[38] Cost–benefit analysis has become popular in the nonprofit sector, where the benefits are often difficult to determine in quantified dollars.

Continuing the example with Wayne: The alternative selected is to have a talk with him to try to determine why his attendance has changed.

Step 5: Plan, Implement the Decision, and Control

Step 5 in the decision-making process has three separate parts, as the title states. Failing to complete step 5 is a major reason why some decisions are never actually used.[39] We will discuss each part separately.

Plan Problem-solving focuses on the future and is about action.[40] After making the decision, you should develop a plan of action with a schedule for its implementation.

Implement the Decision After the decision has been made and the plans developed, they must be implemented. Communication of the plan to all employees is critical for the successful implementation of the plan.[41]

Control As with all plans, controls should be developed while planning. Checkpoints with feedback should be established to determine if the decision is solving the problem.[42] If not, corrective action may be needed. You should not be locked into a decision plan and throw good money after bad. When you make a poor decision, you should admit the mistake and change the decision by going back to previous steps in the decision-making model.

Concluding the example with Wayne: The supervisor plans what she will say to him during the meeting, conducts the meeting, and follows up to be sure that the problem is solved.

Exhibit 13.1 summarizes the five steps in the decision-making model. Notice in Exhibit 13.1 that the steps do not go simply from start to end. At any step, you may have to return to a previous step to make changes. For example, if you are in the fifth step and control and implementation are not going as planned, you may have to backtrack to take corrective action by generating and selecting a new alternative or by changing the objective. If the problem was not defined accurately, you may have to go back to the beginning.

EXHIBIT 13.1 |
Decision-Making Model

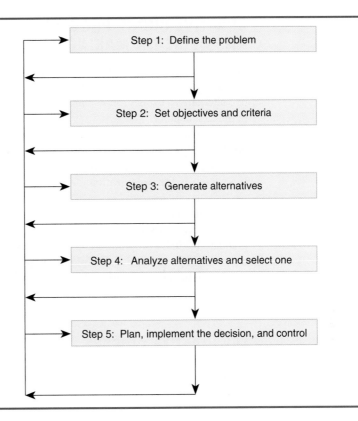

In the opening case, the budget committee should use the decision-making model to allocate the budget among departments.

WORK APPLICATIONS

4. Solve the problem you gave in Work Application (3), following the five steps in the decision-making model. Write it out clearly, labeling each step.

APPLICATION SITUATIONS

Steps in Decision Making

AS 13–1

Match the five statements below with their step in the decision-making model.

A. Step 1: Define the problem

B. Step 2: Set objectives and criteria

C. Step 3: Generate alternatives

D. Step 4: Analyze alternatives and select one

E. Step 5: Plan, implement the decision, and control

_____ 1. "Today we will be using the brainstorming technique."

_____ 2. "Chuck, is the machine still jumping out of sequence?"

_____ 3. "We should state what it is we are trying to accomplish."

_____ 4. "What are the symptoms you have observed?"

_____ 5. "I suggest that we use linear programming to help us in this situation."

CREATIVE GROUP PROBLEM SOLVING AND DECISION MAKING

In the previous section, problem solving and decision making were presented as they apply to individuals and groups. In this section, we examine creativity and how to generate creative alternatives using groups. Innovation is one of the top challenges business leaders face in the 21st century.[43]

Companies are trying to inspire creativity,[44] because competitive advantage is developed through innovation[45] and creativity.[46] New technology leads to innovation.[47] Actually, creativity and innovation are different. Creativity is coming up with new and useful ideas.[48] Innovation is the organizational implementation of the creative ideas.[49] In this chapter, we'll focus on creativity.

Creativity *means the ability to develop unique alternatives to solve problems.* An example of creativity was introduced by Adelphi University when it wanted to expand its graduate business program. People perceived that they did not have time to further their education. The alternative Adelphi developed to solve the problem was the "classroom on wheels," which offers classes four days a week on commuter trains into and out of New York. Today, there are online degree programs.

The Creative Process

To improve your creativity, follow the stages in the creative process. The four **stages in the creative process** *are (1) preparation, (2) possible solutions, (3) incubation, and (4) evaluation.*

1. *Preparation.* You must become familiar with the problem. Get others' opinions, feelings, and ideas, as well as the facts.[50] When solving a problem, look for new angles, use imagination and invention, and don't limit boundaries.[51]

2. *Possible solutions.* Generate as many possible creative solutions as you can think of,[52] without making any judgments. The brainstorming rules (discussed next) will provide details.

3. *Incubation.* After generating alternatives, take a break. It doesn't have to be long, but take time before working on the problem again. During the incubation stage, you may have an insight into the problem's solution. Have you ever worked hard on a problem and become discouraged, but when you had given up or taken a break, the solution came to you?

4. *Evaluation.* Before implementing a solution, you should evaluate the alternative to make sure the idea is practical.[53] Evaluation often leads to more creativity.[54]

Everyone has creative capability.[55] Following these four stages can help you improve your creativity. For a summary of the stages in the creative process, see Exhibit 13.2.

WORK APPLICATIONS

5. Give an example of how you solved a problem using the stages in the creative process, or use the creative process to solve an existing problem.

EXHIBIT 13.2 | Stages in the Creative Process

Stage 1: Preparation
Stage 2: Possible solutions
Stage 3: Incubation
Stage 4: Evaluation

EXHIBIT 13.3 | Responses That Kill Creativity

• It isn't in the budget.	• We're doing the best we can.
• It costs too much.	• We don't have the time.
• We've never done it before.	• That will make other equipment obsolete.
• Has anyone else ever tried it?	• We're too small/big for it.
• It won't work in our company/industry.	• Why change it? It's still working OK.
• That's not our problem.	• We're not ready for that.
• We tried that before.	• You're years ahead of your time.
• It can't be done.	• You can't teach an old dog new tricks.
• That's beyond our responsibility.	• Let's form a committee.
• It's too radical a change.	• Don't be ridiculous.
• We did all right without it.	• Let's get back to reality.

How people respond to creative ideas affects the group's behavior.[56] For a list of responses that kill creativity, see Exhibit 13.3. Avoid these responses and discourage others from using them as well.

Learning Outcome

3. Describe five techniques for generating creative alternatives.

Using Groups to Generate Creative Alternatives

In step 3 of the decision-making process, organizations today are using group input to generate alternatives.[57] There are a variety of techniques to use, including brainstorming, synetics, nominal grouping, consensus mapping, and the Delphi technique.

Brainstorming   **Brainstorming** *is the process of suggesting many alternatives, without evaluation, to solve a problem.* When brainstorming, the group is presented with a problem or opportunity and asked to come up with creative solutions.[58] Brainstorming is commonly used for solving complex problems and for creating new products and to name and market them.[59] For the group product to be greater than the sum of the individual parts (synergy), advertising executive Alex Osborn developed these four interrelated brainstorming rules:[60]

- *Quantity.* Team members should generate as many ideas as possible. More ideas increase the chances of finding an excellent solution. Generating alternatives is step 3 of the decision-making model.

- *No criticism.* Team members should not criticize or evaluate ideas in any way during the solution-generation phase of brainstorming. Evaluation is done in step 4 of decision making—analyze alternatives and select one.

- *Freewheel.* You can't think outside the box when you are in it. You have to get out of the box to see it from new angles or perspectives. Team members should express any idea that comes to mind, no matter how strange, crazy, or weird—thus, the need to avoid criticism that will hinder members' creativity and to avoid responses that kill creativity (see Exhibit 13.3).

- *Extend.* Team members should try to build on the ideas of others and even take them in new directions. Remember that all ideas belong to the group, so everyone gets the credit. Extending helps build quantity and freewheeling, but watch out for criticism.

Brainwriting   Brainwriting is a variation of brainstorming. To eliminate the influence of team peer pressure and other members' suggestions, participants write their ideas down. Then ideas are recorded, and members try to improve and combine ideas.

Electronic Brainstorming   Using the Internet, people from all over the globe can participate in an e-brainstorming session. It can also have the brainwriting benefit of removing team pressure because of greater perceived anonymity. E-brainstorming is commonly used in e-organizations.

Synetics   **Synetics** *is the process of generating novel alternatives through role playing and fantasizing.* Synetics focuses on novel ideas rather than a quantity of ideas. Creativity can come from what seems to be chaos and conflict.[61] At first, to expand the group's thinking process, the leader does not state the exact nature of the situation. For example, when Nolan Bushnell wanted to develop a new concept in family dining, he began by discussing general leisure activities. Bushnell then moved toward leisure activities having to do with eating out. The idea that came out of this synetics process was a restaurant–electronic game complex where families could play games and purchase pizza and hamburgers. The restaurant–electronic game complex is called Pizza Time Theatre and its mascot is Chuck E. Cheese, which is also used as the restaurant's name.

Nominal Grouping   **Nominal grouping** *is the process of generating and evaluating alternatives through a structured voting method.* This process usually involves six steps:

1. Each member individually generates ideas in writing (brainwriting).
2. In a round-robin fashion, members give ideas and the leader records all ideas where everyone can see them.
3. Alternatives are clarified through a guided discussion and any additional ideas are recorded.
4. Each member rates the ideas and votes; the voting eliminates alternatives.
5. An initial vote discussion takes place for clarification, not persuasion. During this time, it is recommended that members present the logic behind the reasons they gave for the various alternatives.
6. The final vote is taken to select the alternative solution presented to the leader. Management may or may not implement the decision. (This is the participative supervisory style.)

Studies have found that nominal grouping outperforms brainstorming.[62] The group can also used multi-voting and affinity grouping.

Consensus Mapping   **Consensus mapping** *is the process of developing a group consensus solution to a problem.* A consensus is a cooperative attempt to develop a solution acceptable to all employees, rather than a competitive battle in which a solution is forced on some members of the group.[63] It is an extension of nominal grouping. The major difference is that the group categorizes or clusters the listed ideas to come to a group consensus solution—rather than voting on one employee's solution. The major benefit of consensus mapping is that since the solution is the group's, members generally are more committed to implementing it. The success of Pizza Hut/KFC is due in part to its CEO's ability to build consensus.

Delphi Technique   The **Delphi technique** *polls a group through a series of anonymous questionnaires.* It is considered a variation of nominal grouping, without face-to-face interaction at any point, and it also includes consensus. The Delphi technique is good to use with teams that have great conflict, but it is time-consuming. The opinions of each round of questionnaires are analyzed and resubmitted to the group in the next round of questionnaires. This process may continue for five or more rounds before a consensus emerges. The Delphi technique is used for technological forecasts, such as what the next computer breakthrough will be.

In the opening case, Sonia Windy used brainstorming to generate alternatives. Group members were not allowed to speak against others' allocations until all had made their presentations. For a review of all five creative techniques, see Exhibit 13.4.

WORK APPLICATIONS

6. Give example situations in which it would be appropriate for a manager to use each of the five techniques for generating creative alternatives (brainstorming, synetics, nominal grouping, consensus mapping, and the Delphi technique).

EXHIBIT 13.4 |

Techniques for Generating Creative Alternatives

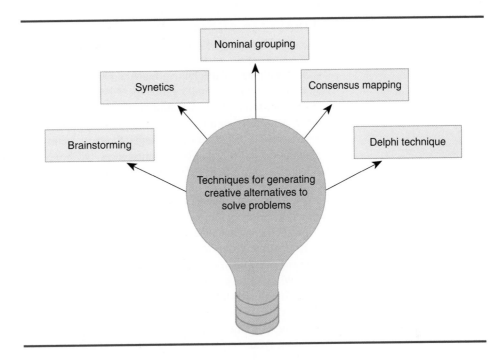

APPLICATION SITUATIONS

Using Groups to Generate Alternatives

AS 13–2

In the five situations below, identify the most appropriate group technique to use to generate alternative solutions.

A. Brainstorming   C. Nominal grouping   E. Delphi technique

B. Synetics   D. Consensus mapping

_____ 6. The supervisor wants to develop some new and different toys. She is meeting with employees and children together.

_____ 7. The department is suffering from morale problems.

_____ 8. The supervisor must decide on new furniture for the office.

_____ 9. The supervisor wants to reduce waste in the department.

_____ 10. The supervisor wants to project future trends of the business.

Learning Outcome

4. Explain the advantages and disadvantages of group decision making.

ADVANTAGES AND DISADVANTAGES OF GROUP DECISION MAKING

In this section, we discuss the advantages and disadvantages of using groups to solve problems and make decisions. But first, you should realize that the trend is clearly toward decentralized decision-making authority.[64] Organizations are sharing power, or empowering employees to make joint decisions,[65] as employees want more responsibility for decision making to solve problems.[66] Employee and customer participative decision making have improved firm performance.[67]

Advantages of Group Decision Making

Some of the advantages of group decision making are the following:

Better Decisions   Participative management is beneficial because groups usually do a better job of solving complex problems.[68] Using groups to solve problems and make decisions is appropriate for nonroutine decisions made under the conditions of risk or uncertainty.[69] Microsoft set up a top decision-making group to improve decision making.

Better decisions result from synergy. Synergy occurs when the total effect is greater than the sum of the individual effects. With synergy, the group solution is superior to that of all individual solutions.[70] Skill-Building Exercise 13–1 compares individual and group decisions.

More Alternatives   Diversity is positive because a diverse group offers different points of view and a variety of alternative solutions.[71] A diverse group offers more creativity.[72] Members can build on each other's ideas to improve the quality of alternatives.[73] The leader can use the creative group techniques discussed earlier. Develop a lot of alternatives during step (3) of the decision-making model.

Another approach to improving the quality of decisions is the devil's advocate approach. The **devil's advocate technique** *requires the individual to explain and defend his or her position before the group.* The group critically asks the presenter questions. They try to shoot holes in the alternative solution to determine any possible problems in its implementation. After a period of time, the group reaches a refined solution. Use it during step (4) of the decision-making model.

Acceptance   The chances of successfully implementing a decision can be greatly increased if those affected are involved in the decision-making process.[74] How the decision is made often means more than the decision itself. When each member contributes to the decision process, it builds ownership, enthusiasm, and a commitment to action.[75]

Morale   Using participation in problem solving and decision making is tangibly rewarding and personally satisfying.[76] Participation results in better understanding of why decisions are made and greater job satisfaction.[77] Better communication within the department results when employees are involved in problem solving and decision making.[78]

Disadvantages of Group Decision Making

Some of the disadvantages of group decision making are these:

Time   It takes longer for a group to make a decision than for an individual. Employees involved in problem solving and decision making are not on the job producing. Therefore, group problem solving and decision making can cost the organization time and money. Cost pressure discourages participation.[79]

Domination   One group member or subgroup coalition may dominate the meeting and nullify the group decision.[80] Subgroups may develop and destructive conflict may result.[81] Conflicting secondary goals also may occur (see the discussion on ulterior transactions in Chapter 7). An individual or subgroup may try to win an argument rather than find the best solution, or the individual may put his or her personal needs before the group's needs.[82]

Conformity and Groupthink   Group members may feel pressured to go along with the group's solution without questioning it out of fear of not being accepted or of being ostracized. The group not willing to use the devil's advocate approach nullifies the advantage of diversity. The phenomenon in which conformity clearly has a negative impact on group problem solving and decision making has been labeled *groupthink*. A charismatic group member may charm others, or an autocratic member may intimidate a group into agreement, especially the shy, introverted personality types. With the use of nominal grouping, domination and conformity can be diminished.

Was Going to China the Right Medicine for Novartis AG or a Formula for Disaster?

Daniel Vasella, chairman and chief executive officer of Novartis AG, would like to feel confident that the firm's decision to open a major research center in China was a good one. Novartis is one of the world's largest pharmaceutical companies in terms of market value. It is among a number of multinationals that are turning to China to conduct more research and development, partly with the aim of leveraging the country's cheaper labor, but mostly in response to the growing importance of the Chinese market. As the Chinese middle class expands, the nation is spending over $100 billion a year on health care.

This growing market comes with increasing problems, however, that may leave CEO Vasella regretting the firm's decision. The Chinese medical market, like the old Wild West, does offer potential rewards for those who can find a rich vein, but its lawless nature regarding intellectual-property theft can lead to a situation akin to claim jumping. Insufficient protection has long been the stumbling block to pharmaceutical-research investment in China, and it is not yet sufficiently enforced. However, authorities are doing a better job of enforcing protections.

Questions

Use the five-step decision-making model to outline and answer the following questions.

1. What are the potential problems associated with Novartis opening a research center in China?

2. Have alternatives been explored? If not, what are some creative suggestions?

3. Why should or shouldn't the firm make this decision through group decision making?

4. If you were CEO Vasella, would you open a research facility in China?

5. Should China help its businesses by letting them copy products that are copyrighted or patented from other countries, or should it stop its businesses from breaking the laws of other countries? Which approach is ethical?

6. Should Novartis and other global companies conduct research in other countries to save money, or should they do their research in their home country? Which approach is ethical?

Source: Novartis Web site, http://www.novartis.com, retrieved October 22, 2008.

Responsibility and Social Loafing   When a group makes a decision, its responsibility is often spread over many people and they can take a less serious attitude, knowing they are not personally responsible. However, managers are responsible for decisions, regardless of how they are made.[83] The manager can delegate the authority to the group to make the decision, but she or he retains responsibility.

Social loafing spreads among team members like the flu, poisoning the decision climate, so prevent it or stop it early. Managers need the necessary skills to effectively use the group.[84]

When the advantages outweigh the disadvantages of using a group, use a group. In the opening case, Sonia decided to use a group. A key question to ask when deciding whether or not to use a group is this: Can the group make a better decision than any one individual? If you feel one individual will make a better decision (the person could be yourself as the manager or a knowledgeable employee), don't use the group. The next section will give you specific guidance on when to use a group, and what level of participation to use.

THE NORMATIVE LEADERSHIP DECISION-MAKING MODEL

Learning Outcome

5. Describe the normative leadership model.

The big issue managers must deal with today is no longer whether groups should be used to solve problems and make decisions; they should.[85] The issues today are *when* managers should use groups and when they should make the decision alone, and when a group is used, what *level of participation* should be used.[86] The normative leadership decision-making model, in this section, and the situational decision-making model, in Skill-Building Exercise 13–3, are used to answer these questions while improving decision-making effectiveness.

The normative and situational models do not take the place of the decision-making model; they tell you when to use a group and what level of participation you should use with the selected decision-making model. In other words, the two models do not tell you how to make the decision; they tell you what level of participation to use when making the decision.

In 1973, Victor Vroom and Philip Yetton published a decision-making model.[87] Vroom and Arthur Jago refined the model and expanded it to four models in 1988.[88] The models were based on two factors: individual versus group decisions and time-driven versus development-driven decisions.

In 2000, Victor Vroom published a revised version of normative leadership with the title, "Leadership and the Decision-Making Process." The current model is based on the research of Vroom and colleagues at Yale University on leadership and decision-making processes with more than 100,000 managers making decisions.[89] We present the latest version with a focus on time- and development-driven decisions.

The **normative leadership model** *has time-driven and development-driven decision trees that enable the user to select one of five leadership styles (decide, consult individually, consult group, facilitate, and delegate) appropriate for the situation.* It is called a normative model because it provides a sequential set of questions that are rules (norms) to follow to determine the best leadership style for the given situation.

EXHIBIT 13.5 |

Normative Leadership Time-Driven Model

The model is a decision tree that works like a funnel. Define the problem statement; then answer the questions from left to right as high (H) or low (L), skipping questions when not appropriate to the situation and avoiding crossing any horizontal lines, until you come to the last column, containing the appropriate leadership participation decision-making style for the situation.

	1 Decision Significance?	2 Importance of Commitment?	3 Leader Expertise?	4 Likelihood of Commitment?	5 Group Support?	6 Group Expertise?	7 Team Competence?	Leadership Style
P R O B L E M S T A T E M E N T	H	H	H	H	—	—	—	Decide
				L	H	H	H	Delegate
							L	Consult (Group)
						L	—	Consult (Group)
					L	—	—	Consult (Group)
			L	H	H	H	H	Facilitate
							L	Consult (Individually)
						L	—	Consult (Individually)
					L	—	—	Consult (Individually)
				L	H	H	H	Facilitate
							L	Consult (Group)
						L	—	Consult (Group)
					L	—	—	Consult (Group)
		L	H	—	—	—	—	Decide
			L	—	H	H	—	Facilitate
						L	—	Consult (Individually)
					L	—	—	Consult (Individually)
	L	H	—	H	—	—	—	Decide
				L	—	—	H	Delegate
							L	Facilitate
		L	—	—	—	—	—	Decide

Source: Adapted from *Organizational Dynamics* 28, Victor H. Vroom, "Leadership and the Decision-Making Process," p. 87. Copyright © 2000 with permission from Elsevier.

To use the normative model, you must have a specific decision to make, the authority to make the decision, and specific potential followers to participate in the decision.

Leadership Participation Styles

Vroom identified five leadership styles based on the level of participation in the decision by the followers.

1. *Decide.* The leader makes the decision alone and announces it, or sells it, to the followers. The leader may get information from others outside the group and within the group without specifying the problem.

2. *Consult individually.* The leader individually tells followers the problem, gets information and suggestions, and then makes the decision.

3. *Consult group.* The leader holds a group meeting and tells followers the problem, gets information and suggestions, and then makes the decision.

4. *Facilitate.* The leader holds a group meeting and acts as a facilitator to define the problem and the limits within which a decision must be made. The leader seeks participation, debate, and concurrence on the decision without pushing his or her ideas. However, the leader has the final say on the decision.

5. *Delegate.* The leader lets the group diagnose the problem and make the decision within stated limits. The role of the leader is to answer questions and provide encouragement and resources.

Model Questions to Determine the Appropriate Leadership Style

To determine which of the five leadership styles is the most appropriate for a given situation, you answer a series of diagnostic questions based on seven variables. The seven variables are listed in the time-driven and development-driven models shown in Exhibits 13.5 and 13.6. We now explain how to answer the questions, based on the variables, when using the two models.

1. *Decision significance.* How important is the decision to the success of the project or organization? Is the decision of high importance (H) or low importance (L)? With highly important decisions, leaders need to be involved.

2. *Importance of commitment.* How important is follower commitment to implementing the decision? If acceptance of the decision is critical to effective implementation, importance is high (H). If commitment is not critical, importance is low (L). With decisions that require high levels of follower commitment to ensure success, followers generally need to be involved in making the decisions.

3. *Leader expertise.* How much knowledge and expertise does the leader have with this specific type of decision? Is expertise high (H) or low (L)? The more expertise the leader has, the less need there is for follower participation.

4. *Likelihood of commitment.* If the leader were to make the decision alone, is it highly likely (H) that the followers would be committed to the decision, or is the likelihood of commitment low (L)? With decisions that followers will like and want to implement, there is less need to involve them in the decision.

5. *Group support.* Do followers have high (H) or low (L) support for the team or organizational goals to be attained in solving the problem? Higher levels of participation are acceptable with high levels of support.

6. *Group expertise.* How much knowledge and expertise do the individual followers have with this specific type of decision? Is expertise high (H) or low (L)? The more expertise the followers have, the greater the individuals' or group's participation can be.

EXHIBIT 13.6 |

Normative Leadership Development-Driven Model

The model is a decision tree that works like a funnel. Define the problem statement; then answer the questions from left to right as high (H) or low (L), skipping questions when not appropriate to the situation and avoiding crossing any horizontal lines, until you come to the last column, containing the appropriate leadership participation decision-making style for the situation.

	1 Decision Significance?	2 Importance of Commitment?	3 Leader Expertise?	4 Likelihood of Commitment?	5 Group Support?	6 Group Expertise?	7 Team Competence?	Leadership Style
P R O B L E M S T A T E M E N T	H	H	—	H	H	H	H	Delegate
							L	Facilitate
						L	—	Consult (Group)
					L	—	—	Consult (Group)
				L	H	H	H	Delegate
							L	Facilitate
						L	—	Facilitate
					L	—	—	Consult (Group)
		L	—	—	H	H	H	Delegate
							L	Facilitate
						L	—	Consult (Group)
					L	—	—	Consult (Group)
	L	H	—	H	—	—	—	Decide
				L	—	—	—	Delegate
		L	—	—	—	—	—	Decide

Source: Adapted from *Organizational Dynamics* 28, Victor H. Vroom, "Leadership and the Decision-Making Process," p. 88. Copyright © 2000 with permission from Elsevier.

7. *Team competence.* Is the ability of the individuals to work together as a team to solve the problem high (H) or low (L)? With high team competence, more participation can be used.

Not all seven questions are relevant to all decisions. All seven or as few as two questions may be needed to select the most appropriate leadership style in a given situation. If questions 1, 3, and 6 are tied together when making important decisions, it is critical to include the leader and/or followers with the expertise to solve the problem. Then the issue of commitment (questions 2 and 4) becomes relevant. If questions 5 to 7 are tied together in decision making, the leader should not delegate decisions to groups with low support for objectives, low group expertise, and low team competence. The great thing about the models is that they tie the relevant variables together as you answer the questions to determine the most appropriate leadership style for the given situation.

Selecting the Time-Driven or Development-Driven Model for the Situation

The first step is to select one of the two models based on whether the situation is being driven by the importance of time or by the development of followers. The characteristics of the decision are focus, value, and orientation.

The Time-Driven Model   See Exhibit 13.5. Its three characteristics are as follows:

- *Focus.* The model is concerned with making effective decisions with minimum cost. Time is costly, because it takes longer for groups to make decisions than the leader alone.

- *Value.* Value is placed on time, and no value is placed on follower development.
- *Orientation.* The model has a short-term horizon.

The Development-Driven Model See Exhibit 13.6. Its three characteristics are as follows:

- *Focus.* The model is concerned with making effective decisions with maximum development of followers. Follower development is worth the cost.
- *Value.* Value is placed on follower development, and no value is placed on time.
- *Orientation.* The model has a long-term horizon, since development takes time.

Computerized Normative Model Vroom has developed a computerized CD-ROM model that is more complex and more precise, yet easier to use. It combines the time- and development-driven models into one model, includes 11 variables/questions (rather than 7), and has five variable measures (rather than H or L). In addition, it guides users through the process of analyzing the situation with definitions, examples, and other forms of help as they use the model. The computerized model is beyond the scope of this course, but you will learn how to use the time- and development-driven models in Application Situation 13–3 and Skill-Building Exercise 13–2.

Determining the Appropriate Leadership Style

To determine the appropriate style for a specific situation, use the best model (time- or development-driven) for the situation and answer the questions, some of which may be skipped, depending on the model used and on previous questions. The questions are sequential and are presented in a decision-tree format, similar to that of the Fiedler model (Exhibit 8.3), in which you end up with the appropriate style to use. If you were to use both models for the same situation, for some decisions the appropriate style would be the same; for other decisions, it would be different.

In the opening case, what normative leadership decision-making style did Sonia use? Is that the style she should have used? The model to use for the budget situation is the development-driven model, in Exhibit 13.6. Use the model to select the style Sonia should have used and the one she did use. Then check your answer below.

- Question 1—(H). The decision is important.
- Question 2—(L). Commitment is actually low; Sonia could just tell departments how much their budgets are, and they would have no choice but to accept them.
- Skip questions 3 and 4.
- Question 5—(L). Group support is not really high because the members have a self-interest in getting more money for their own departments.
- Skip questions 6 and 7.

Sonia should have used and did use the consult group decision-making style. Sonia held a meeting, got information, and let the team debate. Then she made the final allocation decision.

> **WORK APPLICATIONS**
>
> 7. Give examples of situations in which each decision-making style—decide, consult (individually or group), facilitate, and delegate—would be appropriate to use.
>
> 8. Recall a specific decision you or your boss have had to make. Was the decision time- or development-driven? Using Exhibit 13.5 or 13.6, select the appropriate participation style for the situation. Be sure to state the questions you answered and how (H or L) you answered each.

APPLICATION SITUATIONS

The Normative Leadership Model

AS 13–3

A. Decide   C. Consult group   E. Delegate

B. Consult individually   D. Facilitate

Using the time-driven model, Exhibit 13.5, select the leadership style for the following situations:

_____ 11. Someone in your department has been making lots of personal copies, and it is affecting your budget. You want the copying to stop. You are a new manager and are pretty sure you know who is doing it.

_____ 12. Things are going OK in your department, but you know performance could be better. The department members are knowledgeable, have positive work norms, and work well together. You are thinking about having a one-time brainstorming session. You've never led one.

Using the development-driven model, Exhibit 13.6, select the leadership style for the following situations:

_____ 13. You work in purchasing and have to buy five new cars for the sales staff, within a set budget.

_____ 14. You oversee a self-directed team, but you don't provide any supervision; the team is self-managed. One of the seven team members has retired and needs to be replaced.

_____ 15. You supervise five part-time high school–aged employees. You know you have been losing customers, but you don't know why. You want to find out why and improve the situation.

Note: There are more complex and detailed situations in Skill-Building Exercise 13–2.

DOES DECISION MAKING APPLY GLOBALLY?

The *global economy* requires decisions to be made that affect operations worldwide.[90] At the same time, country and cultural differences call for local decisions. New technologies, especially the Internet, have increased the speed and quality of global communications and decisions.[91]

E-organizations are taking advantage of the Internet and, as discussed, using e-brainstorming. E-orgs, being team-based, use more group decision making than the older, traditional organizations.[92] Nevertheless, e-orgs make fast decisions, and the Internet helps speed up the process of gathering data to generate and evaluate alternative solutions. As learning organizations, they value knowledge sharing and learning from mistakes and quickly take corrective action if decisions are not going well.[93]

Decision-making styles and the decision-making model are based on the U.S. approach to decision making. People from different cultures don't necessarily make decisions the same way.[94] In fact, decision-making styles vary with culture.[95] In some countries decisions are made faster than in others. In countries that are not time-sensitive, such as Egypt, decisions are more reflective. In time-sensitive countries, such as the United States, decisions are more reflexive. Countries using participative decision making take longer than do countries that use autocratic decision making. The Japanese, using higher levels of participation than in the United States, often take longer to make decisions.

Some countries are more problem-solving–oriented, such as the United States, whereas others, such as Thailand and Indonesia, accept things the way they are. Culture influences the selection of problems to solve, the depth of analysis, the importance placed on logic and rationality, and the level of participation used in decision making. Thus, in high power distance cultures (for example, Mexico, Venezuela, the Philippines, and Yugoslavia), where more autocratic decisions are made, participation is not acceptable, so the normative leadership decision model would not be used. In low power distance cultures (the United States, Japan, Ireland, Australia, New Zealand, Denmark, Israel, and the Netherlands), there is greater use of participation in decision making—especially in Japan.[96]

Let's close this chapter by discussing in Self-Assessment Exercise 13–2 how your personality may affect your decision-making style and use of participation in decision making.

Self-Assessment Exercise 13–2

Personality Traits and Decision-Making Styles and Participation

Let's discuss how your personality affects how you make decisions.

If you have a high *surgency* personality, with a high need for power, you may make quick, reflexive decisions. Your preferred normative leadership style may tend to be decide or consult. You may need to allow more participation in decision making to be more effective. Participation will also slow down your decision making.

If you are high in *agreeableness* personality traits, with a high need for affiliation, you tend to be a good team player and likely seek out others to participate in decision making. Your preferred normative leadership styles may tend to be facilitate and delegate. However, don't be too reflective and make decisions too slowly because you can miss opportunities.

If you are high in *conscientiousness*, with a high need for achievement, you may know what you want and may make quick, reflexive decisions. You may change normative leadership styles to help get what you want. Being conscientious, you may tend to follow the steps in the decision-making model more than the other personality types.

Being high on *adjustment*, in control of your emotions, helps when making team decisions. If you tend to get too emotional, try to stay calm and help the team.

If you are *open to new experiences*, you are willing to try new things, which helps with creativity. People who are open to new experiences are usually more creative than those who are not. If you are reluctant to try new things, make an effort to continually look for ways to improve and be more creative.

Action Plan: Based on your personality, what specific things will you do to improve your decision-making skills? Should you follow the steps in the decision-making model more often?

_____

_____

_____

_____

Videos

Manager's Hot Seat and Behavior Model Videos are available for this chapter.

Online Learning Center Resources

Go to the Internet (http://mhhe.com/lussier8e) where you will find a broad array of resources to help maximize your learning.

• Review the vocabulary.

• Try a quiz.

R E V I E W

The chapter review is organized to help you master the 6 learning outcomes for Chapter 13. First provide your own response to each learning outcome, and then check the summary provided to see how well you understand the material. Next, identify the final statement in each section as either true or false (T/F). Correct each false statement. Answers are given at the end of the chapter.

1. **Describe the three decision-making styles and know which style is preferred.**

   The three decision-making styles are: (1) the *reflexive* style, in which one makes quick decisions; (2) the *reflective* style, in which one makes slow decisions; and (3) the *consistent* style, in which the speed of decision-making is balanced. The consistent style is preferable, as it balances the speed of decision-making by neither rushing nor wasting time.

   Problem solving and decision making are interrelated because when one is faced with a problem, one must make a decision. T F

2. **List the five steps in the decision-making model.**

   The steps in the decision-making model are: (1) define the problem, (2) set objectives and criteria, (3) generate alternatives, (4) analyze alternatives and select one, and (5) plan, implement the decision, and control.

   The decision-making model should be used when making unimportant recurring decisions. T F

3. **Describe five techniques for generating creative alternatives.**

   Five techniques for generating creative alternatives include: (1) *brainstorming,* the process of suggesting as many alternatives as possible, without evaluation, to solve a problem; (2) *synetics,* the process of generating novel alternatives through role playing and fantasizing; (3) *nominal grouping,* the process of generating and evaluating alternatives using a structured voting method; (4) *consensus mapping,* the process of developing a group consensus to solve a problem; and (5) the *Delphi technique,* which involves using a series of anonymous questionnaires to refine a solution.

   The one thing these five techniques have in common is that they all involve a small group of people who get together to come up with creative ideas. T F

4. **Explain the advantages and disadvantages of group decision making.**

   The advantages of group decision making are: better decisions, more alternatives, acceptance of the team decision, and increased morale. The disadvantages include: group decision making takes more time, one person can dominate the team, conformity and groupthink may occur, and no one person is held responsible for the decision.

   The trend today is to use more group decision making. T F

5. **Describe the normative leadership model.**

   The normative leadership model has time-driven and development-driven decision trees that enable the user to select one of five leadership styles (decide, consult individually, consult group, facilitate, and delegate) appropriate for the situation.

   The normative leadership model is useful because it tells managers which decision to make. T F

Learning Outcome

6. Define the following 14 key terms.

6. **Define the following 14 key terms.**

   Select one or more methods: (1) fill in the missing key terms from memory; (2) match the key terms from the end of the review with their definitions below; and/or (3) copy the key terms in order from the key terms at the beginning of the chapter.

   A _____ exists whenever there is a difference between what is

   actually happening and what the individual or group wants to be happening.

   _____ is the process of taking corrective action in order to meet

   objectives.

_____ is the process of selecting an alternative course of action that will solve a problem.

The steps in the _____ are as follows: step (1) define the problem; step (2) set objectives and criteria; step (3) generate alternatives; step (4) analyze alternatives and select one; and step (5) plan, implement the decision, and control.

_____ is a technique for comparing the cost and benefit of each alternative course of action.

_____ is the ability to develop unique alternatives to solve problems.

The _____ are (1) preparation, (2) possible solutions, (3) incubation, and (4) evaluation.

_____ is the process of suggesting many alternatives, without evaluation, to solve a problem.

_____ is the process of generating novel alternatives through role playing and fantasizing.

_____ is the process of generating and evaluating alternatives through a structured voting method.

_____ is the process of developing a group consensus solution to a problem.

The _____ polls a group through a series of anonymous questionnaires.

The _____ requires the individual to explain and defend his or her position before the group.

The _____ has time-driven and development-driven decision trees that enable the user to select one of five leadership styles (decide, consult individually, consult group, facilitate, and delegate) appropriate for the situation.

K E Y   T E R M S

brainstorming 465	Delphi technique 466	problem solving 459
consensus mapping 466	devil's advocate	stages in the creative
cost–benefit analysis 462	technique 468	process 464
creativity 464	nominal grouping 466	synetics 466
decision making 459	normative leadership	
decision-making	model 470	
model 461	problem 459	

C O M M U N I C A T I O N   S K I L L S

The following critical thinking questions can be used for class discussion and/or as written assignments to develop communication skills. Be sure to give complete explanations for all questions.

1. What is the role of intuition in decision making? Should managers use more objective or subjective intuition techniques when making decisions?

2. Is following the steps in the decision-making model really all that important? Which steps of the model do you tend to follow? Which steps do you tend to not use? Will you use the model in your personal and/or professional life?

3. Should managers be ethical in their decision making? If so, how should ethics be used in decision making?

4. Are creativity and innovation really that important to all types of businesses?

5. Is it important to evaluate a creative idea before it becomes an innovation?

6. Have you used any of the five techniques for generating creative alternatives (Exhibit 13.4)? If yes, which ones?

7. Which of the potential advantages and disadvantags of group problem solving and decision making do you think arise most frequently?

8. Some people say that the normative leadership decision-making model is too complex to use on the job. Do you agree with this statement?

9. How do your personality traits affect your decision-making style and your interest and ability to participate in group decision making?

CASE

Cindi Bigelow and the R.C. Bigelow Tea Company

The R.C. Bigelow Tea Company "blends and markets both traditional black and herbal teas under the Bigelow brand. Constant Comment—a blend of black tea, orange peel, and spices—is the company's original product. Bigelow teas are produced at plants in Connecticut, Idaho, and Kentucky and are widely available through grocery retailers, mass merchandisers, and the food service industry. R.C. Bigelow also sells tea and tea accessories direct to consumers through its Web site and catalog business. Founded by Ruth C. Bigelow in the late 1940s, the company is still owned and operated by the Bigelow family. As a family-owned and -operated business, the company is guided by the following four basic principles, as noted on its Web site:

1. **Satisfied Consumers:** At Bigelow, the consumer is number one. Therefore, it is essential that we provide a product that satisfies all of their expectations. Our primary focus is to produce teas that offer a unique and truly gratifying experience. In this endeavor, we will not allow price to compromise our products. Good flavor and product freshness are the prime considerations in the creations of our teas.

2. **Strong Relationships:** With our customers and suppliers we continually work to build and maintain strong business relationships. We realize that it is through excellent communication and mutual respect that we grow and prosper together.

3. **Satisfied Employees:** Bigelow is an equal opportunity employer dedicated to providing our employees with a challenging and positive environment in which to work. Recognizing that each and every employee plays a pivotal role in the success of our company, we seek to attract and retain outstanding individuals who will take pride in all aspects of their areas of responsibility, and understand the importance of cooperation among their fellow employees. We strive to motivate and satisfy our employees as well as promote individuals based on merit and contribution.

4. **Good Corporate Citizen:** Our company has been, and always will be, based upon strong ethical business practices and is dedicated to only the highest standard of behavior in all areas. We feel an obligation to support the local communities where we reside so as to build a good working relationship as well as to contribute to worthy local and national causes. Furthermore, as a good corporate citizen, we remain committed to protecting the environment by continually striving to improve the environmental responsiveness of our packaging.

As chief operating officer, Cindi Bigelow was charged in part with developing new product concepts for the company and introducing these new ideas into an intensely competitive but slow-growth hot tea category. Cindi was mindful of the importance of retaining her franchise base, women 45 and older. However, she was hopeful that introducing new flavors with more youth-oriented names, like "Berri-Good" and "Tasty Tangerine," and more contemporary packaging would overcome some negative perceptions about hot tea drinking among college-age students and young professionals, aged 18–34. Packaging design became more modern and upbeat than the traditional Bigelow Tea package both to communicate a zestier taste experience and to attract a younger audience to the company's tea product line.

Cindi said, "It would be a breakthrough for us to get younger people to start drinking hot tea in significant numbers. That would represent a real growth market for us." Her vice president of marketing, Robert Kelly, agreed: "We know we do a solid job marketing our product to an older population, but the tea category isn't growing much with our franchise consumers. We could see substantial increases in our year-over-year sales numbers if we could only attract younger professional women *and* men. Unfortunately, we don't know an awful lot about their tea drinking habits."

Interestingly, most tea consumed in the United States is iced, not hot, and iced tea outsells the more traditional variety four to one. Unfortunately for Bigelow, the company decided not to enter the iced tea category until it was saturated by far larger companies with a lot more marketing clout, including Snapple. Bigelow currently offers only five powdered ice tea products, two of which are decaffeinated.

Bigelow is still trying to expand its demographics to include younger tea drinkers. The earlier young adults convert to hot tea and away from soda, iced tea, coffee, and bottled water, the longer Bigelow will have them as customers throughout their lives. That is Bigelow's real marketing challenge. But how do you change young people's perceptions about specialty tea? Does the company need to change its image? Cindi hopes not. To grow, Bigelow really wants to target the 18–34 age segment, without alienating its current loyal customers—older women. How can Bigelow get younger people to drink hot tea?[97]

Go to the Internet: For more information on the R.C. Bigelow Tea Company and to update the information provided in this case, do a name search on the Internet and visit http://www.bigelowtea.com.

Support your answers to the following questions with specific information from the case and text, or with other information you get from the Web or other sources.

1. What style of decision making most accurately depicts Cindi Bigelow's style of decision making?

2. Using the decision-making model (Exhibit 13.1), where is Cindi Bigelow in terms of the decision-making steps?

3. What major alternative has Cindi Bigelow decided not to pursue in order to reach younger tea drinkers? Why?

4. Assume that you want to come up with a creative solution to the firm's problem. What steps would you take in order to facilitate creative problem solving?

5. Assume Cindi Bigelow is thinking of putting together a group to help her solve the company's problem. What disadvantages should she be cognizant of before she does so?

6. How might Cindi Bigelow motivate young people to become more active hot tea drinkers?

Cumulative Questions

7. How do perception (Chapter 2), attitudes, and values (Chapter 3) relate to this case?

8. Assuming the firm wanted to develop a product line just for young tea drinkers, what organizational structure (Chapter 6) would facilitate that strategy?

9. As a leader (Chapter 8), what role should Cindi Bigelow play in the decision-making process?

OBJECTIVE CASE   **Department Meeting**

Juanita, the check-processing supervisor of the Tenth National Bank, has called her five employees together to try to figure out a way to stop the bottleneck in the processing of checks. Below are some of the statements made during the meeting.

JUANITA: (*opening statement*) You are all aware of the bottleneck problem we have. I've called this meeting to try to come up with a solution. I feel that this meeting can help bring us together as a team and help increase our job satisfaction by allowing the group to decide how to solve the problem. I'd like you all to suggest possible solutions. One rule is that no one will make any negative comments about any solution. Any crazy idea is acceptable. Who wants to go first? (*After about four or five minutes, Mary, the informal group leader, interrupts the group meeting.*)

MARY: I've already given the best solution. There is no need to keep asking for ideas.

JUANITA: Mary, we are trying to come up with as many creative ideas as possible.

MARY: For what? I've got a good idea.

JUANITA: Let's continue generating ideas. Who will go next? (*Mary looks around the room with an expression that says, "be quiet." After waiting three or four minutes, which feel like a hundred, no one makes a suggestion, so Juanita speaks.*)

JUANITA: Let's analyze the seven alternatives we have to determine which is the best.

MARY: Mine is the best.

WILL: Wait a minute, Mary, my idea is as good as yours or better. Tell us why yours is so much better than anyone else's.

MARY: I will if everyone else will.

JUANITA: Wait a minute; these ideas are the group's, not just any one person's. We want to work as a team. (*Will and Mary continue to battle it out. Their two ideas seem to be the most popular. With the battle on, Juanita knows the group will not agree to one solution.*)

JUANITA: We are down to two alternatives. Let's vote for the one to use. (*The vote is four for Mary's idea and two for Will's. Will and Juanita vote for his idea, and the rest go with Mary's alternative.*)

Answer the following questions. Then in the space between the questions, state why you selected that answer.

_____ 1. The bank has a problem.

     a. true   *b.* false

_____ 2. Juanita used participative management during the meeting.

     a. true   *b.* false

_____ 3. The group is a _____ group.

     a. functional   *b.* task   *c.* informal

_____ 4. Mary's decision-making style seems to be:

     a. reflexive   *b.* consistent   *c.* reflective

_____ 5. The group used the creative process.

     a. true   *b.* false

_____ 6. Will suggested using the _____ technique.

     a. cost–benefit   *c.* Delphi technique

     b. synetics   *d.* devil's advocate

_____ 7. The major technique Juanita used at the meeting was:

     a. brainstorming   *c.* nominal grouping   *e.* Delphi technique

     b. synetics   *d.* consensus mapping

_____ 8. The major benefit of using a group, which Juanita hoped to accomplish, was:

     a. a better decision   *c.* acceptance

     b. more alternatives   *d.* higher morale

_____ 9. The major disadvantage to using a group was:

     a. time   *c.* conformity and groupthink

     b. domination   *d.* responsibility

_____ 10. Juanita used the _____ normative leadership decision-making style.

     a. decide   *c.* facilitate

     b. consult (individually or group)   *d.* delegate

11. If you were in Juanita's situation, would you have used a group to solve the problem? Why or why not?

12. Assume you decided to use a group. In Juanita's position, how would you have handled the meeting?

Note: The meeting can be role-played in class.

SKILL-BUILDING EXERCISE 13–1

Individual versus Group Decision Making

In-Class Exercise (Group)

Objective: To compare individual and group decision making to better understand when and when not to use a group to make decisions.

AACSB: The primary AACSB learning standard skills developed through this exercise are teamwork and leadership; in addition, communication and analytic skills are developed.

Preparation: You should have completed Application Situations 13–1 and 13–2, or the first 10 questions in the Objective Case, whichever your instructor assigned.

Experience: During class, you will work in a group that will make the same decisions, followed by an analysis of the results.

Procedure 1 (1–2 minutes)

Place your individual answers to Application Situations 13–1 and 13–2 in the "Individual Answer" column below.

Application Situation Question	Individual Answer (A-E)	Group Answer (A-E)	Recommended Answer (A-E)	Score Individual versus Group
1.				
2.				
3.				
4.				
5.				
6.				
7.				
8.				
9.				
10.	＿＿＿	＿＿＿	＿＿＿	＿＿＿
Total score				

Procedure 2
(18–22 minutes)

Break into teams of five; make groups of four or six as necessary. As a group, come to an agreement on the answers to Application Situations 13–1 and 13–2. Place the group answers in the "Group Answer" column above. Try to use consensus rather than the voting technique.

Procedure 3
(4–6 minutes)

Scoring: The instructor will give you the recommended answers to Application Situations 13–1 and 13–2; place the answers in column 4. In column 2, place the number of individual answers you got correct (1–10) on the total score line. In column 3, place the number the group answered correctly (1–10) on the total score line. In column 5, place the number representing the gain/loss of individual versus group answers on the total score line. (For example, if you scored 8 correct and the group scored 6, you beat the group by 2—so put +2 on the total score line. If you scored 5 correct and the group scored 8, the group beat you by 3—so put −3 on the total score line. If you tied, put 0.)

Averaging: Calculate the average individual score by adding all the individual scores and dividing by the number of group members. Average _____ .

Gain or Loss: Find the difference between the average score and the group score. If the group's score is higher than the average individual score, you have a gain of ____ points; if the group's score is lower, you have a loss of ____ points.

Determine the highest individual score _____ .
Determine the number of individuals who scored higher than the group's score _____ .

Integration (4–8 minutes): As a group, discuss which advantages and/or disadvantages your group had while making the decisions in this exercise.

Advantages:

*   *Better decisions.* Did your group make better decisions? Was the group's score higher than the highest individual score? If not, why not? Were the knowledgeable members nonassertive or just not listened to?

*   *More alternatives.* Did the group get members to consider alternatives they did not consider as individuals? Did your group use the devil's advocate approach?

*   *Acceptance.* Did group members accept the answers as a consensus?

*   *Morale.* Were members more satisfied making the decisions and giving the answers in a group?

Disadvantages:

*   *Time.* Did it take the group longer than it took individuals to make the decisions? Was the time spent worth the benefits?

*   *Domination.* Did any one person or subgroup dominate the group? Did everyone participate?

*   *Conformity.* Were members nonassertive in presenting their answers in order to be accepted or because of group pressure to agree with the majority?

*   *Responsibility.* Because no one person was held responsible for the group's answers, did members take an "I don't care" attitude?

Improvements: Overall, were the advantages of using a group greater than the disadvantages of using a group? If your group continues to work together, how could it improve its problem-solving and decision-making abilities? Write out the answer below.

Conclusion: The instructor leads a class discussion and/or makes concluding remarks.

Application (2–4 minutes):   What did I learn from this experience? How will I use this knowledge in the future?

Sharing: Volunteers give their answers to the application section.

Using the Normative Leadership Model

Preparation (Individual and Group)

You should have studied the normative leadership decision-making model text material. Using the appropriate exhibit, either Exhibit 13.5 or 13.6, determine the appropriate leadership style for the given problem statements below. Follow these steps:

1. Determine which of the two normative leadership models to use for the given situation.
2. Answer the variable questions (you will answer between 2 and 7 of the diagnostic questions) for the problem.
3. Select the appropriate leadership style of the model.

   a. *Production department manager.* You are the manager of a mass-produced manufactured product. You have two major machines in your department, with 10 people working on each. You have an important order that needs to be shipped first thing tomorrow morning. Your boss has made it very clear that you must meet this deadline. It's 2:00 and you are right on schedule to meet the order deadline. At 2:15 an employee comes to tell you that one of the machine is smoking a little and making a noise. If you keep running the machine, it may make it until the end of the day and you will deliver the important shipment on time. If you shut down the machine, the manufacturer will not be able to check the machine until tomorrow and you will miss the deadline. You call your boss and there is no answer. You don't know how else to contact the boss or how long it will be before the boss gets back to you if you leave a message. There are no higher-level managers than you or anyone with more knowledge of the machine than you. Which leadership style should you use?

   Step 1. Which model should you use? (____ time-driven ____ development-driven)

   Step 2. Which questions did you answer, and how (H = high, L = low, NA = not answered/skipped)? Circle your answers.

1. H L NA	3. H L NA	5. H L NA	7. H L NA
2. H L NA	4. H L NA	6. H L NA	

   Step 3. Which leadership style is the most appropriate?

   ____ decide ____ consult individually ____ consult group ____ facilitate ____ delegate

b. *Religious leader.* You are the top religious leader of your church, which has 200 members from 125 families. You have a doctorate of religious studies, with just two years' experience as the head of a church, but you have taken no business courses. The church has one paid secretary; three part-time program directors for religious instruction, music, and social activities; plus many volunteers. Your paid staff serves on your advisory board with 10 church members who are primarily top-level business leaders in the community. You make a yearly budget with the board's approval. The church's source of income is members' weekly donations. The board doesn't want to operate in the red, and the church has very modest surplus funds. Your volunteer accountant (CPA), who is a board member, asked to meet with you. During the meeting, she informed you that weekly collections are down 20 percent below budget and that the cost of utilities has increased 25 percent over the yearly budget figure. You are running a large deficit, and at this rate, your surplus will be gone in two months. Which leadership style will you use in this crisis?

Step 1. Which model should you use? (____ time-driven ____ development-driven)

Step 2. Which questions did you answer and how (H = high, L = low, NA = not answered/skipped)? Circle your answers.
1. H L NA   3. H L NA   5. H L NA   7. H L NA
2. H L NA   4. H L NA   6. H L NA

Step 3. Which leadership style is the most appropriate?

____ decide ____ consult individually ____ consult group ____ facilitate ____ delegate

c. *School of business dean.* You are the new dean of the school of business at a small private university. Your faculty includes 20 professors, only 2 of which are nontenured, and the average number of years at the school is 12. On taking the job, you expected to leave for a larger school in three years. Your primary goal is to start a business school faculty advisory board to improve community relations and school alumni relations, and to raise money for financial aid scholarships. You have already done this in your previous job as dean. However, you are new to this area and have no business contacts. You need help to develop a network of alumni and community leaders fairly quickly if you are to show achieved results on your resume in 2½ years. Your faculty gets along well and is talkative, but when you approach small groups of them, they tend to become quiet and to disperse. Which primary leadership style would you use to achieve your objective?

Step 1. Which model should you use? (____ time-driven ____ development-driven)

Step 2. Which questions did you answer and how (H = high, L = low, NA = not answered/skipped)? Circle your answers.
1. H L NA   3. H L NA   5. H L NA   7. H L NA
2. H L NA   4. H L NA   6. H L NA

Step 3. Which leadership style is the most appropriate?

____ decide ____ consult individually ____ consult group ____ facilitate ____ delegate

d. *Dot-com president.* You are the president of a dot-com company that has been having financial problems for a few years. As a result, your top two managers left for other jobs. One left four months ago and the other two months ago. With your networking contacts, you replaced both within a month, so the new managers don't have a lot of time on the job and haven't worked together for very long. Additionally, they currently do their own thing to get their jobs done. However, they are both very bright, hardworking, and dedicated to your vision of what the company can be. You know how to turn the company around and so do your two key managers. To turn the company around, you and your two managers will have to work together, with the help of all your employees. Virtually all the employees are high-tech specialists who want to be included in decision making. Your business partners have no more money to invest. If you cannot turn a profit in four to five months, you will most likely go bankrupt. Which primary leadership style would you use to achieve your objective?

Step 1. Which model should you use? (_____ time-driven _____ development-driven)

Step 2. Which questions did you answer and how (H = high, L = low, NA = not answered/skipped)? Circle your answers.

1. H L NA	3. H L NA	5. H L NA	7. H L NA
2. H L NA	4. H L NA	6. H L NA	

Step 3. Which leadership style is the most appropriate?

_____ decide _____ consult individually _____ consult group _____ facilitate _____ delegate

In-Class Exercise	*Objective:* To develop your skill at determining the appropriate leadership style to use in a given situation using the normative leadership model.
	AACSB: The primary AACSB learning standard skills developed through this exercise are leadership and analytic skills.
	Experience: You will use the normative leadership model in four given problem situations.
Procedure 1 *(10–15 minutes)*	The instructor goes over the normative leadership model and illustrates how to use it to select the appropriate leadership style for problem situation a.
Procedure 2 *(10–20 minutes)*	Break into groups of two or three and use the model to determine the appropriate leadership style for situations b through d in the preparation above. The instructor will then go over or just state the answers to situations b through d.
	Conclusion: The instructor may lead a class discussion and/or make concluding remarks.
	Application (2–4 minutes): What did I learn from this experience? How will I apply the normative leadership model in the future?

Sharing: Volunteers give their answers to the application section.

SKILL-BUILDING EXERCISE 13-3

Using the Situational Decision-Making Model	In this exercise, you will learn how to use the situational decision-making model. You will realize that it is similar to the normative leadership model, but it has only one model and fewer questions.
Preparation (Individual and Group)	Chapter 8 discussed the situational supervision model. Chapter 6 provided a situational communication model to use when communicating. Now you will learn a similar model to use when deciding which supervisory style to use when solving problems and making decisions. Selecting the appropriate situational supervisory style when solving problems and making decisions includes two steps: step (1) diagnose the situation, and step (2) select the appropriate style.
	Step 1: Diagnose the Situation The first step is to diagnose the situational variables, which include time, information, acceptance, and employee capability level. See Exhibit 13.7 for a list of variables.

EXHIBIT 13.7 |
Variables Influencing
Participation

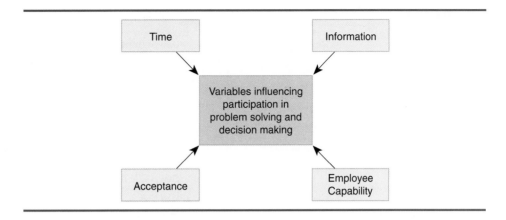

Time   The manager must determine if there is enough time to include the group in decision making. If there is not enough time, managers should use the autocratic style, regardless of their preferred style. In this case the manager should also ignore the other three variables; they are irrelevant if there is no time. If time permits, the manager considers the other three variables and selects the problem-solving and decision-making styles without considering time. When time is short, the manager may use the consultative style, but not the participative or laissez-faire styles. Time, however, is a relative term. In one situation, a few minutes may be considered a short time period, while in another, a month may be a short period of time.

Information   Does the manager have enough information to make a quality decision alone? If the manager has all the necessary information, there is no need to use participation. The autocratic style may be appropriate. When the manager has some information but needs more, the consultative style may be appropriate. However, if the manager has little information, the appropriate style may be participative or laissez-faire.

Acceptance   The manager must decide if the group's acceptance of the decision is critical to its implementation. If the manager makes the decision alone, will the group implement it? If so, the appropriate style may be autocratic. If the group will be reluctant, the appropriate style may be consultative or participative. If the group will probably not implement the decision unless consulted in advance, the participative or laissez-faire style may be appropriate.

Employee Capability   The manager must decide if the group has the ability and willingness to be involved in problem solving and decision making. Does the group have the experience and information needed to be involved in problem solving and decision making? Will the group put the organization's or the department's goals ahead of personal goals? Does the group want to be involved in problem solving and decision making? Employees are more willing to participate when the decisions affect them personally. If the group's level of capability is low, an autocratic style may be appropriate. When a group's capability is moderate, a consultative style may be appropriate. If the group's capability level is high, a participative style may be appropriate. If the group's level of capability is outstanding, the laissez-faire style may be appropriate. Remember that a group's capability level can change from situation to situation.

  The top half of Exhibit 13.8 summarizes step 1.

Step 2: Select the Appropriate Supervisory Style for the Situation   After considering the four variables, a manager uses the analysis to select the appropriate style for the situations at hand. In some situations, all variables suggest the same possible style, while other cases indicate conflicting styles. For example, the manager may have time to use

EXHIBIT 13.8 |
Situational Decision
Making

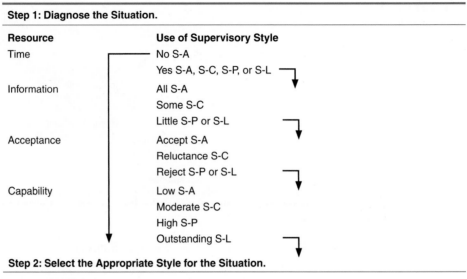

Step 1: Diagnose the Situation.

Resource	Use of Supervisory Style
Time	No S-A
	Yes S-A, S-C, S-P, or S-L
Information	All S-A
	Some S-C
	Little S-P or S-L
Acceptance	Accept S-A
	Reluctance S-C
	Reject S-P or S-L
Capability	Low S-A
	Moderate S-C
	High S-P
	Outstanding S-L

Step 2: Select the Appropriate Style for the Situation.

Autocratic (S-A)

The supervisor makes the decision alone and announces it after the fact. An explanation of the rationale for the decision may be given.

Consultative (S-C)

The supervisor consults individuals or the group for information and then makes the decision. Before implementing the decision, the supervisor explains the rationale for the decision and sells the benefits to the employees. The supervisor may invite questions and have a discussion.

Participative (S-P)

The supervisor may present a tentative decision to the group and ask for its input. The supervisor may change the decision if the input warrants a change. Or the supervisor may present the problem to the group for suggestions. Based on employee participation, the supervisor makes the decision and explains its rationale.

Laissez-Faire (S-L)

The supervisor presents the situation to the group and describes limitations to the decision. The group makes the decision. The supervisor may be a group member.

any style and may have all the information necessary (autocratic); employees may be reluctant (consultative or participative); and the capability may be moderate (consultative). In situations where conflicting styles are indicated for different variables, the manager must determine which variable should be given more weight. In the above example, assume it was determined that acceptance was critical for successful implementation of the decision. Acceptance takes precedence over information. Realizing that employees have a moderate capability, the consultative style would be appropriate. See the bottom half of Exhibit 13.8 for an explanation of how the decision is made using each of the four situational supervisory styles.

Applying the Situational Decision-Making Model

We will apply the model to the following situation:

Ben, a supervisor, can give one of his employees a merit pay raise. He has a week to make the decision. Ben knows how well each employee performed over the past year. The employees really have no option but to accept getting or not getting the pay raise, but they can complain to upper management about the selection. The employees' capability levels vary, but as a group, they have a high capability level under normal circumstances.

Step 1: Diagnose the Situation.

____ time   ____ information   ____ acceptance   ____ capability

Ben, the supervisor, has plenty of time to use any level of participation. He has all the information needed to make the decision (autocratic). Employees have no choice but to accept the decision (autocratic). And the group's level of capability is normally high (participative).

Step 2: Select the Appropriate Style for the Situation.   There are conflicting styles to choose from (autocratic and participative):

____ yes time   ____ S-A information   ____ S-A acceptance   ____ S-P capability

The variable that should be given precedence is information. The employees are normally capable, but in a situation like this, they may not be capable of putting the department's goals ahead of their own. In other words, even if employees know which employee deserves the raise, they may each fight for it anyway. Such a conflict could cause future problems. Some of the possible ways to make the decision are as follows:

- *Autocratic (S-A).* The supervisor would select the person for the raise without discussing it with any employees. Ben would simply announce the decision and explain the rationale for the selection, after submitting it to the payroll department.

- *Consultative (S-C).* The supervisor would consult the employees as to who should get the raise. Ben would then decide who would get the raise. He would announce the decision and explain the rationale for it. The supervisor may invite questions and discussion.

- *Participative (S-P).* The supervisor could tentatively select an employee to get the raise, but be open to change if an employee or group convinces him that someone else should get the raise. Or Ben could explain the situation to the group and lead a discussion of who should get the raise. After considering their input, Ben would make the decision and explain the rationale for it.

- *Laissez-faire (S-L).* The supervisor would explain the situation and allow the group to decide who gets the raise. Ben may be a group member. Notice that this is the only style that allows the group to make the decision.

Selection   The autocratic style is appropriate for this situation because Ben has all the information needed, acceptance is not an issue, and capability is questionable.

Below are 10 situations calling for a decision. Select the appropriate problem-solving and decision-making style. Be sure to use Exhibit 13.8, p. 488, when determining the style to use. On the time, information, acceptance, and capability lines, place S-A, S-C, S-P, or S-L, as indicated by the situation. Based on your diagnoses, select the one style you would use. Note that style on the line preceding the situation.

S-A Autocratic   S-C Consultative   S-P Participative   S-L Laissez-faire

_____   1. You have developed a new work procedure that will increase productivity. Your boss likes the idea and wants you to try it within a few weeks. You view your employees as fairly capable and believe that they will be receptive to the change.

____ time ____ information ____ acceptance ____ capability

_____   2. The industry of your product has new competition. Your organization's revenues have been dropping. You have been told to lay off 3 of your

10 employees in two weeks. You have been the supervisor for over one year. Normally, your employees are very capable.

_____ time _____ information _____ acceptance _____ capability

_____ 3. Your department has been facing a problem for several months. Many solutions have been tried, but all have failed. You have finally thought of a solution, but you are not sure of the possible consequences of the change required or of acceptance by the highly capable employees.

_____ time _____ information _____ acceptance _____ capability

_____ 4. Flextime has become popular in your organization. Some departments let each employee start and end work when he or she chooses. However, because of the cooperative effort of your employees, they must all work the same eight hours. You are not sure of the level of interest in changing the hours. Your employees are a very capable group and like to make decisions.

_____ time _____ information _____ acceptance _____ capability

_____ 5. The technology in your industry is changing so fast that the members of your organization cannot keep up. Top management hired a consultant who has made recommendations. You have two weeks to decide what to do. Your employees are normally capable, and they enjoy participating in the decision-making process.

_____ time _____ information _____ acceptance _____ capability

_____ 6. A change has been handed down from top management. How you implement it is your decision. The change takes effect in one month. It will personally affect everyone in your department. Their acceptance is critical to the success of the change. Your employees are usually not too interested in being involved in making decisions.

_____ time _____ information _____ acceptance _____ capability

_____ 7. Your boss called you on the telephone to tell you that someone has requested an order for your department's product with a very short delivery date. She asked you to call her back in 15 minutes with the decision about taking the order. Looking over the work schedule, you realize that it will be very difficult to deliver the order on time. Your employees will have to push hard to make it. They are cooperative, capable, and enjoy being involved in decision making.

_____ time _____ information _____ acceptance _____ capability

_____ 8. Top management has decided to make a change that will affect all your employees. You know the employees will be upset because it will cause them hardship. One or two may even quit. The change goes into effect in 30 days. Your employees are very capable.

_____ time _____ information _____ acceptance _____ capability

_____ 9. You believe that productivity in your department could be increased. You have thought of some ways that may work, but you are not sure of them. Your employees are very experienced; almost all of them have been in the department longer than you have.

_____ time _____ information _____ acceptance _____ capability

_____ 10. A customer has offered you a contract for your product with a quick delivery date. The offer is open for two days. Meeting the contract deadline would require employees to work nights and weekends for six weeks. You cannot require them to work overtime. Filling this profitable contract could help get you the raise you want and feel you deserve. However, if you take the contract and don't deliver on time, it will hurt your chances of getting a big raise. Your employees are very capable.

_____ time _____ information _____ acceptance _____ capability

In-Class Exercise

Objective: To develop your situational supervisory problem-solving and decision-making skills.

AACSB: The primary AACSB learning standard skills developed through this exercise are leadership and analytic skills.

Preparation: You should have completed the 10 situations from the preparation.

Experience: You will try to select the recommended problem-solving and decision-making style in the 10 preparation situations.

Procedure 1
(5–12 minutes)

The instructor reviews Exhibit 13.8 and explains how to use it for selecting the appropriate supervisory style for situation 1 of the exercise preparation.

Procedure 2
(12–20 minutes)

Break into teams of two or three. Apply the model to situations 2 through 5 as a team. You may change your original answers. It may be helpful to tear the model out of the book so you don't have to keep flipping pages. The instructor goes over the recommended answers and scoring for situations 2 through 5. Do not continue on to situation 6 until after the instructor goes over the answers to situations 2 through 5.

VE 13–1
BMV 13–1

In the same teams, select problem-solving and decision-making styles for situations 6 through 10. The instructor will go over the recommended answers and scoring.

Procedure 2
(12–20 minutes)

Conclusion: The instructor may lead a class discussion and/or make concluding remarks.

Application (2–4 minutes):   What did I learn from this experience? How will I use this knowledge in the future?

Sharing: Volunteers give their answers to the application section.

ANSWERS TO TRUE/FALSE QUESTIONS

1. T.
2. F. The decision-making model should be used when making *important nonrecurring* decisions.
3. F. None of these techniques require that a small group of people get together; in fact, they can be used online. With the Delphi technique, members never get together and often don't even know who else is in the group.
4. T.
5. F. The normative leadership model tells you the level of participation to use when making the decision, not which decision to select.

Organizational Change and Culture

After completing this chapter, you should be able to:

1. Describe the four types of changes.

2. State why people resist change and how to overcome resistance.

3. Explain how to use the Lussier change model when making changes.

4. Explain the two dimensions of an organization's culture.

5. Explain the seven dimensions of an organization's climate.

6. Describe five organizational development techniques.

7. Describe the training cycle and how training is used to increase performance.

8. List and explain the five steps of performance appraisals and state how performance appraisals can lead to increased performance.

9. List the steps in the coaching model.

10. Explain the relationship between organizational culture, climate, and development.

11. Define the following 16 key terms (in order of appearance in the chapter):

types of changes	**training**
management information systems (MIS)	**development**
automation	**performance appraisal**
resistance to change	**standards**
organizational culture	**coaching model**
organizational climate	**survey feedback**
morale	**force field analysis**
organizational development	**team building**

C H A P T E R   O U T L I N E

How Change Affects Behavior, Human Relations, and Performance

Managing Change

    Types of Changes

    Stages in the Change Process

Resistance to Change and How to Overcome It

    Resistance to Change

    Overcoming Resistance to Change

    Responding to Resistance

    Change Models

Organizational Culture

    Learning the Organization's Culture

    Strong and Weak, Positive and Negative Cultures

Organizational Climate

    Dimensions of Climate

Organizational Development

    Managing and Changing Culture and Climate through OD

Training and Development

Performance Appraisal

Survey Feedback

Force Field Analysis

Team Building

The Relationship between Organizational
Culture, Climate, and Development

Global Differences

Ronnie Linkletter now works for the New York City Insurance Company (NYCIC). Ronnie was the manager of the claims department at Rider, a small insurance company in Danbury, Connecticut, until it was bought by NYCIC. Since the purchase of Rider, Ronnie and his peers don't know what to expect. They know there will be many changes, which they don't look forward to. They have been told by the new managers that they are a part of the NYCIC family. "Family" relates to some kind of organizational culture managers keep talking about, which has developed over many years through an ongoing organizational development program. NYCIC has been concerned about its employees' morale. Ronnie feels confused by all these new buzzwords. He wants to know how these changes will affect him. Ronnie knows that at Rider all the managers were white males, and there were very few minorities. But at NYCIC, there are women and minority managers, and more than half of NYCIC employees are minorities.

Is there a way to make changes in organizations so that people don't resist the changes? This is the major topic of Chapter 14.

HOW CHANGE AFFECTS BEHAVIOR, HUMAN RELATIONS, AND PERFORMANCE

Plato said, "Change takes place no matter what deters it." Managing change is a central subject of management.[1] There is a lot of truth in the business world's saying that "change is the only constant. Organizational change and development make innovation a valuable necessity for the new economy.[2]

Organizational success depends on the organization's adaptations to environmental changes.[3] Some of the external environmental forces for organizational change are increased global competition, consumer demands, government laws, economic conditions, and technological advances that increase the speed of conducting business.[4] Internal environmental forces for change include financial position, new and revised mission and strategy, reorganization of formal structure (Chapter 6), and acquisitions and mergers[5]—such as that in the opening case between NYCIC and Rider. All these forces require change, whether it is welcomed or not.

Continental Airlines made internal changes to get employees to change the poor record of late departures to much improved on-time records. The monthly goals set by managers affected behavior and human relations.[6] Employees respond with different behavior to change.[7] With downsizing, there are fewer employees, which changes human relations. You can't improve, and continually improve, without change.[8] To be successful, you have to keep stretching and changing.[9]

The topics of organizational culture, climate, and development are all about making changes to continually improve behavior, human relations, and performance.

WORK APPLICATIONS

1. Give reasons why managing-change skills are important to managers in an organization for which you work or have worked.

MANAGING CHANGE

Successful business is about improving and creating new products and services.[10] However, adapting and changing to meet new market demands is not easy.[11] In this section we discuss types of changes and stages in the change process. Our discussion continues in the next section, in which we examine resistance to change and change models. Before we begin, complete Self-Assessment Exercise 14–1 to determine your openness to change.

Self-Assessment Exercise 14–1

Your Openness to Change

Select the response that best describes what you would do in each situation.

1. In my daily life I:

    _____*a.* Look for new ways of doing things.

    _____*b.* Like things the way they are.

2. If my friends were opposed to a change:

    _____*a.* It would not affect my changing.

    _____*b.* I would resist the change, too.

3. In my work situation I:

    _____*a.* Do things differently.

    _____*b.* Do things the same way.

4. If I had the opportunity to learn to use new computer software to help me in school or at work, I would:

    _____*a.* Take time to learn to use it on my own.

    _____*b.* Wait until required to use it.

5. I like to know about a change:

    _____*a.* Anytime. Short notice is OK with me.

    _____*b.* Well in advance, to have time to plan for it.

6. When a work change is required, I:

    _____*a.* Change as quickly as management wants.

    _____*b.* Want to move slowly to implement change.

7. When leading others, I:

    _____*a.* Use the style appropriate for their capability.

    _____*b.* Use my distinct leadership style.

   The more *a* answers you selected, the more open to change you are. The *b* answers show resistance to change. If you tend to be resistant to change, and want to have a successful career, you may want to change your attitude and behavior. You can begin by looking for different ways to do things more productively. Look at your routine for getting ready for school or work. Could you make any changes to save time?

Learning Outcome

1. Describe the four types of changes.

Types of Changes

There are different types of change, and types of change have various names. Organizations are composed of four interactive variables. The four variables, or **types of changes,** *are technological change, structural change, task change, and people change.* The proper metaphor for the systems effect for managing change is a balanced mobile in which a change in one variable affects the others. Because of the systems effect, you need to consider the repercussions that a change in one variable will have on the other variables, and plan accordingly.[12]

Technological Change   Technological changes, such as the Internet, have increased the rate of speed at which change takes place. Technology is a commonly used method of increasing productivity to gain competitive leverage.[13] For example, Wal-Mart is committed to technology. Wal-Mart's operating costs are less than its nearest competitor's. Consequently, the lower cost structure equals lower prices for customers.

Some of the major areas of technology change are the following:

Machines   New machinery or equipment is introduced on an ongoing basis. The computer is a sophisticated machine that is also a part of many other machines. The fax machine and e-mail have increased the speed of doing business.

Process   *Process* refers to how the organization transforms inputs (raw materials, parts, data, and so on) into outputs (finished goods and services, information). The change in the sequence of work in process is a technology change. With the aid of the computer, organizations have changed the way they process information. **Management information systems (MIS)** *are formal systems for collecting, processing, and disseminating the information necessary to aid managers in decision making.* The MIS attempts to centralize and integrate all or most of the organization's information, such as financial, production, inventory, and sales information. In this way the departments can coordinate their efforts, which leads to improved performance (recall our discussion of the systems effect in chapter 1).[14]

WORK APPLICATIONS

2. Describe the MIS at an organization, preferably one with which you have been associated. If you are not knowledgeable about the organization's MIS, talk with someone who is.

Automation   **Automation** *is the simplification or reduction of human effort required to do a job.* Computers and other machines have allowed some jobs, such as inspecting, cleaning, guarding, and assembling parts, to be done by robots. Automation does not take away jobs; it changes the types of jobs. The need for training and higher levels of skills will continue in the future, while the demand for unskilled jobs will continue to decrease. A college education should help you be flexible and continue to upgrade your skills with technological changes. If you want pay increases and promotions, be the first to volunteer to learn new technologies.

WORK APPLICATIONS

3. Describe an automation change in an organization, preferably one with which you have been associated.

Structural Change   It is important to coordinate structure with technology.[15] *Structure* refers to the type of organization principle and departments used, as discussed in Chapter 6.

Task and People Change   *Task* refers to the day-to-day things that employees do to perform their jobs. Tasks change with technology and structural changes. As tasks change, people's skills must change. Employee retraining is an ongoing process. In some cases, organizations must hire new people with the necessary skills.

It is people that create, manage, and use technology; therefore, people are the most important resource.[16] What people often resist are the social changes brought about by technological changes. Business success is based on optimizing the integration of both

EXHIBIT 14.1 |

Types of Changes

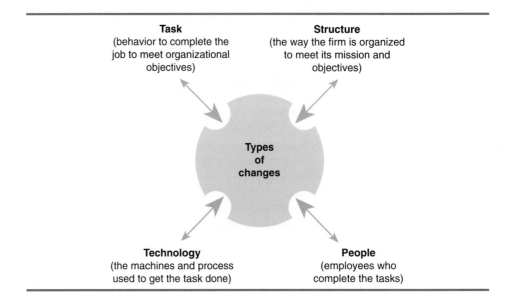

people and technology. This integration is known as *creating a sociotechnical system.* When changing task, structure, or technology, you should never forget the impact of change on people. Changing any of these other variables will not be effective without considering people change.

In the opening case, Rider Insurance has been bought by NYCIC. The primary change is structural. Rider is no longer a separate entity; it is part of NYCIC. NYCIC will most likely change the structure at Rider to match its present structure. With the change in structure, most likely the tasks, technology, and people will also change. See Exhibit 14.1 for a review of the types of changes.

WORK APPLICATIONS

4. Give one or more examples of a type of change you experienced in an organization. (Identify it as task change, structural change, technological change, or people change.)

APPLICATION SITUATIONS

Types of Changes

AS 14–1

Identify the type of change represented in each statement as:

A. Task change

B. Structural change

C. Technological change

D. People change

_____ 1. "Jim, from now on, you have to fill in this new form every time you deliver a package."

_____ 2. "Because of the increase in the size of our department, we will now split into two departments."

_____ 3. "Kelly is taking Ray's place now that he has retired."

_____ 4. "From now on, purchases under $300 will no longer need to be approved by the purchasing manager."

_____ 5. "Kim, report to the training center to learn proper procedures."

EXHIBIT 14.2 |
Stages in the Change
Process

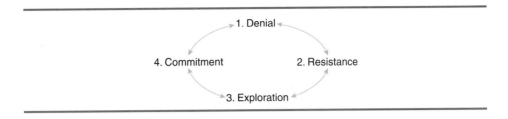

Stages in the Change Process

Managers need to understand the change process. Most people go through four distinct stages in the change process:

1. *Denial.* When people first hear rumors through the grapevine that change is coming, they deny that it will happen at all, or to them. The "it will affect the others, but not me" reaction is common.

2. *Resistance.* Once people get over the initial shock and realize that change is going to be a reality, they resist the change. The next section examines resistance to change and how to overcome it.

3. *Exploration.* When the change begins to be implemented, employees explore the change, often through training, and better understand how it will affect them.[17] Training is an organizational development technique that you will learn about later in this chapter.

4. *Commitment.* Through exploration, employees determine their level of commitment to making the change a success. The level of commitment can change over time.

In the opening case, employees at both Rider and NYCIC will be going through the stages of the change process. How successfully the change process is implemented will affect the behavior, human relations, and performance of the two businesses, which are now one company.

Exhibit 14.2 illustrates the stages in the change process. Notice that the stages are in a circular formation because change is an ongoing process, not a linear one, and people can regress, as the arrows show.

RESISTANCE TO CHANGE AND HOW TO OVERCOME IT

Learning Outcome

2. State why people resist change and how to overcome resistance.

Some workers in any firm actively resist change, and their resistance should be overcome.[18] People resist change for a variety of reasons, some of which include (1) maintaining the *status quo* (people like things the way they are now, view the change as an inconvenience, or don't agree that a change is needed), (2) *uncertainty* (people tend to fear the unknown and wonder how the change will affect them), (3) *learning anxiety* (the prospect of learning something new itself produces anxiety), and (4) *fear* (people often fear they may lose their jobs, that the friends they work with may change, that they will not be successful with learning new ways, or that they may lose control over how they do their jobs). Next you will learn why people resist change and how to overcome it.

Resistance to Change

Before making changes, managers should anticipate how employees will react to or resist the change.[19] **Resistance to change** *involves the variables of intensity, source, and focus, which together explain why people are reluctant to change.* Ken Hultman identifies these three variables as the major variables of resistance to change.[20]

Intensity   People often have four basic reactions to change: acceptance, tolerance, resistance, and rejection. The resistance intensity can vary from strong to weak or somewhere in between. As a manager of change, you should anticipate the intensity of resistance to change so that you can effectively plan to overcome it.

Sources   There are three major sources of resistance: facts, beliefs, and values.

1. *Facts.* The facts (statements that identify reality) of the change are often circulated through the grapevine inaccurately. People tend to use facts selectively to prove their point. Facts used correctly help overcome fear of the unknown.

2. *Beliefs.* Facts can be proved; beliefs cannot. They are subjective. Our beliefs are our opinions that lead us to think and feel that a change is correct or incorrect, good or bad.

3. *Values.* Values are what people believe are worth pursuing or doing. What we value is important to us. Values are priorities. Our values meet our needs and affect our behavior.

People analyze the facts presented from all sources and determine if they believe the change is of value to them. When the facts are clear and logical and people believe the change is of value to them, they tend to have lower resistance to the change.

Focus   There are three major focuses of resistance: self, others, and the work environment.

1. *Self.* It is natural for people to want to know, "What's in it for me? What will I gain or lose?" When the facts of change have a negative effect on an employee's economic well-being, such as lower pay or longer hours without additional compensation, employees tend to resist the change.

2. *Others.* After considering what's in it for them, or when they are not affected by the change, people tend to consider how the change will affect their friends, peers (peer pressure), and colleagues. If employees analyze the facts and believe the change will affect others negatively, they may be resistant to the change.

3. *Work environment.* The work environment includes the job itself and the physical setting and climate. People like to be in control of their environment, and they resist changes that take away their control. Employees' analysis of the facts about the current versus the changed work environment will affect their resistance to the change.

Exhibit 14.3 is an adapted version of Ken Hultman's resistance matrix, with examples of each area of resistance. For instance, in box 1, "Facts about self," note that one reason

EXHIBIT 14.3 | Resistance Matrix

Sources of Resistance (facts → beliefs → values)		
1. Facts about self I never did it before. I failed the last time I tried. All my friends are here.	**4. Beliefs about self** I'm too busy to do it. I'll do it, but I'll mess up. I don't think I can accept the change.	**7. Values pertaining to self** I like the job I have now better. I don't want to change; I'm happy. I like working alone.
2. Facts about others He's on probation. She has two children. Other people told me it's hard to do.	**5. Beliefs about others** She pretends to be busy to avoid extra work. He's better at it than I am; let him do it. She never understands our side.	**8. Values pertaining to others** Let someone else train her; I'm not interested. What you really think really doesn't matter to me. I don't give a . . . about him.
3. Facts about the work environment Why should I do it? I'm not getting paid extra. I haven't been trained to do it. I make less than anyone else in the department.	**6. Beliefs about the work environment** This is a lousy place to work. The pay here is terrible. It's who you know, not what you know around here that counts.	**9. Values pertaining to the work environment** Who cares what the goals are? I just do my job. The salary is more important than the benefits. This job gives me the chance to work outside.

(left margin label: Focus of Resistance (self → others → work))

Source: Adapted from Ken Hultman's resistance matrix, *The Path of Least Resistance* (Austin, Tex.: Learning Concepts, 1979).

given is "I never did it before." Understanding the reasons behind a person's resistance to change will make you better able to anticipate and deal with those reasons. However, resistance may come from more than one focus and source. Use the matrix to identify the intensity, source, and focus of resistance. Once you have identified the probable resistance to change, you can work at overcoming it. Overcoming resistance to change is the next topic.

WORK APPLICATIONS

5. Describe a situation in which you were resistant to change. Identify the intensity, source, and focus. Using Exhibit 14.3, which box (by number and statement) describes your resistance?

APPLICATION SITUATIONS

**Identifying
Resistance to
Change**

AS 14–2

Below are five statements made by employees asked to make a change on the job. Identify the source, focus, and intensity of their resistance using Exhibit 14.3. Place the number of the box (1 to 9) that represents and best describes the major resistance.

_____ 6. The police sergeant asked Sue, the patrol officer, to take a rookie cop as her partner. Sue said, "Do I have to? I broke in the last rookie."

_____ 7. The tennis coach asked Bill, the star player, to have Jim as his doubles partner. Bill said, "Come on, Jim is a lousy player. Peter is better; don't break us up." The coach disagreed and forced Bill to accept Jim.

_____ 8. The supervisor realized that Sharon always uses the accommodating conflict style. The supervisor told her to stop giving in to everyone's wishes. Sharon said, "But I like people, and I want them to like me, too."

_____ 9. The employee went to Sim, the supervisor, and asked him if she could change the work-order form. Sim said, "That would be a waste of time; the current form is fine."

_____ 10. Ann, an employee, is busy at work. The supervisor tells her to stop what she is doing and begin a new project. Ann says, "The job I'm working on now is more important."

Overcoming Resistance to Change

Below are some of the major methods managers can use to overcome resistance to change.

Develop a Positive Climate for Change   Develop and maintain good human relations. Because change and trust are so closely intertwined, the manager's first concern should be to develop mutual trust. Develop cooperation and interdependence within the department. Cooperation carries over into times of change.

Encourage Interest in Improvement   Continually give employees opportunities to develop new skills, abilities, and creativity.[21] Constantly look for better ways to do things. Encouraging employees to suggest changes and listening to and implementing their ideas are important parts of continuous improvement.[22]

Plan   Implementing changes successfully takes good planning. You need to identify the possible resistances to change and plan how to overcome them. Put yourself in the employee's position. Don't consider how you—as manager—would react because a manager perceives things differently. What seems very simple and logical to you may not be to an employee. Set clear objectives. As stated previously, use a systems approach to planning. A change in one variable, such as technology, will also have effects on social relations, and so forth. The next eight methods should be part of your plan.

Give Facts   Get all the facts and plan how you will present them to the employees. Giving half-answers will only make employees more confused and angry, and hiding things and lying is a disaster. But you can't let bad news dribble out in small pieces because then you'll lose credibility. Giving the facts as far in advance as possible helps overcome the fear of the unknown. If the grapevine starts to send incorrect information, correct it as quickly as possible.

Clearly State Why the Change Is Needed and How It Will Affect Employees   As part of giving the facts, you need to remember that employees want and need to know why the change is needed and how it will affect them both positively and negatively. Be open and honest with employees. If employees understand why the change is needed, and it makes sense to them, they will be more willing to change. It is important to create a sense of urgency to kill complacency and get employees to want to change.

Create a Win–Win Situation   Recall that the goal of human relations is to meet the employees' needs while achieving departmental or organizational objectives. To overcome resistance to change, be sure to answer the other parties' unasked question, "What's in it for me?" When people can see the benefits to them, they are more willing to change. If the organization is going to benefit by the change, so should the employees, when possible.[23]

Involve Employees   To create a win–win situation, involve employees. A commitment to change is usually critical to its successful implementation. Employees who participate in developing changes are more committed to them than employees who have changes assigned to them.

Provide Support   Allow employees to express their feelings in a positive way. Since training is very important to successful changes, give as much advance notice and training as possible before the change takes place. Giving thorough training helps reduce learning anxiety and helps employees realize they can be successful with the change.[24]

Stay Calm   Emotional people tend to be defensive. When you are emotional, you may hear, but you don't listen well because you are resistant to change. If managers get emotional, they will likely cause employees to get emotional as well. Try not to do or say things that will make people emotional so that you don't create more resistance to change.

Avoid Direct Confrontation   Confrontation tends to make people emotional and more resistant to change. A subtle approach is preferable to most people.[25] A confrontational debate is risky. Trying to persuade people that their facts, beliefs, and values are wrong leads to resistance. What if you lose the debate? Avoid statements like, "You're wrong; you don't know what you're talking about" and "You're just stubborn."

Use Power and Ethical Politics   Chapter 10 discussed how to get what you want through the use of power and politics. Getting what you want often involves change. So use your power and ethical political skills to implement changes. Remember that the 11 methods for overcoming resistance to change should be a part of your plan for change. Below you will learn about planning for change.

See Exhibit 14.4 for a review of the methods for overcoming resistance to change.

EXHIBIT 14.4 |
Overcoming Resistance
to Change

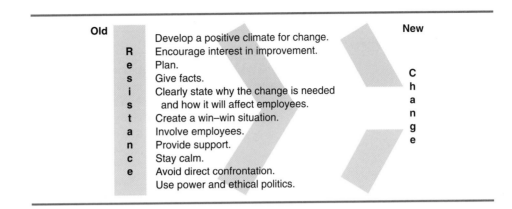

| Old | | New |

R Develop a positive climate for change.
e Encourage interest in improvement.
s Plan.
i Give facts.
s Clearly state why the change is needed
t   and how it will affect employees.
a Create a win–win situation.
n Involve employees.
c Provide support.
e Stay calm.
  Avoid direct confrontation.
  Use power and ethical politics.

C h a n g e

Responding to Resistance

Below are classifications of employee resistance types, resistant statements, and responses a manager could make to the employee to help overcome resistance to change. The following are presented to acquaint you with some of the possible types of resistance you may face, along with some possible responses you could make:

- *The blocker:* "I don't want to do it that way." Manager: "What are your objections to the change? How would you prefer to do it?"
- *The roller:* "What do you want me to do?" Manager: "I want you to . . ." (Be specific and describe the change in detail; use communication skills.)
- *The staller:* "I'll do it when I can." Manager: "What is more important?"
- *The reverser:* "That's a good idea." (But she or he never does it.) Manager: "What is it that you like about the change?"
- *The sidestepper:* "Why don't you have XYZ do it?" Manager: "I asked you to do it because . . ."
- *The threatener:* "I'll do it, but the guys upstairs will not like it." Manager: "Let me worry about it. What are *your* objections?"
- *The politician:* "You owe me one; let me slide." Manager: "I do owe you one, but I need the change. I'll pay you back later."
- *The traditionalist:* "That's not the way we do things around here." Manager: "This is a unique situation; it needs to be done."
- *The assaulter:* "You're a . . . (pick a word)." Manager: "I will not tolerate that type of behavior." Or, "This is really upsetting you, isn't it?"

The above supervisory responses will be helpful in most situations, but not all. If employees persist in resisting the change, they may need to be considered problem employees and handled accordingly.

Change Models

Lewin's Change Model   It is important to know how to implement change. So here are two change models, providing a pro-change orientation. In the early 1950s, Kurt Lewin developed a technique, still used today, for changing people's behavior, skills, and attitudes. Lewin viewed the change process as consisting of three steps:

1. *Unfreezing.* This step usually involves reducing those forces maintaining the status quo. Unfreezing is sometimes accomplished by introducing information that shows discrepancies between desired performance and actual performance.
2. *Moving.* This step shifts the behavior to a new level. This is the change process in which employees learn the new desirable behavior, values, and attitudes. Structural, task, technological, and people changes may take place to reach desirable performance levels.

EXHIBIT 14.5 | Change Models

Lewin's Change Model	Lussier's Change Model
Step 1: Unfreezing	Step 1: Define the change.
Step 2: Moving	Step 2: Identify possible resistance to the change.
Step 3: Refreezing	Step 3: Plan the change.
	Step 4: Implement the change.
	Give the facts.
	Involve employees.
	Provide support.
	Step 5: Control the change (implementation, reinforcement, maintenance).

3. *Refreezing.* The desirable performance becomes the permanent way of doing things. This is the new status quo. Refreezing often takes place through reinforcement and support for the new behavior.

See Exhibit 14.5 for a review of the steps.

Learning Outcome

3. Explain how to use the Lussier change model when making changes.

Lussier's Change Model   Lewin's model provides a general framework for understanding organizational change. Because the steps of change are broad, the author has developed a more specific model. The Lussier change model consists of five steps:

1. *Define the Change.* Clearly state what the change is. Is it a task, structural, technological, or people change? What are the systems effects on the other variables? Set objectives, following the guidelines in Chapter 9.

2. *Identify Possible Resistance to the Change.* Determine the intensity, source, and focus of possible resistance to the change. Use the resistance matrix in Exhibit 14.3.

3. *Plan the Change.* Plan the change implementation. Use the appropriate supervisory style for the situation. We will discuss planned change in more detail later in this chapter.

4. *Implement the Change.* This step has three parts:

   • *Give the facts.* Give the facts about the change and explain why it is necessary, as far in advance of the change as possible. Explain how the change will affect the employees. Relate the change to their values.

   • *Involve employees.* Use as much employee involvement as you can. But use the appropriate supervisory style for the situation. (Follow the guidelines from Chapters 8 and 13.)

   • *Provide support.* Allow employees to express their thoughts and feelings in a positive way. Answer their questions openly and honestly. Make sure that they receive proper training in how to implement the changed method(s).

5. *Control the Change.* Follow up to ensure that the change is implemented, reinforced, and maintained. Make sure the objective is met. If not, take corrective action. For major changes, be sure to change performance appraisals to reflect new jobs accurately.

For a review of the steps, see Exhibit 14.5.

If managers at NYCIC follow the guidelines for overcoming resistance to change and develop an effective plan using the change model, change can be implemented successfully at Rider.

WORK APPLICATIONS

6. Give a specific example of when a change model would be helpful to a specific manager.

It started back in 1999 when Shawn Fanning created Napster and developed the first peer-to-peer (P2P) file sharing system to allow users to swap files of digitized copyrighted material. The recording industry not only denounced the free trading of these files, without any compensation to them or their recording artists, but was able to convince the courts to issue injunctions that prevented Napster (and later, Grokster) from trading copyrighted music on its network. Both Napster and Grokster were forced to shut down. In 2005, the U.S. Supreme Court ruled against free downloading of copyrighted files.

Yet the P2P trend has resumed, with new programs and networks picking up the torch. The new generation of file sharing systems are designed as decentralized networks, which are proving to be much more challenging for copyright owners to pursue in the courts. As you most likely know, file sharing still exists, but the operations are outside of the jurisdiction of the U.S. court system. More recently, file sharing of movies has become a concern for the film industry and actors.

Questions

1. Making illegal copies of music has been an issue since the development of the first tape recorder. Explain in this situation how technology is a driver for change.

2. Why were the recording industry firms and artists so resistant to change that would allow free downloading of their music? Refer to the four reasons people resist change and Hultman's resistance matrix.

3. Is it ethical to own and operate a file sharing company?

4. Is it ethical to download copyrighted material?

5. Do you download copyrighted material?

ORGANIZATIONAL CULTURE

You have heard of national cultures, in which citizens of a country behave in certain ways; organizations have cultures, too.[26] For our purposes, **organizational culture** *consists of the shared values and assumptions of how its members will behave.*

Managers have largely accepted that organizational culture is linked with positive organizational results.[27] Organizations can develop cultures that foster creativity.[28] 3M has developed a culture that values innovation.[29] Although culture can change, it is difficult to change beliefs and values.[30] In this section, we discuss learning the organization's culture as well as the two dimensions—strong and weak, positive and negative—of an organization's culture.

Learning the Organization's Culture

Newcomers need to learn and be integrated into the organizational culture.[31] Organizational culture is learned primarily through observing people and events in the organization and training.[32] Success and shared experiences also shape culture. Five important ways that employees learn about organizational culture are through heroes, stories, slogans, symbols, and ceremonies.

1. *Heroes*—such as founder Tom Watson of IBM, Sam Walton of Wal-Mart, Herb Kelleher of Southwest Airlines, Frederick Smith of FedEx, and others who made outstanding contributions to their organizations.

2. *Stories*—often about founders and others who have made extraordinary efforts, such as Sam Walton visiting every Wal-Mart store yearly or someone driving through a blizzard to deliver a product or service. Public statements and speeches can also be considered stories.

3. *Slogans*—such as "Quality is Job 1" at Ford; McDonald's Q, S, C, V—Quality, Service, Cleanliness, and Value; The H-P Way; FedEx's People—Service—Profit philosophy.

4. *Symbols*—such as plaques, pins, and jackets, or a Mary Kay pink Cadillac. Symbols are used to convey meaning.

5. *Ceremonies*—such as awards dinners for top achievers.

If you hear expressions such as, "That's not how we do things here," or "This is the way we do things here," you are learning the organization's culture.

Strong and Weak, Positive and Negative Cultures

The two dimensions of an organization's culture are strong and weak, and positive and negative.

Learning Outcome

4. Explain the two dimensions of an organization's culture.

Strong and Weak Cultures   Organizations with clear values that are shared to the extent of similar behavior have strong cultures. Organizations that have no stated values and do not enforce behavior have weak cultures. Examples of strong cultures include:

IBM   Although IBM had problems and worked to change its culture, IBM is recognized as having a very strong culture. Having a strong culture, however, does not necessarily mean an organization is successful. Company founder Thomas J. Watson worked to develop IBM's unique culture long before it became popular to do so. Employees identified three core values for IBM, which are stated in its "Our Values at Work on Being an IBMer." They are: (1) dedication to every client's success; (2) innovation that matters, for our company and for the world; and (3) trust and personal responsibility in all relationships.[33]

PepsiCo, Inc.   Unlike IBM's culture, which stresses excellence, Pepsi's organizational culture stresses competition in every aspect of an employee's work life. Pepsi executives are jointly determined to surpass archrival Coca-Cola, while surpassing rival executives at PepsiCo. Managers are continually pressured to increase market share; a small decline can lead to a manager's dismissal. Pepsi also stresses health and wellness.[34]

J. C. Penney Company, Inc.   James Cash Penney established the following seven principles for his company, which serve as its culture base: "(1) to serve the public, as nearly as we can, to its complete satisfaction; (2) to expect, from the service we render, a fair remuneration and not all the profit the traffic will bear; (3) to do all in our power to pack the customer's dollar full of value, quality, and satisfaction; (4) to continue to train ourselves and our associates so that the service we give will be more and more intelligently performed; (5) to improve constantly the human factor in our business; (6) to reward men and women in our organization through participation in what the business produces; and (7) to test policy, methods, and act in this manner: 'Does it square with what is right and just?'"[35]

As you can see, IBM stresses excellence; PepsiCo, competition; and J. C. Penney, fairness. They have different cultures, yet they are all successful organizations, which shows there is no one best organizational culture.

Positive and Negative Cultures   An organizational culture is considered positive when it has norms that contribute to effective performance and productivity. A negative organizational culture is a source of resistance and turmoil that hinders effective performance.

The most effective organizational culture that leads to effective performance is strong and positive. Companies with strong positive cultures, not already listed, include Amdahl, Emerson Electric, Johnson & Johnson, Procter & Gamble, 3M, Dana Corporation, Marriott, and Fluor.

Before accepting a job with an organization, you may want to learn about its culture to determine if it is the kind of organization you will enjoy working in. For example, if you are not competitive, you probably will not enjoy working for PepsiCo.

In the opening case, Ronnie feels that NYCIC has a strong organizational culture, whereas Rider had a weak culture. NYCIC needs to develop the shared values and assumptions of how members behave at Rider. Many firms experience difficulty merging cultures.

The OD team-building program (discussed later in this chapter) would be an excellent way to develop the NYCIC culture at Rider.

> **8.** Describe the organizational culture at a firm for which you work or have worked. Does or did the organization strive to have a strong positive culture? If so, how?

ORGANIZATIONAL CLIMATE

Organizational climate *is the relatively enduring quality of the internal environment of the organization as perceived by its members.* Climate is employees' perception of the atmosphere of the internal environment.[36] Organizational climate is a broad term. Its definition will be explained throughout this section.

The major difference between culture and climate is as follows: Culture is based on shared values and assumptions of "how" things should be done (ideal environment), while climate is based on shared perceptions of the "way" things are done (intangibles of the actual internal environment). An organization can claim to have a strong culture and have a negative climate. Employees can know how things should be, while being dissatisfied with their perception of the way things actually are.[37] For example, in some organizations managers claim that quality is very important; signs are posted telling everyone it is. But if you ask employees if quality is important, they say management only cares about how many units are actually shipped out the door. Successful companies tend to have strong cultures and positive climates.

Organizational climate is important because the employees' perception of the organization serves as the basis for the development of their attitudes toward it. Their attitudes in turn affect their behavior. Climate is concerned with the entire organization or major subunits within it. While the organization has an overall climate, specific work group climates may be different. For example, an entire company may have a positive, friendly climate while one of its departments has a negative climate.

Job satisfaction, discussed in Chapter 3, is based primarily on organizational climate. Morale is also an important part of organizational climate. **Morale** *is a state of mind based on employees' attitudes and satisfaction with the organization.* Morale can be different at various levels within the organization. Morale is commonly measured on a continuum ranging from high to low morale, based on the seven dimensions of climate listed below.

Dimensions of Climate

Learning Outcome

5. Explain the seven dimensions of an organization's climate.

Some of the common dimensions of climate are the following:

- *Structure.* The degree of constraint on members—the number of rules, regulations, and procedures.
- *Responsibility.* The degree of control over one's own job.
- *Rewards.* The degree of being rewarded for one's efforts and being punished appropriately.
- *Warmth.* The degree of satisfaction with human relations.
- *Support.* The degree of being helped by others and of experiencing cooperation.
- *Organizational identity and loyalty.* The degree to which employees identify with the organization and their loyalty to it.
- *Risk.* The degree to which risk-taking is encouraged.

Studies show that poor climate tends to result in lower levels of performance, but not always. Performance tends to be better when climate dimensions are logically consistent

EXHIBIT 14.6 |

Dimensions of Climate

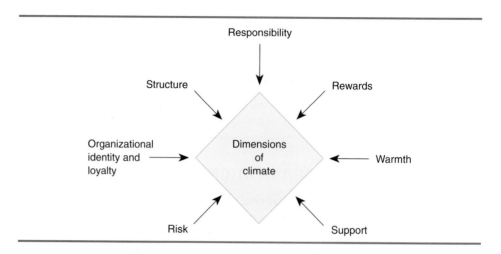

with one another. Like plants, employees require a proper climate to thrive. Working in a climate you enjoy will also affect your performance.

You can develop an effective productive climate by focusing on the dimensions of climate. Often, large companies like NYCIC take over a smaller company like Rider because they are successful. In too many situations, the larger company changes the flexible entrepreneurial climate to one of bureaucracy, resulting in the small company's becoming less productive. NYCIC needs to focus on these seven dimensions of climate. For Rider to have a positive climate, NYCIC should provide a structure that minimizes rules and red tape and encourages employees to take risks. Employees should have control over their own jobs and should be rewarded based on performance. The two companies are becoming one; therefore, warm, supportive human relations should be developed for cooperation and a smooth change. The Rider employees need to shift identity and loyalty to NYCIC.

See Exhibit 14.6 for a list of the dimensions of climate.

WORK APPLICATIONS

9. Describe the organizational climate at a firm for which you work or have worked, based on the seven dimensions of climate. Does or did the organization measure its climate? If so, how?

10. Describe the morale at the organization.

APPLICATION SITUATIONS

Organizational Culture or Climate?

Identify each statement as being associated with:

A. Organizational culture   B. Organizational climate

AS 14–3

_____ 11. Rotary International's motto, "Service above Self."

_____ 12. "Employees were not happy with this year's raise."

_____ 13. "Please fill out this questionnaire and return it to the personnel department when you are done."

_____ 14. "The unwritten dress code is a suit and tie for work."

_____ 15. "From now on, no one but you will check the quality of your work."

ORGANIZATIONAL DEVELOPMENT

Organizations that change and manage culture include Tektronix, Procter & Gamble, TRW, Polaroid, Pacific Telesis, Pacific Mutual, Fiat, and the City of San Diego. These organizations realize that managing culture and climate is not a program within a few departments with starting and ending dates. It is an ongoing organizationwide process called *organizational development (OD)*. **Organizational development** *is the ongoing planned process of change used as a means of improving the organization's effectiveness in solving problems and achieving its objectives.*

Managing and Changing Culture and Climate through OD

To manage organizational culture, top management must define the attitudes, values, and expectations it wants organizational members to share.[38] (Recall IBM's list of three principles and J.C.Penney's list of seven principles discussed earlier.) After values and expectations have been defined, they must be communicated effectively to employees so they can adopt them.[39]

The first step in organizational development is to diagnose the problem(s). Indicators that problems exist, such as conflicts between diverse groups, the need for increased quality and productivity, low profits, and excessive absenteeism or turnover, lead management to call in a change agent to study the organization's problems and needs.[40] A *change agent* is the person responsible for the OD program. The change agent can use a variety of methods to diagnose problems. Some methods are reviewing records, observing, interviewing individuals and work groups, holding meetings, and/or using questionnaires. After the problem has been diagnosed, OD techniques are used to solve it.

This section examines five OD techniques: training and development, performance appraisal, survey feedback, force field analysis, and team building. Training and development is presented first because the other four techniques usually include training.

Training and Development

After a position is staffed, either by a new or an existing employee, there is usually a need to train the person to do the job.[41] **Training** *is the process of developing the necessary skills to perform the present job.* **Development** *is the process of developing the ability to perform both present and future jobs.* Typically, training is used to develop technical skills of nonmanagers, while development is usually less technical and is designed for professional and managerial employees.[42] The terms *training* and *development* are often used together; they are used interchangeably as well.

Organizations are concerned with continuous improvement and use training to bring it about.[43] Corporations are now spending more on training and development than all the universities and colleges in the United States are spending on education. Organizations are offering personal development to change employee behavior, attitudes, skills, and even personalities through continuous learning.[44]

The Training Cycle   Following the steps in the training cycle helps ensure that training is done in a systematic way. The training cycle steps are as follows: step (1) conduct a needs assessment; step (2) set objectives; step (3) prepare for training; step (4) conduct the training; and step (5) measure and evaluate training results. See Exhibit 14.7 for more details about each of the five steps in the training cycle. Exhibit 14.8 summarizes the steps involved in conducting a job instructional training (JIT) session, which is part of steps (3) and (4) of the training cycle.

Management at NYCIC will have to determine the training needs of Rider employees, set objectives, prepare for training, conduct the training, and evaluate results so that the two units can work effectively as one organization.

EXHIBIT 14.7 | The Training Cycle

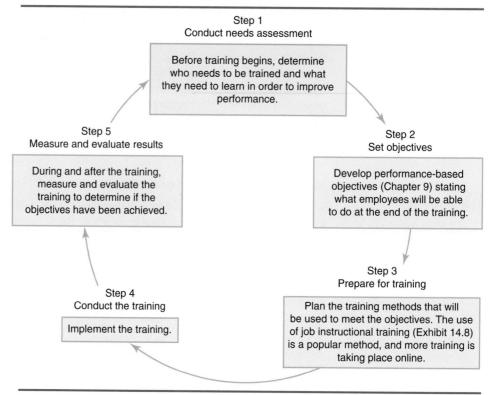

Step 1
Conduct needs assessment

Before training begins, determine who needs to be trained and what they need to learn in order to improve performance.

Step 5
Measure and evaluate results

During and after the training, measure and evaluate the training to determine if the objectives have been achieved.

Step 2
Set objectives

Develop performance-based objectives (Chapter 9) stating what employees will be able to do at the end of the training.

Step 3
Prepare for training

Plan the training methods that will be used to meet the objectives. The use of job instructional training (Exhibit 14.8) is a popular method, and more training is taking place online.

Step 4
Conduct the training

Implement the training.

EXHIBIT 14.8 | Job Instructional Training

Step 1: Preparation of the trainee.
Step 2: Trainer presentation of the job.
Step 3: Trainee performance of the job.
Step 4: Follow-up.

WORK APPLICATIONS

11. State how you were trained to perform a specific job. Explain how the training affected your job performance. How could training at this organization be used to increase performance?

APPLICATION SITUATIONS

The Training Cycle

AS 14–4

Identify each of the five statements below by its step in the training cycle.

A. Step 1: Conduct needs assessment
B. Step 2: Set objectives
C. Step 3: Prepare for training
D. Step 4: Conduct the training
E. Step 5: Measure and evaluate results

_____ 16. "I will now demonstrate the proper technique."

_____ 17. "At the end of this training session, you will be able to operate the machine."

_____ 18. "In reviewing your performance, I've decided that you need more training to increase your speed."

_____ 19. "You passed the test with a perfect score; you're certified."

_____ 20. "Where did I put that JIT sheet? I need to revise it."

Performance Appraisal

After employees are hired, and during and after their training, they must be evaluated. And properly trained employees get better performance reviews.[45] **Performance appraisal** *is the ongoing process of evaluating employee job performance.* Performance appraisal is also called *performance job evaluation, performance review, merit rating,* and *performance audit.* Regardless of the name, because of the relationship between the manager's behavior and the employee's performance, performance appraisal is one of the manager's most important, and most difficult, functions.[46] Managers should provide performance feedback as a daily function, and 360-degree feedback (Chapter 5) is effective.[47] Conducted properly, performance appraisal can decrease absenteeism and turnover and increase morale and productivity.

The performance of employees is appraised according to two sets of objectives: (1) developmental and (2) evaluative. Developmental objectives are used as the basis of decisions to improve future performance. Evaluative objectives are used as the basis of administrative decisions to reward or punish past performance, for example, to make compensation decisions (e.g., wage and salary increases, bonus pay); and to make demotion, termination, transfer, and promotion decisions.[48]

The performance appraisal process has five steps. These are shown in Exhibit 14.9 and steps 2 and 3 are discussed below.

Developing Standards and Measurement Methods   After you determine what it takes to do the job, you should develop standards and methods for measuring performance. This is step (2) in the performance appraisal process. Poor standards are a major problem of performance appraisals. They include vagueness of the performance, poorly defined performance criteria, inappropriate scale measures, and meaningless assessment items.[49]

The term **standards** *describes performance levels in the areas of quantity, quality, time, and cost.* Sample standards for an administrative assistant could be to type 50 words (quantity) per minute (time) with two errors or less (quality) at a maximum salary of $10 per hour (cost). When establishing standards for performance appraisals, you should

Learning Outcome

8. List and explain the five steps of performance appraisals and state how performance appraisals can lead to increased performance.

EXHIBIT 14.9 |
Performance Appraisal
Steps

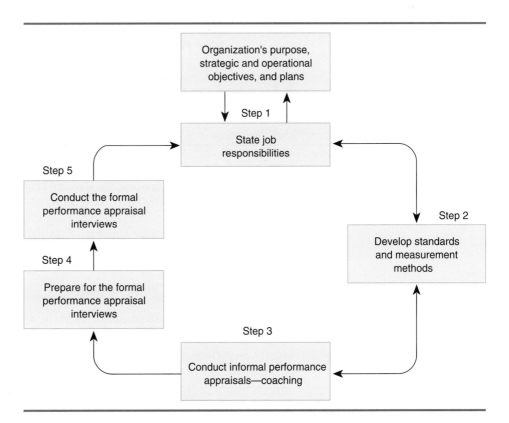

EXHIBIT 14.10 | Performance Appraisal Measurement Methods

The Critical Incidents File

The critical incidents file is a performance appraisal method in which the manager writes down positive and negative performance behavior of employees throughout the performance period. The critical incidents file is a form of documentation that is needed in this litigious environment.

The Rating Scale

The rating scale is a performance appraisal form on which the manager simply checks off the employee's level of performance. Some of the possible areas evaluated are quantity of work, quality of work, dependability, judgment, attitude, cooperation, and initiative.

Behaviorally Anchored Rating Scales (BARS)

BARS is a performance appraisal method combining rating and critical incidents. It is more objective and accurate than the two methods separately. Rather than having categories such as excellent, good, average, and so forth, the form has several statements that describe an employee's performance. The manager selects the one that best describes the employee's performance for that task. Standards are clear when good BARS are developed.

Ranking

Ranking is a performance appraisal method that is used to evaluate employee performance from best to worst. Under the ranking method, the manager compares an employee with another employee, rather than comparing each one with a standard measurement. An offshoot of ranking is the forced distribution method, which is similar to grading on a curve. A predetermined percentage of employees are placed in performance categories: for example, excellent—5 percent, above average—15 percent, average—60 percent, below average—15 percent, and poor—5 percent.

Management by Objectives (MBO)

MBO is a process by which managers and their employees jointly set objectives for the employee, periodically evaluate the performance, and reward according to the results (review Chapter 9 for details).

The Narrative Method

The narrative method requires the manager to write a statement about the employee's performance. The system can vary. Managers may be allowed to write whatever they want, or they may be required to answer questions about employees' performance. The narrative is often combined with another method.

Which Performance Appraisal Method Is the Best?

Determining the best appraisal method depends on the objectives of the system. A combination of methods is usually superior to any one method. For developmental objectives, the critical incidents file and the MBO process work well. For administrative decisions, a ranking method based on rating scales or BARS works well. The real success of performance appraisal does not lie in the method or form used; it depends on the manager's human relations skills.

have a range of performance. For example, the standard range for typing could be 70 words per minute (WPM)—excellent; 60 WPM—good; 50 WPM—average; 40 WPM—satisfactory; and 30 WPM—unsatisfactory. Not communicating standards and not giving feedback are major problems with performance appraisals.[50] In Exhibit 14.10, several commonly used performance appraisal measurement methods are described.

WORK APPLICATIONS

12. Describe the performance standards for a job you hold or have held. How would you improve them?

13. Identify the performance measurement method(s) used to evaluate your job performance. Describe how you would improve the method(s).

APPLICATION SITUATIONS

Performance Appraisal Methods

AS 14–5

Select the major performance appraisal method that should be used in each situation below. Use the information in Exhibit 14.10.

A. Critical incidents file
B. Rating scale

C. BARS
D. Ranking

E. MBO
F. Narrative method

_____ 21. You work for a small organization that does not have a formal performance appraisal system. You are overworked, but you want to develop an evaluation tool.

_____ 22. You have been promoted from a supervisory position to a middle-management position. You have been asked to select your replacement.

_____ 23. Wally is not performing up to standard. You have decided to talk to him in order to improve his performance.

_____ 24. You want to develop a system for developing employees.

_____ 25. You have a master's degree in HR and work in the HR department. You have been assigned to develop an objective performance appraisal system meeting EEO guidelines for the entire organization.

Learning Outcome

9. List the steps in the coaching model.

Conducting Informal Performance Appraisals—Coaching   Performance appraisals should not merely be formal once-a-year, one-hour sessions. Employees need regular informal feedback on their performance.[51] The employee performing below standard may need daily or weekly coaching to reach increased productivity. The supervisor's new emerging role is that of a coach rather than that of a dictator.[52]

The coaching model is designed for use in improving ability and for dealing with motivation problems. The **coaching model** *involves these steps: step (1) refer to past feedback; step (2) describe current performance; step (3) describe desired performance; step (4) get a commitment to the change; and step (5) follow up.* To help you understand each step, we'll use dialogue to illustrate it. In the dialogue situation, Fran is the supervisor of vending machine repair and Dale is a relatively new vending machine repair technician. Fran is coaching Dale.

Step 1: Refer to Past Feedback   This step assumes that the employee was told or trained to do something in the past and never did or no longer does it properly. If the employee has never received feedback, explain the situation.

FRAN: Hi, Dale. I called you into my office because I wanted to discuss your repair record.

DALE: What about it?

FRAN: We haven't discussed your performance since you started, but I've noticed a problem and wanted to correct it quickly.

Step 2: Describe Current Performance   Using specific examples, describe in detail the current performance that needs to be changed.

FRAN: In reviewing the repair reports, I realized that you repaired vending machines at the Big Y Supermarket, the United Cooperative Bank, and the Springfield YMCA. In all three locations, you had to return to repair the same machine within a month.

DALE: That's correct. If you look at my report, you'll see that it was for different problems. I fixed them right the first time.

FRAN: I realize that. That's not the problem. The problem is that the average time before returning for any repair on a machine is three months. Did you realize that?

DALE: Now that you mention it, I did hear it in the training class.

FRAN: I want to determine why you have to return to the same machine more frequently than the average. My guess is that it's because when you go to a machine for repair, you fix only the specific problem, rather than going through the entire machine to perform routine maintenance.

DALE: My job is to fix the machines.

Step 3: Describe Desired Performance   In detail, tell the employee exactly what the desired performance is. Have him or her tell you why it is important. If a skill is needed, teach it, using job instructional training (JIT). Explain why it is important for the performance to be done differently, and model the behavior.

FRAN: At the training program, did they tell you to go through the entire machine for routine maintenance?

DALE: I don't remember them saying that.

FRAN: Do you know why it is important to do maintenance rather than just to fix the machines?

DALE: I guess it's so I don't have to go back within a month and repair the same machine.

FRAN: That's right. You're more productive. From now on, I want you to go through the machines and perform maintenance rather than just fix them.

Step 4: Get a Commitment to the Change   If possible, get the employee to commit to changing his or her performance. The commitment is important because if the employee is not willing to commit to the change, he or she will not make the change. It's better to know now that the employee is not going to change than to wait and find out later, when it may be too late. The employee can commit and not make the change. But at least you have done your job, and you can refer to past commitments without change when you discipline the employee.

FRAN: From now on, will you do maintenance, rather than repairs?

DALE: I didn't do it in the past because I didn't realize I was supposed to. But in the future, I will.

Step 5. Follow Up   The follow-up is important to ensure that the employee realizes that the supervisor is serious about the change. When employees know their performance will be evaluated, they are more likely to make the change. A specific meeting is not always needed. But the employee should be told how the supervisor will follow up.

FRAN: In the future, I will continue to review the records for frequent repairs of the same machine. I don't think it will continue, but if it does, I will call you in again.

DALE: It will not be necessary.

FRAN: Great. I appreciate your cooperation, Dale. This was the only concern about your work that I had. Other than this one area, you're doing a good job. I'll see you later.

DALE: Have a good one.

During the discussion with the employee, preferably near the end, give positive reinforcement while correcting performance. Being positive helps motivate the employee to make the necessary change. For an example, refer to Fran's last statement above. Exhibit 14.11 lists the five steps to increase employee performance through coaching.

EXHIBIT 14.11 | Coaching Model

Step 1: Refer to past feedback.
Step 2: Describe current performance.
Step 3: Describe desired performance.
Step 4: Get a commitment to the change.
Step 5: Follow up.

14. Describe a specific situation in which it would be appropriate to use the coaching model.

Exhibit 14.9 lists the performance appraisal steps. Notice that steps 1 to 3 are double-looped (have two-headed arrows) because the development at one step may require the manager to backtrack and make changes. For example, during an informal appraisal, the manager may realize that environmental changes require a change in the employee's job and/or performance standards. Step 5 brings the manager back to step 1.

If people are performing to expectations, performance appraisals will not help solve productivity problems. However, if employees are performing below expectations, using performance appraisals and the coaching model can lead to higher levels of productivity.

Survey Feedback

Survey feedback *is an OD technique that uses a questionnaire to gather data that are used as the basis for change.* Different change agents will use slightly different approaches; however, a commonly used survey feedback program would include these six steps:

1. Management and the change agent do some preliminary planning to develop an appropriate survey questionnaire.
2. The questionnaire is administered to all members of the organization or unit.
3. The survey data are analyzed to uncover problem areas for improvement.
4. The change agent feeds back the results to management.
5. Managers evaluate the feedback and discuss the results with their subordinates.
6. Corrective action plans are developed and implemented.

As an example, a consultant was called by a large manufacturer to discuss training. He met with the managers of industrial engineering and manufacturing engineering. They informed the consultant of a survey that had been conducted (Steps 1 to 3). The feedback results had shown engineers as being low in organizational performance (Step 4). The three engineering managers had met with their engineers and discussed the reasons for the low rating and ways to change their image (Step 5). They decided to have the engineers go through a human relations/communication skill-building training program to improve their ability to interact more effectively with the organizational members that they served. The consultant developed and conducted a training program that helped correct the situation (Step 6).

Measuring Climate   The survey feedback technique is commonly used to measure the organizational climate. Based on the results, the organization may set up training programs as described above. Some of the signs that an organization may have a climate problem include high rates of tardiness, absenteeism, and turnover. When employees have many complaints, sabotage each other's work, talk about unionization or striking, lack pride in their work, and have low morale, the organization may have a climate problem that should be corrected.

Organizational climate is measured in the same way job satisfaction is (review Chapter 3). Survey feedback is the most common approach. But the dimensions included in the questionnaire vary from organization to organization.

In Skill-Building Exercise 14–2, you are asked to complete a questionnaire. You may want to review it now as a sample climate measurement instrument.

Force Field Analysis

Force field analysis *is a technique that diagrams the current level of performance, the hindering forces against change, and the driving forces toward change.* The process

EXHIBIT 14.12 | Force Field Analysis

Hindering forces	H-1	H-2	H-3	H-4	H-5	H-6
	High production cost	Longevity of product	Slow delivery	High sales-people turnover	Poor performance of three salespeople	Inadequate sales training

Present performance: 1,000 units sold per month

	Good reputation of organization	High-quality product	Quality advertising	Good service	Seven excellent salespeople	Skilled sales supervisor
Driving forces	D-1	D-2	D-3	D-4	D-5	D-6

begins by appraising the current level of performance. As shown in Exhibit 14.12, the present level of performance is shown in the middle of the diagram. The hindering forces holding back performance are listed in the top part of the diagram. The driving forces keeping performance at this level are listed on the bottom of the diagram. After viewing the diagram, you develop strategies for maintaining or increasing the driving forces with simultaneous steps for decreasing hindering forces. For example, in Exhibit 14.12, the solution you select could be to have the salespeople go through a training program. You could spend more time working with the less productive salespeople. Speeding up delivery time could be worked on, while maintaining all the driving forces could lead to higher sales volume.

Force field analysis is particularly useful for group problem solving. After group members agree on the diagram, the solution often becomes clear to them.

Team Building

Team building is a widely used OD technique. Individuals work as part of a unit or department, and each small functional group of individuals that works closely and interdependently makes up a team. The effectiveness of each team and all the teams working together directly affects the results of the entire organization.[53] **Team building** *is an OD technique designed to help work groups operate more effectively.*

Team building is widely used as a means of helping new or existing groups that are in need of improving effectiveness.[54] For example, Dr. Miriam Hirsch was called in as a consultant by a medical center and told that there was a restructuring of administrative responsibility. The medical center changed to a three-member team management approach. Doctors were no longer sole decision makers; they had to work with a management nurse and an administrative person. Because these managers were not used to teamwork, the consultant was asked to propose a team-building program to help them develop their skills.

Team-Building Goals   The goals of team-building programs will vary considerably, depending on the group needs and the change agent's skills. Some of the typical goals are:

- To clarify the objectives of the team and the responsibilities of each team member.
- To identify problems preventing the team from accomplishing its objectives.
- To develop team problem-solving and decision-making, objective-setting, and planning skills.
- To determine a preferred style of teamwork and to change to that style.

- To fully utilize the resources of each individual member.
- To develop open, honest working relationships based on trust and an understanding of group members.

The Change Agent's Responsibilities   Generally, the change agent first meets with the manager to discuss why a team-building program will be conducted. They discuss the goals of the program. The change agent assesses the manager's willingness to get feedback on how the team feels about his or her style and practices. The supervisor's receptiveness to the program will directly affect the team-building results.

The change agent and manager meet with the team. An atmosphere of openness and trust begins with the change agent describing the goals, agenda, and procedures of the team-building program. The change agent describes the agreement with the manager.

The change agent may interview each team member privately and confidentially to identify group problems. In addition to, or in place of, the interviews, a survey feedback questionnaire may be used. A sample questionnaire appears in Skill-Building Exercise 14–2.

The change agent conducts the team-building program in one or more days, depending upon the problems and the number of members.

Team-Building Program Agenda   The team-building agendas vary with team needs and the change agent's skills. Typical agenda topics include the following items:

1. *Climate building.* The program begins with the change agent trying to develop a climate of trust, support, and openness. He or she discusses the program's purpose and objectives. Team members learn more about each other and share what they would like to accomplish in the session.
2. *Process and structure evaluation.* The team evaluates the strengths and weaknesses of its process. The team explores and selects ideal norms.
3. *Problem identification.* The team identifies its strengths, then its weaknesses or areas where improvement is possible. The problems come from the change agent's interviews and/or the feedback survey. The team first lists several areas where improvement is possible. Then it prioritizes them by importance in helping the team improve performance.
4. *Problem solving.* The team takes the top priority and develops a solution. It then moves to the second priority, followed by the third, the fourth, and so on.
5. *Training.* Team building often includes some form of training that addresses the problem(s) facing the group.
6. *Closure.* The program ends by summarizing what has been accomplished. Follow-up responsibility is assigned. Team members commit to improving performance.

At Rider, a good starting place for OD would be team-building sessions. In teams, Rider employees could be made aware of NYCIC's OD program and how Rider will be developed. Through team-building sessions, the planned changes of NYCIC could be implemented at Rider. After a period of months, NYCIC could use survey feedback to determine how the change program at Rider is perceived. The survey could serve as the basis for understanding the need for future change at Rider. As the teams develop at Rider, they can use force field analysis to work out any problems the new changes bring and to reach higher levels of performance as part of their team-building program.

WORK APPLICATIONS

15. Identify an OD technique and explain how it is used by a specific organization, preferably one with which you have been associated.

APPLICATION   SITUATIONS

OD Techniques

AS 14–6

Below are five situations in which an OD technique would be beneficial. Identify the most appropriate technique for each.

A. Force field analysis   D. Team building

B. Survey feedback   E. Performance appraisal

C. Training and development

_____ 26. "We need to teach employees statistical process control techniques."

_____ 27. "We are a progressive company; we believe in developing our people. We'd like to give each employee better feedback to help them improve their performance."

_____ 28. "To improve productivity, we should identify the things that are holding us back and the things that are helping us be productive, too."

_____ 29. "We want an OD program that will enable us to better utilize the input of each manager."

_____ 30. "Morale and motivation are low in our organization. We'd like to know why and change."

THE RELATIONSHIP BETWEEN ORGANIZATIONAL CULTURE, CLIMATE, AND DEVELOPMENT

Learning Outcome

10. Explain the relationship between organizational culture, climate, and development.

Organizational culture, climate, and development are all different, yet related. Climate refers to the shared values and assumptions of the *actual internal* environment, while culture refers to the values and assumptions of the *ideal* environment. Thus, culture informs climate. Often the concept of culture encompasses that of climate. However, in recent years, the concern with culture has increased, while the importance of the concept of climate has decreased.

Organizational development is commonly used as the vehicle to change culture or climate. Organizational development programs to improve performance tend to be wider in scope than culture or climate. Culture and climate changes can be a part of an extensive OD program addressing other issues as well.

NYCIC can overcome the resistance to change at Rider through a planned organizational development program involving team building. The OD program can be based on the change model. Through team building, NYCIC can change the culture and climate at Rider to be the same as that of NYCIC.

GLOBAL DIFFERENCES

As stated, the Big Five personality types are global. Therefore, individuals in all cultures are more or less open to change. However, cultural values can influence openness to change.[55] Countries including the United States value change, whereas other cultures, including some Arab countries, place less value on change and more on tradition and religious beliefs. Diversity in attitude toward time also affects the rate of change. The United States is known for creating urgency and for setting deadlines for implementing change. However, other cultures take a slower approach and are more patient, such as many Asian and Middle Eastern countries.[56]

Collective (i.e., Japan, Mexico) versus individual (United States and much of Western Europe) societies do affect change. Collective societies tend to want to improve the team and organizations, so individuals are often more open to change to help others even when they personally may not gain and even lose, whereas those in individual societies are more concerned about helping themselves and are more willing to resist change that hurts them personally.[57] The Japanese generate a lot more creative ideas for improvement than do United States workers.

The Japanese tend to focus on small incremental changes to improve processes and products, whereas the United States tends to focus on large major changes. The baseball example used is that the Japanese try to get a hit, whereas the United States goes for the home run.

Some cultures are more open to power and following orders for change without questioning authority, such as France, China, and India. However, other cultures are more willing to question and resist change, such as the United States and Scandinavian (Denmark, Sweden, and Norway) cultures, which can cause problems for companies trying to change.[58] Participation in change also varies by culture and country development. For example, in the United States and Japan employees are highly trained and want to participate in planning and implementing change. However, in Third World countries employees are not highly educated and trained and are generally neither capable nor interested in being empowered to participate in the change process.[59]

Multinational corporations are continually seeking best practices to implement at all their global facilities. Too often they have difficulty making the changes and even fail to do so.[60] For example, a French (Western European country) food chain retailer opened stores in Poland (former Communist Central European country) assuming the common Western management practices and "one-best way" work routines would be transferable. Large numbers of Polish managers and employees were trained in the successful Western way of conducting business. However, cultural differences led to disappointing results. The French retailer had to adapt practices to local cultural differences to be successful.[61]

You will read more about global diversity in Chapter 15. As we bring this chapter to a close, complete Self-Assessment Exercise 14–2 to determine how your personality affects your response to change and organizational culture.

Self-Assessment Exercise 14–2

Personality and Organizational Change and Culture

Let's determine how your personality relates to your ability to change and the type of culture you may prefer.

On the Big Five personality traits, if you are *open to new experiences,* you are willing to change and will do well in an adaptive-type culture. If you are closed to new experiences, you will tend to do well in a bureaucratic-type culture that changes slowly.

If you score high on *conscientiousness,* with a high need for achievement, you may tend to be a conformist and will most likely feel comfortable in an organization with a strong culture.

If you have a high *agreeableness* personality, with a high need for affiliation, you tend to get along well with people and can fit into a strong culture. You would do well in a cooperative-type culture that values teamwork and empowerment.

If you have *surgency* traits, with a high need for power, you like to dominate and may not fit into a strong culture that does not reflect the values you have. You would tend to do well in a competitive-type culture that values individualism and high power.

Action plan: Would you like to work in an organization with a weak or a strong culture? What type of cultural values interest you?

_____

_____

_____

_____

Videos

Manager's Hot Seat and Behavior Model Videos are available for this chapter.

Online Learning Center Resources
Go to the Internet (http://mhhe.com/lussier8e) where you will find a broad array of resources to help maximize your learning.

* Review the vocabulary.

* Try a quiz.

R E V I E W

The chapter review is organized to help you master the 11 learning outcomes for Chapter 14. First provide your own response to each learning outcome, and then check the summary provided to see how well you understand the material. Next, identify the final statement in each section as either true or false (T/F). Correct each false statement. Answers are given at the end of the chapter.

1. **Describe the four types of changes.**

    The four types of changes are: (1) technology—machines and processes for creating products and services; (2) structure—organizational principles and departmentalization; (3) task—the way people perform their jobs; and (4) people—their knowledge and skill development.

    Although automation is a technology change, it results in task and people changes. T F

2. **State why people resist change and how to overcome resistance.**

    Four major reasons people resist change are the desire to maintain the status quo, uncertainty, learning anxiety, and fear. To overcome resistance to change, one should first identify three major variables: (1) *intensity*—the strength of the intensity against change; (2) *source*—the source of resistance, whether facts, beliefs, or values; and (3) *focus*—the focus of resistance, which may be self, others, or the work environment. The 11 ways to overcome resistance to change include: (1) develop a positive climate for change; (2) encourage interest in improvement; (3) plan; (4) give facts; (5) clearly state why the change is needed and how it will affect employees; (6) create a win–win situation; (7) involve employees; (8) provide support; (9) stay calm; (10) avoid direct confrontation; and (11) use power and ethical politics.

    The first reaction to rumors of change is resistance to the change. T F

3. **Explain how to use the Lussier change model when making changes.**

    To make a change, follow the steps in the Lussier change model: (1) define the change, (2) identify possible resistance to the change, (3) plan the change, (4) implement the change, and (5) control the change.

    It is common to shorten the Lussier model to unfreezing, moving, and refreezing. T F

4. **Explain the two dimensions of an organization's culture.**

    The two dimensions of an organization's culture are strong and weak, and positive and negative. Organizations with strong cultures have clear values that are shared and enforced; those with weak cultures do not. Positive cultures contribute to effective performance; negative cultures hinder it.

    Employees learn about the organization's culture through its heroes, stories, slogans, symbols, and ceremonies. T F

5. **Explain the seven dimensions of an organization's climate.**

    The seven dimensions of an organization's climate include: (1) structure—the degree of constraint on members; (2) responsibility—the degree of control over one's own job; (3) rewards—the degree of being rewarded for one's efforts and being punished appropriately; (4) warmth—the degree of satisfaction with human relations; (5) support—the degree of being helped by others and cooperation; (6) organizational identity and loyalty—the degree to which employees identify with the organization and feel loyalty toward it; and (7) risk—the degree to which risk-taking behavior is encouraged.

    Morale is used to measure climate as being either high or low, based on the seven dimensions of climate. T F

6. **Describe five organizational development techniques.**

    Organizational development (OD) is the ongoing planned process of change to improve the organization's effectiveness in solving problems and achieving objectives. Five OD techniques are: (1) training and development, used to teach people their jobs; (2) performance appraisal, used to evaluate employee job performance; (3) survey feedback, which uses a questionnaire to gather data that are used as the basis for change; (4) force field analysis, used to diagram the current level of performance as well as the hindering and driving forces; and (5) team building, designed to help work groups operate more effectively.

Survey feedback can be part of other OD techniques, and it can also lead to the use of other techniques. T F

7. **Describe the training cycle and how training is used to increase performance.**

   The five steps of the training cycle are: (1) conduct a needs assessment, (2) set objectives, (3) prepare for training, (4) conduct the training, and (5) measure and evaluate training results. Employees can get more work done when they follow proper procedures.

   The job instructional training (JIT) steps include: (1) preparation of the trainee, (2) trainer presentation of the job, (3) trainee performance of the job, and (4) follow-up. T F

8. **List and explain the five steps of performance appraisals and state how performance appraisals can lead to increased performance.**

   The five steps of performance appraisal are: (1) state job responsibilities, (2) develop standards and measurement methods, (3) conduct informal performance appraisals, (4) prepare for the formal performance appraisal interviews, and (5) conduct the formal performance appraisal interviews. Performance appraisals can provide motivation and feedback to employees on ways to do a better job.

   For developmental objectives, a ranking method based on rating scales or BARS works well. T F

9. **List the steps in the coaching model.**

   The five steps of the coaching model are: (1) refer to past feedback, (2) describe current performance, (3) describe desired performance, (4) get a commitment to the change, and (5) follow up.

   The coaching model is commonly used during the formal yearly performance review. T F

10. **Explain the relationship between organizational culture, climate, and development.**

    Climate refers to shared perceptions of intangible elements in the *actual internal* environment, while culture refers to the values and assumptions of the *ideal* environment. Often the concept of culture encompasses that of climate. Organizational development programs are commonly used to change culture and climate to improve performance.

    As changes take place in the business environment, the organizational culture needs to change, and as culture changes, climate can deteriorate. T F

Learning Outcome

11. Define the following 16 key terms.

11. **Define the following 16 key terms.**

    Select one or more methods: (1) fill in the missing key terms from memory; (2) match the key terms from the end of the review with their definitions below; and/or (3) copy the key terms in order from the key terms list at the beginning of the chapter.

    _____ are technological change, structural change, task change, and people change.

    _____ are formal systems for collecting, processing, and disseminating the information necessary to aid managers in decision making.

    _____ is the simplification or reduction of the human effort required to do a job.

    _____ involves the variables of intensity, source, and focus and explains why people are reluctant to change.

    _____ consists of the shared values and assumptions of how its members will behave.

_____ is the relatively enduring quality of the internal environment of the organization as perceived by its members.

_____ is a state of mind based on attitudes and satisfaction with the organization.

_____ is the ongoing planned process of change used as a means of improving the organization's effectiveness in solving problems and achieving its objectives.

_____ is the process of developing the necessary skills to perform the present job.

_____ is the process of developing the ability to perform both present and future jobs.

_____ refers to the ongoing process of evaluating employee job performance.

_____ is a term used to describe performance levels in the areas of quantity, quality, time, and cost.

The _____ involves these steps: (1) refer to past feedback, (2) describe current performance, (3) describe desired performance, (4) get a commitment to the change, and (5) follow up.

_____ is a technique that uses a questionnaire to gather data that are used as the basis for change.

_____ is a technique that diagrams the current level of performance, the hindering forces toward change, and the driving forces toward change.

_____ is a technique designed to help work groups operate more effectively.

K E Y   T E R M S

automation   495
coaching model   511
development   507
force field analysis   513
management information
  systems (MIS)   495
morale   505

organizational climate   505
organizational
  culture   503
organizational
  development   507
performance
  appraisal   509

resistance to change   497
standards   509
survey feedback   513
team building   514
training   507
types of changes   494

C O M M U N I C A T I O N   S K I L L S

The following critical thinking questions can be used for class discussion and/or as written assignments to develop communication skills. Be sure to give complete explanations for all questions.

1. Which single technology change has had the largest effect on your behavior?
2. Of the four reasons people resist change, which one do you think is the most common?

3. Of the 11 methods for overcoming resistance to change, which one do you think is the best?

4. Describe your college's culture. Is it strong or weak? Are there any good slogans and/or symbols that help to convey your college's culture? Give at least one new way (slogans/symbols, etc.) to promote your college's culture.

5. Using the seven dimensions of climate, describe your college's climate. Rate the morale of students as high or low, explaining your answer in detail.

6. One of the purposes of college is to train and develop students for future careers. How would you rate your overall college education?

7. A professor's job is to facilitate student learning, evaluate student performance, and assign grades. Do you believe your learning performance is evaluated effectively? How could it be improved?

8. Do your professors use consistent standards in terms of the work they require in their courses and the performance appraisal grades they give? Or do some professors require more work than others? Do some give lots of As while others give lots of lower grades? Is this diversity in work requirements and performance appraisal positive or negative? Why does it exist?

9. Which OD technique(s) can be used to improve consistency among professors in terms of work assignments and performance appraisals at your college? Which of the four reasons for resistance would be the dominant reason for faculty resistance to such a change? How would you rate the intensity, focus, and source of their resistance (see Exhibit 14.3, Resistance Matrix)?

10. Can a multinational company have one organizational culture, or does it need to have different cultures based on its business unit in each country?

CASE

Sanyo Electric—Sold to Panasonic

Based in Osaka, Japan, Sanyo Electric Co., Ltd., has more than 200 subsidiaries worldwide. Its products and services are divided among four business segments: consumer, commercial, components, and other. Its companies make a variety of electrical devices and appliances, including industrial and commercial equipment (refrigerated supermarket cases), audio and video equipment (DVD players, TVs, digital cameras), semiconductors, communications equipment (cellular phones, computers), batteries, and home appliances (microwave ovens, air conditioners).

Although Sanyo's name means "three oceans" (representing the three major oceans of the world), Japan accounts for almost 70 percent of the company's sales. This concentration of sales in Japan was not the vision that founder Mr. Toshio Iue had in mind for the firm. "Our belief is to be like the sun that shines on all people regardless of race, creed, religion, or difference in wealth." Along with other Japanese electronics makers, Sanyo is also under pressure as lower-cost manufacturers elsewhere in Asia push down prices of products, while the cost of raw materials rises. The company is paring down its wide-ranging operations to focus on its core strengths such as batteries and industrial refrigeration systems.

In order to remain competitive and reach non-Japanese markets, Sanyo has changed the way it does business and who it does business with. For example, it has formed a pact with IBM to make semiconductors using Big Blue's energy-saving copper-circuit technology, it has allied with Philips to develop semiconductors and related products, it has teamed up with Eastman Kodak to develop flat-panel displays based on next-generation organic electro-luminescent technology, and it has formed an alliance with China's largest consumer electronics maker, Haier Group, whereby Sanyo sells its products through Haier's outlets and service centers and, in turn, selected Haier goods are sold in Japan.

In 2006, Sanyo essentially gave up control of the company with a ¥300 billion ($2.6 billion) capital injection from Goldman Sachs, Daiwa Securities SMBC, and

Sumitomo Mitsui Banking Corp., making Goldman and Daiwa Sanyo's top shareholders, with each holding 24.5 percent of the voting rights in the company. The firm has made some internal changes as well, including a major management reshuffling. First and foremost, its top executive, Chairwoman and Chief Executive Officer Tomoyo Nonaka, has inherited the sole title of chairwoman. Company officials said the move was an effort to simplify the management structure. The company also did away with other Western titles such as chief operating officer and chief financial officer. Furthermore, the company has revamped its board of directors so that two of the nine members are from Goldman Sachs and two others are from Daiwa Securities SMBC. Two of these four also have been named vice presidents of the company. The rest of the board members are from inside Sanyo.

The most recent change has also been the most drastic. In December 2008 Sanyo agreed to be acquired by rival Panasonic Corporation. The boards of both companies in late December agreed to proceed with the combination of their businesses via a tender offer for Sanyo's shares by Panasonic. Panasonic expected to launch its offer as early as February 2009 and to complete the purchase of a majority of Sanyo's shares by the end of March. Sanyo's shares will remain listed and its brand will be retained. Together, Sanyo and Panasonic will create one of the world's largest electronics companies, ahead of Hitachi Ltd. Panasonic has been eyeing Sanyo to secure its spot in both lithium-ion batteries and photovoltaic cells.[62]

Go to the Internet: For more information on Sanyo Electric Company, Ltd., and to update the information provided in this case, do a name search on the Internet and visit http://www.global-sanyo.com.

Support your answers to the following questions with specific information from the case and text, or with other information you get from the Web or other sources.

1. Looking at Exhibit 14.12 (Force Field Analysis), diagram the hindering and driving forces for change at Sanyo Electric Company, Ltd.

2. What types of changes (see Exhibit 14.1) have been implemented based upon these hindering and driving forces?

3. Using Exhibit 14.3 (Resistance Matrix), describe what might be the sources and focus of resistance to these changes.

4. Sanyo's culture and climate are bound by Japanese tradition and the values of its founder. What changes support or challenge the firm's existing culture and climate?

5. How should Sanyo have prepared its employees for the changes it is employing, especially the Panasonic acquisition?

Cumulative Questions

6. What influence do personality, learning, perception (Chapter 2), attitudes, and values (Chapter 3) have in terms of this case?

7. Is the focus of this case interpersonal communications (Chapter 5) or organizational structure and communication (Chapter 6)?

8. Describe the impact of the founder's leadership (Chapter 8) on Sanyo's continuing operations.

9. Which motivation theory (Chapter 9) would you say is most relevant to this case?

10. What type(s) of power and influence (Chapter 10) did Goldman Sachs and Daiwa Securities employ in order to have representatives placed on Sanyo's board of directors?

11. What role did networking (Chapter 11) and team dynamics (Chapter 12) play in this case?

| OBJECTIVE CASE | **Supervisor Carl's Change** |

Carl was an employee at Benson's Corporation. He applied for a supervisor job at Hedges Inc. and got the job. Carl wanted to do a good job. He observed the employees at work to determine ways to improve productivity. Within a week Carl thought of a way.

On Friday afternoon he called the employees together. Carl told them that starting on Monday he wanted them to change the steps they followed when assembling the product. He demonstrated the new steps a few times and asked if everyone understood them. There were no questions. So Carl said, "Great. Start them on Monday, first thing."

On Monday Carl was in his office for about an hour doing the week's scheduling. When he came out to the shop floor, he realized that no one was following the new procedure he had shown them on Friday. Carl called the crew together and asked why no one was following the new steps.

HANK: We've done it this way for years and it works fine.

SANDY: We are all underpaid for this boring job. Why should we improve productivity? (*Several others nod.*)

DEBBIE: On Friday at the tavern we were talking about the change, and we agreed that we are not getting paid more, so why should we produce more?

Answer the following questions. Then in the space between the questions, state why you selected that answer.

_____ 1. The type of change Carl introduced was:

        a. task change   *c.* technological change

        b. structural change   *d.* people change

_____ 2. Using Exhibit 14.3, identify Sandy's major resistance (box) to change.

a. 1	*c.* 3	*e.* 5	*g.* 7	*i.* 9
b. 2	*d.* 4	*f.* 6	*h.* 8	

_____ 3. Using Exhibit 14.3, identify Debbie's major resistance (box) to change.

a. 1	*c.* 3	*e.* 5	*g.* 7	*i.* 9
b. 2	*d.* 4	*f.* 6	*h.* 8	

_____ 4. When implementing his change, Carl should have used which major step to overcome resistance to change?

a. develop a positive climate   e. stay calm
b. encourage interest in improvement   f. avoid direct confrontation
c. plan   g. involve employees
d. give facts   h. provide support

_____ 5. Hank's response was a _____ resistance statement.

a. blocker   d. reverser   g. politician
b. roller   e. sidestepper   h. traditionalist
c. staller   f. threatener   i. assaulter

_____ 6. The best OD technique for Carl to have used for this change was:

a. force field analysis   d. team building
b. survey feedback   e. performance appraisal
c. training

_____ 7. Carl followed the Lussier change model steps.

a. true   b. false

_____ 8. Hank's statement, assuming it is representative of the group, indicates a _____ organizational culture.

a. positive   b. negative

_____ 9. Based on Sandy's response, it appears organizational climate and morale are:

a. positive   c. in need of improvement
b. neutral

_____ 10. The conflict management style (Chapter 7) Carl should use in this situation (employees are not following the procedures) is:

a. forcing   c. compromising   e. collaborating
b. avoiding   d. accommodating

11. Assume you had Carl's job. How would you have made the change?

Note: The meeting between Carl and the employees may be role-played in class.

SKILL-BUILDING EXERCISE 14–1

Coaching

In-Class Exercise
(Group)

Objective: To develop your skill at improving performance through coaching.

AACSB: The AACSB learning standard skills developed through this exercise are analytic skills, communication ability, and leadership.

Preparation: You should have read and understood the chapter.

Experience: You will coach, be coached, and observe coaching using the coaching model.

Procedure 1
(2–4 minutes)

Break into groups of three. Make one or two groups of two, if necessary. Each member selects one of the three situations below in which to be the supervisor, and a different one in which to be the employee. You will role-play coaching and being coached.

BMV 14–1

1. Employee 1 is a clerical worker. He or she uses files, as do the other 10 employees. The employees all know that they are supposed to return the files when they are finished so that others can find them when they need them. Employees should have only one file out at a time. As the supervisor walks by, he or she notices that employee 1 has five files on his or her desk, and another employee is looking for one of the files. The supervisor thinks employee 1 will complain about the heavy workload as an excuse for having more than one file out at a time.

2. Employee 2 is a server in an ice cream shop. He or she knows that the tables should be cleaned up quickly after customers leave so that the new customers do not have to sit at a dirty table. It's a busy night. The supervisor looks at employee 2's tables and finds customers at two of them with dirty dishes. Employee 2 is socializing with some friends at one of the tables. Employees are supposed to be friendly. Employee 2 will probably use this as an excuse for the dirty tables.

3. Employee 3 is an auto technician. All employees know that they are supposed to place a paper mat on the floor of each car to prevent the carpets from getting dirty. When the service supervisor got into a car employee 3 repaired, it did not have a mat, and there was grease on the carpet. Employee 3 does excellent work and will probably make reference to this fact when coached.

Procedure 2
(3–7 minutes)

Prepare for coaching to improve performance. Below, each group member writes a basic outline of what she or he will say when coaching employee 1, 2, or 3, following the steps in coaching below:

Step 1: Refer to past feedback.

Step 2: Describe current performance.

Step 3: Describe desired performance. (Don't forget to have the employee state why it is important.)

Step 4: Get a commitment to the change.

Step 5: Follow up.

Procedure 3
(5–8 minutes)

    A. Role play. The supervisor of employee 1, the clerical worker, coaches him or her (use the actual name of the group member role-playing employee 1) as planned. Talk; do not read your written plan. Employee 1, put yourself in the worker's position. You work hard; there is a lot of pressure to work fast. It's easier when you have more than one file. Refer to the workload while being coached. Both the supervisor and the employee will have to ad-lib.

    The person not role-playing is the observer. He or she writes notes on the preparation steps in procedure 2 about what the supervisor did well and how he or she could improve.

    B. Feedback. The observer leads a discussion on how well the supervisor coached the employee. It should be a discussion, not a lecture. Focus on what the supervisor did well and how he or she could improve. The employee should also give feedback on how he or she felt and what might have been more effective in getting him or her to change.

    Do not go on to the next interview until told to do so. If you finish early, wait for the others to finish.

Procedure 4
(5–8 minutes)

Same as Procedure 3, but change roles so that employee 2, the server, is coached. Employee 2 should make a comment about the importance of talking to customers to make them feel welcome. The job is not much fun if you can't talk to your friends.

Procedure 5
(5–8 minutes)

Same as Procedure 3. But change roles so that employee 3, the auto technician, is coached. Employee 3 should comment on the excellent work he or she does.

Conclusion: The instructor leads a class discussion and/or makes concluding remarks.

Application (2–4 minutes): What did I learn from this experience? How will I use this knowledge in the future?

Sharing: Volunteers give their answers to the application section.

SKILL-BUILDING EXERCISE 14–2

Your College Climate

Preparation
(Individual and Group)

A popular method of determining organizational climate is a survey questionnaire. Below is a survey instrument developed by Dr. Roland E. Holstead, former chairperson of the Department of Social Sciences and Human Services at Springfield College, and adapted with his permission. Answer the questions as they apply to your college. Leave unanswered the questions that do not apply to you or your school.

Academic Life

	Very Satisfied	Somewhat Satisfied	Satisfied	Somewhat Dissatisfied	Very Dissatisfied
1. How satisfied are you with your academic program?	____	____	____	____	____
2. How satisfied are you with your academic adviser?	____	____	____	____	____
3. How satisfied are you with your instructors, in general?	____	____	____	____	____
4. How satisfied are you with the following types of courses?	____	____	____	____	____
All-college requirements	____	____	____	____	____
Major courses	____	____	____	____	____
Elective courses	____	____	____	____	____

5. In your experience, what academic departments offer some of the *most* worthwhile courses?

_____

_____

_____

6. In your experience, what academic departments offer some of the *least* worthwhile courses?

_____

_____

_____

7. A. How difficult are the following types of courses for you personally?

	Very Difficult	Somewhat Difficult	About Right	Somewhat Easy	Very Easy
All-college requirements	____	____	____	____	____
Major courses	____	____	____	____	____
Elective courses	____	____	____	____	____

B. How challenging are the following types of courses for you personally?

	Very Challenging	Somewhat Challenging	About Right	Somewhat Unchallenging	Very Unchallenging
All-college requirements	____	____	____	____	____
Major courses	____	____	____	____	____
Elective courses	____	____	____	____	____

C. How interesting are the following types of courses for you personally?

	Very Interesting	Somewhat Interesting	Interesting	Somewhat Uninteresting	Very Uninteresting
All-college requirements	____	____	____	____	____
Major courses	____	____	____	____	____
Elective courses	____	____	____	____	____

D. *For Juniors and Seniors Only:* Some courses are numbered for freshmen-sophomores, others for juniors-seniors, and others for seniors–graduate students. Would you agree that as the course number increases, the difficulty or demand on your performance also increases? In other words, are junior-senior courses generally harder than freshman-sophomore courses?

_____ Yes   _____ No   _____ No difference—numbering system is useless.

8. A. Where do you study most often?

What Time(s) of Day?

_____ Own room

_____ Library

_____ Student lounge

_____ Empty classrooms

_____ Other

B. How satisfied are you with your ability to study in each of the following places?

	Very Satisfied	Somewhat Satisfied	Satisfied	Somewhat Dissatisfied	Very Dissatisfied
In your room	_____	_____	_____	_____	_____
In the library	_____	_____	_____	_____	_____
In a student lounge	_____	_____	_____	_____	_____
In empty classrooms	_____	_____	_____	_____	_____

9. About how many hours a day, if any, do you spend at each activity?

Completing assignments _____   Reading _____   Studying _____

10. About how many classes do you cut per week, if any? _____

	Very Satisfied	Somewhat Satisfied	Satisfied	Somewhat Dissatisfied	Very Dissatisfied
11. How satisfied are you with your college's library holdings?	_____	_____	_____	_____	_____
12. How satisfied are you with the size of (number of students in) your classes?	_____	_____	_____	_____	_____
13. How satisfied are you with the grading structure?	_____	_____	_____	_____	_____

What is your major? _____

What is your grade-point average? _____

What is your year in college? _____

Student Services

14. Which of the following services have you ever used, and how satisfied were you with them?

	Very Satisfied	Somewhat Satisfied	Satisfied	Somewhat Dissatisfied	Very Dissatisfied
Dean of Students Office	_____	_____	_____	_____	_____
Housing Office	_____	_____	_____	_____	_____
Counseling Center	_____	_____	_____	_____	_____

	Very Satisfied	Somewhat Satisfied	Satisfied	Somewhat Dissatisfied	Very Dissatisfied
Infirmary	____	____	____	____	____
Chaplain	____	____	____	____	____
Security/Campus Police	____	____	____	____	____
Career Planning and Placement Office	____	____	____	____	____
Minority Advisement/ Special Advisement	____	____	____	____	____

Social Life

15. In general, are you satisfied with the social life at your college? _____

16. Are there enough social activities planned on campus during a typical week? _____ If not, what activities should be increased?

_____

_____

_____

17. In which of the following social activities do you engage on a weekly basis, when available?

_____ Dorm parties   _____ Movies

_____ Private parties   _____ Athletic events on campus

_____ Off-campus activities   _____ Cultural events on campus

18. On what night(s) would you be most likely to attend a social/cultural event on the campus? _____

19. A. How often do you go home (if you are living away from home to go to college)?

_____ Usually weekly (weekends)   _____ At least once a month

_____ Twice monthly   _____ At least once a semester

B. For what reason(s) are you most likely to go home during a school term other than a holiday or term break?

_____

_____

_____

20. What types of events would you like to see available on campus?

_____

_____

_____

21. In which of the following activities do you participate?

_____ Newspaper

_____ Yearbook

_____ Radio station

_____ Varsity athletics

_____ Intramural athletics

_____ Student government

_____ Other clubs

_____ Religious activity

_____ Other (specify)

Dorm Life (Skip questions 22–33 if you do not live in a dorm.)

	Very Satisfied	Somewhat Satisfied	Satisfied	Somewhat Dissatisfied	Very Dissatisfied
22. How satisfied are you with your life in the dorm?	_____	_____	_____	_____	_____
23. How satisfied are you with your					
Resident director?	_____	_____	_____	_____	_____
Resident assistant?	_____	_____	_____	_____	_____
24. How satisfied are you with your ability to study in your dorm room?	_____	_____	_____	_____	_____
25. How satisfied are you with your ability to sleep in your dorm room?	_____	_____	_____	_____	_____
26. How satisfied are you with the degree of privacy in your dorm?	_____	_____	_____	_____	_____
27. How satisfied are you with the cleanliness of your dorm?	_____	_____	_____	_____	_____

	Very Effective	Somewhat Effective	Ineffective	Somewhat Ineffective	Very Ineffective
28. How effective is your dorm government?	_____	_____	_____	_____	_____

	Very Fair	Somewhat Fair	Fair	Somewhat Unfair	Very Unfair
29. How fair are your dorm's rules?	_____	_____	_____	_____	_____
30. How fair is the enforcement of your dorm's rules?	_____	_____	_____	_____	_____

31. A. Is there a problem in your dorm with these behaviors/issues?

_____ Drug use   _____ Security

_____ Sexual activity (whether heterosexual or homosexual)   _____ Violence

_____ Sexual harassment   _____ Noise

B. Are there problems in your dorm not identified above? _____ If yes, what are they?

_____

_____

_____

C. To whom did you report any of these problems?

_____ Resident assistant

_____ Resident director

_____ Dean of Students Office

Were you satisfied with the official response to the problem? _____

32. What are the best things about your dorm?

_____

_____

_____

33. If you could change anything about your dorm, what would it be, and why?

_____

_____

_____

In what dorm do you live? _____

Do most of your college friends live in your dorm? _____

In-Class Exercise	*Objectives:* To better understand organizational climate and the climate at your college.

AACSB: The AACSB learning standard skills developed through this exercise are analytic skills, communication ability, and leadership.

Preparation: You should have completed the preparation questionnaire.

Experience: Your class will calculate its climate and discuss it.

Procedure 1
(8–12 minutes)

Tabulate the Class's Survey Responses

Option A: Break up into teams of five or six and tabulate team members' responses to each of the questions selected by your instructor. Each group reports its responses to the instructor, who tabulates the total responses for the entire class. He or she summarizes the results on the board.

Option B: The instructor asks students to indicate their responses to selected questions by raising their hands. The instructor totals the responses to each question and writes them on the board.

Procedure 2
(8–12 minutes)

Discuss School Climate

1. Climate surveys are usually given to an entire organization or to a major unit. Can you assume that your class is representative of the entire college or university? Why or why not?

2. The survey questions were designed for Springfield College. What sections or individual questions should be changed or added to make the survey more reflective of the climate at your school?

3. Is your school's climate consistent with your needs (and with the needs of the student body as a whole)?

4. How does your school's climate affect your behavior and attitudes (and those of the student body)?

5. How does your school's climate affect your (and the student body's) performance and productivity?

6. Would conducting a climate survey of the entire student body be of value at your college or university? Why or why not?

Conclusion: The instructor leads a class discussion and/or makes concluding remarks.

Application (2–4 minutes):   What did I learn from this experience? How will I use this knowledge in the future?

Sharing: Volunteers give their answers to the application section.

SKILL-BUILDING EXERCISE 14–3

Improving the Quality of Student Life

In-Class Exercise (Individual and Group)

Objective: To experience the quality circle approach to increasing the quality of student life at your college.

AACSB: The AACSB learning standard skills developed through this exercise are analytic skills, communication ability, teamwork, and leadership.

Experience: You will experience being part of a quality circle.

Procedure 1 (8–15 minutes)

Break into groups of five or six members. Select a spokesperson. Your group is to come up with a list of the three to five most needed improvements at your college. Rank them in order of priority, from 1—most important to 5—least important. When you are finished, or the time is up, the spokesperson will write the ranking on the board. You may refer to the preparation for Skill-Building Exercise 14–2 for ideas on areas needing improvement.

Procedure 2
(3–10 minutes)

Option A: The instructor determines the class's top three to five priorities for improvement.

Option B: The class achieves consensus on the top three to five priorities for improvement.

Procedure 3
(5–10 minutes)

Each group selects a new spokesperson. The group develops solutions that will improve the quality of student life for the class's three to five priority areas.

Procedure 4
(5–20 minutes)

For the first-priority item, each spokesperson states the group's recommendation for improving the quality of student life. The class votes or comes to a consensus on the best way to solve the problem. Proceed to items 2 to 5 until you finish or time is up.

Discussion:

1. Are survey feedback and quality circles (as used in this exercise) effective ways to improve the quality of student life on campus?

2. Did the class consider that quality of student life is a balance between the college, the students, and society? Are your solutions going to benefit the college and society as well as the students?

Conclusion: The instructor may lead a class discussion and/or make concluding remarks.

Application (2–4 minutes):   What did I learn from this experience? How will I use this knowledge in the future?

Sharing: Volunteers give their answers to the application section.

SKILL-BUILDING EXERCISE 14–4

Team Building
Preparation (Group)

Note: This exercise is designed for permanent class groups. Below is a survey feedback questionnaire. There are no right or wrong answers. Check off the answer to each question as it applies to your class group. All questions have five choices.

Strongly Agree	Agree Somewhat	Neutral	Disagree Somewhat	Strongly Disagree
Conflict or Fight				

1. Our group's atmosphere is friendly.

2. Our group has a relaxed (rather than tense) atmosphere.

3. Our group is very cooperative (rather than competitive).

_____ | _____ | _____ | _____ | _____

4. Members feel free to say what they want.

_____ | _____ | _____ | _____ | _____

5. There is much disagreement in our group.

_____ | _____ | _____ | _____ | _____

6. Our group has problem people (silent member, talker, bored member, wanderer, arguer).

_____ | _____ | _____ | _____ | _____

Apathy

7. Our group is committed to its tasks (all members actively participate).

_____ | _____ | _____ | _____ | _____

8. Our group has good attendance.

_____ | _____ | _____ | _____ | _____

9. Group members come to class prepared (all assignments are complete).

_____ | _____ | _____ | _____ | _____

10. All members do their share of the work.

_____ | _____ | _____ | _____ | _____

11. Our group should consider firing a member for not attending and/or not doing his or her share of the work.

_____ | _____ | _____ | _____ | _____

Decision Making

12. Our group's decision-making ability is good.

_____ | _____ | _____ | _____ | _____

13. All members participate in making decisions.

_____ | _____ | _____ | _____ | _____

14. One or two members influence most decisions.

_____ | _____ | _____ | _____ | _____

15. Our group follows the five steps of the decision-making model (Chapter 13).
    Step 1: Define the problem.

    _____ | _____ | _____ | _____ | _____

    Step 2: Set objectives and criteria.

    _____ | _____ | _____ | _____ | _____

    Step 3: Generate alternatives.

    _____ | _____ | _____ | _____ | _____

    Step 4: Analyze alternatives (rather than quickly agreeing on one) and select one.

    _____ | _____ | _____ | _____ | _____

    Step 5: Plan, implement the decision, and control.

    _____ | _____ | _____ | _____ | _____

16. Our group uses the following ideas:

    a. Members sit in a close circle.

    _____ | _____ | _____ | _____ | _____

    b. We determine the approach to the task before starting.

    _____ | _____ | _____ | _____ | _____

    c. Only one member speaks at a time, and everyone discusses the same question.

    _____ | _____ | _____ | _____ | _____

    d. Each person presents answers with specific reasons.

    _____ | _____ | _____ | _____ | _____

    e. We rotate order for presenting answers.

    _____ | _____ | _____ | _____ | _____

    f. We listen to others rather than rehearse our own answers.

    _____ | _____ | _____ | _____ | _____

    g. We eliminate choices not selected by group members.

    _____ | _____ | _____ | _____ | _____

    h. All members defend their answers (when they believe they are correct) rather than changing to avoid discussion or conflict, or to get the task over with.

    _____ | _____ | _____ | _____ | _____

    i. We identify the answers remaining and reach a consensus on one (no voting).

    _____ | _____ | _____ | _____ | _____

    j. We come back to controversial questions.

_____ | _____ | _____ | _____ | _____

17. We make a list of other relevant questions.

18. Our group uses the _____ conflict management style.

   a. forcing   *c.* avoiding   *e.* collaborating

   b. accommodating   *d.* compromising

19. Our group _____ resolve its conflicts in a manner that is satisfactory to all.

   a. does   *b.* does not

In-Class Exercise

This exercise is designed for groups that have worked together for some time.

Objectives: To experience a team-building session and to improve your group's effectiveness.

AACSB: The AACSB learning standard skills developed through this exercise are reflective thinking and self-management, analytic skills, communication ability, teamwork, and leadership.

Experience: This exercise is discussion-oriented.

Material: Preparation for Skill-Building Exercise 14–4.

Procedure 1-a
(5–30 minutes)

Climate Building

To develop a climate of trust, support, and openness, group members will learn more about each other through a discussion based on asking questions.

Rules:

1. Rotate; take turns asking questions.

2. You may refuse to answer a question as long as you did not ask it (or plan to).

3. You do not have to ask the questions in the order listed below.

4. You may ask your own questions. (Add them to the list.)

As an individual and before meeting with your group, review the questions below and place the name of one or more *group members* to whom you want to ask the question next to it. If you prefer to ask the entire group, put *group* next to the question. When everyone is ready, begin asking the questions.

1. How do you feel about this course? _____

2. How do you feel about this group? _____

3. How do you feel about me? _____

4. How do you think I feel about you? _____

5. What were your first impressions of me? _____

6. What do you like to do? _____

7. How committed to the group are you? _____

8. What do you like most about this course? _____

9. What do you plan to do after you graduate? _____

10. What do you want out of this course? _____

11. How do you react to deadlines? _____

12. Which member in the group are you the closest to? _____

13. Which member in the group do you know the least? _____

Other_____

When the instructor tells you to do so, get together with your group members and ask each other your questions.

Procedure 1-b
(2–4 minutes)

Participants determine what they would like to accomplish during the team-building session. Below are six major goals of team building; you may add to them. Rank them according to your preference.

_____ To clarify the team's objectives.

_____ To identify areas for improving group performance.

_____ To develop team skills.

_____ To determine and utilize a preferred team style.

_____ To fully utilize the resources of each group member.

_____ To develop working relationships based on trust, honesty, and understanding.

_____ Your own goals (list them).

Procedure 1-c
(3–6 minutes)

Participants share their answers to Procedure 1-b. The group can come to a consensus on its goal(s) if it wants to.

Procedure 2
(3–8 minutes)

Process and Structure: As a team, discuss strengths and weaknesses in group process (how the group works and communicates). Below, list norms (do's and don'ts) for the group to abide by.

Procedure 3-a
(10–15 minutes)

Problem Identification: As a team, answer the survey feedback questionnaire. Place a *G* in the box to signify the team's answer. Don't rush; fully discuss the issues and how and why they affect the group.

Procedure 3-b
(3–7 minutes)

Based on the above information, list 8 to 10 ways the team could improve its performance.

Procedure 3-c
(3–6 minutes)

Prioritize the above list (1 = most important).

Procedure 4
(6–10 minutes)

Problem Solving: Take the top-priority item. Then do the following:

1. Define the problem.

   2. Set objectives and criteria.

   3. Generate alternatives.

   4. Analyze alternatives and select one.

   5. Develop an action plan for its implementation.

Follow the same five steps for each area of improvement until time is up. Try to cover at least three areas.

Procedure 5
(1 minute)

Training: Team building often includes training to address the problems facing the group. Because training takes place during most exercises, we will not do any now. Remember that the agendas for team building vary and usually last for one or more full days, rather than one hour.

Procedure 6-a
(3 minutes)

Closure Application:

   1. I intend to implement the team's solutions. Why?

   2. What did I learn from this experience?

   3. How can I apply this knowledge in my daily life?

   4. How can I apply this knowledge as a manager?

Procedure 6-b
(1–3 minutes)

Group members summarize what has been accomplished and state what they will do (commit to) to improve the group.

Sharing (4–7 minutes):   A spokesperson from each team tells the class the group's top three areas for improvement. The instructor records them on the board.

ANSWERS TO TRUE/FALSE QUESTIONS

1. T.
2. F. The first stage of the change process is denial that the change will occur.
3. F. Unfreezing, moving, and refreezing are the steps of the Lewin change model.
4. T.
5. T.
6. T.
7. T.
8. F. Ranking works well for "administrative" decisions. The critical incidents file and MBO methods work well for developmental objectives.
9. F. The coaching model is an informal performance appraisal method commonly used between formal evaluations.
10. T.

Valuing Diversity Globally

A small group of white women at We-Haul in Hartford, Connecticut, were standing around the water cooler talking. These were some of the statements they made: "There is a lot of prejudice and discrimination against women around here." "There are more nonwhite faces around all the time." "We even have handicapped workers now, and it's uncomfortable to look at them and work with them." "There are plenty of women in this company, but very few of them hold professional or managerial positions." "We women here in the offices make only a fraction of what the men in the shop are paid, and with the cutbacks, women are not getting into the higher-paying jobs." "My male supervisor recently made sexual advances, and since I shot him down, he's been giving me all the lousy jobs to do." "I've complained to management about these inequities, but nothing seems to change for us white women."

At the same time, a group of white men were also talking. Some of their statements were these: "There are more nonwhites and women around all the time." "Why can't these minorities learn to speak English like the rest of us?" "These people are always complaining about not being treated fairly, when they *are*." "We've promoted a few to management, even though they are not qualified." "They don't make good managers anyway." "The way management positions are being eliminated, it's tough enough to compete against the men, let alone these others."

Are these statements, which may have been said in many organizations, based on fact or fiction? Do these attitudes help or hurt the individuals, others, and the organization? You will learn about these and other valuing-diversity issues in this chapter.

HOW DIVERSITY AFFECTS BEHAVIOR, HUMAN RELATIONS, AND PERFORMANCE

Diversity refers to the degree to which differences exist among members of a group or an organization. Within the workforce, the major groups include race and ethnicity, religion, gender, age, and ability. *Valuing diversity* means including all groups at all levels in an organization.

Diverse people behave differently and have different human relations in organizations.[1] It is common for people who are similar to group together.[2] However, when groups develop and oppose each other (Caucasian versus non-Caucasian, male versus female, management versus labor), behavior and human relations can suffer, leading to lower performance.[3] Recall (Chapter 12) that groups and organizations that value diversity generally outperform those that do not.[4]

Is Diversity Really Important Globally?   Yes. Companies that value diversity do better than those that don't.[5] In the United States, the population of potential customers is around 306 million people.[6] When a company goes global, it has 1.3 billion potential customers in China,[7] 1.1 billion in India, 237 million in Indonesia, 196 million in Brazil, 141 million in Russia, and 127 million in Japan.[8] The 27 combined countries of the European Union (EU) have a population of potential customers of 496 million.[9] The world population will hit 7 billion in 2012.[10] Clearly, businesses have gone global because they know that is where growth opportunities are. In today's global economy, you have to develop a global mindset to be able to work with diverse people.[11]

Is Diversity Really Important in America?   The United States population is rapidly diversifying. It has been estimated that by the year 2042 less than 50 percent of the U.S. population will be Caucasian[12] (the current level is 66 percent)[13] and in large cities only 40 percent of the population will be Caucasian.[14] The state of California is already less than 50 percent Caucasian. The number of immigrants continues to surge. Hispanics have surpassed African Americans as the largest U.S. minority group at 20 percent.[15] Is it any wonder that CEOs of Fortune 500 companies have said that "diversity is a strategic business imperative"? Managing diverse work groups is one of the most difficult and pressing challenges in modern organizations.[16]

There is a good chance that during your career you will work for companies that compete with global corporations and/or do business with foreign companies. You may work for a foreign-owned corporation in the United States, and you may have the opportunity to go abroad to work. If you haven't already done so, you most likely will interact with people from other countries. You can learn a great deal through interactions at work with others who have different backgrounds, expertise, and seniority.[17] You can develop your human relations skills by collaborating and learning more about employees who are different from you.[18]

PREJUDICE AND DISCRIMINATION

Learning Outcome

1. Define prejudice and discrimination and state common areas of employment discrimination in organizations.

Although progress has been made, prejudice and discrimination based on race, creed, color, and gender still exists in the United States.[19] The use of discrimination prevents equal employment opportunity.[20] Discrimination is usually based on prejudice. **Prejudice** *is the prejudgment of a person or situation based on attitudes.* As stated in Chapter 3, an attitude is a strong belief or feeling. If someone were to ask you, "Are you prejudiced?", you would probably say no. However, we all tend to prejudge people and situations.[21] Recall that Chapter 2 discussed first impressions and the four-minute barrier. In four minutes you don't have time to get to know someone, yet you make assumptions that affect your behavior. Chapter 3 defined stereotyping as the process of generalizing the behavior of all members of a group. Your prejudice is often based on your stereotype of the group.[22] To prejudge or stereotype a person or situation in and of itself is not harmful; we all tend to do this. Although prejudice is not always negative, if you discriminate based on your prejudice, you may cause harm to yourself and other parties.[23] **Discrimination** *is behavior for or against a person or situation.*

To illustrate the difference between prejudice and discrimination, assume that Joan is a supervisor and is in the process of hiring a new employee. There are two qualified candidates: Pete, an African-American male, and Ted, a white male. Joan is white and has a more positive attitude toward whites. She stereotypes blacks as being not as productive on the job as whites. But she also believes that blacks deserve a break. Joan has a few options.

Joan can discriminate based on her prejudice and hire Ted. Selecting an employee based wholly on race or color is clearly illegal discrimination for Ted and against Pete. In the same manner, Joan could be prejudiced for Pete and against Ted.

Joan can be aware of her prejudices, yet try not to let them influence her decision. She can interview both candidates and select the person who is best qualified for the job. Then there would be no discrimination. This option is legal and is the generally recommended approach. When selecting employees, you must examine a wide variety of issues and not base the decision on prejudice.

The statements in the opening case reflect negative prejudice attitudes that can lead to discrimination. Discrimination has negative consequences at the individual, team, and organizational levels.[24]

WORK APPLICATIONS

1. Discuss a situation in which you were discriminated against for some reason.

APPLICATION SITUATIONS

Prejudice or Discrimination

AS 15–1

Identify each statement made by a white male as an example of:

A. Prejudice   B. Discrimination

_____ 1. "Here comes Jamal [a tall black]; I bet he will talk about basketball."

_____ 2. "I select Pete as my partner. Karen, you team up with Betty for this assignment."

_____ 3. "I cannot continue to work with you today, Sue. Is it your time of the month?"

_____ 4. "I do not want to work the night shift. Can you force me to change?"

_____ 5. "The boss hired a good-looking, blonde secretary. I bet she's not very bright."

Common Areas of Employment Discrimination

Historically, the five areas where discrimination in employment is most common are:

- *Recruitment.* People who hire employees fail to actively recruit people from certain groups to apply for jobs within their organization.[25]
- *Selection.* People who select candidates from the recruited applicants fail to hire people from certain groups.[26]
- *Compensation.* White males make more money than other groups.[27]
- *Upward mobility.* Race and gender are significant influences on advancement.[28]
- *Evaluation.* When organizations do not base evaluations on actual job performance, discrimination in compensation and upward mobility occur.[29]

WORK APPLICATIONS

2. Cite an example of employment discrimination in recruitment, selection, compensation, upward mobility, or evaluation, preferably from an organization for which you work or have worked.

Valuing-Diversity Training

To help overcome prejudice and discrimination, organizations of all types are training their employees to value employee differences.[30] For example, LIMRA developed a customized diversity seminar with the following objectives:

1. To understand the current and changing demographics of the workforce.
2. To view the company's business as part of a global workforce and economy.
3. To recognize how prejudice and discrimination can inhibit business success.
4. To recruit from and market to targeted multicultural markets in their territory.

Avon Products began its managing-diversity program in an effort to move away from assimilation as a corporate value and to raise awareness of how negative stereotypes affect the workplace. Avon's success is evident in the number of women who have advanced to management positions. Hewlett-Packard introduced its managing-diversity program as part of the management development curriculum required of all its managers. The program stresses diversity as a competitive advantage. MetLife has a strong diversity program because it knows it affects the bottom line.[31]

To have effective human relations with all types of people who are different from you, you need to be tolerant of people's differences, try to understand why they are different, have empathy for them and their situation, and communicate openly with them. Be aware of the human tendency to prejudge and stereotype others, and avoid discriminating based on your prejudices. Later in this chapter, we will discuss how organizations are helping their diverse workforces.

WORK APPLICATIONS

3. Have you, or has anyone you know, gone through diversity training? If yes, describe the program.

EQUAL EMPLOYMENT OPPORTUNITY FOR ALL

Valuing diversity, equal employment opportunity (EEO), and affirmative action (AA) are different. Diversity differs conceptually from equal employment opportunity, which is primarily concerned with racism and prejudice. By valuing workforce diversity, management seizes the benefits differences bring.[32] Managers in the coming decade will be challenged to manage a slower-growing labor force composed of more female, immigrant, minority, and older workers, as white men decrease as a percentage of the total workforce.[33] Affirmative action is a recruitment tool to bring formerly disadvantaged workers into the workforce and to help them fit into corporate culture. Valuing differences stresses the understanding, respecting, and valuing of differences among employees.[34] Managing and valuing diversity build on the foundations created by EEO and AA. True diversity, unlike AA, is not about quotas but about finding qualified workers of all races.[35] EEO and AA direct attention to laws that guide recruiting, selecting, compensating, promoting, and evaluating employees.

Laws Affecting Employment Opportunity

Learning Outcome

2. State major laws protecting minorities and women.

You are aware that an organization cannot discriminate against a minority. Who is legally considered a minority? A minority is just about anyone who is not a white male, of European heritage, or adequately educated. The Equal Employment Opportunity Commission (EEOC) **minority** *list includes Hispanics, Asians, African Americans, Native Americans, and Alaskan natives.* Women are also protected by law from discrimination in employment, but they are not considered a legal minority because in some situations they are a majority. Disadvantaged young people, disabled workers, and persons over 40 and up to 70 years of age are also protected.

The EEOC has 37 offices across the nation. It offers seminars for employees who feel they aren't getting a fair shake, and it operates a toll-free telephone line (1-800-USA-EEOC) and Web site (www.eeoc.gov) around the clock to provide information on employee rights.[36] Some of the major laws and regulations affecting employment are presented in Exhibit 15.1.

Companies suspected of violating any of these laws may be investigated by the EEOC or become defendants in class-action or specific lawsuits.[37] Discrimination claims filed with the EEOC continue to increase.[38] Despite expensive court settlements and negative public relations, organizations continue to have problems embedding the management of diversity into their daily practices and procedures.[39] There is no one best way to manage workforce diversity.[40] However, clearly, it is important for you to be familiar with the law and your organization's EEO and AA program guidelines.

EXHIBIT 15.1 | Federal Employment Laws

Law	Description
Equal Employment Opportunity	
Equal Employment Opportunity Act of 1972 (Title VII of the Civil Rights Act of 1964)	Prohibits discrimination in all areas of the employment relationship (based on race, religion, color, sex, or national origin).
Civil Rights Act of 1991	Strengthened Civil Rights Act of 1964 by providing possible compensation and punitive damages for discrimination.
Age Discrimination in Employment Act of 1967 (amended 1978, 1984)	Prohibits age discrimination against people older than 40 and restricts mandatory retirement.
Vocational Rehabilitation Act of 1973	Prohibits discrimination based on physical or mental disability.
Americans with Disabilities Act of 1990	Strengthened the Vocational Rehab Act to require employers to provide "reasonable accommodations" to allow disabled employees to work.
Compensation and Benefits	
Equal Pay Act of 1963	Requires men and women to be paid the same for equal work.
Pregnancy Discrimination Act of 1978	Prohibits discrimination against women because of pregnancy, childbirth, or related medical conditions.
Family and Medical Leave Act of 1993	Requires employers (with 50 or more employees) to provide up to 12 weeks unpaid leave for family (childbirth, adoption, eldercare) or medical reasons.
Health and Safety	
Occupational Safety and Health Act of 1970	Establishes mandatory safety and health standards in organizations, regulated by the Occupational Safety and Health Administration (OSHA).

Learning Outcome

3. Identify what employers can and cannot ask job applicants.

Preemployment Inquiries

On the application blank and during interviews, no member of an organization can legally ask discriminatory questions. The two major rules of thumb to follow are:

1. Every question that is asked should be job related. When developing questions, you should have a purpose for using the information. Only ask legal questions you plan to use in your selection process.

2. Any general question that you ask should be asked of all candidates.

Below, we will discuss what you can (lawful information you can use to disqualify candidates) and cannot (prohibited information you cannot use to disqualify candidates) ask during a job interview. Prohibited information is information that does not relate to a bona fide occupational qualification (BFOQ) for the job. A **bona fide occupational qualification** *allows discrimination on the basis of religion, sex, or national origin where it is reasonably necessary to normal operation of a particular enterprise.* In an example of a BFOQ upheld by its supreme court, the state of Alabama required all guards in male maximum-security correctional facilities to be male. People believing that this requirement was sexual discrimination took it to court. The supreme court upheld the male sex requirement on the grounds that 20 percent of the inmates were convicted of sex offenses, and this creates an excessive threat to the security of female guards.

For a list of topics or questions that can and cannot be asked, see Exhibit 15.2.

WORK APPLICATIONS

4. Have you, or has anyone you know, been asked an illegal discriminatory question during the hiring process? If yes, identify the question(s).

EXHIBIT 15.2 | Preemployment Inquiries

Name

Can Ask: Current legal name and whether the candidate has ever worked under a different name.

Cannot Ask: Maiden name or whether the person has changed his or her name.

Address

Can Ask: Current residence and length of residence.

Cannot Ask: If the candidate owns or rents his or her home, unless it is a BFOQ.

Age

Can Ask: If the candidate is between specific age groups, 21 to 70, to meet job specifications. If hired, can you furnish proof of age? For example, an employee must be 21 to serve alcoholic beverages.

Cannot Ask: How old are you? Cannot ask to see a birth certificate. Do not ask an older person how much longer he or she plans to work before retiring.

Sex

Can Ask: Only if sex is a BFOQ.

Cannot Ask: If it is not a BFOQ. To be sure not to violate sexual harassment laws, do not ask questions or make comments remotely considered flirtatious.

Marital and Family Status

Can Ask: If the candidate can meet the work schedule and whether the candidate has activities, responsibilities, or commitments that may hinder meeting attendance requirements. The same question(s) should be asked of both sexes.

Cannot Ask: To state marital status. Do not ask any questions regarding children or other family issues.

National Origin, Citizenship, Race, or Color

Can Ask: If the candidate is legally eligible to work in the United States, and if this can be proved if hired.

Cannot Ask: To identify national origin, citizenship, race, or color (or that of parents and other relatives).

Language

Can Ask: To list languages the candidate speaks and/or writes fluently. Candidates may be asked if they speak and/or write a specific language if it is a BFOQ.

Cannot Ask: The language spoken off the job, or how the applicant learned the language.

Convictions

Can Ask: If the candidate has been convicted of a felony and other information if the felony is job-related.

Cannot Ask: If the candidate has ever been arrested (an arrest does not prove guilt). Do not ask for information regarding a conviction that is not job-related.

Height and Weight

Can Ask: If the candidate meets or exceeds BFOQ height and/or weight requirements, and if it can be proved if hired.

Cannot Ask: The candidate's height or weight if it is not a BFOQ.

Religion

Can Ask: If the candidate is of a specific religion when it is a BFOQ. Candidates can be asked whether they will be able to meet the work schedules or will have anticipated absences.

Cannot Ask: Religious preference, affiliations, or denominations.

Credit Ratings or Garnishments

Can Ask: If it is a BFOQ.

Cannot Ask: If it is not a BFOQ.

Education and Work Experience

Can Ask: For information that is job-related.

Cannot Ask: For information that is not job-related.

References

Can Ask: For the names of people willing to provide references or for the names of people who suggested the candidate apply for the job.

Cannot Ask: For a reference from a religious leader.

Military

Can Ask: For information on education and experience gained that relates to the job.

Cannot Ask: Dates and conditions of discharge. Do not ask about draft classification or other eligibility for military service, National Guard, or reserve units. Do not ask about experience in foreign armed services.

Organizations

Can Ask: To list membership in job-related organizations, such as union or professional or trade associations.

Cannot Ask: To identify membership in any non-job-related organization that would indicate race, religion, and so on.

Disabilities/AIDS

Can Ask: If the candidate has any disabilities that would prevent him or her from performing the specific job.

Cannot Ask: For information that is not job-related. In states where people with AIDS are protected under discrimination laws, you should not ask if the candidate has AIDS.

Legal Questions

AS 15–2

Identify the five questions below as:

A. Legal (can be asked)   B. Illegal (cannot be asked)

_____ 6. "What is your mother tongue or the major language you use?"

_____ 7. "Are you married or single?"

_____ 8. "Are you a member of the Teamsters Union?"

_____ 9. "Have you been arrested for stealing on the job?"

_____ 10. "Can you prove you are legally eligible to work?"

From Affirmative Action to Valuing Diversity

Affirmative action is a 1977 amendment to Executive Orders of 1965 and 1968. It requires that firms doing business with the federal government make special efforts to recruit, hire, and promote women and members of minority groups.

Affirmative action programs *are planned, special efforts to recruit, hire, and promote women and members of minority groups.* AA requires that organizations determine their racial and sexual compositions and compare these ratios with those of the available people in the population of the appropriate recruitment area. Based on these numbers, the organization plans and acts to obtain the proper percentages according to a complex calculation process.

Under the Reagan, Clinton, and Bush administrations, support for AA declined. Some of the many reasons that AA went out of favor were as follows: quotas often worked against minorities, quotas could not be met, and organizations were charged with reverse discrimination. Many believed that forced AA was not the answer to the problem of discrimination. Thus, we went from AA to valuing diversity. Managers now have titles such as manager of diversity at Xerox, and many organizations, including Coca-Cola and IBM, have diversity advisory councils. Many successful organizations are not only offering diversity training, but are truly valuing diversity as they realize that a diverse work group increases the quality of decision making and organizational performance.[41]

5. Describe the affirmative action program at an organization, preferably one for which you work or have worked.

Although global corporations may have boundaryless organizational structures, their legal systems certainly do have boundaries. Imagine the difficulty of meeting the complex, different laws in hundreds of countries at the same time, especially when the laws conflict.

THE LEGALLY PROTECTED AND SEXUAL HARASSMENT

Learning Outcome

4. List the groups that are legally protected by the EEOC.

The previous section presented the laws affecting minorities and other protected groups. This section discusses minorities, employees' religious beliefs, older workers, the disabled, alcohol and drug abuse and testing, AIDS and AIDS testing, sexual orientation, and sexual harassment in more detail.

Minorities

EEO laws prohibit job discrimination on the basis of race, color, national origin, and religion unless discrimination stems from a BFOQ. Therefore, in the following guidelines any of these terms could replace the word *minority*.

Nonminorities should realize that they may unconsciously stereotype minorities, expect them to fail, and set higher performance standards for them; these practices should be consciously avoided.[42] Errors should not be blamed on ethnic background, age, religion, and so on. Nonminorities should realize that minorities may live down to negative expectations. Minorities should not be subject to the negative Pygmalion effect (Chapter 3) and let others' negative expectations become their self-fulfilling prophecy.

It is also helpful to be open to getting to know people who are different from you. Open, honest communication helps to break down negative stereotypes.[43] When your self-concept is high, it tends to be higher in the minds of others. So project a positive image (Chapter 2).

Religious Beliefs   Employers are required by law to make reasonable accommodations for employees' religious beliefs, without undue hardship on the employer.[44] "Undue hardship" is fairly clear. It involves having to pay premium wages or other costs to accommodate an employee's religious rights, defined as "all forms and aspects of religion." However, "reasonable accommodation" is ambiguous. Employers should willingly negotiate with employees and allow them to swap shifts or job dates with consenting colleagues. And employees should be allowed to take religious holidays off in place of other paid days off. Some employers allow employees to select which paid holidays they want to take. Recall (Chapter 3) that spirituality in the workplace is on the rise.[45]

Age   Young and older workers have differences.[46] You will be working with older customers and workers. The fastest-growing segment of the population is adults and elders.[47] There will be 100 million baby boomers in their 50s by 2011.[48]

People age 40 and older are protected from age discrimination. However, the EEOC has been criticized as being shaky in fighting age bias. Criticism may be based on the fact that hiring and promotion discrimination based on age is one of the most difficult types of discrimination for the victim to prove. People over 50 have a difficult time finding a good, full-time job.

Some of the myths about older workers are the following: (1) *They cost more for benefits.* This is not necessarily true, especially when they are healthy. Younger sickly employees are more costly. (2) *They have more absences for sickness.* Older workers are as reliable as anyone. Sick leave is more related to a person's lifetime pattern of sick leave. Many organizations find older employees are absent less frequently than younger employees and recruit them for this reason. (3) *They resist change.* Older workers are not necessarily more rigid in their thinking than younger persons, and 38 percent of people 62 and older are online.[49]

With the shrinking workforce, many organizations are actively recruiting older workers to get the job done right because they are dependable, caring, experienced, and wise—particularly for part-time jobs in the retailing and fast-food industries. Older workers tend to have a strong work ethic. In addition, people over 40 make good mentors, because they have valuable experience to share.[50]

People with Disabilities   The Americans with Disabilities Act (ADA) gives equal access to employment, transportation, and buildings to millions of people in the United States with disabilities. The act is viewed as the most sweeping civil rights measure in over 25 years. A disability used to be commonly called a *handicap*. People with a **disability** *have significant physical, mental, or emotional limitations.* They include people with prison records, major obesity, or a history of heart disease, cancer, or mental illness that others might view as disabling. (One in five Americans has a mental disorder.) Rehabilitated alcoholics and drug abusers are also considered disabled. The law requires that employers make "reasonable accommodations" to hire the disabled. The disabled can be required to meet the same productivity standards as other employees.[51]

Although the U.S. government is working to place more disabled people in jobs, most disabled people are not working. About 62 percent of disabled people are not working (this figure has decreased since 2001), even though most of them would rather have a job. Many of those that do have jobs say coworkers will not socialize with them.[52] This situation exists despite the fact that in some cases, the disability is an advantage. For example, blind people work well in darkrooms. Discrimination continues despite the fact that companies rate disabled employees as good or excellent workers. Most disabled workers want their bosses and coworkers to treat them like everyone else. Open and honest communication is the best policy.[53]

The cost of making "reasonable accommodations" to employ the disabled is to be paid for by the employer. However, there is often no cost and the average cost is only $120; in addition, the government gives a tax credit of up to $5,000 to help pay the costs. Some firms, including Starbucks, are reaching out to employees and customers with disabilities.

ADA legislation states that reasonable accommodation "may include such areas as job restructuring, part-time or flexible work schedules, acquisition or modification of equipment or devices, the provision of readers or interpreters, and other similar actions." American and Canadian employers who need help in assisting the disabled can obtain information by phone from the President's Committee on Employment of the Handicapped (PCEH). The committee has a Job Accommodation Network (JAN) that provides free information on how new technologies can help as well as names and phone numbers of employers who have successfully developed programs of accommodation. In Canada, call voice or TDD, 1-800-526-2262; in the United States (except West Virginia), call voice or TDD, 1-800-526-7234; in West Virginia, call voice or TDD, 1-800-526-4698; the commercial phone number is 1-304-293-7186.

Alcohol and Drug Abuse and Testing   Since October 1986, when the government began to administer drug tests, drug abuse has been given much attention. According to Partnership for a Drug-Free America, one in six Americans has a substance abuse problem. Six out of ten people say they know of someone who has gone to work under the influence of drugs or alcohol. Substance abuse has been estimated to cost American businesses over $86 billion annually in lost productivity, absenteeism, and health care costs.[54] Complete Self-Assessment Exercise 15–1 to see if you may have a potential substance abuse problem.

To help prevent drug abuse, the Federal Drug-Free Workplace Act of 1988 was enacted. Drug testing is on the increase in both the private and public sectors. Almost three-fourths (74.5 percent) of 1,200 companies surveyed said they test employees for drugs. More big companies than small ones test for substances, and more blue-collar than white-collar employees are tested.

Self-Assessment Exercise 15–1

Your Use of Substances

For each of the following statements, select the number from 1 to 5 that best describes the frequency of your actual substance (alcohol or drug) use. Place the number on the line before each statement. You will not be asked to share this information in class.

(5) Usually   (4) Frequently   (3) Occasionally   (2) Seldom   (1) Rarely

_____ 1. I take substances in the morning.

_____ 2. I take substances to calm my nerves or to forget about worries or pressure.

_____ 3. I go to work/school under the influence of substances or take them during work/school hours.

Self-Assessment Exercise 15–1 (*continued*)

_____ 4. I take substances when I'm alone.

_____ 5. I lie about my substance use.

_____ 6. I drive under the influence of substances.

_____ 7. I wake up and don't remember what I did under the influence of substances.

_____ 8. I do things under the influence of substances that I would not do without them.

_____ 9. I'm late for work/school because of substance use.

_____ 10. I miss work/school as a result of substance use.

_____ 11. I take substances to help me sleep.

_____ 12. I've had financial difficulties due to substances.

_____ 13. My friends take substances.

_____ 14. I plan activities around being able to use substances.

_____ 15. When I'm not under the influence of substances, I think about taking them.

_____ Total

Your score will range from 15 to 75. To determine the degree to which you have a substance problem, mark the point that represents your total score on the continuum below.

No substance abuse   15 - - - - 30 - - - - 45 - - - - 60 - - - - 75   Substance abuse

If you do have a substance abuse problem, you should seek professional help.

WORK APPLICATIONS

6. Have you ever seen any employees under the influence of alcohol or drugs at work? How did their substance use affect their ability to work?

7. How do you feel about drug testing by employers? Why do you feel this way?

AIDS and AIDS Testing   Human immunodeficiency virus (HIV) is the virus that causes AIDS. Acquired immune deficiency syndrome (AIDS) is the name for the condition that occurs after HIV has gradually destroyed a person's immune system, making the person prone to life-threatening infections. AIDS is not a disease affecting only homosexuals; 40 percent of all reported cases have occurred among heterosexuals. According to the World Health Organization (WHO), half of the newly infected adults are women.

A person with HIV or AIDS is protected from discrimination under the ADA of 1990 and the Rehabilitation Act of 1973. In 1987, the federal government unveiled a policy barring discrimination against federal government workers who have AIDS. It also authorizes discipline for those who refuse to work with AIDS patients. The ADA approach to contagious diseases is the same as its approach to drug and alcohol abuse. Employers may adopt a standard that disqualifies persons who currently have a contagious disease if they pose a "direct threat to the health or safety of other individuals in the workplace."

There is agreement on the four major ways the AIDS virus is transmitted: (1) through sex, (2) through shared hypodermic needles, (3) by an infected mother to a fetus, and (4) through blood transfusions. Most medical authorities state that the virus is not transmitted through casual contact. Therefore, there is no risk to coworkers or the public from normal social or work contact with an HIV-infected person.

The national Centers for Disease Control (CDC) has a 24-hour AIDS hotline to assist any manager or employee who desires information about AIDS. The hotline has Spanish speakers and a TDD for deaf callers. The hotline number is 1-800-342-AIDS. The CDC also helps sponsor managing- and valuing-diversity programs through a program called "Business Responds to AIDS." The CDC will help establish workplace AIDS policies, train managers to deal with infected employees, educate workers and their families, and encourage community service.

In some states, including California, Wisconsin, and Florida, it is illegal for employers to test for AIDS. Testing is of questionable use because the test does not reveal whether the individual has AIDS—only whether the individual has been exposed to the AIDS virus. If an employer refuses to hire an employee with AIDS, it may be vulnerable to a charge of disability discrimination.

W O R K   A P P L I C A T I O N S

8. How would you feel about working with a person who has AIDS? Why?

Sexual Orientation   A newcomer to the list of diversity groups is based on sexual orientation. *Homophobia* (an aversion to homosexuals) is the term used to refer to discrimination based on a person's sexual orientation. In most situations, companies are not responsible for determining right and wrong behavior off the job. However, all organizations are responsible for providing all workers with an environment that is safe and free of threats, intimidation, harassment, and, especially, violence.[55]

The federal EEOC law that protects against being not hired for or being discharged from a job because of sexual orientation does not offer protection for gays and lesbians. For example, the U.S. military still discriminates against homosexuals. Some states, however, have enacted laws that do protect gays and lesbians from job discrimination. The state of Vermont was the first to legalize not a marriage, but a similar civil union, between gays and lesbians. The state of Massachusetts was the first to legalize homosexual marriage. In California, on the other hand, the court ruled to allow same-sex marriage, but the citizens voted to overturn the court order. However, other states are not required to recognize these marriages and provide marriage benefits. Some states have passed laws to prohibit same-sex marriage. Some government, nonprofit, and private organizations extend medical and other benefits to gay and lesbian partners, as well as unmarried heterosexual partners living together. Some companies, including AT&T, Walt Disney, Polaroid, Lotus, and Xerox, are combating homophobia in the workplace.

Sexual Harassment

Learning Outcome

5. List the six areas of sexual harassment.

Women are a legally protected group. The most common issues that prompt sex discrimination complaints, in order by numbers of cases, are discharge, terms and condition of employment, sexual harassment, wages, pregnancy, promotion, hiring, and intimidation and reprisals. Sexual harassment is one of the most sensitive areas of discrimination because it is often a matter of personal judgment. Sexual harassment charges can be made against either sex; however, the vast majority of cases are against men. Same-sex harassment is also a problem.[56]

Until 25 years ago, there was no label for actions that today are considered sexual harassment. However, it has become an important social and legal concern, and managing sexual harassment at work is important. Although many firms are training workers to avoid sexual harassment, researchers have reported that a high percentage of women have been victims of sexual harassment at work.[57] Part of the problem is that people observe sexual harassment and don't report it because they don't believe their organizations encourage them to do so, or because complaints fall on deaf ears since organizations lack policies and procedures to resolve the problems. For example, Mitsubishi Motors of America had a long history of harassment complaints, but it wasn't until the company was taken to court that strong action was taken. The number of sexual harassment cases taken to the EEOC continues to increase.

The most frequent harassment targets are new employees, people who are on probation in their jobs, and the young and inexperienced. People who have recently experienced a personal crisis, such as separation or divorce, are frequently victims. Women in traditionally male jobs are also more subject to sexual harassment.

Behaviors considered to be sexual harassment by some are not considered harassment by others. To help people know if they have been sexually harassed, the EEOC has defined the term *sexual harassment* as follows: Unwelcome sexual advances, requests for sexual favors, and other unwanted verbal or physical conduct of a sexual nature constitute sexual harassment when (1) submission to such conduct is made either explicitly or implicitly a term or condition of an individual's employment, (2) submission to or rejection of such conduct by an individual is used as the basis for employment decisions affecting such individual, or (3) such conduct has the purpose or effect of unreasonably interfering with an individual's work performance or creating an intimidating, hostile, or offensive environment.[58]

The federal and state courts have defined sexual harassment in six areas as grounds for lawsuits:

1. *Unwelcome sexual advances.* An employee who is repeatedly propositioned by a supervisor or coworker trying to establish an intimate relationship, on or off the job, may sue for sexual harassment even if not overtly threatened.

2. *Coercion.* An employee whose supervisor asks for a date or sexual favor with the stated or unstated understanding that a favor will be bestowed, or a reprisal made, may sue for sexual harassment.

3. *Favoritism.* Courts have ruled that an employer is liable when employees who submit to sexual favors are rewarded, while others who refuse are denied promotions or benefits. One federal court ruled that an employee who wasn't asked for sexual favors, while others were, was a victim of sexual harassment.

4. *Indirect harassment.* Employees who witness sexual harassment on the job can sue even if they are not victims. In a California state court, a nurse complained that a doctor grabbed other nurses in full view of her, causing an environment of sexual harassment.

5. *Physical conduct.* Employees don't have to be touched. Courts have ruled that unseemly gestures may constitute harassment and create a hostile work environment.

6. *Visual harassment.* Courts have ruled that graffiti written on men's bathroom walls about a female employee is sexual harassment. The pervasive display of nude or pornographic pictures also constitutes sexual harassment.

To keep it simple, DuPont tells its people, "It's harassment when something starts bothering somebody." For our purposes, **sexual harassment** *is any unwelcomed behavior of a sexual nature.*

When people find themselves in a sexual harassment situation, they often feel overwhelmed, confused, unproductive, afraid, alone, and unable to find the words to confront the harasser.[59] Some workable responses to the harasser, which can be revised to suit the offense, are as follows:

"I am uncomfortable when you touch me. Don't do it again or I will report you for sexual harassment."

"It is inappropriate for you to show me sexually graphic material. Don't do it again."

"I am uncomfortable with off-color jokes. Don't tell one to me again or I will report you for sexual harassment."

If the behavior is very serious, you may want to report the first offense. If it is less serious, a warning may be given before reporting the offense. If the behavior is repeated, report the offense to your boss or some other authority in the organization. If the people in authority do not take suitable action to stop the harassment, take the complaint to the EEOC.[60]

In the opening case, a woman complained about a male supervisor making sexual advances. Do you think that was sexual harassment?

WORK APPLICATIONS

9. Have you, or has anyone you know, been sexually harassed? If so, describe the situation(s) (use language acceptable to everyone).

10. How do you feel about the fact that certain groups are legally protected against discrimination?

APPLICATION SITUATIONS

Sexual Harassment

AS 15–3

Identify whether each behavior described below is:

A. Sexual harassment   B. Not sexual harassment

_____ 11. Ted tells Clair she is sexy and he'd like to take her out on a date.

_____ 12. Sue tells José he will have to go to a motel with her if he wants to get the job.

_____ 13. Jean's legs are sticking out into the walkway. As Wally goes by, he steps over them and says, "Nice legs."

_____ 14. For the third time, after being politely told no, Pat says to Chris, "You have a real nice (*fill in the missing sexual words for yourself*). Why don't you and I XXXX?"

_____ 15. Ray puts his hand on Lisa's shoulder as he talks to her.

The next section continues the discussion of how women are discriminated against in the workplace.

SEXISM, RACISM, AND WORK AND FAMILY BALANCE

Learning Outcome

6. Explain sexism in organizations and ways to overcome it.

Sexism *refers to discrimination based on sex.* Sexism limits the opportunities of both women and men to choose the lifestyles and careers that best suit their abilities and interests.[61] Men and women face discrimination when they pursue careers traditionally held by the opposite sex. Males still dominate the construction trades and women, the field of nursing, for example. Stereotyping men and women hurts not only the individuals who dare to be different but also the organization, and it holds both back from achieving their full potential.[62]

Culture promotes differences in males and females. Children learn these values by the age of 10. Traditional thinking states that men are aggressive and unemotional, and women are emotional and weak. Men and women will always be different, but their roles can and should be equal.[63] Meanwhile, traditional roles are changing. Similar to sexism, racism is discrimination based on race.

This section examines women in the workforce, minority managers, overcoming sexism and racism, changing sex roles, and work and family balance. Before reading on, determine your attitude toward women at work by completing Self-Assessment Exercise 15–2.

Each of the 10 statements is a commonly held attitude about women at work. However, they have all been shown to be myths through research conducted by various people. Throughout this section, research disproving these attitudes will be cited. There are always exceptions to the rule. However, if you have a negative attitude toward women at work, you are stereotyping them unfairly.[64] You may want to work at changing your negative attitude. Negative stereotypes hold women back from gaining salary increases and promotions to management positions, despite efforts in the areas of EEO, AA, and valuing diversity.[65]

Your Attitude toward Women at Work

For each of the following 10 statements, select the response that best describes your honest belief about women at work. Place the number 1, 2, 3, or 4 on the line before each statement.

(1) Strongly agree   (2) Agree   (3) Disagree   (4) Strongly disagree

——— 1. Women work to earn extra money.

——— 2. Women are out of work more often than men.

——— 3. Women quit work or take long maternity leaves when they have children.

——— 4. Women have a lower commitment to work than men.

——— 5. Women lack motivation to get ahead.

——— 6. Women are not as good at problem solving as men.

——— 7. The increasing number of women in the workforce has caused rising unemployment among men.

——— 8. Women are not strong enough or emotionally stable enough to succeed in high-pressure jobs.

——— 9. Women are too emotional to be effective managers.

——— 10. Women managers have difficulty in situations calling for quick and precise decisions.

——— Total

To determine your attitude score, add your 10 answers and place that number on the total line. On the continuum below, mark the point that represents your total score.

Negative attitude   10 - - - - - - 20 - - - - - - 30 - - - - - - 40   Positive attitude

Women in the Workforce

We now discuss *women in the workforce* as opposed to *working women*. Women who elect to work as homemakers make a great contribution to society.[66] Unfortunately, these women are not commonly referred to as *working women* because they are not rewarded monetarily for their work. However, every female homemaker is a working woman.

How Many Women Are in the Workforce, and Why Are They Employed? Of the labor force 16 years and older, 53.4 percent of males and 49.3 percent of women have jobs.[67] Of married couples with children under the age of 18, 63 percent of both parents work.[68]

Women work for many different reasons, but they can generally be classified by economic necessity and self-concept needs. With the marriage rate of 50.4 percent and the increase in single-parent households headed mostly by women,[69] women work because of economic necessity. Married women contribute 25 to 50 percent of the household income on average, and women's income is critical to the support of the family. In general, women today want both a job and a family, as they are motivated to meet their needs for achievement and affiliation (Chapter 9). Actually, economic and self-concept needs are so highly intertwined that they usually can't be separated.

Do Men and Women Get the Same Pay? Because of the Equal Pay Act, which is over 30 years old, women and men doing the exact same job generally do get paid the same. However, overall, a woman's average earnings are less than those of a man.[70] The median income for men and women is $41,965 and $32,168, respectively.[71] However, the pay difference is not caused simply by discrimination; women tend to work in jobs with lower pay, such as child-care, education, and clerical work.[72] But discrimination is partly to blame for salary disparities, especially in management positions.[73]

Sleepless in Seattle or Sexism in the City: Neither Story Ends Well for Boeing

When W. James (Jim) McNerney, Jr., became the chair and CEO of Boeing Commercial Airplane Group, he wasn't warned by the world's leading aerospace company and the largest manufacturer of commercial jetliners and military aircraft of what was to come. Not even his staff had given him fair warning before a problem hit the court's radar. More than 20,000 current and former female employees out of a potential pool of 29,000 said Boeing discriminated against them at Seattle-area plants. According to company documents obtained by the plaintiffs, women typically earned $1,000 to $2,000 less each year than men for similar jobs—a disparity magnified over time by the company's policy of calculating pay raises based on an employee's salary.

This revelation must have been quite shocking to the new CEO, given Boeing's corporate values and ethical standards. Boeing seemed quite committed to its ethical standards in that it conducted three mandatory and educational activities annually as reminders of its commitment to ethics and business conduct standards. Furthermore, the company's policy on equal employment opportunity prohibited discrimination in all terms and conditions of employment.

What might be more shocking to CEO McNerney than Boeing's apparent hypocrisy? Why, the loss of government contracts for lack of compliance with federal regulations, not to mention the negative press. The only question left for the new CEO was how he was going to make this whole mess fly away. The solution was to settle out of court, paying $72.5 million.

Questions

1. Which common area of employment discrimination does this ethical dilemma highlight?

2. Referring to affirmative action, equal opportunity employment, and comparable worth, define the problem that this ethical dilemma highlights.

3. Presumably, Boeing values the diversity of its workforce. What additional measures does Boeing need to take to ensure that its values are implemented?

4. If you were CEO McNerney, what actions would you take now to ensure equal opportunity for all at Boeing? Why?

Source: Boeing Web site, www.boeing.com, retrieved November 19, 2008.

Comparable Worth   The term **comparable worth** *applies to jobs that are distinctly different but require similar levels of ability and have the same pay scale.* Comparable worth advocates want traditional women's jobs, such as secretaries, to be paid comparable to men's jobs, such as electricians, when they require the same ability. A woman in the opening case complained that men in the shop are paid more than women in the office. People opposed to comparable worth claim that it is the supply and demand for labor that sets the pay rates, not discrimination against women.

Comparable worth has received much attention from certain women's groups, with mixed support from government agencies and the courts. The issue was tabled by the Civil Rights Commission in 1984 as unenforceable. However, women are gaining access to higher-paying professions, including doctors, lawyers, and accountants. But teachers will most likely never earn as much as the other professionals, even though many of them have as much education.

WORK APPLICATIONS

11. How do you feel about making comparable worth a law? Why?

Women and Minority Managers

Myths about Women Managers   Two old myths about women managers are that they will leave the job to have children and that they are too emotional to be managers. Statistics show that women stay on the job. An eight-year study of male and female managers found virtually identical psychological and emotional profiles between the sexes. On all the variables that have to do with good leadership, men and women as a group show no major differences.[74] Men and women are truly equal in management ability. Another popular myth is that women are not as committed to the organization as men; research supports that they are equally committed.[75]

How Women Are Progressing in Management and the Glass Ceiling   Today's successful women managers realize that they do not have to act like men and become "one of the boys" to get ahead. They feel free to be, well, women; they are confident about their business and management skills and are not shy about showing it. Women who perceive they will have problems managing solely because of their sex may be creating a self-fulfilling prophecy. Management is about developing strong relationships, and women are very effective at developing unique relationships with each employee.[76]

Women hold half of the management and professional jobs in the United States, but they hold only 2.4 percent of the CEO positions in Fortune 500 companies,[77] and boardrooms remain almost exclusively the domain of white males, as only 16 percent of board members are women.[78] Also, compared with married men with children, women advance more slowly.[79] In global management representation, women are underrepresented in management. The lack of women and minorities getting into top-level management positions is known as the *glass ceiling,* an invisible barrier to advancement based on bias. The United States has a federal Glass Ceiling Commission to eliminate the problem, but progress has been very slow.

How Minorities Are Progressing in Management and Professional Jobs   Here are comparisons by race:[80]

- African Americans make up 14 percent of the U.S. workforce, but they hold only 6.5 percent of the management jobs and 8 percent of professional jobs.

- Hispanics make up 11 percent of the workforce, but they hold only 5 percent of the management jobs and 4 percent of professional jobs.

- Asian/Pacific Islanders make up 5 percent of the workforce, and they hold 4 percent of the management jobs and 9 percent of professional jobs.

- By contrast, Caucasians make up 70 percent of the workforce, and they hold 84.5 percent of the management jobs and 80 percent of professional jobs.

Minorities are making slow progress into management and professional level jobs. However, their progress has not been rapid enough to make a significant change in the distribution of those jobs. At the same time, many minorities are leaving corporate America to become entrepreneurs. Some leave due to frustration with their lack of progress in management and others leave to be their own bosses and to reap the profits of their work.

African Americans and Hispanics tend to be concentrated in the lower-wage service-sector jobs. Clearly their level of education is a factor keeping them out of professional and management jobs. Some minorities think that the best legal road to prosperity is professional sports. Sports careers are a good route, but the odds of becoming a doctor—or other higher salary professional including lawyer, accountant, or engineer—are much better than making it to a professional sports team. Education also keeps athletes with the ability to play college and professional sports from doing so. Clearly, we need to do a better job of educating all students and making more of an effort to help them advance.

Advancement   Some industries have been more receptive than others to advancing women and minorities. For example, certain industries, including consumer products, financial services, retail, publishing, and media, and certain nonprofit and government sectors, such as health care and education, have more women and minorities in management.[81]

Research has revealed two advancement-related traits: having a strong desire to advance and focusing on getting the job done or solving the problem. Although education and technical knowledge and skills allow entry into lower management, networks and subjective social factors allow advancement to higher levels of management, which is a disadvantage for women and minorities who can't get into the right networks to break the glass ceiling. A good predictor of a woman's advancement to higher levels of management is career encouragement. As we discussed in Chapter 11, networking is critical to advancement. Having a good mentor who can give you career encouragement and get you into the right networks is also helpful. Do you have the aspiration to climb the corporate ladder, and are you willing to network and get a mentor to help your advancement?

WORK APPLICATIONS

12. How do you feel about having a female boss? Why?

APPLICATION SITUATIONS

Women

AS 15–4

Identify each of the following statements about women as:

A. Fact   B. Myth

_____ 16. "Men make better managers than women."

_____ 17. "Women work because they need the money."

_____ 18. "Male managers are more committed to their jobs than female managers."

_____ 19. "Female managers are viewed as more caring for the individual subordinate than male managers."

_____ 20. "About one out of every three managers is female."

Overcoming Sexism and Racism

Hiring and promotion decisions should not be based on sex, though affirmative action plans may be implemented.

Sexist and Racist Language and Behavior   Men and women should avoid using sexist and racist language. Sexist words such as *mailman* and *salesman* should be replaced with non-sexist terms such as *letter carrier* and *salesperson*. In written communication, the use of *he or she* is appropriate, but don't overuse it. Use neutral language and plurals—*supervisors* rather than *the supervisor*, which tends to end up needing a *he or she* as writing progresses. Avoid racist terms and jokes.

Call people by name, rather than by sexist and racist terms. Working women are not girls and should not be called *girls* because this word is used to describe children, not grown women. Working men are not boys, so avoid such racist terms.

Be wary of swearing in the workplace; it is preferable not to use such language. What is really gained through swearing? Are you impressed by people who swear? Are people who do not swear pressured to do so at work?

If anyone uses language that offends you or others, assertively state your feelings about the words used. Many times, people do not use sexist and racist language intentionally and will not use it if they are requested not to. If it continues, however, report the harassment.[82]

Many working men are becoming more sensitive to sexism because they have wives and daughters entering the workforce for whom they want equal opportunities. Exhibit 15.3 illustrates negative sexist stereotyping that needs to be eliminated. Such stereotypes are a barrier to women's breaking the glass ceiling.

In the opening case, there is negative sexist talk. Can these men and women change their attitudes and learn to value diversity?

EXHIBIT 15.3 | A Sexist (Stereotypical) Way to Tell a Businessman from a Businesswoman

Man	Woman
A businessman is aggressive.	A businesswoman is pushy.
He is careful about details.	She's picky.
He loses his temper because he's so involved in his job.	She's bitchy.
He's depressed (or hung over), so everyone tiptoes past his office.	She's moody, so it must be her time of the month.
He follows through.	She doesn't know when to quit.
He's firm.	She's stubborn.
He makes wise judgments.	She reveals her prejudices.
He is a man of the world.	She's been around.
He isn't afraid to say what he thinks.	She's opinionated.
He exercises authority.	She's tyrannical.
He's discreet.	She's secretive.
He's a stern taskmaster.	She's difficult to work for.

How Family Sex Roles Are Changing

The traditional family in which the husband works and the wife doesn't work outside the home is no longer the pattern in the majority of American households. Two-income marriages became the norm back in 1994. Single-parent households now outnumber all other types of households.[83]

Recall the total person approach, which holds that our personal family life affects our work life. If we can have a happier family life, we can also have a happier work life.[84] We will discuss some important family issues that may help improve your family life. For example, people yearn to better understand what makes a successful marriage.[85] So, start with Self-Assessment Exercise 15–3 to check your knowledge of the facts about marriage.

Self-Assessment Exercise 15–3

Your Marriage Knowledge

Answer each question true or false by circling its letter.

T F   1. People prefer a mate who matches them in education, class, religious background, ethnicity, and age.

T F   2. About half of marriages end in divorce.

T F   3. Living together before marriage decreases the chances of getting divorced.

T F   4. Having a baby before marriage increases the chances of getting divorced.

T F   5. Getting married young (under 18 years old vs. 25) increases the chances of getting divorced.

T F   6. Compared to people with some college, high-school dropouts have a higher divorce rate.

T F   7. Most divorces happen in the seventh year—the seven-year itch.

T F   8. Couples who are very unhappy should get divorced so they will be happier in future years.

T F   9. People who go through the stress of divorce and its aftermath have health effects that may not show up until years later.

T F 10. Compared to those who are happily married, people who get divorced have more health problems and symptoms of depression.

T F 11. Compared to those who are happily married, people who get divorced smoke and drink more.

T F 12. Workaholics have a higher divorce rate than nonworkaholics.

T F 13. Arguing is helpful to a marriage.

T F 14. Couples don't need to agree and solve all their problems.

T F 15. Couples that go to church/pray together have a lower divorce rate than those that don't—the family that prays together stays together.

To determine your marriage knowledge, count the number of correct answers, using the answer key below, and place your score here:

Knowledgeable   15 14 13 12 11 10 9 8 7 6 5 4 3 2 1   Not Knowledgeable

Answers[86]

1. True. The statement that "like attracts like" is factual.

2. True. Since the mid-1960s around half of marriages in any given year end in divorce.

3. False. Couples who live together are 50 percent more likely to get divorced. They tend to have a renter's agreement attitude that makes them less committed to sticking around through the hard times that just about all marriages go through.

4. True. People who have babies before marriage (compared to seven months or more afterward) have a 24 percent higher divorce rate.

5. True. The divorce rate is 24 percent higher for people under 18 than for those 25 or more years old.

6. True. High school dropouts have a 13 percent higher divorce rate than those with some college.

7. False. Most divorces occur in the fourth year.

8. False. Of couples that divorced, 50 percent were "happy" five years later. Of couples that were "very unhappy" but stayed together, 80 percent were "happy" five years later.

9. True. Research supports the fact that stress from divorce can show up years later.

10. True. Compared to those who get divorced, research supports the fact that people who are happily married say they are in better health, have fewer chronic health problems, and retain greater mobility in middle age.

11. True. Research supports the fact that divorced people smoke and drink more than happily married people.

12. True. According to Workaholics Anonymous, divorce is common.

13. True. Open-minded fair fighting often leads to resolving conflicts in any relationship. So use your conflict skills (Chapter 7) in your personal relationships.

14. True. Most successful couples never agree and solve all their problems—they outlast them through the marital endurance ethics. Have you heard the expression, "You don't want to go there" in discussions? Avoiding some less important issues helps couples stay together.

15. True. The divorce rate for church/praying couples is significantly lower, and they have better health than those who don't pray.

Marriage and Family Agreements   Before entering marriage, it is very helpful to discuss and agree on career and family plans and the distribution of household and child-care responsibilities.[87] In fact, some couples are creating family plan prenuptial agreements. These agreements are not legal documents; they are simply written lists of items relating to future family and work issues. Such lists might include these plans: We will have two children; the lower-income earner will switch to part-time work to stay home with the kids until they are in school; if the primary breadwinner is laid off, the other spouse will try to make more money; we will not transfer locations for a job while the kids are in school. However, couples must realize the need to be flexible. After having one child, the couple might change the number of children wanted, and after holding and spending time with a newborn, the father's or mother's desire to stay home or go to work can change.[88] For help talking over these issues, three organizations offer premarital exercises: Foccus, Omaha, Nebraska, at 1-877-883-5422; Life Innovations, Roseville, Minnesota, at www.lifeinnovations.com; and Relate Institute, Provo, Utah, at http://relate.byu.edu. For help making a good marriage even better, there is Worldwide Engaged Encounter and Worldwide Marriage Encounter, at www.wwme.org and 1-800-710-WWME.

Although dual-career couples generally agree to split the household and child-care responsibilities evenly, most husbands often spend less time than their wives do in these areas.[89] Some couples elect the split shift, in which one parent does household work while the other works outside the home, to avoid having to make child-care arrangements. However, this results in more time alone, as ships passing.[90]

Fathers' Roles Are Changing   In the old days, most fathers worked long hours and spent little time with their children. Today, research has clearly found that fathers are important in child care.[91] Dads' interactions with their infants and toddlers influence the way their kids relate later to other people and the world at large, and the father's influence can be more powerful than the mother's.[92] Children who were not close to their fathers at age five were more anxious and withdrawn and less self-confident at age nine. They were less likely to be warmly accepted by their peer group and well-adjusted at school. Although there are many reasons people are criminals, one contributing factor is the father's influence—or lack thereof. Fathers play an important role in criminal activity; most criminals have no real relationship with their fathers. Most males in jail don't know who their father is or have no relationship with him. In some cases, a father–child relationship virtually ends with divorce, but it doesn't have to. It's usually a choice fathers make.

Getting married and having children actually does bring about positive changes in a man's life.[93] Today's father is spending more time with his children. However, it is not as much time as the mother spends, even when both parents work the same number of hours. What some parents who work long hours are doing is coming home for dinner and/or bedtime to spend time with their children and then returning to work, usually at home, when the kids are in bed. Some others get up early to spend time with their children before going to work. More fathers routinely stay home to care for their sick children, take them to visit the doctor, and give them medicine.[94] More fathers are also taking advantage of the Family Leave Act of 1993, which allows up to 12 weeks of unpaid leave to care for a family member, but employees are cutting back on pay and time off.[95]

As discussed, in approximately 5 percent of married couples, only the mother works. As moms earn more, more dads are staying home to take care of the children. Like moms, some fathers work part-time or run their own businesses out of the house, and they do return to full-time work when the children get older. The "gender flip" sometimes comes as the result of a layoff or because the wife can make more money than the husband. But there are also more fathers who prefer to stay home with their children. People who have made the gender flip say it does require plenty of planning and discussion, ongoing communication, and marital troubleshooting skills to make it work. Like men in traditional women's jobs, the father needs a positive self-concept to put up with the potential peer pressure to go back to work.

Mothers' Roles Are Changing   In the old days, most mothers stayed home and took care of the children. Today, as discussed, mothers work outside the home. Mothers who do leave the labor force full-time tend to go back in increasing numbers as the children get older.

Working   So the question today is not, Will most mothers work outside the home? The question is, Will she leave work to raise children, and if so, for how long? More mothers are taking maternity leave under the Family Leave Act to spend up to 12 weeks at home with their newborns.[96] To know your legal rights, and for help getting leave, contact the Labor Department Wage and Hour Division at www.wageandhour.dol.gov and the Job

Survival Hotline, operated from 9 to 5 by the National Association of Working Women, at 1-800-522-0925.

Work at Home or in the Labor Force?   An ongoing debate has been called the war between staying at home (or working part-time) versus working outside the home and the good mother–bad mother debate. More women are in fact staying have with their children.[97] Unfortunately, many mothers who decide, for whatever reason, to stay home with the kids or to work outside the home get pressured and are made to feel guilty for the role they have chosen. For example, stay-at-home moms are asked questions like these: "Do you work or do you stay home and take it easy?" "Don't you have a job?" Moms working outside are asked questions like these: "Don't you love your kids?" "Don't you want to be with your kids?"

Why can't we all just let moms, and dads, make their own decisions about where they work? Let's all make an effort to stop judgmental questions and to stop making moms, and dads, feel guilty. Let's congratulate them and make them feel good about their choices and about themselves! As workers, all moms and dads need praise for a job well done. Remember, valuing diversity is about letting people live their own lives. So let's also not pressure people to get married, to have children, or to have more or fewer children than they want.

For the stay-at-home mom, two good resources are www.athomemothers.com for motherhood lifestyle and www.familyandhome.org for tips on transitioning from work to home. For the mom in the workforce, two good resources are www.momsrefuge.com for information on juggling work and family and www.workingmommall.com for strategies to simplify parenting.

Stay-at-Home Moms Need to Plan   Firms are cutting maternity leave pay,[98] and more mothers are happily staying home with their children.[99] On the downside, most women who stay home do diminish their pay (they may not have any and may get less when they return to work) and may miss chances for advancement. Women who stop working to raise kids and then jump back into the workforce need to plan for that circumstance. Career plans can include taking a hiatus to raise kids.[100] When planning a career, try to select and develop portable skills with lots of job openings, such as teaching, and careers that offer good-paying, part-time jobs, such as nursing, accounting, and law, so that you can keep up in your field. Consider starting your own home business; women-owned businesses have increased over the past five years. You can also consider a "hot" occupation, but that choice can be risky. Recall the rise and retrenchment in the dot-com sector.

Parenting   Parenting can be stressful; 67 percent of new parents experience a drop in marital satisfaction after the baby is born, and the stress can spill over onto the baby and the job.[101] If we can avoid stressful parenting, we can better manage the stress at home and work.[102] Children's basic personalities are developed during the first five years of life and affect them all their lives. Here are two simple guidelines to help develop a child's personality with a positive self-concept:[103]

- *Engage in sensitive play.* Touch and hold children, and talk in a way they can understand. Stimulate and encourage them by making appealing suggestions for play. Refrain from unnecessary criticism; the "give more praise than criticism" rule is even more important for children than for employees. Remember that they are children— tell them they are smart and capable, help them when they need it, and praise their accomplishments.

- *Develop a warm, loving bond.* Children need to feel secure and know they are loved; sensitive play helps. Reading to children during these preschool years is a form of play that also helps academic performance in school; the more reading and less TV watching, the better the academic performance. Reading when putting children to bed and talking about their day is a great way to bond. It is much easier to bond and stay close when the child is young than to develop a relationship when they are school-age.[104]

Good child care has its benefits, but it can be costly, and you tend to get what you pay for with professional day care.[105] Child care costs can be 25 percent or more of a young couple's annual income, even for college grads.

Work and Family Balance

In today's reengineered, reorganized, and downsized companies, the employees who remain are being asked to work longer hours, to work more days each week, and to maintain that pace for longer uninterrupted periods. Work is straining families.[106] Parents are feeling guilty about using child care and about not getting home for dinner to eat as a family; they want to spend more time at home.[107] People are searching for fulfillment. Exhausted from nonstop work, many people realize their life is out of balance.[108]

Both men and women are feeling conflict between work and family. Work–family conflict has been defined as a form of interrole conflict in which the role pressures from the work and family are incompatible in some respect, participation in the work (family) role is made more difficult by participation in the family (work) role, and the strain and demand of one's work role spills over into one's family and personal role. Work–family conflict is not as bad for a workaholic, but it is worse for his or her family, and the conflict often results in divorce.[109]

Men and women want a better balance between work and family, with a stable family life.[110] As noted earlier, researchers have shown that the most important years of a person's life are ages 0–5, because this is when one's personality is developed. Many parents want to be around to shape their children's personalities. Tired of long work hours and short family hours, what job candidates really want to know is: Will I have a life? Many men between the ages of 20 and 39 are electing the daddy track; a "family-friendly" schedule is their most important job criterion.[111] And, as discussed, some moms are staying home.

Work and family balance has become so important that *Fortune, BusinessWeek,* and *Working Mother* publish lists of best places to work. Companies compete with each other to earn a place on the list and use their placements as recruiting tools.[112]

Next, we discuss family-friendly and other policies that organizations are using to help employees satisfy their work–life needs.

MANAGING DIVERSITY

In the old days, family-friendly policies (also called *work–family policies* and *work–life benefits*) were not an issue. Family men were expected to have wives who worked at home so the employee could devote his full attention to the job. As the traditional family decreased in number, it was then expected that employees would leave their family issues at home and devote their full attention to the job. Today, employers understand the total person approach and that career satisfaction affects organizational commitment, turnover, and support for organizational change, and that satisfaction with the work–family balance clearly affects career satisfaction.[113] Many organizations believe that providing family-friendly benefits helps motivate employees to work harder in return for the "extra" benefits.[114] Some of the many benefits don't even cost the employer anything, such as flexible working hours and on-site child care that employees pay for. Employees like being able to work around their children's schedules; they appreciate the convenience of on-site child care and enjoy being close to their children while at work.[115] Research supports that organizations with more extensive work–family policies have higher levels of perceived performance.[116] Let's face it; businesses don't just give things away. Many businesses believe in the goal of human relations, so they are giving work–family benefits because they are also benefiting.

However, managing diversity is not just about family-friendly benefits. *Managing diversity* emphasizes helping *all* employees meet their work–life needs, or improving the quality of work and life.[117] Many organizations are offering work–life benefits packages that let the employees choose the benefits they want; these packages are also called *cafeteria benefits.* For example, one employee may select a child-care benefit, another a membership at a local gym, life insurance, or more money in a retirement account.

In addition to the many standard benefits, such as health care and retirement, here are some of the many work–life benefits being offered (the first two items describe flexible work arrangements):

- *Telecommuting,* letting employees work at home; *telecenters,* working at remote locations; and *mobile work,* working from anywhere with a laptop and cellular telephone to communicate with the office.

- *Flextime,* which allows employees to set, within limits, their starting and ending times, and sometimes to determine which days to work and which days to take off and the number of hours to work (for example, five 8-hour days or four 10-hour days). Within flextime, some organizations allow employees to take a few hours off during the day for personal reasons, such as attending a child's school activity, as long as they make up the hours.

- *Work–life,* or cafeteria, *benefits,* as discussed above.

- *Child care,* on-site or at nearby centers. This can include financial assistance and help finding child care. Some firms pay for sick child care so the employee can work. Some people are calling for a significant national child care program to cut individual costs.

- *Work–life balance classes,* to learn techniques to improve the quality of life.

- *Wellness programs,* at a company-owned facility. These programs can include payment of all or part of the cost to join a health club as well as diet and nutrition and smoking-cessation programs.

- *Tuition reimbursement,* paying all or part of educational expenses. If you want to get an advanced degree, you may want to work for a company that offers this benefit.

- *Employee assistance programs.* These programs offer professional counseling for personal, family, and/or substance abuse problems.

Some of the many organizations that offer diversity programs and benefits are: Levi Strauss, McDonald's, Nestlé, Avon, Prudential, Hewlett-Packard, and LIMRA. Some companies, including AC Nielsen, are tying managers' bonuses partly to employee satisfaction scores on a wide range of issues, including work–life balance. Work and family balance and quality of life are also global concerns.[118]

GLOBAL DIVERSITY

Because globalization is the number one challenge to business leaders in the 21st century, we have been discussing it in every chapter. In this section we discuss more areas of global diversity and cross-cultural relations; we begin with multinational corporations.

Multinational Companies

Advances in technology have allowed the world to become smaller through rapid communication and travel.[119] Technology has made it practical to conduct business in more than one country, and competition has made it necessary for the survival of some firms.[120] As a result, countries are becoming more interdependent.[121] A **multinational company (MNC)** *conducts a large part of its business outside the country of its headquarters.*

MNCs link many cultures.[122] They operate in virtually every major country. Complete Self-Assessment Exercise 15–4 to determine if you know in which country each MNC is headquartered.

Self-Assessment Exercise 15–4

MNC Country of Ownership

For each item, select the country of ownership. If your answer is the United States, check the USA column. If it's another country, write in the name of that country.

Company/Brand Product	USA	Other; List Country
1. Shell gasoline	_____	_____
2. Nestlé candy	_____	_____
3. Unilever Dove soap	_____	_____
4. Prudential insurance	_____	_____
5. Barclays banking	_____	_____
6. LimeWire File sharing	_____	_____
7. CBS records	_____	_____
8. Aiwa stereos	_____	_____
9. Bayer aspirin	_____	_____
10. Kia cars	_____	_____
11. Nokia cameras	_____	_____
12. L'oréal facial products	_____	_____
13. Samsung stereos/phones	_____	_____

Answers:

1. The Netherlands (Royal Dutch/Shell)
2. Switzerland (Nestlé Swiss Chocolate)
3. England
4. England
5. England
6. South Korea
7. Japan
8. Japan
9. Germany
10. South Korea
11. Finland
12. France
13. South Korea

How many did you get correct? Place your score here _____.

One thing you should understand about MNCs is that the management functions of planning, organizing, leading, and controlling are essentially the same in all countries. Running an auto plant in Detroit is no different from running one in a European or Asian country. Good training of employees in these countries is almost exactly the same. It's the human relations that can be very different between workers, workers and managers, and levels of managers, as well as between employees and customers, suppliers, and people in other organizations.[123] So effective human relations do vary globally.[124] We will discuss more about the differences in cross-cultural human relations after we discuss expatriates, who have to deal with diversity.

Expatriates *are people who live and work in a country other than their native country.* Expatriates often experience culture shock, a state of confusion, and anxiety when they are first exposed to an unfamiliar culture. There are changes with any move, but the changes compound tremendously when the move is to another country. U.S. managers using traditional American management styles often fail in an overseas business culture because managing diversity goes well beyond business etiquette.[125] Companies need to train expatriates in language, local culture, and local business practices so they can be successful globally.[126] The trend today is to hire more local managers to run the company unit in their country.

Cross-Cultural Relations

Learning Outcome

7. List seven areas of global diversity.

Effectively managing diversity promotes performance.[127] When conducting business with foreign firms and, more importantly, in foreign countries, be aware of cultural differences. To have successful human relations, you must be flexible and adapt to other people's ways of behaving; you are the foreigner and cannot expect others to change for you.[128] This section examines diversity in customs, attitudes toward time, work ethics, pay, laws and politics, ethics, and participative management. As you read, realize that you are being presented with stereotyped generalizations to which there are exceptions. The examples are not meant to judge "right" and "wrong" behavior. They are intended to illustrate cross-cultural differences that do affect human relations.

Diversity in Customs   The Japanese place a high priority on human relations, participative management, and teamwork. If you try to be an individual star, you will not be successful in Japan. However, the French do not place high importance on team effort. If you are very outspoken, you will be considered impolite in Japan. If you refuse to be involved in receiving and giving gifts, you will offend Japanese people. However, don't wrap gifts in white paper because white is a sign of death. Also, don't place chopsticks straight up and down; doing so imitates an offering to the dead. Many Japanese companies start the day with exercises and company cheers. If you do not actively participate, you will be an outsider.

In Europe, management has more cultural than technical aspects and deals with value systems and religious background; it is organized more as a language than a set of techniques. While power and politics (Chapter 10) are important in the United States, they are even more important in France. It is important for a French manager to be perceived as very powerful.

Americans prefer to speak face-to-face from a greater distance than people of most other countries. If you back away or turn to the side from others, they may follow you and create a dance, and you may be considered cold and standoffish. During face-to-face communication, Latinos tend to touch each other more than Americans. Jumping when unexpectedly touched could create an embarrassing situation.

Gestures vary from country to country. For example, Americans prefer eye contact. However, the Japanese tend to look at the knot in a Japanese colleague's tie, or at the neck, to show respect. In Australia, making the "V" sign with the hand is considered an obscenity rather than a sign for victory.

Diversity in Attitudes toward Time   Americans typically view time as a valuable resource that is not to be wasted, and socializing is often considered a waste of time. However, it would be considered impolite to start a business meeting with Hispanics without engaging in a certain amount of relaxed small talk.

American and Swiss businesspeople usually expect you to be precisely on time for an appointment. However, in several countries, you could find yourself going to an appointment with a manager on time, only to be kept waiting. In some countries, if you call a meeting, most members will be late. If you get angry and yell, you could harm human relations.

Diversity in Work Ethics   The work ethic, viewing work as a central life interest and a desirable goal in life, varies around the world. Generally, the Japanese have a stronger work ethic than Americans and Europeans. With a strong work ethic, and the acceptance of automation, many Japanese plants are the most productive in the world. Although there is not much difference in work ethics between Americans and Europeans, Americans work more hours than Europeans.[129]

Americans are relatively good at getting poorly prepared workers to be productive, which is important when working with illiterate people all over the world. However, in some cultures, managers and employees have little interest in being productive. These relaxed attitudes do not do much for the bottom line of global businesses that are trying to change work ethics.

Diversity in Pay   Americans, in general, are no longer the world's highest-paid employees. The Japanese and Europeans have caught up and earn as much as Americans. However, employees in Third World countries continue to be paid much less than employees in developed countries.

Pay systems also vary to meet employee values.[130] One of the pay trends in the United States is pay for performance. However, some cultures value being paid for loyalty and following orders. Paying a salary works well in some countries, but not in others.

Diversity in Laws and Politics   The legal and political environment becomes increasingly complex as multinationals do business all over the world. Employee health and safety laws are generally more protective in developed countries than in Third World countries. Labor laws also vary widely from country to country. Western European nations offer good benefits, including a required four- to six-week vacation, paid holidays, and sick and family leave. The amount of time employees work varies from country to country:[131] Such differences change the actual labor cost per hour. It is also easier to terminate employees in some countries than in others.

In some countries, government structure and politicians are more stable than in others. A change in government can mean changes in business practices overnight. Some countries, such as Cuba, have literally taken away the plants and equipment owned by U.S. companies and sent the Americans home without any compensation.

Diversity in Ethics   When conducting global business, you must rethink business ethics. In the United States and some other countries, it is illegal to take and give bribes for doing business. However, in some countries, bribing is a standard practice of doing business. For example, an American businessperson complained to a local telephone company manager that the service person showed up and asked for a bribe, which was refused, so the telephone worker left without installing the phone. The businessperson was told by the telephone company manager that the matter would be investigated, for a fee (bribe). MNCs, including GE, are working to develop global ethics codes.[132]

Diversity in Participative Management   In Third World nations, employees need basic skills training and may not be capable of participating in management decisions. Some cultures, like those of Japan and the United States, value participation in management whereas others do not. In some cultures, employees simply want to be told what to do.[133]

Management–labor relations vary globally. In France relations are more polarized than in the United States, whereas in Japan they are more cooperative. You should realize that management and human relations become more complex as styles change from country to country.

WORK APPLICATIONS

13. Have you experienced any cultural differences in human relations with others? If so, explain.

HANDLING COMPLAINTS

Learning Outcome

8. List the steps in
    handling a complaint.

The EEOC's job is to handle complaints that are brought to it, many of which result in lawsuits. Effective management can be measured by the lack of complaints. As a manager, you should strive to meet the goal of human relations by creating a win–win situation for all employees. However, no matter how hard you try to satisfy employees' needs, complaints will arise covering a range of topics, which may include discrimination. Use the open-door policy and let employees feel as though they can come to you with a complaint.[134] It is much better to get complaints out in the open and try to resolve them than to have employees complaining to everyone else about you.

You can use the complaint model to help you resolve employee complaints in either a union or nonunion organization. The **complaint model** *involves these steps: step (1) listen to the complaint and paraphrase it; step (2) have the complainer recommend a solution;*

step (3) schedule time to get all the facts and/or make a decision; and step (4) develop and implement a plan, and follow up. Each step is discussed below.

Step 1: Listen to the Complaint and Paraphrase It

Listening is probably the most important step.[135] Listen to the full story without interruptions, and paraphrase it to ensure accuracy. When employees come to you with a complaint, try not to take it personally; even the best supervisors have to deal with complaints. Do not become defensive and try to talk the employee out of the complaint.

Step 2: Have the Complainer Recommend a Solution

After the supervisor has paraphrased the complaint and the employee has agreed with the paraphrasing, the supervisor should ask the complainer to recommend a solution that will resolve the complaint. Requesting a solution does not mean that the supervisor has to implement it.

In some cases, the recommended solution may not solve the problem. Or the solution may not be fair to others. Some recommendations may not be possible for the supervisor to implement. In such cases, the supervisor should let the employee know that the solution is not possible and explain why.

Step 3: Schedule Time to Get All the Facts and/or Make a Decision

Since employee complaints often involve other people, you may find it necessary to check records or to talk to others. It is often helpful to talk to your boss or your peers, who may have had a similar complaint; they may be able to offer you some good advice on how best to resolve the complaint. Even when you have all the facts, it is usually advisable to take some time to weigh the facts before making a decision.

Schedule a specific period of time. In many cases, it does not have to be long. Generally, the more quickly a complaint is resolved, the fewer the negative side effects. Too many supervisors simply say, "I'll get back to you on this," without specifying a time period. This response is very frustrating to the employee. Some supervisors are purposely vague because they have no intention of getting back to the employee. They are hoping the employee will forget about the complaint. This tactic may get the employee to stop complaining, but it may also cause productivity and turnover problems.

Step 4: Develop and Implement a Plan, and Follow Up

After getting all the necessary facts and advice from others, the supervisor should develop a plan. The plan may be developed by simply using the complainer's recommended solution. However, when supervisors do not agree with the complainer's solution, they should explain why and either work with the employee to find an alternative or present their own plan. The level of the employee's participation can change with capability level.

In cases in which supervisors decide not to take any action to resolve the complaint, they should clearly explain why they chose not to do so. They should also state that if employees are not satisfied, they can appeal the decision to another level. The complainer should be told how to appeal the decision. In the nonunion organization, the usual step is to go to the supervisor's boss. In the union organization, the next step is often to go to the union steward.

As with all plans, it is important for the supervisor to make sure that the plan is implemented through follow-up methods. It may be appropriate to set a follow-up meeting. It is also advisable to document all meetings and action.

Exhibit 15.4 lists the four steps in the complaint model.

EXHIBIT 15.4 | Complaint Model

Step 1: Listen to the complaint and paraphrase it.
Step 2: Have the complainer recommend a solution.
Step 3: Schedule time to get all the facts and/or make a decision.
Step 4: Develop and implement a plan, and follow up.

WORK APPLICATIONS

14. Identify a complaint you brought to a supervisor. If you have never complained, interview someone who has. State the complaint and identify the steps in the complaint model the supervisor did and/or did not follow.

In the opening case, both the men and the women are complaining to each other about each other. A woman states that she did complain to management, but nothing happened. The minorities are also complaining about not being treated fairly. For things to change, management and the union have to work to resolve complaints.

Customer Complaints   Handling a customer complaint is somewhat different from handling an employee complaint, especially when it involves something you and your company did wrong. The steps to follow are:

1. Admit you made a mistake.

2. Agree that it should not have happened.

3. Tell the customer what you are going to do about it, or ask what the customer recommends you do about it.

4. Take the action to make it up to the customer.

5. Take precautions to prevent the mistake in the future.

As we bring this chapter to a close, complete Self-Assessment Exercise 15–5 to determine how your personality affects your ability to deal with diversity in the workplace.

Self-Assessment Exercise 15–5

Personality and Diversity

If you are *open to new experiences,* you are probably interested in learning about people who are different from you.

If you have a high *agreeableness* personality, with a high need for affiliation, you tend to get along well with diverse people. You most likely do not judge peoples' behavior negatively simply because it is different. But you may need to be assertive so that you are not taken advantage of.

If you scored high in *conscientiousness,* with a high need for achievement, you may tend to be a conformist and will most likely adjust to diverse situations.

If you have a high *surgency* personality, with a high need for power, you like to dominate and may not want to accept diversity. You may need to remember, as the conscientious may too, that your ways are not always correct and are not always the best ways of doing things.

Action plan: Based on your personality, what specific things can you do to improve your ability to value and manage diversity? If you are well adjusted, you are better at dealing with a diversity of people.

_____

_____

_____

_____

Videos

Manager's Hot Seat and Behavior Model Videos are available for this chapter.

Online Learning Center Resources
Go to the Internet (http://mhhe.com/lussier8e) where you will find a broad array of resources to help maximize your learning.

• Review the vocabulary.

• Try a quiz.

R E V I E W

The chapter review is organized to help you master the 9 learning outcomes for Chapter 15. First provide your own response to each learning outcome, and then check the summary provided to see how well you understand the material. Next, identify the final statement in each section as either true or false (T/F). Correct each false statement. Answers are given at the end of the chapter.

1. **Define prejudice and discrimination and state common areas of employment discrimination in organizations.**

   Prejudice is a prejudgment of a person or situation based on attitudes. *Discrimination* is behavior for or against a person or situation. Common areas of employment discrimination include: recruitment, selection, compensation, upward mobility, and evaluation.

   We all prejudge people and situations. T F

2. **State major laws protecting minorities and women.**

   Some of the major laws passed to protect minorities and women in the workplace include: the Equal Employment Opportunity (EEO) Act, the Civil Rights Act, the Age Discrimination in Employment Act, the Americans with Disabilities Act, the Equal Pay Act, the Pregnancy Discrimination Act, and the Family and Medical Leave Act.

   The Justice Commission has the primary responsibility of ensuring equal opportunity for all. T F

3. **Identify what employers can and cannot ask job applicants.**

   To avoid breaking the law, employers interviewing job applicants should follow two major rules of thumb: (1) Every question that is asked should be job related, and (2) any general question that is asked should be asked of all candidates.

   An organization can discriminate as long as it can prove that it is reasonably necessary to normal operation of the enterprise. T F

4. **List the groups that are legally protected by the EEOC.**

   Those legally protected by the EEOC include: minorities (Hispanics, Asians, African Americans, Native Americans, and Alaskan natives), women, disadvantaged young people, the disabled, and persons over 40.

   The law states that the protected groups must be given special consideration in employment practices. T F

5. **List the six areas of sexual harassment.**

   The six areas of sexual harassment are: (1) unwelcome sexual advances, (2) coercion, (3) favoritism, (4) indirect harassment, (5) physical conduct, and (6) visual harassment.

   Physical conduct refers to keeping your hands to yourself; touching is sexual harassment. T F

6. **Explain sexism in organizations and ways to overcome it.**

   Sexism is discrimination based on sex. To help overcome sexism, we should not use sexist language and behavior and we should discourage others from doing so.

   Women who have been discriminated against based on gender can file a complaint with the EEOC. T F

7. **List seven areas of global diversity.**

   Seven areas of global diversity are: (1) diversity in customs, (2) attitudes toward time, (3) work ethics, (4) pay, (5) laws and politics, (6) ethics, and (7) participative management.

   In general, American workers are the highest paid in the world. T F

8. **List the steps in handling a complaint.**

   The complaint model involves the following steps: step (1) listen to the complaint and paraphrase it; step (2) have the complainer recommend a solution; step (3) schedule time to get all the facts and/or make a decision; and step (4) develop and implement a plan, and follow up.

Managers don't always need to use step (3) of the complaint model. T F

Learning Outcome

9.   Define the following
     12 key terms.

9. **Define the following 12 key terms.**

Select one or more methods: (1) fill in the missing key terms from memory; (2) match the key terms from the end of the review with their definitions below; and/or (3) copy the key terms in order from the key terms list at the beginning of the chapter.

_____ is the prejudgment of a person or situation based on attitudes.

_____ is behavior for or against a person or situation.

The EEOC _____ list includes Hispanics, Asians, African Americans, Native Americans, and Alaskan natives.

A _____ allows discrimination on the basis of religion, sex, or national origin where it is reasonably necessary to normal operation of a particular enterprise.

_____ are planned, special efforts to recruit, hire, and promote women and members of minority groups.

A _____ refers to a significant physical, mental, or emotional limitation.

_____ is any unwelcomed behavior of a sexual nature.

_____ is discrimination based on sex.

_____ applies to jobs that are distinctly different but require similar levels of ability and have the same pay scale.

A _____ conducts a large part of its business outside the country of its headquarters.

_____ are people who live and work in a country other than their native country.

The _____ involves these steps: step (1) listen to the complaint and paraphrase it; step (2) have the complainer recommend a solution; step (3) schedule time to get all the facts and/or make a decision; and step (4) develop and implement a plan, and follow up.

K E Y   T E R M S

affirmative action programs 547	complaint model 566	multinational company (MNC) 563
bona fide occupational qualification 545	disability 548	prejudice 542
comparable worth 555	discrimination 542	sexism 553
	expatriates 564	sexual harassment 552
	minority 544	

C O M M U N I C A T I O N   S K I L L S

The following critical thinking questions can be used for class discussion and/or as written assignments to develop communication skills. Be sure to give complete explanations for all questions.

1. Clearly, women and minorities were held back from employment opportunities in the past. So shouldn't we give them special consideration today (like giving them jobs when they are qualified even though there are better qualified white males)? Should we be increasing or decreasing affirmative action programs?

2. Do we really need laws to get organizations to give equal opportunities to all? Should the current employment laws be changed? How?

3. Should religious people be given breaks and a special place to pray during their work time?

4. Some companies and jobs have a mandatory retirement age. Should the government pass a law stating a mandatory retirement age?

5. Do you feel comfortable being around people with disabilities? Should organizations make special efforts to hire the disabled? Are organizations that hire the disabled just being socially responsible, or are the disabled productive workers?

6. Do you agree that people who work together can date? How might dating lead to sexual harassment? Should organizations have policies about employee dating? If they have policies, what should the policies include?

7. Only a small percentage of Fortune 500 companies have female CEOs. One solution to increase the number of women CEOs would be to have co-CEOs, one male and one female. Do you think this would work? Do you have any other ideas on how to break the glass ceiling?

8. Consider the statement, "Sexist and racist jokes are just meant to be funny and no one gets hurt anyway." Do you agree?

9. The traditional family hasn't been the norm for several years. Instead, it is being overtaken by dual-income earners and single parents. Are we better off today, or should we return to the traditional family?

10. The percentage of married people has declined over the years due to divorce and people living together. Also, male and female roles have changed. Do these trends help or hurt society?

11. Consider the statement, "With the global economy, people around the world are becoming more and more alike, so why be concerned about diversity?" Do you agree? Should organizations conduct diversity training?

CASE

Employee Diversity at McDonald's

"Billions served," indeed. McDonald's is the world's number one fast-food company by sales, with more than 31,000 restaurants serving burgers and fries in almost 120 countries. (Nearly 14,000 Golden Arches locations are in the U.S.) The popular chain is well known for its Big Macs, Quarter Pounders, and Chicken McNuggets. Most of its outlets are free-standing units, but McDonald's also has many quick-service kiosk units located in airports and retail areas. Each unit gets its food and packaging from approved suppliers and uses standardized procedures to ensure that a Big Mac purchased in Pittsburgh tastes the same as one bought in Beijing. More than 75 percent of its restaurants are run by franchisees or affiliates.[136]

To run one of the largest workforces in the world, McDonald's has embraced and empowered a diverse workforce, which has been a part of the McDonald's culture for decades. In the mid-1970s, McDonald's then-CEO Fred Turner established an initial diversity program, and in 1980, McDonald's hired the first official manager for the program. Back then, as now, encouraging diversity both at McDonald's and within its supply chain is not only the right thing to do but good for business.

Another critical component to diversity and inclusion for McDonald's is teaching people how to work with others who are different from themselves. The core of its education framework includes formal presentations, workshops, seminars, and informal training designed to practice the skills and behaviors needed to collaborate with and lead people in an inclusive, diverse workforce. The U.S.-based seminars and workshops include: Winning with Inclusion and Diversity; GenderSpeak—Working Together Successfully; Asian Career Development; Hispanic Career Development; and Diversity & Inclusion from a White Male Perspective. McDonald's also has a number of employee networks based at its U.S. headquarters, including: McDonald's African American Council; Women's Leadership Network; Gays, Lesbians and Allies at McDonald's; the Asian Employee Network; and the Hispanic Employee Network.

While the definition of "inclusion" remains relatively constant across geographic boundaries, the word "diversity" has very different implications from place to place. For example, McDonald's approach to sexual orientation has not gone unnoticed, both positively and negatively.[137]

McDonald's Corporation scored an 85 percent ranking on the Human Rights Campaign's (HRC) Corporate Equality Index. HRC, the nation's leading homosexual lobby group, [which] publishes the corporate survey every year, [found that] . . . McDonald's passed all but one test (a gender-identity 'nondiscrimination' policy—criterion 2a).[138] This rating, however, has led to a boycott by the AFT (Americans for Truth) and AFTAH (Americans for Truth About Homosexuality), two right-wing organizations that are sick and tired of rewarding and subsidizing corporations that promote homosexuality.[139]

Go to the Internet: For more information on McDonald's Corporation and to update the information provided in this case, do a name search on the Internet and visit http://www.crmcdonalds.com.

Support your answers to the following questions with specific information from the case and text, or with other information you get from the Web or other sources.

1. After reading the case and visiting McDonald's Web site, in what ways has McDonald's taken a proactive approach toward supporting and valuing diversity?

2. What structures and systems has McDonald's established in order to ensure that it leverages its diversity as part of the business strategy?

3. How does McDonald's propose to overcome prejudice and discrimination within the firm?

4. What actions would you recommend that McDonald's take relative to the boycott and statements made by the AFA and AFTAH?

Cumulative Questions

5. How do perception (Chapter 2), attitudes, values, and ethics (Chapter 3) help us to understand the dynamics within this case?

6. The case indicates that the AFA and AFTAH are in conflict with McDonald's over its inclusive diversity policy (inclusion of sexual preference). What are the alternative management styles McDonald's could use to address this conflict? (Chapter 7)

7. Should McDonald's use a team approach (Chapter 13) for solving this problem?

8. How might McDonald's organizational culture (Chapter 14) have led to the problems described in this case?

Lilly's Promotion

The Carlson Mining and Manufacturing Company needs a new vice president of human resources. Its headquarters are in Detroit, but the company has mining and manufacturing plants in three states and five different countries. Foreign plants account for about 70 percent of total operations.

The president, Ron Carlson, is meeting with some of the vice presidents and the board of directors to decide who will be promoted to vice president. The following are excerpts from their discussion:

RON: As you know, we are meeting today to promote someone to vice president. Ted, tell us about the candidates.

TED: We have narrowed the list of candidates to two people. You all know the two candidates. They are Rich Martin and Lilly Jefferson. Rich is 38 and has been with us for 15 years, and he has worked in human resources for 10 years. He has an M.B.A. from a leading business school. Lilly is 44 and has been with us for 10 years. She recently finished her B.S. in business going to school nights at the local state college.

JIM: Lilly is an African-American female with older children. She is perfect for the job, fitting into two AA classifications. We can meet our AA quotas without promoting Lilly, but it would help. Besides, there are a lot of African Americans here in Detroit; we could get some great publicity.

ED: Wait a minute. We cannot have any girls at the VP level. You know they are emotional and cannot take the pressure of the job.

CARL: Their performance records are about the same, but Rich has been with us longer, and is better educated.

The discussion ended in a vote. Lilly won by a large margin. Off the record: It was because she is a qualified African American female. If she were a white male, Rich would have been promoted.

Answer the following questions. Then in the space between questions, state why you selected that answer.

_____ 1. Discrimination was used in the promotion process.
   a. true   b. false

_____ 2. The primary area discussed in this case is:
   a. recruitment   c. compensation   e. evaluation
   b. selection   d. upward mobility

_____ 3. Affirmative action affected the decision to promote Lilly.
   a. true   b. false

_____ 4. Rich may have a case for reverse discrimination.
   a. true   b. false

_____ 5. Sexism occurred in this case.

   a. true   *b.* false

_____ 6. Ed's statement was:

   a. factual   *b.* myth

_____ 7. Ed used sexist language.

   a. true   *b.* false

_____ 8. With Lilly being a minority member, she will most likely encounter cross-cultural relations problems.

   a. true   *b.* false

_____ 9. Carlson is a multinational company.

   a. true   *b.* false

_____ 10. The most help Lilly got in getting to the vice president position was from:

   a. AAP   *d.* child care   *f.* wellness programs

   b. training   *e.* role models and

   c. flexible work schedule   mentors

11. Who would you have voted for? Why?

12. How would you feel in Lilly's position, knowing that you are qualified for the job but that you have been selected because you are a minority? Lilly's response can be role-played.

SKILL-BUILDING EXERCISE 15–1

Sexism

In-Class Exercise
(Individual and Group)

Objective: To better understand sexist language and behavior and how it affects human relations.

AACSB: The AACSB learning standard skills developed through this exercise are reflexive thinking and diversity.

Experience: You will discuss sexism.

Procedure 1
(7–15 minutes)

Option A: Students give sample words and behaviors found in the workplace that are sexist (for example, [words] foreman and [behaviors] a woman being required to get the coffee). The instructor or a class member writes the headings "words" and "behaviors" on the board and records the class members' examples. Discuss how these sexist words and behaviors affect people's behavior in organizations.

Option B: Break into teams of five or six, making the number of males and females as even as possible. As in option A, develop a list of sexist words and behaviors and discuss how they affect people's behavior in organizations.

Procedure 2
(7–15 minutes)

Option A: As a class, select a few sexist words and behaviors. Discuss how to overcome this sexism.

Option B: As a group, select a few sexist words and behaviors. Discuss how to overcome this sexism.

Conclusion: The instructor may lead a class discussion and/or make concluding remarks.

Application (2–4 minutes):   What did I learn from this exercise? How will I use this knowledge in the future?

Sharing: Volunteers give their answers to the application section.

Male and Female Small Group Behavior

In-Class Exercise (Group)

For this exercise, some of the class members will need to bring tape recorders to class to record small group discussions. Small tape recorders are suggested. Your instructor may assign specific people to bring them. If not, bring a tape recorder if you have one.

Objective: To see if there are any differences in male and female behavior in small groups.

AACSB: The AACSB learning standard skills developed through this exercise are analytic skills, reflexive thinking, and diversity.

Preparation: Some of the class members need to bring tape or digital recorders to class to record the small group discussion.

Experience: In a small group, you will make a decision that will be recorded, and then you will analyze the recording to determine if there are differences in male and female behavior.

Procedure 1 (15–20 minutes)

Break into teams of five or six. Make the number of males and females as even as possible in each group. Be sure each group has a recorder. As a group, you will select a candidate for a job opening. As an individual, read the information below and think about whom you would hire in this situation. When all group members are ready, begin your discussion of whom to hire. *Be sure to record the conversation.* Discuss each candidate's qualifications fully, coming to a group consensus on whom to hire. Do not vote, unless the time is almost up. You must make a decision by the deadline stated by your instructor. Try not to finish very early, but if you do, wait for the rest of the class to finish before going on to the next procedure.

You are a member of the local school board. The board is making the decision on which candidate to hire for the open position of girls' high school tennis coach. The following is information on each candidate.

Mary Smith: Mary has been a history teacher at a nearby high school for 10 years. She was the tennis coach for one year. It has been five years since she coached the team. Mary says she stopped coaching because it was too time-consuming with her young daughter, but she misses it and wants to return. Mary's performance was rated as 3 on a scale of 1 to 5. Mary never played competitive tennis, but she says she plays regularly. You guess she is about 35 years old.

Tom Jones: Tom works as a supervisor on the 11 P.M. to 7 A.M. shift for a local business. He has never coached before. However, Tom was a star player in high school and college. He still plays in local tournaments, and you see his name in the paper now and then. You guess Tom is about 25 years old.

Wendy Clark: Wendy has been a basketball coach and a teacher of physical education classes for a nearby high school for the past five years. She has a bachelor's degree in physical education. Wendy has never coached tennis, but she did play on the high school team. She says she plays tennis about once a week. You guess she is about 40 years old.

Lisa Williams: Lisa has been an English teacher at your school for the past two years. She has never coached, but she did take a course in college on how to coach tennis. She is popular with her students. Lisa plays tennis regularly, and you have heard she is a pretty good player. She is an African American. You guess Lisa is about 24 years old.

Hank Chung: Hank has been teaching math at your school for seven years. He was a star player in high school in Japan, and he played tennis for a successful U.S. college team. He still plays for fun regularly. He has never coached or had any type of coaching courses. He applied for the job the last time it was open four years ago but was not selected. You guess Hank is about 30 years of age.

Sally Carson: Sally has taught physical education classes at your school for the past four years. She never played competitive tennis but has a master's degree in physical education and has had courses regarding how to coach tennis. Sally taught and coached field hockey at a high school for 15 years before moving to your city. You guess she is about 48 years old.

Procedure 2
(1–2 minutes)

As an individual, answer the following questions. Circle the letter of your response.

1. Who spoke more?
   a. males   *b.* females   *c.* equal time

2. The one individual with the most influence in the group was:
   a. male   *b.* female

3. The one individual with the least influence in the group was:
   a. male   *b.* female

4. Overall, who had the most influence on the group?
   a. males   *b.* females   *c.* equal influence

5. Interruptions came more frequently from:
   a. males interrupting females

   b. females interrupting males

   c. equal interruption from both

6. Of the total discussion time, I spoke for about _____ minutes.

Procedure 3
(2–4 minutes)

Total the group's answers to the six questions in procedure 2. All members should write the totals next to the questions above.

Procedure 4
(20–30 minutes)

Play back the recorded discussion. As it plays, write down who talks and for how long they talk. If one person interrupts another, note it as "male interrupts female," or vice versa. When the tape finishes, add up the number of minutes each person spoke. Total the male and female times. As a team, answer the six questions in procedure 2 above. Were the answers the same before and after listening to the recorded discussion?

Conclusion: The instructor may lead a class discussion and/or make concluding remarks.

Application (2–4 minutes):   What did I learn from this experience? How can I use this knowledge in the future?

Sharing: Volunteers give their answers to the application section.

Source: The idea to develop this exercise came from Susan Morse, University of Massachusetts at Amherst, in "Gender Differences in Behavior in Small Groups: A Look at the OB Class," paper presented at the 25th Annual Meeting of the Eastern Academy of Management, May 12, 1988.

SKILL-BUILDING EXERCISE 15-3

Handling Complaints

Preparation (Group)

During class you will be given the opportunity to role-play handling a complaint. Select a complaint. It may be one you brought to a supervisor, one that was brought to you, one you heard about, or one you made up. Fill in the information below for the person who will role-play bringing you a complaint to resolve.

Explain the situation and complaint.

List pertinent information about the other party that will help him or her play the role of the complainer (relationship with supervisor, knowledge, years of service, background, age, values, and so on).

Review Exhibit 15.4 (complaint model) and think about what you will say and do when you handle this complaint.

Complaint Observer Form

During the role play, observe the handling of the complaint. Determine whether the supervisor followed the steps below, and how well. Try to have both a positive and an improvement comment for each step in the complaint model. Be specific and descriptive. For all improvement comments, have an alternative positive behavior (APB). What could have been done or said that was not?

Step 1.   How well did the supervisor listen? Was the supervisor open to the complaint? Did the supervisor try to talk the employee out of the complaint? Was the supervisor defensive? Did the supervisor get the full story without interruptions? Did the supervisor paraphrase the complaint?

　　　　　(positive)　　　　　　　　(improvement)

Step 2.   Did the supervisor have the complainer recommend a solution? How well did the supervisor react to the solution? If the solution could not be used, did the supervisor explain why?

(positive)   (improvement)

Step 3.   Did the supervisor schedule time to get all the facts and/or make a decision? Was it a specific date? Was it a reasonable length of time?

(positive)   (improvement)

Step 4.   Did the supervisor develop and implement a plan, and schedule a follow-up? (This step may not have been appropriate at this time.)

In-Class Exercise

Objective: To experience and develop skills in resolving complaints.

AACSB: The AACSB learning standard skills developed through this exercise are analytic skills, communication ability, and leadership.

Preparation: You should have prepared to handle a complaint.

Experience: You will initiate, respond to, and observe a complaint role play. Then you will evaluate the effectiveness of its resolution.

Procedure 1
(2–3 minutes)

Break into as many groups of three as possible. (You do not have to be with members of your permanent team.) If there are any people not in a triad, make one or two groups of two. Each member selects a number 1, 2, or 3. Number 1 will be the first to initiate a complaint role play, then 2, followed by 3.

Procedure 2
(8–15 minutes)

A. Number 1 (the supervisor) gives his or her preparation complaint information to number 2 (the complainer) to read. Once number 2 understands, role-play the complaint (step B). Number 3 is the observer.

B. Role-play the complaint. Put yourself in this person's situation; ad-lib. Number 3, the observer, writes his or her observations on the complaint observer form.

C. Integration. When the role play is over, the observer leads a discussion on the effectiveness of the conflict resolution. All three should discuss the effectiveness; Number 3 is not a lecturer.

Do not go on until told to do so.

Procedure 3
(8–15 minutes)

Same as Procedure 2, only number 2 is now the supervisor, number 3 is now the complainer, and number 1 is the observer.

Procedure 4
(8–15 minutes)

Same as Procedure 2, only number 3 is now the supervisor, number 1 is now the complainer, and number 2 is the observer.

Conclusion: The instructor leads a class discussion and/or makes concluding remarks.

Application (2–4 minutes):   What did I learn from this experience? How will I use this knowledge in the future?

Sharing: Volunteers give their answers to the application section.

Periodical Articles

Preparation (Individual and Group)

Select a human relations topic that you would like to learn more about. It can be any topic covered in this book or a topic not covered, if related to human relations.

Now go to the library (usually the reference section) or online. If you are using the library, find the computer database that has business journals. Search your topic by typing it in the computer. The index should list periodical titles with the name of the author(s) and the name of the periodical in which the article appears, with its date and page number(s). You may also get an abstract of the article and a full article in the database, which you can download and/or print. Select one of the articles to read. Be sure the library has the publication in some form.

Write down the following information:

Author's name(s): _____

Title of article: _____

Title of the periodical: _____

Date of publication and page number(s): _____

Now get the periodical and read the article. Then answer the following questions. (Use additional paper if needed.)

Be sure to write neatly. You may be asked to report to the class or pass this assignment in to the instructor. Be prepared to give a three- to five-minute talk on your article.

What did the article say?   (Give a summary of the most important information in the article.)

How does this information relate to me and/or my interests?

How will I use this information in the future?

When reading articles of interest to your career, always answer the three questions. Answering these questions will help you use the information rather than forget it and will develop your abilities and skills.

To continue to improve on your human relations skills after the course is over, read more articles of interest to you. When you can afford it, subscribe to a periodical of interest to you. Many employers have copies of periodicals related to their business available to employees, and they are willing to pay for employee subscriptions.

In-Class Exercise

Objectives: To become familiar with various publications. To gain some specific knowledge regarding a topic of your choice and the choices of other students in the class.

AACSB: The AACSB learning standard skills developed through this exercise are analytic skills and communication ability.

Preparation: You should have read an article of interest to you and answered the three questions in the preparation section.

Experience: Class members will share their articles.

Procedure 1
(5–50 minutes)

One at a time, students come to the front of the room and give a three- to seven-minute speech on the article they read.

Conclusion: The instructor leads a class discussion and/or makes concluding remarks.

Application (2–4 minutes):   What did I learn from this experience? How will I use this knowledge in the future?

Sharing: Volunteers give their answers to the application section.

ANSWERS TO TRUE/FALSE QUESTIONS

1. T.

2. F. The Equal Employment Opportunity Commission (EEOC), not the Justice Commission, is responsible for ensuring equal opportunity for all.

3. T. (It is called a bona fide occupational qualification [BFOQ]).

4. F. The law states that protected groups must not be *discriminated* against.

5. F. Physical conduct states that a person does not have to be touched to be sexually harassed. Touching is not harassment when it is welcomed.

6. T.

7. F. The pay of Japanese and European workers is similar to that of U.S. workers.

8. T.

Applying Human Relations Skills

After completing this appendix, you should be able to:

1. State why human relations skills are important.

2. Identify the most important human relations concepts from the entire book.

3. Determine your strongest and weakest areas of human relations.

4. Compare your present skills assessment with the one you did in Chapter 1.

5. Explain three options in handling human relations problems.

6. Describe the four steps of changing behavior.

7. Develop your own human relations plan.

Pat O'Conner and David Fredrick, two students nearing the completion of a human relations course, were talking about the course:

PAT: This course has a lot of good practical advice that can help me develop effective human relations.

DAVID: I agree. Have you been using the information on a regular basis in your daily life?

PAT: Some of it. I'm so busy that I don't always have time to think about and actually do these things, even though I know they will help me. Have you been using it?

DAVID: Most of it. I figure that if I use these skills now rather than wait until I get a full-time job, I'll be that much ahead of the game.

PAT: Is there a way to do this?

DAVID: Yes, I've already read the appendix. It explains how to develop a human relations plan that you can put into action immediately.

PAT: Guess I'll go read it now.

DAVID: Good luck, see you in class.

Whether you are more like Pat or David, this appendix will help you develop your own human relations plan.

A REVIEW OF SOME OF THE MOST IMPORTANT HUMAN RELATIONS CONCEPTS

Learning Outcome

1. State why human relations skills are important.

Learning Outcome

2. Identify the most important human relations concepts from the entire book.

Let's highlight some of the most important information from each chapter in the book to tie things all together. If you cannot recall the information covered in any of the chapters, please return to the chapter for a review of the material.

Part 1. Intrapersonal Skills: Behavior, Human Relations, and Performance Begin with You
Chapter 1 defined some of the important concepts used throughout the book. Can you define the following: human relations, the goal of human relations, behavior, levels of behavior, group behavior, organizational behavior, and performance? Please return to Chapter 1 and review the first few pages that state the many reasons why human relations are so important.

Can you define and discuss personality, stress, intelligence, learning styles, perception, and first impressions? If not, return to Chapter 2.

Can you define and discuss attitudes, job satisfaction, self-concept, and values? If not, return to Chapter 3.

Can you define and discuss time management and career management? If not, return to Chapter 4.

Part 2. Interpersonal Skills: The Foundation of Human Relations   Can you define and discuss the importance of communications; the communication process; message transmission channels; and how to send, receive, and respond to messages? If not, return to Chapter 5.

Can you define and discuss organizational structure and communication, communication barriers and how to overcome them, and situational communications? If not, return to Chapter 6.

Can you define and discuss transactional analysis, assertiveness, conflict management styles, how to resolve conflict with the collaborating conflict style, and interpersonal dynamics? If not, return to Chapter 7.

Part 3. Leadership Skills: Influencing Others   Can you define and discuss trait leadership theory, behavioral leadership theories, contingency leadership theories, situational supervision, and substitutes for leadership? If not, return to Chapter 8.

Can you define and discuss content motivation theories, process motivation theories, reinforcement theory, and motivation techniques? If not, return to Chapter 9.

Can you define and discuss power, organizational politics, vertical politics, and horizontal politics? If not, return to Chapter 10.

Can you define and discuss networking and negotiating? If not, return to Chapter 11.

Part 4. Leadership Skills: Team and Organizational Behavior, Human Relations, and Performance   Can you define and discuss team dynamics, group development stages, and how to lead groups and meetings? If not, return to Chapter 12.

Can you define and discuss problem-solving and decision-making approaches and models, and creative group problem-solving and decision-making techniques? If not, return to Chapter 13.

Learning Outcome

3. Determine your strongest and weakest areas of human relations.

Learning Outcome

4. Compare your present skills assessment with the one you did in Chapter 1.

Can you define and discuss resistance to change and how to overcome it; organizational culture and climate; and organizational development? If not, return to Chapter 14.

Can you define and discuss prejudice and discrimination, equal employment opportunity, legally protected groups, sexual harassment, sexism in organizations, global diversity and cross-cultural relations, and how to handle complaints? If not, return to Chapter 15.

ASSESSING YOUR HUMAN RELATIONS ABILITIES AND SKILLS

For each of the 43 statements that follow, record in the blank the number from 1 to 7 that best describes your level of ability or skill. You are not expected to have all high numbers.

Low ability/skill						High ability/skill
1	2	3	4	5	6	7

_____ 1. I understand how personality and perception affect people's behavior, human relations, and performance.

_____ 2. I can describe several ways to handle stress effectively.

_____ 3. I know my preferred learning style (accommodator, diverger, converger, assimilator) and how it affects my behavior, human relations, and performance.

_____ 4. I understand how people acquire attitudes and how attitudes affect behavior, human relations, and performance.

_____ 5. I can describe self-concept and self-efficacy and how they affect behavior, human relations, and performance.

_____ 6. I can list several areas of personal values and state how values affect behavior, human relations, and performance.

_____ 7. I understand how to use a time management system.

_____ 8. I understand how to use time management techniques to get more done in less time with better results.

_____ 9. I know how to develop a career plan and manage my career successfully.

_____ 10. I can describe the communication process.

_____ 11. I can list several transmission media and when to use each.

_____ 12. I can identify and use various message response styles.

_____ 13. I understand organizational communications and networks.

_____ 14. I can list barriers to communications and how to overcome them.

_____ 15. I know my preferred communication style and how to use other communication styles to meet the needs of the situation.

_____ 16. I can describe transactional analysis.

_____ 17. I can identify the differences between aggressive, passive, and assertive behavior. I am assertive.

_____ 18. I can identify different conflict resolution styles. I understand how to resolve conflicts in a way that does not hurt relationships.

_____ 19. I can identify behavioral leadership theories.

_____ 20. I can identify contingency leadership theories.

_____ 21. I know my preferred leadership style and how to change it to meet the needs of the situation.

_____ 22. I understand the process people go through to meet their needs.

_____ 23. I know several content and process motivation theories and can use them to motivate people.

_____ 24. I can list and use motivation techniques.

_____ 25. I can identify bases and sources of power.

_____ 26. I know how to gain power in an organization.

_____ 27. I can list political techniques to increase success.

_____ 28. I have 100 people I can call on for career help.

_____ 29. I know how to open a conversation to get people to give me career assistance.

_____ 30. I know two critical things to do during a negotiation to get what I want.

_____ 31. I understand how to plan and conduct effective meetings.

_____ 32. I can identify components of group dynamics and how they affect behavior, human relations, and performance.

_____ 33. I know the stages groups go through as they develop.

_____ 34. I understand the roles and various types of groups in organizations.

_____ 35. I can help groups make better decisions through consensus.

_____ 36. I know when, and when not, to use employee participation in decision making.

_____ 37. I understand why people resist change and know how to overcome that resistance.

_____ 38. I can identify and use organizational development techniques.

_____ 39. I understand how to develop a positive organizational culture and climate.

_____ 40. I understand equal employment opportunity (EEO) and the rights of legally protected groups such as minorities, people with disabilities, alcohol and drug addicts, and people with AIDS.

_____ 41. I can define sexism and sexual harassment in organizations.

_____ 42. I can handle a complaint using the complaint model.

_____ 43. I understand how to plan for improved human relations.

To use the profile form below, place an X in the box whose number corresponds to the score you gave each statement above.

Profile Form

	Your Score							Parts and Chapters in Which the Information Will Be Covered in the Book
	1	**2**	**3**	**4**	**5**	**6**	**7**	
								Part 1. Intrapersonal Skills: Behavior, Human Relations, and Performance Begin with You
1.								2. Personality, Stress, Learning, and Perception
2.								
3.								
4.								3. Attitudes, Self-Concept, Values, and Ethics
5.								
6.								
7.								4. Time and Career Management
8.								
9.								
								Part 2. Interpersonal Skills: The Foundation of Human Relations
10.								5. Interpersonal Communication
11.								
12.								
13.								6. Organizational Structure and Communication
14.								
15.								
16.								7. Dealing with Conflict
17.								
18.								
								Part 3. Leadership Skills: Influencing Others
19.								8. Leading and Trust
20.								
21.								

(*continued*)

Profile Form (*continued*)

	Your Score							Parts and Chapters in Which the Information Will Be Covered in the Book
	1	2	3	4	5	6	7	
22.								9. Motivating Performance
23.								
24.								
25.								10. Ethical Power and Politics
26.								
27.								
28.								11. Networking and Negotiating
29.								
30.								
								Part 4. Leadership Skills: Team and Organizational Behavior, Human Relations, and Performance
31.								12. Team Dynamics and Leadership
32.								
33.								
34.								13. Teams and Creative Problem Solving and Decision Making
35.								
36.								
37.								14. Organizational Change and Culture
38.								
39.								
40.								15. Valuing Diversity Globally
41.								
42.								
43.								Appendix A. Applying Human Relations Skills

Recall that in Chapter 1 you answered these same 43 questions. At that time you were told that you would compare your scores at the beginning and end of the course. Do so now. Turn back to your profile form in Chapter 1. Either tear it out or flip back and forth as you place your scores from Chapter 1 on the profile form here. You were asked to place an X in the boxes above. To distinguish your responses from Chapter 1, place a check or some other mark in the boxes above. If you have the same box marked for both, don't bother to check the box above. You will know it was the same response because there is only one score.

When you have finished, you will have your early and your present assessment of your human relations abilities and skills on one form. This will allow you to make an easy comparison of your scores, which represent your strong and weak areas of human relations. You will be using your profile form in the next section.

HUMAN RELATIONS PLANNING

In this section, you will learn about handling human relations problems, changing one's behavior, and developing a human relations plan.

Learning Outcome

5. Explain three options in handling human relations problems.

Handling Human Relations Problems

In any organization, there are bound to be times when you disagree with other employees. You may be assigned to work with a person you do not like. When you encounter these human relations problems, you have to choose either to avoid resolving the problem or to confront the person to solve it. In most cases, it is advisable to solve human relations problems, rather than to ignore them. Problems usually get worse rather than better, and they do not solve themselves. When you decide to resolve a human relations problem, you have at least three alternatives:

1. *Change the other person.* Whenever there is a human relations problem, it is easy to blame the other party and expect that person to make the necessary changes in behavior to meet our expectations. In reality, few human relations problems can be blamed entirely on one party. Both parties usually contribute to the human relations problem. Blaming the other party without taking some responsibility usually results in resentment and defensive behavior. The more we force people to change to meet our expectations, the more difficult it is to maintain effective human relations.

2. *Change the situation.* If you have a problem getting along with the person or people you work with, you can try to change the situation by working with another person or people. You may tell your boss you cannot work with so-and-so because of a personality conflict and ask for a change in jobs. There are cases where this is the only solution; however, when you complain to your boss, the boss often figures that you are the problem, not the other party. Blaming the other party and trying to change the situation enables us to ignore our behavior, which may be the actual cause of the problem.

3. *Change yourself.* Throughout this book, particularly in Part I, the focus has been on personal behavior. In many situations, your own behavior is the only thing you can control. In most human relations problems, the best alternative is to examine others' behavior and try to understand why they are doing and saying the things they are, and then examine your own behavior to determine why you are behaving the way you are. In most cases, the logical choice is to change your behavior. We are not saying to simply do what other people request. In fact, you should be assertive, as discussed in Chapter 7. You are not being forced to change; you are changing your behavior because you elect to do so. When you change your behavior, the other party may also change. Remember to create a win–win situation for all stakeholders.

Changing One's Behavior

Improving human relations generally requires a change in one's behavior. It is hoped that over the time period of this course, you have made changes in your behavior that have improved your human relations abilities and skills. In changing behavior, it is helpful to follow a four-step approach: step (1) assess your abilities and skills; step (2) develop new skills; step (3) change your behavior; and step (4) get feedback and reward yourself.

Step 1: Assess Your Abilities and Skills   You should consistently be aware of your behavior and assess it. Without becoming aware of your behavior and being committed to changing it, you cannot improve. You may know someone who has annoying behavior. The person is aware of it, yet does nothing to change. Without that commitment, this person will not change. Think about your own behavior; others may find you annoying, but do you change? What can you gain from changing? Can you make the change successfully?

You assessed your human relations abilities and skills at the beginning of the course and at the present. To continue your assessment, answer the following questions in the space provided, using your profile form.

1. Have your profile numbers (1 to 7) gotten higher compared to what they were at the beginning of the course? Why or why not?

2. Review your five objectives from Chapter 1, following your profile form. Did you meet them? Why or why not?

3. What are your strongest areas of human relations (highest numbers on your profile form)?

4. What human relations areas do you need to improve the most (lowest numbers on your profile form)?

5. What are the most important abilities and skills you have developed and/or things you have learned through this course?

Step 2. Develop New Skills   The development of new skills can come in a variety of ways. In this course, you had a text to read. This information gives you the basis for new skills. In life, when there is no textbook, you can refer to libraries for periodicals and books that can give you the knowledge you need to change your behavior. You can also refer to friends and experts in the areas in which you need to improve. There may be workshops, seminars, and courses in these areas as well.

Step 3: Change Your Behavior   Try to find safe, nonthreatening situations to try out your new behavior. Friends are usually willing to help; try your new behavior on them to see how it works.

Progressively change your behavior as you develop skill and confidence. For example, if you want to develop your ability to speak in front of people, volunteer and speak in class when the instructor gives you the opportunity. Take a speech class or join Toastmasters.

As with anything else in life, developing new skills takes time. Try not to be discouraged. For example, if you want to develop more positive, or less emotional, behavior, be patient; it will not happen overnight. If you catch yourself acting emotionally, be aware of it and change to more controlled behavior. With time and persistence, you will have to catch yourself less often.

Step 4: Get Feedback and Reward Yourself   Being aware of people's nonverbal communication will give you feedback on your behavior, as will their intentional behavior toward you. However, others' direct feedback requested by you is often more accurate

EXHIBIT A.1 |
Changing Behavior
Model

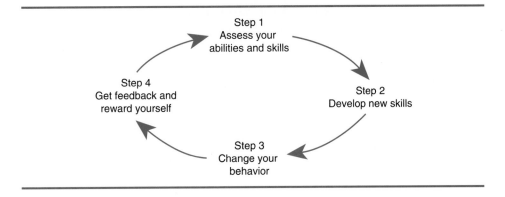

and unbiased. After trying new behavior, ask people you trust if they have noticed any difference. Get their advice on what you can do to improve. For example, if you are trying to be more positive and to give less negative feedback to others, ask them if they have noticed any difference. Ask them to recall the last time they remember hearing you make a put-down statement. People are often willing to help you, especially when it benefits them.

You should also reward yourself for your efforts. Notice we said efforts, not total success. Build on small successes; take one step at a time. As the saying goes, "Success by the yard is hard . . . but a cinch by the inch." Your rewards do not have to be big or expensive; you can treat yourself to a snack, take a walk, or do anything you enjoy. For example, say you want to stop putting people down, and you catch yourself in the act. Stop yourself in the middle and end by complimenting the person. Focus on the success, not the failure. Reward yourself rather than be disappointed in yourself.

Exhibit A.1 illustrates these four steps.

My Human Relations Plan

Learning Outcome

7. Develop your own human relations plan.

Follow the changing behavior model and develop a plan to change your behavior. Write in the space provided.

Step 1: Assess Your Abilities and Skills   Select the one human relations area in most need of improvement. Use the information from step 1, question 4 on page 588. Write it below.

Step 2: Develop New Skills   Review the material in the text that will help you develop the skill to improve your behavior. You may also talk to others for ideas, and go to the library to find articles and books on the skill. You can even look into taking a workshop or course on the subject. Below, write down some helpful notes on these skills.

Step 3: Change Your Behavior   Describe what you will have to do to change your behavior. Try to be specific.

Step 4: Get Feedback and Reward Yourself   How will you get feedback on your changed behavior? How will you know if you have succeeded in changing your behavior? When will you reward yourself? How will you reward yourself?

Additional Plans   If you feel you can handle working on more than one change in human relations, follow the changing behavior steps and develop another plan. However, don't try to make too many changes too quickly.

Human Relations Plan
In-Class Exercises
(Individual and Group)

Objectives: To share your human relations plan with others in order to get feedback on it.

AACSB: The primary AACSB learning standard skills developed through this exercise are reflective thinking and self-management, analytic skills, and communication abilities.

Preparation: You should have completed the human relations plan in the chapter.

Experience: This exercise is discussion-oriented.

Procedure 1
(5–15 minutes)

Break into groups of two to six persons and share your answers to the first four questions under step 1, assessing your abilities and skills. You may also look at and discuss each other's profiles, if you wish to do so. Share your human relations plans, offering each other positive feedback on your plans.

Conclusion: The instructor may lead a class discussion and/or make concluding remarks.

Application (2–4 minutes):   What did I learn from this experience? How will I use this knowledge in the future?

Sharing: Volunteers give their answers to the application situation.

Course Learning
In-Class Exercise
(Individual and Group)

Objectives: To share your human relations abilities and skills developed through this course.

AACSB: The primary AACSB learning standard skills developed through this exercise are reflective thinking and self-management, analytic skills, and communication abilities.

Preparation: You should have answered the question, "What are the most important abilities and skills you developed and/or things you learned through this course?"

Experience: This exercise is discussion-oriented.

Procedure 1
(5–30 minutes)

Volunteers tell the class the most important abilities and skills developed and/or things they learned through this course.

Conclusion: The instructor may lead a class discussion and/or make concluding remarks.

ENDNOTES

Chapter 1

1. IBM Web site www.ibm.com, retrieved June 24, 2008.

2. A.M. Grant, M.K. Christianson, and R.H. Price, "Happiness, Health, or Relationships? Managerial Practices and Employee Well-Being Tradeoffs," *Academy of Management Perspectives* 21(3) (2007): 51–63.

3. J.C. Santora, "Managing Open Employees: Do Resources and Leadership Style Matter?" *Academy of Management Perspectives* 21(3) (2007): 83–84.

4. D.A. Wren, J.R.B. Halbesleben, and M.R. Buckley, "The Theory-Application Balance in Management Pedagogy: A Longitudinal Update," *Academy of Management Learning & Education* 6(4) (2007): 484–492.

5. H. Lancaster, "Managing Your Career, How You Can Make Your M.B.A. Degree Even More Valuable," *The Wall Street Journal* (July 16, 1997): B1.

6. R.T. Harrison, C.M. Leitch, and R. Chia, "Developing Paradigmatic Awareness in University Business Schools: The Challenge for Executive Education," *Academy of Management Learning & Education* 6(3) (2007): 332–343.

7. R. Cropanzano, D.E. Bowen, and S.W. Gilliland, "The Management of Organizational Justice," *Academy of Management Perspectives* 21(4) (2007): 34–48.

8. D.A. Wren, J.R.B. Halbesleben, and M.R. Buckley, "The Theory-Application Balance in Management Pedagogy: A Longitudinal Update," *Academy of Management Learning & Education* 6(4) (2007): 484–492.

9. J.C. Santora, "Managing Open Employees: Do Resources and Leadership Style Matter?" *Academy of Management Perspectives* 21(3) (2007): 83–84.

10. F. Shipper, R.C. Hoffman, and D.M. Rotondo, "Does the 360 Feedback Process Create Actionable Knowledge Equally Across Cultures?" *Academy of Management Learning & Education* 6(1) (2007): 33–50.

11. R. Alsop, "Playing Well with Others," *The Wall Street Journal* (September 9, 2002): R11.

12. A.M. Grant, M.K. Christianson, and R.H. Price, "Happiness, Health, or Relationships? Managerial Practices and Employee Well-Being Tradeoffs," *Academy of Management Perspectives* 21(3) (2007): 51–63.

13. R. Cropanzano, D.E. Bowen, and S.W. Gilliland, "The Management of Organizational Justice," *Academy of Management Perspectives* 21(4) (2007): 34–48.

14. A.M. Grant, "Relational Job Design and the Motivation to Make a Prosocial Difference," *Academy of Management Review* 32(2) (2007): 393–417.

15. D.C. Hambrick, "Upper Echelons Theory: An Update," *Academy of Management Review* 32(2) (2007): 334–343.

16. C. Barzantny, "Managing Diversity: Toward a Globally Inclusive Workplace," *Academy of Management Learning & Education* 6(2) (2007): 285–286.

17. MetLife, "The Power of Diversity," *Fortune* (March 17, 2008): 118.

18. S.D. Sidle, "Do Teams Who Agree to Disagree Make Better Decisions?" *Academy of Management Perspectives* 21(2) (2007): 74–75.

19. A.J. Wefald and J.P. Katz, "Leaders: The Strategies for Taking Charge," *Academy of Management Perspectives* 21(3) (2007): 105–106.

20. D.C. Hambrick, "Upper Echelons Theory: An Update," *Academy of Management Review* 32(2) (2007): 334–343.

21. G.J. Jolley, "Leadership Can Be Taught: A Bold Approach for a Complex World," *Academy of Management Learning & Education* 6(1) (2007): 149–150.

22. J.B. Carson, P.E. Tesluck, and J.A. Marrone, "Shared Leadership in Teams: An Investigation of Antecedent Conditions and Performance," *Academy of Management Journal* 50(5) (2007): 1217–1234.

23. O. Gottschalg and M. Zollo, "Interest Alignment and Competitive Advantage," *Academy of Management Review* 32(2) (2007): 418–437.

24. R. Cropanzano, D.E. Bowen, and S.W. Gilliland, "The Management of Organizational Justice," *Academy of Management Perspectives* 21(4) (2007): 34–48.

25. A.M. Grant, "Relational Job Design and the Motivation to Make a Prosocial Difference," *Academy of Management Review* 32(2) (2007): 393–417.

26. J.E. Jennings and M.S. McDougald, "Work-Family Interface Experiences and Coping Strategies: Implications for Entrepreneurship Research and Practice," *Academy of Management Review* 32(3) (2007): 747–760.

27. J.R. Harrison, Z. Lin, G.R. Carroll, and K.M. Carley, "Simulation Modeling in Organizational and Management Research," *Academy of Management Review* 32(4) (2007): 1229–1245.

28. J. Weber, "Bribery: Not Only Wrong, But Costly Too?" *Academy of Management Perspectives* 21(3) (2007): 86–87.

29. D.C. Hambrick, "Upper Echelons Theory: An Update," *Academy of Management Review* 32(2) (2007): 334–343.

30. R. Gulati and M. Sytch, "The Dynamic of Trust," *Academy of Management Review* 32(1) (2007): 276–277.

31. F. Shipper, R.C. Hoffman, and D.M. Rotondo, "Does the 360 Feedback Process Create Actionable Knowledge Equally Across Cultures?" *Academy of Management Learning & Education* 6(1) (2007): 33–50.

32. A.M. Grant, M.K. Christianson, and R.H. Price, "Happiness, Health, or Relationships? Managerial Practices and Employee Well-Being Tradeoffs," *Academy of Management Perspectives* 21(3) (2007): 51–63.

33. R.L. Ackoff, Interview by G. Detrick, *Academy of Management Learning & Education* 1(1) (2002): 56–63.

34. A.M. Grant, M.K. Christianson, and R.H. Price, "Happiness, Health, or Relationships? Managerial Practices and Employee Well-Being Tradeoffs," *Academy of Management Perspectives* 21(3) (2007): 51–63.

35. M.L. Tushman, C.A. O'Reilly, A. Fenollosa, A.M. Kleinbaum, and D. McGrath, "Relevance and Rigor: Executive Education as a Lever in Shaping Practice and Research," *Academy of Management Learning & Education* 6(3) (2007): 345–362.

36. J.B. Carson, P.E. Tesluck, and J.A. Marrone, "Shared Leadership in Teams: An Investigation of Antecedent Conditions and Performance," *Academy of Management Journal* 50(5) (2007): 1217–1234.

37. J.R. Harrison, Z. Lin, G.R. Carroll, and K.M. Carley, "Simulation Modeling in Organizational and Management Research," *Academy of Management Review* 32(4) (2007): 1229–1245.

38. J.B. Carson, P.E. Tesluck, and J.A. Marrone, "Shared Leadership in Teams: An Investigation of Antecedent Conditions and Performance," *Academy of Management Journal* 50(5) (2007): 1217–1234.

39. J.R. Hackman and R. Wageman, "A Theory of Team Coaching," *Academy of Management Review* 30(2) (2005): 269–287.

40. D.M. Rousseau and S. McCarthy, "Educating Managers from an Evidence-Based Perspective," *Academy of Management Learning & Education* 6(1) (2007): 84–101.

41. G.P. Latham, "A Speculative Perspective on the Transfer of Behavioral Science Findings to the Workplace: The Times They Are A-Changin," *Academy of Management Journal* 50(5) (2007): 1027–1032.

42. T.G. Cummings, "Quest for an Engaged Academy," *Academy of Management Review* 32(2) (2007): 355–360.

43. F.W. Taylor, *Principles of Scientific Management* (New York: Harper & Brothers, 1911).

44. D. Jacobs, "Critical Biography and Management Education," *Academy of Management Learning & Education* 6(1) (2007): 104–108.

45. L. Frankel and A. Fleisher, *The Human Factor in Industry* (New York: Macmillan, 1920): 8.

46. F. Roethlisberger and W. Dickson, *Management and the Worker* (Boston: Harvard University Press, 1939): 15–86.

47. D. McGregor, *The Human Side of Enterprise* (New York: McGraw-Hill, 1960).

48. W. Ouchi, *Theory Z—How American Business Can Meet the Japanese Challenge* (Reading, MA: Addison-Wesley, 1981).

49. T. Peters and R. Waterman, *In Search of Excellence: Lessons from America's Best Run Companies* (New York: Harper & Row, 1982).

50. F. Shipper, R.C. Hoffman, and D.M. Rotondo, "Does the 360 Feedback Process Create Actionable Knowledge Equally Across Cultures?" *Academy of Management Learning & Education* 6(1) (2007): 33–50.

51. O. Gottschalg and M. Zollo, "Interest Alignment and Competitive Advantage," *Academy of Management Review* 32(2) (2007): 418–437.

52. C. Barzantny, "Managing Diversity: Toward a Globally Inclusive Workplace," *Academy of Management Learning & Education* 6(2) (2007): 285–286.

53. M. Williams, "Building Genuine Trust through Interpersonal Emotion Management: A Threat Regulation Model of Trust and Collaboration across Boundaries," *Academy of Management Review* 32(2) (2007): 595–621.

54. R.A. Giacalone, "Taking a Red Pill to Disempower Unethical Students: Creating Ethical Sentinels in Business Schools," *Academy of Management Learning & Education* 6(4) (2007): 534–542.

55. M.F.R. Kets de Vries and K. Korotov, "Creating Transformational Executive Education Programs," *Academy of Management Learning & Education* 6(3) (2007): 375–387.

56. S. Maitlis and T. B. Lawrence, "Triggers and Enablers of Sensegiving in Organizations," *Academy of Management Journal* 50(1) (2007): 57–84.

57. D.J. Cohen, "The Very Separate Worlds of Academic and Practitioner Publications in Human Resource Management: Reasons for the Divide and Concrete Solutions for Bridging the Gap," *Academy of Management Journal* 50(5) (2007): 1013–1019.

58. I. Nooyi, "The Best Advice I Ever Got," *Fortune* (May 12, 2008): 74.

59. G. Kawasaki, "Gimme Some Love," *Entrepreneur* (June 2007): 24.

60. B. Farber, "Some Like It Hot," *Entrepreneur* (December 2007): 100.

61. C. Newmark, "The Best Advice I Ever Got," *Fortune* (May 12, 2008): 78.

62. M. Beck, "The Science Behind Senior Moments," *The Wall Street Journal* (May 27, 2007): D1.

63. S. Barlyn, "Tricks of the Trade," *The Wall Street Journal* (May 31, 2006): D1.

64. "Making Sales Presentations," *Entrepreneur* (June 2007): 105.

65. B. Farber, "Some Like It Hot," *Entrepreneur* (December 2007): 100.

66. O. Gottschalg and M. Zollo, "Interest Alignment and Competitive Advantage," *Academy of Management Review* 32(2) (2007): 418–437.

67. D. Geddes and R.R. Callister, "Crossing the Lines: A Dual Threshold Model of Anger in Organizations," *Academy of Management Review* 32(3) (2007): 721–746.

68. M. Bloomberg, "The Best Advice I Ever Got," *Fortune* (May 12, 2008): 72.

69. R. Cropanzano, D.E. Bowen, and S.W. Gilliland, "The Management of Organizational Justice," *Academy of Management Perspectives* 21(4) (2007): 34–48.

70. O. Gottschalg and M. Zollo, "Interest Alignment and Competitive Advantage," *Academy of Management Review* 32(2) (2007): 418–437.

71. R. Cropanzano, D.E. Bowen, and S.W. Gilliland, "The Management of Organizational Justice," *Academy of Management Perspectives* 21(4) (2007): 34–48.

72. J.C. Santora, "Managing Open Employees: Do Resources and Leadership Style Matter?" *Academy of Management Perspectives* 21(3) (2007): 83–84.

73. M.F.R. Kets de Vries and K. Korotov, "Creating Transformational Executive Education Programs," *Academy of Management Learning & Education* 6(3) (2007): 375–387.

74. J.A. Raelin, "Toward an Epistemology of Practice," *Academy of Management Learning & Education* 6(4) (2007): 495–519.

75. "Introduction: Promoting the Practice of Learning from Practice," *Academy of Management Learning & Education* 6(4) (2007): 493–494.

76. R.B. Kaiser and R.B. Kaplan, "The Deeper Work of Executive Development: Outgrowing Sensitivities," *Academy of Management Learning & Education* 5(4) (2006): 463–483.

77. P. Navarro, "The Hidden Potential of Managerial Macroeconomics for CEO Decision Making in MBA Programs," *Academy of Management Learning & Education* 5(2) (2006): 463–483.

78. Information taken for the AACSB Web site (www.aacsb.edu), accessed June 25, 2008.

79. "Building the 21st Century Leader," *Entrepreneur* (February 2007): 64–69.

80. R.B. Kaiser and R.B. Kaplan, "The Deeper Work of Executive Development: Outgrowing Sensitivities," *Academy of Management Learning & Education* 5(4) (2006): 463–483.

81. S.G. Barsade and D.E. Gibson, "Why Does Affect Matter in Organizations?" *Academy of Management Perspectives* 21(1) (2007): 36–59.

82. R. Cropanzano, D.E. Bowen, and S.W. Gilliland, "The Management of Organizational Justice," *Academy of Management Perspectives* 21(4) (2007): 34–48.

83. J.M. Wilson, P.S. Goodman, and M.A. Cronin, "Group Learning," *Academy of Management Review* 32(4) (2007): 1041–1059.

84. R.B. Kaiser and R.B. Kaplan, "The Deeper Work of Executive Development: Outgrowing Sensitivities," *Academy of Management Learning & Education* 5(4) (2006): 463–483.

85. R. Kark and D. Van Dijk, "Motivation to Lead, Motivation to Follow: The Role of the Self-Regulatory Focus in Leadership Process," *Academy of Management Review* 32(2) (2007): 500–528.

86. C.B. Gibson and P.C. Earley, "Collective Cognition in Action: Accumulation, Interaction, Examination, and Accommodation in the Development and Operation of Group Efficacy Beliefs in the Workplace," *Academy of Management Review* 32(2) (2007): 438–458.

87. R.B. Kaiser and R.B. Kaplan, "The Deeper Work of Executive Development: Outgrowing Sensitivities,"
Academy of Management Learning & Education 5(4) (2006): 463–483.

88. http://premium.hoovers.com/subscribe/co/overview.xhtml?ID=ffffcrkhrtkhrtkskh, retrieved September 8, 2008.

89. D. Jolly, "New Alcatel-Lucent Leaders Vow to Move Ahead," *The New York Times* (September 2, 2008). Retrieved from http://www.nytimes.com/2008/09/03/technology/03alcatel.html?_r=1&ref=worldbusiness&oref=slogin, September 8, 2008.

Chapter 2

1. "The Fortune 500," *Fortune* (May 5, 2008): F1–F60.

2. C.C. Berk, "PepsiCo's CEO Sees No Need to Change Strategy," *The Wall Street Journal* (October 24, 2006): B4.

3. B. Morris, "The Pepsi Challenge," *Fortune* (March 3, 2008): 55–66.

4. "The Fortune 500," *Fortune* (May 5, 2008): F1–F60.

5. K. Benner, E. Levenson, and R. Arora, "50 Most Powerful Women," *Fortune* (October 15, 2007): 107–116.

6. PepsiCo Web site (www.pepsico.com), retrieved June 27, 2008.

7. S.G. Barsade and D.E. Gibson, "Why Does Affect Matter in Organizations?" *Academy of Management Perspectives* 21(1) (2007): 36–59.

8. H. Le, I.S. Oh, J. Shaffer, and F. Schmidt, "Implications of Methodological Advances for the Practice of Personnel Selection: How Practitioners Benefit from Meta-analysis," *Academy of Management Perspectives* 21(3) (2007): 6–15.

9. L.W. Hunter and S.M.B. Thatcher, "Feeling the Heat: Effects of Stress, Commitment, and Job Experience on Job Performance," *Academy of Management Journal* 50(4) (2007): 953–968.

10. B.J. Tepper, S.E. Moss, D.E. Lockhart, and J.C. Carr, "Abusive Supervision, Upward Maintenance Communication, and Subordinates' Psychological Distress," *Academy of Management Journal* 50(5) (2007): 1169–1180.

11. S.L. Rynes, T.L. Giluk, and K.G. Brown, "The Very Separate Worlds of Academic and Practitioner Periodicals in Human Resource Management: Implications for Evidence-Based Management," *Academy of Management Journal* 50(5) (2007): 987–1008.

12. D.C. Hambrick, "Upper Echelons Theory: An Update," *Academy of Management Review* 32(2) (2007): 334–343.

13. R.B. Kaiser and R.B. Kaplan, "The Deeper Work of Executive Development: Outgrowing Sensitivities," *Academy of Management Learning & Education* 5(4) (2006): 463–483.

14. Ibid.

15. S.G. Barsade and D.E. Gibson, "Why Does Affect Matter in Organizations?" *Academy of Management Perspectives* 21(1) (2007): 36–59.

16. C.M. Vance, K.S. Groves, Y. Paik, and H. Kindler, "Understanding and Measuring Linear-Nonlinear Thinking Style for Enhanced Management Education and Professional Practice," *Academy of Management Learning & Education* 6(2) (2007): 167–185.

17. S.L. Rynes, T.L. Giluk, and K.G. Brown, "The Very Separate Worlds of Academic and Practitioner Periodicals in Human Resource Management: Implications for Evidence-Based Management," *Academy of Management Journal* 50(5) (2007): 987–1008.

18. A.J. Wefald and J.P. Katz, "Leaders: The Strategies for Taking Charge," *Academy of Management Perspectives* 21(3) (2007): 105–106.

19. T.A. Judge, R. Ilies, J.E. Bono, and M.W. Gerhardt, "Personality and Leadership: A Qualitative and Quantitative Review," *Journal of Applied Psychology* 87(4) (2002): 765–768.

20. S.G. Barsade and D.E. Gibson, "Why Does Affect Matter in Organizations?" *Academy of Management Perspectives* 21(1) (2007): 36–59.

21. T.A. Judge, R. Ilies, J.E. Bono, and M.W. Gerhardt, "Personality and Leadership: A Qualitative and Quantitative Review," *Journal of Applied Psychology* 87(4) (2002): 765–768.

22. C.M. Vance, K.S. Groves, Y. Paik, and H. Kindler, "Understanding and Measuring Linear-Nonlinear Thinking Style for Enhanced Management Education and Professional Practice," *Academy of Management Learning & Education* 6(2) (2007): 167–185.

23. J.C. Santora, "Managing Open Employees: Do Resources and Leadership Style Matter?" *Academy of Management Perspectives* 21(3) (2007): 83–84.

24. Statement made by Reviewer Robert Losik, Southern New Hampshire University.

25. T.A. Judge, R. Ilies, J.E. Bono, and M.W. Gerhardt, "Personality and Leadership: A Qualitative and Quantitative Review," *Journal of Applied Psychology* 87(4) (2002): 765–768.

26. A.J. Wefald and J.P. Katz, "Leaders: The Strategies for Taking Charge," *Academy of Management Perspectives* 21(3) (2007): 105–106.

27. T.A. Judge, R. Ilies, J.E. Bono, and M.W. Gerhardt, "Personality and Leadership: A Qualitative and Quantitative Review," *Journal of Applied Psychology* 87(4) (2002): 765–768.

28. Ibid.

29. M.G. Seo and L.F. Barrett, "Being Emotional During Decision Making—Good or Bad? An Empirical Investigation," *Academy of Management Journal* 50(4) (2007): 923–940.

30. T.A. Judge, R. Ilies, J.E. Bono, and M.W. Gerhardt, "Personality and Leadership: A Qualitative and Quantitative Review," *Journal of Applied Psychology* 87(4) (2002): 765–768.

31. J.A. Detert and E.R. Burris, "Leadership Behavior and Employee Voice: Is the Door Really Open?" *Academy of Management Journal* 50(4) (2007): 869–884.

32. H. Le, I.S. Oh, J. Shaffer, and F. Schmidt, "Implications of Methodological Advances for the Practice of Personnel Selection: How Practitioners Benefit from Meta-analysis," *Academy of Management Perspectives* 21(3) (2007): 6–15.

33. T.A. Judge, R. Ilies, J.E. Bono, and M.W. Gerhardt, "Personality and Leadership: A Qualitative and Quantitative Review," *Journal of Applied Psychology* 87(4) (2002): 765–768.

34. J.C. Santora, "Managing Open Employees: Do Resources and Leadership Style Matter?" *Academy of Management Perspectives* 21(3) (2007): 83–84.

35. S.L. Rynes, T.L. Giluk, and K.G. Brown, "The Very Separate Worlds of Academic and Practitioner Periodicals in Human Resource Management: Implications for Evidence-Based Management," *Academy of Management Journal* 50(5) (2007): 987–1008.

36. A. Gupta, "Leadership in a Fast-Paced World: An Interview with Ken Blanchard," *Mid-American Journal of Business* 20(1) (2005): 7–10.

37. S.L. Rynes, T.L. Giluk, and K.G. Brown, "The Very Separate Worlds of Academic and Practitioner Periodicals in Human Resource Management: Implications for Evidence-Based Management," *Academy of Management Journal* 50(5) (2007): 987–1008.

38. S.G. Barsade and D.E. Gibson, "Why Does Affect Matter in Organizations?" *Academy of Management Perspectives* 21(1) (2007): 36–59.

39. D.C. Hambrick, "Upper Echelons Theory: An Update," *Academy of Management Review* 32(2) (2007): 334–343.

40. T.A. Judge, R. Ilies, J.E. Bono, and M.W. Gerhardt, "Personality and Leadership: A Qualitative and Quantitative Review," *Journal of Applied Psychology* 87(4) (2002): 765–768.

41. Ibid.

42. H. Le, I.S. Oh, J. Shaffer, and F. Schmidt, "Implications of Methodological Advances for the Practice of Personnel Selection: How Practitioners Benefit from Meta-analysis," *Academy of Management Perspectives* 21(3) (2007): 6–15.

43. C.M. Vance, K.S. Groves, Y. Paik, and H. Kindler, "Understanding and Measuring Linear-Nonlinear Thinking Style for Enhanced Management Education and Professional Practice," *Academy of Management Learning & Education* 6(2) (2007): 167–185.

44. R.L. Hotz, "Scientists are Still Searching in the Dark for the Secrets of Sleep," *The Wall Street Journal* (January 18, 2008): B1.

45. D. Geddes and R.R. Callister, "Crossing the Lines: A Dual Threshold Model of Anger in Organizations," *Academy of Management Review* 32(3) (2007): 721–746.

46. L.W. Hunter and S.M.B. Thatcher, "Feeling the Heat: Effects of Stress, Commitment, and Job Experience on Job Performance," *Academy of Management Journal* 50(4) (2007): 953–968.

47. "How to Manage Anger," *TopHealth* (May 2007): 2.

48. "Hidden Ways to Help Your Heart," *TopHealth* (February 2007): 1.

49. "5 Common Headache Triggers," *TopHealth* (October 2007): 1.

50. "Obesity May Increase," *The Wall Street Journal* (February 15, 2008): A1.

51. "How to Manage Anger," *TopHealth* (May 2007): 2.

52. C. Mamberto, "Companies Aim to Combat Job-Related Stress," *The Wall Street Journal* (August 13, 2007): B6.

53. B.J. Tepper, S.E. Moss, D.E. Lockhart, and J.C. Carr, "Abusive Supervision, Upward Maintenance Communication, and Subordinates' Psychological Distress," *Academy of Management Journal* 50(5) (2007): 1169–1180.

54. D. Geddes and R.R. Callister, "Crossing the Lines: A Dual Threshold Model of Anger in Organizations," *Academy of Management Review* 32(3) (2007): 721–746.

55. L.W. Hunter and S.M.B. Thatcher, "Feeling the Heat: Effects of Stress, Commitment, and Job Experience on Job Performance," *Academy of Management Journal* 50(4) (2007): 953–968.

56. "People Who Feel Chronic Stress," *The Wall Street Journal* (October 4, 2007): A1.

57. D. Geddes and R.R. Callister, "Crossing the Lines: A Dual Threshold Model of Anger in Organizations," *Academy of Management Review* 32(3) (2007): 721–746.

58. "The Right Prescription," *Fortune* (February 12, 2007): S7.

59. B. Iger, "How I Work," *Fortune* (December 10, 2007): 38.

60. C. Mamberto, "Companies Aim to Combat Job-Related Stress," *The Wall Street Journal* (August 13, 2007): B6.

61. "About 70% of Americans Don't Exercise," *The Wall Street Journal* (April 8, 2002): A1.

62. "Earth's Easiest Exercise," *TopHealth* (October 2007): 1.

63. "Simple Tips to Slimmer Waists," *TopHealth* (May 2007): 1.

64. Front page news, AOL.com (May 22, 2003).

65. "Obesity and Related Illnesses," *The Wall Street Journal* (May 22, 2003): A1.

66. T.P. Pope, "Exploring a Surprising Link between Obesity and Diet Soda," *The Wall Street Journal* (July 27, 2007): D1.

67. M. Beck, "Gut Check: Why Doctors Say Not All Fat Is Created Equal," *The Wall Street Journal* (April 15, 2008): D1.

68. "Simple Tips to Slimmer Waists," *TopHealth* (May 2007): 1.

69. Ibid.

70. "Healthy Food Shopping Dos & Don'ts," *TopHealth* (February 2007): 2.

71. "Simple Tips to Slimmer Waists," *TopHealth* (May 2007): 1.

72. S. Shellenbarger, "Americans Get Too Little Sleep and Everyone Has an Excuse," *The Wall Street Journal* (May 31, 2007): D1.

73. R.L. Hotz, "Scientists Are Still Searching in the Dark for the Secrets of Sleep," *The Wall Street Journal* (January 18, 2008): B1.

74. S. Shellenbarger, "Americans Get Too Little Sleep and Everyone Has an Excuse," *The Wall Street Journal* (May 31, 2007): D1.

75. "How to Get That Second Wind," *TopHealth* (February 2007): 1.

76. Ibid.

77. B.M. Wiesenfeld, W.B. Swann, J. Brockner, and C.A. Bartel, "Is More Fairness Always Preferred? Self-Esteem Moderates Reactions to Procedural Justice," *Academy of Management Journal* 50(5) (2007): 1235–1253.

78. C. Penttila, "Time Out," *Entrepreneur* (April 2007): 71.

79. B.J. Tepper, S.E. Moss, D.E. Lockhart, and J.C. Carr, "Abusive Supervision, Upward Maintenance Communication, and Subordinates' Psychological Distress," *Academy of Management Journal* 50(5) (2007): 1169–1180.

80. "Exercise, Quitting Smoking," *The Wall Street Journal* (January 8, 2008): A1.

81. A.J. Wefald and J.P. Katz, "Leaders: The Strategies for Taking Charge," *Academy of Management Perspectives* 21(3) (2007): 105–106.

82. H. Le, I.S. Oh, J. Shaffer, and F. Schmidt, "Implications of Methodological Advances for the Practice of Personnel Selection: How Practitioners Benefit from Meta-analysis," *Academy of Management Perspective* 21(3) (2007): 6–15.

83. R.B. Kaiser and R.B. Kaplan, "The Deeper Work of Executive Development: Outgrowing Sensitivities," *Academy of Management Learning & Education* 5(4) (2006): 463–483.

84. S.L. Rynes, T.L. Giluk, and K.G. Brown, "The Very Separate Worlds of Academic and Practitioner Periodicals in Human Resource Management: Implications for Evidence-Based Management," *Academy of Management Journal* 50(5) (2007): 987–1008.

85. B. Schlender, "Gates After Microsoft," *Fortune* (July 7, 2008): 110–116.

86. C. Barzantny, "Managing Diversity: Toward a Globally Inclusive Workplace," *Academy of Management Learning & Education* 6(2) (2007): 285–286.

87. D. Petraeus, "The Best Advice I Ever Got," *Fortune* (May 12, 2008): 75.

88. "On the Football Field This Season," *The Wall Street Journal* (September 30, 2005): W1.

89. S.G. Barsade and D.E. Gibson, "Why Does Affect Matter in Organizations?" *Academy of Management Perspectives* 21(1) (2007): 36–59.

90. D. Goleman, *Emotional Intelligence: Why It Can Matter More Than IQ* (New York: Bantam Books, 1995).

91. C.M. Vance, K.S. Groves, Y. Paik, and H. Kindler, "Understanding and Measuring Linear-Nonlinear Thinking Style for Enhanced Management Education and Professional Practice," *Academy of Management Learning & Education* 6(2) (2007): 167–185.

92. L.W. Hunter and S.M.B. Thatcher, "Feeling the Heat: Effects of Stress, Commitment, and Job Experience on Job Performance," *Academy of Management Journal* 50(4) (2007): 953–968.

93. O. Gottschalg and M. Zollo, "Interest Alignment and Competitive Advantage," *Academy of Management Review* 32(2) (2007): 418–437.

94. "Making Sales Presentations," *Entrepreneur* (June 2007): 105.

95. W. Lam, X. Huang, and E. Snape, "Feedback-Seeking Behavior and Leader-Member Exchange: Do Supervisor-Attributed Motives Matter?" *Academy of Management Journal* 50(2) (2007): 348–363.

96. R.B. Kaiser and R.B. Kaplan, "The Deeper Work of Executive Development: Outgrowing Sensitivities," *Academy of Management Learning & Education* 5(4) (2006): 463–483.

97. J. Houde, "Analogically Situated Experiences: Creating Insight through Novel Contexts," *Academy of Management Learning & Education* 6(3) (2007): 321–331.

98. Kolb Web site (www.learningfromexperience.com), retrieved June 30, 2008.

99. L. Proserpio, "Teaching the Virtual Generation," *Academy of Management Learning & Education* 6(1) (2007): 69–80.

100. D. Dimov, "From Opportunity Insight to Opportunity Intention: The Importance of Person-Situation Learning Match," *Entrepreneurship Theory and Practice* 31(6) (2007): 1121–1243.

101. N. Anand, H.K. Gardner, and T. Morris, "Knowledge-Based Innovation: Emergence and Embedding of New Practice Areas in Management Consulting Firms," *Academy of Management Journal* 50(2) (2007): 406–428.

102. D.J. Miller, M.J. Fern, and L.B. Cardinal, "The Use of Knowledge for Technological Innovation within Diversified Firms," *Academy of Management Journal* 50(2) (2007): 308–326.

103. J.C. Santora, "Managing Open Employees: Do Resources and Leadership Style Matter?" *Academy of Management Perspectives* 21(3) (2007): 83–84.

104. M.A. Cronin and L.R. Weingart, "Representational Gaps, Information Processing, and Conflict in Functionally Diverse Teams," *Academy of Management Review* 32(3) (2007): 761–773.

105. F.C. Brodbeck, R. Kerschreiter, A. Mojzisch, and S. Schulz-Hardt, "Improving Group Decision Making Under Conditions of Distributed Knowledge: The Information Asymmetries Model," *Academy of Management Review* 32(2) (2007): 459–479.

106. D.J. Miller, M.J. Fern, and L.B. Cardinal, "The Use of Knowledge for Technological Innovation within Diversified Firms," *Academy of Management Journal* 50(2) (2007): 308–326.

107. B. Farber, "No Pain, No Gain," *Entrepreneur* (July 2007): 78.

108. N. Anand, H.K. Gardner, and T. Morris, "Knowledge-Based Innovation: Emergence and Embedding of New Practice Areas in Management Consulting Firms," *Academy of Management Journal* 50(2) (2007): 406–428.

109. C.W. Langfred, "The Downside of Self-Management: A Longitudinal Study of the Effects of Conflict on Trust, Autonomy, and Task Interdependence in Self-Managing Teams," *Academy of Management Journal* 50(4) (2007): 885–900.

110. N. Anand, H.K. Gardner, and T. Morris, "Knowledge-Based Innovation: Emergence and Embedding of New Practice Areas in Management Consulting Firms," *Academy of Management Journal* 50(2) (2007): 406–428.

111. M.A. Cronin and L.R. Weingart, "Representational Gaps, Information Processing, and Conflict in Functionally Diverse Teams," *Academy of Management Review* 32(3) (2007): 761–773.

112. R.B. Kaiser and R.B. Kaplan, "The Deeper Work of Executive Development: Outgrowing Sensitivities," *Academy of Management Learning & Education* 5(4) (2006): 463–483.

113. J. Sandberg, "People Can't Resist Doing a Big Favor—Or Asking for One," *The Wall Street Journal* (December 18, 2007): B1.

114. S. Maitlis and T. B. Lawrence, "Triggers and Enablers of Sensegiving in Organizations," *Academy of Management Journal* 50(1) (2007): 57–84.

115. C. Hymowitz, "Sometimes, Moving Up Makes It Harder to See What Goes On Below," *The Wall Street Journal* (October 15, 2007): B1.

116. S. Covel, "How to Get Workers to Think and Act Like Owners," *The Wall Street Journal* (February 7, 2008): B6.

117. M.G. Seo and L.F. Barrett, "Being Emotional During Decision Making—Good or Bad? An Empirical Investigation," *Academy of Management Journal* 50(4) (2007): 923–940.

118. L. Roberson and C.T. Kulik, "Stereotype Threat at Work," *Academy of Management Perspectives* 21(2) (2007): 24–40.

119. E. White, "Deloitte Tries a Different Sales Pitch for Women," *The Wall Street Journal* (October 8, 2007): B1.

120. M. Sonfield and R.N. Lussier, "Family Business Ownership and Management: A Gender Comparison," *Journal of Small Business Strategy* 15(2) (2005): 59–76.

121. C.T. Kulik, H.T.J. Bainbridge, and C. Cregan, "Known by the Company We Keep: Stigma-by-Association Effects in the Workplace," *Academy of Management Review* 33(1) (2008): 216–230.

122. S.E. Page, "Making the Difference: Applying a Logic of Diversity," *Academy of Management Perspectives* 21(4) (2007): 6–20.

123. S. Covel, "How to Get Workers to Think and Act Like Owners," *The Wall Street Journal* (February 7, 2008): B6.

124. L. Roberson and C.T. Kulik, "Stereotype Threat at Work," *Academy of Management Perspectives* 21(2) (2007): 24–40.

125. M.A. Cronin and L.R. Weingart, "Representational Gaps, Information Processing, and Conflict in Functionally Diverse Teams," *Academy of Management Review* 32(3) (2007): 761–773.

126. S. Maitlis and T. B. Lawrence, "Triggers and Enablers of Sensegiving in Organizations," *Academy of Management Journal* 50(1) (2007): 57–84.

127. M.G. Seo and L.F. Barrett, "Being Emotional During Decision Making—Good or Bad? An Empirical Investigation," *Academy of Management Journal* 50(4) (2007): 923–940.

128. Z. Xin, "The Best Advice I Ever Got," *Fortune* (May 12, 2008): 77.

129. S. Maitlis and T. B. Lawrence, "Triggers and Enablers of Sensegiving in Organizations," *Academy of Management Journal* 50(1) (2007): 57–84.

130. L. Roberson and C.T. Kulik, "Stereotype Threat at Work," *Academy of Management Perspectives* 21(2) (2007): 24–40.

131. W. Lam, X. Huang, and E. Snape, "Feedback-Seeking Behavior and Leader-Member Exchange: Do Supervisor-Attributed Motives Matter?" *Academy of Management Journal* 50(2) (2007): 348–363.

132. S. Bing, "How Fred Got His First Job," *Fortune* (March 31, 2008): 126.

133. C. Binkley, "Rejected: Readers Reveal Interview Don'ts," *The Wall Street Journal* (January 17, 2008): D8.

134. L. Zuin and N. Zuin, *Contact—The First Four Minutes* (New York: Ballantine Books, 1972).

135. J. Elsea, *The Four Minute Sell* (New York: Simon & Schuster, 1984).

136. S. Bing, "How Fred Got His First Job," *Fortune* (March 31, 2008): 126.

137. C. Seda, "First Impressions," *Entrepreneur* (October 2006): 64.

138. Ibid.

139. S. Bing, "How Fred Got His First Job," *Fortune* (March 31, 2008): 126.

140. C. Binkley, "Rejected: Readers Reveal Interview Don'ts," *The Wall Street Journal* (January 17, 2008): D8.

141. Ibid.

142. Ibid.

143. Retrieved from http://en.wikipedia.org/wiki/Ted_Turner, September 15, 2008.

144. David D. Kirkpatrick and Jim Rutenberg, "The Media Business: Turner Plans Role of Gadfly Without Portfolio," *The New York Times*. Retrieved from http://query.nytimes.com/gst/fullpage.html?res=9F00E6DF153DF933A157 51C0A9659C8B63&sec=&spon=&pagewanted=2, September 22, 2008.

Chapter 3

1. Red Cross Web site (www.redcross.org), retrieved July 8, 2008.

2. R.B. Kaiser and R.B. Kaplan, "The Deeper Work of Executive Development: Outgrowing Sensitivities," *Academy of Management Learning & Education* 5(4) (2006): 463–483.

3. S.G. Barsade and D.E. Gibson, "Why Does Affect Matter in Organizations?" *Academy of Management Perspectives* 21(1) (2007): 36–59.

4. S. Shellenbarger, "Rules of Engagement," *The Wall Street Journal* (October 1, 2007): R3.

5. A.M. Grant, M.K. Christianson, and R.H. Price, "Happiness, Health, or Relationships? Managerial Practices and Employee Well-Being Tradeoffs," *Academy of Management Perspectives* 21(3) (2007): 51–63.

6. P. Dvorak, "Hotelier Finds Happiness Keeps Staff Checked In," *The Wall Street Journal* (December 17, 2007), B3.

7. R.M.J. Wells, "Outstanding Customer Satisfaction: The Key to a Talented Workforce? *Academy of Management Perspectives* 21(3) (2007): 87–89.

8. S. Bing, "How Fred Got His First Job," *Fortune* (March 31, 2008): 126.

9. B. Farber, "Take a Swing," *Entrepreneur* (September 2007): 84.

10. R. Ely and I. Padavic, "A Feminist Analysis of Organizational Research on Sex Differences," *Academy of Management Review* 32(4) (2007): 1121–1143.

11. J. Weber, "Bribery: Not Only Wrong, But Costly Too?" *Academy of Management Perspectives* 21(3) (2007): 86–87.

12. J.A. Detert and E.R. Burris, "Leadership Behavior and Employee Voice: Is the Door Really Open?" *Academy of Management Journal* 50(4) (2007): 869–884.

13. R. Cropanzano, D.E. Bowen, and S.W. Gilliland, "The Management of Organizational Justice," *Academy of Management Perspectives* 21(4) (2007): 34–48.

14. Y. Zhu, "Do Cultural Values Shape Employee Receptivity to Leadership Styles?" *Academy of Management Perspectives* 21(3) (2007): 89–90.

15. P. Dvorak, "Hotelier Finds Happiness Keeps Staff Checked In," *The Wall Street Journal* (December 17, 2007), B3.

16. R.M.J. Wells, "Outstanding Customer Satisfaction: The Key to a Talented Workforce? *Academy of Management Perspectives* 21(3) (2007): 87–89.

17. S.G. Barsade and D.E. Gibson, "Why Does Affect Matter in Organizations?" *Academy of Management Perspectives* 21(1) (2007): 36–59.

18. C. Seda, "First Impressions," *Entrepreneur* (October 2006): 64.

19. S.G. Barsade and D.E. Gibson, "Why Does Affect Matter in Organizations?" *Academy of Management Perspectives* 21(1) (2007): 36–59.

20. D. Jacobs, "Critical Biography and Management Education," *Academy of Management Learning & Education* 6(1) (2007): 104–108.

21. J.A. Detert and E.R. Burris, "Leadership Behavior and Employee Voice: Is the Door Really Open?" *Academy of Management Journal* 50(4) (2007): 869–884.

22. P. Osterman, "Comments on Le, Oh, Shaffer, and Schmidt," *Academy of Management Perspectives* 21(3) (2007): 16–18.

23. S. Shellenbarger, "Rules of Engagement," *The Wall Street Journal* (October 1, 2007): R3.

24. R. Cropanzano, D.E. Bowen, and S.W. Gilliland, "The Management of Organizational Justice," *Academy of Management Perspectives* 21(4) (2007): 34–48.

25. P. Osterman, "Comments on Le, Oh, Shaffer, and Schmidt," *Academy of Management Perspectives* 21(3) (2007): 16–18.

26. D. Reynolds, "Restraining Golem and Harnessing Pygmalion in the Classroom: A Laboratory Study of Managerial Expectations and Task Design," *Academy of Management Learning & Education* 6(4) (2007): 475–483.

27. Ibid.

28. L. Roberson and C.T. Kulik, "Stereotype Threat at Work," *Academy of Management Perspectives* 21(2) (2007): 24–40.

29. Ibid.

30. B. Farber, "No Pain, No Gain," *Entrepreneur* (July 2007): 78.

31. P. Dvorak, "Hotelier Finds Happiness Keeps Staff Checked In," *The Wall Street Journal* (December 17, 2007), B3.

32. R. Cropanzano, D.E. Bowen, and S.W. Gilliland, "The Management of Organizational Justice," *Academy of Management Perspectives* 21(4) (2007): 34–48.

33. D. Reynolds, "Restraining Golem and Harnessing Pygmalion in the Classroom: A Laboratory Study of Managerial Expectations and Task Design," *Academy of Management Learning & Education* 6(4) (2007): 475–483.

34. P. Dvorak, "Hotelier Finds Happiness Keeps Staff Checked In," *The Wall Street Journal* (December 17, 2007), B3.

35. D. Reynolds, "Restraining Golem and Harnessing Pygmalion in the Classroom: A Laboratory Study of Managerial Expectations and Task Design," *Academy of Management Learning & Education* 6(4) (2007): 475–483.

36. B. Farber, "No Pain, No Gain," *Entrepreneur* (July 2007): 78.

37. Ibid.

38. A.M. Grant, M.K. Christianson, and R.H. Price, "Happiness, Health, or Relationships? Managerial Practices and Employee Well-Being Tradeoffs," *Academy of Management Perspectives* 21(3) (2007): 51–63.

39. S.G. Barsade and D.E. Gibson, "Why Does Affect Matter in Organizations?" *Academy of Management Perspectives* 21(1) (2007): 36–59.

40. F. Shipper, R.C. Hoffman, and D.M. Rotondo, "Does the 360 Feedback Process Create Actionable Knowledge Equally Across Cultures?" *Academy of Management Learning & Education* 6(1) (2007): 33–50.

41. S. Shellenbarger, "Rules of Engagement," *The Wall Street Journal* (October 1, 2007): R3.

42. O. Gottschalg and M. Zollo, "Interest Alignment and Competitive Advantage," *Academy of Management Review* 32(2) (2007): 418–437.

43. D. Reynolds, "Restraining Golem and Harnessing Pygmalion in the Classroom: A Laboratory Study of Managerial Expectations and Task Design," *Academy of Management Learning & Education* 6(4) (2007): 475–483.

44. J. Sandberg, "For Many Employees, A Dream Job Is One That Isn't a Nightmare," *The Wall Street Journal* (April 15, 2007): B1.

45. P. Dvorak, "Hotelier Finds Happiness Keeps Staff Checked In," *The Wall Street Journal* (December 17, 2007), B3.

46. S. Shellenbarger, "Rules of Engagement," *The Wall Street Journal* (October 1, 2007): R3.

47. J.B.O. Buchanan and W.R. Boswell, "An Integrative Model of Experiencing and Responding to Mistreatment at Work," *Academy of Management Review* 33(1) (2008): 75–96.

48. S.G. Barsade and D.E. Gibson, "Why Does Affect Matter in Organizations?" *Academy of Management Perspectives* 21(1) (2007): 36–59.

49. J. Sandberg, "For Many Employees, A Dream Job Is One That Isn't a Nightmare," *The Wall Street Journal* (April 15, 2007): B1.

50. S. Shellenbarger, "Rules of Engagement," *The Wall Street Journal* (October 1, 2007): R3.

51. M. Henricks, "The Best of the Best," *Entrepreneur* (September 2007): 34.

52. "More Bonuses Tied to Job Performance," *The Wall Street Journal* (August 15, 2007): D5.

53. M. Henricks, "The Best of the Best," *Entrepreneur* (September 2007): 34.

54. J.C. Santora, "Managing Open Employees: Do Resources and Leadership Style Matter?" *Academy of Management Perspectives* 21(3) (2007): 83–84.

55. Y. Zhu, "Do Cultural Values Shape Employee Receptivity to Leadership Styles?" *Academy of Management Perspectives* 21(3) (2007): 89–90.

56. S. Shellenbarger, "Rules of Engagement," *The Wall Street Journal* (October 1, 2007): R3.

57. S.G. Barsade and D.E. Gibson, "Why Does Affect Matter in Organizations?" *Academy of Management Perspectives* 21(1) (2007): 36–59.

58. U. Raja, G. Johns, and F. Ntalianis, "The Impact of Personality on Psychological Contracts," *Academy of Management Journal* 47(3) (2004): 350–367.

59. J. Sandberg, "For Many Employees, A Dream Job Is One That Isn't a Nightmare," *The Wall Street Journal* (April 15, 2007): B1.

60. Ibid.

61. S. Shellenbarger, "Rules of Engagement," *The Wall Street Journal* (October 1, 2007): R3.

62. B.L. Kirkman and D.L. Shapiro, "The Impact of Cultural Values on Job Satisfaction and Organizational Commitment in Self-Managing Work Teams: The Mediating Role of Employee Resistance," *Academy of Management Journal* 44(3) (2001): 557–569.

63. Based on a Princeton University study reported in *The Wall Street Journal* (January 10, 2002): A1.

64. B.M. Wiesenfeld, W.B. Swann, J. Brockner, and C.A. Bartel, "Is More Fairness Always Preferred? Self-Esteem

Moderates Reactions to Procedural Justice," *Academy of Management Journal* 50(5) (2007): 1235–1253.

65. S. Bing, "How Fred Got His First Job," *Fortune* (March 31, 2008): 126.

66. T.A. Judge, R. Ilies, J.E. Bono, and M.W. Gerhardt, "Personality and Leadership: A Qualitative and Quantitative Review," *Journal of Applied Psychology* 87(4) (2002): 765–768.

67. J. Sandberg, "If That Guy Got a Promotion, Mine Can't Be Far Behind," *The Wall Street Journal* (September 18, 2007): B1.

68. D. Reynolds, "Restraining Golem and Harnessing Pygmalion in the Classroom: A Laboratory Study of Managerial Expectations and Task Design," *Academy of Management Learning & Education* 6(4) (2007): 475–483.

69. S. Bing, "How Fred Got His First Job," *Fortune* (March 31, 2008): 126.

70. J. Sandberg, "If That Guy Got a Promotion, Mine Can't Be Far Behind," *The Wall Street Journal* (September 18, 2007): B1.

71. Ibid.

72. P. Osterman, "Comments on Le, Oh, Shaffer, and Schmidt," *Academy of Management Perspectives* 21(3) (2007): 16–18.

73. L. Roberson and C.T. Kulik, "Stereotype Threat at Work," *Academy of Management Perspectives* 21(2) (2007): 24–40.

74. S. Bing, "How Fred Got His First Job," *Fortune* (March 31, 2008): 126.

75. J.B. Carson, P.E. Tesluck, and J.A. Marrone, "Shared Leadership in Teams: An Investigation of Antecedent Conditions and Performance," *Academy of Management Journal* 50(5) (2007): 1217–1234.

76. B. Farber, "Take a Swing," *Entrepreneur* (September 2007): 84.

77. J. Zaslow, "In Praise of Less Praise," *The Wall Street Journal* (May 3, 2007): D1.

78. B. Kotick, "The Three-Minute Manager," *Fortune* (July 7, 2008): 28.

79. J. Dyson, "The Three-Minute Manager," *Fortune* (July 7, 2008): 28.

80. T. Koczmarski, "The Three-Minute Manager," *Fortune* (July 7, 2008): 28.

81. L.W. Hunter and S.M.B. Thatcher, "Feeling the Heat: Effects of Stress, Commitment, and Job Experience on Job Performance," *Academy of Management Journal* 50(4) (2007): 953–968.

82. B. Farber, "Take a Swing," *Entrepreneur* (September 2007): 84.

83. J. Sandberg, "If That Guy Got a Promotion, Mine Can't Be Far Behind," *The Wall Street Journal* (September 18, 2007): B1.

84. L.A. Mainiero and S.E. Sullivan, *The Opt-Out Revolt: Why People Are Leaving Companies to Create Kaleidoscope Careers* (Mountain View, CA: Davies-Black, 2006).

85. S. Waddock, "Leadership Integrity in a Fractured Knowledge World," *Academy of Management Learning & Education* 6(4) (2007): 543–557.

86. R. Ely and I. Padavic, "A Feminist Analysis of Organizational Research on Sex Differences," *Academy of Management Review* 32(4) (2007): 1121–1143.

87. K.K. Metters and R. Metters, "Misunderstanding the Chinese Worker," *The Wall Street Journal* (July 7, 2008): R11.

88. R.A. Giacalone, "Taking a Red Pill to Disempower Unethical Students: Creating Ethical Sentinels in Business Schools," *Academy of Management Learning & Education* 6(4) (2007): 534–542.

89. K. Basu and G. Palazzo, "Corporate Social Responsibility: A Process Model of Sensemaking," *Academy of Management Review* 33(1) (2008): 122–136.

90. A.G. Scherer and G. Palazzo, "Toward a Political Conception of Corporate Responsibility: Business and Society Seen from a Habermasian Perspective," *Academy of Management Review* 32(4) (2007): 1096–1120.

91. J. Clements, "No Satisfaction: Why What You Have Is Never Enough," *The Wall Street Journal* (May 2, 2007): D1.

92. J. Clements, "The Pursuit of Happiness: Six Experts Tell What They've Done to Achieve It," *The Wall Street Journal* (December 6, 2006): D1.

93. T. Petzinger, "Edward O. Wilson: Human Nature, Dr. Wilson Believes, Has Changed Little in Many Millennia. And It Will Change Very Little in the Millennia Ahead," *The Wall Street Journal* (January 1, 2000): R16.

94. Spirit at Work Web site (www.spiritatwork.com), retrieved July 15, 2008.

95. K. Helliker, "Body and Spirit: Why Attending Religious Services May Benefit Your Health," *The Wall Street Journal* (May 3, 2005): D1.

96. D. Seidman, "The Case for Ethical Leadership," *Academy of Management Executive* 18(2) (2004): 134–138.

97. M. Learmonth, "Critical Management Education in Action: Personal Tales of Management Unlearning," *Academy of Management Learning & Education* 6(1) (2007): 109–113.

98. D. M. Rousseau and S. McCarthy, "Educating Managers from an Evidence-Based Perspective," *Academy of Management Learning & Education* 6(1) (2007): 84–101.

99. J. Weber, "Bribery: Not Only Wrong, But Costly Too?" *Academy of Management Perspectives* 21(3) (2007): 86–87.

100. R.A. Giacalone, "Taking a Red Pill to Disempower Unethical Students: Creating Ethical Sentinels in Business Schools," *Academy of Management Learning & Education* 6(4) (2007): 534–542.

101. G. Probst and S. Raisch, "Organizational Crisis: The Logic of Failure," *Academy of Management Executive* 19(1) (2005): 90–105.

102. G. Kawasaki, "Lies, Lies, Lies!" *Entrepreneur* (March 2007): 34.

103. B. Farber, "Basic Instincts," *Entrepreneur* (August 2007): 66.

104. G. Kawasaki, "Go for the Gold," *Entrepreneur* (April 2007): 20.

105. H. Le, I.S. Oh, J. Shaffer, and F. Schmidt, "Implications of Methodological Advances for the Practice of Personnel Selection: How Practitioners Benefit from Meta-analysis," *Academy of Management Perspectives* 21(3) (2007): 6–15.

106. M. Learmonth, "Critical Management Education in Action: Personal Tales of Management Unlearning," *Academy of Management Learning & Education* 6(1) (2007): 109–113.

107. J.A. Detert and E.R. Burris, "Leadership Behavior and Employee Voice: Is the Door Really Open?" *Academy of Management Journal* 50(4) (2007): 869–884.

108. S. Sonenshein, "The Role of Construction, Intuition, and Justification in Responding to Ethical Issues at Work: The Sensemaking Intuition Model," *Academy of Management Review* 32(4) (2007): 1022–1028.

109. J. Houde, "Analogically Situated Experiences: Creating Insight through Novel Contexts," *Academy of Management Learning & Education* 6(3) (2007): 321–331.

110. S. Sonenshein, "The Role of Construction, Intuition, and Justification in Responding to Ethical Issues at Work: The Sensemaking Intuition Model," *Academy of Management Review* 32(4) (2007): 1022–1028.

111. R.A. Giacalone, "Taking a Red Pill to Disempower Unethical Students: Creating Ethical Sentinels in Business Schools," *Academy of Management Learning & Education* 6(4) (2007): 534–542.

112. Ibid.

113. R.V. Aguilera, D.E. Rupp, C.A. Williams, and J. Ganapathi, "Putting the S Back in Corporate Social Responsibility: A Multilevel Theory of Social Change in Organization," *Academy of Management Review* 32(3) (2007): 836–863.

114. J.L. Campbell, "Why Would Corporations Behave in Socially Responsible Ways? An Institutional Theory of Corporate Social Responsibility," *Academy of Management Review* 32(3) (2007): 946–967.

115. J. Weber, "Bribery: Not Only Wrong, But Costly Too?" *Academy of Management Perspectives* 21(3) (2007): 86–87.

116. A. Mackey, T.B. Mackey, and J.B. Barney, "Corporate Social Responsibility and Firm Performance: Investor Preferences and Corporate Strategies," *Academy of Management Review* 32(3) (2007): 817–835.

117. J. B. Cullen, K P. Parboteeah, and M. Hoegl, "Cross-National Differences in Managers: Willingness to Justify Ethically Suspect Behaviors: A Test of Institutional Anomie Theory," *Academy of Management Journal* 47(3) (2004): 411–421.

118. R.J. Bies, J.M. Bartunek, T.L. Fort, and M.N. Zaid, "Corporations as Social Change Agents: Individual, Interpersonal, Institutional, and Environmental Dynamics," *Academy of Management Review* 32(3) (2007): 788–793.

119. http://premium.hoovers.com/subscribe/co/overview.xhtml?ID=ffffrfyhsffytsjrkh, retrieved September 22, 2008.

120. http://www.thecoca-colacompany.com/citizenship/strategic_vision.html, retrieved September 22, 2008.

121. http://www.thecoca-colacompany.com/ourcompany/manifesto_for_growth.html, retrieved September 22, 2008.

122. http://www.thecoca-colacompany.com/ourcompany/meet_our_people.html, retrieved September 22, 2008.

123. http://www.thecoca-colacompany.com/ourcompany/manifesto_for_growth.html, retrieved September 22, 2008.

Chapter 4

1. J. Sandberg, "Why Learn and Grow on the Job? Easier to Feign Infallibility," *The Wall Street Journal* (January 22, 2008): B1.

2. J.E. Jennings and M.S. McDougald, "Work-Family Interface Experiences and Coping Strategies: Implications for Entrepreneurship Research and Practice," *Academy of Management Review* 32(3) (2007): 747–760.

3. L.W. Hunter and S.M.B. Thatcher, "Feeling the Heat: Effects of Stress, Commitment, and Job Experience on Job Performance," *Academy of Management Journal* 50(4) (2007): 953–968.

4. B. Iger, "How I Work," *Fortune* (December 10, 2007): 38.

5. Spirit at Work Web site (www.spiritatwork.com), retrieved July 17, 2008.

6. J. Sandberg, "Had It Up to Here? Despite Risk, Some Say Quitting Is Way to Go," *The Wall Street Journal* (August 14, 2007): B1.

7. L. Uchitelle, "Employer-Employee Social Contracts: Fashioning a New Compact for Workers," *Academy of Management Perspectives* 21(2) (2007): 5–9.

8. A. Fisher, "How to Get Hired by a Best Company," *Fortune* (February 4, 2008): 96.

9. S. Shellenbarger, "How to Fix Your Life in 2008," *The Wall Street Journal* (December 27, 2007): D3.

10. C. Penttila, "Time Out," *Entrepreneur* (April 2007): 71.

11. Ibid.

12. J. Sandberg, "Why Learn and Grow on the Job? Easier to Feign Infallibility," *The Wall Street Journal* (January 22, 2008): B1.

13. S. Shellenbarger, "Multitasking Makes You Stupid: Studies Show Pitfalls of Doing Too Much at Once," *The Wall Street Journal* (February 27, 2003): D1.

14. C. Hymowitz, "Crowded Calendars Rule Executives' Days," *The Wall Street Journal* (June 16, 2008): B1.

15. S. Shellenbarger, "Rules of Engagement," *The Wall Street Journal* (October 1, 2007): R3.

16. C. Penttila, "Time Out," *Entrepreneur* (April 2007): 71.

17. S. Shellenbarger, "Multitasking Makes You Stupid: Studies Show Pitfalls of Doing Too Much at Once," *The Wall Street Journal* (February 27, 2003): D1.

18. C. Hymowitz, "Crowded Calendars Rule Executives' Days," *The Wall Street Journal* (June 16, 2008): B1.

19. R. Rico, M.S. Manzanares, F. Gil, and G. Gibson, "Team Implicit Coordination Process: A Team Knowledge-Based Approach," *Academy of Management Review* 33(1) (2008): 163–184.

20. M. Beck, "The Science Behind Senior Moments," *The Wall Street Journal* (May 27, 2007): D1.

21. C. Hymowitz, "Crowded Calendars Rule Executives' Days," *The Wall Street Journal* (June 16, 2008): B1.

22. M. Beck, "The Science Behind Senior Moments," *The Wall Street Journal* (May 27, 2007): D1.

23. D. Newman, "How to Motivate Your Sales Team," *Entrepreneur* (June 2007): 73.

24. R. Rico, M.S. Manzanares, F. Gil, and G. Gibson, "Team Implicit Coordination Process: A Team Knowledge-Based Approach," *Academy of Management Review* 33(1) (2008): 163–184.

25. Ibid.

26. C. Hymowitz, "Crowded Calendars Rule Executives' Days," *The Wall Street Journal* (June 16, 2008): B1.

27. J. Sandberg, "I'm Not Really Late, I'm Just Indulging in Magical Thinking," *The Wall Street Journal* (October 13, 2007): B1.

28. C. Hymowitz, "Crowded Calendars Rule Executives' Days," *The Wall Street Journal* (June 16, 2008): B1.

29. Ibid.

30. B. Iger, "How I Work," *Fortune* (December 10, 2007): 38.

31. K. Tindell, "The Professional Organizer," *Fortune* (September 3, 2007): 26.

32. J. Sandberg, "I'm Not Really Late, I'm Just Indulging in Magical Thinking," *The Wall Street Journal* (October 13, 2007): B1.

33. C. Penttila, "Time Out," *Entrepreneur* (April 2007): 71.

34. L. Uchitelle, "Employer-Employee Social Contracts: Fashioning a New Compact for Workers," *Academy of Management Perspectives* 21(2) (2007): 5–9.

35. J. Sandberg, "Why Learn and Grow on the Job? Easier to Feign Infallibility," *The Wall Street Journal* (January 22, 2008): B1.

36. L.M. Roth, "Women on Wall Street: Despite Diversity Measures, Wall Street Remains Vulnerable to Sex Discrimination Charges," *Academy of Management Perspectives* 21(1) (2007): 24–33.

37. L. Osburn, "Youthful Expectations Clash with Work Reality," *Sunday Republican* (October 14, 2007): E10.

38. Ibid.

39. S. Palmisano, "The Best Advice I Ever Got," *Fortune* (May 12, 2008): 74.

40. A. Malhotra, A. Majchrzak, and B. Rosen, "Leading Virtual Teams," *Academy of Management Perspectives* 21(1) (2007): 60–70.

41. L.L. Brennan, "Working Around the Family: Is There a Gender Divide?" *Academy of Management Perspectives* 21(2) (2007): 81–82.

42. B.M. Wiesenfeld, K.A. Wurthmann, and D.C. Hambrick, "The Stigmatization and Devaluation of Elites Associated with Corporate Failures: A Process Model," *Academy of Management Review* 33(1) (2008): 231–251.

43. L. Uchitelle, "Employer-Employee Social Contracts: Fashioning a New Compact for Workers," *Academy of Management Perspectives* 21(2) (2007): 5–9.

44. Ibid.

45. S. Shellenbarger, "Grad Tidings: Can a Test Steer You to the Ideal Career?" *The Wall Street Journal* (June 18, 2008): B1.

46. Ibid.

47. L. Osburn, "Youthful Expectations Clash with Work Reality," *Sunday Republican* (October 14, 2007): E10.

48. J.S. Lublin, "Talking Too Much on a Job Interview May Kill Your Chances," *The Wall Street Journal* (October 30, 2007): B1.

49. S.E. Needleman, "It Pays to Plan Ahead When Taking a New Job," *The Wall Street Journal* (May 20, 2008): D4.

50. Ibid.

51. J.S. Lublin, "Silence Is Golden Rule for Resume of People Who Have Broken It," *The Wall Street Journal* (October 2, 2007): B1.

52. A. Fisher, "How to Get Hired by a Best Company," *Fortune* (February 4, 2008): 96.

53. Ibid.

54. Ibid.

55. Some of the questions were developed by the author and others were taken from the *Quintessential Careers* Web site, www.quintcareers.com, retrieved July 17, 2008.

56. J.S. Lublin, "Talking Too Much on a Job Interview May Kill Your Chances," *The Wall Street Journal* (October 30, 2007): B1.

57. C. Binkley, "Rejected: Readers Reveal Interview Don'ts," *The Wall Street Journal* (January 17, 2008): D8.

58. J.S. Lublin, "Notes to Interviewers Should Go Beyond a Simple Thank You," *The Wall Street Journal* (February 5, 2008): B1.

59. S.E. Needleman, "It Pays to Plan Ahead When Taking a New Job," *The Wall Street Journal* (May 20, 2008): D4.

60. Ibid.

61. B. Iger, "How I Work," *Fortune* (December 10, 2007): 38.

62. B. Farber, "Now Presenting," *Entrepreneur* (June 2007): 76.

63. S. Shellenbarger, "How to Fix Your Life in 2008," *The Wall Street Journal* (December 27, 2007): D3.

64. J. Sandberg, "Had It Up to Here? Despite Risk, Some Say Quitting Is Way to Go," *The Wall Street Journal* (August 14, 2007): B1.

65. G. Kawasaki, "Gimme Some Love," *Entrepreneur* (June 2007): 24.

66. L. Osburn, "Youthful Expectations Clash with Work Reality," *Sunday Republican* (October 14, 2007): E10.

67. J. Sandberg, "Had It Up to Here? Despite Risk, Some Say Quitting Is Way to Go," *The Wall Street Journal* (August 14, 2007): B1.

68. L. Osburn, "Youthful Expectations Clash with Work Reality," *Sunday Republican* (October 14, 2007): E10.

69. J.T. Battenberg, "In New Worker Compact, Competitiveness Is Job One," *Academy of Management Perspectives* 21(2) (2007): 9–13.

70. C. Binkley, "Rejected: Readers Reveal Interview Don'ts," *The Wall Street Journal* (January 17, 2008): D8.

71. C. Binkley, "Want to Be CEO? You Have to Dress the Part," *The Wall Street Journal* (January 10, 2008): D1.

72. Margin Note, *Entrepreneur* (April 2007): 26.

73. C. Binkley, "Rejected: Readers Reveal Interview Don'ts," *The Wall Street Journal* (January 17, 2008): D8.

74. C. Binkley, "Want to Be CEO? You Have to Dress the Part," *The Wall Street Journal* (January 10, 2008): D1.

75. C. Binkley, "Business Casual: All Business, Never Casual," *The Wall Street Journal* (April 17, 2008): D1.

76. C. Binkley, "Want to Be CEO? You Have to Dress the Part," *The Wall Street Journal* (January 10, 2008): D1.

77. C. Binkley, "Rejected: Readers Reveal Interview Don'ts," *The Wall Street Journal* (January 17, 2008): D8.

78. C. Binkley, "Business Casual: All Business, Never Casual," *The Wall Street Journal* (April 17, 2008): D1.

79. C. Binkley, "Rejected: Readers Reveal Interview Don'ts," *The Wall Street Journal* (January 17, 2008): D8.

80. C. Binkley, "Want to Be CEO? You Have to Dress the Part," *The Wall Street Journal* (January 10, 2008): D1.

81. C. Binkley, "Risky Business: Decolletage at a Work Dinner," *The Wall Street Journal* (May 8, 2008): D10.

82. http://www.buildabear.com/aboutus/ourcompany/default.aspx, retrieved September 29, 2008.

83. http://www.buildabear.com/babw/us/pages/aboutus/ourcompany/factsheet.pdf, retrieved September 29, 2008.

84. http://www.buildabear.com/aboutus/ourcompany/ourfounder.aspx, retrieved September 29, 2008.

Chapter 5

1. Sara and David are not actual employees of Sears. However, their delegation communication is typical in all organizations.

2. M.A. Cronin and L.R. Weingart, "Representational Gaps, Information Processing, and Conflict in Functionally Diverse Teams," *Academy of Management Review* 32(3) (2007): 761–773.

3. Staff, "Brush Up Your Shakespeare," *The Wall Street Journal* (October 5, 2004): B1.

4. R. Alsop, "Playing Well with Others," *The Wall Street Journal* (September 9, 2002): R11.

5. D.J. Miller, M.J. Fern, and L.B. Cardinal, "The Use of Knowledge for Technological Innovation within Diversified Firms," *Academy of Management Journal* 50(2) (2007): 308–326.

6. S. Bing, "How Fred Got His First Job," *Fortune* (March 31, 2008): 126.

7. D. Mattioli, "Next on the Agenda: Kisses from Honey Bunny," *The Wall Street Journal* (June 10, 2008): D1.

8. J.M. Brett, M. Olekalns, R. Friedman, N. Goates, C. Anderson, and C.C. Lisco, "Sticks and Stones: Language, Face, and Online Dispute Resolution," *Academy of Management Journal* 50(1) (2007): 85–99.

9. Ibid.

10. J.T. Battenberg, "In New Worker Compact, Competitiveness Is Job One," *Academy of Management Perspectives* 21(2) (2007): 9–13.

11. D.J. Miller, M.J. Fern, and L.B. Cardinal, "The Use of Knowledge for Technological Innovation within Diversified Firms," *Academy of Management Journal* 50(2) (2007): 308–326.

12. S.G. Barsade and D.E. Gibson, "Why Does Affect Matter in Organizations?" *Academy of Management Perspectives* 21(1) (2007): 36–59.

13. F. Shipper, R.C. Hoffman, and D.M. Rotondo, "Does the 360 Feedback Process Create Actionable Knowledge Equally Across Cultures?" *Academy of Management Learning & Education* 6(1) (2007): 33–50.

14. M. Henricks, "Buddy System," *Entrepreneur* (June 2007): 26.

15. F.D. Schoorman, R.C. Mayer, and J.H. Davis, "An Integrative Model of Organizational Trust: Past, Present, and Future," *Academy of Management Review* 32(2) (2007): 344–354.

16. G. Kawasaki, "Go for the Gold," *Entrepreneur* (April 2007): 20.

17. C. Feldman, "Game Changers," *Fortune* (July 21, 2008): 54.

18. B. Farber, "Some Like It Hot," *Entrepreneur* (December 2007): 100.

19. P. Dvorak, "Hotelier Finds Happiness Keeps Staff Checked In," *The Wall Street Journal* (December 17, 2007), B3.

20. D. Geddes and R.R. Callister, "Crossing the Lines: A Dual Threshold Model of Anger in Organizations," *Academy of Management Review* 32(3) (2007): 721–746.

21. M.G. Seo and L.F. Barrett, "Being Emotional During Decision Making—Good or Bad? An Empirical Investigation," *Academy of Management Journal* 50(4) (2007): 923–940.

22. S.G. Barsade and D.E. Gibson, "Why Does Affect Matter in Organizations?" *Academy of Management Perspectives* 21(1) (2007): 36–59.

23. R. Rico, M.S. Manzanares, F. Gil, and G. Gibson, "Team Implicit Coordination Process: A Team Knowledge-Based Approach," *Academy of Management Review* 33(1) (2008): 163–184.

24. P. Osterman, "Comments on Le, Oh, Shaffer, and Schmidt," *Academy of Management Perspectives* 21(3) (2007): 16–18.

25. C. Hymowitz, "Sometimes, Moving Up Makes It Harder to See What Goes on Below," *The Wall Street Journal* (October 15, 2007): B1.

26. G. Kawasaki, "Go for the Gold," *Entrepreneur* (April 2007): 20.

27. J. Sandberg, "Why Learn and Grow on the Job? Easier to Feign Infallibility," *The Wall Street Journal* (January 22, 2008): B1.

28. J. Gray, *Men Are from Mars, Women Are from Venus* (New York: HarperCollins, 1992).

29. D. Tannen, *You Just Don't Understand: Women and Men in Conversation* (New York: Ballantine Books, 1991); and *Talking from 9 to 5* (New York: William Morrow, 1995).

30. F. Shipper, R.C. Hoffman, and D.M. Rotondo, "Does the 360 Feedback Process Create Actionable Knowledge Equally Across Cultures?" *Academy of Management Learning & Education* 6(1) (2007): 33–50.

31. J.T. Battenberg, "In New Worker Compact, Competitiveness Is Job One," *Academy of Management Perspectives* 21(2) (2007): 9–13.

32. C. Binkley, "Americans Learn the Global Art of the Cheek Kiss," *The Wall Street Journal* (March 27, 2008): D1.

33. N.J. Adler, *International Dimensions of Organizational Behavior*, 6e (Mason, OH: South-Western, 2008).

34. Ibid.

35. G. Kawasaki, "The Art of Execution," *Entrepreneur* (September 2007): 26.

36. R. Wolter, "Make It Happen," *Entrepreneur* (June 2007): 126.

37. C. Hymowitz, "Crowded Calendars Rule Executives' Days," *The Wall Street Journal* (June 16, 2008): B1.

38. "Making Sales Presentations," *Entrepreneur* (June 2007): 105.

39. G. Kawasaki, "The Art of Execution," *Entrepreneur* (September 2007): 26.

40. R. Wolter, "Make It Happen," *Entrepreneur* (June 2007): 126.

41. P. Dvorak, "Hotelier Finds Happiness Keeps Staff Checked In," *The Wall Street Journal* (December 17, 2007), B3.

42. R. Wolter, "Make It Happen," *Entrepreneur* (June 2007): 126.

43. S. Palmisano, "The Best Advice I Ever Got," *Fortune* (May 12, 2008): 74.

44. B. Farber, "Basic Instincts," *Entrepreneur* (August 2007): 66.

45. B. Farber, "Some Like It Hot," *Entrepreneur* (December 2007): 100.

46. M.A. Cronin and L.R. Weingart, "Representational Gaps, Information Processing, and Conflict in Functionally Diverse Teams," *Academy of Management Review* 32(3) (2007): 761–773.

47. "Making Sales Presentations," *Entrepreneur* (June 2007): 105.

48. A.M. Grant, M.K. Christianson, and R.H. Price, "Happiness, Health, or Relationships? Managerial Practices and Employee Well-Being Tradeoffs," *Academy of Management Perspectives* 21(3) (2007): 51–63.

49. "Making Sales Presentations," *Entrepreneur* (June 2007): 105.

50. P. Dvorak, "Hotelier Finds Happiness Keeps Staff Checked In," *The Wall Street Journal* (December 17, 2007), B3.

51. C. Feldman, "Game Changers," *Fortune* (July 21, 2008): 54.

52. R. Wolter, "Make It Happen," *Entrepreneur* (June 2007): 126.

53. B. Farber, "Sell as Easy as 1-2-3," *Entrepreneur* (January 2008): 82.

54. B. Farber, "Basic Instincts," *Entrepreneur* (August 2007): 66.

55. R. Wolter, "Make It Happen," *Entrepreneur* (June 2007): 126.

56. "Making Sales Presentations," *Entrepreneur* (June 2007): 105.

57. B. Farber, "Some Like It Hot," *Entrepreneur* (December 2007): 100.

58. B. Farber, "Basic Instincts," *Entrepreneur* (August 2007): 66.

59. J.M. Brett, M. Olekalns, R. Friedman, N. Goates, C. Anderson, and C.C. Lisco, "Sticks and Stones: Language, Face, and Online Dispute Resolution," *Academy of Management Journal* 50(1) (2007): 85–99.

60. C. Hymowitz, "Crowded Calendars Rule Executives' Days," *The Wall Street Journal* (June 16, 2008): B1.

61. S.L. Rynes, T.L. Giluk, and K.G. Brown, "The Very Separate Worlds of Academic and Practitioner Periodicals in Human Resource Management: Implications for Evidence-Based Management," *Academy of Management Journal* 50(5) (2007): 987–1008.

62. F. Shipper, R.C. Hoffman, and D.M. Rotondo, "Does the 360 Feedback Process Create Actionable Knowledge Equally Across Cultures?" *Academy of Management Learning & Education* 6(1) (2007): 33–50.

63. C. Hymowitz, "Sometimes, Moving Up Makes It Harder to See What Goes on Below," *The Wall Street Journal* (October 15, 2007): B1.

64. R. Rico, M.S. Manzanares, F. Gil, and G. Gibson, "Team Implicit Coordination Process: A Team Knowledge-Based Approach," *Academy of Management Review* 33(1) (2008): 163–184.

65. J. Sandberg, "Performance Reviews Need Some Work, Don't Meet Potential," *The Wall Street Journal* (November 20, 2007): B1.

66. R. Rico, M.S. Manzanares, F. Gil, and G. Gibson, "Team Implicit Coordination Process: A Team Knowledge-Based Approach," *Academy of Management Review* 33(1) (2008): 163–184.

67. C. Hymowitz, "Sometimes, Moving Up Makes It Harder to See What Goes on Below," *The Wall Street Journal* (October 15, 2007): B1.

68. F. Shipper, R.C. Hoffman, and D.M. Rotondo, "Does the 360 Feedback Process Create Actionable Knowledge Equally Across Cultures?" *Academy of Management Learning & Education* 6(1) (2007): 33–50.

69. R. Wolter, "Make It Happen," *Entrepreneur* (June 2007): 126.

70. F. Shipper, R.C. Hoffman, and D.M. Rotondo, "Does the 360 Feedback Process Create Actionable Knowledge Equally Across Cultures?" *Academy of Management Learning & Education* 6(1) (2007): 33–50.

71. "Making Sales Presentations," *Entrepreneur* (June 2007): 105.

72. Information taken from personal interviews with the Clarks (updated on July 23, 2008) and the Ranch Web site (www.theranchgolfclub.com).

Chapter 6

1. C.W. Langfred, "The Downside of Self-Management: A Longitudinal Study of the Effects of Conflict on Trust, Autonomy, and Task Interdependence in Self-Managing Teams," *Academy of Management Journal* 50(4) (2007): 885–900.

2. N. Anand, H.K. Gardner, and T. Morris, "Knowledge-Based Innovation: Emergence and Embedding of New Practice Areas in Management Consulting Firms," *Academy of Management Journal* 50(2) (2007): 406–428.

3. D.J. Miller, M.J. Fern, and L.B. Cardinal, "The Use of Knowledge for Technological Innovation within Diversified Firms," *Academy of Management Journal* 50(2) (2007): 308–326.

4. G. Hamel, "Break Free!" *Fortune* (October 1, 2007): 119–126.

5. "Novartis's CEO Said," *The Wall Street Journal* (December 11, 2007): A1, A21.

6. C. Mamberto, "Companies Aim to Combat Job-Related Stress," *The Wall Street Journal* (August 13, 2007): B6.

7. J.M. Brett, M. Olekalns, R. Friedman, N. Goates, C. Anderson, and C.C. Lisco, "Sticks and Stones: Language, Face, and Online Dispute Resolution," *Academy of Management Journal* 50(1) (2007): 85–99.

8. J. Sandberg, "Why Learn and Grow on the Job? Easier to Feign Infallibility," *The Wall Street Journal* (January 22, 2008): B1.

9. N. Anand, H.K. Gardner, and T. Morris, "Knowledge-Based Innovation: Emergence and Embedding of New Practice Areas in Management Consulting Firms," *Academy of Management Journal* 50(2) (2007): 406–428.

10. C.W. Langfred, "The Downside of Self-Management: A Longitudinal Study of the Effects of Conflict on Trust, Autonomy, and Task Interdependence in Self-Managing Teams," *Academy of Management Journal* 50(4) (2007): 885–900.

11. D.M. Bergeron, "The Potential Paradox of Organizational Citizenship Behavior: Good Citizens at What Cost?" *Academy of Management Review* 32(4) (2007): 1078–1095.

12. A.M. Grant, "Relational Job Design and the Motivation to Make a Prosocial Difference," *Academy of Management Review* 32(2) (2007): 393–417.

13. A.M. Grant, M.K. Christianson, and R.H. Price, "Happiness, Health, or Relationships? Managerial Practices and Employee Well-Being Tradeoffs," *Academy of Management Perspectives* 21(3) (2007): 51–63.

14. N. Anand, H.K. Gardner, and T. Morris, "Knowledge-Based Innovation: Emergence and Embedding of New Practice Areas in Management Consulting Firms," *Academy of Management Journal* 50(2) (2007): 406–428.

15. R. Cross, A. Hargadon, S. Parise, and R.J. Thomas, "Together We Innovate," *The Wall Street Journal* (September 15, 2007): R6.

16. M.A. Cronin and L.R. Weingart, "Representational Gaps, Information Processing, and Conflict in Functionally Diverse Teams," *Academy of Management Review* 32(3) (2007): 761–773.

17. C. Hymowitz, "Sometimes, Moving Up Makes It Harder to See What Goes on Below," *The Wall Street Journal* (October 15, 2007): B1.

18. G. Hamel, "Break Free!" *Fortune* (October 1, 2007): 119–126.

19. "Novartis's CEO Said," *The Wall Street Journal* (December 11, 2007): A1, A21.

20. R.A. Guth, "Microsoft's Online Chief Is Departing for Juniper," *The Wall Street Journal* (July 24, 2008): B1.

21. G. Hamel, "Break Free!" *Fortune* (October 1, 2007): 119–126.

22. "Novartis's CEO Said," *The Wall Street Journal* (December 11, 2007): A1, A21.

23. R. Rico, M.S. Manzanares, F. Gil, and G. Gibson, "Team Implicit Coordination Process: A Team Knowledge-Based Approach," *Academy of Management Review* 33(1) (2008): 163–184.

24. G. Hamel, "Break Free!" *Fortune* (October 1, 2007): 119–126.

25. C.W. Langfred, "The Downside of Self-Management: A Longitudinal Study of the Effects of Conflict on Trust, Autonomy, and Task Interdependence in Self-Managing Teams," *Academy of Management Journal* 50(4) (2007): 885–900.

26. G. Hamel, "Break Free!" *Fortune* (October 1, 2007): 119–126.

27. C.W. Langfred, "The Downside of Self-Management: A Longitudinal Study of the Effects of Conflict on Trust,

Autonomy, and Task Interdependence in Self-Managing Teams," *Academy of Management Journal* 50(4) (2007): 885–900.

28. G. Hamel, "Break Free!" *Fortune* (October 1, 2007): 119–126.

29. D.J. Miller, M.J. Fern, and L.B. Cardinal, "The Use of Knowledge for Technological Innovation within Diversified Firms," *Academy of Management Journal* 50(2) (2007): 308–326.

30. N. Anand, H.K. Gardner, and T. Morris, "Knowledge-Based Innovation: Emergence and Embedding of New Practice Areas in Management Consulting Firms," *Academy of Management Journal* 50(2) (2007): 406–428.

31. R. Rico, M.S. Manzanares, F. Gil, and G. Gibson, "Team Implicit Coordination Process: A Team Knowledge-Based Approach," *Academy of Management Review* 33(1) (2008): 163–184.

32. M.A. Cronin and L.R. Weingart, "Representational Gaps, Information Processing, and Conflict in Functionally Diverse Teams," *Academy of Management Review* 32(3) (2007): 761–773.

33. C.W. Langfred, "The Downside of Self-Management: A Longitudinal Study of the Effects of Conflict on Trust, Autonomy, and Task Interdependence in Self-Managing Teams," *Academy of Management Journal* 50(4) (2007): 885–900.

34. G. Hamel, "Break Free!" *Fortune* (October 1, 2007): 119–126.

35. W. L. Gore & Associates Web site (www.gore.com), retrieved August 7, 2008.

36. G. Hamel, "Break Free!" *Fortune* (October 1, 2007): 119–126.

37. R. Cross, A. Hargadon, S. Parise, and R.J. Thomas, "Together We Innovate," *The Wall Street Journal* (September 15, 2007): R6.

38. D.J. Miller, M.J. Fern, and L.B. Cardinal, "The Use of Knowledge for Technological Innovation within Diversified Firms," *Academy of Management Journal* 50(2) (2007): 308–326.

39. R. Cross, A. Hargadon, S. Parise, and R.J. Thomas, "Together We Innovate," *The Wall Street Journal* (September 15, 2007): R6.

40. R. Rico, M.S. Manzanares, F. Gil, and G. Gibson, "Team Implicit Coordination Process: A Team Knowledge-Based Approach," *Academy of Management Review* 33(1) (2008): 163–184.

41. N. Anand, H.K. Gardner, and T. Morris, "Knowledge-Based Innovation: Emergence and Embedding of New Practice Areas in Management Consulting Firms," *Academy of Management Journal* 50(2) (2007): 406–428.

42. S. Bing, "How Fred Got His First Job," *Fortune* (March 31, 2008): 126.

43. N. Anand, H.K. Gardner, and T. Morris, "Knowledge-Based Innovation: Emergence and Embedding of New Practice Areas in Management Consulting Firms," *Academy of Management Journal* 50(2) (2007): 406–428.

44. R. Rico, M.S. Manzanares, F. Gil, and G. Gibson, "Team Implicit Coordination Process: A Team Knowledge-Based Approach," *Academy of Management Review* 33(1) (2008): 163–184.

45. O. Gottschalg and M. Zollo, "Interest Alignment and Competitive Advantage," *Academy of Management Review* 32(2) (2007): 418–437.

46. B.J. Tepper, S.E. Moss, D.E. Lockhart, and J.C. Carr, "Abusive Supervision, Upward Maintenance Communication, and Subordinates' Psychological Distress," *Academy of Management Journal* 50(5) (2007): 1169–1180.

47. Ibid.

48. Ibid.

49. R. Rico, M.S. Manzanares, F. Gil, and G. Gibson, "Team Implicit Coordination Process: A Team Knowledge-Based Approach," *Academy of Management Review* 33(1) (2008): 163–184.

50. Margin Note, *Entrepreneur* (January 2004): 23.

51. C.T. Kulik, H.T.J. Bainbridge, and C. Cregan, "Known by the Company We Keep: Stigma-by-Association Effects in the Workplace," *Academy of Management Review* 33(1) (2008): 216–230.

52. Ibid.

53. R. Cross, A. Hargadon, S. Parise, and R.J. Thomas, "Together We Innovate," *The Wall Street Journal* (September 15, 2007): R6.

54. Ibid.

55. Ibid.

56. A. Hwang, E.H. Kessler, and A.M. Francesco, "Student Networking Behavior, Culture, and Grade Performance: An Empirical Study and Pedagogical Recommendations," *Academy of Management Learning & Education* 3(2) (2004): 139–150.

57. C. Hymowitz, "Crowded Calendars Rule Executives' Days," *The Wall Street Journal* (June 16, 2008): B1.

58. Ibid.

59. B. Farber, "Sell as Easy as 1-2-3," *Entrepreneur* (January 2008): 82

60. R. Rico, M.S. Manzanares, F. Gil, and G. Gibson, "Team Implicit Coordination Process: A Team Knowledge-Based Approach," *Academy of Management Review* 33(1) (2008): 163–184.

61. C. Hymowitz, "Crowded Calendars Rule Executives' Days," *The Wall Street Journal* (June 16, 2008): B1.

62. Ibid.

63. B. Farber, "Now Presenting," *Entrepreneur* (June 2007): 76.

64. C. Penttila, "Time Out," *Entrepreneur* (April 2007): 71.

65. M. Henricks, "Pen to Paper," *Entrepreneur* (July 2007): 85.

66. Ibid.

67. B. Farber, "Now Presenting," *Entrepreneur* (June 2007): 76.

68. C. Seda, "First Impressions," *Entrepreneur* (October 2006): 64.

69. C. Penttila, "Time Out," *Entrepreneur* (April 2007): 71.

70. C. Hymowitz, "Companies Need CEOs to Stop Spinning and Start Thinking," *The Wall Street Journal* (December 17, 2007): B1.

71. J.S. Lublin, "Talking Too Much on a Job Interview May Kill Your Chances," *The Wall Street Journal* (October 30, 2007): B1.

72. Ibid.

73. M.G. Seo and L.F. Barrett, "Being Emotional During Decision Making—Good or Bad? An Empirical Investigation," *Academy of Management Journal* 50(4) (2007): 923–940.

74. S.G. Barsade and D.E. Gibson, "Why Does Affect Matter in Organizations?" *Academy of Management Perspectives* 21(1) (2007): 36–59.

75. D. Geddes and R.R. Callister, "Crossing the Lines: A Dual Threshold Model of Anger in Organizations," *Academy of Management Review* 32(3) (2007): 721–746.

76. S.G. Barsade and D.E. Gibson, "Why Does Affect Matter in Organizations?" *Academy of Management Perspectives* 21(1) (2007): 36–59.

77. D. Geddes and R.R. Callister, "Crossing the Lines: A Dual Threshold Model of Anger in Organizations," *Academy of Management Review* 32(3) (2007): 721–746.

78. J.M. Brett, M. Olekalns, R. Friedman, N. Goates, C. Anderson, and C.C. Lisco, "Sticks and Stones: Language, Face, and Online Dispute Resolution," *Academy of Management Journal* 50(1) (2007): 85–99.

79. S.P. Robbins and T. Judge, *Essentials of Organizational Behavior* 9e (Upper Saddle River, NJ: Prentice-Hall, 2008).

80. J. Sandberg, "Do You Hear What I Hear? Telling Off a Colleague—Silently," *The Wall Street Journal* (October 23, 2007): B1.

81. D. Geddes and R.R. Callister, "Crossing the Lines: A Dual Threshold Model of Anger in Organizations," *Academy of Management Review* 32(3) (2007): 721–746.

82. J.M. Brett, M. Olekalns, R. Friedman, N. Goates, C. Anderson, and C.C. Lisco, "Sticks and Stones: Language, Face, and Online Dispute Resolution," *Academy of Management Journal* 50(1) (2007): 85–99.

83. S.G. Barsade and D.E. Gibson, "Why Does Affect Matter in Organizations?" *Academy of Management Perspectives* 21(1) (2007): 36–59.

84. "Making Sales Presentations," *Entrepreneur* (June 2007): 105.

85. J. Sandberg, "Why Learn and Grow on the Job? Easier to Feign Infallibility," *The Wall Street Journal* (January 22, 2008): B1.

86. G. Kawasaki, "Gimme Some Love," *Entrepreneur* (June 2007): 24.

87. J.M. Brett, M. Olekalns, R. Friedman, N. Goates, C. Anderson, and C.C. Lisco, "Sticks and Stones: Language, Face, and Online Dispute Resolution," *Academy of Management Journal* 50(1) (2007): 85–99.

88. J. Sandberg, "Why Learn and Grow on the Job? Easier to Feign Infallibility," *The Wall Street Journal* (January 22, 2008): B1.

89. G. Kawasaki, "Gimme Some Love," *Entrepreneur* (June 2007): 24.

90. R. Rico, M.S. Manzanares, F. Gil, and G. Gibson, "Team Implicit Coordination Process: A Team Knowledge-Based Approach," *Academy of Management Review* 33(1) (2008): 163–184.

91. G. Kawasaki, "Gimme Some Love," *Entrepreneur* (June 2007): 24.

92. D. Geddes and R.R. Callister, "Crossing the Lines: A Dual Threshold Model of Anger in Organizations," *Academy of Management Review* 32(3) (2007): 721–746.

93. R. Rico, M.S. Manzanares, F. Gil, and G. Gibson, "Team Implicit Coordination Process: A Team Knowledge-Based Approach," *Academy of Management Review* 33(1) (2008): 163–184.

94. G. Kawasaki, "At Their Service," *Entrepreneur* (August 2007): 24.

95. http://premium.hoovers.com/subscribe/co/overview.xhtml?ID=ffffrfktyffsrtthyt, retrieved September 29, 2008.

96. http://www.melcrum.com/offer/hsic/08a/HSIC08A_XS.pdf, retrieved September 29, 2008.

Chapter 7

1. R. Cropanzano, D.E. Bowen, and S.W. Gilliland, "The Management of Organizational Justice," *Academy of Management Perspectives* 21(4) (2007): 34–48.

2. D. Geddes and R.R. Callister, "Crossing the Lines: A Dual Threshold Model of Anger in Organizations," *Academy of Management Review* 32(3) (2007): 721–746.

3. R.B. Kaiser and R.B. Kaplan, "The Deeper Work of Executive Development: Outgrowing Sensitivities," *Academy of Management Learning & Education* 5(4) (2006): 463–483.

4. S.G. Barsade and D.E. Gibson, "Why Does Affect Matter in Organizations?" *Academy of Management Perspectives* 21(1) (2007): 36–59.

5. C.W. Langfred, "The Downside of Self-Management: A Longitudinal Study of the Effects of Conflict on Trust, Autonomy, and Task Interdependence in Self-Managing Teams," *Academy of Management Journal* 50(4) (2007): 885–900.

6. J.M. Brett, M. Olekalns, R. Friedman, N. Goates, C. Anderson, and C.C. Lisco, "Sticks and Stones: Language, Face, and Online Dispute Resolution," *Academy of Management Journal* 50(1) (2007): 85–99.

7. M.A. Cronin and L.R. Weingart, "Representational Gaps, Information Processing, and Conflict in Functionally Diverse Teams," *Academy of Management Review* 32(3) (2007): 761–773.

8. E. Berne, *Transactional Analysis in Psychotherapy* (New York: Grove Press, 1961).

9. T. Newton, "The Health System: Metaphor and Meaning," *Transactional Analysis Journal* 37(3) (2007): 195–205.

10. K. Tudor, "Take It: A Sixth Driver," *Transactional Analysis Journal* 38(1) (2008): 43–57.

11. R.G. Erskine, "Cooperation, Relationship, and Change," *Transactional Analysis Journal* 38(1) (2008): 31–35.

12. E. Berne, *Games People Play* (New York: Grove Press, 1964).

13. R.G. Erskine, "Cooperation, Relationship, and Change," *Transactional Analysis Journal* 38(1) (2008): 31–35.

14. M. Widdowson, "Metacommunicative Transactions," *Transactional Analysis Journal* 38(1) (2008): 58–71.

15. C. Steiner, "Stroking: What's Love Got to Do with It?" *Transactional Analysis Journal* 37(4) (2007): 307–310.

16. S. Ligabue, "Being in Relationship: Different Languages to Understand Ego States, Script, and the Body," *Transactional Analysis Journal* 37(4) (2007): 294–306.

17. G. Petriglieri, "Stuck in a Moment: A Developmental Perspective on Impasses," *Transactional Analysis Journal* 37(3) (2007): 85–194.

18. B. Schmid, "The Role Concept of Transactional Analysis and Other Approaches to Personality, Encounter, and Cocreativity for All Professional Fields," *Transactional Analysis Journal* 38(1) (2008): 17–30.

19. G. Petriglieri, "Stuck in a Moment: A Developmental Perspective on Impasses," *Transactional Analysis Journal* 37(3) (2007): 85–194.

20. W.F. Cornell, "The Inevitability of Uncertainty, the Necessity of Doubt, and the Development of Trust," *Transactional Analysis Journal* 37(1) (2007): 8–16.

21. M. Mazzetti, "Supervision in Transactional Analysis: An Operational Model," *Transactional Analysis Journal* 37(2) (2007): 93–103.

22. S. van Beekum, "Supervision as a Metamodality and a Multiarea Activity, *Transactional Analysis Journal* 37(2) (2007): 140–149.

23. R.U. Priya, "Transactional Analysis and the Mind/Body Connection," *Transactional Analysis Journal* 37(4) (2007): 278–285.

24. T. Newton and R. Napper, "The Bigger Picture: Supervision as an Educational Framework for All Fields," *Transactional Analysis Journal* 37(2) (2007): 150–158.

25. R.G. Erskine, "Cooperation, Relationship, and Change," *Transactional Analysis Journal* 38(1) (2008): 31–35.

26. B. Schmid, "The Role Concept of Transactional Analysis and Other Approaches to Personality, Encounter, and Cocreativity for All Professional Fields," *Transactional Analysis Journal* 38(1) (2008): 17–30.

27. W.F. Cornell, "The Inevitability of Uncertainty, the Necessity of Doubt, and the Development of Trust," *Transactional Analysis Journal* 37(1) (2007): 8–16.

28. C. Steiner, "Stroking: What's Love Got to Do with It?" *Transactional Analysis Journal* 37(4) (2007): 307–310.

29. K. Tudor, "Take It: A Sixth Driver," *Transactional Analysis Journal* 38(1) (2008): 43–57.

30. C. Steiner, "Stroking: What's Love Got to Do with It?" *Transactional Analysis Journal* 37(4) (2007): 307–310.

31. M. Widdowson, "Metacommunicative Transactions," *Transactional Analysis Journal* 38(1) (2008): 58–71.

32. Ibid.

33. C. Steiner, "Stroking: What's Love Got to Do with It?" *Transactional Analysis Journal* 37(4) (2007): 307–310.

34. J. Zaslow, "The Most-Praised Generation Goes to Work," *The Wall Street Journal* (April 20, 2007): W1.

35. S. Ligabue, "Being in Relationship: Different Languages to Understand Ego States, Script, and the Body," *Transactional Analysis Journal* 37(4) (2007): 294–306.

36. A. Lazarus, "On Assertive Behavior: A Brief Note," *Behavior Theory* 4 (October 1973): 697–699.

37. J.C. Santora, "Assertiveness and Effective Leadership: Is There a Tipping Point?" *Academy of Management Perspectives* 21(3) (2007): 84–86.

38. J.M. Brett, M. Olekalns, R. Friedman, N. Goates, C. Anderson, and C.C. Lisco, "Sticks and Stones: Language, Face, and Online Dispute Resolution," *Academy of Management Journal* 50(1) (2007): 85–99.

39. C. L. Porath and A. Erez, "Does Rudeness Really Matter? The Effects of Rudeness on Task Performance and Helpfulness," *Academy of Management Journal* 50(5) (2007): 1181–1197.

40. J.C. Santora, "Assertiveness and Effective Leadership: Is There a Tipping Point?" *Academy of Management Perspectives* 21(3) (2007): 84–86.

41. Ibid.

42. R. Cropanzano, D.E. Bowen, and S.W. Gilliland, "The Management of Organizational Justice," *Academy of Management Perspectives* 21(4) (2007): 34–48.

43. "How to Manage Anger," *TopHealth* (May 2007): 2.

44. B.J. Tepper, S.E. Moss, D.E. Lockhart, and J.C. Carr, "Abusive Supervision, Upward Maintenance Communication, and Subordinates' Psychological Distress," *Academy of Management Journal* 50(5) (2007): 1169–1180.

45. D. Geddes and R.R. Callister, "Crossing the Lines: A Dual Threshold Model of Anger in Organizations," *Academy of Management Review* 32(3) (2007): 721–746.

46. C.L. Porath and A. Erez, "Does Rudeness Really Matter? The Effects of Rudeness on Task Performance and Helpfulness," *Academy of Management Journal* 50(5) (2007): 1181–1197.

47. B.J. Tepper, S.E. Moss, D.E. Lockhart, and J.C. Carr, "Abusive Supervision, Upward Maintenance Communication, and Subordinates' Psychological Distress," *Academy of Management Journal* 50(5) (2007): 1169–1180.

48. Ibid.

49. R. Cropanzano, D.E. Bowen, and S.W. Gilliland, "The Management of Organizational Justice," *Academy of Management Perspectives* 21(4) (2007): 34–48.

50. J.C. Santora, "Assertiveness and Effective Leadership: Is There a Tipping Point?" *Academy of Management Perspectives* 21(3) (2007): 84–86.

51. B.J. Tepper, S.E. Moss, D.E. Lockhart, and J.C. Carr, "Abusive Supervision, Upward Maintenance Communication, and Subordinates' Psychological Distress," *Academy of Management Journal* 50(5) (2007): 1169–1180.

52. R. Lussier, "Dealing with Anger and Preventing Workplace Violence," *Clinical Leadership & Management Review* 18(2) (2004): 117–119.

53. B.J. Tepper, S.E. Moss, D.E. Lockhart, and J.C. Carr, "Abusive Supervision, Upward Maintenance Communication, and Subordinates' Psychological Distress," *Academy of Management Journal* 50(5) (2007): 1169–1180.

54. R. Cropanzano, D.E. Bowen, and S.W. Gilliland, "The Management of Organizational Justice," *Academy of Management Perspectives* 21(4) (2007): 34–48.

55. J.M. Brett, M. Olekalns, R. Friedman, N. Goates, C. Anderson, and C.C. Lisco, "Sticks and Stones: Language, Face, and Online Dispute Resolution," *Academy of Management Journal* 50(1) (2007): 85–99.

56. C. Steiner, "Stroking: What's Love Got to Do with It?" *Transactional Analysis Journal* 37(4) (2007): 307–310.

57. J.C. Santora, "Assertiveness and Effective Leadership: Is There a Tipping Point?" *Academy of Management Perspectives* 21(3) (2007): 84–86.

58. O. Gottschalg and M. Zollo, "Interest Alignment and Competitive Advantage," *Academy of Management Review* 32(2) (2007): 418–437.

59. R. Losik, Southern New Hampshire University, reviewer suggestion, January 23, 2006.

60. R. Lussier, "Dealing with Anger and Preventing Workplace Violence," *Clinical Leadership & Management Review* 18(2) (2004): 117–119.

61. R. Lussier, "Maintaining Civility in the Laboratory," *Clinical Leadership & Management Review* 19(62) (2005): E 4–7.

62. R. Lussier, "Dealing with Anger and Preventing Workplace Violence," *Clinical Leadership & Management Review* 18(2) (2004): 117–119.

63. R. Lussier, "Maintaining Civility in the Laboratory," *Clinical Leadership & Management Review* 19(62) (2005): E 4–7.

64. "How to Manage Anger," *TopHealth* (May 2007): 2.

65. D. Geddes and R.R. Callister, "Crossing the Lines: A Dual Threshold Model of Anger in Organizations," *Academy of Management Review* 32(3) (2007): 721–746.

66. Ibid.

67. R. Lussier, "Dealing with Anger and Preventing Workplace Violence," *Clinical Leadership & Management Review* 18(2) (2004): 117–119.

68. Ibid.

69. Ibid.

70. Ibid.

71. C.W. Langfred, "The Downside of Self-Management: A Longitudinal Study of the Effects of Conflict on Trust, Autonomy, and Task Interdependence in Self-Managing Teams," *Academy of Management Journal* 50(4) (2007): 885–900.

72. M.A. Cronin and L.R. Weingart, "Representational Gaps, Information Processing, and Conflict in Functionally Diverse Teams," *Academy of Management Review* 32(3) (2007): 761–773.

73. S.G. Barsade and D.E. Gibson, "Why Does Affect Matter in Organizations?" *Academy of Management Perspectives* 21(1) (2007): 36–59.

74. J.B.O. Buchanan and W.R. Boswell, "An Integrative Model of Experiencing and Responding to Mistreatment at Work," *Academy of Management Review* 33(1) (2008): 75–96.

75. A. Mehra, "Symposium: Handbook of Trust Research," *Academy of Management Review* 33(1) (2008): 271–272.

76. W.F. Cornell, "The Inevitability of Uncertainty, the Necessity of Doubt, and the Development of Trust," *Transactional Analysis Journal* 37(1) (2007): 8–16.

77. J.B.O. Buchanan and W.R. Boswell, "An Integrative Model of Experiencing and Responding to Mistreatment at Work," *Academy of Management Review* 33(1) (2008): 75–96.

78. D. Geddes and R.R. Callister, "Crossing the Lines: A Dual Threshold Model of Anger in Organizations," *Academy of Management Review* 32(3) (2007): 721–746.

79. C. Steiner, "Stroking: What's Love Got to Do with It?" *Transactional Analysis Journal* 37(4) (2007): 307–310.

80. C.L. Porath and A. Erez, "Does Rudeness Really Matter? The Effects of Rudeness on Task Performance and Helpfulness," *Academy of Management Journal* 50(5) (2007): 1181–1197.

81. B.J. Tepper, S.E. Moss, D.E. Lockhart, and J.C. Carr, "Abusive Supervision, Upward Maintenance Communication, and Subordinates' Psychological Distress," *Academy of Management Journal* 50(5) (2007): 1169–1180.

82. K. Tudor, "Take It: A Sixth Driver," *Transactional Analysis Journal* 38(1) (2008): 43–57.

83. J.M. Brett, M. Olekalns, R. Friedman, N. Goates, C. Anderson, and C.C. Lisco, "Sticks and Stones: Language, Face, and Online Dispute Resolution," *Academy of Management Journal* 50(1) (2007): 85–99.

84. G. Petriglieri, "Stuck in a Moment: A Developmental Perspective on Impasses," *Transactional Analysis Journal* 37(3) (2007): 85–194.

85. R. Cropanzano, D.E. Bowen, and S.W. Gilliland, "The Management of Organizational Justice," *Academy of Management Perspectives* 21(4) (2007): 34–48.

86. T. Newton, "The Health System: Metaphor and Meaning," *Transactional Analysis Journal* 37(3) (2007): 195–205.

87. C. Steiner, "Stroking: What's Love Got to Do with It?" *Transactional Analysis Journal* 37(4) (2007): 307–310.

88. J.C. Santora, "Assertiveness and Effective Leadership: Is There a Tipping Point?" *Academy of Management Perspectives* 21(3) (2007): 84–86.

89. J.M. Brett, M. Olekalns, R. Friedman, N. Goates, C. Anderson, and C.C. Lisco, "Sticks and Stones: Language, Face, and Online Dispute Resolution," *Academy of Management Journal* 50(1) (2007): 85–99.

90. Ibid.

91. J.B.O. Buchanan and W.R. Boswell, "An Integrative Model of Experiencing and Responding to Mistreatment at Work," *Academy of Management Review* 33(1) (2008): 75–96.

92. J.M. Brett, M. Olekalns, R. Friedman, N. Goates, C. Anderson, and C.C. Lisco, "Sticks and Stones: Language, Face, and Online Dispute Resolution," *Academy of Management Journal* 50(1) (2007): 85–99.

93. J.K. Williams, "Facilitating with Ease! Core Skills for Facilitators, Team Leaders and Members, Managers, Consultants, and Trainers," *Academy of Management Learning & Education* 6(2) (2007): 294–295.

94. Case sources: http://premium.hoovers.com; http://www.Nike.com; Michael Barbaro, "Slightly Testy Nike Divorce Came Down to Data vs. Feel," *New York Times* (January 28, 2006): C4; Michael Barbaro, "Cricket Anyone? Sneakers Makers on Fresh Turf," *New York Times* (January 28, 2006): C1, C4.

Chapter 8

1. R.B. Kaiser and R.B. Kaplan, "The Deeper Work of Executive Development: Outgrowing Sensitivities," *Academy of Management Learning & Education* 5(4) (2006): 463–483.

2. R. Kark and D. Van Dijk, "Motivation to Lead, Motivation to Follow: The Role of the Self-Regulatory Focus in Leadership Process," *Academy of Management Review* 32(2) (2007): 500–528.

3. D.C. Hambrick, "Upper Echelons Theory: An Update," *Academy of Management Review* 32(2) (2007): 334–343.

4. G.J. Jolley, "Leadership Can Be Taught: A Bold Approach for a Complex World," *Academy of Management Learning & Education* 6(1) (2007): 149–150.

5. R.B. Kaiser and R.B. Kaplan, "The Deeper Work of Executive Development: Outgrowing Sensitivities," *Academy of Management Learning & Education* 5(4) (2006): 463–483.

6. J.C. Santora, "Assertiveness and Effective Leadership: Is There a Tipping Point?" *Academy of Management Perspectives* 21(3) (2007): 84–86.

7. W. Lam, X. Huang, and E. Snape, "Feedback-Seeking Behavior and Leader-Member Exchange: Do Supervisor-Attributed Motives Matter?" *Academy of Management Journal* 50(2) (2007): 348–363.

8. C. Hymowitz, "Companies Need CEOs to Stop Spinning and Start Thinking," *The Wall Street Journal* (December 17, 2007): B1.

9. A.J. Wefald and J.P. Katz, "Leaders: The Strategies for Taking Charge," *Academy of Management Perspectives* 21(3) (2007): 105–106.

10. B. Jackson and K. Parry, "A Very Short, Fairly Interesting and Reasonably Cheap Book about Studying Leadership," *Academy of Management Perspectives* 21(4) (2007): 90–92.

11. C. Feldman, "Game Changers," *Fortune* (July 21, 2008): 54.

12. R.B. Kaiser and R.B. Kaplan, "The Deeper Work of Executive Development: Outgrowing Sensitivities," *Academy of Management Learning & Education* 5(4) (2006): 463–483.

13. S. Friedman, "My Employees Are Burned Out from Too Much Work. How Can I Create a Better Environment?" *Fortune* (July 21, 2008): 58.

14. M.F.R. Kets de Vries and K. Korotov, "Creating Transformational Executive Education Programs," *Academy of Management Learning & Education* 6(3) (2007): 375–387.

15. M. Williams, "Building Genuine Trust through Interpersonal Emotion Management: A Threat Regulation Model of Trust and Collaboration across Boundaries," *Academy of Management Review* 32(2) (2007): 595–621.

16. R. Kark and D. Van Dijk, "Motivation to Lead, Motivation to Follow: The Role of the Self-Regulatory Focus in Leadership Process," *Academy of Management Review* 32(2) (2007): 500–528.

17. J.C. Santora, "Managing Open Employees: Do Resources and Leadership Style Matter?" *Academy of Management Perspectives* 21(3) (2007): 83–84.

18. W. Lam, X. Huang, and E. Snape, "Feedback-Seeking Behavior and Leader-Member Exchange: Do Supervisor-Attributed Motives Matter?" *Academy of Management Journal* 50(2) (2007): 348–363.

19. G.J. Jolley, "Leadership Can Be Taught: A Bold Approach for a Complex World," *Academy of Management Learning & Education* 6(1) (2007): 149–150.

20. D.C. Hambrick, "Upper Echelons Theory: An Update," *Academy of Management Review* 32(2) (2007): 334–343.

21. D. Jacobs, "Critical Biography and Management Education," *Academy of Management Learning & Education* 6(1) (2007): 104–108.

22. T.A. Judge, R. Ilies, J.E. Bono, and M.W. Gerhardt, "Personality and Leadership: A Qualitative and Quantitative Review," *Journal of Applied Psychology* 87(4) (2002): 765–768.

23. J. Houde, "Analogically Situated Experiences: Creating Insight through Novel Contexts," *Academy of Management Learning & Education* 6(3) (2007): 321–331.

24. S.G. Barsade and D.E. Gibson, "Why Does Affect Matter in Organizations?" *Academy of Management Perspectives* 21(1) (2007): 36–59.

25. B. Bass, *Handbook of Leadership* 2e (New York: Free Press, 2000).

26. G.J. Jolley, "Leadership Can Be Taught: A Bold Approach for a Complex World," *Academy of Management Learning & Education* 6(1) (2007): 149–150.

27. A.J. Wefald and J.P. Katz, "Leaders: The Strategies for Taking Charge," *Academy of Management Perspectives* 21(3) (2007): 105–106.

28. E. Ghiselli, *Exploration in Management Talent* (Santa Monica, CA: Goodyear, 1971).

29. C.M. Vance, K.S. Groves, Y. Paik, and H. Kindler, "Understanding and Measuring Linear-Nonlinear Thinking Style for Enhanced Management Education and Professional Practice," *Academy of Management Learning & Education* 6(2) (2007): 167–185.

30. T. Bacon, "Personality Conflict," *Entrepreneur* (March 2007): 78.

31. A.J. Wefald and J.P. Katz, "Leaders: The Strategies for Taking Charge," *Academy of Management Perspectives* 21(3) (2007): 105–106.

32. T.A. Judge, R. Ilies, J.E. Bono, and M.W. Gerhardt, "Personality and Leadership: A Qualitative and Quantitative Review," *Journal of Applied Psychology* 87(4) (2002): 765–768.

33. P. Dvorak and J. Badal, "This Is Your Brain on the Job," *The Wall Street Journal* (September 20, 2007): B1.

34. Staff, "What Are the Most Important Traits for Success as a Supervisor?" *The Wall Street Journal* (November 14, 1980): 33.

35. W. Lam, X. Huang, and E. Snape, "Feedback-Seeking Behavior and Leader-Member Exchange: Do Supervisor-Attributed Motives Matter?" *Academy of Management Journal* 50(2) (2007): 348–363.

36. J.A. Detert and E.R. Burris, "Leadership Behavior and Employee Voice: Is the Door Really Open?" *Academy of Management Journal* 50(4) (2007): 869–884.

37. J.C. Santora, "Managing Open Employees: Do Resources and Leadership Style Matter?" *Academy of Management Perspectives* 21(3) (2007): 83–84.

38. R. Likert, *New Patterns of Management* (New York: McGraw-Hill, 1961).

39. R.M. Stogdill and A.E. Coons (eds.), *Leader Behavior: The Description and Measurement* (Columbus: The Ohio State University Bureau of Business Research, 1957).

40. C. Hymowitz, "Effective Management Remains an Art Steeped in Good Relationships," *The Wall Street Journal* (August 11, 2008): B6.

41. M. Cox, "On Doing Supervision," *Transactional Analysis Journal* 37(2) (2007): 104–114.

42. R. Blake and J. Mouton, *The Managerial Grid* (Houston: Gulf Publishing, 1964).

43. R. Blake and J. Mouton, *The New Managerial Grid* (Houston: Gulf Publishing, 1978).

44. R. Blake and J. Mouton, *The Managerial Grid III: Key to Leadership Excellence* (Houston: Gulf Publishing, 1985).

45. R. Blake and A.A. McCanse, *Leadership Dilemmas— Grid Solutions* (Houston: Gulf Publishing, 1991).

46. M.F.R. Kets de Vries and K. Korotov, "Creating Transformational Executive Education Programs," *Academy of Management Learning & Education* 6(3) (2007): 375–387.

47. A.J. Wefald and J.P. Katz, "Leaders: The Strategies for Taking Charge," *Academy of Management Perspectives* 21(3) (2007): 105–106.

48. R. Kark and D. Van Dijk, "Motivation to Lead, Motivation to Follow: The Role of the Self-Regulatory Focus in Leadership Process," *Academy of Management Review* 32(2) (2007): 500–528.

49. B. Jackson and K. Parry, "A Very Short, Fairly Interesting and Reasonably Cheap Book about Studying Leadership," *Academy of Management Perspectives* 21(4) (2007): 90–92.

50. R. Kark and D. Van Dijk, "Motivation to Lead, Motivation to Follow: The Role of the Self-Regulatory Focus in Leadership Process," *Academy of Management Review* 32(2) (2007): 500–528.

51. B. Jackson and K. Parry, "A Very Short, Fairly Interesting and Reasonably Cheap Book about Studying Leadership," *Academy of Management Perspectives* 21(4) (2007): 90–92.

52. Y. Zhu, "Do Cultural Values Shape Employee Receptivity to Leadership Styles?" *Academy of Management Perspectives* 21(3) (2007): 89–90.

53. D. Jacobs, "Critical Biography and Management Education," *Academy of Management Learning & Education* 6(1) (2007): 104–108.

54. C. Hambrick, "Upper Echelons Theory: An Update," *Academy of Management Review* 32(2) (2007): 334–343.

55. F. Fiedler, *A Theory of Leadership Effectiveness* (New York: McGraw-Hill, 1967).

56. R. Tannenbaum and W. Schmidt, "How to Choose a Leadership Pattern," *Harvard Business Review* (May–June 1973): 166.

57. V.H. Vroom and P. Yetton, *Leadership and Decision Making* (Pittsburgh: University of Pittsburgh Press, 1973).

58. V.H. Vroom, "Leadership and the Decision Making Process," *Organizational Dynamics* 28 (Spring, 2000): 82–94.

59. P. Hersey, K. Blanchard, and D. Johnson, *Management of Organizational Behavior: Leading Human Resources* 9e (Upper Saddle River, NJ: Prentice-Hall, 2008).

60. M. Cox, "On Doing Supervision," *Transactional Analysis Journal* 37(2) (2007): 104–114.

61. J.A. Detert and E.R. Burris, "Leadership Behavior and Employee Voice: Is the Door Really Open?" *Academy of Management Journal* 50(4) (2007): 869–884.

62. W. Lam, X. Huang, and E. Snape, "Feedback-Seeking Behavior and Leader-Member Exchange: Do Supervisor-Attributed Motives Matter?" *Academy of Management Journal* 50(2) (2007): 348–363.

63. J.C. Santora, "Assertiveness and Effective Leadership: Is There a Tipping Point?" *Academy of Management Perspectives* 21(3) (2007): 84–86.

64. C. Hymowitz, "Effective Management Remains an Art Steeped in Good Relationships," *The Wall Street Journal* (August 11, 2008): B6.

65. Y. Zhu, "Do Cultural Values Shape Employee Receptivity to Leadership Styles?" *Academy of Management Perspectives* 21(3) (2007): 89–90.

66. W. Lam, X. Huang, and E. Snape, "Feedback-Seeking Behavior and Leader-Member Exchange: Do Supervisor-Attributed Motives Matter?" *Academy of Management Journal* 50(2) (2007): 348–363.

67. J.A. Detert and E.R. Burris, "Leadership Behavior and Employee Voice: Is the Door Really Open?" *Academy of Management Journal* 50(4) (2007): 869–884.

68. S. Kerr and J.M. Jermier, "Substitutes for Leadership: Their Meaning and Measurement," *Organizational Behavior and Human Performance* 22(1978): 375–403.

69. Reviewer Robert Losik, New Hampshire University, January 24, 2006.

70. S. Waddock, "Leadership Integrity in a Fractured Knowledge World," *Academy of Management Learning & Education* 6(4) (2007): 543–557.

71. Y. Zhu, "Do Cultural Values Shape Employee Receptivity to Leadership Styles?" *Academy of Management Perspectives* 21(3) (2007): 89–90.

72. J. Keyton, "Nascent and Complex: What Is the Focus of Trust Research?" *Academy of Management Review* 32(1) (2007): 274–275.

73. A. Malhotra, A. Majchrzak, and B. Rosen, "Leading Virtual Teams," *Academy of Management Perspectives* 21(1) (2007): 60–70.

74. C.L. Pearce, "Follow the Leaders," *The Wall Street Journal* (July 7, 2008): R8, R12.

75. Ibid.

76. A. Malhotra, A. Majchrzak, and B. Rosen, "Leading Virtual Teams," *Academy of Management Perspectives* 21(1) (2007): 60–70.

77. S. Waddock, "Leadership Integrity in a Fractured Knowledge World," *Academy of Management Learning & Education* 6(4) (2007): 543–557.

78. K.K. Metters and R. Metters, "Misunderstanding the Chinese Worker," *The Wall Street Journal* (July 7, 2008): R11.

79. S. Friedman, "My Employees Are Burned Out from Too Much Work. How Can I Create a Better Environment?" *Fortune* (July 21, 2008): 58.

80. Y. Zhu, "Do Cultural Values Shape Employee Receptivity to Leadership Styles?" *Academy of Management Perspectives* 21(3) (2007): 89–90.

81. W.F. Cornell, "The Inevitability of Uncertainty, the Necessity of Doubt, and the Development of Trust," *Transactional Analysis Journal* 37(1) (2007): 8–16.

82. R. Gulati and M. Sytch, "The Dynamic of Trust," *Academy of Management Review* 32(1) (2007): 276–277.

83. C.W. Langfred, "The Downside of Self-Management: A Longitudinal Study of the Effects of Conflict on Trust, Autonomy, and Task Interdependence in Self-Managing Teams," *Academy of Management Journal* 50(4) (2007): 885–900.

84. A. Malhotra, A. Majchrzak, and B. Rosen, "Leading Virtual Teams," *Academy of Management Perspectives* 21(1) (2007): 60–70.

85. C. Feldman, "Game Changers," *Fortune* (July 21, 2008): 54.

86. B. Farber, "Basic Instincts," *Entrepreneur* (August 2007): 66.

87. R. Cropanzano, D.E. Bowen, and S.W. Gilliland, "The Management of Organizational Justice," *Academy of Management Perspectives* 21(4) (2007): 34–48.

88. F.D. Schoorman, R.C. Mayer, and J.H. Davis, "An Integrative Model of Organizational Trust: Past, Present, and Future," *Academy of Management Review* 32(2) (2007): 344–354.

89. M. Williams, "Building Genuine Trust through Interpersonal Emotion Management: A Threat Regulation Model of Trust and Collaboration across Boundaries," *Academy of Management Review* 32(2) (2007): 595–621.

90. A.M. Grant, M.K. Christianson, and R.H. Price, "Happiness, Health, or Relationships? Managerial Practices and Employee Well-Being Tradeoffs," *Academy of Management Perspectives* 21(3) (2007): 51–63.

91. S.P. Robbins and T. Judge, *Essentials of Organizational Behavior* 9e (Upper Saddle River, NJ: Prentice-Hall, 2008).

92. A. Mehra, "Symposium: Handbook of Trust Research," *Academy of Management Review* 33(1) (2008): 271–272.

93. M. Henricks, "Buddy System," *Entrepreneur* (June 2007): 26.

94. D. Amos, "My Employees Are Burned Out from Too Much Work. How Can I Create a Better Environment?" *Fortune* (July 21, 2008): 58.

95. A. Mehra, "Symposium: Handbook of Trust Research," *Academy of Management Review* 33(1) (2008): 271–272.

96. M. Williams, "Building Genuine Trust through Interpersonal Emotion Management: A Threat Regulation Model of Trust and Collaboration across Boundaries," *Academy of Management Review* 32(2) (2007): 595–621.

97. A. Malhotra, A. Majchrzak, and B. Rosen, "Leading Virtual Teams," *Academy of Management Perspectives* 21(1) (2007): 60–70.

98. R. Ely and I. Padavic, "A Feminist Analysis of Organizational Research on Sex Differences," *Academy of Management Review* 32(4) (2007): 1121–1143.

99. R. Cropanzano, D.E. Bowen, and S.W. Gilliland, "The Management of Organizational Justice," *Academy of Management Perspectives* 21(4) (2007): 34–48.

100. S. Waddock, "Leadership Integrity in a Fractured Knowledge World," *Academy of Management Learning & Education* 6(4) (2007): 543–557.

101. G. Kawasaki, "Lies, Lies, Lies!" *Entrepreneur* (March 2007): 34.

102. R. Cropanzano, D.E. Bowen, and S.W. Gilliland, "The Management of Organizational Justice," *Academy of Management Perspectives* 21(4) (2007): 34–48.

103. W. Lam, X. Huang, and E. Snape, "Feedback-Seeking Behavior and Leader-Member Exchange: Do Supervisor-Attributed Motives Matter?" *Academy of Management Journal* 50(2) (2007): 348-363.

104. R. Cropanzano, D.E. Bowen, and S.W. Gilliland, "The Management of Organizational Justice," *Academy of Management Perspectives* 21(4) (2007): 34–48.

105. Mehra, "Symposium: Handbook of Trust Research," *Academy of Management Review* 33(1) (2008): 271–272.

106. A. Malhotra, A. Majchrzak, and B. Rosen, "Leading Virtual Teams," *Academy of Management Perspectives* 21(1) (2007): 60–70.

107. M. Williams, "Building Genuine Trust through Interpersonal Emotion Management: A Threat Regulation Model of Trust and Collaboration across Boundaries," *Academy of Management Review* 32(2) (2007): 595–621.

108. C.W. Langfred, "The Downside of Self-Management: A Longitudinal Study of the Effects of Conflict on Trust, Autonomy, and Task Interdependence in Self-Managing Teams," *Academy of Management Journal* 50(4) (2007): 885–900.

109. J. Luft, *Of Human Interaction* (Palo Alto, CA: National Press, 1969).

110. M. Henricks, "Buddy System," *Entrepreneur* (June 2007): 26.

111. Starbucks Web site (www.starbucks.com), retrieved September 9, 2008.

112. Ibid.

Chapter 9

1. S.G. Barsade and D.E. Gibson, "Why Does Affect Matter in Organizations?" *Academy of Management Perspectives* 21(1) (2007): 36–59.

2. R. Kark and D. Van Dijk, "Motivation to Lead, Motivation to Follow: The Role of the Self-Regulatory Focus in Leadership Process," *Academy of Management Review* 32(2) (2007): 500–528.

3. C.B. Cadsby, F. Song, and F. Tapon, "Sorting and Incentive Effects of Pay for Performance: An Experimental Investigation," *Academy of Management Journal* 50(2) (2007): 387–405.

4. R. Kark and D. Van Dijk, "Motivation to Lead, Motivation to Follow: The Role of the Self-Regulatory Focus in Leadership Process," *Academy of Management Review* 32(2) (2007): 500–528.

5. R.B. Kaiser and R.B. Kaplan, "The Deeper Work of Executive Development: Outgrowing Sensitivities," *Academy of Management Learning & Education* 5(4) (2006): 463–483.

6. J.A. Detert and E.R. Burris, "Leadership Behavior and Employee Voice: Is the Door Really Open?" *Academy of Management Journal* 50(4) (2007): 869–884.

7. S. Shellenbarger, "Rules of Engagement," *The Wall Street Journal* (October 1, 2007): R3.

8. B. Kotick, "The Three-Minute Manager," *Fortune* (July 7, 2008): 28.

9. W. Lam, X. Huang, and E. Snape, "Feedback-Seeking Behavior and Leader-Member Exchange: Do Supervisor-Attributed Motives Matter?" *Academy of Management Journal* 50(2) (2007): 348–363.

10. S. Shellenbarger, "Rules of Engagement," *The Wall Street Journal* (October 1, 2007): R3.

11. C.B. Cadsby, F. Song, and F. Tapon, "Sorting and Incentive Effects of Pay for Performance: An Experimental Investigation," *Academy of Management Journal* 50(2) (2007): 387–405.

12. R. Kark and D. Van Dijk, "Motivation to Lead, Motivation to Follow: The Role of the Self-Regulatory Focus in Leadership Process," *Academy of Management Review* 32(2) (2007): 500–528.

13. S.G. Barsade and D.E. Gibson, "Why Does Affect Matter in Organizations?" *Academy of Management Perspectives* 21(1) (2007): 36–59.

14. J.A. Detert and E.R. Burris, "Leadership Behavior and Employee Voice: Is the Door Really Open?" *Academy of Management Journal* 50(4) (2007): 869–884.

15. W. Lam, X. Huang, and E. Snape, "Feedback-Seeking Behavior and Leader-Member Exchange: Do Supervisor-Attributed Motives Matter?" *Academy of Management Journal* 50(2) (2007): 348–363.

16. S. Shellenbarger, "Rules of Engagement," *The Wall Street Journal* (October 1, 2007): R3.

17. R. Kark and D. Van Dijk, "Motivation to Lead, Motivation to Follow: The Role of the Self-Regulatory Focus in Leadership Process," *Academy of Management Review* 32(2) (2007): 500–528.

18. S. Shellenbarger, "Rules of Engagement," *The Wall Street Journal* (October 1, 2007): R3.

19. R. Kark and D. Van Dijk, "Motivation to Lead, Motivation to Follow: The Role of the Self-Regulatory Focus in Leadership Process," *Academy of Management Review* 32(2) (2007): 500–528.

20. P. Dvorak, "Hotelier Finds Happiness Keeps Staff Checked In," *The Wall Street Journal* (December 17, 2007), B3.

21. S. Shellenbarger, "Rules of Engagement," *The Wall Street Journal* (October 1, 2007): R3.

22. Y. Zhu, "What Drives Differences in Reward Allocation Principles across Countries and Organizations," *Academy of Management Perspectives* 21(3) (2007): 90–92.

23. A. Maslow, "A Theory of Human Motivation," *Psychological Review* 50(1943): 370–396; and *Motivation and Personality* (New York: Harper & Row, 1954).

24. L.A. Mainiero and S.E. Sullivan, *The Opt-Out Revolt: Why People Are Leaving Companies to Create Kaleidoscope Careers* (Mountain View, CA: Davies-Black, 2006).

25. P. Dvorak, "Hotelier Finds Happiness Keeps Staff Checked In," *The Wall Street Journal* (December 17, 2007), B3.

26. A.J. Wefald and J.P. Katz, "Leaders: The Strategies for Taking Charge," *Academy of Management Perspectives* 21(3) (2007): 105–106.

27. Ibid.

28. Ibid.

29. Y. Zhu, "What Drives Differences in Reward Allocation Principles across Countries and Organizations," *Academy of Management Perspectives* 21(3) (2007): 90–92.

30. F. Herzberg, "One More Time: How Do You Motivate Employees?" *Harvard Business Review* (January–February 1968): 53–62.

31. J. Clements, "No Satisfaction: Why What You Have Is Never Enough," *The Wall Street Journal* (May 2, 2007): D1.

32. Y. Zhu, "What Drives Differences in Reward Allocation Principles across Countries and Organizations," *Academy of Management Perspectives* 21(3) (2007): 90–92.

33. L.A. Mainiero and S.E. Sullivan, *The Opt-Out Revolt: Why People Are Leaving Companies to Create Kaleidoscope Careers* (Mountain View, CA: Davies-Black, 2006).

34. J. Clements, "Down the Tube: The Sad Stats on Happiness, Money and TV," *The Wall Street Journal* (April 2, 2008): D1.

35. M. Henricks, "The Best of the Best," *Entrepreneur* (September 2007): 34.

36. H. Murray, *Explorations in Personality* (New York: Oxford Press, 1938).

37. J. Atkinson, *An Introduction to Motivation* (New York: Van Nostrand Reinhold, 1964).

38. D. McClelland, *The Achieving Society* (New York: Van Nostrand Reinhold, 1961); and D. McClelland and D.H. Burnham, "Power Is the Great Motivator," *Harvard Business Review* (March–April 1978): 103.

39. M. Henricks, "The Best of the Best," *Entrepreneur* (September 2007): 34.

40. T.A. Judge, R. Ilies, J.E. Bono, and M.W. Gerhardt, "Personality and Leadership: A Qualitative and Quantitative Review," *Journal of Applied Psychology* 87(4) (2002): 765–768.

41. M. Henricks, "The Best of the Best," *Entrepreneur* (September 2007): 34.

42. L.A. Mainiero and S.E. Sullivan, *The Opt-Out Revolt: Why People Are Leaving Companies to Create Kaleidoscope Careers* (Mountain View, CA: Davies-Black, 2006).

43. Ibid.

44. S.L. Rynes, T.L. Giluk, and K.G. Brown, "The Very Separate Worlds of Academic and Practitioner Periodicals in Human Resource Management: Implications for Evidence-Based Management," *Academy of Management Journal* 50(5) (2007): 987–1008.

45. S. Covel, "How to Get Workers to Think and Act Like Owners," *The Wall Street Journal* (February 7, 2008): B6.

46. C.B. Cadsby, F. Song, and F. Tapon, "Sorting and Incentive Effects of Pay for Performance: An Experimental Investigation," *Academy of Management Journal* 50(2) (2007): 387–405.

47. W. Lam, X. Huang, and E. Snape, "Feedback-Seeking Behavior and Leader-Member Exchange: Do Supervisor-Attributed Motives Matter?" *Academy of Management Journal* 50(2) (2007): 348–363.

48. S.L. Rynes, T.L. Giluk, and K.G. Brown, "The Very Separate Worlds of Academic and Practitioner Periodicals in Human Resource Management: Implications for Evidence-Based Management," *Academy of Management Journal* 50(5) (2007): 987–1008.

49. A.M. Grant, M.K. Christianson, and R.H. Price, "Happiness, Health, or Relationships? Managerial Practices and Employee Well-Being Tradeoffs," *Academy of Management Perspectives* 21(3) (2007): 51–63.

50. R. Cropanzano, D.E. Bowen, and S.W. Gilliland, "The Management of Organizational Justice," *Academy of Management Perspectives* 21(4) (2007): 34–48.

51. V.H. Vroom, *Work and Motivation* (New York: Wiley, 1964).

52. C.B. Gibson and P.C. Earley, "Collective Cognition in Action: Accumulation, Interaction, Examination, and Accommodation in the Development and Operation of Group Efficacy Beliefs in the Workplace," *Academy of Management Review* 32(2) (2007): 438–458.

53. J.C. Santora, "Assertiveness and Effective Leadership: Is There a Tipping Point?" *Academy of Management Perspectives* 21(3) (2007): 84–86.

54. J. Sandberg, "For Many Employees, a Dream Job Is One That Isn't a Nightmare," *The Wall Street Journal* (April 15, 2007): B1.

55. S. Covel, "How to Get Workers to Think and Act Like Owners," *The Wall Street Journal* (February 7, 2008): B6.

56. P. Keegan, "Get a Life!" *Fortune* (September 1, 2008): 115–120.

57. C.B. Cadsby, F. Song, and F. Tapon, "Sorting and Incentive Effects of Pay for Performance: An Experimental Investigation," *Academy of Management Journal* 50(2) (2007): 387–405.

58. W. Lam, X. Huang, and E. Snape, "Feedback-Seeking Behavior and Leader-Member Exchange: Do Supervisor-Attributed Motives Matter?" *Academy of Management Journal* 50(2) (2007): 348–363.

59. S. Adams, "Toward an Understanding of Inequity," *Journal of Abnormal and Social Psychology* 67(4) (1963): 422–436.

60. B.M. Wiesenfeld, W.B. Swann, J. Brockner, and C.A. Bartel, "Is More Fairness Always Preferred? Self-Esteem Moderates Reactions to Procedural Justice," *Academy of Management Journal* 50(5) (2007): 1235–1253.

61. Ibid.

62. S.G. Barsade and D.E. Gibson, "Why Does Affect Matter in Organizations?" *Academy of Management Perspectives* 21(1) (2007): 36–59.

63. B.M. Wiesenfeld, W.B. Swann, J. Brockner, and C.A. Bartel, "Is More Fairness Always Preferred? Self-Esteem Moderates Reactions to Procedural Justice," *Academy of Management Journal* 50(5) (2007): 1235–1253.

64. C.B. Cadsby, F. Song, and F. Tapon, "Sorting and Incentive Effects of Pay for Performance: An Experimental Investigation," *Academy of Management Journal* 50(2) (2007): 387–405.

65. S.G. Barsade and D.E. Gibson, "Why Does Affect Matter in Organizations?" *Academy of Management Perspectives* 21(1) (2007): 36–59.

66. C.B. Cadsby, F. Song, and F. Tapon, "Sorting and Incentive Effects of Pay for Performance: An Experimental Investigation," *Academy of Management Journal* 50(2) (2007): 387–405.

67. Ibid.

68. D.M. Bergeron, "The Potential Paradox of Organizational Citizenship Behavior: Good Citizens at What Cost? *Academy of Management Review* 32(4) (2007): 1078–1095.

69. B.F. Skinner, *Beyond Freedom and Dignity* (New York: Alfred Knopf, 1971).

70. P. Osterman, "Comments on Le, Oh, Shaffer, and Schmidt," *Academy of Management Perspectives* 21(3) (2007): 16–18.

71. G. Kawasaki, "The Art of Execution," *Entrepreneur* (September 2007): 26.

72. J. Sandberg, "Performance Reviews Need Some Work, Don't Meet Potential," *The Wall Street Journal* (November 20, 2007): B1.

73. P. Dvorak, "Hotelier Finds Happiness Keeps Staff Checked In," *The Wall Street Journal* (December 17, 2007), B3.

74. J. Sandberg, "I'm Not Really Late, I'm Just Indulging in Magical Thinking," *The Wall Street Journal* (October 13, 2007): B1.

75. D.M. Bergeron, "The Potential Paradox of Organizational Citizenship Behavior: Good Citizens at What Cost? *Academy of Management Review* 32(4) (2007): 1078–1095.

76. S.L. Rynes, T.L. Giluk, and K.G. Brown, "The Very Separate Worlds of Academic and Practitioner Periodicals in Human Resource Management: Implications for Evidence-Based Management," *Academy of Management Journal* 50(5) (2007): 987–1008.

77. C.B. Cadsby, F. Song, and F. Tapon, "Sorting and Incentive Effects of Pay for Performance: An Experimental Investigation," *Academy of Management Journal* 50(2) (2007): 387–405.

78. Y. Zhu, "What Drives Differences in Reward Allocation Principles across Countries and Organizations," *Academy of Management Perspectives* 21(3) (2007): 90–92.

79. J. Zaslow, "In Praise of Less Praise," *The Wall Street Journal* (May 3, 2007): D1.

80. D. Newman, "How to Motivate Your Sales Team," *Entrepreneur* (June 2007): 73.

81. S. Shellenbarger, "What Makes a Company a Great Place to Work Today," *The Wall Street Journal* (October 4, 2007): D1.

82. R. Kark and D. Van Dijk, "Motivation to Lead, Motivation to Follow: The Role of the Self-Regulatory Focus in Leadership Process," *Academy of Management Review* 32(2) (2007): 500–528.

83. T. Petzinger, "Edward O. Wilson: Human Nature, Dr. Wilson Believes, Has Changed Little in Many Millennia. And It Will Change Very Little in the Millennia Ahead," *The Wall Street Journal* (January 1, 2000): R16.

84. D. Newman, "How to Motivate Your Sales Team," *Entrepreneur* (June 2007): 73.

85. C. Hymowitz, "Sometimes, Moving Up Makes It Harder to See What Goes on Below," *The Wall Street Journal* (October 15, 2007): B1.

86. Y. Zhu, "What Drives Differences in Reward Allocation Principles across Countries and Organizations," *Academy of Management Perspectives* 21(3) (2007): 90–92.

87. P. Dvorak and J. Badal, "This Is Your Brain on the Job," *The Wall Street Journal* (September 20, 2007): B1.

88. K. Blanchard and S. Johnson, *The One-Minute Manager* (New York: Wm. Morrow, 1982).

89. B. Iger, "How I Work," *Fortune* (December 10, 2007): 38.

90. D.M. Rousseau and S. McCarthy, "Educating Managers from an Evidence-Based Perspective," *Academy of Management Learning & Education* 6(1) (2007): 84–101.

91. E.A. Locke, "Guest Editor's Introduction: Goal-Setting Theory and Its Applications to the World of Business," *Academy of Management Executive* 18 (4) (2004): 124–125.

92. A.J. Wefald and J.P. Katz, "Leaders: The Strategies for Taking Charge," *Academy of Management Perspectives* 21(3) (2007): 105–106.

93. D.M. Rousseau and S. McCarthy, "Educating Managers from an Evidence-Based Perspective," *Academy of Management Learning & Education* 6(1) (2007): 84–101.

94. G. Kawasaki, "The Art of Execution," *Entrepreneur* (September 2007): 26.

95. P. Keegan, "Get a Life!" *Fortune* (September 1, 2008): 115–120.

96. D.M. Bergeron, "The Potential Paradox of Organizational Citizenship Behavior: Good Citizens at What Cost? *Academy of Management Review* 32(4) (2007): 1078–1095.

97. S.L. Rynes, T.L. Giluk, and K.G. Brown, "The Very Separate Worlds of Academic and Practitioner Periodicals in Human Resource Management: Implications for Evidence-Based Management," *Academy of Management Journal* 50(5) (2007): 987–1008.

98. J. Adamy, "Will a Twist on an Old Vow Deliver for Domino's Pizza?" *The Wall Street Journal* (December 17, 2007): A1.

99. A. Chozick, "Toyota's Goal: First to Sell 10 Million," *The Wall Street Journal* (September 12, 2007): A3.

100. "BMW Revamped," *The Wall Street Journal* (September 28, 2007): A1.

101. C.W. Langfred, "The Downside of Self-Management: A Longitudinal Study of the Effects of Conflict on Trust, Autonomy, and Task Interdependence in Self-Managing Teams," *Academy of Management Journal* 50(4) (2007): 885–900.

102. Ibid.

103. E.A. Locke, "Guest Editor's Introduction: Goal-Setting Theory and Its Applications to the World of Business," *Academy of Management Executive* 18(4) (2004): 124–125.

104. D.M. Rousseau and S. McCarthy, "Educating Managers from an Evidence-Based Perspective," *Academy of Management Learning & Education* 6(1) (2007): 84–101.

105. C.B. Cadsby, F. Song, and F. Tapon, "Sorting and Incentive Effects of Pay for Performance: An Experimental Investigation," *Academy of Management Journal* 50(2) (2007): 387–405.

106. R. Kark and D. Van Dijk, "Motivation to Lead, Motivation to Follow: The Role of the Self-Regulatory Focus in Leadership Process," *Academy of Management Review* 32(2) (2007): 500–528.

107. A.M. Grant, "Relational Job Design and the Motivation to Make a Prosocial Difference," *Academy of Management Review* 32(2) (2007): 393–417.

108. P. Keegan, "Get a Life!" *Fortune* (September 1, 2008): 115–120.

109. C.W. Langfred, "The Downside of Self-Management: A Longitudinal Study of the Effects of Conflict on Trust, Autonomy, and Task Interdependence in Self-Managing Teams," *Academy of Management Journal* 50(4) (2007): 885–900.

110. A.M. Grant, "Relational Job Design and the Motivation to Make a Prosocial Difference," *Academy of Management Review* 32(2) (2007): 393–417.

111. R. Kark and D. Van Dijk, "Motivation to Lead, Motivation to Follow: The Role of the Self-Regulatory Focus in Leadership Process," *Academy of Management Review* 32(2) (2007): 500–528.

112. Y. Zhu, "What Drives Differences in Reward Allocation Principles across Countries and Organizations," *Academy of Management Perspectives* 21(3) (2007): 90–92.

113. C.B. Cadsby, F. Song, and F. Tapon, "Sorting and Incentive Effects of Pay for Performance: An Experimental Investigation," *Academy of Management Journal* 50(2) (2007): 387–405.

114. Ibid.

115. E. A. Locke, "Guest Editor's Introduction: Goal-Setting Theory and Its Applications to the World of Business," *Academy of Management Executive* 18(4) (2004): 124–125.

116. Revere Group Web site (www.reveregroup.com), retrieved September 15, 2008.

Chapter 10

1. G.J. Jolley, "Leadership Can Be Taught: A Bold Approach for a Complex World," *Academy of Management Learning & Education* 6(1) (2007): 149–150.

2. D.C. Hambrick, "Upper Echelons Theory: An Update," *Academy of Management Review* 32(2) (2007): 334–343.

3. B.J. Tepper, S.E. Moss, D.E. Lockhart, and J.C. Carr, "Abusive Supervision, Upward Maintenance Communication, and Subordinates' Psychological Distress," *Academy of Management Journal* 50(5) (2007): 1169–1180.

4. Ibid.

5. G. Kawaski, "Get in Good," *Entrepreneur* (October 2007): 46.

6. S.G. Barsade and D.E. Gibson, "Why Does Affect Matter in Organizations?" *Academy of Management Perspectives* 21(1) (2007): 36–59.

7. M. Learmonth, "Critical Management Education in Action: Personal Tales of Management Unlearning," *Academy of Management Learning & Education* 6(1) (2007): 109–113.

8. F.D. Schoorman, R.C. Mayer, and J.H. Davis, "An Integrative Model of Organizational Trust: Past, Present, and Future," *Academy of Management Review* 32(2) (2007): 344–354.

9. D.C. Hambrick, "Upper Echelons Theory: An Update," *Academy of Management Review* 32(2) (2007): 334–343.

10. C.L. Pearce, "Follow the Leaders," *The Wall Street Journal* (July 7, 2008): R8, R12.

11. B.J. Tepper, S.E. Moss, D.E. Lockhart, and J.C. Carr, "Abusive Supervision, Upward Maintenance Communication, and Subordinates' Psychological Distress," *Academy of Management Journal* 50(5) (2007): 1169–1180.

12. R. Kark and D. Van Dijk, "Motivation to Lead, Motivation to Follow: The Role of the Self-Regulatory Focus in Leadership Process," *Academy of Management Review* 32(2) (2007): 500–528.

13. G.J. Jolley, "Leadership Can Be Taught: A Bold Approach for a Complex World," *Academy of Management Learning & Education* 6(1) (2007): 149–150.

14. D.C. Hambrick, "Upper Echelons Theory: An Update," *Academy of Management Review* 32(2) (2007): 334–343.

15. M. Williams, "Building Genuine Trust through Interpersonal Emotion Management: A Threat Regulation Model of Trust and Collaboration across Boundaries," *Academy of Management Review* 32(2) (2007): 595–621.

16. J. French and B. Raven, "A Comparative Analysis of Power and Preference," in J.T. Tedeschi (ed.), *Perspectives on Social Power* (Hawthorne, NY: Aldine Publishing, 1974).

17. B.J. Tepper, S.E. Moss, D.E. Lockhart, and J.C. Carr, "Abusive Supervision, Upward Maintenance Communication, and Subordinates' Psychological Distress," *Academy of Management Journal* 50(5) (2007): 1169–1180.

18. Ibid.

19. B.P. Matherne, "Does Whom You Know Matter in Venture Capital Networks?" *Academy of Management Perspectives* 21(4) (2007): 85–86.

20. R. Cross, A. Hargadon, S. Parise, and R.J. Thomas, "Together We Innovate," *The Wall Street Journal* (September 15, 2007): R6.

21. B. Farber, "Some Like It Hot," *Entrepreneur* (December 2007): 100.

22. B.A. Hudson, "Against All Odds: A Consideration of Core-Stigmatized Organizations," *Academy of Management Review* 33(1) (2008): 252–266.

23. S.G. Barsade and D.E. Gibson, "Why Does Affect Matter in Organizations?" *Academy of Management Perspectives* 21(1) (2007): 36–59.

24. R. Cross, A. Hargadon, S. Parise, and R.J. Thomas, "Together We Innovate," *The Wall Street Journal* (September 15, 2007): R6.

25. S. Shellenbarger, "Rules of Engagement," *The Wall Street Journal* (October 1, 2007): R3.

26. M. Williams, "Building Genuine Trust through Interpersonal Emotion Management: A Threat Regulation Model of Trust and Collaboration across Boundaries," *Academy of Management Review* 32(2) (2007): 595–621.

27. Ibid.

28. J.D. Westphal and I. Stern, "Flattery Will Get You Everywhere (Especially If You Are a Male Caucasian): How Ingratiation, Boardroom Behavior, and Demographic Minority Status Affect Additional Board Appointments at U.S. Companies," *Academy of Management Journal* 50(2) (2007): 267–288.

29. S.G. Barsade and D.E. Gibson, "Why Does Affect Matter in Organizations?" *Academy of Management Perspectives* 21(1) (2007): 36–59.

30. S. Shellenbarger, "Rules of Engagement," *The Wall Street Journal* (October 1, 2007): R3.

31. B.A. Hudson, "Against All Odds: A Consideration of Core-Stigmatized Organizations," *Academy of Management Review* 33(1) (2008): 252–266.

32. M. Williams, "Building Genuine Trust through Interpersonal Emotion Management: A Threat Regulation Model of Trust and Collaboration across Boundaries," *Academy of Management Review* 32(2) (2007): 595–621.

33. M. Learmonth, "Critical Management Education in Action: Personal Tales of Management Unlearning," *Academy of Management Learning & Education* 6(1) (2007): 109–113.

34. M. Boyle, "Questions for Carly Fiorina," *Fortune* (October 29, 2007): 68.

35. M. Diener, "Fair Share?" *Entrepreneur* (March 2007): 86.

36. J.B. Carson, P.E. Tesluck, and J.A. Marrone, "Shared Leadership in Teams: An Investigation of Antecedent Conditions and Performance," *Academy of Management Journal* 50(5) (2007): 1217–1234.

37. J. Sandberg, "For Many Employees, a Dream Job Is One That Isn't a Nightmare," *The Wall Street Journal* (April 15, 2007): B1.

38. J.D. Westphal and I. Stern, "Flattery Will Get You Everywhere (Especially If You Are a Male Caucasian): How Ingratiation, Boardroom Behavior, and Demographic Minority Status Affect Additional Board Appointments at U.S. Companies," *Academy of Management Journal* 50(2) (2007): 267–288.

39. G. Kawaski, "Get in Good," *Entrepreneur* (October 2007): 46.

40. F.D. Schoorman, R.C. Mayer, and J.H. Davis, "An Integrative Model of Organizational Trust: Past, Present, and Future," *Academy of Management Review* 32(2) (2007): 344–354.

41. E. Cassoni, "Parallel Process in Supervision and Therapy: An Opportunity for Reciprocity," *Transactional Analysis Journal* 37(2) (2007): 130–139.

42. J. Sandberg, "People Can't Resist Doing a Big Favor—Or Asking for One," *The Wall Street Journal* (December 18, 2007): B1.

43. G. Kawaski, "Get in Good," *Entrepreneur* (October 2007): 46.

44. F.D. Schoorman, R.C. Mayer, and J.H. Davis, "An Integrative Model of Organizational Trust: Past, Present, and Future," *Academy of Management Review* 32(2) (2007): 344–354.

45. M. Learmonth, "Critical Management Education in Action: Personal Tales of Management Unlearning," *Academy of Management Learning & Education* 6(1) (2007): 109–113.

46. B.J. Tepper, S.E. Moss, D.E. Lockhart, and J.C. Carr, "Abusive Supervision, Upward Maintenance Communication, and Subordinates' Psychological Distress," *Academy of Management Journal* 50(5) (2007): 1169–1180.

47. A.G. Scherer and G. Palazzo, "Toward a Political Conception of Corporate Responsibility: Business and Society Seen from a Habermasian Perspective," *Academy of Management Review* 32(4) (2007): 1096–1120.

48. F.D. Schoorman, R.C. Mayer, and J.H. Davis, "An Integrative Model of Organizational Trust: Past, Present, and Future," *Academy of Management Review* 32(2) (2007): 344–354.

49. T. Bacon, "Personality Conflict," *Entrepreneur* (March 2007): 78.

50. D.C. Hambrick, "Upper Echelons Theory: An Update," *Academy of Management Review* 32(2) (2007): 334–343.

51. J. Sandberg, "Your Boss's Obsession Too Often Becomes Your Job Obligation," *The Wall Street Journal* (December 12, 2007): B1.

52. B.J. Tepper, S.E. Moss, D.E. Lockhart, and J.C. Carr, "Abusive Supervision, Upward Maintenance Communication, and Subordinates' Psychological Distress," *Academy of Management Journal* 50(5) (2007): 1169–1180.

53. S. Shellenbarger, "Rules of Engagement," *The Wall Street Journal* (October 1, 2007): R3.

54. S.E. Needleman, "It Pays to Plan Ahead When Taking a New Job," *The Wall Street Journal* (May 20, 2008): D4.

55. S. Shellenbarger, "Rules of Engagement," *The Wall Street Journal* (October 1, 2007): R3.

56. S.E. Needleman, "It Pays to Plan Ahead When Taking a New Job," *The Wall Street Journal* (May 20, 2008): D4.

57. Ibid.

58. F.D. Schoorman, R.C. Mayer, and J.H. Davis, "An Integrative Model of Organizational Trust: Past, Present, and Future," *Academy of Management Review* 32(2) (2007): 344–354.

59. S. Shellenbarger, "Rules of Engagement," *The Wall Street Journal* (October 1, 2007): R3.

60. B. Farber, "Some Like It Hot," *Entrepreneur* (December 2007): 100.

61. S.E. Needleman, "It Pays to Plan Ahead When Taking a New Job," *The Wall Street Journal* (May 20, 2008): D4.

62. R. Cross, A. Hargadon, S. Parise, and R.J. Thomas, "Together We Innovate," *The Wall Street Journal* (September 15, 2007): R6.

63. C.L. Pearce, "Follow the Leaders," *The Wall Street Journal* (July 7, 2008): R8, R12.

64. Ibid.

65. R. Cross, A. Hargadon, S. Parise, and R.J. Thomas, "Together We Innovate," *The Wall Street Journal* (September 15, 2007): R6.

Chapter 11

1. Toyota Web site (www.toyota.com), retrieved September 26, 2008.

2. C.T. Kulik, H.T.J. Bainbridge, and C. Cregan, "Known by the Company We Keep: Stigma-by-Association Effects in the Workplace," *Academy of Management Review* 33(1) (2008): 216–230.

3. K.E. Kram and M.C. Higgins, "A New Approach to Mentoring," *The Wall Street Journal* (September 22, 2008): R10.

4. R. Cross, A. Hargadon, S. Parise, and R.J. Thomas, "Together We Innovate," *The Wall Street Journal* (September 15, 2007): R6.

5. S.E. Needleman, "It Pays to Plan Ahead When Taking a New Job," *The Wall Street Journal* (May 20, 2008): D4.

6. R. Cross, A. Hargadon, S. Parise, and R.J. Thomas, "Together We Innovate," *The Wall Street Journal* (September 15, 2007): R6.

7. S.E. Needleman, "It Pays to Plan Ahead When Taking a New Job," *The Wall Street Journal* (May 20, 2008): D4.

8. S.E. Needleman, "Tough Times Don't Mean Tough Luck on Salary," *The Wall Street Journal* (April 15, 2008): D6.

9. B. Farber, "Sell as Easy as 1-2-3," *Entrepreneur* (January 2008): 82.

10. M. Diener, "Asking for It," *Entrepreneur* (September 2007): 86.

11. M. Diener, "Fair Share?" *Entrepreneur* (March 2007): 86.

12. A. Gumbus and R.N. Lussier, "Career Development: Enhancing Your Networking Skills," *Clinical Leadership & Management Review* 17(1) (2003): 16–20.

13. G. Kawaski, "Get in Good," *Entrepreneur* (October 2007): 46.

14. K.E. Kram and M.C. Higgins, "A New Approach to Mentoring," *The Wall Street Journal* (September 22, 2008): R10.

15. R. Cross, A. Hargadon, S. Parise, and R.J. Thomas, "Together We Innovate," *The Wall Street Journal* (September 15, 2007): R6.

16. A. Gumbus and R.N. Lussier, "Career Development: Enhancing Your Networking Skills," *Clinical Leadership & Management Review* 17(1) (2003): 16–20.

17. Ibid.

18. B.P. Matherne, "Does Whom You Know Matter in Venture Capital Networks?" *Academy of Management Perspectives* 21(4) (2007): 85–86.

19. A. Gumbus and R.N. Lussier, "Career Development: Enhancing Your Networking Skills," *Clinical Leadership & Management Review* 17(1) (2003): 16–20.

20. K. E. Kram and M.C. Higgins, "A New Approach to Mentoring," *The Wall Street Journal* (September 22, 2008): R10.

21. R. Cross, A. Hargadon, S. Parise, and R.J. Thomas, "Together We Innovate," *The Wall Street Journal* (September 15, 2007): R6.

22. K.E. Kram and M.C. Higgins, "A New Approach to Mentoring," *The Wall Street Journal* (September 22, 2008): R10.

23. G. Kawaski, "Get in Good," *Entrepreneur* (October 2007): 46.

24. A. Gumbus and R.N. Lussier, "Career Development: Enhancing Your Networking Skills," *Clinical Leadership & Management Review* 17(1) (2003): 16–20.

25. G. Kawaski, "Get in Good," *Entrepreneur* (October 2007): 46.

26. B. Farber, "Some Like It Hot," *Entrepreneur* (December 2007): 100.

27. A. Gumbus and R.N. Lussier, "Career Development: Enhancing Your Networking Skills," *Clinical Leadership & Management Review* 17(1) (2003): 16–20.

28. Ibid.

29. G. Kawasaki, "The Art of Execution," *Entrepreneur* (September 2007): 26.

30. A. Gumbus and R.N. Lussier, "Career Development: Enhancing Your Networking Skills," *Clinical Leadership & Management Review* 17(1) (2003): 16–20.

31. B. Farber, "Some Like It Hot," *Entrepreneur* (December 2007): 100.

32. Ibid.

33. A. Gumbus and R.N. Lussier, "Career Development: Enhancing Your Networking Skills," *Clinical Leadership & Management Review* 17(1) (2003): 16–20.

34. B. Farber, "Some Like It Hot," *Entrepreneur* (December 2007): 100.

35. M. Diener, "Asking for It," *Entrepreneur* (September 2007): 86.

36. B. Farber, "Some Like It Hot," *Entrepreneur* (December 2007): 100.

37. G. Kawaski, "Get in Good," *Entrepreneur* (October 2007): 46.

38. Ibid.

39. Ibid.

40. S. Shellenbarger, "Tucking the Kids in—in the Dorm: Colleges Ward Off Overinvolved Parents," *The Wall Street Journal* (July 28, 2005): D1.

41. B. Farber, "Some Like It Hot," *Entrepreneur* (December 2007): 100.

42. S.E. Needleman, "Tough Times Don't Mean Tough Luck on Salary," *The Wall Street Journal* (April 15, 2008): D6.

43. B. Farber, "Some Like It Hot," *Entrepreneur* (December 2007): 100.

44. M. Henricks, "Buddy System," *Entrepreneur* (June 2007): 26.

45. "Making Sales Presentations," *Entrepreneur* (June 2007): 105.

46. M. Diener, "Asking for It," *Entrepreneur* (September 2007): 86.

47. B. Farber, "Sell as Easy as 1-2-3," *Entrepreneur* (January 2008): 82.

48. A. Mehra, "Symposium: Handbook of Trust Research," *Academy of Management Review* 33(1) (2008): 271–272.

49. B. Farber, "Sell as Easy as 1-2-3," *Entrepreneur* (January 2008): 82.

50. M. Henricks, "Buddy System," *Entrepreneur* (June 2007): 26.

51. B. Farber, "Some Like It Hot," *Entrepreneur* (December 2007): 100.

52. D. Petraeus," "The Best Advice I Ever Got," *Fortune* (May 12, 2008): 75.

53. M. Bloomberg, "The Best Advice I Ever Got," *Fortune* (May 12, 2008): 72.

54. B. Farber, "Sell as Easy as 1-2-3," *Entrepreneur* (January 2008): 82.

55. S.E. Needleman, "Tough Times Don't Mean Tough Luck on Salary," *The Wall Street Journal* (April 15, 2008): D6.

56. B. Farber, "Some Like It Hot," *Entrepreneur* (December 2007): 100.

57. B. Farber, "Sell as Easy as 1-2-3," *Entrepreneur* (January 2008): 82.

58. B. Farber, "Some Like It Hot," *Entrepreneur* (December 2007): 100.

59. M. Diener, "Fair Share?" *Entrepreneur* (March 2007): 86.

60. C.J. Prince, "Currency Time Bomb," *Entrepreneur* (January 2008): 66.

61. M. Bloomberg, "The Best Advice I Ever Got," *Fortune* (May 12, 2008): 72.

62. C.J. Prince, "Currency Time Bomb," *Entrepreneur* (January 2008): 66.

63. M. Henricks, "Buddy System," *Entrepreneur* (June 2007): 26.

64. Ibid.

65. B. Farber, "Some Like It Hot," *Entrepreneur* (December 2007): 100.

66. "Making Sales Presentations," *Entrepreneur* (June 2007): 105.

67. M. Diener, "Asking for It," *Entrepreneur* (September 2007): 86.

68. B. Farber, "Sell as Easy as 1-2-3," *Entrepreneur* (January 2008): 82.

69. A. Mehra, "Symposium: Handbook of Trust Research," *Academy of Management Review* 33(1) (2008): 271–272.

70. B. Farber, "Sell as Easy as 1-2-3," *Entrepreneur* (January 2008): 82.

71. Ibid.

72. M. Henricks, "Buddy System," *Entrepreneur* (June 2007): 26.

73. B. Spector, "An Interview with Roger Fisher and William Ury," *Academy of Management Executive* 18(3) (2004): 101–108.

74. B. Farber, "Sell as Easy as 1-2-3," *Entrepreneur* (January 2008): 82.

75. "Making Sales Presentations," *Entrepreneur* (June 2007): 105.

76. A. Mehra, "Symposium: Handbook of Trust Research," *Academy of Management Review* 33(1) (2008): 271–272.

77. R. Ely and I. Padavic, "A Feminist Analysis of Organizational Research on Sex Differences," *Academy of Management Review* 32(4) (2007): 1121–1143.

78. D. Dimov, "From Opportunity Insight to Opportunity Intention: The Importance of Person-Situation Learning Match," *Entrepreneurship Theory and Practice* 31(6) (2007): 1121–1243.

79. M. Diener, "Asking for It," *Entrepreneur* (September 2007): 86.

80. A. Mehra, "Symposium: Handbook of Trust Research," *Academy of Management Review* 33(1) (2008): 271–272.

81. WFCR Public Radio, "News Story," aired June 8, 2005.

82. "Making Sales Presentations," *Entrepreneur* (June 2007): 105.

83. B. Farber, "Some Like It Hot," *Entrepreneur* (December 2007): 100.

84. C.J. Prince, "Currency Time Bomb," *Entrepreneur* (January 2008): 66.

85. B. Farber, "Sell as Easy as 1-2-3," *Entrepreneur* (January 2008): 82.

86. M. Diener, "Asking for It," *Entrepreneur* (September 2007): 86.

87. C.J. Prince, "Currency Time Bomb," *Entrepreneur* (January 2008): 66.

88. M. Henricks, "Buddy System," *Entrepreneur* (June 2007): 26.

89. A. Mehra, "Symposium: Handbook of Trust Research," *Academy of Management Review* 33(1) (2008): 271–272.

90. B. Farber, "Sell as Easy as 1-2-3," *Entrepreneur* (January 2008): 82.

91. Ibid.

92. Ibid.

93. C.J. Prince, "Currency Time Bomb," *Entrepreneur* (January 2008): 66.

94. N.J. Adler, *International Dimensions of Organizational Behavior* 6e (Cincinnati: South-Western, 2008).

95. Ibid.

96. Ibid.

97. Avon Web site (www.avon.com), retrieved October 3, 2008.

Chapter 12

1. R. Cross, A. Hargadon, S. Parise, and R.J. Thomas, "Together We Innovate," *The Wall Street Journal* (September 15, 2007): R6.

2. J.B. Carson, P.E. Tesluck, and J.A. Marrone, "Shared Leadership in Teams: An Investigation of Antecedent Conditions and Performance," *Academy of Management Journal* 50(5) (2007): 1217–1234.

3. R. Rico, M.S. Manzanares, F. Gil, and G. Gibson, "Team Implicit Coordination Process: A Team Knowledge-Based Approach," *Academy of Management Review* 33(1) (2008): 163–184.

4. J. Sandberg, "I'm Not Really Late, I'm Just Indulging in Magical Thinking," *The Wall Street Journal* (October 13, 2007): B1.

5. M. Learmonth, "Critical Management Education in Action: Personal Tales of Management Unlearning," *Academy of Management Learning & Education* 6(1) (2007): 109–113.

6. J. Sandberg, "Another Meeting? Good, Another Chance to Hear Myself Talk," *The Wall Street Journal* (March 11, 2008): B1.

7. C. Hymowitz, "Effective Management Remains an Art Steeped in Good Relationships," *The Wall Street Journal* (August 11, 2008): B6.

8. J.M. Wilson, P.S. Goodman, and M.A. Cronin, "Group Learning," *Academy of Management Review* 32(4) (2007): 1041–1059.

9. J.B. Carson, P.E. Tesluck, and J.A. Marrone, "Shared Leadership in Teams: An Investigation of Antecedent Conditions and Performance," *Academy of Management Journal* 50(5) (2007): 1217–1234.

10. R. Rico, M.S. Manzanares, F. Gil, and G. Gibson, "Team Implicit Coordination Process: A Team Knowledge-Based Approach," *Academy of Management Review* 33(1) (2008): 163–184.

11. R. Cross, A. Hargadon, S. Parise, and R.J. Thomas, "Together We Innovate," *The Wall Street Journal* (September 15, 2007): R6.

12. J.B. Carson, P.E. Tesluck, and J.A. Marrone, "Shared Leadership in Teams: An Investigation of Antecedent Conditions and Performance," *Academy of Management Journal* 50(5) (2007): 1217–1234.

13. J.M. Wilson, P.S. Goodman, and M.A. Cronin, "Group Learning," *Academy of Management Review* 32(4) (2007): 1041–1059.

14. R. Cross, A. Hargadon, S. Parise, and R.J. Thomas, "Together We Innovate," *The Wall Street Journal* (September 15, 2007): R6.

15. A. Malhotra, A. Majchrzak, and B. Rosen, "Leading Virtual Teams," *Academy of Management Perspectives* 21(1) (2007): 60–70.

16. J.B. Carson, P.E. Tesluck, and J.A. Marrone, "Shared Leadership in Teams: An Investigation of Antecedent Conditions and Performance," *Academy of Management Journal* 50(5) (2007): 1217–1234.

17. M.A. Cronin and L.R. Weingart, "Representational Gaps, Information Processing, and Conflict in Functionally Diverse Teams," *Academy of Management Review* 32(3) (2007): 761–773.

18. S.D. Sidle, "Do Teams Who Agree to Disagree Make Better Decisions?" *Academy of Management Perspectives* 21(2) (2007): 74–75.

19. J. Sandberg, "Another Meeting? Good, Another Chance to Hear Myself Talk," *The Wall Street Journal* (March 11, 2008): B1.

20. J.B. Carson, P.E. Tesluck, and J.A. Marrone, "Shared Leadership in Teams: An Investigation of Antecedent Conditions and Performance," *Academy of Management Journal* 50(5) (2007): 1217–1234.

21. A. Malhotra, A. Majchrzak, and B. Rosen, "Leading Virtual Teams," *Academy of Management Perspectives* 21(1) (2007): 60–70.

22. Ibid.

23. C. Hymowitz, "Effective Management Remains an Art Steeped in Good Relationships," *The Wall Street Journal* (August 11, 2008): B6.

24. C. Barzantny, "Managing Diversity: Toward a Globally Inclusive Workplace," *Academy of Management Learning & Education* 6(2) (2007): 285–286.

25. R. Cross, A. Hargadon, S. Parise, and R.J. Thomas, "Together We Innovate," *The Wall Street Journal* (September 15, 2007): R6.

26. G. Hamel, "Break Free!" *Fortune* (October 1, 2007): 119–126.

27. R. Rico, M.S. Manzanares, F. Gil, and G. Gibson, "Team Implicit Coordination Process: A Team Knowledge-Based

Approach," *Academy of Management Review* 33(1) (2008): 163–184.

28. C. Hymowitz, "Effective Management Remains an Art Steeped in Good Relationships," *The Wall Street Journal* (August 11, 2008): B6.

29. C.L. Pearce, "Follow the Leaders," *The Wall Street Journal* (July 7, 2008): R8, R12.

30. S.D. Sidle, "Do Teams Who Agree to Disagree Make Better Decisions?" *Academy of Management Perspectives* 21(2) (2007): 74–75.

31. J.B.O. Buchanan and W.R. Boswell, "An Integrative Model of Experiencing and Responding to Mistreatment at Work," *Academy of Management Review* 33(1) (2008): 75–96.

32. M.A. Cronin and L.R. Weingart, "Representational Gaps, Information Processing, and Conflict in Functionally Diverse Teams," *Academy of Management Review* 32(3) (2007): 761–773.

33. C.L. Porath and A. Erez, "Does Rudeness Really Matter? The Effects of Rudeness on Task Performance and Helpfulness," *Academy of Management Journal* 50(5) (2007): 1181–1197.

34. J.M. Wilson, P.S. Goodman, and M.A. Cronin, "Group Learning," *Academy of Management Review* 32(4) (2007): 1041–1059.

35. C.B. Gibson and P.C. Earley, "Collective Cognition in Action: Accumulation, Interaction, Examination, and Accommodation in the Development and Operation of Group Efficacy Beliefs in the Workplace," *Academy of Management Review* 32(2) (2007): 438–458.

36. J.M. Wilson, P.S. Goodman, and M.A. Cronin, "Group Learning," *Academy of Management Review* 32(4) (2007): 1041–1059.

37. A. Malhotra, A. Majchrzak, and B. Rosen, "Leading Virtual Teams," *Academy of Management Perspectives* 21(1) (2007): 60–70.

38. M. Learmonth, "Critical Management Education in Action: Personal Tales of Management Unlearning," *Academy of Management Learning & Education* 6(1) (2007): 109–113.

39. G. Hamel, "Break Free!" *Fortune* (October 1, 2007): 119–126.

40. J.B. Carson, P.E. Tesluck, and J.A. Marrone, "Shared Leadership in Teams: An Investigation of Antecedent Conditions and Performance," *Academy of Management Journal* 50(5) (2007): 1217–1234.

41. D. Newman, "How to Motivate Your Sales Team," *Entrepreneur* (June 2007): 73.

42. C.B. Gibson and P.C. Earley, "Collective Cognition in Action: Accumulation, Interaction, Examination, and Accommodation in the Development and Operation of Group Efficacy Beliefs in the Workplace," *Academy of Management Review* 32(2) (2007): 438–458.

43. G. Hamel, "Break Free!" *Fortune* (October 1, 2007): 119–126.

44. M.A. Cronin and L.R. Weingart, "Representational Gaps, Information Processing, and Conflict in Functionally Diverse Teams," *Academy of Management Review* 32(3) (2007): 761–773.

45. A. Terlaak, "Order without Law? The Role of Certified Management Standards in Shaping Socially Desired Firm Behaviors," *Academy of Management Review* 32(3) (2007): 968–985.

46. Ibid.

47. Ibid.

48. Ibid.

49. J.B. Carson, P.E. Tesluck, and J.A. Marrone, "Shared Leadership in Teams: An Investigation of Antecedent Conditions and Performance," *Academy of Management Journal* 50(5) (2007): 1217–1234.

50. MetLife, "The Power of Diversity," *Fortune* (March 17, 2008): 118.

51. J.B. Carson, P.E. Tesluck, and J.A. Marrone, "Shared Leadership in Teams: An Investigation of Antecedent Conditions and Performance," *Academy of Management Journal* 50(5) (2007): 1217–1234.

52. A. Malhotra, A. Majchrzak, and B. Rosen, "Leading Virtual Teams," *Academy of Management Perspectives* 21(1) (2007): 60–70.

53. M.A. Cronin and L.R. Weingart, "Representational Gaps, Information Processing, and Conflict in Functionally Diverse Teams," *Academy of Management Review* 32(3) (2007): 761–773.

54. J.D. Westphal and I. Stern, "Flattery Will Get You Everywhere (Especially If You Are a Male Caucasian): How Ingratiation, Boardroom Behavior, and Demographic Minority Status Affect Additional Board Appointments at U.S. Companies," *Academy of Management Journal* 50(2) (2007): 267–288.

55. C.T. Kulik, H.T.J. Bainbridge, and C. Cregan, "Known by the Company We Keep: Stigma-by-Association Effects in the Workplace," *Academy of Management Review* 33(1) (2008): 216–230.

56. B.M. Wiesenfeld, W.B. Swann, J. Brockner, and C.A. Bartel, "Is More Fairness Always Preferred? Self-Esteem Moderates Reactions to Procedural Justice," *Academy of Management Journal* 50(5) (2007): 1235–1253.

57. Ibid.

58. M.A. Cronin and L.R. Weingart, "Representational Gaps, Information Processing, and Conflict in Functionally Diverse Teams," *Academy of Management Review* 32(3) (2007): 761–773.

59. G. Hamel, "Break Free!" *Fortune* (October 1, 2007): 119–126.

60. M.A. Cronin and L.R. Weingart, "Representational Gaps, Information Processing, and Conflict in Functionally Diverse Teams," *Academy of Management Review* 32(3) (2007): 761–773.

61. G. Hamel, "Break Free!" *Fortune* (October 1, 2007): 119–126.

62. D.M. Bergeron, "The Potential Paradox of Organizational Citizenship Behavior: Good Citizens at What Cost?" *Academy of Management Review* 32(4) (2007): 1078–1095.

63. S. Bing, "The Seven Ages of Business," *Fortune* (March 17, 2008): 174.

64. S.D. Sidle, "Do Teams Who Agree to Disagree Make Better Decisions?" *Academy of Management Perspectives* 21(2) (2007): 74–75.

65. J. Houde, "Analogically Situated Experiences: Creating Insight through Novel Contexts," *Academy of Management Learning & Education* 6(3) (2007): 321–331.

66. J.M. Wilson, P.S. Goodman, and M.A. Cronin, "Group Learning," *Academy of Management Review* 32(4) (2007): 1041–1059.

67. B.M. Wiesenfeld, W.B. Swann, J. Brockner, and C.A. Bartel, "Is More Fairness Always Preferred? Self-Esteem Moderates Reactions to Procedural Justice," *Academy of Management Journal* 50(5) (2007): 1235–1253.

68. R.B. Lacoursiere, *The Life Cycle of Groups: Group Development Stage Theory* (New York: Human Services Press, 1980).

69. K. Woods, "Surrender as a Group Norm," *Transactional Analysis Journal* 37(3) (2007): 235–239.

70. M.A. Cronin and L.R. Weingart, "Representational Gaps, Information Processing, and Conflict in Functionally Diverse Teams," *Academy of Management Review* 32(3) (2007): 761–773.

71. J.B. Carson, P.E. Tesluck, and J.A. Marrone, "Shared Leadership in Teams: An Investigation of Antecedent Conditions and Performance," *Academy of Management Journal* 50(5) (2007): 1217–1234.

72. M.A. Cronin and L.R. Weingart, "Representational Gaps, Information Processing, and Conflict in Functionally Diverse Teams," *Academy of Management Review* 32(3) (2007): 761–773.

73. A. Malhotra, A. Majchrzak, and B. Rosen, "Leading Virtual Teams," *Academy of Management Perspectives* 21(1) (2007): 60–70.

74. K. Woods, "Surrender as a Group Norm," *Transactional Analysis Journal* 37(3) (2007): 235–239.

75. M.A. Cronin and L.R. Weingart, "Representational Gaps, Information Processing, and Conflict in Functionally Diverse Teams," *Academy of Management Review* 32(3) (2007): 761–773.

76. C.B. Gibson and P.C. Earley, "Collective Cognition in Action: Accumulation, Interaction, Examination, and Accommodation in the Development and Operation of Group Efficacy Beliefs in the Workplace," *Academy of Management Review* 32(2) (2007): 438–458.

77. A. Terlaak, "Order without Law? The Role of Certified Management Standards in Shaping Socially Desired Firm Behaviors," *Academy of Management Review* 32(3) (2007): 968–985.

78. A. Malhotra, A. Majchrzak, and B. Rosen, "Leading Virtual Teams," *Academy of Management Perspectives* 21(1) (2007): 60–70.

79. J.B. Carson, P.E. Tesluck, and J.A. Marrone, "Shared Leadership in Teams: An Investigation of Antecedent Conditions and Performance," *Academy of Management Journal* 50(5) (2007): 1217–1234.

80. C.B. Gibson and P.C. Earley, "Collective Cognition in Action: Accumulation, Interaction, Examination, and Accommodation in the Development and Operation of Group Efficacy Beliefs in the Workplace," *Academy of Management Review* 32(2) (2007): 438–458.

81. B.M. Wiesenfeld, W.B. Swann, J. Brockner, and C.A. Bartel, "Is More Fairness Always Preferred? Self-Esteem Moderates Reactions to Procedural Justice," *Academy of Management Journal* 50(5) (2007): 1235–1253.

82. M.A. Cronin and L.R. Weingart, "Representational Gaps, Information Processing, and Conflict in Functionally Diverse Teams," *Academy of Management Review* 32(3) (2007): 761–773.

83. A. Malhotra, A. Majchrzak, and B. Rosen, "Leading Virtual Teams," *Academy of Management Perspectives* 21(1) (2007): 60–70.

84. M.A. Cronin and L.R. Weingart, "Representational Gaps, Information Processing, and Conflict in Functionally Diverse Teams," *Academy of Management Review* 32(3) (2007): 761–773.

85. A. Terlaak, "Order without Law? The Role of Certified Management Standards in Shaping Socially Desired Firm Behaviors," *Academy of Management Review* 32(3) (2007): 968–985.

86. S. Bing, "The Seven Ages of Business," *Fortune* (March 17, 2008): 174.

87. J. Sandberg, "Another Meeting? Good, Another Chance to Hear Myself Talk," *The Wall Street Journal* (March 11, 2008): B1.

88. D. Mattioli, "Next on the Agenda: Kisses from Honey Bunny," *The Wall Street Journal* (June 10, 2008): D1.

89. K. Roberts, "My Employees Are Burned out from Too Much Work. How Can I Create a Better Environment?" *Fortune* (July 21, 2008): 58.

90. J.B. Carson, P.E. Tesluck, and J.A. Marrone, "Shared Leadership in Teams: An Investigation of Antecedent Conditions and Performance," *Academy of Management Journal* 50(5) (2007): 1217–1234.

91. D. Mattioli, "Next on the Agenda: Kisses from Honey Bunny," *The Wall Street Journal* (June 10, 2008): D1.

92. A. Malhotra, A. Majchrzak, and B. Rosen, "Leading Virtual Teams," *Academy of Management Perspectives* 21(1) (2007): 60–70.

93. J.B. Carson, P.E. Tesluck, and J.A. Marrone, "Shared Leadership in Teams: An Investigation of Antecedent Conditions and Performance," *Academy of Management Journal* 50(5) (2007): 1217–1234.

94. D. Mattioli, "Next on the Agenda: Kisses from Honey Bunny," *The Wall Street Journal* (June 10, 2008): D1.

95. M.A. Cronin and L.R. Weingart, "Representational Gaps, Information Processing, and Conflict in Functionally Diverse Teams," *Academy of Management Review* 32(3) (2007): 761–773.

96. C. Hymowitz, "Effective Management Remains an Art Steeped in Good Relationships," *The Wall Street Journal* (August 11, 2008): B6.

97. M.A. Cronin and L.R. Weingart, "Representational Gaps, Information Processing, and Conflict in Functionally Diverse Teams," *Academy of Management Review* 32(3) (2007): 761–773.

98. J. Sandberg, "I'm Not Really Late, I'm Just Indulging in Magical Thinking," *The Wall Street Journal* (October 13, 2007): B1.

99. C. Barzantny, "Managing Diversity: Toward a Globally Inclusive Workplace," *Academy of Management Learning & Education* 6(2) (2007): 285–286.

100. C.L. Pearce, "Follow the Leaders," *The Wall Street Journal* (July 7, 2008): R8, R12.

101. Ibid.

102. Case sources: http://www.mondaymemo.net/030512feature.htm; http://www.strategy-business.com/press/article/05408?pg=all; http://semco.locaweb.com.br/ingles/; http://semco.locaweb.com.br/en/content.asp?content=1&contentID=610. Retrieved October 24, 2008.

Chapter 13

1. D. Jacobs, "Critical Biography and Management Education," *Academy of Management Learning & Education* 6(1) (2007): 104–108.

2. C. Hymowitz, "Companies Need CEOs to Stop Spinning and Start Thinking," *The Wall Street Journal* (December 17, 2007): B1.

3. F.C. Brodbeck, R. Kerschreiter, A. Mojzisch, and S. Schulz-Hardt, "Improving Group Decision Making Under Conditions of Distributed Knowledge: The Information Asymmetries Model," *Academy of Management Review* 32(2) (2007): 459–479.

4. R.N. Lussier and C.E. Halabi, "An Analysis of Small Business: A Correlational Study," *Journal of Small Business and Enterprise Development,*" 15(3) (2008): 490–503.

5. D.M. Rousseau and S. McCarthy, "Educating Managers from an Evidence-Based Perspective," *Academy of Management Learning & Education* 6(1) (2007): 84–101.

6. C.L. Pearce, "Follow the Leaders," *The Wall Street Journal* (July 7, 2008): R8, R12.

7. J.S. Lublin, "Notes to Interviewers Should Go Beyond a Simple Thank You," *The Wall Street Journal* (February 5, 2008): B1.

8. S. Sonenshein, "The Role of Construction, Intuition, and Justification in Responding to Ethical Issues at Work: The Sensemaking Intuition Model," *Academy of Management Review* 32(4) (2007): 1022–1028.

9. J. Weber, "Bribery: Not Only Wrong, But Costly Too?" *Academy of Management Perspectives* 21(3) (2007): 86–87.

10. Ibid.

11. B. Farber, "Basic Instincts," *Entrepreneur* (August 2007): 66.

12. L. Proserpio, "Teaching the Virtual Generation," *Academy of Management Learning & Education* 6(1) (2007): 69–80.

13. C. Hymowitz, "Sometimes, Moving Up Makes It Harder to See What Goes on Below," *The Wall Street Journal* (October 15, 2007): B1.

14. G. Kawasaki, "At Their Service," *Entrepreneur* (August 2007): 24.

15. M.G. Seo and L.F. Barrett, "Being Emotional During Decision Making—Good or Bad? An Empirical Investigation," *Academy of Management Journal* 50(4) (2007): 923–940.

16. Z. Xin, "The Best Advice I Ever Got," *Fortune* (May 12, 2008): 77.

17. M.G. Seo and L.F. Barrett, "Being Emotional During Decision Making—Good or Bad? An Empirical Investigation," *Academy of Management Journal* 50(4) (2007): 923–940.

18. J. Zweig, "Train Your Brain to Win Big," *Fortune* (December 24, 2007): 100–102.

19. D. Ariely, "The Irrationalities of Product Pricing," *The Wall Street Journal* (September 22, 2008): R2.

20. S.L. Rynes, T.L. Giluk, and K.G. Brown, "The Very Separate Worlds of Academic and Practitioner Periodicals in Human Resource Management: Implications for Evidence-Based Management," *Academy of Management Journal* 50(5) (2007): 987–1008.

21. D.P. Forbes, "Reconsidering the Strategic Implications of Decision Comprehensiveness," *Academy of Management Review* 32(2) (2007): 361–376.

22. C.M. Vance, K.S. Groves, Y. Paik, and H. Kindler, "Understanding and Measuring Linear-Nonlinear Thinking Style for Enhanced Management Education and Professional Practice," *Academy of Management Learning & Education* 6(2) (2007): 167–185.

23. D.C. Hambrick, "Upper Echelons Theory: An Update," *Academy of Management Review* 32(2) (2007): 334–343.

24. C.M. Vance, K.S. Groves, Y. Paik, and H. Kindler, "Understanding and Measuring Linear-Nonlinear Thinking Style for Enhanced Management Education and Professional Practice," *Academy of Management Learning & Education* 6(2) (2007): 167–185.

25. L. Trigeorgis, R. Brosch, and H. Smit, "Stay Loose," *The Wall Street Journal* (September 15–16, 2008): R4.

26. D.P. Forbes, "Reconsidering the Strategic Implications of Decision Comprehensiveness," *Academy of Management Review* 32(2) (2007): 361–376.

27. S.L. Rynes, T.L. Giluk, and K.G. Brown, "The Very Separate Worlds of Academic and Practitioner Periodicals in Human Resource Management: Implications for

Evidence-Based Management," *Academy of Management Journal* 50(5) (2007): 987–1008.

28. G. Kawasaki, "At Their Service," *Entrepreneur* (August 2007): 24.

29. D. Newman, "How to Motivate Your Sales Team," *Entrepreneur* (June 2007): 73.

30. J.B. Carson, P.E. Tesluck, and J.A. Marrone, "Shared Leadership in Teams: An Investigation of Antecedent Conditions and Performance," *Academy of Management Journal* 50(5) (2007): 1217–1234.

31. R. Rico, M.S. Manzanares, F. Gil, and G. Gibson, "Team Implicit Coordination Process: A Team Knowledge-Based Approach," *Academy of Management Review* 33(1) (2008): 163–184.

32. L. Trigeorgis, R. Brosch, and H. Smit, "Stay Loose," *The Wall Street Journal* (September 15–16, 2008): R4.

33. P. Georgescu, "Creativity to the Rescue," *Fortune* (October 15, 2007): 74.

34. D.J. Miller, M.J. Fern, and L.B. Cardinal, "The Use of Knowledge for Technological Innovation within Diversified Firms," *Academy of Management Journal* 50(2) (2007): 308–326.

35. L. Trigeorgis, R. Brosch, and H. Smit, "Stay Loose," *The Wall Street Journal* (September 15–16, 2008): R4.

36. D.C. Hambrick, "Upper Echelons Theory: An Update," *Academy of Management Review* 32(2) (2007): 334–343.

37. D. Ariely, "The Irrationalities of Product Pricing," *The Wall Street Journal* (September 22, 2008): R2.

38. C.M. Vance, K.S. Groves, Y. Paik, and H. Kindler, "Understanding and Measuring Linear-Nonlinear Thinking Style for Enhanced Management Education and Professional Practice," *Academy of Management Learning & Education* 6(2) (2007): 167–185.

39. D.P. Forbes, "Reconsidering the Strategic Implications of Decision Comprehensiveness," *Academy of Management Review* 32(2) (2007): 361–376.

40. D.M. Rousseau and S. McCarthy, "Educating Managers from an Evidence-Based Perspective," *Academy of Management Learning & Education* 6(1) (2007): 84–101.

41. R. Rico, M.S. Manzanares, F. Gil, and G. Gibson, "Team Implicit Coordination Process: A Team Knowledge-Based Approach," *Academy of Management Review* 33(1) (2008): 163–184.

42. D.M. Rousseau and S. McCarthy, "Educating Managers from an Evidence-Based Perspective," *Academy of Management Learning & Education* 6(1) (2007): 84–101.

43. D.J. Miller, M.J. Fern, and L.B. Cardinal, "The Use of Knowledge for Technological Innovation within Diversified Firms," *Academy of Management Journal* 50(2) (2007): 308–326.

44. G. Colvin, "Here It Is. Now, You Design It!" *Fortune* (May 26, 2008): 34.

45. B. Iger, "How I Work," *Fortune* (December 10, 2007): 38.

46. P. Georgescu, "Creativity to the Rescue," *Fortune* (October 15, 2007): 74.

47. G. Colvin, "Here It Is. Now, You Design It!" *Fortune* (May 26, 2008): 34.

48. P. Gloor and S. Cooper, "The New Principles of a Swarm Business," *Sloan Management Review* (Spring 2007): 18–24.

49. R. Cross, A. Hargadon, S. Parise, and R.J. Thomas, "Together We Innovate," *The Wall Street Journal* (September 15, 2007): R6.

50. Ibid.

51. L. Trigeorgis, R. Brosch, and H. Smit, "Stay Loose," *The Wall Street Journal* (September 15–16, 2008): R4.

52. R.D. Austin, L. Devin, and E. Sullivan, "Oops!" *The Wall Street Journal* (July 7, 2008): R6.

53. D.J. Miller, M.J. Fern, and L.B. Cardinal, "The Use of Knowledge for Technological Innovation within Diversified Firms," *Academy of Management Journal* 50(2) (2007): 308–326.

54. J. Dyson, "The Three-Minute Manager," *Fortune* (July 7, 2008): 28.

55. R.G. Erskine, "Cooperation, Relationship, and Change," *Transactional Analysis Journal* 38(1) (2008): 31–35.

56. R. Cross, A. Hargadon, S. Parise, and R.J. Thomas, "Together We Innovate," *The Wall Street Journal* (September 15, 2007): R6.

57. S.E. Page, "Making the Difference: Applying a Logic of Diversity," *Academy of Management Perspectives* 21(4) (2007): 6–20.

58. R. Wolter, "Make It Happen," *Entrepreneur* (June 2007): 126.

59. C. Seda, "First Impressions," *Entrepreneur* (October 2006): 64.

60. L. Thompson, "Improving the Creativity of Organizational Work Groups," *Academy of Management Executive* 17(1) (2003): 96–109.

61. J.K. Williams, "Facilitating with Ease! Core Skills for Facilitators, Team Leaders and Members, Managers, Consultants, and Trainers," *Academy of Management Learning & Education* 6(2) (2007): 294–295.

62. L. Thompson, "Improving the Creativity of Organizational Work Groups," *Academy of Management Executive* 17(1) (2003): 96–109.

63. R. Cross, A. Hargadon, S. Parise, and R.J. Thomas, "Together We Innovate," *The Wall Street Journal* (September 15, 2007): R6.

64. C.L. Pearce, "Follow the Leaders," *The Wall Street Journal* (July 7, 2008): R8, R12.

65. J.B. Carson, P.E. Tesluck, and J.A. Marrone, "Shared Leadership in Teams: An Investigation of Antecedent Conditions and Performance," *Academy of Management Journal* 50(5) (2007): 1217–1234.

66. R. Cross, A. Hargadon, S. Parise, and R.J. Thomas, "Together We Innovate," *The Wall Street Journal* (September 15, 2007): R6.

67. G. Colvin, "Here It Is. Now, You Design It!" *Fortune* (May 26, 2008): 34.

68. F.C. Brodbeck, R. Kerschreiter, A. Mojzisch, and S. Schulz-Hardt, "Improving Group Decision Making Under Conditions of Distributed Knowledge: The Information Asymmetries Model," *Academy of Management Review* 32(2) (2007): 459–479.

69. A. Mehra, "Symposium: Handbook of Trust Research," *Academy of Management Review* 33(1) (2008): 271–272.

70. S.E. Page, "Making the Difference: Applying a Logic of Diversity," *Academy of Management Perspectives* 21(4) (2007): 6–20.

71. A. Malhotra, A. Majchrzak, and B. Rosen, "Leading Virtual Teams," *Academy of Management Perspectives* 21(1) (2007): 60–70.

72. S.E. Page, "Making the Difference: Applying a Logic of Diversity," *Academy of Management Perspectives* 21(4) (2007): 6–20.

73. R. Cross, A. Hargadon, S. Parise, and R.J. Thomas, "Together We Innovate," *The Wall Street Journal* (September 15, 2007): R6.

74. D.M. Rousseau and S. McCarthy, "Educating Managers from an Evidence-Based Perspective," *Academy of Management Learning & Education* 6(1) (2007): 84–101.

75. F.C. Brodbeck, R. Kerschreiter, A. Mojzisch, and S. Schulz-Hardt, "Improving Group Decision Making Under Conditions of Distributed Knowledge: The Information Asymmetries Model," *Academy of Management Review* 32(2) (2007): 459–479.

76. C.L. Pearce, "Follow the Leaders," *The Wall Street Journal* (July 7, 2008): R8, R12.

77. F.C. Brodbeck, R. Kerschreiter, A. Mojzisch, and S. Schulz-Hardt, "Improving Group Decision Making Under Conditions of Distributed Knowledge: The Information Asymmetries Model," *Academy of Management Review* 32(2) (2007): 459–479.

78. R. Cross, A. Hargadon, S. Parise, and R.J. Thomas, "Together We Innovate," *The Wall Street Journal* (September 15, 2007): R6.

79. F.C. Brodbeck, R. Kerschreiter, A. Mojzisch, and S. Schulz-Hardt, "Improving Group Decision Making Under Conditions of Distributed Knowledge: The Information Asymmetries Model," *Academy of Management Review* 32(2) (2007): 459–479.

80. Ibid.

81. C.W. Langfred, "The Downside of Self-Management: A Longitudinal Study of the Effects of Conflict on Trust, Autonomy, and Task Interdependence in Self-Managing Teams," *Academy of Management Journal* 50(4) (2007): 885–900.

82. S.D. Sidle, "Do Teams Who Agree to Disagree Make Better Decisions?" *Academy of Management Perspectives* 21(2) (2007): 74–75.

83. C.L. Pearce, "Follow the Leaders," *The Wall Street Journal* (July 7, 2008): R8, R12.

84. J.B. Carson, P.E. Tesluck, and J.A. Marrone, "Shared Leadership in Teams: An Investigation of Antecedent Conditions and Performance," *Academy of Management Journal* 50(5) (2007): 1217–1234.

85. J.M. Wilson, P.S. Goodman, and M.A. Cronin, "Group Learning," *Academy of Management Review* 32(4) (2007): 1041–1059.

86. C. Hymowitz, "Effective Management Remains an Art Steeped in Good Relationships," *The Wall Street Journal* (August 11, 2008): B6.

87. V.H. Vroom and P.W. Yetton, *Leadership and Decision Making* (Pittsburgh: University of Pittsburgh Press, 1973).

88. V.H. Vroom and A.G. Jago, *The New Leadership: Managing Participation in Organizations* (Englewood Cliffs, NJ: Prentice-Hall, 1988).

89. V.H. Vroom, "Leadership and the Decision Making Process," *Organizational Dynamics* 28 (Spring, 2000): 82–94.

90. F.C. Brodbeck, R. Kerschreiter, A. Mojzisch, and S. Schulz-Hardt, "Improving Group Decision Making Under Conditions of Distributed Knowledge: The Information Asymmetries Model," *Academy of Management Review* 32(2) (2007): 459–479.

91. D.J. Miller, M.J. Fern, and L.B. Cardinal, "The Use of Knowledge for Technological Innovation within Diversified Firms," *Academy of Management Journal* 50(2) (2007): 308–326.

92. F.C. Brodbeck, R. Kerschreiter, A. Mojzisch, and S. Schulz-Hardt, "Improving Group Decision Making Under Conditions of Distributed Knowledge: The Information Asymmetries Model," *Academy of Management Review* 32(2) (2007): 459–479.

93. C. Hymowitz, "Effective Management Remains an Art Steeped in Good Relationships," *The Wall Street Journal* (August 11, 2008): B6.

94. J. Weber, "Bribery: Not Only Wrong, But Costly Too?" *Academy of Management Perspectives* 21(3) (2007): 86–87.

95. C.L. Pearce, "Follow the Leaders," *The Wall Street Journal* (July 7, 2008): R8, R12.

96. Ibid.

97. L. Weinstein and C. Bigelow, "The R.C. Bigelow Tea Company Case Study," *The CASE Journal* 2(1) (2005); the Bigelow Web site, www.bigelowtea.com, accessed January 4, 2009.

Chapter 14

1. S. Maitlis and T. B. Lawrence, "Triggers and Enablers of Sensegiving in Organizations," *Academy of Management Journal* 50(1) (2007): 57–84.

2. D.J. Miller, M.J. Fern, and L.B. Cardinal, "The Use of Knowledge for Technological Innovation within Diversified Firms," *Academy of Management Journal* 50(2) (2007): 308–326.

3. R. Cross, A. Hargadon, S. Parise, and R.J. Thomas, "Together We Innovate," *The Wall Street Journal* (September 15, 2007): R6.

4. M.F.R. Kets de Vries and K. Korotov, "Creating Transformational Executive Education Programs," *Academy of Management Learning & Education* 6(3) (2007): 375–387.

5. V. Jayaraman and Y. Luo, "Creating Competitive Advantages through New Value Creation: A Reverse Logistics Perspective," *Academy of Management Perspectives* 21(2) (2007): 55–73.

6. Continental Airlines Web site (www.continentalairlines.com), retrieved October 31, 2008.

7. R.U. Priya, "Transactional Analysis and the Mind/Body Connection," *Transactional Analysis Journal* 37(4) (2007): 278–285.

8. R.D. Austin, L. Devin, and E. Sullivan, "Oops!" *The Wall Street Journal* (July 7, 2008): R6.

9. J. Dyson, "The Three-Minute Manager," *Fortune* (July 7, 2008): 28.

10. D.J. Miller, M.J. Fern, and L.B. Cardinal, "The Use of Knowledge for Technological Innovation within Diversified Firms," *Academy of Management Journal* 50(2) (2007): 308–326.

11. R.D. Austin, L. Devin, and E. Sullivan, "Oops!" *The Wall Street Journal* (July 7, 2008): R6.

12. R.L. Ackoff, Interview by G. Detrick, *Academy of Management Learning & Education* 1(1) (2002): 56–63.

13. D.J. Miller, M.J. Fern, and L.B. Cardinal, "The Use of Knowledge for Technological Innovation within Diversified Firms," *Academy of Management Journal* 50(2) (2007): 308–326.

14. R.L. Ackoff, Interview by G. Detrick, *Academy of Management Learning & Education* 1(1) (2002): 56–63.

15. D.J. Miller, M.J. Fern, and L.B. Cardinal, "The Use of Knowledge for Technological Innovation within Diversified Firms," *Academy of Management Journal* 50(2) (2007): 308–326; S. Michel, D. Bowen and R. Johnson, "Making the Most of Customer Complaints," *The Wall Street Journal* (September 22, 2008): R4.

16. R. Cross, A. Hargadon, S. Parise, and R.J. Thomas, "Together We Innovate," *The Wall Street Journal* (September 15, 2007): R6.

17. M.F.R. Kets de Vries and K. Korotov, "Creating Transformational Executive Education Programs," *Academy of Management Learning & Education* 6(3) (2007): 375–387.

18. S. Maitlis and T. B. Lawrence, "Triggers and Enablers of Sensegiving in Organizations," *Academy of Management Journal* 50(1) (2007): 57–84.

19. Ibid.

20. K. Hultman, *The Path of Least Resistance* (Austin, TX: Learning Concepts, 1979).

21. R.D. Austin, L. Devin, and E. Sullivan, "Oops!" *The Wall Street Journal* (July 7, 2008): R6.

22. R. Cross, A. Hargadon, S. Parise, and R.J. Thomas, "Together We Innovate," *The Wall Street Journal* (September 15, 2007): R6.

23. Ibid.

24. M.F.R. Kets de Vries and K. Korotov, "Creating Transformational Executive Education Programs," *Academy of Management Learning & Education* 6(3) (2007): 375–387.

25. C.W. Langfred, "The Downside of Self-Management: A Longitudinal Study of the Effects of Conflict on Trust, Autonomy, and Task Interdependence in Self-Managing Teams," *Academy of Management Journal* 50(4) (2007): 885–900.

26. N.E. Boudette, "Nardelli Tries to Shift Chrysler's Culture," *The Wall Street Journal* (June 18, 2008): B1.

27. Ibid.

28. R. Cross, A. Hargadon, S. Parise, and R.J. Thomas, "Together We Innovate," *The Wall Street Journal* (September 15, 2007): R6.

29. 3M Web site, www.3M.com, retrieved November 3, 2008.

30. N.E. Boudette, "Nardelli Tries to Shift Chrysler's Culture," *The Wall Street Journal* (June 18, 2008): B1.

31. R.A. Giacalone, "Taking a Red Pill to Disempower Unethical Students: Creating Ethical Sentinels in Business Schools," *Academy of Management Learning & Education* 6(4) (2007): 534–542.

32. T. Newton and R. Napper, "The Bigger Picture: Supervision as an Educational Framework for All Fields," *Transactional Analysis Journal* 37(2) (2007): 150–158.

33. IBM Web site, http://www.ibm.com/ibm/values/us/, retrieved November 3, 2008.

34. PepsiCo Web site, http://www.pepsico.com/index.cfm, retrieved November 3, 2008.

35. J. C. Penney Web site, www.jcpenny.com, retrieved November 3, 2008.

36. S. Shellenbarger, "Rules of Engagement," *The Wall Street Journal* (October 1, 2007): R3.

37. N.E. Boudette, "Nardelli Tries to Shift Chrysler's Culture," *The Wall Street Journal* (June 18, 2008): B1.

38. A.M. Grant, M.K. Christianson, and R.H. Price, "Happiness, Health, or Relationships? Managerial Practices and Employee Well-Being Tradeoffs," *Academy of Management Perspectives* 21(3) (2007): 51–63.

39. M.F.R. Kets de Vries and K. Korotov, "Creating Transformational Executive Education Programs," *Academy of Management Learning & Education* 6(3) (2007): 375–387.

40. S. Shellenbarger, "Rules of Engagement," *The Wall Street Journal* (October 1, 2007): R3.

41. D.M. Rousseau and S. McCarthy, "Educating Managers from an Evidence-Based Perspective," *Academy of Management Learning & Education* 6(1) (2007): 84–101.

42. M. Mazzetti, "Supervision in Transactional Analysis: An Operational Model," *Transactional Analysis Journal* 37(2) (2007): 93–103.

43. T. Newton and R. Napper, "The Bigger Picture: Supervision as an Educational Framework for All Fields," *Transactional Analysis Journal* 37(2) (2007): 150–158.

44. M.F.R. Kets de Vries and K. Korotov, "Creating Transformational Executive Education Programs," *Academy of Management Learning & Education* 6(3) (2007): 375–387.

45. P. Osterman, "Comments on Le, Oh, Shaffer, and Schmidt," *Academy of Management Perspectives* 21(3) (2007): 16–18.

46. G. Hamel, "Break Free!" *Fortune* (October 1, 2007): 119–126.

47. J. Sandberg, "Performance Reviews Need Some Work, Don't Meet Potential," *The Wall Street Journal* (November 20, 2007): B1.

48. C.B. Cadsby, F. Song, and F. Tapon, "Sorting and Incentive Effects of Pay for Performance: An Experimental Investigation," *Academy of Management Journal* 50(2) (2007): 387–405.

49. S.L. Rynes, T.L. Giluk, and K.G. Brown, "The Very Separate Worlds of Academic and Practitioner Periodicals in Human Resource Management: Implications for Evidence-Based Management," *Academy of Management Journal* 50(5) (2007): 987–1008.

50. J. Sandberg, "Performance Reviews Need Some Work, Don't Meet Potential," *The Wall Street Journal* (November 20, 2007): B1.

51. G. Hamel, "Break Free!" *Fortune* (October 1, 2007): 119–126.

52. M. Mazzetti, "Supervision in Transactional Analysis: An Operational Model," *Transactional Analysis Journal* 37(2) (2007): 93–103.

53. C.W. Langfred, "The Downside of Self-Management: A Longitudinal Study of the Effects of Conflict on Trust, Autonomy, and Task Interdependence in Self-Managing Teams," *Academy of Management Journal* 50(4) (2007): 885–900.

54. J. Houde, "Analogically Situated Experiences: Creating Insight through Novel Contexts," *Academy of Management Learning & Education* 6(3) (2007): 321–331.

55. J.C. Santora, "Managing Open Employees: Do Resources and Leadership Style Matter?" *Academy of Management Perspectives* 21(3) (2007): 83–84.

56. C.L. Pearce, "Follow the Leaders," *The Wall Street Journal* (July 7, 2008): R8, R12.

57. K.K. Metters and R. Metters, "Misunderstanding the Chinese Worker," *The Wall Street Journal* (July 7, 2008): R11.

58. C.L. Pearce, "Follow the Leaders," *The Wall Street Journal* (July 7, 2008): R8, R12.

59. K.K. Metters and R. Metters, "Misunderstanding the Chinese Worker," *The Wall Street Journal* (July 7, 2008): R11.

60. D. Friel, "Transferring a Lean Production Concept from Germany to the United States: The Impact of Labor Laws and Training Systems," *Academy of Management Executive* 19(2) (2005): 50–61.

61. M. and S. Hurt, "Transfer of Managerial Practices by French Food Retailers to Operations in Poland," *Academy of Management Executive* 19(2) (2005): 36–49.

62. G.P. Woods and K. Ishibashi, "Goldman Sachs to Gain 2 Seats On Sanyo's Board," *The Wall Street Journal* (January 26, 2006): B4; http://online.wsj.com; http://www.global-sanyo.com; http://premium.hoovers.com. All three Web sites accessed January 6, 2009.

Chapter 15

1. A. Malhotra, A. Majchrzak, and B. Rosen, "Leading Virtual Teams," *Academy of Management Perspectives* 21(1) (2007): 60–70.

2. C.T. Kulik, H.T.J. Bainbridge, and C. Cregan, "Known by the Company We Keep: Stigma-by-Association Effects in the Workplace," *Academy of Management Review* 33(1) (2008): 216–230.

3. S. Waddock, "Leadership Integrity in a Fractured Knowledge World," *Academy of Management Learning & Education* 6(4) (2007): 543–557.

4. MetLife, "The Power of Diversity," *Fortune* (March 17, 2008): 118.

5. C. Barzantny, "Managing Diversity: Toward a Globally Inclusive Workplace," *Academy of Management Learning & Education* 6(2) (2007): 285–286.

6. http://www.census.gov/main/www/popclock.html, retrieved November 10, 2008.

7. http://www.chinability.com/China%20population%20clock.htm, retrieved November 10, 2008.

8. https://www.cia.gov/library/publications/the-world-factbook/geos/in.html#People, retrieved November 10, 2008.

9. http://epp.eurostat.ec.europa.eu/portal/page?_pageid=2053,71798984&_dad=portal&_schema=PORTAL, retrieved November 10, 2008.

10. "The World Population," *The Wall Street Journal* (June 20, 2008): A1.

11. C. Hymowitz, "Effective Management Remains an Art Steeped in Good Relationships," *The Wall Street Journal* (August 11, 2008): B6.

12. "Whites Will Constitute," *The Wall Street Journal* (August 14, 2008): A1.

13. C. Dougherty, "The End of White Flight," *The Wall Street Journal* (July 19–20, 2007): B1.

14. Ibid.

15. NPR radio broadcast, January 18, 2008.

16. S.E. Page, "Making the Difference: Applying a Logic of Diversity," *Academy of Management Perspectives* 21(4) (2007): 6–20.

17. A. Malhotra, A. Majchrzak, and B. Rosen, "Leading Virtual Teams," *Academy of Management Perspectives* 21(1) (2007): 60–70.

18. S. Waddock, "Leadership Integrity in a Fractured Knowledge World," *Academy of Management Learning & Education* 6(4) (2007): 543–557.

19. B.R. Ragins, "Disclosure Disconnects: Antecedents and Consequences of Disclosing Invisible Stigmas Across Life Domains," *Academy of Management Review* 33(1) (2008): 194–215.

20. C.T. Kulik, H.T.J. Bainbridge, and C. Cregan, "Known by the Company We Keep: Stigma-by-Association Effects in the Workplace," *Academy of Management Review* 33(1) (2008): 216–230.

21. L. Roberson and C.T. Kulik, "Stereotype Threat at Work," *Academy of Management Perspectives* 21(2) (2007): 24–40.

22. Ibid.

23. R. Parloff, "The War Over Unconscious Bias," *Fortune* (October 1, 2007): 90–93.

24. B.R. Ragins, "Disclosure Disconnects: Antecedents and Consequences of Disclosing Invisible Stigmas Across Life Domains," *Academy of Management Review* 33(1) (2008): 194–215.

25. Ibid.

26. "Bridging the Age Gap," *Fortune* (July 21, 2008): 70.

27. F.D. Blau and L.M. Kahn, "The Gender Pay Gap," *Academy of Management Perspectives* 21(1) (2007): 7–23.

28. R. Parloff, "The War Over Unconscious Bias," *Fortune* (October 1, 2007): 90–93.

29. Ibid.

30. S.E. Page, "Making the Difference: Applying a Logic of Diversity," *Academy of Management Perspectives* 21(4) (2007): 6–20.

31. MetLife, "The Power of Diversity," *Fortune* (March 17, 2008): 118.

32. L. Roberson and C.T. Kulik, "Stereotype Threat at Work," *Academy of Management Perspectives* 21(2) (2007): 24–40.

33. https://www.cia.gov/library/publications/the-world-factbook/geos/in.html#People, retrieved November 10, 2008.

34. A. Malhotra, A. Majchrzak, and B. Rosen, "Leading Virtual Teams," *Academy of Management Perspectives* 21(1) (2007): 60–70.

35. MetLife, "The Power of Diversity," *Fortune* (March 17, 2008): 118.

36. EEOC Web site, www.eeoc.gov, retrieved November 10, 2008.

37. R. Parloff, "The War Over Unconscious Bias," *Fortune* (October 1, 2007): 90–93.

38. EEOC Web site, www.eeoc.gov, retrieved November 10, 2008.

39. R. Parloff, "The War Over Unconscious Bias," *Fortune* (October 1, 2007): 90–93.

40. C. Barzantny, "Managing Diversity: Toward a Globally Inclusive Workplace," *Academy of Management Learning & Education* 6(2) (2007): 285–286.

41. S.E. Page, "Making the Difference: Applying a Logic of Diversity," *Academy of Management Perspectives* 21(4) (2007): 6–20.

42. C.T. Kulik, H.T.J. Bainbridge, and C. Cregan, "Known by the Company We Keep: Stigma-by-Association Effects in the Workplace," *Academy of Management Review* 33(1) (2008): 216–230.

43. L. Roberson and C.T. Kulik, "Stereotype Threat at Work," *Academy of Management Perspectives* 21(2) (2007): 24–40.

44. EEOC Web site, www.eeoc.gov, retrieved November 10, 2008.

45. Spirit at Work Web site, www.spiritatwork.org, retrieved November 10, 2008.

46. "Bridging the Age Gap," *Fortune* (July 21, 2008): 70.

47. "AARP 2008 Exclusive News for AARP Members," *AARP Magazine* (September & October 2008): 94–95.

48. "Because We Are Powerful," *AARP Magazine* (September & October 2008): 53.

49. "AARP 2008 Exclusive News for AARP Members," *AARP Magazine* (September & October 2008): 94–95.

50. "Bridging the Age Gap," *Fortune* (July 21, 2008): 70.

51. EEOC Web site, www.eeoc.gov, retrieved November 10, 2008.

52. K. Maher, "Disabled Face Scarcer Jobs, Data Show," *The Wall Street Journal* (October 5, 2005): D2.

53. R.N. Lussier, K. Say, and J. Corman, "Improving Job Satisfaction of Employees Who Are Deaf and Hearing," *Mid-American Journal of Business* 14(1) (1999): 69–73.

54. M. Corkery, "A Special Effort," *The Wall Street Journal* (November 14, 2005): R8.

55. B.R. Ragins, "Disclosure Disconnects: Antecedents and Consequences of Disclosing Invisible Stigmas Across Life Domains," *Academy of Management Review* 33(1) (2008): 194–215.

56. J.L. Berdahl, "Harassment Based on Sex: Protecting Social Status in the Context of Gender Hierarchy," *Academy of Management Review* 32(2) (2007): 641–658.

57. L.M. Roth, "Women on Wall Street: Despite Diversity Measures, Wall Street Remains Vulnerable to Sex Discrimination Charges," *Academy of Management Perspectives* 21(1) (2007): 24–33.

58. EEOC Web site, www.eeoc.gov, retrieved November 12, 2008.

59. J.L. Berdahl, "Harassment Based on Sex: Protecting Social Status in the Context of Gender Hierarchy," *Academy of Management Review* 32(2) (2007): 641–658.

60. L.B. Sperry and A.M.O. Kelly, "To Act or Not to Act: The Dilemma Faced by Sexual Harassment Observers," *Academy of Management Review* 30(2) (2005): 288–306.

61. B.R. Ragins, "Disclosure Disconnects: Antecedents and Consequences of Disclosing Invisible Stigmas Across Life Domains," *Academy of Management Review* 33(1) (2008): 194–215.

62. L. Roberson and C.T. Kulik, "Stereotype Threat at Work," *Academy of Management Perspectives* 21(2) (2007): 24–40.

63. R. Ely and I. Padavic, "A Feminist Analysis of Organizational Research on Sex Differences," *Academy of Management Review* 32(4) (2007): 1121–1143.

64. Ibid.

65. F.D. Blau and L.M. Kahn, "The Gender Pay Gap," *Academy of Management Perspectives* 21(1) (2007): 7–23.

66. S. Shellenbarger, "How Stay-at-Home Moms Are Filling an Executive Niche," *The Wall Street Journal* (April 30, 2008): D1.

67. U.S. Census Bureau Web site, www.census.gov, retrieved November 12, 2008.

68. S. Shellenbarger, "Please Send Chocolate: Moms Now Face Stress Moving In and Out of Work Force," *The Wall Street Journal* (May 9, 2002): D1.

69. U.S. Census Bureau Web site, www.census.gov, retrieved November 12, 2008.

70. F.D. Blau and L.M. Kahn, "The Gender Pay Gap," *Academy of Management Perspectives* 21(1) (2007): 7–23.

71. U.S. Census Bureau Web site, www.census.gov, retrieved November 12, 2008.

72. Ibid.

73. F.D. Blau and L.M. Kahn, "The Gender Pay Gap," *Academy of Management Perspectives* 21(1) (2007): 7–23.

74. M.C. Sonfield and R.N. Lussier, "Family Business Ownership and Management: A Gender Comparison," *Journal of Small Business Strategy* 15(2) (2005): 59–75.

75. L.L. Brennan, "Working Around the Family: Is There a Gender Divide?" *Academy of Management Perspectives* 21(2) (2007): 81–82.

76. L.A. Mainiero and S.E. Sullivan, *The Opt-Out Revolt: Why People Are Leaving Companies to Create Kaleidoscope Careers* (Mountain View, CA: Davies-Black, 2006).

77. M. Marr, "The 50 Women to Watch 2008," *The Wall Street Journal* (November 10, 2008): R1–R8.

78. P. Sellers, "Women on Boards (Not!)," *Fortune* (October 15, 2007): 105.

79. L.L. Brennan, "Working Around the Family: Is There a Gender Divide?" *Academy of Management Perspectives* 21(2) (2007): 81–82.

80. J. Preciphs, "Moving Ahead . . . But Slowly," *The Wall Street Journal* (November 14, 2005): R3.

81. U.S. Census Bureau Web site, www.census.gov, retrieved November 19, 2008.

82. J.L. Berdahl, "Harassment Based on Sex: Protecting Social Status in the Context of Gender Hierarchy," *Academy of Management Review* 32(2) (2007): 641–658.

83. U.S. Census Bureau Web site, www.census.gov, retrieved November 12, 2008.

84. S. Shellenbarger, "What Makes a Company a Great Place to Work Today," *The Wall Street Journal* (October 4, 2007): D1.

85. S. Shellenbarger, "In Search of Wedded Bliss: What Research Can Tell Us," *The Wall Street Journal*, (March 20, 2008): D1.

86. Question and answer for 1: S. Begley, "Evolution Psychology May Not Help Explain Our Behavior After All," *The Wall Street Journal* (April 29, 2005): B1.

Questions and answers for 2, 3, 7, 8, 12–15: The study was conducted by the Universities of Wisconsin and Minnesota and reported by Jeffrey Zaslow, "Divorce Makes a Comeback," *The Wall Street Journal* (January 14, 2003): D1, D10.

Questions and answers for 4, 5, 6: S. Shellenbarger, "No Comfort in Numbers: Divorce Rate Varies Widely From Group to Group," *The Wall Street Journal* (April 22, 2004): D1.

Questions and answers for 9, 10, 11: S. Shellenbarger, "Another Argument for Marriage: How Divorce Can Put Your Health at Risk," *The Wall Street Journal* (June 16, 2005): D1.

Questions and more current answer references supporting 2, 4, 5, 15: "The National Marriage Project," *AFA Journal* (February 2007): 12–13; S. Shellenbarger, "In Search of Wedded Bliss: What Research Can Tell Us," *The Wall Street Journal* (March 20, 2008): D1.

87. L.L. Brennan, "Working Around the Family: Is There a Gender Divide?" *Academy of Management Perspectives* 21(2) (2007): 81–82.

88. S. Shellenbarger, "More New Mothers Are Staying Home Even When It Causes Financial Pain," *The Wall Street Journal* (November 30, 2006): D1.

89. L.L. Brennan, "Working Around the Family: Is There a Gender Divide?" *Academy of Management Perspectives* 21(2) (2007): 81–82.

90. S. Shellenbarger, "More Couples Find Marriage Leaves Them Alone Together," *The Wall Street Journal* (July 2, 2008): D1.

91. T. McMahon, "Dads Important to Children in So Many Ways," *The Republican* (June 16, 2008): E1.

92. K. Helliker, "A Father's Tough Love," *The Wall Street Journal* (June 14–15, 2008): W1, W9.

93. E. Vitagliano, "Heirs to the Past and Ancestors to the Future," *AFA Journal* (June 2008): 14–15.

94. S. Shellenbarger, "What Makes a Company a Great Place to Work Today," *The Wall Street Journal* (October 4, 2007): D1.

95. S. Shellenbarger, "Downsizing Maternity Leave: Employers Cut Pay, Time Off," *The Wall Street Journal* (June 11, 2008): D1.

96. Ibid.

97. J. Adamy, "Restaurants Feel the Bite of Stay-at-Home Moms," *The Wall Street Journal* (March 14, 2008): B1.

98. S. Shellenbarger, "Downsizing Maternity Leave: Employers Cut Pay, Time Off," *The Wall Street Journal* (June 11, 2008): D1.

99. S. Shellenbarger, "More New Mothers Are Staying Home Even When It Causes Financial Pain," *The Wall Street Journal* (November 30, 2006): D1.

100. S. Shellenbarger, "How Stay-at-Home Moms Are Filling an Executive Niche," *The Wall Street Journal* (April 30, 2008): D1.

101. S. Shellenbarger, "Not in Front of the Kids: Documenting the Emotional Toll of Parental Tension," *The Wall Street Journal* (June 23, 2005): D1.

102. S.D. Sidle, "Pain or Gain: Is There a Bright Side to Juggling Work and Family Roles?" *Academy of Management Perspectives* 21(4) (2007): 80–82.

103. S. Shellenbarger, "Move Over, Mom: Research Suggests Dad's Role Sometimes Matters More," *The Wall Street Journal* (June 12, 2003): D1.

104. J. Trelease, *The Read Aloud Handbook* 6e (New York: Penguin, 2006).

105. S. Shellenbarger, "More New Mothers Are Staying Home Even When It Causes Financial Pain," *The Wall Street Journal* (November 30, 2006): D1.

106. S.D. Sidle, "Pain or Gain: Is There a Bright Side to Juggling Work and Family Roles?" *Academy of Management Perspectives* 21(4) (2007): 80–82.

107. L.L. Brennan, "Working Around the Family: Is There a Gender Divide?" *Academy of Management Perspectives* 21(2) (2007): 81–82.

108. L.A. Mainiero and S.E. Sullivan, *The Opt-Out Revolt: Why People Are Leaving Companies to Create Kaleidoscope Careers* (Mountain View, CA: Davies-Black, 2006).

109. J. Zaslow, "Divorce Makes a Comeback," *The Wall Street Journal* (January 14, 2003): D1, D10.

110. S. Shellenbarger, "Another Casualty Emerges from the Crises: Family Time," *The Wall Street Journal* (October 15, 2008): D1.

111. S. Shellenbarger, "What Makes a Company a Great Place to Work Today," *The Wall Street Journal* (October 4, 2007): D1.

112. R. Levering and M. Moskowitz, "The Ranking," *Fortune* (February 4, 2008): 75–80.

113. S.E. Page, "Making the Difference: Applying a Logic of Diversity," *Academy of Management Perspectives* 21(4) (2007): 6–20.

114. L.L. Brennan, "Working Around the Family: Is There a Gender Divide?" *Academy of Management Perspectives* 21(2) (2007): 81–82.

115. S. Shellenbarger, "Another Casualty Emerges from the Crises: Family Time," *The Wall Street Journal* (October 15, 2008): D1.

116. S.E. Page, "Making the Difference: Applying a Logic of Diversity," *Academy of Management Perspectives* 21(4) (2007): 6–20.

117. C. Barzantny, "Managing Diversity: Toward a Globally Inclusive Workplace," *Academy of Management Learning & Education* 6(2) (2007): 285–286.

118. S.E. Page, "Making the Difference: Applying a Logic of Diversity," *Academy of Management Perspectives* 21(4) (2007): 6–20.

119. S. Waddock, "Leadership Integrity in a Fractured Knowledge World," *Academy of Management Learning & Education* 6(4) (2007): 543–557.

120. J.T. Battenberg, "In New Worker Compact, Competitiveness Is Job One," *Academy of Management Perspectives* 21(2) (2007): 9–13.

121. F. Shipper, R.C. Hoffman, and D.M. Rotondo, "Does the 360 Feedback Process Create Actionable Knowledge Equally Across Cultures?" *Academy of Management Learning & Education* 6(1) (2007): 33–50.

122. Y. Zhu, "What Drives Differences in Reward Allocation Principles Across Countries and Organizations," *Academy of Management Perspectives* 21(3) (2007): 90–92.

123. K.K. Metters and R. Metters, "Misunderstanding the Chinese Worker," *The Wall Street Journal* (July 7, 2008): R11.

124. Y. Zhu, "Do Cultural Values Shape Employee Receptivity to Leadership Styles?" *Academy of Management Perspectives* 21(3) (2007): 89–90.

125. C.L. Pearce, "Follow the Leaders," *The Wall Street Journal* (July 7, 2008): R8, R12.

126. C. Binkley, "Americans Learn the Global Art of the Cheek Kiss," *The Wall Street Journal* (March 27, 2008): D1.

127. C. Barzantny, "Managing Diversity: Toward a Globally Inclusive Workplace," *Academy of Management Learning & Education* 6(2) (2007): 285–286.

128. C. Rhoads, "U.S. Olympic Training Features a New Requirement: Etiquette 101," *The Wall Street Journal* (August 6, 2008): A1, A12.

129. G. Colvin, "Not So Lazy, After All," *Fortune* (August 18, 2008): 32.

130. Y. Zhu, "What Drives Differences in Reward Allocation Principles Across Countries and Organizations," *Academy of Management Perspectives* 21(3) (2007): 90–92.

131. G. Colvin, "Not So Lazy, After All," *Fortune* (August 18, 2008): 32.

132. GE Web site, www.ge.com, retrieved November 21, 2008.

133. C.L. Pearce, "Follow the Leaders," *The Wall Street Journal* (July 7, 2008): R8, R12.

134. M.A. Cronin and L.R. Weingart, "Representational Gaps, Information Processing, and Conflict in Functionally Diverse Teams," *Academy of Management Review* 32(3) (2007): 761–773.

135. C. Hymowitz, "Sometimes, Moving Up Makes It Harder to See What Goes On Below," *The Wall Street Journal* (October 15, 2007): B1.

136. Hoovers Web site (http://premium.hoovers.com/subscribe/co/overview.xhtml?ID=ffffrfskcfcrhyctjc), retrieved November 10, 2008.

137. http://www.crmcdonalds.com/publish/csr/home/report/employment_experience/inclusion_and_diversity.html, retrieved November 10, 2008.

138. http://americansfortruth.com/news/mcdonalds-scores-85-percent-on-homosexual-lobby-group-hrcs-corporate-scorecard.html, retrieved November 10, 2008.

139. http://americansfortruth.com/news/americans-for-truth-supports-afas-boycott-of-mcdonalds.html, retrieved November 10, 2008.

INDEX